The Goodriches

James P. Goodrich

Pierre F. Goodrich

The Goodriches

An American Family

By Dane Starbuck

LIBERTY FUND

Indianapolis

This book is published by Liberty Fund, Inc., a foundation established to encourage study of the ideal of a society of free and responsible individuals.

The cuneiform inscription that serves as our logo and as the design motif for our endpapers is the earliest-known written appearance of the word "freedom" (*amagi*), or "liberty." It is taken from a clay document written about 2300 B.C. in the Sumerian city-state of Lagash.

Printed in the United States of America

C 10 9 8 7 6 5 4 3

Library of Congress Cataloging-in-Publication Data

Starbuck, Dane, 1956–

The Goodriches: an American family/Dane Starbuck.

p. cm.

Includes bibliographical references and index.

ISBN 0-86597-184-6 (cloth: alk. paper).—

ISBN 0-86597-185-4 (pbk.: alk. paper)

1. Goodrich, James P. (James Putnam), 1864–1940.
2. Governors—Indiana—Biography. 3. Goodrich, Pierre F.
4. Businessmen—Indiana—Biography. 5. Goodrich family.
I. Title.

F526.G67S83 2001

977.2′042′092—dc21

[B] 98-24458

Liberty Fund, Inc.

8335 Allison Pointe Trail, Suite 300

Indianapolis, IN 46250-1684

I know of no more encouraging fact than the unquestionable ability of man to elevate his life by conscious endeavor. It is something to be able to paint a particular picture, or to carve a statue, and so to make a few objects beautiful. But it is far more glorious to carve and paint the very atmosphere and medium through which we look which morally we can do. To affect the quality of the day, that is the highest of arts.

HENRY DAVID THOREAU, *Walden*

What a stupendous, what an incomprehensible machine is man! Who can endure toil, famine, stripes, imprisonment or death itself in vindication of his own liberty, and the next moment be deaf to all those motives whose power supported him thro' his trial, and inflict on his fellow men a bondage, one hour of which is fraught with more misery than ages of that which he rose in rebellion to oppose. . . .

THOMAS JEFFERSON, *Papers*

I must study politics and war, that my sons may have liberty to study mathematics and philosophy, geography, natural history and naval architecture, navigation, commerce, and agriculture, in order to give their children a right to study painting, poetry, music, architecture, statuary, tapestry, and porcelain.

JOHN ADAMS, *Letters of John Adams Addressed to His Wife*

Our civilization is still in a middle stage, scarcely beast, in that it is no longer wholly guided by instinct; scarcely human, in that it is not yet wholly guided by reason.

THEODORE DREISER, *Sister Carrie*

Contents

PART V

The Goodriches Assayed

APPENDIXES

Illustrations

Foreword

James M. Buchanan

THE Indiana Goodriches are an American family whose leading members, James and Pierre, helped to shape the American century. The book becomes, primarily, the necessary biography of Pierre Goodrich, but the life of such a man could never be understood were he not centrally placed within the family heritage. And, particularly, attention must be paid to the personal saga of James P. Goodrich, Pierre's father, which, when accomplished, converts this biographical effort into the sequential narrative of two lives. James P. Goodrich was a business and political leader whose credits include a term as Indiana's governor during World War I, official United States missions to the famine-stricken and collectivized chaos that was the Soviet Union in the 1920s, and both state and national prominence in Republican Party affairs—all of this while building the foundations for the far-flung business network that Pierre brought to fruition. In its turn, however, James Goodrich's own history is not readily separated from that of the Goodrich brothers, who were all among Indiana's movers and shakers during the first half of the twentieth century.

I was fascinated when I learned about the family's early connection with Blacksburg, Virginia, my adopted hometown, and with Virginia Polytechnic Institute, an institution with which I was affiliated. And what a story! The matriarch of the clan, the widowed Rebecca Pearse Goodrich, who married at thirteen and had given birth to fourteen children by the time she was thirty-nine, set out from Blacksburg in 1831 to cross the mountains and rivers for Indiana. We can only stand in awe of such persons, who did indeed make our land.

This biography makes us recognize what is missing from the millennial setting in which we find ourselves. We have lost the "idea of America," both as a motivation for action and as a source of emotional self-confidence. We have lost that which the Goodriches possessed.

Pierre Goodrich was a highly successful entrepreneur whose efforts were a unique combination of divergent activities (agriculture, communication, finance, law, mining, publishing, utilities) and locational concentration (Indiana). So long as politicized constraints are kept within reasonable limits, a few comparably successful business leaders will emerge in the least expected places. But who among them will appreciate the specific philosophical foundations of the institutional environment that sustains their own flourishing? Further, who among them might emulate Pierre Goodrich in the recognition that these very foundations must be continually renewed and reinvigorated in public understanding?

Liberty Fund is the permanent embodiment of Pierre Goodrich's faith in the power of ideas and his personal belief that ideas are more exciting and more important than things. The biographer appropriately distinguishes between Pierre Goodrich as the man of ideas who both created Liberty Fund and remains its inspiration, and Pierre Goodrich as the directing force behind an extended network of business enterprises. It is both appropriate and helpful in our understanding to describe Goodrich's own interpretation of his business activity as a "calling," which more or less necessarily embodied the Calvinist virtues of work and accumulation, virtues that he imputed as norms and evaluative standards for others than himself. While he was not actively religious in any personal sense, it is interesting to learn that both Luther and Calvin are on Goodrich's recommended short reading list. The family's Presbyterian heritage was surely important in allowing Pierre Goodrich to ward off all temptations toward profligacy.

When he established Liberty Fund, however, Pierre Goodrich went well beyond his calling even as a creator of economic value. The institution has, indeed, made a difference in the world of ideas. I am cited as noting that the philosophical dialogue has shifted over the century's last quarter. Liberty Fund's conferences are owed at least some part of the causal credit for that shift. The "Great Books" are now exhaustively discussed, both exegetically and extensively, and well beyond the confines of a few college and university programs. And the foundational origins of the ideas and ideals of a free society are being examined in depth. Their numbers are legion: those who have, finally, been exposed firsthand to the ideas of Acton, Althusius, Hobbes, Hume, Locke, Maine, Mandeville, Montesquieu, Smith, and Spinoza, along with those of their twentieth-century successors. In this skeptical age, is it not really a bit marvelous that Liberty Fund has lived up to its name? If academic, political, and public understanding fails to reckon the potential dangers of inattention to the classical norms, Pierre Goodrich and Liberty Fund have absolved themselves of any share of the responsibility.

I commenced this foreword by reference to Pierre and James Goodrich as leading members of an American family in the American century. But more precise temporal and locational identification seems to be possible here. There is only one natural setting from which such men could have emerged: the great American Midwest during the early years of the twentieth century. The contrasting cultures of the effete, elitist, establishment-minded East and the caste-bound South could never have bred and nurtured such spirits.

Personally, I recall seeing Pierre Goodrich on a few occasions at early Mont Pelerin Society meetings in the late 1950s and the 1960s. He was one of a very small number of business leaders (three or four) who seemed fully at home in the company of his generation's classical liberals, who have now become legends: F. A. Hayek, Frank Knight, Ludwig von Mises, Karl Popper, Wilhelm Röpke. I am sure that none of these men could have made nearly so comfortable a comparative shift from the realm of ideas to that of practical reality.

I have participated in many Liberty Fund conferences. I have always been impressed at the efforts made by Liberty Fund's program officers to adhere rigorously to the guidelines laid out in the foundation's *Basic Memorandum.* In this respect, Pierre Goodrich has been posthumously blessed. In some provisional comparative reckoning, he outdistances

Carnegie, Ford, Lilly, MacArthur, Rockefeller, Sage, and others in the dispositional efficiency of his legacy. The ratio between final usage and original intent is surely much greater for the Goodrich endowment than it is for many of his peers whose fortunes far surpassed his own.

It is good to have this biography, because it now becomes easier for us to understand and appreciate how Liberty Fund's surprisingly comprehensive *Basic Memorandum* came into being, and to sense its intent and purpose. Pierre Goodrich was not so naïve as to think that the linkage between ideas and their consequences is direct along either the temporal or the intellectual dimension. He was, himself, no "policy wonk," and he would have considered support of policy-oriented think tanks to be relatively less productive than alternative investment in the stimulation of discussion of basic ideas.

Should he have lived out his own full century, Pierre Goodrich would surely have rejoiced at the demise of the fatal conceit that was socialism. He would also have sensed that the postsocialist pragmatic drift that we currently experience guarantees disaster. The millennial politics of situational response demands, more than ever, attention to navigational guidepoles in the ideas and ideals of those classical liberals who laid the foundation from which America rose to greatness.

It is no fault of Liberty Fund, or of this biography, that we are left with an obvious and continuing query: Where can Pierre Goodrich's true successors be found? Who will emerge to combine the passion for ideas and the ability to offer incentives for others to take time out to think beyond quotidian limits?

James M. Buchanan is advisory general director of the Center for the Study of Public Choice at George Mason University and a Nobel Laureate (1986) in Economics.

Preface

So many people go through life thinking all that's around us just happened; that it didn't take initiative, and imagination and effort. And it can be blown away, it can be discarded . . . very rapidly, never ever to come back again. It's not just ignorant to be indifferent to history. It's rude. It is being ungrateful . . . toward all those people who worked so hard to give us what we have here in this nation. And we have to not only be the custodians of that; we have to improve upon it.

DAVID MCCULLOUGH, "Chautauqua and Its Place in American Culture"

On the southern edge of Winchester, Indiana, lies the town's main cemetery. If you wander through the oldest section, you come across hundreds of headstones engraved with many of the names of those who used to be the most prominent citizens of this community: Davises, Edgers, Goodriches, Jaquas, Kitselmans, Macys, McCamishes, Millers, and Moormans. Yet few of today's local inhabitants recognize these names, let alone associate them with the establishment of the town. For the most part, either the individual descendants of these families have moved away or the families themselves have died out. It is sad that they are gone. It is sadder still that they have been mostly forgotten.

This book is about one of those families. While the primary focus is on James P. Goodrich, the twenty-eighth governor of Indiana, and his son, Pierre F. Goodrich, businessman extraordinaire and founder of Liberty Fund, Inc., the following pages also discuss these two men's extended families and provide a narrative about the civic, economic, intellectual, and religious milieu in which the Goodriches thrived. The research I have undertaken in writing this book has increased my own appreciation of just how special this time period was in the formation of our nation's character. I have also gained at least a partial understanding of how much the Goodriches' story reflects "America's story" of the latter half of the nineteenth century and the first half of the twentieth century.

As a result of learning about this one family, I now see the community where the Goodriches gained their prominence in a completely different light: The east portico of the county courthouse not only is an entrance to a building, but also is the platform from which former President Theodore Roosevelt addressed a crowd of proud Americans at the turn of the present century; downtown Washington Street in Winchester is where Hoosier poet laureate James Whitcomb Riley amused children and adults alike with his homespun verse; the recently restored Civil War monument on the courthouse square is where Union veterans marched from surrounding villages in memory of the "Great Conflict" between the North and South; the steepled churches that are prominently located in this community are where Protestant values have been passed down to succeeding generations from early pioneer families.

It is within this context that the Goodrich family, and specifically James and Pierre Goodrich, are explored. It was not my original intent to draw from such a broad landscape. Indeed, this book was initially conceived as a biography of Pierre Goodrich. Given the achievements of the man, let alone his complexity, that would have been a sufficiently daunting task. Yet as I learned more about Pierre Goodrich, it became evident to me that it was next to impossible to comprehend him and his incredible range of interests without closely examining his father, his family, and his times. One example illustrates the need for a dual biography of father and son: It puzzled me why an attorney, businessman, and intellectual like Pierre Goodrich would take such an incredible interest in environmental matters, specifically land management. After I learned about his father's ambitious conservation record both as governor and private citizen, however, Pierre's interest in ecology made much greater sense. In addition, Pierre's religious beliefs, his deep commitment to liberty, and his convictions about work, business, and virtue also stem largely, I believe, from his father's tutelage, as well as from his extended family and the teachings of earlier generations of Goodriches.

The later chapters of this book are as much a social commentary on American life in the twentieth century as parts of a biography of two accomplished men. This is not an accident. It reflects my analysis of how James and Pierre Goodrich fit into the larger scheme of things. Biography is more than the recording of significant facts, dates, names, and events. It also involves placing the subject's life in context—showing how the subject was shaped by his environment and vice versa—and it requires a considerable amount of interpretation. Moreover, writing history (and biography) is an attempt to analyze the origin and meaning of individuals' ideals, motives, and wills. Sometimes the individual prevails; more often societal forces thwart individual initiative. This is the struggle that characterizes every life, and it is one that both James and Pierre Goodrich engaged in constantly on extraordinary fronts.

One caveat. As will become apparent, Pierre Goodrich's thinking was somewhat convoluted and elaborate; still, an examination of his thought is crucial to understanding him and understanding why he believed that Liberty Fund—the institution he established and to which he bequeathed most of his fortune—was so important. I am mindful, however, that every "author who writes on a very complex topic is faced with a dilemma. If he writes simply, he is likely to be misunderstood. If he takes the greatest care not to be misunderstood by making his material formidable, he may not be read at all."[1] I have attempted in the latter chapters to describe Pierre Goodrich's philosophical beliefs and the intellectual influences to which he was exposed. I have tried to strike a balance—not using so much technical language as to overwhelm the general reader or being so superficial in my analysis as to deprive Goodrich's thinking of the serious study it deserves. It is not an easy balance to strike, and I ask in advance for the reader's indulgence.

I would like to take this opportunity to express my gratitude to the

1. John C. Kemeny, *A Philosopher Looks at Science* (Princeton, N.J.: D. Van Nostrand, 1959), p. 3.

directors of Liberty Fund and the Winchester Foundation for their support and assistance in the writing of this book. I would also like to acknowledge two authors who preceded me in examining the Goodrich family: Richard E. Wise, former publisher of the *Winchester (Ind.) News-Gazette,* who wrote a series of articles in 1984 about early generations of Goodriches;[2] and Professor Benjamin D. Rhodes of the University of Wisconsin at Whitewater, who wrote an informative article about James Goodrich's various trips to the Soviet Union in a 1989 issue of the *Indiana Magazine of History.*[3] Professor Rhodes later expanded the article into a book.[4] Although I was raised in Winchester and was familiar with the Goodrich family, it was not until I read these articles that I began to gain some insight into the Goodriches' achievements and contributions. I hope that the following text will add to the public's knowledge and appreciation of this family's remarkable members.

I will close this preface with an anecdote. In July 1954, after years of debate on the subject, the commissioners of Randolph County, Indiana, decided to renovate the local courthouse, the very center, physically and civically, of this county's activities. The decision was controversial because it involved tearing down the upper third of the building. This part contained a beautiful bell tower with four clocks and turrets—the ornamental structure that made the building especially handsome and visible for many miles in all directions. Over the years, local authorities had allowed the tower to deteriorate, and the commissioners believed that it was beyond restoration. Indiana is known for its beautiful

2. Richard E. Wise, "Family Has Had Profound Effect Locally," *Winchester (Ind.) News-Gazette,* February 15, 1984, p. 4, col. 1; "Goodrich Grandfather Lived Eventful Life," *Winchester (Ind.) News-Gazette,* February 16, 1984, p. 1, col. 2; "Goodrich Father Was a Public Spirited Citizen," *Winchester (Ind.) News-Gazette,* February 17, 1984, p. 1, col. 2.

3. Benjamin D. Rhodes, "Governor James P. Goodrich of Indiana and the 'Plain Facts' About Russia, 1921–1933," *Indiana Magazine of History* 85 (March 1989): 1–30.

4. Rhodes's book, which evolved from his article about James P. Goodrich's various trips to the Soviet Union, is *James P. Goodrich, Indiana's "Governor Strangelove"* (Selinsgrove, Pa.: Susquehanna University Press, 1996; London: Associated University Press, 1996).

courthouses, and Randolph County's was a grand example of exquisite Victorian architecture, having been built in 1876. Though the commissioners lamented the decision, they believed that the upper third of the courthouse was structurally unsafe and should be removed.

When the wrecking crew went to tear down the tower, however, the task proved to be monumental. The tower was more structurally sound than anyone had realized. In fact, the tower was balanced on steel cables that, if properly tightened and periodically adjusted, could have supported the tower for decades to come. Over the years, however, no one had thought to convey this information to the later custodians of the building. Thus, a perfectly good and beautiful landmark was needlessly lost because no one had bothered to preserve the work of an earlier time or pass on "the story" to succeeding generations. I'll not bother to explain my obvious point. I simply hope that the reader may find in the following pages that much of the "tower" of a particular family has been preserved—and that the effort was worthwhile.

Acknowledgments

THIS WORK would have been impossible to write without the assistance of not only the more than one hundred people I interviewed and corresponded with but also countless others. I am especially grateful to Sandy Truitt, Margaret Hyre, and W. W. Hill, who read an early draft of the manuscript and made helpful suggestions for improvement. Also, I want to thank Ruth E. Connolly, William C. Dennis, Jeanne Shendel, and Martin Seyfert for their comments on chapters they read.

A writer of history and biography is indebted to those who have helped preserve valuable resources and materials. Research for this book took me to libraries and archives in a number of states, including California, Connecticut, Illinois, Indiana, Iowa, New York, and Washington, D.C. Throughout these travels, I was fortunate to have the help of dozens of archivists and librarians who generously assisted me in obtaining information. I would like especially to thank the following for their kindness and assistance: Dale C. Mayer, Senior Archivist, Herbert Hoover Presidential Library in West Branch, Iowa; Carol Leadenham, Archives, Hoover Institution, Stanford, California; Dennis Kovener, Archivist, Hanover College, Hanover, Indiana; David DeLorenzo of the Harvard Law School Archives and Stephen Smith, Curator of Art at the Harvard Law School, Cambridge, Massachusetts; Pam Wasmer and David Lewis, Indiana Division, Indiana State Library; Stephen Towne and Jennifer Wigley, State Archives, Indiana Commission on Public Records; Stephen Fletcher, Librarian, Indiana Historical Society, Indianapolis; Johanna Herring, Director, Archives, Wabash College, Crawfordsville, Indiana; Hans Sennholz and Bettina Bien Greaves of the

Foundation for Economic Education, Irvington-on-Hudson, New York; Leslie A. Simmer and Sharon Crowley, the Great Books Foundation, Chicago, Illinois; Phil Wagner, Center for East Asian Studies, Wesleyan University, Middletown, Connecticut; reference librarians, the Library of Congress, Washington, D.C.; Monisa Wisener of the Randolph County, Indiana, Historical and Genealogical Society; Gordon W. Greigh of the Adams County, Indiana, Historical Society; Marianna Reed, volunteer historian of the First Presbyterian Church, Winchester, Indiana; Jenny Stonerock of the Winchester, Indiana, Public Library; Suzanne Robinson, Librarian, Washington Township Public Library in Lynn, Indiana. There are many other librarians and archivists whose names are too numerous for me to mention, but to whom I am also grateful. I would also like to thank Jamie Bronstein of Stanford University for her assistance in conducting research for me, Jerry Wyatt for his assistance in helping me organize the Goodrich family genealogy, Charles Bragg for our many conversations about the importance of the Civil War to east-central Indiana, and federal judge William C. Lee for the interesting insights he offered about the Goodrich family.

Finally, I would like to thank the boards of directors and staffs of the Winchester Foundation and Liberty Fund, Inc., as well as the Goodrich family members who generously donated their time to this project: Elizabeth Goodrich Terry and the late Perce G. Goodrich and Florence Goodrich Dunn.

This work contains thousands of dates, places, and events, as well as hundreds of impressions of various people. I have tried to be as accurate as possible in using this material. I am aware that, despite all efforts, inaccuracies may exist for which only I am responsible. I hope they are few.

I
Family Life and Early Background

Chapter 1
An American Family

> The [early] Americans were tough men fighting for a very tough idea. How they won their battles is a story for the schoolbooks, studied by scholars, wrapped in myths by historians and poets.
>
> THEODORE H. WHITE, "The American Idea"

WHO WERE James P. Goodrich and his son, Pierre F. Goodrich? What about their family? No, they didn't manufacture automobile tires. They were not related, at least not directly, to the B. F. Goodrich tire clan of Akron, Ohio. They were highly ambitious businessmen from Indiana, a breed emblematic of the American ideal that began with the Founding Fathers: men who possessed a vision of success and independence for themselves and their country and went out and worked hard to realize it.

It is understandable if you have never heard of them. Indeed, it would be surprising if you had. Both James and Pierre valued privacy. In James Goodrich's case, this was highly unusual, because he had a public profile in politics during most of his life. As for Pierre, he eschewed attention even more than his father did. Just months before his death in 1973, Pierre told an interviewer, "I just never saw any need to have publicity. What good is publicity unless you plan to run for public office? And I never did."[1]

Pierre was in many ways elusive, a person with a pattern of so little

1. Thomas R. Keating, "He's Unknown—and Remarkable," *Indianapolis Star*, April 12, 1973, p. 21, col. 1.

self-disclosure that even people who "knew him" were puzzled by the man. The late Henry Regnery, a longtime Chicago publisher, remarked, "I saw Mr. Goodrich on a good many occasions, traveled with him for several days in Europe, but I am beginning to wonder how well I really knew him."[2] Fred Young, a retired vice-president of Harris Bank in Chicago, responded in a similar manner:

> As many times as he came to see me and as much time as I spent with him I now realize that I did not know the gentleman very well. He always came to the Harris Bank prepared to discuss what he wanted to discuss. He did not come to discuss Pierre Goodrich. . . .
>
> Back in those days I was traveling extensively through Indiana selling our Investment Service to bank trust departments and insurance companies. I would look for occasions when it seemed advantageous to me to mention my good friend Pierre Goodrich. But the response invariably was, "Who?" I did not understand how a man could be so rich and so influential in his state yet seem to be so little known among people that you would expect to know him well. . . . [I]t is too bad that more people didn't know him because he was one of the most phenomenal people that I have ever met.[3]

Similarly, James Goodrich preferred accomplishment to recognition. His brother Percy wrote in 1948, several years after James's death:

> [James] was an indefatigable worker and very earnest in everything he did and was one of the three greatest Governors the State ever had. . . . It is strange when there are so many school houses, roads, parks, etc. [in Indiana] that nothing was ever named in his honor and I am not desiring to blame anyone for it. I believe it was his reticence to appear in the limelight. . . . He would organize a crowd to go someplace to have a political rally and then at the last minute would slip out to do some obscure work elsewhere.[4]

2. Letter to author, April 29, 1992.
3. Letter to author, October 12, 1992.
4. Percy E. Goodrich, "Governor Jim," *Down in Indiana* 61 (December 4, 1948): 1, Indiana Historical Society Library, Indianapolis.

James P. and Pierre F. Goodrich were members of a family that built a financial dynasty in Indiana that began with five Goodrich brothers in the 1880s and continued for nearly one hundred years. Both were attorneys and businessmen, and both were public-minded, but in different ways. Beyond being an entrepreneurial genius, James served as head of the Indiana Republican Party for nearly ten years (1901–10); as the twenty-eighth governor of Indiana (1917–21); and as an adviser to Presidents Warren G. Harding, Calvin Coolidge, and Herbert Hoover, and to the national Republican Party. Pierre's achievements were more restricted to business and intellectual pursuits. He was chairman of the board of the Ayrshire Collieries Corporation (1946–69), president and CEO of the Indiana Telephone Corporation (1934–73), president and CEO of Peoples Loan and Trust Company (1940–73), and director of dozens of other companies. He also served as an officer and director of numerous educational foundations, including the one that he established himself, Liberty Fund, Inc., of Indianapolis, Indiana.

Both men were driven, ambitious, stubborn, and indefatigable. For both, twelve- and even fourteen-hour workdays were not uncommon. In later life, Pierre occasionally worked all night just to prove to himself that he could still do it.[5] "Pierre was one of the hardest working people I ever knew," said Richard Swallow, chief engineer at Ayrshire Collieries for thirty-seven years.[6]

"It was hard to live up to his expectations," stated Gilbert Snider, an attorney in Goodrich's law firm, adding: "Pierre was so brilliant. What most people thought was the norm was the bottom for him. You sometimes got dismayed that you worked like a dog and to find it just barely reached his minimum standard."[7]

After James Goodrich's death, the former Indiana Appellate Court judge Charles F. Remy recalled the former governor's work habits:

5. Irwin H. Reiss, interview, June 29, 1996.
6. Richard Swallow, telephone interview, December 20, 1992.
7. Gilbert Snider, interview, December 23, 1991.

> I was one of the judges of the Appellate Court, with offices in the Statehouse, and, therefore, was very familiar with the work of his administration. During [James Goodrich's] term as governor, he was usually the first state officer to arrive at the Statehouse. Much of the time he was at his desk in the governor's office at seven o'clock in the morning. . . . He gave his best he had every day, every week, every month, and every year of his four-year term.[8]

If the two men shared many similarities, they also possessed many differences: James Goodrich was a hard-hitting, decisive man, quick to analyze a situation and then to act.[9] It was these qualities that made him such an imposing governor.[10]

> Pierre . . . by contrast was, or appeared to others to be, laborious and tedious in arriving at decisions, often ambivalent and equivocal, sometimes mysterious. He worried and stewed about problems, consulted others, disregarded their advice once given, explored alternatives, checked and double-checked his own tentative conclusions. It was an exhausting process for those who worked with him. But when he acted finally, the results, for him at least, were almost always beneficial.[11]

The painstaking, almost soul-searching process by which Pierre made even the simplest of decisions revealed a man who, although essentially shy, desired to remain in control. A more charitable assessment of Pierre's decision-making style suggests a conscious reason for his deliberateness. Professor Benjamin A. Rogge, who delivered the eulogy at

8. Charles F. Remy, "Governor Goodrich and Indiana Tax Legislation," *Indiana Magazine of History* 43 (March 1947): 43.

9. An example of James Goodrich's decisiveness is his 1939 appointment of Francis Simpson and Claude Barnes, both of whom were directors of Peoples Loan and Trust Company, to investigate the value of a bank in Ridgeville, Indiana, that Goodrich was interested in purchasing. Before Simpson and Barnes could report to the former governor, Goodrich had already made the owners of the Ridgeville Bank an offer that they had accepted (Perce G. Goodrich, interview, November 9, 1992).

10. Byron K. Trippet, *Wabash on My Mind: Wabash College 1832–1982* (Crawfordsville, Ind.: Wabash College, 1982), p. 183.

11. Ibid.

Pierre's funeral in 1973, stated at the memorial service, "[Mr. Goodrich] recognized that only when we were pressing him for a decision could he command our attention sufficiently to make us truly listen to and try to understand the philosophy behind *all* of his decision-making—a philosophy that he believed we, too, must understand and know how to apply if we were to be fully useful in our joint endeavors."[12] Alan Russell, who worked for Goodrich in the telephone industry and is now chairman of Liberty Fund, gave a slightly different response: "Pierre never made a decision. The proposer made the decision in the end. But you had a dialogue with Pierre until he knew you were going to reach the *right* answer."[13]

In other words, Goodrich used the Socratic method of inquiry to induce the proposer to reach a conclusion. This approach could be maddening to traditional management types who simply wanted a yes or no answer. Pierre was no less enigmatic when it came to his demeanor. He could be taciturn or engage in a discussion for hours if the topic was about some business decision or, more likely, some philosophical insight that interested him. His father had little time for scholastic exercises. James Goodrich's confident, aggressive, risk-taking nature would not tolerate such a roundabout approach. He looked for quick results. Thus, in terms of personality, the two men seemed, in many ways, to be opposites.

Their temperaments were also different. As a boy growing up in post–Civil War times, James Goodrich could be confrontational and a bit of a roughhouser. He was not afraid to get into neighborhood scraps when the need arose. Pierre, despite a tough-minded and businesslike exterior, was more sensitive and less prone to confrontation. He found it nearly impossible to fire an employee. Rather, he took a cautious approach when hiring employees, preferring to interview dozens of potential candidates for several hours each (sometimes for several days) in

12. Benjamin Rogge, eulogy delivered at First Presbyterian Church, Winchester, Indiana, October 28, 1973. Copy in author's possession.

13. T. Alan Russell, interview, July 2, 1994.

the hope that he could find just the right person for the position.[14] Moreover, Pierre had an aesthetic appreciation far greater than that of his father. A close cousin of Pierre's described his love of beauty as almost feminine.[15] He knew all about cats, how they liked to be petted and nurtured. He had a love of music, art, and flowers, and was able to identify dozens of species of flowers by their botanical as well as common names. He became an aficionado of gemstones, coffees, and fine wines (despite being a teetotaler most of his life).[16]

James Goodrich was described by some as a peculiar man, balding, of medium height, bespectacled, and with searching eyes that seemed to hide what he was thinking. During the last twenty years of his life, he walked with the use of a cane as the result of an automobile accident that almost killed him while he was governor. James Goodrich was unquestionably driven, even up to the time of his death. In 1940, ill but having weathered the worst of the Great Depression, he was quoted as saying, "I know I am very sick and I know I am going to die. And I hate it terribly because I know there will be a lot of money made in the next few years."[17] The former governor was clearly aware of his money-

14. Lovett C. Peters, who worked briefly for Pierre Goodrich in negotiating the sale of the Ayrshire Collieries Corporation in the late 1960s, said that Goodrich had a very difficult time firing anyone (telephone interview, June 25, 1994). "Before Pierre Goodrich would hire a new person—and it didn't make any difference what kind of job—he would interview them personally and sometimes the interview would go on for hours," said Rosanna Amos (interview, December 23, 1991). Alan Russell stated that, for a top management position in one of his companies, Goodrich would interview a candidate for two to three days (interview, July 2, 1994).

15. Florence Dunn, interview, July 18, 1992.

16. Observations about cats—Anna Marie Gibbons, interview, December 23, 1991; observation about flowers—Don Welch, interview, December 16, 1991. Henry Regnery, a Chicago publisher, claims that he introduced Goodrich to wine in the mid or late 1940s (interview, October 3, 1992). Helen Fletcher confirms that claim in her letter to the author, June 18, 1996.

17. The quote is taken from Benjamin D. Rhodes's *James P. Goodrich, Indiana's "Governor Strangelove,"* p. 14 (citing *Indianapolis News,* June 24, 1950). Irwin H. Reiss also told the author the same story, saying that Norman Kelb, a former president of the Ayrshire Collieries Corporation, had told Reiss that James Goodrich had told Kelb the same thing (interview, June 26, 1996).

making skills. In retirement, Goodrich once told an interviewer he had "to check on himself to keep from making too much."[18]

Pierre was more distinguished and robust than his father. He had a mop of white hair, a rough complexion, somewhat cherubic cheeks, and a youthful disposition that lasted into his later years. He was generally serious, having what many described as a "strong personality" and a reserved, malcontent attitude. Yet Pierre would occasionally display a lighter side.[19] Pierre, like his father, had a penchant for making money, but he was driven by other motives as well. Nobel Prize–winning economist Milton Friedman, now a senior fellow with the Hoover Institution, fondly remembers Pierre for his depth of thought and strongly held views:

> I was a personal friend of Pierre Goodrich and a great admirer of him. The occasion for my meeting him was a series of summer programs at Wabash College. . . . I recall many an exciting and pleasant evening spent discussing issues ranging over a very wide area with Pierre Goodrich. He was extraordinarily widely read, very knowledgeable, and deeply interested in a great variety of issues.
>
> He had thought deeply about philosophical issues and was a convinced libertarian who believed in minimal government. Indeed, he would have liked a world in which there was no government involvement at all, in which primary reliance was placed on the free market as the best defender of human liberty. [H]e also was a remarkably keen student of current politics and economics. . . . That was the respect in which I enjoyed our conversations the most.[20]

The late Russell Kirk, prominent scholar and lecturer, remembered Pierre's demeanor as noteworthy:

18. "Former Indiana Gov. James P. Goodrich Is Dead," *Winchester (Ind.) Journal-Herald,* August 16, 1940, p. 2, col. 5; see also Benjamin D. Rhodes, *James P. Goodrich, Indiana's "Governor Strangelove,"* p. 14.

19. Most of these impressions of Pierre Goodrich's appearance and demeanor were given by Professor Stephen Tonsor (interview, December 5, 1992), although a number of interviewees said many of the same things.

20. Letter to author, December 19, 1991.

> A certain austerity, a dry humor, and an uprightness of character were joined in him with a passion for booklearning. . . . He was what would be called in Europe a high bourgeois; but we have in Britain and America no proper equivalent of that term. Although very civil and interesting in conversation, he always maintained a dignity of demeanor and a certain reserve.
>
> A stickler for punctuality, [Mr. Goodrich] once informed me that he had telephoned my library about nine o'clock in the morning, and nobody answered; he thought I might like to know that, since it suggests that my assistants might be unpunctual.[21]

Harold Rogers, a former history teacher at Winchester High School, Pierre's alma mater, once remarked that a sign of Goodrich's intelligence was that he knew his limitations and stayed within them.[22] Rosanna Amos, a secretary to Goodrich, echoed Rogers's observation: "Mr. Goodrich was not a speechmaker and he knew it."[23]

Both James and Pierre had lilting voices that were not suited to public speaking. James abhorred making a speech and preferred the backroom maneuvering that made him such an effective businessman and political strategist.[24] In this regard, father and son were alike. When Pierre did preside, he had the annoying habit of jumping from topic to topic in a stream-of-consciousness manner. It often made it nearly impossible for listeners to follow him. Jack Charles, a retired Wabash College history professor, recalls:

> My chief involvement with Pierre was in connection with his enthusiasm for "Great Books" discussion groups. For a couple of years in the

21. Letter to author, February 8, 1992.

22. Anna Marie Gibbons, interview, December 23, 1991. Rogers had made the comment to Anna Marie Gibbons after a Winchester Great Books meeting in 1948 or 1949.

23. Rosanna Amos, interview, December 10, 1991.

24. James Goodrich wrote in 1918 to his good friend Will Hays, Sr., then chairman of the national Republican Party: "I have reached the point where I despise, above all things to undertake to make a speech. It is drudgery to me and . . . I can be of so much greater service in other directions and let those who know how and like to, do the talking" (June 20, 1918, Will H. Hays Papers, box 4, Indiana State Library, Manuscript Section, Indianapolis).

> late '40s I was driving all over Indiana to lead groups that Pierre had persuaded local citizens to organize; frequently he would decide to be my co-leader. The result was disastrous. He was a very poor [discussion] leader, and when he intervened with some complicated and rambling question or comment the discussion ground to a halt.[25]

Fortunately, Goodrich learned, at least in business situations, to let others do the talking—men like his longtime law partners Albert Campbell and Claude Warren. "But as I quickly learned," said Gilbert Snider, "Pierre Goodrich made all the decisions. In the meetings prior to the court or utility hearings it was very clear who had thought out what was to be said and the strategy that the presenting lawyer was to follow."[26]

Despite this brief introduction, the questions remain: Why should we care about James and Pierre Goodrich and the Goodrich family? What about them should interest us to the point that it is worth our time to read a book about a family dynasty that is essentially gone? How does a study of them deepen our understanding beyond simple knowledge of the family itself?

I believe there are several answers to these questions. They are, however, not self-evident. They can be answered only after one has answered still other questions. First, how did five brothers raised as farm boys shortly after the Civil War create a financial dynasty that included various industries: agriculture, natural gas, coal, oil, telephones, bank-

25. Jack Charles, letter to author, January 28, 1993. Moreover, Anna Marie Gibbons recalled another time when Pierre tried to give a talk at a Peoples Loan and Trust Company banquet. The banquet was probably on December 4, 1970, at the dedication dinner of the new Peoples Loan and Trust Company bank building. She said that the talk turned into a Socratic dialogue in which Goodrich started asking questions of the audience. To her recollection, no one responded but her. The "speech" finally evolved into a discourse between her and Goodrich, quite to the bewilderment of the other audience members (interview, December 22, 1992). A reference to Goodrich's talk was made in a local newspaper. See "Economist Warns of Economic Dangers of Coming Decades," *Winchester (Ind.) News-Gazette* and *Journal-Herald,* December 5, 1970, p. 1, col. 3.

26. Gilbert Snider, interview, December 23, 1991.

ing, securities, newspapers, transportation? Second, to what degree did the circumstances and beliefs of the times—political, economic, ethical, and religious—contribute to these five brothers' achievements? Third, what was James Goodrich's role in leading the Republican Party in Indiana during the first twenty years of the twentieth century and the state generally during World War I, when he served as governor (1917–21)? Fourth, what essential role did James Goodrich play in the great Russian famine-relief program and in furthering diplomatic relations between the United States and the Soviet Union in the 1920s? Fifth, what tremendous social changes took place in the United States in the twentieth century that compelled Pierre Goodrich to establish Liberty Fund from the profits of the sale of the Goodrich companies? Sixth, why did Pierre Goodrich believe that the study of liberty is of central importance if our society is to withstand the growing political, economic, and social dependency that has earmarked the last half of the twentieth century?

An exploration of the above questions, I believe, enables us to gain greater insight into more than just the Goodriches. An exploration into these questions facilitates a greater appreciation for how the business, political, religious, and ethical values of a quintessentially American family were largely responsible for that family's financial success, James Goodrich's own political ambitions, and the belief systems of nineteenth- and early twentieth-century Americans in general. I believe that, for the Goodrich family, work in the business arena amounted to a calling. James's and Pierre's identities were largely shaped by what they did. The reader will also learn how family and physical location held a special place in the hearts of the Goodriches, helping to define their sense of identity both publicly and privately.

Chapter 2
Origins

> We arrived at our Present place of abode on White River, Randolph County, Ind., . . . after a long and Tedious journey. We arrived here without any Lives lost or Limbs broke, and that is all we can say. If I was to tell you of the many Difficulties we have encountered in moving here, extreme bad weather, dangerous Roads in consequence of Ice, you would hardly believe me, and, therefore, I shall say nothing about it. We are all in good health and spirits at Present, and we are well Pleased with the country as far as we have yet seen. . . .
>
> EDMUND B. GOODRICH, grandfather of James P. Goodrich, letter, 1832

JAMES PUTNAM GOODRICH was born on February 18, 1864, in Winchester, Indiana, toward the end of arguably the most significant event in American history: the Civil War. His middle name was taken from the name of his maternal grandmother, Jane Gray Putnam Edger, a common practice at the time. James's delivery into the world occurred just two weeks before President Abraham Lincoln appointed a little-known general and former tanner, Ulysses S. Grant, commander in chief of the Union forces. The future Indiana governor was preceded by two older brothers: Ernest, who died shortly after birth in 1860; and Percy Edgar "P. E.," who was born in 1861. Three younger Goodrich

Edmund B. Goodrich, James Goodrich's grandfather, was one of approximately fourteen Goodrich family members who made the harrowing trip from Blacksburg, Virginia, to Randolph County, Indiana, from December 1831 to January 1832. His letter was sent to a relative in Virginia. It is quoted in full in Calvin Goodrich and Percy E. Goodrich, *A Great-Grandmother and Her People* (Winchester, Ind.: privately printed, 1950), pp. 24–26.

brothers followed: John Baldwin (1866), Edward Shields (1868), and William Wallace (1871).

The origins of the Goodrich family are worth noting. More than one hundred years earlier, in the mid 1700s, three Goodrich brothers crossed the Atlantic Ocean from England to the United States. The three men were descendants of an aristocratic clan that had sided with the Royalists and King Charles, fighting Oliver Cromwell at Goodrich Castle on the River Tyne in the mid 1600s. Ruins of Goodrich Castle exist even to this day.[1] Regarding the origin of their family name, Calvin and Percy Goodrich wrote: "The meaning usually given to Goodrich is 'rich in Godliness.' Yet an early definition of 'good' was 'gather.' That which was gathered was 'goods.' So a Goodrich of the Saxon day in England may have been a notable accumulator of personal possessions rather than a man distinguished for sanctity and good works."[2] The possible dual origin of the name seems appropriate for a family who would build a financial dynasty in the midst of post-Reformation religious values.

The three Goodrich brothers arrived in Massachusetts, but one, Edmund B. Goodrich, eventually settled in Petersburg, Virginia. The sequence of generations from there is complicated because of the number of children who are named for a father or mother.

Edmund B. Goodrich had eight children, including a son, John Baldwin Goodrich. John Baldwin Goodrich, born in 1783, became a teacher, lawyer, and land conveyor. He practiced law with Baldwin Pearse, soon to be his father-in-law, beginning in approximately 1800. John B. Goodrich later became president of the Blacksburg Virginia Academy. Today, the successor of that institution is known as Virginia Polytechnic Institution (VPI). In 1802, Goodrich married Rebecca Pearse of Ambrose County, Virginia, the daughter of Baldwin Pearse. Rebecca was just thirteen when the couple married. Between 1803 and 1828, they had four-

1. James P. Goodrich, "Autobiography," James P. Goodrich Papers, box 4, pp. 1–2, Herbert Hoover Presidential Library, West Branch, Iowa.

2. Calvin Goodrich and Percy E. Goodrich, *A Great-Grandmother and Her People* (Winchester, Ind.: privately printed, 1950), p. 60.

teen children, including Edmund Baldwin, who was born about 1805 and was named for his paternal grandfather.

John Baldwin Goodrich died from a fall from a horse in September 1828. His death left Rebecca, at age thirty-nine, a widow with fourteen children. The sale of John Baldwin's assets occurred in February 1829. After his debts were paid off, Rebecca was left with only two hundred dollars. Two and a half years later, Rebecca decided to leave Blacksburg to join other family members near Fort Wayne, Indiana. Therefore, in December 1831, the Goodriches sold their one slave and packed up all the personal possessions they could load onto two horse-drawn wagons. Led by Rebecca, a willowy woman who never weighed more than ninety pounds, the Goodriches left Blacksburg and headed northwest by foot, destined for northeastern Indiana, a distance of almost four hundred miles. One of the grandchildren in the Goodrich clan was a three-month-old baby, John B. Goodrich, who would become James Goodrich's father.[3]

The Goodriches had crossed the western tip of West Virginia, the frozen Ohio River, and much of southern Ohio before they entered eastern Indiana in January 1832. The "roads" were little more than muddy Indian trails and animal paths. As one Hoosier "poet" wrote about the poor traveling conditions in a local tavern registry:

> *The Roads are impassable—*
> *Hardly jackassable;*
> *I think those that travel 'em*
> *Should turn out and gravel 'em.*[4]

It was not a road, however, but a *river* that kept the Goodrich family in east-central Indiana. They were traveling northwest of Winchester,

3. John Baldwin Goodrich was the son of Edmund B. Goodrich and the grandson of John Baldwin and Rebecca Goodrich. See Goodrich and Goodrich, *A Great-Grandmother and Her People,* pp. 21–23, and Ebenezer Tucker, "The Goodrich Family," in *History of Randolph County, Indiana* (Chicago: A. L. Kingman, 1882), p. 313.

4. From the reminiscence of J. H. B. Knowland, cited by George S. Cottman in "Internal Improvement in Indiana," *Indiana Magazine of History* 3 (1907): 20.

Indiana, on their way to Fort Wayne, when one of their wagons broke down as they attempted to ford the White River. Winchester served as the county seat of Randolph County, which, until 1823, stretched clear to the Michigan state line, some 120 miles northward. It was on the outskirts of Winchester that the family chose to settle, some seventy miles south of Fort Wayne. According to legend, when the broken wagon impeded the Goodriches' journey north, the diminutive matriarch, Rebecca Goodrich, exclaimed to her family that she had had enough of the arduous journey and they would go no farther, "one swamp being as good as another."[5]

The Goodrich family settled in Randolph County only sixteen years after Indiana had become a state. Thickly wooded and sparsely populated, the county had been occupied by Miami and Delaware Indians until the 1840s. In 1846, the federal government marched the tribes' remaining members to Toledo, Ohio, to begin what was known as the Trail of Tears. They were subsequently loaded on rafts and floated down the canal system to Cincinnati, Ohio, and from there to St. Louis, Missouri, on the Ohio and Mississippi rivers. Many died along the way. Eventually, the Miamis were transported to Kansas and, later, to Oklahoma, where they ended up on reservations.[6]

In the early 1800s, the Goodriches were one of several hundred pioneer families that had come to eastern Indiana from the Carolinas and Virginia. Winchester was a deeply religious community. In February 1832, it was the site of the largest branch of the Church of Jesus Christ of Latter-Day Saints in Indiana. The founder of the Mormon Church, Joseph Smith, visited the Winchester branch of more than one hundred believers in July 1834. He performed several baptisms of converts in the Mississinewa River, north of Winchester. When several

5. Goodrich, "Autobiography," pp. 23–24. The Goodrich wagon broke down on what is now the Fidler Farm, last owned by Eugene Fidler.

6. See Stewart Rafert, *The Miami Indians of Indiana: A Persistent People, 1654–1994* (Indianapolis: Indiana Historical Society, 1996), pp. 108–13.

members of the Mormon congregation left for Missouri in the spring of 1832, the Goodrich family bought land northeast of Winchester from a departing Mormon farmer.[7]

One of the first written references to a Goodrich family member is contained in a history of Jay County, just north of Randolph County. The reference reads: "In 1834, the families scattered over the south part of the county began to think their settlement of sufficient importance to be under the restraint of law. Prior to this they had enjoyed unlimited freedom. When Mr. Goodrich, Collector of Randolph County, came to collect taxes, every man positively refused to pay. The collector laughed, said that any one who dared come out there to open a forest, ought not to pay tax, and returned."[8]

Edmund B. Goodrich, who was James Goodrich's grandfather, may well have been the tax collector referred to. He also studied law and served as judge of the Randolph County Probate Court. He is described by an early Randolph County history as "a strong temperance man, and a leading member of the Methodist Episcopal Church."[9] His son, John Baldwin Goodrich, who was just three months old when the Goodriches left Virginia for Indiana, also grew up to become a lawyer in Randolph County. In the 1850s, John Goodrich practiced law with his uncle, Carey Goodrich, and with Enos L. Watson. Enos Watson would become the father of James E. Watson, future United States Senate majority leader and lifelong friend of James P. Goodrich.

7. Many members of the Mormon faith left Winchester in the fall of 1831 and the spring of 1832 to join fellow believers in Missouri, but some of them remained in Winchester until at least the end of the 1830s before heading west. For a history of the Winchester branch of the Mormon Church, see LaRene Gaunt, "The Pioneer Saints of Winchester, Indiana," *Ensign* (of the Church of Jesus Christ of Latter-Day Saints), October 1992, pp. 56–59; "Blooming Where Planted," *Ensign,* July 1993, p. 68; and "Mormons Led by Joseph Smith Through City in May of 1834," *Winchester (Ind.) News-Gazette,* September 22, 1984, p. 3, col. 6.

8. M. W. Montgomery, *History of Jay County* (Chicago: Church, Goodman, and Cushing, 1864), p. 6.

9. Tucker, *History of Randolph County, Indiana,* p. 313.

In addition to practicing law, John B. Goodrich became politically active, serving as county Republican chairman and road commissioner. He was elected Randolph County clerk in 1861 and was reelected in 1865. In 1859, John B. Goodrich married Elizabeth Edger, who had grown up in nearby Deerfield, Indiana. They had both attended the Winchester Seminary in the 1850s. At that time, public schools for general education had not yet been established; in many communities, seminaries provided both basic secular and religious education. Before her marriage, Elizabeth Edger had also attended Liber College in Portland, Indiana, a small academy begun in 1853 by a zealous Presbyterian minister.[10] She was a redheaded beauty whose Protestant father, Edward Edger, was born in county Derry, Ireland, before his family immigrated to the United States in 1807.[11] Edger had married Jane Putnam in November 1833, and they had two sons and five daughters, including Elizabeth.[12]

James Goodrich's maternal grandfather, Edward Edger, lived a remarkable pioneer life. In the 1820s, prior to locating in Indiana, he piloted steamboats down the Mississippi and Ohio rivers. In the 1830s, he drove hogs from Indiana to the Carolinas. And for many years he traded with local Indians in northern Randolph County, floating the goods he traded for down the Indiana river system by raft to the Ohio and Mississippi rivers and eventually to St. Louis. There he would sell the goods, pocket the gold payment, and walk hundreds of miles back to his home in Randolph County. Edward Edger also became a small-time banker. He even dabbled in politics, serving one term in the Indiana General Assembly (1843–45). In 1860, he started a grain operation

10. For a brief history of Liber College, see Michael McBride, "College Long Gone, But History Still Strong," *Muncie (Ind.) Star Press,* January 13, 1997, sec. D, p. 1, col. 1. From 1859 to 1868, more than 850 students, mostly from Jay County, attended Liber College.

11. Goodrich, "Autobiography," pp. 3–8. In his autobiography, James Goodrich repeatedly refers to the strong religious convictions of his parents.

12. "Edward Edger," in *Randolph County History: 1818–1990* (Paducah, Ky.: Turner Publishing, 1991), p. 504.

on the very spot on which his grandsons would establish in 1898 the Goodrich Brothers Grain and Hay Company. His wife, Jane Putnam Edger, was a devoted member of the Presbyterian Church.[13]

James Goodrich's father, John B. Goodrich, was a deeply religious Congregationalist who was the superintendent of his local church's Sunday school. He was also the father of five surviving sons. In 1938, James Goodrich wrote about his father in his unpublished autobiography: "Often men would come to me in the early years of my life and say to me, 'if you are half as good a man as your father was, you will be all right.'"[14] Thus, the seeds of political involvement and religious heritage were planted early in the Goodrich family history. The significance of this religious heritage may be illustrated by a vignette. When James Goodrich was campaigning for governor in 1916, a local man by the name of John Callahan came to him and said that he owed his life to Goodrich's father. Callahan told James Goodrich,

> I met your father in the woods on the Goodrich farm, Northeast of Winchester, one Sunday afternoon, and he spoke to me about my excessive drinking. I told your Father I had tried very hard to quit but it seemed I was unable to do so. I have time and again resolved never to touch it again only to yield when liquor was available. Your father said to me, "The trouble with you, John, is you are depending upon your own strength. If you will ask the help of God you will be able to overcome your habit," and he then asked me to get down on my knees with him in the woods and ask God's help. Your father put his arm around me and asked God to help and strengthen me, and from that day to this I have never touched liquor in any form.[15]

13. Richard Wise, "Goodrich Grandfather Lived Eventful Life," *Winchester (Ind.) News-Gazette,* February 17, 1984, p. 1, col. 2.

14. James Goodrich's memories of his father were few and vague because of his father's early death. He does mention in his unfinished autobiography, however, that he was constantly reminded by local citizens of his father's outstanding character. Goodrich, "Autobiography," p. 5.

15. Ibid., pp. 5–6.

Toward the end of 1871, John B. Goodrich became ill with tuberculosis. He finally left his family in October 1872 to travel south in the hope of regaining his health, but he died in Atlanta, Georgia, on November 2. John B. Goodrich, deceased at forty-one, left his widow, Elizabeth, thirty-two, with five sons: Percy Edgar, eleven; James Putnam, eight; John Baldwin, six; Edward Shields, four; and William Wallace, sixteen months.[16]

The Goodrich family owned approximately five hundred acres of Randolph County farm ground at the time of John Goodrich's death. Nonetheless, the Goodriches were far from being a wealthy family. It was through the strength of Elizabeth Edger Goodrich, who never remarried but raised five rambunctious and strong-willed sons by herself, that the family slowly gained wealth and influence in Indiana. The Goodrich brothers were known throughout their lives as tough business competitors. They worked in concert for their mutual benefit. This sense of familial protection, of looking out for each other, had been instilled in the brothers from their childhood. James Goodrich recounts the stability his mother brought to these five fatherless boys:

> My mother was a woman of wonderful character, great common sense, and with faith as firm as my father's. . . . Her life was devoted entirely to her children. Her sons were not all alike. She was continually looking out for those of us who needed assistance. Above all else she urged us to stand together. I remember one circumstance when she had the five boys around her and handed to us a bundle of five sticks, bound tightly together, and asked us to break the bundle. This we had not strength enough to do. She untied the bundle and handed us the separate sticks and we had no difficulty in breaking them one by one. She used this as an illustration emphasizing the importance of standing by each other and said to us, "As long as you boys do so no one can harm you; should you become divided failure will be your lot."[17]

16. Ibid., pp. 3–5.
17. Ibid., p. 8.

All the Goodrich brothers enjoyed successful business careers, but none of them had the financial acumen or ambition that James possessed. Even as a small boy, James Goodrich had learned to turn a profit through painstaking physical labor. He worked long, hard hours on the family's farms in the 1870s and 1880s: He planted and harvested crops, ditched fields, sawed and piled wood for neighbors for fifty cents a cord, ran a threshing machine, and baled hay.[18] Life on a farm in post–Civil War times was difficult, requiring unusual ingenuity and frugality. James Goodrich recalled:

> Money was scarce and hard to get. We produced everything we possibly could. We ran our lye and made our own soap. We planted a bit of sugar cane and made our own sorghum. We also planted a little patch of broom corn and made our own broom. We tapped the trees in what we then called the "sugar camp," on which is now located the Goodrich Experimental Farm, and made our own syrup and sugar. We molded our own candles using tallow from the sheep we killed, hardened with bees wax, which came from the hives of bees we always kept.[19]

Life was not all hard work and drudgery, however. In the Goodrich brothers' free time, they managed to entertain themselves by playing cards and marbles, attending local dances, and attempting to play musical instruments. In July 1876, when James Goodrich was just twelve years old, he and his older brother Percy, who was just fourteen, traveled alone to Philadelphia to attend the country's Centennial Exposition. They stayed for ten days, visited Liberty Hall and the Liberty Bell, and saw what was then considered a bawdy performance by a woman who appeared on stage "clad [only] in tights from head to foot."[20] Roughhousing was not uncommon for the boys either. James Goodrich recalled:

18. Ibid., pp. 14–18.
19. Ibid., p. 11.
20. Ibid., pp. 21–22.

> Winchester was then divided into two sections by what is now the Big Four Railroad—that part along the north side of the road was called "Goose Pasture" and south of the road was called "Dog Town," and rivalry between the two sections very great. In Goose Pasture there was a lot of Irish, Fitzgeralds, Lavins, Currans, Radys, Ryans, and I was one-quarter Irish myself—we could usually lick the fellows on the south side and did so when the provocation seemed to justify a resort to physical force.[21]

James Goodrich's boyhood seems to have been marked by hard work, study, and a desire to get ahead. In only a few years, he would be exposed to the most important activities of his successful life: business and politics.

21. Ibid., p. 20.

Chapter 3

Youth and Experience

Life [in the 1870s] was hard but it was wholesome. There was plenty of work to do and the problem of how to keep the child busy didn't exist in those days.

JAMES P. GOODRICH, "Autobiography"

IN THE SUMMER of 1880, between his junior and senior years at Winchester High School, James Goodrich worked to develop the Fountain Park Cemetery, located on the south edge of Winchester. The forty-acre site had recently been purchased and donated to the town by Asahel Stone, a former Civil War general. Stone had achieved recognition by serving as quartermaster general for Indiana during the war. His responsibilities included securing supplies, provisions, and medical attention for Hoosier soldiers in the field. He became a legend in his own right, building one of the largest mansions in east-central Indiana, at the south end of Meridian Street in Winchester. General Stone also served in Indiana's General Assembly (1848–49, 1871–73) and was the third president of the Randolph County Bank.[1]

For all his hard manual labor in the cemetery, James Goodrich earned only slightly more than a dollar a day for ten hours of labor.[2] Yet the future Indiana governor was able to save enough that summer not only to meet his own personal expenses but also to make small loans

1. See entry on A. Stone in Ebenezer Tucker, *History of Randolph County, Indiana* (Chicago: A. L. Kingman, 1882), pp. 324–25.

2. Goodrich, "Autobiography," pp. 20–21.

to "less industrious companions."[3] One such companion was James E. Watson, a classmate of Jim Goodrich's from the time they were small children. Jim Goodrich was pleased to have the work and decided to ask James Watson if he would be interested in a job as well. Goodrich recorded the incident in his autobiography:

> Jim Watson never had any money and at my suggestion he agreed to work at the cemetery and I got Uncle Billy to give him a job. He worked until noon the first day—didn't show up at 1 o'clock. I went to see what the trouble was. Watson lived then at the old home place two blocks north of the cemetery [on South Main Street next to the Winchester Nazarene Church]. I found him lying under a cherry tree, face sunburned, hands blistered, and thoroughly disgusted with physical work. He told me he would not go back to that "damn place" for all the money in the world.[4]

James Goodrich and James Watson attended the local Winchester schools together and graduated from Winchester High School in 1881. Their studies were rigorous and included geometry, trigonometry, higher algebra, Stoddard's Mental Arithmetic, literature, history, and Virgil. Among the other seven graduating classmates were James Goodrich's older brother Percy; John Commons, who later obtained a doctorate in economics and served as head of the economics department at the University of Wisconsin; and Cora J. Frist, whom James Goodrich would marry seven years later.[5] The school had no library at the time and no visible means of raising funds to establish one. Therefore, in 1880, the students relied on their ingenuity and decided to establish a lecture series in order to raise money for a library. Joseph Farrand Tuttle, president of Wabash College in Crawfordsville, Indiana, delivered the first lecture. The second presenter was Indiana's beloved poet James Whitcomb Riley. Riley returned to lecture in 1881, although nei-

3. Ibid., p. 22.
4. Ibid., p. 21.
5. Ibid., p. 23.

ther time did the class raise enough money to pay the total amount of his fees.[6]

James Watson and James Goodrich remained lifelong friends, although their friendship was often marred by political rivalry and jealousy. For example, in his memoirs, written in 1936, Watson does not mention James Goodrich even once.[7] Watson later served in the United States House of Representatives and Senate for nearly thirty years. In addition to being the United States Senate majority leader from 1929 to 1933, Watson held the position of majority whip under the well-known Speaker of the House Joseph Cannon from 1904 to 1908. Moreover, in 1908, eight years before James Goodrich would win the office himself, Watson was the Republican candidate for governor of Indiana.

Cora Frist, an attractive and bright young woman, had moved to Winchester in 1879 from Lynn, Indiana, a small town ten miles south of Winchester. Cora was born in Middleborough, in Wayne County, Indiana, in 1861. She was more than two years older than James Goodrich. Her parents were Jonas Frist, a native of Preble County, Ohio, and the former Amy Stidham, who had been reared in Philadelphia, Pennsylvania. Cora had a younger sister by the name of Toda ("Todie"). Her father had operated a tile company in Lynn before moving to Winchester. Cora would be courted by both James Goodrich and James Watson.[8]

In 1881, after graduating from Winchester High School, James Goodrich, James Watson, and Cora Frist took the Indiana state teacher's licensing examination. At the time, neither a college degree nor course work was required in order to teach in Indiana. All three passed the

6. Percy E. Goodrich, "James Whitcomb Riley," *Down in Indiana* 57 (October 9, 1948).

7. James E. Watson, *As I Knew Them* (Indianapolis: Bobbs-Merrill, 1936).

8. According to the records, Cora was born on June 26, 1861. This would make her more than two and a half years older than Goodrich. It is puzzling that she would have graduated in his class. James's brother Percy was three years older than James, however, and James wrote in his autobiography that Percy also graduated in the Winchester High School class of 1881. Pierre's middle name, Frist, was his mother's maiden name.

examination and subsequently began teaching in Randolph County schools. James Watson, however, quit teaching after only a week to attend Asbury College in Greencastle, Indiana, which, within a year, was to be renamed DePauw University. Ironically, James Goodrich was asked by the local school superintendent to replace Watson. He took the position and began teaching twelve students in a one-room schoolhouse five miles southwest of Winchester. At the time, more than one hundred one-room schoolhouses dotted the Randolph County countryside.[9]

James Goodrich had planned to teach for only one year. From childhood, Goodrich had dreamed of a naval career. He had long been fascinated by the prospects of a life at sea, largely because of the stories of relatives, especially those of an uncle, Will Gilpatrick. Gilpatrick had become a rear admiral in the United States Navy shortly after the Civil War.[10] In the autumn of 1881, James Goodrich received an appointment to the United States Naval Academy from Congressman Thomas M. Browne of Winchester. Browne had represented the Sixth Congressional District since 1876; he had served as a brigadier general in the Civil War and was the Republican gubernatorial candidate in the election of 1872. He was also a first cousin to James Watson's mother.[11]

In 1881, James Goodrich had passed the written examination and was waiting for formal admission to the Naval Academy at Annapolis, Maryland. Sadly, the young man was forced to give up his dream. Just four weeks after he began teaching, a tree limb fell on him while he was shaking free hickory nuts. James was knocked temporarily unconscious,

9. See "Schools in Randolph County 1900–1926," in *Randolph County History: 1818–1990,* p. 334.

10. Goodrich, "Autobiography," p. 23. James Goodrich also discussed his plans to enter the Naval Academy in an extensive article about the future governor in Earl Mushlitz's "Issues of the Indiana Campaign as James P. Goodrich Sees Them," *Indianapolis Star,* September 1916, magazine section, p. 2, col. 1.

11. For a summary of Thomas Browne's life, see *Randolph County History: 1818–1990,* p. 211.

and his right hip was badly broken, which made it impossible for him to pass the Naval Academy's rigorous physical examination.[12]

Goodrich farmed and taught another year at a schoolhouse of sixty students three miles east of Winchester. Then, in September 1883, after two years of teaching, James Goodrich followed his good friend James Watson to DePauw University. Because of his advanced studies in high school, Goodrich was admitted as a conditional sophomore. At DePauw, he joined the Phi Kappa Psi Fraternity and became the friend of another brilliant student and orator by the name of Albert Beveridge. Beveridge, like James Watson, would become a prominent United States senator from Indiana and a gubernatorial candidate.[13] Goodrich noted an intense rivalry and jealousy between Watson and Beveridge that would last the rest of their lives. "Beveridge was tireless in his work," Goodrich recalled, while "Watson was lazy but his great natural ability and amazing memory carried him through."[14]

Goodrich and Watson left DePauw in 1885 before either obtained a degree. James Goodrich was forced to quit after only two years because he had exhausted his finances, and James Watson was expelled just days before he was scheduled to graduate, because he had written and published an obscene pamphlet about the male students of the sophomore class.[15]

Unsure of his future, Goodrich decided to pursue farming. He sought his fortune in the Red River Valley in a territory that was simply known as "Dakota." It would not be until four years later that the territory became divided into the separate states of North Dakota and South Da-

12. Goodrich, "Autobiography," p. 23.

13. Ibid., p. 26. Beveridge was also a national leader of the Progressive Party and the author of a number of serious political biographies. Watson was the Republican candidate for governor in 1908, Beveridge was the Progressive candidate for governor in 1912, and James Goodrich was the Republican candidate for governor in 1916. Goodrich was the only one of the three to reach the statehouse, although both Watson and Beveridge had long and distinguished careers in the United States Senate and in national politics in general.

14. Ibid., p. 26.

15. A copy of the bawdy pamphlet that got James Watson expelled from DePauw University is located in the Indiana State Library, James E. Watson Papers, box 2.

kota. During the latter part of the summer of 1885, he and his uncle, John "Ches" Macy, worked on a farm about twenty miles southwest of Big Stone Lake in what is now South Dakota. The two men lived in a sod house and stayed long enough to harvest a wheat crop and plant five hundred acres of spring wheat. In the fall of 1885, Goodrich attempted to buy a wheat ranch from a Swedish farmer by the name of Johnny Gustason, but the deal fell through when they could not agree upon a price. Upon the advice of Ches Macy, James returned to Indiana and took up the study of law.[16]

Expelled from DePauw in May, James Watson had already returned to Winchester by this time. Goodrich joined him, and the two became students together again, this time studying law under the former Randolph circuit court judge John J. Cheney and Enos Watson, James Watson's father. For fifteen months, James Watson and James Goodrich recited each morning from such great common-law writers as Blackstone, Chitty, and Kent, and then served their apprenticeships in the afternoons. They were admitted to Indiana's bar on November 2, 1886.[17]

The two future politicians practiced law for the next seven years (1887–94) in offices above the old Randolph County Bank at the northeast corner of Washington and Meridian streets in Winchester. Watson first practiced with his father, while James Goodrich became a partner with his uncle Ches Macy and Ed Jaqua in the firm of Macy, Jaqua and Goodrich. Goodrich learned the rudiments of lawyering by drafting deeds, mortgages, and contracts, and by representing clients before the justice of the peace.[18] In 1892, the small firm merged with that of Enos

16. Goodrich, "Autobiography," p. 27.

17. Ibid.

18. James Goodrich claimed in his autobiography that he and James Watson practiced law together from 1887 to 1894, but it appears that they worked in the same office only in 1893, when James Watson's father, Enos, retired, giving his place in the firm of Macy, Watson and Goodrich to his son. James Watson and Goodrich had, however, practiced in adjacent offices during the previous six years. Because of their proximity, they would have consulted with each other on a regular basis regarding legal and political matters even though they did not work for the same firm. In January 1894, a newly married James Watson moved to Rushville, Indiana, where he practiced law. In November 1894, he was elected to the United States House of Representatives.

and James Watson and became known as Watson, Macy and Goodrich. In November 1892, Enos Watson became ill and was forced to retire. He passed away in January 1893. James Watson took his father's position in the firm and practiced with Macy and Goodrich until the end of 1893.[19]

Through all these changes, John Winchester "Ches" Macy remained the constant figure in James Goodrich's life. Macy was extremely important to the Goodrich family, and his ties extended back to James Goodrich's father and mother. Macy's wife, the former Sarah Edger, and James Goodrich's mother, Elizabeth Edger, were sisters. At the age of nineteen, Macy had joined the Eighty-fourth Indiana Volunteer Infantry, and he fought and was wounded at the Battle of Chickamauga in Georgia. When he returned to Winchester after the Civil War, he first worked under James Goodrich's father, John B. Goodrich, in the county clerk's office. He later was elected clerk himself before being elected senator to the Indiana State Assembly for one term (1885–89). At one time or another, Macy held the positions of Randolph County Republican chairman, Republican chairman of the Eighth Congressional District, and Randolph Circuit Court judge (1902–8).[20] He became the chief mentor and surrogate father to James Goodrich. The relationship between the two families continued into the next generation. Macy was the father of John Macy, Jr., who became Pierre Goodrich's first law partner.

By 1885, James Goodrich had had Cora Frist on his mind for several years but had failed to act. The two had many mutual interests, including books, music, and art. Finally, after a whirlwind courtship, James proposed. Still, it would be three years before they would marry. As he wrote to Pierre in his autobiography: "I became engaged to your mother when I was twenty-one years old, and I am sure that the wish to consummate that engagement had much to do with my desire to get into

19. Leander J. Monks, "James P. Goodrich," in *Courts and Lawyers of Indiana*, vol. 3 (Indianapolis: Federal Publishing, 1916), p. 1397. Macy and Goodrich practiced law with John Cheney for five years (1893–98). After that, Cheney retired, and his position in the firm was filled by Alonzo L. Nichols.

20. For a brief sketch of John Winchester Macy's early life, see Ebenezer Tucker, *History of Randolph County, Indiana*, p. 319.

something whereby I could earn an income sufficient to justify our marriage." The couple married on March 15, 1888, in Cora's hometown of Lynn. The other four Goodrich brothers would also take brides: Percy married Susan Engle, John married Charlotte Martin, Edward married Elizabeth Neff, and William Wallace married Charlotte Moore. The marriage of James and Cora would last until James Goodrich's death more than fifty-two years later.[21]

21. Mary Waldon, "Only Son Fondly Remembers Baking in Home at Winchester," *Indianapolis Star,* September 27, 1964, sec. 7, p. 4, col. 1.

Chapter 4

Initiation into Politics

I became interested in politics at a very early age. I remember as far back as 1876, the campaign when [Rutherford B.] Hayes was really defeated for President by [Samuel J.] Tilden but through maneuvering of Oliver P. Morton and others Hayes was counted in. I was only twelve years old at that time but I distinctly remember one great rally that they held in Winchester.

JAMES P. GOODRICH, "Autobiography"

IN THE EARLY 1890s, James Goodrich was described in a Randolph County history as "a rising young lawyer of Winchester." [1] He had been appointed city attorney by the town council at the "huge" salary of $50 per year. In 1888, James's share in his private legal practice with Macy and Jaqua amounted to $720; he wrote to Pierre that only "by the practice of the most rigid economy [were we] able to save a small portion of that." [2]

Although James Goodrich was extremely busy practicing law, he also took an interest in a number of community and fraternal groups. The first was the Granger movement, which he had first joined locally in 1881. The National Grange of the Patrons of Husbandry was established in 1867 to broaden the educational awareness of America's farmers and to further their interests. By 1875, the National Grange claimed more

1. "James P. Goodrich," *History of Delaware and Randolph Counties* (Chicago: A. W. Bowen, 1894), p. 886.

2. Goodrich, "Autobiography," p. 28.

than 800,000 members in 20,000 local chapters.[3] Goodrich also took part in the Knights of Labor, which he was a member of from 1882 until 1894. His association with the labor organization was significant. It gave him an appreciation for the common worker. Goodrich found that while the laborer might not be able to articulate why he thought as he did, he generally reached the right conclusion by instinct. Once a month, James Goodrich would join members of the local chapter on the third floor of the Knights of Labor building, located on the south side of the town square. There the local body debated the issues of the day: secret ballot, woman suffrage, child labor, prohibition, workmen's compensation, and other matters.[4] Goodrich was also a member, along with James Watson, of the Winchester chapter of the Knights of Pythias, a secret fraternal order that engaged in philanthropic activities. James Watson became even more active in this organization than Goodrich, rising to the position of grand chancellor of the order in Indiana in June 1893, the youngest head of the order up to that time. In 1892, Goodrich became a Mason, joining the Winchester Lodge, No. 56.[5]

In the late 1880s, James Goodrich became deeply involved with politics. Through his uncle Ches Macy, Goodrich learned the art of politicking. Besides serving in the Indiana General Assembly as the joint senator from Delaware and Randolph counties from 1885 to 1889, Macy served at the time as Randolph County Republican chairman. James Goodrich recalls his political indoctrination:

3. For a more extensive discussion of the significance of the Granger movement, see T. Harry Williams, Richard N. Current, and Frank Freidel, *A History of the United States: Since 1865* (New York: Alfred A. Knopf, 1959), pp. 180–84.

4. Goodrich, "Autobiography," pp. 24–25. There is a discrepancy regarding when Goodrich ended his association with the Knights of Labor. On page 25 of his autobiography, he writes that he ceased to be a member in 1894, when he was forced to resign because he had become a member of the Randolph County Bar. Goodrich actually became a member of the bar in November 1886.

5. "James E. Watson," *History of Delaware and Randolph Counties*, pp. 996–98; regarding James Goodrich's connections to Freemasonry, see "Indiana's Masonic Governors," *The Indiana Freemason* 40 (October 1962): 9.

> [Uncle Ches] was interested in young men and had a lot of young fellows around him all the time doing the "leg work" and acquiring experience in politics. Nearly all of those in active political life were then members of the Grand Army of the Republic. They were still fighting the Civil War. . . . I was invited into political meetings, or caucuses as we called them, after my uncle became County Chairman and I had great fun hauling in voters and running errands for the County Organization.[6]

Goodrich's early participation in politics and law enabled him to associate with local men, mostly attorneys, of great talent and ambition. Besides Macy, these men included Thomas Browne, former general, Republican gubernatorial candidate, and Sixth District congressman; James Watson and his father, Enos Watson, who served in the Indiana General Assembly (1867–69, 1879–81); James S. Engle, who served in the Indiana General Assembly during the time that he was law mentor to Goodrich and James Watson (1885–87); Silas Canada, who served in the General Assembly during the four years in which James acted as Republican county chairman (1896–1900); Union B. Hunt, elected secretary of state (1899–1903); Leander J. Monks, who served as judge on the Indiana Supreme Court from 1895 to 1913; and Frederick S. Caldwell, who would serve as a judge on the Indiana Court of Appeals from 1913 to 1919. Moreover, Isaac P. Gray, who lived just ten miles east of Winchester in Union City, was a former Civil War general, state senator (1868–70), lieutenant governor of Indiana (1876–80), and governor (1880–81, 1885–89). Gray went on to become a Democratic presidential candidate in 1892 and 1896, and United States ambassador to Mexico from 1893 to 1895.[7] All of these men from Randolph County were active in law or politics when James Goodrich was just getting his start.

In 1886, Goodrich began his own foray into politics. He was elected

6. Goodrich, "Autobiography," p. 30.

7. "Isaac P. Gray," in *Randolph County History: 1818–1990,* pp. 518–19; Wilber D. Peat, "Isaac P. Gray," *Portraits and Painters of the Governors of Indiana, 1800–1978* (Indianapolis: Indiana Historical Society, 1978), p. 50.

precinct councilman and practiced pragmatic politics as he had been taught. Clearly, it was a time before election laws and political ethics as we know them today. Goodrich writes:

> Those were the days of open ballot. There was no hesitancy about buying votes and men such as I have mentioned not only countenanced it but engaged in it either directly or indirectly [as a] patriotic duty [where] ends equalled means. The floaters would be with "spirits" and led to the polls early in the morning. It was with a great deal of pride that occasionally I was permitted to lead one of the floaters down to the polls and when there handed him a ticket which he gave to the election clerk and then returned to the headquarters to receive his reward.[8]

By this time, James Goodrich had become intoxicated himself, not with alcohol, but with the "spirits" of politics. He followed national, state, and local elections with keen interest, but without any apparent desire to become a candidate himself. In 1890, Ches Macy was elected Republican chairman of Indiana's Eighth Congressional District. As Macy had been Goodrich's most important mentor in law, so he was in politics. During these early years, James Goodrich met such national political figures as Benjamin Harrison, who was elected president in 1888; William Jennings Bryan, Democratic presidential nominee in 1896, 1900, and 1908; Mark Hanna, a wealthy Ohio industrialist who became national Republican Party chairman; William McKinley, who was elected president in 1896; and Theodore Roosevelt, vice-president under McKinley and later the twenty-sixth president of the United States.[9]

8. Goodrich, "Autobiography," p. 31.

9. Goodrich states in his autobiography that he met Harrison, McKinley, and Hanna. See "Autobiography," pp. 33, 41. Florence Dunn, niece of James Goodrich and ninety-seven years old when she was interviewed in 1992, told the author that she and James Goodrich had met William Jennings Bryan when he came to speak in Winchester at around the turn of the century. She said that she had, in fact, ridden on Bryan's lap on the train from Union City to Winchester (interview, July 18, 1992). Since Goodrich was Republican chairman of the Eighth Congressional District when Theodore Roosevelt spoke at a rally in Winchester on October 11, 1900, the author assumes that Goodrich had met Roosevelt by that time.

Contact with these national figures would cause James Goodrich to think about his own political future.

There was another rising young attorney and political star of Winchester by the name of James who had his sights on statewide and national office. By the early 1890s, James Watson had already confided in James Goodrich that he wanted someday to become governor of Indiana and, later, president of the United States. Watson's first two ventures in politics, however, were complete failures. He withdrew in 1892 as a candidate for joint senator of Randolph and Delaware counties when a Republican Party leader threatened to disclose an incriminating letter that Watson had written to him. Recognizing that he had made too many enemies in Randolph County to pursue a successful political career there, James Watson left his law practice with Macy and Goodrich at the end of 1893.

Watson moved to Rushville, Indiana, the county seat of Rush County, approximately sixty miles southeast of Winchester. He next sought election as Indiana's secretary of state in 1894. His nomination, made by Goodrich, failed at the state Republican convention. Shortly after his attempt to gain the secretary of state's post, Watson announced himself as a Republican candidate for Congress. Miraculously, Watson beat a popular thirty-year incumbent in the November 1894 election. Watson's success was partially a result of his indefatigable campaigning: He had been speaking for the Indiana Republican Party since the age of twenty; in one year alone (1888), he had given more than one hundred political speeches in some forty-six Indiana counties. Watson also attributed his success partially to his ability to address in their native language the large German constituency of his new district. In support of his childhood chum, James Goodrich garnered the backing of the Republican National Committee, and he personally contributed five hundred dollars to Watson's congressional campaign.[10]

Ironically, once Watson made it to Washington, D.C., he was none

10. Goodrich, "Autobiography," pp. 34–35.

too pleased with the position he had campaigned so exhaustively to gain. In a typically humorous letter to Goodrich, Watson dispels the idea that any glamour was involved in the position.

> My Dear Friend:
> . . . I am disgusted with the entire life of a Congressman. A member from Indiana is no more than a Fourth-rate Pension Attorney and a distributer of garden seeds and public documents. He has no time to give to questions of great interests. He has no time in which to study the needs of the people or to devote to matters of public legislation. He is simply a dog, and every fellow in his district in the whole state can bawl: "Sic! sic! Take him Towzer!" And he is compelled to take him or lose his job.
>
> The fact is that Congressional life is not what it is supposed to be. Distance lends enchantment to the view. There is a glamor about it which conceals its real character. I came here, expecting something of that kind, because Tom Brown had opened my eyes to it, but it is much worse than I anticipated. . . . We have no time for study. We have no time for intellectual pursuits. We simply answer letters, frank documents and send out garden seeds. It is a life of drudgery and there is nothing easy or delightful about it.
>
> At the same time, I may desire to return. If I do, I shall simply do the best I can when the race comes. If I am beaten, I am out of politics forever. If I win, Heaven only knows what my future will be, but whatever comes, Jim, and whatever may be the changes or mutations of the future, I have never had a friend of whom I have thought more than yourself, and no matter what the days to come may bring forth, that friendship shall remain unchanged.[11]

Goodrich began to experience politics firsthand himself, making his maiden political speech in 1896. He addressed a crowd of some two thousand in Winchester. He spoke on the issue of whether the country should have two standards of monetary value—one gold, the other silver. The topic now seems archaic and of little consequence. Yet at the time, the "subject of the Gold Standard vs Free Silver at the ratio of 16

11. Letter from Watson to Goodrich, February 4, 1897, James P. Goodrich Papers, box 28.

to 1 was discussed everywhere where two or more people were gathered together," Goodrich claimed. He went on to state that the national debate was "the greatest educational campaign ever held in America."[12]

James Goodrich's exposure to local politicking would provide him with experience and lead to bigger opportunities in the realm of politics—leading the Indiana state Republican Party, serving on the national Republican Party's executive committee, and gaining the governor's office. He had thrust himself into what was then the great American pastime.

12. Goodrich, "Autobiography," pp. 40–41.

Chapter 5

The Early Years, 1894–1900

July 30, 1901

Pierre,

I got your letter. I have been looking after the cellar and it is all right and the water did not get into it. Muggins came over to the house this morning and I gave her some milk and a piece of meat. She was glad to get it and hunted around as if she were hunting for a little boy about the size of Pierre.

I want you to be sure and write to Uncle Percy for he wants to get a letter from you. Keep out as much as you can and play and have a good time. Good bye, dear and write to papa, he is always glad to hear from you and Mamma.

Papa (letter from James Goodrich to Pierre, in Colorado Springs)

JAMES AND CORA GOODRICH had been married for five years when they expected the birth of their first child. Their anticipation was, however, met with deep sadness. On May 16, 1893, the baby (a girl to whom the couple had already given the name Jean) was born dead. Less than sixteen months later, however, on September 10, 1894, a much happier event occurred when the Goodriches' son Pierre was born at their East Franklin Street home in Winchester.

On the local scene in Winchester, Pierre's birth coincided with the "Colossal" Lemen Brothers' traveling circus. The circus featured Rajah, claimed to be the biggest "brute" (elephant) on earth (circuses, then, as today, were known to do a bit of puffing).[1] On the national front, 1894 marked the year that President Grover Cleveland first gave civil servants Christmas Day off. It was also a time when a man was not a substantial

1. See "Lemen Bros. New Colossal Shows" (advertisement), *Winchester (Ind.) Journal,* September 7, 1894, p. 5, col. 1.

member of society unless he wore a mustache. While upcoming years would justify the decade's being remembered as the "gay nineties," in September 1894 there was little to be happy about. The country was plunged into one of the worst depressions in its history.[2]

The causes of the disastrous economic times were many and complicated: The 1880s had been a boom period in which overexpansion and overinvestment in railroads and industry had occurred. Moreover, farmers were suffering greatly because of extremely depressed farm prices and decreased demand from Europe for their produce. Inflation had increased substantially as a result of the Sherman Silver Purchase Act, legislation that required the federal government to buy increased amounts of silver.[3] President Cleveland was confronted with a failed economy and a disenchanted electorate. Within a six-month period, 156 railroads went into receivership, 400 banks suspended operations, and more than 8,000 businesses went bankrupt. As many as one million workers found themselves thrown out of jobs.[4]

Except for signs of modern culture at its edges (a strip of highway on the east end of town, complete with McDonald's, Pizza Hut, Wal-Mart, and Taco Bell), the appearance of Winchester, Indiana, today differs little from what it was at the turn of the century. Its streets are lined with stately sycamores, elms, and hard maples. The town serves as the county seat of a rural community area. A community of approximately five thousand residents, Winchester is much like those small towns nostalgically described by the Indiana poet James Whitcomb Riley. In fact, three of Riley's grandparents are buried in area cemeteries, and his parents were reared and later married in Randolph County.[5] Riley himself

2. See H. W. Brand, *The Reckless Decade: America in the 1890s* (New York: St. Martin's Press, 1995), p. 47.

3. Williams, Current, and Freidel, *A History of the United States: Since 1865*, p. 200.

4. Brand, *The Reckless Decade*, p. 47.

5. Riley's parents, Reuben Alexander Riley and Elizabeth Marine, were married in 1844 in Unionport, Indiana. See "Unionport," in *Randolph County History: 1818–1990*, p. 69. According to Florence Dunn, Pierre's first cousin, when Riley visited Winchester, her father, Ed Goodrich (Pierre's uncle), would always have her memorize one of Riley's poems and recite it to the master as a special gift (interview, July 18, 1992).

worked in the county as a sign painter and printer for a year in the 1870s. In later life, he occasionally returned to Winchester to deliver his homespun verse. He also occasionally played in a medicine show on the town square. Riley would sing comic songs and draw pictures to entertain the crowds while his companion, a Dr. Sears, lectured and tried to sell a medicinal elixir that was commonly sold during those times to treat all kinds of ailments.[6]

At the turn of the century, Winchester still had a large number of Quakers as well as several hundred Civil War veterans. Randolph County sent nearly twenty-four hundred men to fight for the Northern cause, including fifty black soldiers. Despite the strong pacifist sentiments of the Quaker population, most of the county's Quakers supported the war because of their even stronger abolitionist beliefs.[7] For runaway slaves, Winchester was a stop along a major route leading from the deep South to Canada. Levi Coffin, chief engineer of this fabled Underground Railroad, lived just four miles south of Randolph County in Newport (now Fountain City), Indiana. He helped provide safe passage for more than three thousand black fugitives.[8] Randolph County was also home to the Union Literary Institute, which was founded in 1845 to educate black children as well as students of other races. The importance of the Civil War to local people is still evident today: the tallest county Civil War monument in the state of Indiana, dedicated in July 1892, is located on the town's square.[9]

6. Percy Goodrich's memories of the Hoosier poet are contained in "James Whitcomb Riley," *Down in Indiana* 57 (October 9, 1948). According to Florence Dunn, Riley and Percy Goodrich shared the same birthday, October 7, and Riley would often stay with Percy and his wife Claudia when he visited Winchester (interview, July 18, 1992). Percy Goodrich makes mention of none of this, however, in his brief memoir of Riley, which calls Florence Dunn's memory into question.

7. See Jacqueline S. Nelson, *Indiana Quakers Confront the Civil War* (Indianapolis: Indiana Historical Society, 1991).

8. See Eric Rodenberg, "The Levi Coffin Home: Story of the Underground Railroad," *Winchester (Ind.) News-Gazette*, October 9, 1976, historical supplement, pp. 4–5.

9. Former United States senator James E. Watson documents this in his memoirs, *As I Knew Them*, p. 13. The Civil War monument in Winchester was primarily the responsibility of two men: Jimmy Moorman, who, at his death, donated two thousand dollars toward the cost, and John W. Macy, Sr. Macy had legislation passed through the

Even as a small boy, Pierre Goodrich always preferred to be called "Peer" rather than the French pronunciation of his name.[10] He was born with a very weak right eye and wore glasses from a young age. The late Helen Engle Hart, who was 101 at the time she was interviewed, described the Winchester of the 1890s and early 1900s as an idyllic small town in which to grow up. She remembered Pierre as a shy, quiet, and studious boy. She further recalled that as children they used to visit each other's homes, attend each other's birthday parties, and exchange gifts. Their families also attended the same Presbyterian Church. Pierre and Mrs. Hart's younger brother, Russell Engle, were childhood friends and remained close throughout their lives.[11]

In 1894, Emily Isabelle "Belle" Edger, James Goodrich's aunt, returned to Winchester after having worked under Jane Addams at Hull House in Chicago. She persuaded Winchester's school board, on which James Goodrich served, to start a public kindergarten for the town's four- and five-year-old children. For the next fifty-five years, Aunt Belle taught kindergarten to hundreds of Winchester schoolchildren. From 1898 to 1900, Pierre attended public kindergarten, where his teacher was "Miss Belle"—his great aunt.[12]

Indiana General Assembly that made it possible for Randolph County residents to raise an additional twenty-three thousand dollars for the monument by means of a municipal bond.

10. Elizabeth Terry, interview, November 16, 1991. Richard Dennis, former president of the Great Books Foundation in Chicago, remembers that Pierre never liked to be called by the French pronunciation of his name and corrected Dennis on one occasion for doing so (telephone interview, September 30, 1992).

11. Helen Engle Hart, interview, May 10, 1992. Russell Engle attended Wabash College (1915–17) and the First Presbyterian Church of Winchester with Goodrich. The two men also served together for several years on the boards of the Peoples Loan and Trust Co. and Standard Securities. See "Dr. Russell B. Engle Dies; Was Medical Doctor in Randolph County for 46 Years," *Winchester (Ind.) News,* April 4, 1966, p. 1, col. 1.

12. Emily Isabelle Edger was the sister of James Goodrich's mother, Elizabeth Edger Goodrich. Aunt Belle, as she was affectionately known by the entire town, became an icon in Randolph County education. She taught kindergarten to several hundred schoolchildren, including her own five grandnieces and -nephews, over a span of nearly fifty-five years. See "Emily Isabelle Edger," in *Randolph County History: 1818–1990,* p. 330.

The following year further sadness struck the family: On September 10, 1901, Pierre's seventh birthday, his first cousin, James, the son of John and Charlotte Goodrich, died at the age of four. Another tragedy struck the family soon after. William Wallace, the youngest of the five Goodrich brothers, suffered a terrible loss when his wife, also named Charlotte, died during childbirth.

Despite these losses, growing up in the Goodrich household at the turn of the twentieth century was, for the most part, warm and joyous. In a 1964 interview, Pierre recounted fond memories of his early childhood. "Growing up at Winchester meant a wonderful boyhood," he recalled. "The first memory I have of my mother is of a dark enthusiastic woman sitting on the floor of our library with a friend of hers, both of them completely surrounded by books. . . . Saturday was a wonderful day in our house at Winchester. Mother assembled great hordes of relatives for Sunday dinner and Saturday was the day when pies, cakes, and bread were baked.

"Unless you have experienced it as a small boy, you can never know the wonderful baking aromas of Saturday at Winchester in the early 1900s," Pierre added.[13]

It is revealing that Pierre's first memory of his mother was associated with books. Cora was a passionate reader and was clearly the more intellectual of Pierre's parents, but James Goodrich was interested in books all his life as well. As a student at DePauw University, James had studied literature, certainly not an obvious major for a man whose life was dominated by more practical disciplines, such as agriculture, business, banking, politics, and law. James and Cora Goodrich had one of the finest private libraries in east-central Indiana.

During Pierre's boyhood, the family lived across from the First Presbyterian Church on Franklin Street. In 1913, after Pierre had left to study at Wabash College, James and Cora moved one block to South

13. Mary Waldon, "Only Son Fondly Remembers Baking in Home in Winchester," *Indianapolis Star,* September 27, 1964, sec. 7, p. 4, col. 1. The article, which is about Cora Goodrich, is one in a series of articles about wives of Indiana governors.

Street, where their newly built French Provincial mansion stood as a landmark in Winchester for the next sixty-five years.[14] At both homes, James and Cora had libraries filled with books on economics, religion, history, music, and literature. The Goodriches' new house reflected the interests of its occupants. A large reception hall was the first room that visitors entered from the front door. On the left was the library and to the right was the music room. On the ground level there were also a sunroom, a large dining area, a kitchen, and a back porch. The walls and fixtures were made of cherry, oak, or mahogany, and the wood of the dark walls came from trees south of Winchester owned by Cora's parents.[15] On the second floor were five bedrooms and two bathrooms; on the third floor was a ballroom where James and Cora did most of their entertaining.[16]

Pierre's childhood was much like those of other boys in small midwestern towns, although his mother constantly hovered over him. The death of Cora's firstborn may well explain her protective attitude toward Pierre. While he was still quite young, Cora Goodrich bought him a violin. Pierre took lessons and played occasionally throughout his life. He also had a pet cat by the name of Muggins and a pony named Bessie.

14. Cora Goodrich told John Kidder that it was at her instigation that the building of the well-known Goodrich mansion on South Street was begun in 1912. She was tired of renting, but her husband was traveling so much as state director of the Republican Party and on business that he did not want to be bothered with building a house. Finally, after many pleas from his wife, the future governor consented to the building of the large mansion on three acres of property just three blocks from downtown. Salt Creek, a small creek that runs into the White River, is adjacent to the property, and it was there that James Goodrich and James Watson used to fish when they were boys. Kidder said that Cora Goodrich told him that James Goodrich finally gave in to his wife's requests to have the house built, but on one condition: that he would have to write only one check to pay for all of the work when it was completed (interview, October 10, 1991).

15. Ibid. According to John Kidder, when the Goodrich mansion was torn down in 1977, the paneling from the library was used in the basement of the newly constructed Peoples Loan and Trust Bank.

16. The description of the Goodriches' home at 226 East South Street in Winchester is taken from "James Putnam Goodrich," in *Randolph County History: 1818–1990*, p. 517.

His favorite pet, however, was a rooster. Pierre regularly placed his feathered pet in cockfights, which were fairly common at the time.[17]

Pierre was a member of a group of boys who called themselves the Six Jolly Urchins. The group was begun by Ida Kitselman McCamish, mother of Pierre's closest childhood friend, Carl McCamish. The young troupe included Pierre, Tom Veech, Carl McCamish, Ralph Bales, and several other Winchester boys. The boys had their own outfits and later became known as simply the S.J.U. club. For several years they sponsored monthly dances in the community.[18]

As Pierre grew older, his father's absence from the house grew more frequent because of his extensive political and business involvements. The traveling started even before Pierre's birth. For instance, in April 1893, James Goodrich went to Independence, Missouri, for several days to inquire about investing in gas exploration. A rumor had gone around the town that Goodrich was a representative from the Standard Oil Company and that he was there for the express purpose of buying up all the leasing rights. He was amused by the tremendous interest his presence had created among the townspeople.[19]

Travels two years later took James Goodrich south. In March 1895, Goodrich made an extensive tour of several southern states, visiting Louisiana, Alabama, Tennessee, and North Carolina. While hiking in the Smoky Mountains, "jumping from rock to rock," he fell forty feet down a mountainside, reinjuring the hip that he had broken in 1881. James later traveled down the Mississippi River on the steamship *Paul Tulane* and toured Baton Rouge and New Orleans. While he admired the architecture of New Orleans, the filth and odors of the southern city repulsed him. His southern exposure aroused in him a particular interest in the plight of the "Negro." He predicted in a letter to his wife that it would not be long before southern "Negroes" would be relocating in

17. Perce G. Goodrich, interview, May 2, 1993.

18. A brief remembrance of the S.J.U. club can be found in *Randolph County History: 1818–1990*, p. 379.

19. Letter from James P. Goodrich to Cora Goodrich, April 24, 1893 (in the possession of Priscilla Klosterman, R.R. 2, Box 265, Ridgeville, Indiana).

northern cities because so few opportunities were available to them in the South.[20]

In June 1901, Cora and Pierre traveled to Colorado Springs, Colorado, to stay with cousins for several weeks while Pierre recovered from an illness. James remained in Indiana. In early August, after he had just been appointed chairman of the state Republican Party, James traveled to Colorado to be with his wife and son.[21] The family visited Pikes Peak and toured the Pike National Forest in the Rocky Mountains by stagecoach. The experience left quite an impression on Pierre. In a letter he wrote some sixty years later to the great Austrian economist Friedrich Hayek, Pierre referred to the visit nostalgically. He was concerned that modern development and modes of travel were destroying the beautiful preserves he had seen as a child.[22]

Nothing in Pierre Goodrich's childhood was remarkable except that he was perhaps more dedicated to study and devoted to family than most boys his age. Yet these early years were a critical time in the formation of Pierre's character. They were years in which a strong sense of family, security, ingenuity, and other influences left lasting impressions. These influences helped to shape Pierre Goodrich's entrepreneurial drive, intellectual curiosity, and, probably most directly, his deep libertarian beliefs.

20. Letter from James P. Goodrich to Cora Goodrich, March 13, 1895 (in the possession of Priscilla Klosterman, R.R. 2, Box 265, Ridgeville, Indiana).

21. Letters from James P. Goodrich to Cora Goodrich in Colorado Springs: June 27, 1901; July 12, 1901; and July 22, 1901. Letters from James P. Goodrich to Pierre F. Goodrich in Colorado Springs: July 20, 1901; July 27, 1901; and July 30, 1901 (in the possession of Priscilla Klosterman, R.R. 2, Box 265, Ridgeville, Indiana).

22. Letter to Friedrich A. Hayek, February 18, 1959, F. A. Hayek Collection, box 22, folder 6, Hoover Institution on War, Revolution and Peace, Stanford, California.

Chapter 6

Entering the Business World

No agency of modern times has ever affected such marvelous transformations in business or wrought such rapid and easy fortunes for investors as Natural Gas. . . . Especially are these favoring conditions true in the Natural Gas Fields in and around . . . Indiana, a State notably enterprising and wealthy before her people had learned of the boundless reservoir of riches that lay beneath the surface of many of her oldest and richest counties, and a commonwealth that is since leaping forward to a destiny so great and near that it fairly dazzles the imagination to contemplate.

Gas Boom of Gas City, Indiana

They were exciting times. By the end of 1888, thousands of people came daily from all over the state to east-central Indiana on excursion trains to see the wonder. There, in fields where the most notable sights had previously been shocks of wheat and corn, beautiful flaming torches of light poured forth. The countryside was ablaze with the burning of millions of cubic feet of the best fuel in the world. What limestone had done for such communities as Bedford, Bloomington, and Ellettsville in the 1880s and 1890s and coal had done, during the same period, for Vigo, Sullivan, Vermillion, Knox, and Greene counties, natural gas did for small Indiana towns such as Dunkirk, Elwood, Fairmount, Farmland, Hartford City, Jonesboro, Knightstown, Muncie, Redkey, Portland, Salem, and Winchester.

In March 1892, one small town in Grant County, Harrisburg, took formal action in recognizing the transformation, renaming itself "Gas City."[1]

In the years from 1886 to 1892, the "natural gas craze" occurred. It started on March 14, 1886, in Portland, Indiana, when a well struck gas at a depth of 990 feet. The boom was on, with a frenzy reminiscent of a gold rush. By the following April, a local well was producing 5 million cubic feet daily. By January 1891, another well's daily output was nearly 15 million cubic feet. Wells by the hundreds were being drilled. By 1892, it was estimated that the gas fields of east-central Indiana were several times larger than the known combined size of all other gas fields in the United States. The fuel spouted from the ground with such ease that the state geologist estimated that by the latter half of 1887 there had been an average waste of one hundred million cubic feet of it a day.[2]

The cheap energy seemed unlimited. It brought to the area trainloads of newspaper reporters, capitalists, and the curious from such faraway places as Cincinnati, Buffalo, and New York City. In the late 1880s, three hundred members of the American Association for the Advancement of Science visited to witness the phenomenon. The find created unprecedented growth. By 1900, the population of Muncie, Indiana, just twenty-five miles west of the Goodriches' hometown, had grown to more than twenty thousand, quadrupling in size since 1880. Real estate speculation was at its zenith. One man who shied away from buying an eight-acre plot in Delaware County in 1888 for $1,600 found that only

1. See Logan Esarey, *A History of Indiana* (Indianapolis: Hoosier Heritage Press, 1970), pp. 910–12. Harrisburg, Indiana, officially changed its name to Gas City on March 21, 1892. See also *Gas Boom of Gas City, Indiana* (Indianapolis: Department of Geology and Natural Resources, 1892), pp. 4–5 (a souvenir book located in the Gas City Middle Township Public Library).

2. See *Gas Boom of Gas City,* pp. 5–6. There is a minor dispute regarding where the first gas well was struck. The town of Eaton, Indiana, only a few miles west of Jay County, claims that the first significant gas well was struck near there. See Keith Roysdon, "Eaton Market Tells of Town's Gas Boom Past," *Muncie (Ind.) Star Press,* August 12, 1996, sec. A, p. 3, col. 1.

sixty days later the property had changed hands five times and had doubled in price.[3]

The gas craze fueled nearly boundless growth in the Goodriches' hometown of Winchester. Around the town square, a dozen or more two-, three-, and four-story buildings popped up that are still the mainstay of the town's commercial center. Because of its cheap energy, the area attracted businesses in an unprecedented way. The result was an industrial explosion that was only slightly less dramatic than the natural gas find itself. The discovery of natural gas resulted in the relocation of dozens of industries, particularly foundries, that relied upon the cheap fuel to melt iron and other metals. The largest industry to exploit the gas resources was the glass industry, which relied upon the seemingly inexhaustible fuel to heat large demanding furnaces. In 1880, only 4 glass factories existed in Indiana; by 1900, there were 110, most of which were in east-central Indiana. The best-known, and ultimately the largest, glass company in the Midwest would be in Muncie. In 1887, five brothers, about the same ages as the five Goodrich brothers, had moved their company from Buffalo, New York, to Muncie to take advantage of the gas boom. They were the Ball family, and the corporation they founded is today a Fortune 500 company with more than thirteen thousand employees and $2 billion in annual sales.[4]

The Goodrich brothers were too savvy not to take advantage of the great gas boom. One of the first companies that the family held a substantial

3. See Robert S. Lynd and Helen Merrell Lynd, *Middletown: A Study in Contemporary American Culture* (New York: Harcourt, Brace, 1929), p. 15, n. 4.

4. For one of the best studies of the significance of the gas boom in transforming east-central Indiana from an agrarian area into a modern industrial area, see Dwight W. Hoover's *Magic Middletown* (Bloomington: Indiana University Press, 1986), pp. 1–5. Just a few of the many glass companies that located in east-central Indiana are the Woodbury Glass Company (later known as Anchor Hocking), in Winchester; Kerr Glass and Indiana Glass, in Hartford City; Owens-Illinois Glass Company, in Gas City; and Ball Brothers, Muncie Glass, and the Port Glass Works, in Muncie. For a discussion of the importance of glass in east-central Indiana, see Wiley W. Spurgeon, "Jarred Memories: Local Glass Industry Faded as Markets, Companies Changed," *Muncie (Ind.) Star Press,* October 6, 1996, sec. F, p. 1, col. 1.

interest in was the Rock Oil Company, which was located in Winchester. The Rock Oil Company was formed on June 8, 1886, less than two months after gas was discovered in Jay County. It had thirty-three founding investors who issued a capital stock of $50,000. It was established to incorporate a gas, oil, and mining company. Although drilling for oil was done almost as aggressively in the area as for natural gas, the anticipated oil boom was never realized.[5]

Percy Goodrich was one of the original investors in the Rock Oil Company. Within a short time, Ed and James, along with Percy, became directors of the company. James also served as corporate secretary, becoming responsible for filing the company's annual reports and maintaining records.[6] Three of the remaining four directors and officers of the company were A. L. Kitselman, D. M. Kitselman, and E. F. Kitselman. These three brothers, along with a fourth Kitselman brother, were from Ridgeville, a small town in northwestern Randolph County. The Kitselman brothers began a company that manufactured, beginning in 1883, roller skates and, beginning in 1887, wire fences. The Kitselman brothers moved their operations to Muncie in 1900. In 1901, they formed what would become one of the largest wire-making companies in the country, the Indiana Steel and Wire Company.[7]

By 1886, the Goodriches had recognized the tremendous growth opportunities associated with the natural gas fields. As a result, they pooled the wealth they had garnered from farming and retail and entered into the utility business. At the turn of the century, it was not uncommon for the Goodrich brothers to help locate natural gas fields and actually

5. See "Remembrance of 'The Great Oil Boom' of Parker City," *Winchester (Ind.) News-Gazette,* June 29, 1976, p. 1, col. 1.

6. The Rock Oil Company was located at 7 South Meridian Street. Article 2 of its bylaws states: "The object and purpose of said company was the production of gas either natural or manufactured for lighting, heating, and fuel purposes and purposes of mining petroleum, oil, rock, and minerals." Bylaws of the Rock Oil Company, State Archives, Indiana Commission on Public Records, Indianapolis, Indiana, 1701–30 1/2.

7. Information about the Kitselmans was taken from a family-history paper in the author's possession, "The Starbucks and the Kitselmans," pp. 9–11.

do some of the legwork in drilling the wells.[8] This was their start in the public utilities business.

On July 30, 1901, the Goodrich brothers formed, with a capital stock of $50,000, a second natural gas company known as the Union Heat, Light and Power Company of Union City, Indiana. James, Percy, John, and Edward were four of the six directors. Union Heat provided heat, light, and electricity to consumers in both eastern Randolph County and western Darke County, Ohio. It also operated for the purposes of drilling, buying, and selling natural gas and oil. James's initial investment in the company was $12,400, which entitled him to 248 shares. By 1915, he owned 956 of the total of 3,000 shares. The other brothers owned a total of 760 shares between them, and the remaining investors were business associates of the Goodrich family: Jesse "Jett" Moorman, William E. Miller, and James W. McCamish. For several years, James Goodrich served as president of this company. In 1915, Union Heat purchased the Portland Gas Company.[9]

Besides the Rock Oil Company and Union Heat, the Goodrich brothers had controlling interest in the Lynn Gas Company and the Indiana-Ohio and the Western Ohio Public Services Companies (electric companies). These utilities also served communities in east-central Indiana and west-central Ohio, including Union City, Indiana; Union City, Ohio; and Greenville, Ohio.

During this time, the Goodrich brothers maintained their interest in their farm operations. After graduating from high school in 1881 with his brother James, Percy Goodrich began with the other brothers a farming operation called simply Goodrich Farms. Eight years later, in

8. Perce G. Goodrich, interview, November 9, 1992.

9. See "The Union Heat, Light and Power Company of Union City, Indiana," pp. 36–53, Dissolved Corporations, State Archives, Indiana Commission on Public Records, Indianapolis. The articles of incorporation for Union Heat were filed on July 30, 1901. In 1915, the Goodrich brothers owned more than half of the 3,000 shares: James, 956; William Wallace, 354; Percy, 171; Edward, 165; and John B., 70. The Peoples Loan and Trust Company owned 63 shares. The last annual report filed with the secretary of state's office showing ownership by the Goodriches of Union Heat, Light and Power was dated June 21, 1926.

1889, Percy quit farming to sell furniture and hardware. John and Ed Goodrich were also involved in this business known as the Goodrich Brothers. The three of them operated stores both in Winchester and Maxville, the latter a small town six miles west of Winchester that has disappeared. Nine years later, on January 5, 1898, the five brothers established the Goodrich Brothers Hay and Grain Company. It bought and sold grain, seed, and farm implements in the area. By 1917, the company (which had by then become the Goodrich Brothers Company) was the largest grain dealer in Indiana. A forerunner of the company had been established by the brothers' maternal grandfather, Edward Edger, in 1860. The only stockholders of Goodrich Brothers were the five brothers and their wives. John was president. Percy, the oldest brother, became secretary and general manager of the hay and grain business. He later also assumed the title of chairman of the board.[10]

The Goodrich brothers also invested heavily in electric companies, such as Citizens Heat, Light and Power Company, based in Winchester. Reorganized on July 21, 1913, Citizens Heat was the successor to the Citizens Water and Light Company, which had been established on June 6, 1899. Citizens Heat provided electricity to approximately nine thousand Randolph County residents. Citizens Heat also owned the water company in Winchester. Edward Goodrich managed Citizens, while William Wallace served on the board of directors with Edward. Several other businessmen with whom the Goodrich brothers would form financial alliances in banking, coal, and other ventures served as directors, including Jesse Moorman, William E. Miller, and Thomas L. Ward, all of Winchester, and Edwin F. Kitselman of Muncie.[11]

10. See "Ninetieth Annual Goodrich Brothers Anniversary Luncheon," a program pamphlet in the possession of the Columbia Club, Indianapolis. See *Percy Goodrich,* vol. 36 in the Indiana Biography Series, pp. 96–97.

11. The Goodrich brothers held a large interest in Citizens Heat, Light and Power Company from 1913 to 1927. Citizens provided electricity to residences, offices, stores, livery stables, hotels, restaurants, theaters, churches, lodge halls, schools, and other establishments in Winchester, Farmland, Lynn, Saratoga, and Ridgeville. Later, it expanded its service area to include other Randolph County communities such as Spartansburg, Carlos City, Modoc, Losantville, and Deerfield, as well as Blountsville in

Around the turn of the century, a remarkable new invention, previously found only in large cities, became available in people's homes—the telephone. The Goodrich brothers pooled their money and became directors of several local telephone companies: Investors Telephone Company, Interstate Telephone and Telegraph Company, and the Eastern Indiana Telephone Company. The latter company was one of the first the brothers invested in. The Eastern Indiana Telephone Company was also located in the family's hometown of Winchester. James, Percy, and Edward were three of the original eighteen investors in Eastern Indiana Telephone when it was formed on January 5, 1899, with a capital stock of $150,000. Percy Goodrich was treasurer of the company.[12] These three telephone companies served east-central Indiana and west-central Ohio. From the late 1800s to 1920, the Goodrich brothers established or bought into one small-town utility after another. These included the Washington Water, Light and Power Company in Washington (Daviess County, Indiana) and the Jeffersonville Water Company in Jeffersonville

Henry County and Fountain City in Wayne County. Citizens also provided water to the residents of Winchester. In 1913, Jesse Moorman was president of Citizens, Thomas L. Ward served as vice-president, and Edward Goodrich served as secretary and treasurer. In 1927, Citizens was sold to the United Public Utilities Company of Chicago, Illinois. All officers and directors except William Wallace Goodrich (who remained a director for three years) were located in Chicago. Citizens sold power to the Greenville Electric Light and Power Company of Ohio and the Indiana-Ohio Public Service Company. Interestingly, fuel oil, not natural gas or coal, was the original energy source. Citizens' gross income in 1926 was derived from electricity (89.7 percent) and water (10.3 percent) production. The last full year that the Goodrich brothers owned a substantial share of Citizens was 1926, when the company's assets were $556,099.52. See Indiana Public Service Commission, annual reports of the Citizens Heat, Light and Power Company—Winchester, Indiana, 1912 to 1927, especially for the year 1926, Re 4950, box 4, State Archives, Indiana Commission on Public Records, Indianapolis.

12. The Eastern Indiana Telephone Company was located at 114 East Franklin Street. The articles of association were filed on November 16, 1905. The company had a capital stock of six thousand shares at $25 per share. At an initial offering, Percy Goodrich purchased a total of fifty-five shares for $1,375. The Eastern Indiana Telephone Company was purchased by General Telephone and Electric (GTE) in approximately 1969 in a deal wherein each share of Eastern Indiana stock was exchanged for two and a half shares of GTE stock. William Fitts, interview, December 28, 1991.

(Clark County, Indiana). James Goodrich obtained both companies through serving as receiver of the Cincinnati, Chicago and Louisville Railroad from 1908 to 1912.

At the turn of the century, there were no state or federal agencies regulating gas, electric, telephone, or other utilities. Anyone who could raise the funds to buy pipelines or put in telephone poles and wire could do business. This resulted in fierce competition. Often, several gas, electric, and telephone companies began to operate in the same area. It was not uncommon to have two or three gas lines running down the same city street; the same was true of telephone poles and lines. But, as with nearly any industry, only the efficient survive, and the Goodrich companies were efficient. In 1920, the Goodriches' gas company put out of business the Monarch Gas Company in Winchester. Within a short time, the Goodriches held a monopoly in most basic utilities: coal, electric, water, natural gas, and telephones. Percy Goodrich ran the coal and grain operations of the various companies, Ed operated the electric and water, and William Wallace, the natural gas. The brothers all served as directors or officers of the various telephone companies.

James's business interests far exceeded east-central Indiana. At one time or another over the next twenty years, he would assume several other positions: president of the Patoka Coal Company in Pike County, the Railway Service and Supply Company in Indianapolis, and the National City Bank of Indianapolis; secretary-treasurer of the Winona Railway Company in southern Indiana; treasurer of the Union Reduction Company; and director of dozens of other companies, including the Red River Refining Company, an oil refining company in Chicago, as well as the Goodrich brothers' utility and grain companies in east-central Indiana.

Shortly after the turn of the century, the family became involved in the business that they would be most closely associated with in their home community—banking. On June 1, 1901, James founded, along with thirty-four other local stockholders, the Peoples Loan and Trust Company. James served as president of Peoples until his death in 1940. In 1901, the amount of the capital stock was set at $30,000. Within one year of opening, Peoples had total assets of $115,000. By 1907, the bank had outgrown its original location and moved to its present location at the corner of Meridian and Washington streets in Winchester. Early loans were made for everything from the purchase of local businesses to teams of horses for farmwork. Over the years, the Goodrich brothers bought interests in various other small-town Indiana banks, including banks in Eaton, Farmland, Modoc, Redkey, Ridgeville, and Tipton, and Citizens Bank in LaCrosse. The banks in Farmland and Modoc were converted into branches of Peoples Loan and Trust in 1931, as was the Ridgeville bank in 1939. Peoples Loan and Trust eventually eclipsed in assets the much older Randolph County Bank, which had been established in 1865. Peoples Loan and Trust became the flagship of the Goodrich family's later business enterprises.[13]

Most, but not all, of the business ventures taken on by the Goodrich brothers became successful. Shortly after the turn of the century, James and Percy had become friends with a farmer and businessman in Huntington, Indiana, by the name of Edward Wasmuth. Wasmuth had been a political associate of James Goodrich's, serving as state Republican chairman during the time that Goodrich was governor. He had earlier served as president of the National Hay Association, where Wasmuth became good friends with Percy. It was through these connections that the Goodrich brothers invested in Wasmuth's business, a furniture company in Peru, Indiana. The Wasmuth-Goodrich Company came into being on July 16, 1919. It mostly made and sold kitchen cabinets. Percy Goodrich was vice-president of the company, while James and, later, Pierre, were directors. By the 1930s, however, the Depression had hit hard, making luxury items such as kitchen cabinets expendable. The company was dissolved in October 1936 by the Miami County Circuit Court.[14]

13. See "Trust Company Begins Its Fifty-first Year," *Winchester (Ind.) News,* June 29, 1951, p. 1, col. 2; "Winchester Bank Observes 75th Birthday This Month," *Richmond (Ind.) Palladium-Item,* June 22, 1976, p. 2, col. 1; and "Peoples Loan and Trust Marking 75th Anniversary," *Muncie (Ind.) Star,* June 23, 1976, p. 20, col. 1.

14. The Wasmuth-Goodrich Company had originally been the Booth Furniture Company, which was incorporated on April 6, 1906, in Peru, Indiana. The change of

On another occasion, the Goodrich brothers failed to capitalize on a golden opportunity to gain an even larger share of the midwestern agribusiness. Harold W. McMillen, a Fort Wayne native, had approached Percy in the early 1930s about merging the Goodriches' grain business with his sugar-beet operation in Decatur, Indiana. McMillen proposed that he would purchase and store sugar beets and the Goodrich Brothers would expand their operations in grains: corn, wheat, soybeans, and oats. For some reason, the brothers rejected McMillen's merger offer.[15] McMillen decided to establish his own grain company and formed Central Soya, which has become one of the largest agribusinesses in the country.[16] Instead of merging with McMillen, the Goodriches made one of their few poor business decisions when they merged many years later, in 1947, with the Acme-Evans Milling Company in Indianapolis. The merger would ultimately involve a lengthy court battle by Pierre in the 1960s and the demise of the Goodrich brothers' grain operations. Still, the Goodrich brothers enjoyed phenomenal success in the business world. By the 1920s, their family's financial dynasty was just beginning to be formed.

---

name was granted by the secretary of state on July 16, 1919. At various times, Edward, Percy, James, and Pierre served on the company's board of directors. The company experienced difficult financial times in the late 1920s, failing to file annual reports with the secretary of state's office in 1928, 1932, and 1933. Because of this failure, Philip Lutz, Jr., Indiana's attorney general at the time, brought an action to dissolve the company. The petition was granted by the Miami Circuit Court judge Val Phelps on October 7, 1936. See Wasmuth-Goodrich Company, 2424–19, Dissolved Corporations, State Archives, Indiana Commission on Public Records, Indianapolis; Perce G. Goodrich, interview, November 9, 1992; and Percy E. Goodrich, "Ed Wasmuth," *Down in Indiana* 27 (September 20, 1947), Indiana Historical Society Library, Indianapolis. Edward Wasmuth was also president of the Wasmuth Grain and Coal Company and the Wasmuth Realty Corporation in Huntington County, Indiana.

15. Perce G. Goodrich, interview, November 9, 1992.

16. See Dick D. Heller, Jr., ed., "Vo-Ag," in *1979 History of Adams County, Indiana,* vol. 2 ([Decatur, Ind.]: Adams County Historical Society, 1980–89), pp. 154–55. The article contains the history of Harold W. McMillen's establishment of Central Soya.

Chapter 7
The Early Years, 1901–1916

We sat on the old-fashioned benches
Beguiled with our pencils and slate,
We thought of the opening future,
And dreamed of our manhood's estate;
O days of my boyhood! I bless you,
While looking from life's busy prime,
The treasures are lingering with me
I gathered in life's early time.

"OLD NO. 21"

AFTER having served on the Winchester School Board for thirteen years, James Goodrich was one of three local men appointed in July 1912 to the Winchester Library Board. In 1906, a group of nine women, including Elizabeth and Cora Goodrich, had established the Winchester Association for the purpose of raising funds to build a town library. They began soliciting subscriptions but fell far short of raising a sufficient amount. Finally, in 1916, the Andrew Carnegie Foundation contributed $12,000 to the local library board, and a library was built on East Street on the site of the old Winchester High School, which the five Goodrich brothers had attended. Today, a new addition to the library houses the James P. Goodrich Room, built with funds contributed by the Winchester Foundation, which Pierre established in 1945.[1]

1. "The Winchester Community Library," in *Randolph County History: 1818–1990*, p. 179.

Pierre Goodrich was introduced to politics at a very early age. By the time he was five, his father had already served as Randolph County Republican chairman and had been appointed Republican chairman of Indiana's Eighth Congressional District. In 1901, when Pierre was seven, James Goodrich was selected chairman of the Indiana Republican Party, a position he held for the next decade. During Pierre's formative years, he was almost certainly exposed to dozens, if not hundreds, of local, state, and national political figures.

According to those who still remember Pierre when he was a teenager, he was not particularly athletic, and his mother was constantly fearful that he would take on some sort of dangerous activity. Cora Goodrich often admonished Pierre to safeguard himself from even the most benign activities. For instance, she was strongly opposed to her son's swimming. She would relent to his pleas to go to a nearby pond only if he promised not to get wet,[2] and she would grant permission for Pierre to play baseball only if he promised he would not run.[3] Cora Goodrich could be gracious, but she was also a worrier when it came to the expenditure of money or anything to do with Pierre. It was Cora who directed Pierre into such safe activities as reading, music, and dancing.[4]

"Pierre's mother would often call and ask, 'Do you know where the boys are at?'" said the late Mrs. Francis (Mary) Simpson, a lifelong resident of Winchester. Simpson's two older brothers, John and George Jaqua, were Pierre's childhood friends. "Cora's constant checking up on Pierre aggravated Jim Goodrich," said Mrs. Simpson. "He would say to Cora, 'Why don't you just leave the boys alone?'"[5] James Goodrich had

2. This story was mentioned by three people whom the author interviewed: Ralph Litschert, November 10, 1991; Mary Johnson, January 1, 1992; and Elizabeth Goodrich Terry, November 16, 1991.

3. Perce G. Goodrich, interview, May 2, 1993.

4. Florence Dunn, interview, July 18, 1992.

5. Mary Simpson, interview, April 12, 1992. Mary Simpson's husband Francis served on the board of directors of the Peoples Loan and Trust for more than fifty years under both James and Pierre Goodrich and was a lifelong friend of Pierre.

experienced and survived all kinds of youthful bumps and bruises.[6] He did not think that a little of the same thing would hurt his son.[7]

A comical account of Goodrich family relations was published in a local Winchester newspaper in 1911. According to the article, James Goodrich had presented his wife with a new car on her fiftieth birthday (June 26, 1911). Jim had invited Cora and Pierre to go touring in Indianapolis, where Jim Goodrich had set up a law practice in 1910 under the firm name of Robbins, Starr and Goodrich. After spending the afternoon riding and viewing urban Indianapolis, the three headed eastward toward Winchester, barely escaping disaster.

> Pierre, [only sixteen], who has had quite a deal of experience as a driver, wanted to take the wheel, but Jim insisted, that upon their first voyage, they would have an older head, and a steadier and more experienced hand at the helm. . . .
>
> . . . Unfortunately he was not careful in his choice of roads, and presently discovered that they were well out on the Rushville road. . . . Jim promptly executed a forward turning movement then a backward movement in the direction of the sign board, the speed increased despite his frantic manipulation of the wilderness of levers, brakes, wheels, screws and other trigger work about him, and the machine collided with and bore down upon sign board, fence and all obstructions, and plunged into the cornfield up to the hub. . . . By the united efforts of Jim and Pierre, aided by the somewhat incoherent instruction of Mrs. Goodrich, and the yielding earth, the machine finally came to a full stop. A council of war was held, Mrs. Goodrich held the balance of power and Pierre was installed at the wheel and Jim, the indomitable, but outvoted, was relegated to a back seat, where he sat chafing at the monotony of a 30 mile speed.[8]

6. James Goodrich recalled the rough games that he and his classmates used to play during recess at school. He and his brothers were also very independent. See Goodrich, "Autobiography," pp. 21–22.

7. Moreover, James Goodrich often became upset with Pierre because of the latter's hesitant, indecisive nature (Henry Regnery, interview, October 3, 1992; Perce Goodrich, interview, May 2, 1993).

8. *Winchester (Ind.) Journal,* June 29, 1911, p. 1, col. 5. There was no byline indicating authorship of this account. It is likely, however, that the article was written by either

James Goodrich later regained the driver's seat only to wreck the new car in Anderson, Indiana. The elder Goodrich was a poor and impatient driver, obtaining countless speeding tickets in racing about the state: He would speed until caught, pay the fine, and then race off again until the next encounter with a patrolman. He also experienced several automobile accidents, the most serious being in 1918 when he collided with a streetcar in Indianapolis, which nearly cost him his life.[9] One anecdote about James Goodrich's driving habits may say it all. One weekday, he was returning from Indianapolis to Winchester when he picked up a hitchhiker. The following week, on his return to Winchester along the very same route, the same hitchhiker appeared beside the roadside. Goodrich stopped to give the man another ride, but the hitchhiker refused, stating that he would be crazy to ever get in a car again with James Goodrich behind the wheel.[10]

Pierre Goodrich had, from childhood, an almost insatiable curiosity about everything. During Pierre's teenage years, his father once bought a used car. Pierre methodically took the vehicle apart to see how it was built and then put it back together.[11] In this sense, father and son were

---

John Macy, Jr., or Jesse T. Moorman, both of whom were close friends of the Goodriches' (Moorman is also mentioned in the article). The article is too lengthy to quote in full, but it concludes humorously: "This morning [James Goodrich] started for the City [Indianapolis] in his machine. J. T. Moorman wired Dr. Conrad as follows: 'Goodrich leaves this city [Winchester] at 8 A.M. per motor, bound for Indianapolis via Anderson. Will arrive at Anderson at 8:30, keep the children and automobiles off street.'"

9. Many accounts of James Goodrich's driving habits exist. One can be found in "James Putnam Goodrich," in *Randolph County History: 1818–1990,* p. 517: "The Governor did . . . have an inclination to exceed the highway speed limits, and perhaps was a bit aristocratic in his approach to tickets. It was said that he simply paid as he went, speeding down the highway until a patrolman would stop him, paying the fine, and then speeding on until the next patrolman stopped him."

10. Carl "Barney" Thompson, interview, April 18, 1996.

11. Pierre Goodrich told the story about taking the car apart to Rosanna Amos when she worked for him as a secretary in the 1960s. "I've never met anybody who had the curiosity that Mr. Goodrich had about everything under the sun," said Amos (interview, December 10, 1991).

much alike. James Goodrich once lit with a match gasoline that had spilled out over his automobile's gas tank. After extinguishing the fire, the garage owner asked Goodrich why he would do such a stupid thing. Jim Goodrich's response was that he was curious to see what would happen.[12]

As a youth, Pierre was a constant visitor to the town's excellent bookstore. The store was operated by a succession of retired school superintendents who, Pierre remembered, were rather broadly educated.[13] He traveled to Mexico during the Christmas holidays of his senior year in high school, and the southern adventure gave him an opportunity to play cowboy when he donned a "38-40 Winchester-Carbine rifle," with which he shot down coconuts, and to explore by horseback Guadalajara and southwestern Mexico near Manzanillo.[14]

On the evening of June 3, 1912, Pierre received his diploma from Winchester High School as one of twenty-one graduating students. Goodrich, like his classmates, had to write a graduation composition based on an assigned topic. His friends Ralph Bales and Tom Veech were given the topics of, respectively, trade relations with South America and the 1857 Dred Scott Supreme Court decision. Carl McCamish and Pierre were assigned the more esoteric subjects of, respectively, the evolution of nations and universal peace.[15] The commencement speaker was Dr. E. H. Lindley of Indiana University, whose address to the thirty-

12. Perce G. Goodrich, interview, May 2, 1993.

13. Letter from Pierre F. Goodrich to Felix Morley, May 1, 1959, Felix Morley Collection, Herbert Hoover Presidential Library, West Branch, Iowa. At the time, Winchester did not have a public library, although it was common for the wealthy citizens of a community to have substantial private libraries. The Winchester town library was not established until July 18, 1911. That was the summer between Pierre's junior and senior years at Winchester High School. Even then, the library's collection consisted of 970 books located in a front room of a residence on Franklin Street. See "The Winchester Community Library," in *Randolph County History: 1818–1990,* pp. 179–80.

14. Pierre recounted his Mexico trip as a high school student in a letter to Gustavo R. Velasco, February 16, 1969, Pierre F. Goodrich Papers, box 2, Hoover Institution.

15. "Commencement Day Is Named," *Winchester (Ind.) Democrat,* May 2, 1912, p. 1, col. 3.

seventh graduating class of Winchester High School was "The Power of Man."[16]

After graduation, Pierre's close friend Carl McCamish went to Ohio State University to study medicine. Tom Veech journeyed with Pierre to Crawfordsville, Indiana, to matriculate at Wabash College. Pierre would be gone from his hometown to college, law school, and the military for the next eight years. At Wabash College in September 1912, Goodrich pledged with Phi Gamma Delta Fraternity, one of the few social organizations in which he took any long-term interest.[17] The fraternity, then located at 217 College Street, housed approximately twenty young men from other small communities throughout the Midwest, including several close friends of Pierre's: Phil Magner of Morris, Illinois; Howard Plummer of Kokomo, Indiana; and Fred Van Buskirk of Roann, Indiana. Goodrich was known as "Frisky" to his schoolmates, a group of young men with whom Pierre fit in well.

Wabash College would play an important part in the Goodrich family's lives. James Goodrich served as a trustee of the college from 1904 to 1940 and held the position of chairman of the board from 1924 to 1940. John Goodrich, Pierre's first cousin, attended Wabash briefly in 1912 before returning to Winchester. Perce G. Goodrich, Pierre's youngest first cousin, graduated from Wabash in 1930. Others who later became associated with Pierre also had strong Wabash connections: John Macy, Jr., Goodrich's first law partner (B.A., 1912); Dr. Russell Engle (1915–17), a lifelong friend and business partner; Bill Hunter, Pierre's personal attorney in Winchester (B.A., 1937); and Albert Campbell, Pierre's longtime law partner, who later became director of development at Wabash from 1962 to 1976 and was selected nonalumnus of the year in 1974.[18]

16. "Commencement Exercises Held," *Winchester (Ind.) Democrat,* June 6, 1912, p. 1, col. 6.

17. It is probable that Goodrich chose Phi Gamma Delta because John Macy, Jr., Pierre's close friend and second cousin, had pledged to the fraternity. Macy had matriculated at Wabash four years before Pierre, in 1908.

18. "Wabash Honorary Alumnus Award Goes to Campbell," *Indianapolis Star,* May 23, 1974, p. 43, col. 7.

Wabash left an indelible impression on Pierre. Published in a college pamphlet at about the time Pierre became a student, Wabash's creed reflected the rigorous educational approach applied at the small liberal arts college: "[Wabash] believes that the best foundation for culture and for vocational pursuits is thorough training in a few studies rather than a smattering of many things. Habits of mind, rather than mere information, count largest in the long run. The foundation of the educational process is Discipline, and Discipline is not secured by superficial pursuit of many studies."[19]

During Goodrich's undergraduate days, he participated in several extracurricular activities. In addition to writing for the school's newspaper, *The Bachelor,* he participated in the Shakespeare Club, Greek Chorus, the YMCA cabinet, and the Wabash Board (the school's student government body). Goodrich was especially fond of Professor Jasper Asaph Cragwell, who taught mathematics and apparently was at his best during the time Pierre studied under him. Cragwell, a true individualist, often walked around campus in his bare feet.[20]

In May 1915, Goodrich was one of two juniors elected to Phi Beta Kappa, the national honorary fraternity. A year later, in May 1916, Pierre graduated at the top or near the top of his class (out of sixty-two graduating seniors) with a B.A. in Humanities.[21] Receiving his degree was not

19. Wabash's creed further stated: "The patience to be thorough, the concentration to understand and the persistence to grasp and to apply, are traits that most clearly mark off the truly educated and disciplined fellows; and they are precisely the three traits which are most overlooked and neglected in the modern school and college curriculum. When discipline is withdrawn, dawdling quickly enters and the habit of dawdling is as corrupting to the intellect as it is to the morals" ("Creed," *Wabash College: Pure American* [Crawfordsville, Ind.: Wabash College, 1918], p. 4).

20. See Byron K. Trippet, *Wabash on My Mind* (Crawfordsville, Ind.: Wabash College, 1982), p. 185. A list of extracurricular activities Goodrich participated in, as well as his picture, appeared in the June 1916 issue of *The Wabash.* Cragwell was known for his unconventional thinking and individualistic views. Norman Baxter, interview, February 15, 1993.

21. Wabash does not disclose the rank of graduating students. It is fairly clear, however, that Goodrich was at the top of his class, at least in his junior year, because the tradition at Wabash was that election to Phi Beta Kappa was based primarily on class

the end of his relationship with Wabash. In 1940, Pierre assumed his father's position on the board of trustees, a position he would hold for nearly thirty years. Wabash held a special place in Pierre's heart, because it was there that he established close friendships with such people as the college's eighth and ninth presidents, Frank Sparks and Byron Trippet, and dean and economics professor Benjamin A. Rogge.

At Wabash, Pierre was required to watch his money closely.[22] Goodrich's secretary Rosanna Amos recalls, "I remember Mr. Goodrich telling me that apparently his parents were not given to just letting him have money just because they had money. . . . They knew how hard the

---

rank. In 1914, the year before Goodrich's election to Phi Beta Kappa, the only two juniors who were selected to the honor fraternity were ranked first and second in their class, according to an article in the May 15, 1914, issue of *The Bachelor*. Therefore, Goodrich's selection as one of two juniors would seem to indicate that he was either first or second in his class. See "Phi Beta Kappa Honors to Twelve Wabash Men," *The Bachelor* 8 (May 15, 1915), p. 1, col. 1 ("P. F. Goodrich and W. L. Kessinger, members of the present Junior class, also made the society with high honors"). The division of Humanities that existed when Goodrich attended Wabash included the departments of classical languages and literatures, German, Romance languages and literatures, English, and philosophy.

Although Goodrich was extremely bright and well read, he apparently did have trouble early on with a particular mathematics course. Janet Fuller, former city editor of the *Winchester (Ind.) News-Gazette*, recalled that James Goodrich had sought out her aunt, Wanda Way Harrison, a mathematics teacher at Winchester High School, to tutor Pierre in one of his courses at Wabash. Way, according to Fuller, would tutor Pierre on the train back to Crawfordsville after he had visited his parents in Winchester. "My aunt would often laugh later when Pierre became this prominent intellectual and economist that she had earlier been his tutor," said Ms. Fuller (telephone interview, October 29, 1991).

22. Mary Miller Johnson, who lived next door to the Goodriches in Winchester when Pierre attended Wabash, remembers a particularly curious event when Pierre was an undergraduate. In addition to being neighbors, the Goodriches and the Millers are related. "I remember Aunt Cora coming to my mother with a letter in her hand from Pierre who was at college. Aunt Cora said that Pierre had written to her and one of the things he had asked was whether it would be all right for him to have ice cream after his Sunday evening meal," said Mrs. Johnson (interview, January 1, 1992).

Whether it was the expense or that Goodrich felt that he could not indulge in such a pleasure on Sunday without his mother's permission is open to question. Both interpretations indicate the degree of control that Cora Goodrich had over her son.

wealth came, and they didn't just let him run free with it." At Wabash and later at Harvard, Pierre had to keep a written ledger of literally every penny he spent.[23] Cora Goodrich, who was primarily responsible for her son's strict accounting of expenditures, was known for her extreme frugality. In fact, Cora Goodrich's efforts to economize were renowned among her family and friends and were often humorous.[24] Yet, interestingly, her parsimonious attitude centered mostly on her family's personal expenditures. There were many other instances throughout her life in which Cora Goodrich was extremely generous.[25] Emma Lieber, wife of the former Indiana conservation commissioner Richard Lieber, remembers Cora as a charming, self-confident, "very straight-laced lady" who was amazingly naïve at times.[26]

23. Rosanna Amos, interview, December 10, 1991.

24. At the Goodrich mansion, there was a natural spring in the basement that ran all the time. Mrs. Goodrich believed that it was wasteful for the spring to run continuously. She repeatedly turned off the spring despite her husband's warnings that if she continued to do so, she would kill it (that is, divert the water elsewhere underground). She refused to listen, and eventually the spring stopped flowing. Perce G. Goodrich, interview, November 9, 1992. According to Harry Fraze, undertaker, former mayor of Winchester, and town gossip, Cora Goodrich was known to wear undergarments with holes in them and would refuse to buy new ones (interview, October 26, 1991). Cora Goodrich's niece, Elizabeth Goodrich Terry, recalls, "Aunt Cora would walk several blocks just to return a penny if it was owing to someone" (interview, November 16, 1991). Mary Simpson, a longtime member of the Winchester Presbyterian Church, recalls that Cora Goodrich had a fur coat that she would wear only to church, after which she would return it to a cedar chest. The coat smelled so much of cedar that its smell soon permeated the church when Cora Goodrich entered the sanctuary. Moreover, Mrs. Goodrich continued to wear black lisle stockings long after they were out of fashion, because she had purchased many of them before World War I (interview, April 12, 1992).

25. Apparently, Cora Goodrich's largest individual contribution was eleven thousand dollars toward the cost of building a library in 1940 in Lynn, Indiana, in honor of her parents, Jonas and Amy Frist. She also contributed toward the statue of the doughboy on the Winchester Courthouse square and to the church (Elizabeth Goodrich Terry, interview, November 16, 1991).

26. To illustrate Cora Goodrich's naïveté, Lieber recalls one occasion when she and her husband and the Goodriches were in Germany: "Once when ordering a ticket at a railroad station, Mrs. Goodrich made this remark: 'Isn't it too stupid that they call the

Pierre's own thrifty nature was an eccentricity that many early friends and associates recall. For instance, Pierre was notorious for wearing old scuffed shoes and rumpled suits,[27] and in the early days, when the collars of his dress shirts became frayed, Goodrich would have them turned and resewn rather than buy new ones.[28] John Thompson of Winchester remembers that Goodrich attended the opening of a branch office of the Peoples Loan and Trust Company on May 18, 1968, wearing pleated pants and suspenders. The suit had been out of style for more than a decade. "When Pierre was jokingly asked by Bob Oliver [a Winchester attorney] where he got his suit," Thompson recalled, "Pierre told us that he had found it in the attic the night before."[29]

On another occasion in the early 1920s, Goodrich asked Russell "Buss" Moorman, a Winchester dentist, to repair and clean a saxophone for him. It purportedly took Moorman a couple of days to tear apart, clean, and overhaul the instrument. When Moorman returned it to Goodrich, Pierre gave him twenty-five cents.[30] But like his parents, Pierre could also be generous for a cause that he believed in. Goodrich's underlying attitudes about wealth and its proper use reveal much about the influences on him as a youth and the things he thought truly important.

---

city of Cologne Köln in Germany, when everybody knows it to be Cologne?'" Emma Lieber, *Richard Lieber* (Indianapolis: privately printed, 1947), pp. 97–98.

27. Many people interviewed recalled that Goodrich often wore rumpled clothes. Dale Braun, February 17, 1992; John Kidder, October 10, 1991; Arlene Metz, November 10, 1992. Janet Fuller recalled her parents' telling her that they had seen Goodrich at the Claypool Hotel in Indianapolis, sitting on a bench reading a newspaper. They thought he looked more like a homeless person than an individual who was probably the richest citizen in Indianapolis (Janet Fuller, telephone interview, October 29, 1991).

28. Rosanna Amos, interview, December 10, 1991.

29. John Thompson, interview, December 20, 1991.

30. Mary Thompson, telephone interview, July 11, 1992.

Jonas and Amy Powell Frist and their daughters, Toda (Mrs. Dan Hecker) and Cora (Mrs. James Goodrich). (Randolph County [Ind.] Historical and Genealogical Society)

The original Goodrich brothers and their mother at the turn of the century. *Left to right:* Percy, Edward, William Wallace (behind Elizabeth Goodrich), John, and James. (Courtesy Mary Miller Johnson, Liberty, Ind.)

Winchester, Indiana. Randolph Hotel and City Building–Fire Station, looking west on Franklin Street, circa 1920s. (Randolph County [Ind.] Historical and Genealogical Society)

Winchester, Indiana. Looking south on Main Street and west on Washington Street, circa 1920s. (Randolph County [Ind.] Historical and Genealogical Society)

James P. Goodrich, 1881, when he graduated from Winchester High School. (Courtesy Mrs. Perce G. Goodrich, Portland, Ind.)

James P. Goodrich when he first assumed the position of Randolph County Republican Party chairman, circa 1897. (Courtesy Mrs. Perce G. Goodrich, Portland, Ind.)

Pierre Goodrich at approximately age three. (Courtesy Mrs. Perce G. Goodrich, Portland, Ind.)

Pierre Goodrich at approximately five years old. (Courtesy Mary Miller Johnson, Liberty, Ind.)

John, *left,* and Pierre Goodrich with their maternal grandmother, Elizabeth, circa 1896. (Randolph County [Ind.] Historical and Genealogical Society)

"Five dancing sailors!" circa 1900. *Left to right:* Don Irvin, John Goodrich, Carl McCamish, Pierre Goodrich, and Walter Klinck. (Randolph County [Ind.] Historical and Genealogical Society)

James, Cora, and Pierre Goodrich, *center,* on Pikes Peak, Colorado, August 10, 1901. (Randolph County [Ind.] Historical and Genealogical Society)

Cousins John, *left,* and Pierre Goodrich, circa 1904. (Courtesy Mrs. Perce G. Goodrich, Portland, Ind.)

Pierre Goodrich belonged to the "Six Jolly Urchins," a boys club fondly referred to as the SJU club. Pierre Goodrich is in front row, farthest right. (Courtesy Miriam Halbert Bales, Muncie, Ind.)

Pierre Goodrich as a fisherman, circa 1906. (Courtesy Mrs. Perce G. Goodrich, Portland, Ind.)

The Goodrich family in 1907. *Front row:* Elizabeth Neff Goodrich, wife of Edward; Susan Engle Goodrich, wife of Percy; Louise Gordon Goodrich, wife of William Wallace, and Elizabeth, their child; Elizabeth Edger Goodrich, mother of the five brothers; Cora Frist Goodrich, wife of James; and Lottie Martin Goodrich, wife of John B. *Second row:* Edward; Florence, Ed and Elizabeth's daughter; William Wallace; Percy; Pierre, son of James and Cora; James; John B.; and John, son of John B. and Lottie. (Courtesy Mrs. Perce G. Goodrich, Portland, Ind.)

Pierre Goodrich's high school graduation picture, 1912. (Courtesy Mrs. Perce G. Goodrich, Portland, Ind.)

In 1914 Cora Goodrich formed a women's Bible class called the "Madonna Class" at the Presbyterian church in Winchester. Cora is in the center of the picture, second row, sixth from left. (First Presbyterian Church, Winchester, Ind.)

II

James P. Goodrich

The Consummate Politician

Chapter 8

The Political Years

> I might say without egotism here that from that time [1901] on down until 1921, the general policy of the [Indiana] Republican party so far as the organization was concerned was directed by me.
>
> JAMES P. GOODRICH, "Autobiography"

IT WAS the most exciting day in Randolph County's history. It was bigger than the day the Civil War Monument was dedicated in July 1892 or the day that the former president Benjamin Harrison addressed thousands from the courthouse lawn in 1888. It would be even more important than Republican presidential candidate William Howard Taft's tour of Winchester in 1908 or former President Herbert Hoover's visit to the Goodriches in 1939. The crowd was enormous—at least ten thousand people clustered around the train depot. Bands stirred up the people for two hours. Campaign posters and handbills were tacked to anything that did not move and some things that did. Boys were perched in trees and on telephone poles along the train tracks, straining their eyes to be the first to glimpse the smoke pouring from the Special. It was a political rally, but not just any political rally. It was October 11, 1900, the day Teddy Roosevelt came to town.[1]

It seemed that every Republican within a hundred miles was present, including United States Senator Charles W. Fairbanks, United States Congressman George W. Cromer, and the Republican candidate for

1. "Randolph County's Teddy Roosevelt Rally Day," *Randolph County History: 1818–1990*, p. 48.

governor, Winfield T. Durbin. The welcoming committee, composed of the Indiana Supreme Court justice Leander Monks (from Winchester), John W. Macy, Sr., and others, waited patiently. Then the Special was sighted, and within no more than a minute, the train stopped at the platform and the great man himself appeared. "As big as life," one of the committee men said later, "and twice as natural!" The welcoming committee, gaining composure, suddenly sang out: "Welcome to our city, Governor Roosevelt."[2]

"De-e-eelighted!" roared Teddy, and Randolph County's greatest day had officially begun.

The governor of New York, who would become the nation's twenty-sixth president within the year by virtue of a combination of talent and fate, was escorted to the courthouse square. After several enthusiastic introductions of dignitaries, the irrepressible Teddy Roosevelt rose from the platform to address the multitude. The governor first thanked the county for its devoted support of the Union cause in the Civil War. He then made reference to a matter of more topical importance—the 1900 national election. With only three weeks left until voting day, Teddy blasted the opposition for thirty minutes, deprecating the claims and accusations of the Democratic presidential candidate, William Jennings Bryan. It was said that Teddy became so enraged that he "beat to pieces" his new Stetson hat on the platform railing as he delivered his oration.[3]

Although Governor Roosevelt departed shortly after his vitriolic speech, the day's events had barely begun: There was a parade lasting more than two hours in which military regiments and others marched before the speakers' stand; Rafe Murray and George Bright led their "Deerfield Rough Riders" up "San Juan Hill" (actually, in pancake-flat Winchester, it was a small incline known as Kettle Hill); bands that had come from as far as fifty miles away played patriotic music; glee clubs sang; and spectacular floats, representing patriotic, temperance, and labor union themes, were pulled by horses throughout the town. The

2. Ibid.
3. Ibid.

largest delegation, from nearby Portland, Indiana, had brought twelve hundred marchers. The day's celebratory events ended when a Randolph County native, Congressman James Watson, delivered an eloquent speech to a packed house. At midnight, the "Old 44" cannon on the courthouse square was fired and the Artillery Company bugler sounded "taps."[4]

As was typical, James P. Goodrich, now the Republican chairman of the Eighth Congressional District, was so busy organizing the whole affair that he took little part in the official activities of the day. Staying in the background was a habit of his. Nonetheless, his work for the Republican Party did not go unnoticed by such men as Senator Fairbanks and even the great Teddy Roosevelt himself. James Goodrich's rise in the party had begun about four years earlier, when William W. Canada, a Winchester attorney, resigned his position as Randolph County Republican chairman to accept a position in Washington, D.C. Immediately John Macy put James Goodrich's name forward as Canada's successor. Despite objections by local senior Republicans that James Goodrich was too young, Goodrich was elected chairman by a unanimous vote of the committee in 1897. He was only thirty-three years old.[5]

Goodrich was reelected in 1898. Soon afterward, he headed the statewide campaign of Union B. Hunt, a Winchester lawyer who sought the position of Indiana's secretary of state. Hunt was nominated by the Republican Party and was elected in November. Political debutant Goodrich quickly learned the game of patronage and was consulted regarding numerous unfilled federal and state positions. In early 1898, Goodrich was encouraged by United States Congressman George Cromer to seek the chairmanship of the Eighth Congressional District. Despite a plot

4. Ibid., pp. 48–49.

5. Goodrich, "Autobiography," pp. 42–44. Those who opposed Goodrich's selection for local party chairman were the former Randolph Circuit Court judges Leander J. Monks, who had recently been appointed to Indiana's Supreme Court, and Albert O. Marsh. They both claimed that Goodrich was too young. Goodrich was convinced, however, that Marsh's objection was a result of Goodrich's support of his former law mentor, James S. Engle, for the local judgeship when Monks resigned.

to derail his bid, Goodrich prevailed by traveling throughout the district to meet with nearly every voting delegate. He received more than 90 percent of the delegate vote and assumed the chairmanship of Indiana's Eighth Congressional District at the age of thirty-six.[6]

After James Goodrich's election as Eighth District chairman in 1898, his political work increased substantially. John Macy agreed to take over much of James's law practice so that the loss of income would not be substantial. As Eighth District chairman, Goodrich became intimately involved with state politics; he was wooed by the state's two powerful Republican United States senators—Charles W. Fairbanks, who would become vice-president to Theodore Roosevelt in 1905, and Albert J. Beveridge, Goodrich's former classmate at DePauw University. Fairbanks and Beveridge courted his support because their own political futures depended largely on the ability of the state, district, and county chairmen to deliver a Republican legislature: Until 1912, when Article XVII of the Constitution was ratified, United States senators were not elected directly by popular vote, but were selected by the state's legislature. Goodrich worked tirelessly in the campaign of 1900 to obtain a Republican victory in the Eighth District. The hard work paid off. A Republican landslide occurred: William McKinley was elected president over William Jennings Bryan (only to be assassinated in September 1901 and succeeded by Theodore Roosevelt); Winfield T. Durbin was elected governor, and a Republican majority was maintained in the state's General Assembly.[7]

In late July 1901, Fairbanks approached Goodrich with the idea that Goodrich should seek the chairmanship of the Republican state committee. Fairbanks was a political power not only within Indiana, but nationally as well. He had been offered the vice-presidential nomination by McKinley in 1900 and had refused it, but he accepted it when Roosevelt offered it to him again in the 1904 election. Goodrich re-

6. Ibid., pp. 45–48.

7. See Clifton J. Phillips, *Indiana in Transition: The Emergence of an Industrial Commonwealth, 1880–1920* (Indianapolis: Indiana Historical Bureau and Indiana Historical Society, 1968), pp. 50–84.

turned to Winchester and consulted with Macy about Fairbanks's desire to see him as state party chairman. Macy encouraged his nephew to accept the post. To show his support, Macy offered to divide the earnings of their law practice while James was working on party activities.[8] Goodrich met with Fairbanks the following day. He agreed to take the position on condition that no contributions would be accepted by the party from corporations that had direct dealings with the state. Fairbanks acceded to the request. On the following day, August 1, a meeting was held in Indianapolis with the state committee members and Goodrich was elected unanimously.[9]

In his autobiography, James Goodrich appraised his political responsibilities in Indiana over the next twenty years: "I might say without egotism here that from that time on down until 1921, the general policy of the Republican party so far as the organization was concerned was directed by me."[10] Within thirty days of his election as the state's Republican Party chief, Goodrich was offered a retainer of five thousand dollars a year to represent the J. P. Morgan interests in Indiana. The true intent of the company, Goodrich realized, was "to employ the

8. Goodrich practiced law with a number of attorneys after Enos and James Watson. From 1895 to 1900, Goodrich practiced with Macy and John J. Cheney. Cheney, who had previously served as Randolph Circuit Court judge, retired in 1900 and was replaced in the firm by Alonzo L. Nichols. In January 1902, Macy was appointed Randolph Circuit Court judge, and Macy's position in the firm was filled by Alonzo L. Bales. The firm's name was changed to Nichols, Goodrich and Bales. In 1908, Macy resigned as judge and rejoined Goodrich in the firm of Macy, Nichols, Goodrich and Bales. After Macy's death in 1912, his son, John W. Macy, Jr., left Columbia Law School and replaced his father in the firm. In 1910, Goodrich opened a law office in Indianapolis under the name Robbins, Starr and Goodrich. In 1913, Leander Monks, originally from Winchester, resigned from the supreme court of Indiana and joined the firm, which became Monks, Robbins, Starr and Goodrich. See John L. Smith and Lee L. Driver, "James P. Goodrich," in *Past and Present of Randolph County Indiana* (Indianapolis: A. W. Bowen, 1914), pp. 1521–24; "Judge John Winchester Macy," *Past and Present of Randolph County Indiana*, pp. 1048–51.

9. See "New Republican Chairman: J. P. Goodrich Slated to Succeed Hernly," *Indianapolis News*, July 26, 1901, p. 8, col. 2; "J. P. Goodrich Chosen to Succeed Hernly as Republican State Chairman," *Indianapolis Journal*, August 8, 1901, p. 8, col. 2.

10. Goodrich, "Autobiography," pp. 53–54.

Chairman of the State Committee and not a country lawyer from over at Winchester." The new party chief declined the offer, thwarting the first of many corporate intents to use his new powerful position.[11]

In 1902, Goodrich was again elected state chairman by the Republican Party. Almost all higher state officeholders went Republican: Daniel E. Storms of Stockwell won election as secretary of state, Charles W. Miller of Goshen was elected attorney general, and David E. Sherrick of Noblesville was elected auditor.

In 1904, James Watson chaired the Republican State Convention. James Goodrich was again elected state Republican chairman, despite an attempt by Albert Beveridge to defeat him. During most of their political lives, Goodrich and Beveridge had a guarded relationship. Beveridge, a man of great abilities, served in the United States Senate from 1889 to 1911. He is still considered one of the greatest orators in the history of the Senate, in the company of Daniel Webster of New Hampshire and John C. Calhoun of South Carolina. He was also a writer of some repute, especially in the area of biography, having written the life histories of Abraham Lincoln and the former United States Supreme Court justice John Marshall. For his biography of Marshall, Beveridge received the Pulitzer Prize in 1920. Goodrich held Indiana's young senator in some esteem:

> I have had from the time I knew him in college a great admiration for Senator Beveridge. He was intellectually honest, he had firm convictions on public questions and followed through on them. He had courage and intelligence of a very high order. I know that he never accepted a dollar as contribution from anyone. I saw him return to George Perkins [senior partner of J. P. Morgan Company and national chairman of the Progressive Party], a personal check for $25,000.00, to aid in his election but he was a profound egotist, believed in his inherent greatness and he was not bound by the limitations that surround men of lesser ability.[12]

11. Ibid., p. 55; see also Rhodes, *James P. Goodrich, Indiana's "Governor Strangelove,"* pp. 21–22.

12. Goodrich, "Autobiography," p. 65. For a more extensive account of the life of Albert J. Beveridge, see Claude G. Bowers, *Beveridge and the Progressive Era* (Cambridge, Mass.: Houghton Mifflin, 1932).

Goodrich had a difficult time stroking the egos of Fairbanks, Beveridge, and Watson while maintaining party unity. He wrote of the task: "There was a great deal of jealousy among the men prominent in Indiana politics during the period I was State Chairman. Fairbanks, Beveridge, [and] Watson all had their eyes on the presidency, each was jealous of the other and it was somewhat of a job for the organization to steer a course that would give the least possible offense to any one of the three and yet be fair to all."[13]

It was shortly after the 1904 election that an embarrassing situation occurred for the Indiana Republican Party. A number of state Republican officeholders, most notably Daniel Storms, who was secretary of state after Hunt, and David Sherrick, state auditor, were accused of embezzling state funds. While neither Goodrich nor the Republican governor, Harold Hanley, was implicated in the misappropriations, it was during their watch that Storms, Sherrick, and the others were elected. The result of the fiasco was mixed: Storms and Sherrick were forced to resign, but a depository law was passed by the legislature that required the state to adopt modern auditing practices.[14]

In December 1905, James Watson was elected majority whip in Congress under the powerful Speaker of the House Joseph Cannon.[15] Despite his rise in Congress, Watson still dreamed of running for governor of Indiana. James Goodrich was again elected state party chairman in 1906 and 1908. At that time, Indiana law limited a governor to one term. In 1907, toward the end of Governor Hanley's term, Hanley became very interested in anointing a successor. Goodrich recalled that Hanley sought him out to run for governor for two reasons: first, Hanley believed that the Winchester lawyer and businessman was qualified, and, second, and perhaps more important, Hanley knew that if Goodrich ran, James Watson would not. When Goodrich refused to be a candidate, the expected happened: Watson threw his hat into the political ring, seeking the top state post as a stepping-stone to the presi-

13. Goodrich, "Autobiography," p. 65.

14. Ibid., pp. 70–77.

15. "Watson's Duties as House Whip," *Indianapolis News,* December 16, 1905, p. 7, col. 4.

dency. Watson received the Republican nomination on April 2, 1908.[16] Goodrich, who had persuaded Watson not to run for governor in 1904, again strongly discouraged his close friend from running in 1908. Goodrich's reason was that Watson had shot himself in the foot by flip-flopping on the all-important issue of temperance. Goodrich recalled that Watson was not committed to either position and played each against the other. "The trouble was that while [Watson] would whoop it up for the dry cause when with the Epworth Leaguers [members of a temperance society] and Anti-Saloon League, when he got with the boys at Terre Haute, Evansville, Lake County and other places he would put in his time drinking beer with the boys and assuring them he would be all right in case he was elected. The result was that neither side trusted him."[17]

Watson's equivocation on the temperance issue was his downfall. In the November 1908 election, he lost to the Democratic candidate, attorney Thomas Marshall of Columbia City, by a meager eight thousand votes. Marshall, who would become vice-president in 1913 under Woodrow Wilson, was essentially handed the governor's seat by Watson's blunder. Interestingly, the 1908 governor's race caused Goodrich and his wife Cora to start thinking about their own political future. After the 1908 state Republican convention, James Goodrich recorded in his diary that Cora was quite smitten by the political maneuvering she had wit-

16. "Watson Nominated for Governor," *Indianapolis Star,* April 3, 1908, p. 1, col. 3; "Rushville, Watson's Home Town and That of Hall, Democrat, Will Hold a Jollification Night over Both Candidates, Regardless of Party," *Indianapolis News,* April 4, 1908, p. 14, col. 1. In a letter from James Watson to James P. Goodrich dated January 25, 1901, Watson wrote: "Your advice on the Governorship question is timely and I shall abide by it. I am a candidate for renomination [to Congress] and shall say nothing about my ever-living ambition to be Governor of Indiana." James P. Goodrich Papers, Herbert Hoover Presidential Library, West Branch, Iowa.

17. Goodrich, "Autobiography," p. 80. See also "Watson and Bingham Cry Saloon-Democracy Bond: Liquor Issue Put First by Watson," *Indianapolis Star,* June 5, 1908, p. 1, col. 7; "Watson Defends County Unit Plan," *Indianapolis News,* June 5, 1908, p. 1, col. 3; and "Watson Penetrates Enemy's Territory: Nominee in Special Train Makes Option Stand in Southern Indiana," *Indianapolis Star,* October 30, 1908, p. 1, col. 1.

nessed. "What caused me to record this I do not remember," he wrote to Pierre. "[I]n fact, I was astonished when I found it there [in my diary], at the conclusion of the record of the day's [Convention] fight: 'From the expression upon her face, I believe that Mrs. Goodrich wants to be "Mrs. Governor" some day.'"[18]

At the 1908 Republican National Convention, held in Chicago from June 16 to June 19, Goodrich was a delegate from Indiana serving on the Committee on Credentials.[19] William Howard Taft of Ohio was nominated for president by the Republicans, and he easily defeated the Democratic nominee, William Jennings Bryan, in the November general election. In anticipation of the 1910 presidential election off year, Goodrich begged to be relieved of his duties as state Republican chairman to return full time to his legal practice and business interests. Fairbanks, Watson, and even Beveridge asked him to continue, but he declined. Deferring to his wishes, the three politicians in January 1910 honored Goodrich at a farewell dinner at the Claypool Hotel in Indianapolis.[20]

During the next several years, Goodrich had to bail Watson out of one scrape after another. In 1908, Watson had given up his seat in Congress to run for governor and had lost. Once William Howard Taft took office as president, he offered the defeated gubernatorial candidate the position of either ambassador to Cuba or governor of Puerto Rico.[21] Watson wanted to return to politics, however, and he hoped to make some quick money by working as a lobbyist in Washington, D.C., before seeking political office again in Indiana. Watson turned down Taft's offers, which paid only ten thousand dollars a year, in favor of the more lucrative prospect of lobbying his former colleagues in Congress.[22]

No sooner had Watson returned to Washington as a lobbyist in 1909

18. Goodrich, "Autobiography," p. 79.

19. "Indiana Will Storm Chicago," *Indianapolis News*, p. 3, col. 1.

20. Goodrich, "Autobiography," p. 83.

21. "Watson Offered Choice of Two Plums by Taft," *Indianapolis Star*, July 22, 1913, p. 5, col. 2.

22. Goodrich, "Autobiography," p. 84.

than he became embroiled in a scam for which he was nearly prosecuted. Two states—California and Louisiana—were fighting for the right to host the Panama Exposition (promoting the construction of the Panama Canal). Watson had taken five thousand dollars as a retainer from a California delegation to promote the exhibition's being held there. Soon afterward, the California delegation learned that Watson had also taken ten thousand dollars from a New Orleans delegation that believed that he was promoting their city as the site. Goodrich received a telegram from the former United States senator James A. Hemenway of Indiana, who had opened a law office with Watson, begging Goodrich to come to Washington to the aid of their mutual friend. Once there, Goodrich relates, it "took everything that [Vice-President] Fairbanks, Joe Cannon [Speaker of the House of Representatives], Hemenway, McKinley of Illinois and myself could do to prevent publicity and prosecution." According to Goodrich, "Watson finally refunded the money to California and the matter was quieted down."[23]

In an equally serious controversy in 1913, Watson was alleged to have received during his 1908 run for governor personal funds that were purportedly raised for his campaign by a lobbyist for the National Association of Manufacturers. The investigation of the Mulhall Affair, named for the lobbyist, resulted in weeks of hearings before both the United States Senate and the House.[24] Again, Goodrich had to make statements in defense of his friend, given that he was state Republican chairman when the alleged "slush fund" money had been raised. Time and again, Goodrich came to Watson's defense, especially in financial matters.[25]

23. Ibid., p. 85.

24. Louis Ludlow, "Raised $22,000 in Campaign to Elect Watson," *Indianapolis Star,* July 16, 1913, p. 1, col. 1; Louis Ludlow, "Watson Pleads Vainly to Take Witness Stand," *Indianapolis Star,* July 25, 1913, p. 1, col. 1; "Spurns Watson In Last Appeal," *Indianapolis Star,* July 26, 1913, p. 2, col. 3; Louis Ludlow, "Where Did Fund Go? Is Mystery Up to Mulhall: Goodrich and Parry Join in Charge that Manufacturers' Gift Went Astray," *Indianapolis Star,* July 28, 1913, p. 1, col. 1.

25. Letters from Goodrich to Watson, January 31, 1918, and February 20, 1918 (regarding Goodrich's cosigning for an overdue loan by Watson from National City Bank of Indianapolis), James P. Goodrich Papers, box 28.

Watson was simply too caught up in politics to take the time necessary to make money without involving himself in scandals.[26]

It is clear that Goodrich's involvement in Republican politics did not extinguish his business desires. Although he would not allow himself to be employed as a paid lobbyist while he was state chairman, he apparently saw nothing wrong with taking on other business that came to him as a result of his political position. In 1908, Albert Barnes Anderson, federal judge of the Southern District of Indiana, appointed Goodrich receiver of the Chicago, Cincinnati and Louisville Railroad (CC&L). Goodrich was still serving as state Republican Party chief at the time. Many of the New England bondholders of the railroad were none too impressed that the chairman of the state Republican Party, who had no experience running a railroad, had been appointed to such an important position. It was well known that appointments to receiverships were political plums generally reserved for the party in power.

Despite the criticisms, Goodrich pressed ahead. The position required him to spend considerable time in Chicago, where he had an office from 1908 to 1912. "I never worked harder in my life than I did in the four years when I was actively running the railroad," Goodrich recalled.[27] Over the next four years, Goodrich was able to turn the operations of the railroad around to the point that it was handling traffic at 90 percent of the gross income for operating expenses. Soon afterward, he opened negotiations to sell the CC&L to the Chesapeake and Ohio Railroad (C&O). The merger was finally consummated in 1912, with the bondholders of the C&O taking on the debts of the CC&L. When the bonds of the CC&L were finally sold, the first bondholders (now the C&O bondholders) received the payment of par value for their stock plus interest while the second bondholders received eighty cents on the dollar.[28]

26. The assistance was not always one way. There were a few times when Watson came to Goodrich's aid. Once, Watson tried to protect Shields Edger, James Goodrich's uncle and an ardent Democrat, from being fired from his position as Winchester's postmaster in June 1918 because of drunkenness. See letter from Watson to Goodrich, June 11, 1918, James P. Goodrich Papers, box 28.

27. Goodrich, "Autobiography," pp. 86–87.

28. Ibid., pp. 87–88.

The bondholders of the Chesapeake and Ohio Railroad were so pleased with the early results of Goodrich's work that they offered him another opportunity to expand his family's interests in public utilities. These bondholders also owned the Jeffersonville Water Company and the Washington Water and Gas Company in Indiana. In 1908, both companies were in receivership. Goodrich could purchase the Washington Water and Gas Company if he would pay the price of the receivership certificates. He was also offered the opportunity to purchase the Jeffersonville Water Company if he would pay fifty cents on the dollar for the bonds. Goodrich accepted both offers. Goodrich purchased the Washington Water and Gas Company and filed a certificate of incorporation with the secretary of state's office on June 30, 1908. The new company was named the Washington Water, Light and Power Company. Goodrich remained president of the company until 1919, when he stepped down and Jesse "Jett" Moorman, a business associate from Winchester, became head of the utility. At that same time, Pierre took his father's position on the board. In 1913, the Washington Water, Light and Power Company purchased the Citizens Light and Fuel Company, thus expanding its area of service in Daviess County, Indiana.[29]

In January 1910, after resigning as state Republican chairman, Goodrich entered into a law partnership in Indianapolis with John Robbins and Henry Starr, both of whom were from Richmond, Indiana. In January 1913, Leander J. Monks resigned from the Indiana Supreme Court after serving for eighteen years and joined the firm, which came to be called Monks, Robbins, Starr and Goodrich. Its offices were located on the ninth floor of the Pythian Building in Indianapolis. Good-

29. Ibid., pp. 88–89. See also "Washington Water, Light and Power Company," AR 2601–3, Dissolved Corporations, State Archives, Indiana Commission on Public Records. Other officers of the company were Henry Starr, vice-president, Chicago; Carl R. Semans, secretary, who also served as general manager of the company, Washington, Indiana; and Edwin H. Cates, treasurer, Richmond, Indiana. We know from the company's 1913 annual report, dated April 30, 1913, that Washington Water, Light and Power Company purchased the Citizens Light and Fuel Company. The corporate office headquarters of Washington Water, Light and Power Company was Goodrich's law office, located at 931–939 Pythian Building, Indianapolis.

rich served as general counsel for the insurance department of the Knights of Pythias and performed other legal work. Goodrich practiced with the three attorneys until 1914, when he quit the practice of law to devote himself full time to his extensive business interests: banking, farming, mining, oil refining, railroads, public utilities, grain elevators, and bond houses.[30]

In 1912, as a result of his success in operating the Chicago, Cincinnati and Louisville Railroad while it was in receivership, Goodrich was appointed by a federal judge Renster, a Democrat, receiver of the Noelke-Richards Iron Works. Noelke-Richards had plants in both Indianapolis and Pittsburgh, Pennsylvania. The company had contracts to provide structural steel extending from Portland, Maine, to Seattle, Washington. Many of the creditors wanted to see Noelke-Richards go into bankruptcy. One of the company's largest creditors was Bethlehem Steel Corporation of Pennsylvania. Goodrich met with the president of Bethlehem Steel, Charles Schwab. Schwab wanted bankruptcy, not an operating receivership. When Goodrich told Schwab that he thought that Noelke-Richards could pay fifty cents on the dollar if it were allowed to operate under a receivership arrangement, Schwab told Goodrich that the company would be fortunate to pay half that much. This prompted Goodrich to negotiate a deal with Schwab to accept twenty-five cents on the dollar. Only a year later, at the end of 1913, Goodrich disposed of all the assets of the company, paying creditors 87.5 cents on the dollar. Goodrich recalled, "Judge Renster did me the honor when the matter was closed up by stating publicly in open court that it was the most satisfactory trust that he had ever experienced either as a lawyer or judge."[31]

Although James Goodrich had resigned from the chairmanship of the Indiana Republican Party in 1910, his political involvement continued. At the 1912 Republican National Convention in Chicago, he became a key

30. See "Goodrich, James Putnam," *The National Cyclopaedia of American Biography* (New York: J. T. White, 1926), p. 76.

31. Goodrich, "Autobiography," pp. 91–92.

player in an attempt to select a presidential nominee who could defeat the Democratic presidential candidate, Woodrow Wilson. In 1912, Goodrich had been appointed to the Republican National Committee as the Indiana delegate, succeeding Harry S. New of Indianapolis. New would become a United States senator in 1916 and postmaster general for President Warren G. Harding in 1923. Beginning in 1912, Goodrich was also selected to serve on the Republican National Executive Committee.

The Indiana Republican Party was in disarray at this time, and it looked to Goodrich for leadership. In an unprecedented situation, a former president, Theodore Roosevelt, was challenging the incumbent president, William Howard Taft, for the Republican nomination. Both desperately wanted to capture Indiana's delegates at the national convention. Goodrich told Roosevelt that he would support Taft, because Taft was the incumbent. Goodrich knew, however, that the state strongly favored Roosevelt. When the vote was tallied at Indiana's Eighth Congressional District Convention, Roosevelt won by a mere two votes. Taft personally asked Goodrich to contest the election, but Goodrich refused; instead, he made a motion that the selection of the Roosevelt delegates be unanimous, and that motion was carried. At the Indiana state convention in March, however, the Taft forces came out on top with a majority of 105.[32]

The fight between Taft and Roosevelt continued at the national convention in Chicago in June. James Watson, Charles Fairbanks, and Harry New served there as delegates-at-large from Indiana. Goodrich was a delegate by virtue of being a national committeeman. At that time, state party primaries did not precede the national convention. Therefore, at the convention, the selection of the party's nominee for president was the primary task of the delegates. At the 1912 convention, however, the Republican National Committee, made up almost entirely of loyal Taft supporters, allowed Roosevelt only 19 out of 254 contested seats. The anomaly was that Roosevelt, in the minds of the American public, was by far the more popular figure of the two. Roosevelt let it be known in advance that he would not be bound by the convention

32. Ibid., pp. 93–94.

results. It soon became evident to Goodrich that the fight between Taft and Roosevelt had become so acrimonious that the bloodbath would greatly decrease the chances of the eventual nominee's defeating the Democrat presidential nominee, Woodrow Wilson. On June 22, Goodrich met with Roosevelt in the Florentine Room of the Congress Hotel and confronted the former president. Goodrich knew that Roosevelt would never step aside to allow Taft to be the nominee, but he believed that Roosevelt might accept the Missouri governor Herbert S. Hadley, a close friend of Roosevelt's, as a compromise candidate. Goodrich was willing to nominate Hadley if Roosevelt conceded to the dealmaking. After waiting for two hours for Roosevelt to discuss the proposal with his top advisers, Goodrich was summoned into the former president's suite: "I went to Roosevelt's room on his invitation. He was alone. He told me the result of the conference. He said, 'There can be no question but that I am the choice of the Republican party today. If Taft steals this nomination from me, the fight has only begun.'"[33]

Roosevelt overestimated his support among the delegates, who were bound to Taft. Taft prevailed as the Republican nominee after Roosevelt and his throng ultimately walked out of the convention. The irrepressible "Teddy," however, was true to his word. He proceeded to form the Progressive Party (better known as the Bull Moose Party, because Roosevelt said that he was as fit as a bull moose when questions about his health were raised), and he fought Taft till the end. Just as Goodrich and the political pundits had predicted, the resulting bitter campaign between Roosevelt and Taft split the traditional Republican vote. This resulted in Wilson's winning by a large electoral margin in the November election. Taft came in a distant third.[34]

33. Ibid., p. 95.

34. Woodrow Wilson won the 1912 presidency by gaining 6,293,453 popular votes, while Roosevelt received 4,119,538 votes and Taft received 3,484,980 votes. Eugene V. Debs, the Socialist Party candidate, received 900,672 votes. Wilson, however, achieved a major electoral college victory—435 to Roosevelt's 88. Taft received only 8 electoral votes, and Debs received none. An excellent summary of the 1912 split between Taft and Roosevelt is contained in Will H. Hays, *The Memoirs of Will H. Hays* (Garden City, N.Y.: Doubleday, 1955), pp. 79–81.

At that point, Goodrich turned his political attention to his home state, where the Democratic Party had also prevailed by electing two successive governors (Thomas P. Marshall in 1908 and Samuel M. Ralston in 1912) and two United States senators (Benjamin F. Shively and John W. Kern). In an attempt to restore the state Republican Party machinery to its previous dominance, Goodrich sought out a young, bright lawyer from Sullivan, Indiana, to serve as party chairman. His name was Will Hays. The two men had first become acquainted in 1902, when Hays had become Sullivan County Republican chairman. Goodrich was greatly impressed with Hays's energy, his Presbyterian values, and his ability to "dramatize things." He wrote years later that Hays was "the best publicity man that ever lived."[35]

By 1906, Goodrich had appointed Hays head of the Republican Party State Speakers Bureau, responsible for organizing more than one hundred speakers in ninety-two counties and thirteen congressional districts.[36] In 1912, Hays received the appointment of vice-chairman of the state Republican Central Committee. In 1914, he was finally elected, with Goodrich's assistance, state Republican Party chairman. At age thirty-five, he was two years younger than Goodrich had been when Goodrich had assumed the position in 1901. Hays's selection as state party chief was significant to Goodrich's own personal political ambitions. It served as the first stepping-stone toward reuniting the Indiana Republican Party and paved the way for Goodrich's run for the governor's seat in 1916.

35. Goodrich, "Autobiography," p. 110.

36. See Hays, *The Memoirs of Will H. Hays*, p. 70.

Chapter 9
The 1916 Campaign

You give me the power and I'll be responsible for the results.
James P. Goodrich's campaign slogan

As the new chairman of the Indiana Republican Party, William Harrison Hays had a tremendous challenge before him. In the election of 1912, the Republican Party had come in a distant third behind the Democrats and the Progressives (the Bull Moose Party) in Indiana as well as nationally. Only twice since 1860 had the Republican Party failed to place its candidate in the White House. Hays's approach was to return traditional Republican voters to the GOP fold by inviting Progressive Party members from throughout the state to participate in Republican meetings. He also flooded state newspapers with columns and editorials on major issues, cleverly promoting the Republican point of view. He worked closely with James Goodrich and Harry S. New, a former Republican Party national chairman and United States Senate candidate in 1916, to meet with large numbers of precinct committee members in nearly every county in Indiana.[1]

Hays's diligence and brilliance paid big dividends for Goodrich's political aspirations. In the autumn of 1915, James Watson had approached

1. Walden S. Freeman, "Will H. Hays and the Politics of Party Harmony," in *Their Infinite Variety: Essays on Indiana Politicians* (Indianapolis: Indiana Historical Society, 1981), pp. 336–39; Hays, *The Memoirs of Will H. Hays,* p. 146. Hays's organization of the 1916 campaign is discussed in detail in James O. Robertson's "Progressives Elect Will H. Hays Republican National Chairman, 1918," *Indiana Magazine of History* 64 (September 1968): 173–90.

James Goodrich to inquire whether his longtime friend was serious about running for governor in 1916. Watson encouraged Goodrich to seek the office. Watson let it be known that if Goodrich did not run he would. If Goodrich did run, Watson would challenge the incumbent United States senator from Indiana, Democrat John W. Kern, who was up for reelection. Watson began pressing his former schoolmate for an early decision.[2]

Never one to react to someone else's timing, James Goodrich first decided to test the political waters to see what interest a candidacy might generate throughout the state. He had political friends from South Bend to Evansville mention his name as a prospective candidate. Goodrich initially had serious qualms about running for governor. "I had always had a pretty high regard for the office, and was inclined to think of it in terms of [Oliver P.] Morton, [Henry S.] Lane, and men of that type, and I had no exaggerated notions about my own ability to fill that office," he wrote.[3] When the response throughout the state was highly favorable, however, he reached the conclusion that "there was nothing for me to do but to make the race."[4]

Goodrich pursued the state's top governmental position with intense energy and work. The first thing Goodrich did was to write a personal check for $40,000 and give it to his campaign manager, John McCardla. Goodrich admonished McCardla not to accept any contributions from any other individuals or groups. Goodrich believed that by bankrolling his own campaign he could avoid obligations to political contributors.[5]

Despite his twenty years of devoted service to the Indiana Republican Party and his hefty campaign war chest, Goodrich's nomination was by no means certain. He would have to defeat two formidable candidates in the first state Republican primary: Warren McCray, a wealthy farmer from Kentland and the Tenth Congressional District, and Quincy Myers, a former judge of the Indiana Supreme Court, from Logansport.

2. Goodrich, "Autobiography," pp. 99–100.
3. Ibid., p. 99.
4. Ibid., p. 102.
5. Ibid.

Goodrich acknowledged that he was no speechmaker, but he did not allow this weakness to hinder his pursuit of the office. He opened his campaign by delivering an announcement address in Greencastle, Indiana, the home of his alma mater, DePauw University, on December 29, 1915.[6] While McCray relied heavily on advertising in newspapers, Goodrich took his campaign directly to the people in cities, towns, and rural areas across the state. He wrote approximately twenty-five thousand precinct chairmen whom he had met during the five political campaigns in which he had headed the state Republican Party; furthermore, Goodrich traveled and campaigned in every precinct in the state except four counties in McCray's own Tenth Congressional District. Goodrich's approach worked. He took the primary on March 7, 1916, in a landslide, winning the popular vote in eighty-seven out of the state's ninety-two counties.[7]

With Goodrich in the governor's race, Watson was determined to dethrone Kern, who was finishing his first term as the junior senator from Indiana. Watson, considered a favorite for the senate seat, unexpectedly lost to Harry New by a few thousand votes in the Republican primary. Strangely, Goodrich claimed that it was well known that Watson had aligned himself with McCray in the primary. It was an odd alliance, given that it was Watson who had encouraged Goodrich to run for the Republican nomination in the first place. Goodrich was convinced that had Watson made the race on his own, he could have defeated Harry New by fifty thousand votes.[8]

Shocked by his defeat, Watson alleged voter fraud and urged Governor Samuel Ralston, a Democrat, to appoint a special grand jury to investigate the primary election results in Marion County. No sooner had this occurred than a fortuitous event happened that affected Watson's political future: Indiana's senior United States senator, Benjamin F. Shively, unexpectedly died of a heart attack on March 14. Shively's death occurred

6. "Goodrich Announces Candidacy for Governor on Republican Ticket," *Indianapolis Star,* December 30, 1915, p. 6, col. 3.

7. Goodrich, "Autobiography," p. 103.

8. Ibid., p. 104.

just a week after the primary election but before the state Republican convention. Thus, the Republican Party had the task of nominating two senatorial candidates, not just one, at the state convention in May.

Goodrich met with Will Hays the day after Shively's death. He let Hays know that, should he desire Shively's senate seat, he would support him over Watson. The next day, March 16, Hays sent to Goodrich, who was in New York on a business trip, a telegram to inform him that he wanted to remain chairman of the Indiana Republican Party. Shively's death and Hays's decision renewed Watson's senatorial hopes. Watson dropped the allegations of voter fraud and lobbied his Republican colleagues for the chance to become a United States senator after all. Watson and New were formally nominated as the Republican Party's senate candidates at the state convention.[9]

At the national level, Charles Evans Hughes received the Republican Party's presidential nomination at the Chicago convention on June 8. He won over Indiana's Charles Fairbanks. Hughes, a former governor of New York, resigned as an associate justice of the United States Supreme Court to accept his party's candidacy. James Goodrich would become quite familiar with Hughes when Goodrich served with the American Relief Administration in the Soviet Union in the 1920s. Hughes then held the position of United States secretary of state. The 1916 election in Indiana drew national attention. Both major parties' vice-presidential candidates were from Indiana (Fairbanks on the Republican ticket with Hughes, and Thomas Marshall on the Democrat ticket with Woodrow Wilson). The Prohibition Party candidate for president, J. Frank Hanly, was also from Indiana.

With the Republican Party nomination for governor sewed up, Goodrich still had to defeat the Democratic gubernatorial nominee, John Adair, to reach the statehouse. Adair hailed from Portland, Indiana, the county seat of Jay County, just twenty miles north of Winchester. He had served in Congress for the previous ten years. One of the criticisms of Adair's gubernatorial candidacy, brought by Republican

9. Ibid., p. 106.

critics such as Will Hays, was that Adair had lived in Washington, D.C., for so long that he no longer was familiar with the pressing issues in Indiana.[10]

James Goodrich had his own criticisms to overcome, however, because of a perceived conflict between his business interests and his political pursuits. Goodrich was president of Washington Heat, Power and Light Company in Daviess County, Indiana; Union Heat, Light and Power Company of Union City, Indiana; and Peoples Loan and Trust Company in Winchester. He also served as a director of Jeffersonville Heat and Water Company, Citizens Heat, Light and Power Company, and several other public utilities in east-central Indiana. Opponents of Goodrich's candidacy argued that he aspired to the governor's seat so that he could increase his public utility holdings and wealth even more. A Republican announcement in the *Winchester Herald* a week before the election attempted to summarize and deflect the argument:

> They are saying that James P. Goodrich wants to be Governor so he can appoint the Public Service Commission, which will fix the rates to be charged for gas, water and light in the companies in which he is interested. Did you ever stop to think, Mr. Voter, that this commission shall consist of five members and that Mr. Goodrich can not appoint more than three Republicans on it if he wants to? Then did you ever stop to think that if the rates fixed by this commission are unjust the Supreme Court or the Appellate Court will finally pass on the question and determine it? If you believe he will control the commission then you must believe he will control the Supreme and Appellate Courts. Fred S. Caldwell [a Winchester Democrat] is a member of the latter court. Do you believe HE will be controlled by Mr. Goodrich?[11]

In an adroit political maneuver, Goodrich intentionally limited his campaign to the prominent state issues of the day: revision of the tax laws, abolition or consolidation of state positions and departments, workmen's compensation, and centralization of power in the governor's

10. Hays, *The Memoirs of Will H. Hays,* p. 146.

11. "The Republican County Ticket," *Winchester (Ind.) Herald,* November 1, 1916, p. 1, col. 4.

office.[12] He also supported a measure that went against his own interests as an investor in two coal companies. Goodrich favored the "shot-firers" bill (a safety provision for the mining of coal) and the adoption of workmen's compensation. This pleasantly surprised many labor leaders and aroused the ire of corporate officers. Because of Goodrich's position on these issues, John Hewitt, then president of the Indiana Coal Operators Association, wrote a scathing letter to association members stating that Goodrich was not a man to be trusted. Goodrich secured a copy of the letter from Hewitt's son and used it to his political advantage. He released copies of it to various labor organizations throughout the state, thus obtaining the support of many voters who traditionally would have opposed a wealthy Republican candidate.[13]

Goodrich proceeded to turn another potential liability into an asset in his bid for the governorship. Early in the campaign, Adair learned that Goodrich had paid only thirteen dollars in personal income taxes the year before (1915). Adair complained that Goodrich was hypocritical to suggest that the tax laws should be changed when Goodrich had paid so little. Goodrich admitted that he had paid only thirteen dollars in personal taxes, but he argued that was why he supported legislation that would levy a tax on intangible property such as stocks, bonds, interest income—the source of his wealth. Under the existing system, it was primarily tangible property, real and personal, that bore the burden of taxation.[14] In an even more sophisticated deflection of Adair's criticism, Goodrich attempted to make Adair appear to be the wealthier of the two candidates, when clearly the Democrat was not. In a speech to a group of railway workers in Logansport, Goodrich stated:

> Now John [Adair] said that because I pay only thirteen dollars tax I have no right to express myself on the tax question. John Adair is a rich man. He pays a lot of taxes. The amount of tax I pay represents less than a day's

12. Hays, *The Memoirs of Will H. Hays*, p. 108.

13. Ibid., p. 109.

14. See Earl Mushlitz, "Issues of the Indiana Campaign as James P. Goodrich Sees Them," *Indianapolis Star,* September 24, 1916, magazine section, p. 2, col. 1.

> pay that John received from the government [as a United States congressman] while he is chasing around over the state running for governor. Thirteen dollars doesn't amount to much to John, but it does amount to three or four days of hard work while you are driving your trains over the road. . . . I insist that whether you pay one dollar tax, thirteen dollars as I do, or hundreds of dollars as John Adair does, you have the right to insist that the small amount you and I pay shall be expended with care and economy and not wasted in maintaining hundreds of useless persons upon the public pay roll.[15]

James Goodrich claimed that Adair never raised the tax issue again after this pronouncement.[16] But Goodrich continued to hit the inequitable taxation issue hard wherever he campaigned, as he did when he spoke before the LaGrange County Corn Growers Association on October 7, 1916, and before three thousand supporters in Anderson on November 3.[17]

A survey of Goodrich's campaign record makes evident that he was not an inflexible purist on the issues, but a very practical politician. He was far more interested in obtaining results if the means were acceptable to him. For example, he claimed that he had never taken a drink of alcohol and had repeatedly supported local remonstrances against liquor establishments. Yet time and again throughout the campaign, Goodrich entered taverns and saloons to court votes, much to the chagrin of his temperance supporters.[18] Interestingly, however, Goodrich avoided, when at all possible, commenting on two of the most controversial issues of the day: prohibition and the vote for women.

Adair did not stick strictly to state issues, but raised the biggest ques-

15. Goodrich, "Autobiography," p. 112.

16. Ibid.

17. See "Speech of James P. Goodrich," Indiana State Library, Indiana Division, Ip 336.2, no. 6; "Many March in Rain in Goodrich Parade," *Indianapolis Star,* November 4, 1916, p. 1, col. 4. On Saturday, November 4, a day-long Republican rally was planned for "Goodrich Day" in Winchester. See "Goodrich Day" (paid announcement), *Winchester (Ind.) Herald,* November 1, 1916, p. 8, col. 1.

18. Goodrich, "Autobiography," p. 103.

tion on the minds of most Hoosiers: Should the United States enter the European war against Germany? "In his major speech of the campaign, Adair told his Fort Wayne audience that because the President [Wilson] had avoided war the German-Americans were not faced with the necessity of fighting their Fatherland."[19] Adair's appeal to the German-American vote was not sufficient to offset a Democratic campaign that was seriously underfunded and woefully unorganized. In fact, Adair's alignment with President Wilson apparently hurt him, since many German districts in the state were incensed by Wilson's unwillingness to take a strong stance against Germany's aggression.[20] These occurrences, combined with Goodrich's highly effective campaign strategy, resulted in a victory for the Republican candidate, but not by a large margin. On November 7, 1916, Goodrich captured the governor's seat by garnering 337,831 votes, 14,609 more than Adair received. Goodrich led the Republican ticket, while New and Watson also won their senate seats by about 9,000 votes over their Democratic opponents. Moreover, the Republican Party in Indiana also carried both houses of the General Assembly and nine of thirteen congressional seats. In the presidential race, Hughes also carried the state, defeating Wilson by a plurality of 8,779 votes. Nationally, however, Wilson narrowly defeated Hughes in one of the closest presidential elections in the twentieth century, capturing just twenty-three more electoral college votes than Hughes.[21]

19. *Fort Wayne (Ind.) Sentinel,* August 19, 1916, p. 1, col. 3; *Indianapolis News,* August 19, 1916, p. 18, col. 2.

20. According to one Democratic participant in the 1916 state election, the Democratic campaign "was a cross between a comedy and a tragedy. A political battle had never before been so miserably mismanaged in the history of the state accustomed for half a century to fierce fights." Claude Bowers, *The Life of John Worth Kerns* (Indianapolis: Hollenbeck, 1918), p. 377. See also Jacob P. Dunn, *Indiana and Indianans—A History of Aboriginal and Territorial Indiana and the Century of Statehood* (Chicago: American Historical Society, 1919), p. 785.

21. The Wilson-Hughes race was so close that Hughes's running mate, Hoosier Charles Fairbanks, was convinced that he and Hughes had won. It was reported that he had won in at least one newspaper. See "Fairbanks Happy in G.O.P. Revival," *Indianapolis Star,* November 8, 1916, p. 8, col. 1.

James Goodrich remained in Winchester on November 6 and voted the following day. Pierre had returned from Massachusetts, where he was then a student at Harvard Law School, to be with his father on election day. On November 7, James and Cora left for Indianapolis to be present in the state capital for the election results. With victory achieved, on Saturday, November 11, James and Cora returned to Winchester on the Knickerbocker Express to be greeted at the train station by hundreds of well-wishers. A one-hundred-car caravan escorted the Goodriches around the town square and to their home on East South Street. There, the governor-elect, his wife, and his mother addressed the joyous crowd that had gathered around the home in freezing temperatures.[22]

Just a few days before Goodrich took office, another local gathering was held to honor the governor-to-be. On December 29, Goodrich's men's Sunday school class presented him with a chalice honoring him for his many years of service and wishing him well in his new position of leadership. It was a warm send-off that James Goodrich would greatly savor. As the new governor would quickly learn, colleagues and friends in the statehouse were not nearly so numerous or supportive.

22. "Great Reception Given Goodrich," *Winchester (Ind.) Herald,* November 13, 1916, p. 1, col. 1. Harry Fraze, one-time Winchester mayor, was present for the parade and celebration, and he described the euphoric welcome that James Goodrich received (interview, October 26, 1991). We know that Pierre was present for election day from a sentence on the front page of the *Winchester Journal:* "Pierre Goodrich left Tuesday [November 7] to resume his studies at Harvard University" (November 8, 1916, p. 1, col. 3).

Chapter 10

Years as Governor, 1917–1921

We may well aspire to the distinction of establishing as the "Indiana idea" in state government the maintenance of the same standards of economy, efficiency and service which prevail in the conduct of the most efficiently managed private business. . . .

JAMES P. GOODRICH, Address to Indiana General Assembly, January 8, 1917

NO SOONER had he been elected governor in November 1916 than James Goodrich "was besieged upon every hand by persons who wished to receive appointments in [his] administration."[1] He put off filling most positions until after the General Assembly had met in the winter and early spring of 1917. Soon afterward, however, Goodrich made appointments that filled two of the most important offices in his administration: Fred Sims, state Republican chairman after Goodrich, was appointed chairman of the Board of Tax Commissioners; and Ernest Lewis, a reporter who had covered Goodrich's campaign for the *Indianapolis Star,* was selected as chairman of the Public Service Commission. In almost all departments, Goodrich advocated a nonpartisan makeup of employees. He believed that many members of the previous administration—that of Democrat Samuel Ralston—had done a competent job, and he saw no need to replace them.[2]

1. Goodrich, "Autobiography," p. 114.

2. Ibid., p. 121. Goodrich's decision to take a relatively nonpartisan approach toward his appointments is also discussed in his obituary, *Indianapolis News,* August 16, 1940, p. 2, col. 1.

Goodrich took office on January 8, 1917. A special train from Winchester was chartered to Indianapolis. All of Goodrich's family members, including his mother, his brothers and their wives, members of Goodrich's Presbyterian Bible class, and hundreds of others were present for the swearing-in ceremony at the statehouse rotunda. Pierre briefly left his studies at Harvard to attend.[3] James Watson, newly elected as a United States senator, wrote from Washington, D.C., congratulating Goodrich for achieving the political position he had longed for for himself.

January 5, 1917

My dear Governor:

If I were not so taken up here with matters of public interest, I should certainly come to Indiana to see you inaugurated. I am a bit sentimental, and it would be a source of unqualified pleasure to me to see my old boyhood friend and chum made Governor of the great state of Indiana. . . .

Your friend,
James E. Watson[4]

At noon on January 8, James Goodrich was administered the oath of office by Moses B. Lairy, chief justice of the Supreme Court of Indiana. The new governor's inaugural address immediately followed, and it reflected his no-nonsense approach to governing. He stated that the number-one goal of his four-year term would be "efficiency and econ-

3. "Goodrich Ready to Take Seat," *Indianapolis Star,* January 8, 1917, p. 1, col. 6.

4. Letter from James Watson to James Goodrich, James P. Goodrich Papers, box 28. Goodrich's response to his boyhood chum is indicative of his no-nonsense personality:

January 15, 1917

Dear Jim:

Please cut out the "Governor" business. Am glad that you approve of the start made. Wish you might be out here to help along with the work. I find it a difficult task to shake fellows loose from their job. I intend, however, to keep pegging away at it and try to give Indiana a good business administration and make it easier for the boys who are to come after me to be elected.

Sincerely yours,
James P. Goodrich

omy" in the administration of the state's duties. He proceeded to prove it by the brevity of his remarks: Goodrich's entire inaugural address was not five minutes long.[5] Moreover, in order to devote all of his energies to his new position, Goodrich had announced that he would not host an inaugural ball.[6]

On the afternoon of his inauguration, Goodrich did allow himself a longer time to address the General Assembly, a full thirty-six minutes. He outlined the plans of his administration: abolishing the oil inspection department, the state's statistician department, and several minor departments; creating a highway commission, a conservation commission, and banking and insurance commissions; amending the workmen's compensation laws and providing for absentee balloting; and making several offices, such as those of state geologist and superintendent of schools, appointive rather than elective. One of his most pressing concerns was to overhaul the unjust tax system, making it more equitable between real property owners and owners of nontangible property.[7]

While both parties generally favored the recommendations, some Democrats were afraid that all of the consolidations might result in giving the state's top executive too much appointive power. These few Democrats had reason to be concerned. During his gubernatorial campaign speeches, Goodrich had repeatedly shouted the slogan, "You give me the power and I'll be responsible for the results."[8] Goodrich recalled that Democratic-leaning newspapers were even more "venomous" in

5. Goodrich, "Autobiography," pp. 115–19; "Goodrich Counsels Economy: Recommends in Message Many Reforms to Reduce Public Expenditures," *Indianapolis Star,* January 9, 1917, p. 1, col. 4; "Governor Outlines Program," *Indianapolis Star,* November 11, 1916, p. 1, col. 1.

6. "Inauguration of Goodrich to Be Simple," *Indianapolis Star,* November 26, 1916, p. 1, col. 1.

7. Goodrich, "Autobiography," pp. 119–20; "Governor Goodrich's Message," *Indianapolis News,* January 9, 1917, p. 6, col. 2.

8. See David Mannweiler, "Governors of Indiana," *Indianapolis News,* March 16, 1964, p. 5, col. 8.

attacking his policies, referring to him as a "would-be Czar with a desire to centralize in the hands of the Governor complete control of the state's affairs."[9]

There was no official governor's residence in Indianapolis when Goodrich took office. Therefore, James and Cora arranged somewhat makeshift accommodations. During their four years in the state's capital, they lived in three different Indianapolis locations: 1828 North Meridian Street (1917); 2710 Sutherland Avenue (1918–19), and the Claypool Hotel (1920–21).[10] Despite James's hectic schedule, there was hardly a Sunday that he missed traveling back to Winchester, a distance of some eighty miles, to teach his men's Sunday school class at the Presbyterian Church. He either took the Saturday evening train back to Winchester, during which time he would work on his lesson, or drove from Indianapolis on the poor roads between the capital and his hometown.

During the first session of the General Assembly, a prohibition bill had been passed and Goodrich had signed it. An excise tax on corporations promoted by Goodrich, however, was defeated in the senate by "men of small mind and narrow vision," Goodrich claimed.[11] Similarly, Democrats defeated Goodrich's plan to abolish the oil inspector's position, a position that employed sixty-seven inspectors around the state in what Goodrich considered totally useless government jobs. Since it was the Democratic members of the senate who defeated the bill, Goodrich did not hesitate to force the existing chief oil inspector to resign. Goodrich alleged that he had evidence of repeated graft by the chief oil inspector and threatened to see him prosecuted if he did not leave "voluntarily." The governor replaced him with Carl Mote, a Randolph County native who had served as Goodrich's press secretary during his

9. Goodrich, "Autobiography," p. 121. See also "Governor's Czarism," *Indianapolis News,* January 15, 1917, p. 6, col. 1.

10. Indianapolis City Directory (1917–21), Indiana State Library, Indiana Division; see also "Goodrich Selects Home Where He Will Live While Governor," *Indianapolis Star,* December 28, 1916, p. 1, col. 2.

11. Goodrich, "Autobiography," p. 125.

gubernatorial campaign. Mote subsequently fired the remaining oil inspectors—all Democrats—and replaced them with Republicans.[12]

While the Democratic attacks against his legislative agenda were anticipated, Republican opposition was not. The newly elected governor never enjoyed a honeymoon period with the legislature. Instead, he encountered repeated and open opposition, mostly from members of his own party. This included criticism by his own lieutenant governor, Edward Bush, a Republican.[13] "Goodrich could not, however, deny that he was himself responsible for having selected Bush, a dry, to run for lieutenant governor instead of John Lewis of Seymour, a wet. 'As it turned out,' recalled Goodrich, 'I would have been better off with John Lewis drunk than Ed Bush sober.' "[14]

Goodrich wrote about difficulty he encountered in getting the General Assembly to approve his proposals: "It was a strange situation in which I found myself. The men who had been associated with party politics ever since 1900 complimented me during the campaign on the promises made and almost invariably said that it was 'good stuff.' But after my inauguration, they began to express grave doubts as to the wisdom and political expedience of so many new and unusual things."[15]

James Goodrich took office just three months before the United States declared war against Germany. The European conflict indelibly marked his four years in the statehouse, as he would from that time thereafter be referred to as the "war governor." Goodrich had been opposed to the United States' entering the war, describing himself as initially "pro-German."[16] Indeed, the nation itself and Hoosiers in particular had

12. Ibid., pp. 124–27. Regarding Goodrich's tax revision proposals, see Ernest I. Lewis, "Governor Appeals to State's People: Inequalities of Taxation," *Indianapolis News,* March 14, 1917, p. 5, col. 4.

13. Goodrich, "Autobiography," p. 122.

14. Benjamin D. Rhodes, *James P. Goodrich, Indiana's "Governor Strangelove,"* p. 31, quoting in part Goodrich, "Autobiography," p. 107.

15. Goodrich, "Autobiography," p. 120. See also John A. Lapp, "Legislation Is Branded Failure," *Indianapolis Star,* January 1, 1918, p. 20, col. 7.

16. Goodrich, "Autobiography," p. 127.

been greatly divided regarding which side the United States should fight on if it did enter the conflict.[17] By the end of March 1917, however, Goodrich had concluded that the United States' entry on the side of the Allied powers was the moral thing to do. He proclaimed publicly that America "can not with honor stay out any longer."[18]

On the evening of April 2, President Wilson delivered his war message to Congress. Knowing that a declaration of war was imminent, Goodrich held a conference on April 5 in Indianapolis with leading farmers, grain dealers, canners, and county agents from throughout the state. An increase in food production was the foremost topic. On the following day, April 6, Congress passed the War Declaration Act and Wilson signed it. Immediately, Goodrich's office in the statehouse was besieged by eager young men who offered themselves for service in any capacity that was needed. By June, registration of available men was 100.6 percent of the census estimate for the state prepared by the United States Department of War. By July 1918, 88,500 men from Indiana had volunteered to serve in the army and navy, on the basis of percentage of population, more than from any other state.[19] By the war's conclusion, Indiana had supplied more than 130,000 troops, of which 3,354 Indiana soldiers and 15 nurses had been killed or had died of diseases, chiefly influenza and pneumonia.[20] Hoosiers of all backgrounds supported the war effort. For instance, James A. Allison, owner of the Indianapolis Motor Speedway, declared in the spring of 1917 that there would be no more Indianapolis 500 races un-

17. See Cedric C. Cummins, *Indiana Public Opinion and the World War, 1914–1917* (Indianapolis: Indiana Historical Bureau, 1945), pp. 17–41.

18. *Indianapolis News*, March 28, 1917, p. 1, col. 3.

19. Jeannette Covert Nolan, *Hoosier City: The Story of Indianapolis* (New York: Julian Messner, 1943), p. 262; Goodrich, "Autobiography," p. 150. For a summary of Indiana's involvement in World War I, see Charles Roll, *Indiana* (Chicago: Lewis Publishing, 1931), pp. 449–67.

20. *Indiana State News Bulletin*, August 1, 1928, p. 4; see also *Indiana War Records, Gold Star Honor Roll* (Indianapolis, 1921); Clifton J. Phillips, *Indiana in Transition: The Emergence of an Industrial Commonwealth, 1880–1920*, vol. 4 of *The History of Indiana* (Indianapolis: Indiana Historical Bureau and Indiana Historical Society, 1968), pp. 610–11.

til the war was over; he further turned over his manufacturing companies to the army to be used to produce munitions.[21]

Hoosiers with more modest resources also contributed significantly to the war effort. At the request of Governor Goodrich and Indiana's mayors, Hoosiers planted 500,000 home gardens in 1917 to produce necessary vegetables and crops. Senators Harry New and James Watson sent fifty thousand packages of seeds to Hoosiers, who spaded up every available backyard and vacant lot to produce food for the "boys overseas." The next year, 640,000 gardens were planted.[22] Goodrich also signed and promoted several "Liberty Loan Proclamations" whereby he challenged Hoosiers to lend money to the government to support the war effort.[23] Perhaps most important, Goodrich established a State Council of Defense Committee to organize and direct the resources of the state for national use. On May 17, 1917, Goodrich placed his good friend, Will Hays, the state Republican Party chairman, in charge of the council. It proved to be one of the most successful statewide organizations of its kind in the country.[24] Within months, Indiana

21. Nolan, *Hoosier City: The Story of Indianapolis,* pp. 262–64.

22. "Governor Calls Meeting in Each County to Urge Increase in Food Crops," *Indianapolis Star,* April 6, 1917, p. 1, col. 1. See also George S. Cottman, *Centennial History and Handbook of Indiana* (Indianapolis: State of Indiana, 1917), with supplement, "Highlights of Indiana in the World War," edited by Edith Margaret Evans and Freeman T. Felt, pp. 9–11. Goodrich's belief in the importance of increasing the food supply is evident in a speech he delivered to two thousand farmers in Anderson, Indiana, on February 5, 1918, "2,000 Farmers Hear Goodrich," *Indianapolis Star,* February 6, 1918, p. 5, col. 4.

23. See "The Fourth 'Liberty Loan Proclamation' by James P. Goodrich, Governor of Indiana," *Indianapolis Star,* September 28, 1918, p. 5, col. 5; James P. Goodrich, "Indiana Patriot League Articles," *Indianapolis News,* March 16, 1918, p. 8, col. 2; and "Duty Calls to Every Hoosier: Each Loyal Indianian Must Do His Share, Goodrich Says in Message," *Indianapolis Star,* January 1, 1918, p. 20, col. 2.

24. Goodrich, "Autobiography," pp. 130–31; Richard M. Clutter, "Indiana and the First World War," *Indiana Military History Journal* 1 (July 1976), pp. 20–22; George S. Cottman, *Centennial History and Handbook of Indiana* (Indianapolis: State of Indiana, 1917), with supplement, "Highlights of Indiana in the World War," edited by Edith Margaret Evans and Freeman T. Felt, pp. 9–11. Will Hays devotes an entire chapter to the State Council of Defense in his *Memoirs of Will H. Hays* (Garden City, N.Y.: Doubleday, 1955), pp. 114–38.

led every other state in terms of production, conservation, volunteers, and service abroad. The state was so successful that Newton D. Baker, secretary of war in the Woodrow Wilson administration, requested that other state councils go to Indiana and study the Hoosier council's methods.[25]

Despite the large percentage of people of German ancestry in the state and nation, American citizens of German blood were ridiculed, discriminated against, and even lynched.[26] In Indianapolis, most street names that were German or even German sounding were anglicized. By the winter of 1919, the state legislature, with the encouragement of the Indiana State Teachers Association, banned the teaching of German in all Indiana grade and high schools.[27] James Goodrich contested the legislation, but to no effect. As governor, he was limited to issuing a proclamation outlawing any conduct directed against any citizen because of his or her ancestry.[28]

In the face of general criticism of Hoosiers of German ancestry, Goodrich made one of his most difficult but most successful appointments. On March 17, 1917, Goodrich named German-born Richard Lieber secretary of the Forestry Board. Lieber was later appointed director of the Indiana State Parks Committee and chairman of the Department of Conservation. Additionally, just four days after the United States declared war against Germany, Goodrich extended to Lieber the

25. For instance, Goodrich claimed that by July 1917 Fort Wayne, Indiana, had sent more men as soldiers and sailors to the European war than the entire state of New York had. Goodrich, "Autobiography," pp. 133–34. See also Richard M. Clutter, "Indiana and the First World War," pp. 20–23; Clifton J. Phillips, *Indiana in Transition: The Emergence of an Industrial Commonwealth, 1880–1920,* pp. 608–9; and Jeannette Covert Nolan, *Hoosier City: The Story of Indianapolis,* pp. 260–68.

26. Goodrich, "Autobiography," pp. 142–43.

27. *Laws of Indiana,* 1919, pp. 50–51, 822–23. The Board of School Commissioners of Indianapolis even inserted into teachers' contracts a clause stating that disloyalty to the United States in spoken or written word (that is, the use of German) constituted cause for dismissal. The Indiana State Teachers Association passed a resolution on April 13, 1918, forbidding the teaching of German in Indiana schools. See Frances H. Ellis, "German Instruction in the Public Schools of Indianapolis, 1869–1919," *Indiana Magazine of History* 50 (1954): 372, 374–78.

28. Goodrich, "Autobiography," p. 142.

position of military secretary to the governor.[29] In addition to being a native of Germany, Lieber had three brothers who were colonels in the German army. James Goodrich bestowed upon Lieber the rank of colonel. Lieber went on to become the father of Indiana's state parks system, serving three successive governors and helping to establish and preserve some of Indiana's most scenic and historic land: Brown County State Park (1930), Clifty Falls State Park in Jefferson County (1920), Indiana Dunes in Porter County (1925), and Mounds State Park in Madison County (1930).[30]

Richard Lieber was a favorite of Cora Goodrich. For example, Lieber was the only man whom Cora would allow to smoke and drink alcohol in her home. Her fondness for the colonel is evident in the fact that she brought back from a trip to Cuba a box of cigars for him and always kept fresh cigars for whenever he visited the Goodriches' Winchester home. Like James Goodrich, Lieber was an accomplished man with diverse interests. His greatest passion was conservation. In 1908, after attending a conservation conference at the White House called by President Theodore Roosevelt, Lieber became enamored of the preservation of natural resources. He returned to Indiana, and his official conserva-

29. Emma Lieber, *Richard Lieber* (Indianapolis: privately printed, 1947), p. 90; "Governor Names Military Staff," *Indianapolis News,* April 11, 1917, p. 1, col. 6. Goodrich wrote in his autobiography that he first met Lieber accidentally when he was campaigning in Indianapolis for governor. He ran into Lieber on Monument Circle. At the time, Lieber was a wholesale liquor distributor. "I was struck with his knowledge, his spirit of liberality and broad vision with respect to the public service," wrote Goodrich ("Autobiography," p. 143).

30. By the time Lieber left office in 1933, Indiana had sixteen state parks, all established during Lieber's tenure as state parks director except two that had been created in 1916: Turkey Run in Parke County and McCormick's Creek in Owen County. See "Indiana State Parks" (Indiana Department of Conservation, 1932; copy located in Indiana Division of the Indiana State Library). For more background information about Lieber, see "Richard Lieber, State Park System Founder, Dies at McCormick's Creek," *Indianapolis Star,* April 16, 1944, p. 1, col. 2; Harold Sabin, "Indiana Indebted to Richard Lieber for Excellent Park System," *Indianapolis Star,* August 28, 1966, sec. 2, p. 10, col. 2; and Wayne Guthrie, "Father of Indiana State Parks," *Indianapolis News,* October 22, 1965, p. 11, col. 6.

tion efforts continued in the state for the next twenty-five years. After he resigned in July 1933 as chairman of the State Conservation Commission, he served on national ecology committees. The deep friendship between the Goodriches and Lieber and his wife Emma continued long after Goodrich left the governor's office. After James's and Cora's deaths, Lieber advised Pierre in the early 1940s on conservation measures in association with the Ayrshire Collieries Corporation.[31]

Despite the numerous state issues that the new governor had to contend with, it was the European war that most concerned James Goodrich in the spring of 1917. He agonized over how best to support the boys overseas. Finally, knowing that the nation was experiencing an emergency, Goodrich made an appeal to all county commissioners, township trustees, school boards, merchants, and mayors to suspend building contracts until the war was over. In the meantime, however, the Wilson administration had advocated "business as usual." Goodrich called the president to explain that he was "satisfied that the country could not carry on its business as usual [policy] and wage a war at the same time."[32]

Goodrich added that the matter did not extend to construction contracts alone, but to the production of energy as well. Goodrich attempted to get the coal companies to commit to a fixed price for coal; demand had increased as much as 30 percent since the war had begun, and there was a fairly broad sentiment by coal operators, according to Goodrich, that this was a prime opportunity to maximize coal profits. Goodrich was in an embarrassing situation himself because he had, at the time, a large interest in two coal companies. He met with the coal operators of Indiana on June 15, 1917, asking them to make sacrifices. On July 9, he met in Bloomington, Indiana, with William Jennings Bryan, the former Democratic presidential candidate. He sought Bryan's support to encourage President Wilson to fix a fair price for coal. Dissatisfied with his long-distance communications with the president, on

31. Emma Lieber, *Richard Lieber,* pp. 95–103, 161.
32. Goodrich, "Autobiography," pp. 129–30.

July 16 Goodrich traveled to Washington, D.C. He first testified before the Interstate Commerce Commission and then held a private meeting with Wilson. He urged the president "to use his influence with the Congress . . . to pass a law regulating and reducing the price of coal."[33]

On his return to Indiana at the end of July, Goodrich put all his efforts into governing the state and assisting the State Council of Defense in its efforts to raise resources for the war. Goodrich maintained a grueling schedule, and after he had been in office less than eight months, his health began to deteriorate. In August 1917, he contracted typhoid fever after visiting a northern Indiana prison.[34] His condition was severely worsened when he contracted pneumonia. For several weeks, the governor was bedridden at Methodist-Episcopal Hospital in Indianapolis, at times bordering on death.[35] He finally recovered after returning to Winchester in October and then spending a month in convalescence in Florida along the Gulf of Mexico.[36]

Back in the statehouse on November 26, Goodrich pursued his official duties. For the next several months, the state's coal shortage occupied much of his time. On January 22, 1918, he again traveled to Washington, D.C., this time testifying before the Senate. There, Indiana's governor claimed that the coal crisis was really a transportation crisis caused by the shortage of railroad cars and engines.[37]

Unfortunately, Goodrich's attention to the state's problems kept being diverted by personal crises. Three weeks earlier, on December 29,

33. Ibid., pp. 131–33.

34. Ibid., p. 135. See also "Governor Ill at Methodist Hospital," *Indianapolis Star,* August 25, 1917, p. 1, col. 7; "Goodrich Little Better; Friends Not Admitted," *Indianapolis Star,* August 25, 1917, p. 1, col. 7; and "Has Typhoid Fever," *Indianapolis News,* August 27, 1917, p. 1, col. 4.

35. "Governor Takes Turn for Worse," *Indianapolis Star,* September 10, 1917, p. 1, col. 7; "Governor Leaves Hospital for Home at Winchester," *Indianapolis Star,* October 22, 1917, p. 1, col. 2.

36. See Goodrich, "Autobiography," p. 136; "Governor Leaves Hospital for Home at Winchester," *Indianapolis Star,* October 10, 1917, p. 1, col. 7; and "Goodrich Resumes Duties at State House," *Indianapolis News,* October 29, 1917, p. 1, col. 4.

37. Everett C. Watkins, "Goodrich Gives Coal Testimony," *Indianapolis Star,* January 23, 1918, p. 1, col. 4.

1917, James's mother, Elizabeth Edger Goodrich, died of heart failure in Winchester after a very brief illness. A little more than a year before her death, in October 1916, Mrs. Goodrich donated twenty acres of land to Winchester. In consideration of the gift, the town was to maintain the land as a park in the name of Mrs. Goodrich's deceased husband, John B. Goodrich, and to impose a levy that generated at least nine hundred dollars annually for that purpose. The gift was bequeathed on the condition that alcohol would not be sold on the parkland and that no activities would be allowed on Sundays with the exception of religious, charitable, or educational entertainments.[38]

After his mother's death, the governor's own misfortunes continued as well. Almost exactly one year after his bout with typhoid, James Goodrich was in an automobile accident in Indianapolis. On the evening of August 28, 1918, Goodrich attended a dinner party, hosted by Dr. Amelia Keller, for a number of medical officers who were going abroad. Shortly after he left the party in his car, he was struck by a streetcar and critically injured. At the time of the mishap, Pierre was a second lieutenant stationed at the quartermaster depot in Jeffersonville, Indiana. He came immediately to Indianapolis to be with his father at St. Vincent's Hospital. The governor had fractures of the hip, skull, ribs, and collarbone and experienced internal bleeding. Although Goodrich made a relatively quick recovery, his left leg was placed in a cast for several weeks. He had to walk with the aid of a cane for the rest of his life.[39]

The large victory of the Republican Party in Indiana in the 1916 election had given Will Hays a certain mystique in Republican circles throughout the country. Hays had achieved phenomenal success in returning Progressive Party supporters (Bull Moosers) to the Grand Old Party.

38. Donald P. Whitted, "Recollections," *Winchester News-Gazette,* January 6, 1998, p. 8, col. 6.

39. "Governor Seriously Hurt in Automobile Accident," *Indianapolis Star,* August 29, 1918, p. 1, col. 4; "Goodrich Has Peaceful Day; Is Improving," *Indianapolis Star,* August 30, 1918, p. 1, col. 1; "Governor's Progress Pleases Physicians," *Indianapolis Star,* August 31, 1918, p. 1, col. 5; Goodrich, "Autobiography," pp. 150–51.

For instance, whereas 162,000 Hoosiers had voted for the Bull Moose presidential candidate, Theodore Roosevelt, in the 1912 election, fewer than 4,000 voted for the Progressive Party candidate in 1916. Similarly, the Republican Party had garnered 190,000 more votes for presidential candidate Charles Evans Hughes in 1916 than it had for William Howard Taft in 1912. "Immediately there were calls for Hays to consult with national leaders to determine how the Indiana magic could be worked nationally."[40]

Goodrich recognized that Hays had an excellent chance of gaining the national chairmanship of the Republican Party when the position became available at the end of 1917. Hays's name had been mentioned for the position ever since the 1916 election. Goodrich personally lobbied every influential Republican he knew to support Hays's candidacy.[41] In November he traveled to New York and met with Theodore Roosevelt. According to Goodrich, Roosevelt agreed to support Hays. The former president started contacting "men by long distance all over the country, men who would respond to any request he made."[42] Over the years, Goodrich and Roosevelt had established a political and personal friendship. For instance, when Goodrich had met with President Wilson the preceding July in Washington, D.C., he traveled on to New York City at Roosevelt's invitation. There, Goodrich met with the former president at the Harvard Club. At that time, Roosevelt discussed with Goodrich his plans to raise a military division and lead it into France. In a highly controversial and public decision, President Wilson rebuffed Roosevelt's offer.[43]

With regard to Hays's candidacy for chairmanship of the national Republican Party, Goodrich also lobbied Albert Beveridge. Beveridge had rejoined the Republican Party in June 1916 after having left it in 1911

40. Walden S. Freeman, "Will H. Hays and the Politics of Party Harmony," in *Their Infinite Variety: Essays on Indiana Politicians* (Indianapolis: Indiana Historical Society, 1981), p. 340.

41. "Will Hays Boomed to Head G.O.P.: National Leaders Launch Move to Displace Wilcox with Indiana Chairman," *Indianapolis Star*, January 9, 1917, p. 1, col. 3.

42. Goodrich, "Autobiography," p. 140.

43. Ibid., p. 133.

to become a highly prominent leader of the Bull Moose Party. Beveridge was asked by Goodrich to solicit Roosevelt and others on behalf of Hays. Once Roosevelt's support was obtained, the former president lobbied other influential Republicans across the country. Roosevelt's efforts were not totally selfless. He had plans to seek the 1920 Republican presidential nomination. He knew that if he helped Hays, Hays could be counted on to return the favor.

The strong lobbying effort paid off. On February 13, 1918, Hays was elected to the top national Republican position. Hays, just thirty-eight, was the youngest Republican National Committee chairman up to that time. Hays resigned his position as chairman of the Indiana Council on Defense on February 21, and Goodrich was forced to name a successor. Concerned that the subsequent appointment not be seen as solely partisan, Goodrich appointed a top Democrat, Michael Foley.[44]

Within weeks, Goodrich had to contend with one of the most controversial issues ever to be debated and acted upon in the United States—prohibition. At midnight on March 30, 1918, the sale, transportation, and consumption of alcoholic beverages in Indiana were prohibited by state legislation. Immediately, 3,500 Indiana taverns and saloons were closed, 547 of them in Indianapolis alone. By January 1919, the Eighteenth Amendment to the Constitution, outlawing the sale and consumption of alcohol nationally, had been ratified. Fifteen years later, in 1933, the amendment was repealed, replaced by the Twenty-first Amendment.

Before his automobile accident, James Goodrich had been pressed by his brother Percy to ask Will Hays to be the keynote speaker at the National Hay Association's annual convention in Chicago. Percy Goodrich was president of the national agricultural organization. Former Republican presidents William Howard Taft and Theodore Roosevelt had served as keynote speakers in previous years. Therefore, Percy believed that it was not too much to think that the new chairman of the national Republican Party might accept their invitation. Besides, Percy knew of

44. Ibid., p. 141. Hays's account of his selection as national Republican chairman is contained in his *Memoirs of Will H. Hays,* pp. 153–68.

the close friendship between his brother and Hays. He obviously believed that if James were to offer the invitation, the likelihood of a favorable response would be increased. In response to James Goodrich's solicitation, Hays turned the tables. He wrote that the governor himself should address the large convention, since it would be "an opportunity to get into intimate personal touch with all of them."[45] Hays went on to encourage Goodrich to speak nationally and become known beyond Indiana's borders. Hays wrote:

> I want to take this opportunity to make another suggestion: I think you ought to get a good many such trips around the country. You have done the work literally of a hundred men since you have been Governor, and things are moving great. It will interest you to know that your administration is the greatest asset we have got in Indiana. I say this officially and not because of my personal affection. I think for the sake of the whole proposition, and your own health, you ought to run around a good deal—quietly go to important points.[46]

Hays's suggestion stemmed from his desire to groom Goodrich for national office, but Indiana's governor, if he was aware of Hays's ulterior motive, did not take the bait. He responded to Hays:

> I have your letter of June 17th. I may be able to meet you in Chicago. Will see what I can do and advise you later. . . . Sorry you cannot attend the Grain Dealer's meeting, as it is almost out of the question for me to do this. I have reached the point where I despise, above all things, to undertake to make a speech. It is drudgery to me and anything I say seems to be of so little consequence any way.
>
> I can be of so much greater service in other directions and let those

45. Letter from Will H. Hays to James Goodrich, June 13, 1918 (in response to Goodrich's letter to Hays dated June 11, 1918), Will H. Hays Collection, James P. Goodrich file, Indiana State Library, Manuscript Section, Indianapolis.

46. Letter from Will H. Hays to James Goodrich, June 10, 1918, Will H. Hays Collection, James P. Goodrich file, Indiana State Library, Manuscript Section, Indianapolis.

> who know how and like to, do the talking. . . . There are many things I want to talk over when I see you and hope you will have seen Teddy [Roosevelt] before you come west.[47]

Soon afterward, Goodrich's term in office was disrupted by his automobile accident in August. Still another health crisis loomed, this one national—the great influenza epidemic of October 1918. Goodrich recalled that the disease "swept the country like wildfire," killing many. On October 10, the governor issued a statewide prohibition against all public meetings, educational, political, and religious.[48]

The election of November 1918 preoccupied him next. The previous May, Goodrich had presided over the Republican state convention as the temporary chairman.[49] In late October, still recovering from his automobile accident, Goodrich appealed to the voters in Indiana to support the Republican Party. He declared that it had been only Republican leaders who had made a "demand for an unconditional surrender and against peace [with Germany] through compromise and negotiation."[50] The appeal was well received. At the general election two weeks later, Republicans swept offices at the state and federal levels in an unprecedented fashion: eighty-nine out of one hundred Republicans were elected to the Indiana House, thirty-three out of fifty Republicans were elected in the Senate, and Republicans garnered all thirteen of Indiana's United States congressional seats. On November 15, Goodrich called a special two-day meeting of all newly elected Republican members of the legislature. His purpose was to lay before them the proposals he would be submitting to the General Assembly in January 1919. At Goodrich's invitation, United States senators Harry

47. Letter from Goodrich to Hays, June 20, 1918, Will H. Hays Collection, James P. Goodrich file, Indiana State Library, Manuscript Section, Indianapolis.

48. Goodrich, "Autobiography," p. 151.

49. "Goodrich Delivers Speech at Republican Convention," *Indianapolis News,* May 29, 1918, p. 9, col. 1.

50. "Governor Pleads Republican Cause," *Indianapolis News,* October 23, 1918, p. 1, col. 3.

New and James Watson, along with Will Hays, met with the Republican majority in Indianapolis.[51]

On January 6, 1919, just before the General Assembly was to meet, news came that Theodore Roosevelt had died at the relatively young age of sixty. That sad fact "upset all the plans Will Hays and I had for nominating Roosevelt for the presidency [in 1920]," Goodrich recalled.[52] Just four days later, on January 10, Goodrich addressed the General Assembly. He appealed to the legislature to support his platform, which, he believed, had been overwhelmingly endorsed by the voters, as the large Republican victory in November indicated. By January 14, the General Assembly had ratified the Eighteenth Amendment to the Constitution (Prohibition), which had been an accomplished fact in Indiana since the previous March. The General Assembly also passed a joint resolution on one of the other great national issues to be debated in this country's history—woman suffrage. Although Goodrich admitted he was opposed to it, he signed the legislation, apparently submitting to legislative and public pressure.[53]

Through a hard fight, Goodrich next created a state highway commission. This placed control of the construction and maintenance of highways in the hands of the state. More than thirty-five hundred miles of roadway were taken over by the commission. Local contractors had been strongly opposed to the legislation.[54] Moreover, during the waning days of the 1919 legislative session, Goodrich succeeded in getting passed a "shot-firers" bill, which compelled coal operators to hire experienced men to "shoot down" the coal as opposed to making miners do it themselves. Legislation was also approved that reduced the number of oil inspectors from sixty-seven to five, resulting in a net savings to the state, according to Goodrich, of $300,000 per annum. Fi-

51. Goodrich, "Autobiography," pp. 152–53. See also "Governor Will Pen Bi-Ennial Message Soon," *Indianapolis Star,* December 18, 1918, p. 13, col. 8.

52. Goodrich, "Autobiography," p. 154.

53. Ibid., pp. 180–81.

54. Ibid., pp. 157–58.

nally, on March 10, the day before the legislative session ended, a tax bill was passed, although it did not contain all the reforms that the governor had offered.[55]

With the 1919 legislative session behind him, Goodrich could once again focus on the state's efforts to support America's war efforts overseas. As the war was winding down, Goodrich established a Reconstruction Committee to explore how best to manage the return of more than 130,000 Hoosier veterans. An early action of the committee was to send a letter to every employer of an enlisted soldier. The letter inquired whether the soldier's previous job would be available upon his return; approximately 98 percent of the employers responded affirmatively.[56]

The end of World War I marked one of the highlights of James Goodrich's administration. When the armistice was announced on November 11, 1918, Indianapolis was ablaze with fireworks. Anything that could make noise was employed to mark the occasion. The evening of November 11 found thousands crowded around Monument Circle in downtown Indianapolis singing "The Star-Spangled Banner," "Nearer My God to Thee," and other popular patriotic and religious songs.

The delays in transporting some two million men stateside from Europe were many.[57] The following spring, on April 28, Goodrich traveled to New York City to welcome the first contingent of Indiana soldiers home. Ten days later, on May 7, 1919, a crowd estimated at 175,000 filled the sidewalks of downtown Indianapolis. Twenty thousand returned soldiers and others participated in the parade marching under a large Victory Arch and before Governor and Mrs. Goodrich in

55. Ibid., pp. 163–65.

56. See "Governor Will Pen Bi-Ennial Message Soon," *Indianapolis Star,* December 18, 1918, p. 13, col. 8. Goodrich discussed the committee's correspondence with soldiers' employers in an exchange of letters between Goodrich and Seymour Avery, president of the Wheeler-Schebler Carburetor Company, Indianapolis. Letter from Avery to Goodrich, December 6, 1918; letter from Goodrich to Avery, December 9, 1918, Goodrich files, Archives, Indiana State Library. See also "Governor Thinks Surplus Labor After War May Be Used for Road Building," *Indianapolis News,* October 23, 1918, p. 5, col. 3.

57. Roll, *Indiana,* p. 460.

the stands.[58] Goodrich later proclaimed September 22 as "Heroes Day" when the martyred were commemorated with a ceremony at Monument Circle.[59]

Just two weeks before, on September 4, President Woodrow Wilson had visited Indianapolis to seek support for his proposed League of Nations. Goodrich made it well known that he opposed the League, but he entertained the president while Wilson was in Indianapolis and introduced him at a packed rally at the state fairgrounds.[60] In October, Goodrich had to contend with a serious coal strike in Lake County. On October 5, he declared martial law and ordered state troops to quell the labor uprisings.[61] He met with John L. Lewis, the newly elected leader of the United Mine Workers of America. Negotiations between the two men failed because of their disagreement regarding guarantees to provide coal for state institutions and public utilities. The strike, which eventually became nationwide and continued through the months of November and December, resulted in price gouging. Goodrich met with governors from seven other coal-producing states in an attempt to resolve the problem, but the whole situation only grew more "chaotic."[62]

In the fall and winter of 1919, Goodrich made two noteworthy speeches in New York state. Goodrich's willingness to address gatherings so far

58. See Hazel E. Crawford, "Indiana's Victory Celebration of World War I," *Indiana Military History Journal* 4 (October 1979): 16–20; "Governor Proclaims Welcome Home Day," *Indianapolis News,* March 29, 1919, p. 44, col. 7.

59. "Governor Proclaims Heroes' Day," *Indianapolis Star,* September 23, 1918, p. 4, col. 2.

60. Ibid., p. 177; "Governor's Address Welcomes President Wilson to the State," *Indianapolis News,* September 5, 1919, p. 3, col. 3.

61. "Governor Issues Statement Regarding the Keeping of Militia in Calumet Strike Region," *Indianapolis News,* October 28, 1919, p. 5, col. 1.

62. In August 1919, the nation experienced a large increase in inflation, which led to extremely high prices for basic commodities. On August 5, Goodrich proposed government intervention to stop those who were manipulating the markets in order to enjoy excessive profits. There is no indication that any of Goodrich's proposals were ever adopted at the state or federal level. See "Governor Seeks Method to Lower Basic Commodities," *Indianapolis Star,* August 6, 1919, p. 1, col. 3.

from Indiana raises the question of whether he had, at that time, national political aspirations. On September 22, he addressed the National Security League in Albany, New York, and on December 21, he spoke in Brooklyn, New York, before the New England Society. To both, his advice was much the same: America should focus its attention on problems at home and not become involved in international entanglements. The addresses were in obvious response to President Wilson's promotion of the entrance of the United States into the League of Nations.[63] In Washington, D.C., at that time, James Watson was carrying water for the Republican Party against Senate ratification of both the League of Nations and the Versailles Treaty. Watson had been appointed to serve as floor whip by the minority leader, Senator Henry Cabot Lodge of Massachusetts, to manage the defeat of both measures.[64]

By the end of December, Goodrich had decided to call a special session of the General Assembly for the purpose of ratifying the constitutional amendment extending suffrage to women. Clearly, views on women's rights at the time were archaic, and Goodrich's own were hardly enlightened ones. He wrote years later: "I was never very strongly for [woman suffrage]; I did not believe it would accomplish a small percentage of the good claimed by the supporters of the movement. I maintained that it would increase the expense; that women when once engaged in politics would not in any way raise the morals of a campaign; women would adopt themselves to a political situation just the same as men."[65]

The special session on the Nineteenth Amendment was held on January 17, 1920. Despite Goodrich's lack of enthusiasm for the measure, it was ratified in the Indiana Senate by a vote of forty-three to three and in the House by a unanimous vote of ninety-three.

Soon afterward, a financial crisis confronted the state. State Auditor

63. Goodrich, "Autobiography," pp. 177–80; "Goodrich Addresses New England Society in Brooklyn," *Indianapolis News,* December 22, 1919, p. 23, col. 1.

64. James E. Watson, *As I Knew Them,* pp. 189–203, 214–16 (League of Nations); pp. 190–203 (Versailles Treaty).

65. Goodrich, "Autobiography," pp. 180–81.

Otto K. Klaus reported in March that appropriations for state institutions would be exhausted within ninety days unless the General Assembly authorized money for the deficit. The war had placed an inordinate drain on the financial resources of these institutions. Ironically, the state had ample monies in the general fund, but these monies could not be transferred to pay for institutional debts without the General Assembly's approval. Therefore, Goodrich called a special session, beginning July 12, 1920, to deal with the financial emergency.[66]

One of the final activities that Goodrich became involved in as governor involved a twenty-eight-acre memorial site that was constructed on a five-block area north of downtown Indianapolis. In 1919, the state legislature authorized $15 million (to be raised both publicly and privately) for the erection of the World War Memorial Plaza. The construction of the plaza first meant the razing or moving of some forty-five buildings. Goodrich was one of fifteen trustees appointed to oversee the raising of private money and the design of the plaza. The plaza ultimately included Memorial Hall; a fountain; Obelisk Square; and the statues of former presidents Abraham Lincoln and Benjamin Harrison, and a former vice-president from Indiana, Schuyler Colfax. The state's decision to construct the plaza ultimately led to the relocation of the permanent national headquarters of the American Legion in Indianapolis. This seemed quite appropriate, since an earlier brotherhood of veterans, the Grand Army of the Republic (GAR), had had its birthplace in Indianapolis shortly after the Civil War.[67]

On December 30, 1919, Will Hays, James Watson, James Goodrich, and James Hemenway, the latter a former United States senator from Indiana, met at the Hotel Severin in Indianapolis for lunch. The meeting had been arranged by Hays to encourage Goodrich to submit his name on Indiana's primary ballot for president in the 1920 national election. More than a year earlier, Hays, Watson, Goodrich, and United

66. Ibid., p. 184.

67. Nolan, *Hoosier City: The Story of Indianapolis,* pp. 269–75.

States senator Harry New of Indiana had made a private pact that none of them would seek a change in political office without first consulting the others.[68] With former President Theodore Roosevelt deceased, there was no clear front-runner for president. Hays was convinced that Goodrich stood a good chance of gaining the 1920 Republican nomination. On April 25, 1919, the Indianapolis mayor, Charles W. Jewett, who was in New York City to welcome home Hoosier veterans in the Rainbow Division, announced that Goodrich would be the choice for the nomination for president from Indiana's delegation.[69] Several other political insiders encouraged Goodrich to run for president at the Republican National Convention in Chicago in June 1920. Moreover, on January 27, 1920, in Washington, D.C., Senators New and Watson held a meeting with members of Indiana's congressional delegation in an attempt to get them to commit to a Goodrich presidency.[70]

James Goodrich certainly had the credentials to be a legitimate presidential candidate. He was a highly successful and wealthy lawyer and businessman. Moreover, he had been deeply involved in Republican politics for twenty-five years, being everything from the local county chairman to a senior and respected member of the National Republican Committee. He personally knew most top-level Republican leaders throughout the country. Moreover, Goodrich had the right connections. He could clearly count on Hays's influential support as national chairman of the Republican Party. Furthermore, Harry New and James Watson, now highly influential United States senators in their own right, promoted a Goodrich run. In fact, Watson was chairman of the Committee on Resolutions; Senator Henry Cabot Lodge was chairman of the Republican convention. Watson had pledged his total support for a Goodrich presidential run. He announced that in deference to his childhood chum he would not seek the one office he had

68. Watson makes reference to this agreement in a letter to Goodrich dated January 7, 1919, James P. Goodrich Papers, James E. Watson file, box 28.

69. "All on Goodrich Wagon," *Indianapolis Star,* April 26, 1919, p. 1, col. 4.

70. E. C. Watkins, "Solons Shy at Goodrich Boom," *Indianapolis Star,* January 28, 1920, p. 4, col. 1.

cherished all his life.[71] With the illness of Woodrow Wilson and the general dissatisfaction with Wilson's post–World War I policies, the Republican presidential nominee stood an excellent chance of gaining the White House.[72]

James Goodrich, however, never threw his hat into the presidential ring. On January 27, 1920, he publicly announced that he would not be a candidate for president.[73] When he would not consider taking a run at the top post, there were attempts to make him a vice-presidential candidate. In fact, Theodore Roosevelt had asked Goodrich to be his running mate when Goodrich met with the former president in November 1917.[74] When Roosevelt died, General Leonard Wood, former governor of the Philippines and a conservative nationalist, commanded most of Roosevelt's following. Wood had also built up a huge campaign chest of nearly $2 million. General Wood let it be known that he desired a Wood-Goodrich ticket. In fact, when Goodrich went to New York on April 28 to welcome home the first contingent of returning Indiana soldiers, a number of leading newspapers, including the *New York Times* and the *New York Tribune,* were proposing Wood and Goodrich for the ticket.[75]

The selection of Goodrich would have upheld the Indiana tradition of being the nation's number-one supplier of vice-presidents. As previously noted, Hoosiers Charles Fairbanks and Thomas Marshall had served as vice-presidents to Presidents Theodore Roosevelt and Wood-

71. See Goodrich, "Autobiography," pp. 179–80. See also "Indiana Republicans for Goodrich for President," *Indianapolis Star,* April 26, 1919, p. 1, col. 4. For a brief account of Watson's presidential opportunities at the 1920 convention, see "Indiana Senator Refused Republican Nomination for President in 1920," *Indianapolis News,* March 2, 1964, p. 28, col. 7. He did run, however, against Herbert Hoover for the 1928 Republican nomination.

72. Had Goodrich seriously sought the Republican nomination, he would have been a very strong contender. James Goodrich discusses briefly being suggested as a presidential candidate in his "Autobiography," pp. 179–80.

73. "Goodrich Announces He Will Not Be Candidate for President," *Indianapolis Star,* January 28, 1920, p. 1, col. 8.

74. Goodrich, "Autobiography," p. 141.

75. Ibid., p. 167.

row Wilson, respectively. As early as July 1917, Goodrich was considered vice-presidential material:

> WASHINGTON, July 22—The first 1920 Republican vice presidential boom has made its appearance.
>
> Following the visit here of James P. Goodrich, Governor of Indiana, during the last few days when he appeared before the Senate committee on interstate commerce and fought the coal barons to a standstill, information has leaked out that friends of the Indiana governor are preparing to groom him for the office that has been held by four Hoosiers—[Schuyler] Colfax, [T. A.] Hendricks, [Charles] Fairbanks, [Thomas] Marshall, and which Indianans have almost become accustomed to regarding as part of their political preserves.[76]

At the time, Indiana was an important center for geopolitical reasons. This did not go unrecognized by those seeking the White House, such as Roosevelt, Wood, and another New York politician, United States senator James W. Wadsworth.[77]

Despite Goodrich's successes as governor, the call to higher office fell on deaf ears. Goodrich had already decided by the spring of 1920 that he was through with politics. He wrote to Harry New in April: "I have no desire or ambition to do anything but finish my administration as best I can and then go back to my business. I am done with politics for ever and a day."[78] And in November, with only two months to go as governor, he wrote another close friend: "I will be the happiest man in Indiana when the tenth day of January [1921] comes and I can once more be free. Never again will I even think of rendering any service to the people in an official capacity."[79] Even if Goodrich had wished to stay in the governor's office, the position was closed to him. Under Indiana's constitution at the time, a governor was limited to one term.

76. "Goodrich Boom Stirs for 1920," *Indianapolis Star,* July 23, 1917, p. 1, col. 2.

77. Goodrich, "Autobiography," p. 141.

78. Letter from Goodrich to Senator Harry S. New, April 3, 1920, James P. Goodrich Papers, box 13.

79. Letter from Goodrich to Ezra Mattingly, November 6, 1920, James P. Goodrich Papers, box 7.

At the 1920 Republican National Convention in Chicago, none of the candidates, among whom were General Leonard Wood, Illinois governor Frank O. Lowden, and Senator Hiram Johnson of California (Goodrich's pick), could muster enough support to gain the nomination for president in early balloting. James Watson was offered the nomination on the sixth ballot. In a moment he almost certainly regretted for the rest of his life, he turned down the chance. His wife, whom he telephoned back in Rushville, Indiana, about the offer, told him she had absolutely no desire to be first lady.[80] Finally, on the tenth ballot, the convention nominated a former newspaper man and mediocre United States senator from Ohio, Warren G. Harding. The governor of Massachusetts, Calvin Coolidge, was slated as Harding's running mate. Will Hays managed the national Republican team of Harding and Coolidge in a masterly fashion, but it was a lackluster ticket. The country was so opposed to the Democratic Party, however, that the pair easily defeated the Democratic ticket of James M. Cox and Franklin D. Roosevelt, winning by a margin of two to one.[81]

Goodrich returned to Indiana from the convention with the feeling of relief that the remaining few months of his gubernatorial term would soon be over. His frustrations with the job stemmed partly from the failure of his own Republican Party to support him in many of the reforms he had hoped to bring to state government. Perhaps Goodrich's biggest disappointment was opposition by lobbyists and the General Assembly to his attempt to make the tax code more equitable. Goodrich believed that property owners were still bearing a disproportionate burden of state taxation. The tax package passed in 1919 addressed this inequity only partially.[82] It was not until the 1930s that James Goodrich

80. For a brief account of Watson's presidential opportunities at the 1920 convention, see "Indiana Senator Refused Republican Nomination for President in 1920," *Indianapolis News,* March 2, 1964, p. 28, col. 7.

81. Williams, Current, and Freidel, *A History of the United States: Since 1865,* pp. 421, 730.

82. See Charles F. Remy, "Governor Goodrich and Indiana Tax Legislation," *Indiana Magazine of History* 43 (March 1947): 41–55.

was praised for his attempts to revamp Indiana's tax code. In 1931, the *Indianapolis News* won a Pulitzer Prize for advocating tax reforms, most of which Goodrich had pushed for during his years as governor. Finally, the Democratic governor Paul V. McNutt, during his four years in office (1933–37), succeeded in getting passed the tax reforms that James Goodrich had proposed some fifteen years before.[83]

Another apparent reason for Goodrich's disappointment with the job had been his health problems. The fact that he spent several months during his tenure recovering from both typhoid and a nearly fatal automobile accident certainly did not bring back any fond memories for him. Finally, Goodrich's approach to governing was seen by many to be high-handed. For example, he was attacked as the "Hoosier Caesar" by the editor of the Fort Wayne *Journal-Gazette* at the 1920 Democratic state convention.[84] Goodrich knew that governing entails more consensus-building than does the arena of business, where decisions from the top are expected to be followed, yet he seemed to have difficulty making the transition from business executive to coalition-builder.

Despite these frustrations with the job, James Goodrich achieved a formidable record as Indiana's twenty-eighth governor. He had established the State Highway Commission, the Department of Banking, and the Department of Conservation.[85] Under the latter, many of Indiana's existing state parks were created. James Goodrich had also directed through the state's General Assembly legislation reorganizing the Public Service Commission, extending prohibition, improving workmen's compensation, consolidating or eliminating several positions, consolidating most state publications into one annual yearbook, and providing for absentee voting. Moreover, his revamping of the tax law in 1919 in-

83. Also, in 1933, the Indiana General Assembly adopted a gross income tax, combining income and sales tax, to help finance poor relief during the Great Depression. See *Encyclopedia of Indiana,* 2d ed. (New York: Somerset Publishers, 1993), pp. 83–84.

84. Goodrich, "Autobiography," p. 185.

85. For a description of the establishment and operations of the state departments of highways, conservation, and banking, see *Indiana* (Indianapolis: State Board of Public Printing, 1930), pp. 148–64.

corporated the "Indiana Plan," which controlled public expenditures and is estimated to have saved state taxpayers more than $100 million. Most important, during Goodrich's tenure as governor, women won the right to vote, even though Goodrich was, at most, a lukewarm proponent of woman suffrage.[86] On top of all of this, Goodrich had initiated the state's Civil Defense Council, which was essential in the support of the European war effort, and had signed charters establishing two important state institutions of higher education: Indiana State Normal School—Eastern Division (later Ball State University) in 1918 and Evansville College (later Evansville University) in 1919. James Goodrich was known for being the first Indiana governor to introduce modern business principles and methods into state government. He was the epitome of the modern executive.[87]

Goodrich's commitment as governor was admired by many. Thirty-five years after Goodrich's tenure in office, Will Hays wrote in his memoirs: "The reader may already have gathered that Governor James P. Goodrich was one of my political ideals. He was a man of complete unselfishness and devotion to the service of our people."[88] Although James Goodrich would never again be a candidate for elective office, his accomplishments were far from over. Some of his most successful work in the business world and contributions in the public sphere were still to come.

86. Goodrich, "Autobiography," pp. 180–81.

87. Goodrich's term as governor is briefly treated in James H. Madison, *The Indiana Way: A State History* (Bloomington: Indiana University Press, 1986), pp. 221–22; Clifton J. Phillips, *Indiana in Transition: The Emergence of an Industrial Commonwealth,* pp. 126–27, 611–12; Philip R. VanderMeer, *The Hoosier Politician: Officeholding and Political Culture in Indiana, 1896–1920* (Urbana: University of Illinois Press, 1985), pp. 19, 65, 196–97; Will H. Hays, *The Memoirs of Will H. Hays,* pp. 106–38; and Charles F. Remy, "Governor Goodrich and Indiana Tax Legislation," pp. 41–56.

88. Hays, *The Memoirs of Will H. Hays,* p. 138.

Chapter 11

The Middle Years, 1916–1923

In September 1916, in the thick of James Goodrich's gubernatorial campaign, Pierre matriculated at Harvard Law School. There, in Cambridge, Massachusetts, he was exposed to some of the best minds in American jurisprudence: the great scholar Roscoe Pound, who taught Pierre torts (noncontractual liabilities); Austin Wakeman Scott, a renowned professor of trusts, who taught him legal procedure; and Felix Frankfurter, who taught him public utility law. Frankfurter later became one of the most prominent United States Supreme Court justices of the twentieth century.[1]

At that time, Harvard required every student to participate in a sport. Although he did not possess the physical dexterity demanded by sports such as tennis, basketball, and golf, Pierre found rowing to be an activity in which he could excel.[2] At Harvard, Pierre was extremely studious. His cousin Florence Goodrich Dunn, who was then a student at nearby Wellesley College, remembers Pierre as a "grisly grind," seldom willing to take a break from his studies even for social outings.[3] After only a

1. Goodrich mentions Scott in a letter to Dr. Solomon Fabricant of New York University (January 3, 1972, Pierre F. Goodrich Collection, Archives, Wabash College). Goodrich mentions Frankfurter in a letter to Frederick Hayek (March 31, 1959, F. A. Hayek Collection, box 34, folder 17, Hoover Institution) and in a memorandum to the employees of the Indiana Telephone Corporation (March 5, 1970; in author's possession). Frankfurter was an associate justice of the Supreme Court from 1939 to 1962.

2. "I remember Mr. Goodrich telling me about losing his swimming trunks once while rowing on the Harvard row team," said Rosanna Amos. "He always had some kind of tale to tell" (interview, December 10, 1991).

3. Florence Dunn, interview, July 18, 1992.

year at Harvard, however, Pierre was forced to take a reprieve from his books at the behest of a summoner he could not refuse—the draft board. In the summer of 1917, he received notice that he would be a soldier in the United States Army, and later he learned that he would be commissioned to serve in the army's Quartermaster Corps. Pierre was one of 1,345 men and women from Randolph County who served during World War I.[4] While Pierre never served abroad, because of his defective eye, his cousin John Goodrich fought in France.[5]

While Pierre was at Harvard and in the military (1916–20), his father occupied the governorship of Indiana. By January 1919, Pierre was back at Harvard, having received an honorable discharge from the army. To meet the needs of returning soldiers, Roscoe Pound, by then dean of the law school, had devised a special course for the semester that began in February 1919. The course continued through the summer, fitting in with the regular courses that began that fall.[6]

At a ceremony in June 1919, Pierre and Tom Veech, who were both students at Harvard, and another close friend of theirs, Ralph Bales, who was a law student at the University of Michigan, returned to Winchester to be admitted into the local bar. The event was recorded locally:

> A ceremony of interest to many Winchester people took place Saturday morning when three of this city's most prominent young men were admitted to the Randolph County Bar with appropriate ceremony. The young men were Pierre Goodrich, Tom Veech and Ralph Bales.
>
> These three young men have been life long friends and their record is

4. *Randolph County History: 1818–1990*, pp. 223–27.

5. John Goodrich, Pierre's first cousin, returned to Winchester after World War I. He first worked at the Peoples Loan and Trust Company and later established Standard Securities, Inc. He took a particular interest in furthering the activities of Winchester's American Legion Post 39 and contributed a considerable sum of money toward that end. See "W.W. I John B. Goodrich 'Survivors' Trust," *Randolph County History: 1818–1990*, p. 228.

6. Paul Sayre, *The Life of Roscoe Pound* (Iowa City: College of Law Committee, 1948), p. 210.

> rather an unusual one. They entered kindergarten at the same time and after two years' course received their diplomas and were transferred to the first grade of the public schools, where they were classmates throughout the twelve years and graduated in June 1912.
>
> Messrs. Goodrich and Veech went to Wabash College and again graduated together in 1916. The following September they went to Harvard to take a four years' course in law. They left school to enter the United States Army Service and took their training at the same time. Mr. Veech was commissioned second lieutenant in the aviation corps. Mr. Goodrich, who also had the rank of lieutenant, was transferred from military service to the quartermaster department because of a defective eye. The two young men received their honorable discharge last January and in February re-entered Harvard and made up their credits.[7]

In the summer of 1919, an event even more significant to Pierre occurred—he met Dorothy Dugan, who would become his first wife. Pierre was introduced to her by his cousin Florence Goodrich, who was then teaching French at Central High School in Fort Wayne, Indiana.[8] Pierre and Florence had grown up only a block from each other in Winchester and were more like brother and sister than first cousins. Florence's maternal grandparents were the Neffs, who lived in Decatur, Indiana. As a young girl, Florence would visit her grandparents for long periods. There, she became close to two girls, Winnifer Ellingham and Dorothy Dugan. Florence, Winnifer, and Dorothy had much in common: Their families were all stalwart members of the Presbyterian Church and were deeply involved in politics and business in Decatur and Winchester.[9]

Dorothy's parents were Charles A. Dugan and the former Fanny B.

7. The source of the article is unknown, but a copy of the article is contained in a scrapbook of the Goodrich and Miller families kept by Mary Miller of Liberty, Indiana.

8. Florence Dunn, interview, July 18, 1992.

9. Winnifer's father was Lewis G. Ellingham. He owned several newspapers, including the *Winchester Democrat* and the Fort Wayne *Journal-Gazette*. He was also Indiana's secretary of state from 1910 to 1914 and a well-known state Democratic Party leader.

Dorwin. Charles Dugan, like James Goodrich, was a banker by profession. He served as president of Decatur's oldest bank, First State Bank, from 1922 until his death in 1935.[10] Dugan had formerly been superintendent of the City Schools of Decatur and a professor of mathematics at Carlinville College in Illinois.[11] The Dugan house on Monroe Street was a place of great joy, since the Dugans were known in the community for entertaining.[12] When the house was completed in 1902, the local newspaper reported that it was probably the most costly home in the city.[13] The Dugans also had a private library of approximately nine hundred books, reflecting the intellectual interests of its occupants. The house is now the home of the Adams County Historical Society.

Both the Goodriches and the Dugans valued education highly and sent their children to prestigious eastern schools. Dorothy had graduated from Vassar College in 1918; two of her sisters, Frances and Helen, also graduated from Vassar. Florence Goodrich had graduated from Wellesley College in the spring of 1919.[14] Dorothy Dugan was an attractive young woman who especially enjoyed social gatherings and sports. She was known for her high spirit, stubbornness, and strong opinions.

10. See Dick D. Heller, Jr., ed., *1979 History of Adams County, Indiana,* vol. 1 ([Decatur, Ind.]: Adams County Historical Society, 1979), p. 272.

11. "Charles A. Dugan, Deceased, Decatur, Indiana," *Biographical Sketches of Adams County, Indiana Citizens* (Indianapolis: Citizens Historical Association, 1977), pp. 70–71.

12. On one occasion, however, the imposing mansion was the location of great sadness for the family. The year before Dorothy's marriage to Pierre, her older sister, Naomi ("Billie"), died in childbirth, and her funeral was at the home, as were the funerals of Charles Dorwin Porter (Dorothy's great-uncle and the husband of Hoosier novelist and naturalist Gene Stratton-Porter) and Dorothy's father, Charles. In 1968, the Dugan home was purchased by the Adams County Historical Society and converted into the county museum. See Heller, ed., *1979 History of Adams County, Indiana,* p. 336.

13. See *Decatur (Ind.) Democrat,* July 17, 1902, p. 1, col. 4. The *Decatur Democrat* even reported when the Dugan family moved into the house on November 10, 1902. See "Dugans Occupy New House," November 12, 1902, p. 2, col. 3.

14. Dorothy's other sister, Naomi, graduated from Northwestern University. Dorothy's father, Charles Dugan, had undertaken two years of graduate study in astronomy and mathematics at Johns Hopkins University in Baltimore.

After graduating from Decatur High School in 1914, she received her bachelor of arts degree from Vassar. She then returned to teach at her hometown high school during the 1919–20 school year.[15]

Pierre and Dorothy had many things in common, especially a love of learning and books. Little is known of their courtship, but their wedding announcement was prominently placed in the *Indianapolis News.*[16] Pierre was the Harvard Law–educated son of the governor of Indiana. Dorothy Dugan was the Vassar-educated daughter of one of the most prominent families in northeastern Indiana.

The two were married on Saturday afternoon, July 17, 1920. The wedding was a private affair, taking place in the large foyer of the Dugans' home in Decatur. Carl McCamish, Pierre's boyhood friend, served as best man. Dorothy's sister Helen served as bridesmaid.[17] After their wedding, Pierre and his bride went on a two-month honeymoon to the West coast. They camped in Yosemite Valley for two weeks and then took an ocean trip to the Canadian coast.[18]

Beginning in September 1920, they moved into their temporary home on East Street in Winchester. The back of their property abutted Salt Creek, the small stream that meanders through Winchester. On the east side of the creek directly behind Pierre and Dorothy's house stood the imposing governor's mansion of James and Cora Goodrich. Within the immediate neighborhood lived all four of Pierre's uncles and their wives. By all accounts, Pierre and Dorothy lived a happy and quiet life

15. Dorothy Dugan had spent the summer of 1918 at the National Training School of the Young Men's Christian Association in New York City. The school was established to train young women for overseas work in World War I. Dorothy Dugan did not go to Europe, but during the latter part of 1919 she performed "club work" for women employees at the DuPont munitions plants at Pompton Lake, New Jersey, and Lowell, Massachusetts. See "Decatur Young Woman and Son of Governor Are to Wed July 17," *Indianapolis News,* July 1, 1920, p. 21, col. 6.

16. Ibid.

17. "Leave on a Trip: Mr. and Mrs. Pierre Goodrich Left Saturday Evening Following Wedding," *Decatur (Ind.) Democrat,* July 19, p. 1, col. 3.

18. Ibid.

in Winchester. Their only child, Frances "Nancy" Dorwin, was born in October 1921, in Dorothy's parents' home in Decatur.[19] Back in Winchester, Pierre was able to reestablish childhood friendships and begin life as a small-town lawyer.

In January 1921, James Goodrich returned to Winchester to resume his duties as president of the Peoples Loan and Trust Company and pursue his many business interests. The previous September, Pierre had begun practicing law with his cousin John Macy, Jr. They maintained an office in Winchester above the old Randolph County Bank, in the same place that their fathers, James Goodrich and John Macy, Sr., had practiced law together for fifteen years around the turn of the century. John Macy, Jr., a man of substantial intellect, had graduated from Wabash College Phi Beta Kappa in 1908. He attended Columbia University Law School in New York City for one year before returning to Winchester.[20]

In Winchester, Pierre and Dorothy played in a local bridge club. Their closest friends included George and Evelyn Jaqua, John and Matilda Jaqua, Francis and Mary Simpson, Alice and Sarah Miller, and Marie Moorman. Pierre and Dorothy also went on long walks on Sun-

19. Frances was born on October 10, 1921, in the Dugan home at 420 Monroe Street, Decatur.

20. John Macy, Jr., had attended Winchester High School and was admitted to Wabash College in 1904. Macy never received his diploma from Winchester High School; he was denied the parchment for refusing to give the class oration required of every graduating senior. He was admitted into Wabash on the condition that he maintain high grades. Macy pledged with Phi Gamma Delta fraternity and four years later graduated Phi Beta Kappa, earning a bachelor of arts degree in languages and literature. He attended Columbia University Law School for one year but in 1909 was summoned by his father to return to Winchester without a law degree. John Macy, Sr., was forced to resign as Randolph Circuit Court judge because of ill health. Father and son practiced law together until 1912, when John Macy, Sr., passed away. John Macy, Jr., then practiced law with a number of law partners, including Jim Goodrich, until 1920, when Pierre returned to Winchester. Macy and Pierre practiced together for the next three years above the old Randolph County Bank at the intersection of Washington and Meridian streets. See Anna Marie Gibbons, "John W. Macy Retiring as Judge of Randolph Circuit Court," *Winchester (Ind.) News*, December 2, 1966, p. 1, col. 3.

day afternoons.[21] Just three blocks due north of their house was the town's new library, which Pierre's father, mother, and grandmother had helped to establish. Pierre and Dorothy attended the First Presbyterian Church, which was located only two blocks away from their home.

The members of the Goodrich family were and continue to this day to be pillars of the Presbyterian Church. Pierre's grandmother, Elizabeth Goodrich, was a founding board member in 1882. Pierre's uncle Percy served as superintendent of the Sunday school for a number of years, and his father, James Goodrich, served as an elder of the church for more than twenty-five years and, beginning in 1910, taught a men's Sunday school class that met until the former governor's death.[22] Pierre's mother, Cora, also active in the Presbyterian Church, founded the Madonna Class in 1914. Women who were members met both for regular Sunday school and socially at the Goodrich mansion, just a block from the church. Pierre taught an all-boys Sunday school class from 1920 until approximately 1922.

At that time, each of the churches of Winchester had a baseball team. Local contests served as one of the main forms of entertainment.[23] Pierre once explained the reason he stopped attending church regularly.

21. Mary Simpson, interview, April 12, 1992. Accounts of the local bridge parties and the names of those who attended were published in the local newspaper. See "Bridge Party," *Winchester (Ind.) Journal-Herald*, August 27, 1925, p. 5, col. 4.

22. Jim Goodrich seldom missed a Sunday, and he would drive back to Winchester from Indianapolis late on Saturday nights during his years as governor just to teach the class on Sunday mornings. The class would have as many as 100 to 125 men each Sunday morning. It grew so big that the only place large enough to hold it was the church's sanctuary. James Goodrich was a much-admired Sunday school teacher. Even years after the former governor's death, his reputation as a religious instructor continued, although the effectiveness of his message may be questioned. Jack Davidson, a former Randolph County Republican chairman, told Claude Barnes, a one-time employee of the governor, "Jim Goodrich was the best goddamn Sunday school teacher I've ever had" (Don Welch, interview, December 16, 1991).

23. Ralph Litschert was one of Pierre's students in the Sunday school class. He remembers playing for several summers on the Winchester Presbyterian baseball team, along with Fred Oxley, Johnny Copeland, and others, all of whom also attended Pierre's Sunday school class (interview, November 10, 1991).

He and others on the Presbyterian team had gone to the congregation's minister, the Reverend Gustav A. Papperman. They sought approval for the church baseball team to play in a Sunday afternoon league. Mr. Papperman refused the young men's request on the grounds that the day was the Sabbath. Pierre thought the decision totally ridiculous and illogical. He did not think much of the viewpoint that adhered to such a rigid observance. After that, Pierre lost interest in organized religion and did not attend church regularly. He did, however, remain on his hometown church's membership roll for the rest of his life, but he often called himself a "backslid Presbyterian."[24]

By 1923, Pierre had tired of small-town practice in Winchester. He had larger ambitions, especially in the area of corporate law, than he thought his hometown could accommodate. Therefore, against his parents' wishes, he and Dorothy moved to Indianapolis, where they lived on the affluent north side of the city.[25] Pierre had tried to persuade his law partner, John Macy, Jr., to move to Indianapolis also so that they could establish a law practice together. Macy, however, had no desire to leave Winchester. Macy continued to practice law in Winchester until 1939, when he was elected Randolph Circuit Court judge, an office his father had also held. Macy was reelected to the position for the next twenty-eight years and retired in 1966 at the age of eighty.[26]

James and Cora were disappointed to see their only child, daughter-

24. Pierre talked often about his "backsliding" to his two secretaries, Rosanna Amos and Ruth Connolly, though he did occasionally attend church when in Winchester (Rosanna Amos, interview, December 10, 1991; Ruth Connolly, interview, October 25, 1991).

25. According to Goodrich's first cousins, Elizabeth Terry and Florence Dunn, their uncle James and aunt Cora tried to persuade Pierre and Dorothy to stay in Winchester, but Pierre had plans that he believed were too big for Winchester. The couple moved to 1529 Park Avenue, Indianapolis (Elizabeth Goodrich Terry, interview, November 16, 1991; Florence Dunn, interview, July 18, 1992).

26. Anna Marie Gibbons, interview, December 22, 1992. See also "John W. Macy Retiring as Judge of Randolph Circuit Court," *Winchester (Ind.) News*, December 2, 1966, p. 1, col. 2.

in-law, and granddaughter leave Winchester shortly after the couple had returned from four years in the governor's office.[27] Pierre's decision to move to Indianapolis in 1923 was an astute one, however, at least professionally. It became pivotal in his becoming one of Indiana's leading corporate lawyers.

27. Florence Dunn, interview, July 18, 1992. Florence Dunn was excited at the prospect of living again near her cousin and Dorothy. In 1921, Florence had married Francis Dunn of Marion, Indiana, who had recently graduated from Harvard. The two moved to Indianapolis, where Francis was a manager with the W. H. Gossard Company.

Chapter 12
The Great Russian Famine, 1921–1923

In 1921, one of the worst famines in history threatened the lives of millions of Russians as well as the continuance of Soviet rule. On 13 July of that year, the [Russian] writer Maxim Gorky appealed to the world for help. On 20 August the American Relief Administration (ARA), a private organization directed by Herbert Hoover, then secretary of commerce, concluded an agreement with the Soviet government to provide famine relief in the stricken area. For the next twenty-two months, a small group of Americans representing the ARA fed the starving throughout most of Russia. . . . the mission was in many ways the most intimate engagement between the two countries to date.

BENJAMIN M. WEISSMAN,
Herbert Hoover and Famine Relief to Soviet Russia: 1921–1923

In the midst of returning to his many business interests after serving as governor, James Goodrich experienced an interesting diversion. In mid August 1921, James and Cora were on vacation in New York State. They were staying at the upscale Hotel McAlpin in New York City when Goodrich received a letter from Will Hays. Hays was now United States postmaster general in President Warren G. Harding's administration. Hays asked whether Goodrich would be interested in undertaking a special assignment to the Soviet Union. The purpose would be to investigate the terrible famine that plagued Russia's central region.[1] Goodrich was immediately excited about the prospect, especially

1. For information on Goodrich's role in the relief efforts during the Russian famine, see Benjamin D. Rhodes, "Governor James P. Goodrich of Indiana and the 'Plain

since the invitation originated from Herbert Hoover, then secretary of the United States Department of Commerce and chairman of the American Relief Administration (ARA).

While awaiting further word about the possible mission, the Goodriches continued their vacation, arriving in Albany, New York, on August 24. There, Goodrich found waiting for him a telegram from Hoover that read simply: "Would be glad if you could conveniently come to Washington to discuss Russian situation."[2] Goodrich immediately abandoned his vacation and left for Washington, D.C. It would be the start of what the former governor later recalled as the most remarkable adventure of his life.[3] As Goodrich records in his manuscript about his various trips to the Soviet Union:

Facts' About Russia, 1921–1933," *Indiana Magazine of History* 85 (March 1989): 1–30; Rhodes, *James P. Goodrich, Indiana's "Governor Strangelove"*; Harold H. Fisher, *The Famine in Soviet Russia, 1919–1923: The Operations of the American Relief Administration* (New York: Macmillan, 1927), pp. 143–50; Frank Alfred Golder and Lincoln Hutchinson, *On the Trail of the Russian Famine* (Stanford, Calif.: Stanford University Press, 1927), pp. 75–89; and James K. Libbey, *Alexander Gumberg and Soviet-American Relations, 1917–1933* (Lexington: University Press of Kentucky, 1977), pp. 79–84.

2. Letter from Herbert Hoover to Goodrich, August 23, 1921, ARA Personnel Records, box 276, Hoover Institution.

3. James P. Goodrich, "Manuscript on Various Trips to Russia, 1921–1922" (referred to hereafter as "Russia Manuscript"), James P. Goodrich Papers, box 16, chap. A, pp. 6–7, Herbert Hoover Presidential Library, West Branch, Iowa. James Goodrich's personal papers (filling twenty-eight boxes) are kept at the Herbert Hoover Presidential Library. They were sent there in 1982 from the estate of Pierre F. Goodrich. Apparently, James Goodrich's papers were placed at the Hoover Presidential Library because of the close association between Goodrich and Hoover, especially in the ARA's Russian famine-relief effort of 1921 and 1922. Almost all of James Goodrich's accounts of his trips to the Soviet Union are recorded in his diaries and in a three-hundred-page manuscript that he wrote later. Goodrich apparently intended to publish the manuscript but never put it into final form. Also contained in Goodrich's materials are more than one hundred articles about his four trips to the Soviet Union from various national and international newspapers. Most of them are undated. There are several other primary source materials that are related to the ARA relief efforts. The most extensive is contained in the ARA's records at the Hoover Institution. For a much more thorough discussion of the resource materials related to Goodrich's various trips to the Soviet Union, see Rhodes, preface to *James P. Goodrich, Indiana's "Governor Strangelove,"* pp. 7–10.

> I had never been in Russia and I knew nothing about the country of the Great Bear excepting what I had learned at school and what I had read since in the American newspapers and magazines.
>
> But as a boy like most American youth the romantic literature about Russia with its Czars, its terrible Cossacks and its more terrible Nihilists had made a strong appeal to me, and I had long since resolved to visit the wonderland of Eastern Europe and learn for myself what was really there.[4]

Arriving in Washington, D.C., on August 25, Goodrich met with Hoover and army colonel William N. Haskell. Haskell, a native of New Jersey, served as director of the Russian unit of the ARA. He had previously acted as a technical adviser to the Polish government in Warsaw and had supervised ARA operations in Romania and Armenia. He was considered an expert in food relief. Before the meeting, Goodrich knew little about the famine except that millions of Russians were near death from starvation. By the end of his meeting with Hoover and Haskell, however, it was decided that the former governor would leave as soon as possible "with an open mind to investigate the entire famine situation, learn the truth about Russia and return as soon as the preliminary investigation was completed."[5]

Goodrich knew of Hoover by reputation, but he had never met the commerce secretary before the meeting of August 25. Goodrich's name had been brought to the future president's attention by Hays during a cabinet meeting. Hoover's written response to Hays's recommendation was positive: "I believe it would be of substantial benefit for this country to have a man of such experience as Governor Goodrich to obtain a real knowledge of what the real difficulties of this foolish economic system are."[6] From the tenor of the letter, it is obvious that Hoover was not familiar with Goodrich at the time Hays made the suggestion. This might seem odd, given Goodrich's long-term national Republican Party

4. Goodrich, "Russia Manuscript," chap. A, p. 6.

5. Ibid., p. 7.

6. Letter from Herbert Hoover to Will Hays, August 22, 1921, ARA Personnel Records, box 276, Hoover Institution.

ties. Considering Hoover's background, however, it is understandable. Hoover was a political party neophyte. He had not even announced himself as a Republican until February 1920.[7] Therefore, Goodrich's upcoming trips to the Soviet Union not only gave the former governor an opportunity to participate in an extraordinary undertaking, but also resulted in the establishment of a close friendship between Hoover and Goodrich.

The facts confronting Hoover, Goodrich, Haskell, and the ARA relief effort were as follows: In the summer of 1921, millions of peasants in central Russia were suffering from what would become the worst famine in modern Russian history. Immediate foreign relief was critical if the famine situation was to be stemmed before the country entered into the long winter of 1921–22. An internal Soviet evaluation team estimated that the Russian government would be able to provide no more than 20 percent of the food that would be needed in the worst-off provinces—Samara and Saratov—in central Russia.[8] Goodrich's mission was to examine the accuracy of the internal Soviet evaluation team. He was then to report back to Hoover, Congress, and, ultimately, the American people in hopes of obtaining relief.

To some degree, Hoover was a self-appointed overseer of the project, but he clearly had the qualifications for the momentous task. He had headed the ARA, a private relief agency based in New York City, since 1918. Hoover had previously directed food-relief efforts for victims of the Boxer Rebellion in China in 1900 and for victims in Belgium (1915–19) through the United States Committee for Relief in Belgium. From 1917 to 1919, Hoover had served as the United States food administrator. In 1921, Hoover held the position of United States secretary of commerce.[9]

In retrospect, Hoover's selection of James Goodrich to lead the ARA

7. Williams, Current, and Freidel, *A History of the United States: Since 1865*, p. 420.

8. A. Morozanov, "Famine in the Volga Region," *Ekonomicheskaya Zhizn*, June 30, 1921, from a translation in ARA Personnel Records, box 5, folder 2, Hoover Institution.

9. See "Hoover, Herbert Clark," *World Book Encyclopedia*, vol. 9 (Chicago: World Book, 1989), pp. 312–15.

fact-finding mission was unorthodox but excellent. Although Goodrich had very little foreign policy knowledge and no firsthand experience of the Soviet Union, he did have a working understanding of some of the causes of the economic and political upheavals going on in the country: the roles of banking, railroads, commodities, infrastructure, utilities, and government, generally. It was, however, perhaps Goodrich's earliest experiences as a farmer and his knowledge of human nature that were most useful to him in analyzing the immediate crisis. As Benjamin Rhodes observes in his book on Goodrich's ARA trips: "At the age of fifty-seven, having achieved financial security and having attained all he desired in politics, Goodrich was at peace with himself and politically obligated to no one, Hoover included. He took literally Hoover's request that he approach the subject with an open mind. And as a result of his observations he was soon to begin a campaign to enlighten the American mind, but not quite in the direction anticipated by Hoover."[10]

After his meeting in Washington, D.C., with Hoover and Haskell, Goodrich returned to Winchester and got his affairs in order as quickly as possible so that he could begin his arduous journey. On September 15, 1921, Goodrich left New York City on the ship *Kroonland* to make the first of four trips to the Soviet Union. The transatlantic crossing took two weeks, and Goodrich made valuable use of his time. Armed with voluminous records from the British Parliamentary Commission, which had monitored the famine for several months, Goodrich studied about Russia as much as he could: its government, the revolution of 1917, the counterrevolution, and the causes of the famine.[11] Goodrich well understood ahead of time, however, that his mission was to be strictly humanitarian in nature. When Hoover had negotiated with the Russian authorities to allow the ARA to enter the Soviet Union, Bolshe-

10. Rhodes, *James P. Goodrich, Indiana's "Governor Strangelove,"* p. 49.

11. Goodrich mentions how he spent his time on the trip from New York to England in his letter to Secretary of State Charles E. Hughes, November 2, 1921, James P. Goodrich Papers, box 24; see also "Former Governor Leaves for Russia as Member of Hoover Commission," *Indianapolis News,* September 13, 1921, p. 5, col. 2.

vik leaders demanded that no ARA officials could become involved in political matters. The Bolsheviks feared that anticommunist propaganda, which was known to be widespread in the United States, would be attempted in Russia itself.

Goodrich arrived in England on September 30. He first visited Plymouth and then traveled to London to meet with ARA officials and to tour the British capital's historic buildings, including Westminster Abbey. Cora remained with her husband until she left for Paris to allow James to begin his work. On October 3, he left for Moscow, traveling across the English Channel and then by train through France, Germany, and Lithuania to the Russian frontier. Along the way, Goodrich read that one British source estimated that as many as thirty-five million Russians were starving.[12] He believed that to be an exaggerated figure, yet conditions in the Volga region, three hundred miles southwest of Moscow, were even worse than the reports he had received had indicated. In the heart of the Volga region, where drought had destroyed the crops, Goodrich observed that no dogs could be found. He was told on the train to Moscow that in the village of Saratov all the dogs had been butchered for sausage. When colts were foaled, the peasants killed and ate them immediately; the same was true of newborn calves and piglets.[13] Peasants in the Samara region were eating grass, leaves, bark, and clay in an attempt to stave off starvation.[14]

On the way to Moscow, Goodrich and his small party, which included an interpreter and a courier, came across a small group of émigrés who described some of the horrific scenes Goodrich was yet to encounter. Because the Bolshevik government was reluctant to admit how bad things really were, physicians had been forced to certify

12. Letter from Wheeler to Charles Hughes, August 14, 1921, U.S. National Archives, file 861.48/1529.

13. Goodrich, "Russia Manuscript," chap. A, p. 3.

14. This news was contained in a report from Admiral Mark Bristol to Secretary of State Hughes, dated July 21, 1921, which is contained in *Records of the Department of State Relating to the Internal Affairs of Russia and the Soviet Union: 1910–1929,* U.S. National Archives, file 861.48/1562.

Western Soviet Union in Early 1920s (map by Heidi Perov Perry)

peasant deaths as caused not by starvation, but by an epidemic of typhus and cholera. One of the refugee women told Goodrich how desperate the times had become: "Last year and the year before they [government workers] took our grain. They did not even leave our men enough to sow. If we tried to keep what we needed for our children or our next crop they threatened to kill our men if we did not give up all. So our people were discouraged and each year they planted less. This year when the sun burnt up everything, starvation and death came and we had to leave or die."[15]

Goodrich was so moved by the refugees' story that he gave them five American dollars and some chocolate bars for the children. The mother of the children said that the youngest two had never tasted candy. When Goodrich finally arrived in Moscow on the evening of October 5, no one was there to greet him at the train station, because the telegram announcing his arrival had never been received.[16] When he finally arrived at the ARA headquarters on his own, he found a palace, "a veritable museum of art," that was one of only three buildings in the entire city that were heated by steam. The room he was assigned had paintings that he estimated were worth no less than half a million dollars, including portraits and landscapes from some of the great masters: Rubens, Van Dyke, Raphael, Mignard, Bonheur, and other notables. Leon Trotsky's wife had intervened to see that the palace was not destroyed during the Revolution, although the government had taken it from the original owner. The former owner was allowed to remain as the caretaker of the art collection.[17]

Goodrich spent two days in Moscow preparing for the demanding trip to the Volga region. During this time, he received a cholera vaccination, attended an opera, and visited an unofficial market. The sale of furs was not permitted, yet both men and women who had obviously seen better times paraded in the makeshift market area with their ex-

15. Goodrich, "Russia Manuscript," chap. B, p. 3.

16. Goodrich, "Russia Diary," September 30 to October 5, 1921, James P. Goodrich Papers, box 17.

17. Ibid., chap. B, pp. 9–10.

pensive fur coats, waiting to be propositioned for a quick sale. Measured in American money, Goodrich recalled that the items seemed ridiculously cheap.[18] As he wrote in his diary, on that day he also exchanged "90 good American Dollars for 8,920,000 worthless Russian Rubles."[19] He also paid a taxi driver 5,000 rubles to give him a tour of Moscow. "To me it was only six cents but to him it seemed to mean almost a fortune," he recorded.[20]

On Saturday, October 8, Goodrich was packing in anticipation of the train's leaving at 6:00 P.M. At noon, however, he was advised that the government had decided that the train should leave at 1:30 P.M. Racing to the station, he boarded the train along with his traveling companion, Dr. Frank Golder, chairman of the history department of Stanford University. Golder proved to be an invaluable resource and friend to Goodrich. He was a native of Odessa, Russia, who held a Ph.D. from Harvard University. Golder's fluency in Russian and practical traveling skills were put to good use by Goodrich. The Stanford professor was on leave from the university, serving as a special investigator for the ARA. Goodrich's own title was lead special investigator.

The train's early departure caused Goodrich's interpreter, his courier, and all his belongings to be left behind. "As the train pulled out of Moscow I did not find the prospect a pleasing one," Goodrich recalled. "Here I was going into a famine and disease stricken country, without an interpreter, dependent on what food I could forage along the way."[21]

Goodrich and Golder managed to fend for themselves. They bought food and supplies from peasants at the various train stops. Even though it was only early October, the weather was already like that in December in the northern United States: Snow covered the ground, and the ditches were filled with ice.

18. Ibid.

19. Goodrich, "Russia Diary," October 6, 1921. See also Rhodes, *James P. Goodrich, Indiana's "Governor Strangelove,"* p. 57.

20. Goodrich, "Russia Manuscript," chap. A, pp. 9–10. See also Rhodes, *James P. Goodrich, Indiana's "Governor Strangelove,"* p. 57.

21. Goodrich, "Russia Manuscript," chap. B, p. 2.

Goodrich had managed to take along a sleeping bag and two army blankets. Both he and Golder did not rise from sleep until late on Sunday, October 9. On the trip, Goodrich was able to make several observations about the lifestyle of the peasants: The cattle and land were held by the villagers communally, and schools were considered taboo, except for private institutions where the rich, under the old regime, provided their children with an education. Moreover, Goodrich was intrigued at the physical prominence of Greek Orthodox churches. Their golden domes and steeples appeared everywhere, it seemed.

He and Golder struck up a conversation with some young Communist sympathizers who criticized capitalism and the church. Goodrich countered that the Soviet government had itself adopted some capitalistic practices, such as authorizing rents and wages and allowing the opening of retail stores for profit. The "Reds," as Goodrich called them, admitted that certain capitalistic concessions had been made. But capitalistic governments themselves, they declared, often made concessions to socialism, too.

> This argument set me [Goodrich] to reflecting on the slow processes of human evolution in government and it occurred to me that it would be indeed strange if this experiment in Russia, starting as it did with pure Marxian government with its rule of the workers through a dictatorship should evolve into the capitalistic form, as was the experience of our ancestors in progressing from barbarism to civilization, while our capitalistic form should after long ages slowly disintegrate into socialism as it now shows evidences of doing in America and in England.[22]

After the heated discussion, Goodrich and Golder bundled up in their blankets and sang all the patriotic songs they could recall: "America," "The Star-Spangled Banner," and "Glory, Glory, Hallelujah." Goodrich wrote in his diary how he thought of the notable contrast between "our blessed country" and the Russia of Lenin. Before going to sleep, Goodrich "prayed God to give us men and women with a vision big enough

22. Ibid., p. 6.

to measure up to the task of saving our country from the awful blight that has fallen on Russia."[23]

Eyewitness to Suffering

The following day, October 10, Goodrich and Golder woke to find that they had entered a "land of snow." They had also arrived in the famine district. Goodrich wrote, "the squalor and the suffering are indescribable."[24] It was important for him and Golder to keep away from the throngs of refugees who crowded the platforms of the train stations, for they "would have given the sufferers all our rubles and [we would have had] nothing left to continue our way."[25]

Goodrich and Golder arrived at Samara on the evening of October 10. They saw on the outskirts of the city thousands of new graves of refugees who had died on their way out of the region and been buried along the dirt road in improvised potters' fields. Samara was a city of about 175,000 inhabitants and the grain capital of the Volga region. The flourishing grain business had been ruined, however, by the government's confiscation of the grain mills. One such grain mill in Samara had produced fifteen thousand pounds of grain per day under private ownership; whereas under government control the same mill produced only two thousand pounds a day.[26]

Wages for common laborers and railroad workers alike were shockingly low, being only between three thousand and five thousand rubles (approximately three to five cents in American money) a month. As Goodrich noted, because no one could live on so small a wage, workers were engaged on the side in the black market.[27] Goodrich found traveling conditions primitive. Before the Revolution of 1917, Russia had

23. Goodrich, "Russia Diary," October 9, 1921; Rhodes, *James P. Goodrich, Indiana's "Governor Strangelove,"* pp. 59–60.

24. Goodrich, "Russia Manuscript," chap. B, p. 7.

25. Ibid., pp. 7–8.

26. Ibid., chap. C, p. 2.

27. Ibid.

thirty-nine thousand railroad engines. In 1921, there were only nine thousand engines; the rest had been stripped for parts and stood rusting and idle in the repair shops. The locomotives burned wood. Second- and third-class coaches were simply boxcars without heat. They had holes cut out of their sides to allow in light. Second-class coaches were equipped with a few crude wooden benches; passengers in third-class cars had to stand.

In 1921 and 1922, the drought-afflicted areas included all of the Volga region and much of the Ukraine, an area of more than a thousand miles across the eastern and central parts of the Soviet Union and more than three hundred miles north and south. The average peasant of that time, during the best of conditions, was barely able to scratch out a living for himself and his family. For instance, in Samara Gubenia, one of the most fertile of the Russian provinces where Goodrich traveled, more than 60 percent of the population did not produce enough to support themselves even during years of average rainfall.

Drought, however, was not the only cause of the famine. Political, social, and economic upheavals in the aftermath of the revolution laid the foundation for the terrible human suffering. Both Communists and those seeking an overturn of the Communist regime, mainly foreign sympathizers from Britain and France, engaged in acts of terrorism.

Approximately one hundred thousand on both sides were executed or killed in battle. As many as two million Russians, mainly of the middle and upper educated classes, emigrated to escape communistic rule. The civil strife took place on some of the most productive land in the Volga and Ukraine regions, not only destroying crops but also preventing the planting of new ones. The Russian peasants were accustomed to droughts and had traditionally stored excess grain from productive years in anticipation of lean ones. The government, however, had established "grain patrols" to scour the countryside and confiscate any grain surpluses for distribution among the starving city workers.

These grain patrols acted in the belief that the peasants were hoarding grain to undermine the collective farm policies of the Communist government. The search-and-seizure methods were so thorough that even much of the seed grain was taken, thus depriving the peasants of the ability to plant new crops. As Goodrich wrote in summarizing what he had learned: "The civil war of 1919 swept the Volga valley clean of its surplus grain supply. To quote a Volga peasant, 'The Reds took all they could get and then the Whites [soldiers supporting the former Czarist regime] came along and took what was left.'"[28]

When Goodrich and Golder arrived in Samara, the cold weather had killed off the cholera bacteria. Typhus raged, however, and no vaccine had yet been discovered. The plague is transmitted from person to person by body lice, which seemed common to everyone in Russia according to Goodrich. The thousands of new graves in Samara were separated into two groups: those who had died from starvation, and those who had died from cholera and typhus. When the deaths came too quickly and individual graves could not be dug, Goodrich noted that as many as a half-dozen bodies were placed in a single grave or bodies were simply put in piles and burned.[29]

Not surprisingly, Goodrich observed that despair and a strong sense of fatalism were the predominant attitudes of the people. This was true even among the Soviet officials. One official reiterated to Goodrich the brutality that he had personally experienced. His father had tried to conceal from the government some food for his starving family, and the soldiers had bludgeoned him to death for the "crime."[30]

Goodrich found that a small relief effort was already under way. Approximately seventy-five ARA workers were in the Volga region, along with a handful of members from the Society of Friends. Malnourished children were given food tickets that entitled them to two ounces of bread each day, nine ounces of milk each week, five ounces of beans on one day per week, and two ounces of rice four times a week. At one railroad station, Goodrich poked a bundle of rags with his cane, only to find that the rags moved. Three children were underneath, using the

28. Ibid., chap. J, p. 11.
29. Ibid., chap. C, p. 3.
30. Ibid., chap. C, p. 5.

rags as protection from the cold while their parents searched for food.[31] Abandoned children were everywhere on the streets and in lots where refugees were huddled together. Goodrich counted seventy-six abandoned children in one relief kitchen. In most instances, their parents had died; in other instances, the parents had decided that

> they could not go on with the children and had left the youngsters in the hope that somebody would pick them up and care for them. They were the most pitiable objects I have ever seen—dirty, ragged, almost naked, lousy, emaciated little souls left to live or die according to whatever fate chance might bring to them.
>
> But raggedness and nakedness were not confined to the children, and the vermin was everywhere. It was no uncommon thing to see one refugee engaged monkey like, in searching the head of a fellow traveler for lice, and the search was rarely in vain.[32]

On Thursday, October 13, Goodrich left Samara with Professor Golder and Professor Lincoln Hutchinson, the latter the head of the economics department at the University of California at Berkeley. The three men traveled next to the province of Penza, where Golder and Hutchinson were to make a complete statistical survey of the whole of eastern and southwestern Russia. There was a need for a survey, according to Goodrich, because the "Russians are proverbially careless in everything, and this includes gathering facts," and the Russian peasant, "with true oriental cunning," had concealed significant reserves from governmental confiscation.[33]

At Penza, the capital of the province, Goodrich found another desperate situation. Medical supplies were essentially nonexistent. The administrator of an eight-hundred-bed hospital confided to Goodrich that because he had no drugs available to treat cholera and typhus, the mortality rate from the two diseases was twice as great as it should have

31. Goodrich, "Russia Diary," October 9, 1921; Goodrich, "Russia Manuscript," chap. B, p. 8; Rhodes, *James P. Goodrich, Indiana's "Governor Strangelove,"* p. 60.

32. Goodrich, "Russia Manuscript," chap. C, p. 7.

33. Ibid., chap. D, pp. 8–9.

been. The hospital had only two thermometers, and many doctors had succumbed to the hardships. The administrator's best assistant, thoroughly discouraged by the situation, had committed suicide just the day before.[34]

On Friday, October 14, Goodrich's team traveled to Rtischtschere, "the city with the unpronounceable name." The conditions there, if anything, were even worse than at Penza. The local peasants were barefooted or had made sandals out of birch bark. Their clothing was a patchwork of materials or simply grain sacks.

From Rtischtschere, Goodrich, Golder, and Hutchinson traveled to Saratov on Saturday, October 15, in the heart of the Volga region. Conditions there were much better than they had been in the Russian cities they had visited previously. Goodrich attributed this change in appearance to the fact that Saratov had a university of approximately five thousand students. Also, "its business life is dominated largely by the Volga Germans and their descendants, who seem to have retained some of that efficiency and desire for orderliness for which the Germans are noted."[35] Still, food was difficult to come by because of expense: A month's supply of staple items such as bread, meat, cheese, potatoes, eggs, and beans was selling for less than one American dollar, but few peasants had that much money. As mentioned, common laborers were paid but pennies a month. A highly distinguished professor who met briefly with Goodrich reported that his salary was one hundred thousand rubles a month (about one American dollar) and that he had not been paid in more than four months.[36]

At Saratov, Goodrich witnessed Bolshevik justice firsthand. When Russian workers refused to unload cargo from an ARA ship without receiving some of the food, the local Cheka officer gave the workers a simple ultimatum: Be back to work in thirty minutes or face summary execution. Just days before, a band of robbers had been caught, and

34. Ibid., chap. C, pp. 9–10.
35. Ibid., chap. E, p. 3.
36. Ibid., chap. E, p. 5.

all nine were shot and buried along a roadside. Goodrich recounted: "Everybody that I talked to seemed to approve of this summary justice, even the peasants. The Central Government, I was told, justified the arbitrary power conferred on the Cheka on the theory that in no other way could countless counter-revolutions and raids have been prevented during the early days of the Soviet regime. They held that it was a case of 'the end justified the means.'"[37]

Goodrich experienced another element unique to Russian society: the peasant communal system. Goodrich stayed in many peasants' homes and became familiar with their customs. In his diary, he recounts much of what he learned about the communal way of living and describes how antithetical it was to Bolshevik Communism itself. The communal peasant, a staunch individualist, derived his political existence not from the central government, but from the Mir, the local governing body. Under that system, the commune owned the land. Yet the peasant could market and thereby benefit from his surplus crops beyond what was due the central government and commune. Each commune was a unit composed of a few hundred to a few thousand peasants. At the time Goodrich first toured the Soviet Union in 1921, some eighty million peasants belonged to communes of various sizes and complexities. Goodrich noted that the intellectuals could predict all that they wanted to about how the old form of the commune and the family were passing away, "but the Russian Peasant will go his way marrying and giving in marriage and rearing his family pretty much as the American farmer rears his family."[38]

On October 20, Goodrich and his small entourage traveled to Markstadt, a small town of approximately four thousand northwest of Saratov. As Goodrich relates, death had been busy there. More than five thousand people in the immediate region had died since the first of the year, and the death toll continued each day: thirty-five on Monday, October 17; twenty on Tuesday; twenty-two on Wednesday. The story of

37. Ibid., chap. E, p. 5B.
38. Ibid., chap. E, p. 8.

abandoned children was much the same as it had been in the other towns and villages he had visited:

> There were abandoned homes in the communes by the score, the roofs and wooden parts taken off for fuel, and the walls of mud and straw falling into decay. Everywhere we found emaciated starving children, with stomachs distended from eating melon rinds, cabbage leaves and anything that could be found, things which filled the stomach but did not nourish. . . .
>
> In one shack we found two little orphan girls. Their parents had been taken from them three days before by the dreaded typhus. Barefoot, half-naked, destitute, with that same helpless haunted look, sobbing as they spoke, they told us they had had nothing but a few cabbage and carrot leaves to eat for three days and they were hungry, oh, so hungry! These two poor youngsters we took to the soup kitchen, gave them what there was to eat and left 500,000 rubles to get them to Markstadt.[39]

The Volga region, which was the heart of the famine and of Goodrich's travels, had a population of approximately eighteen million. The average family had nine children. Put in comparable terms, about 15,000 to 20,000 persons lived in an area that was the size of a large Indiana township. In Saratov, there were 105 persons per square mile; in Kazan, 118; in Simbursk, 111; and in Samara, 69. Because the densely populated area was totally dependent upon agriculture, there being virtually no industry, it is easy to understand why a crop failure of two years' duration would bring about such devastation.

Goodrich, Golder, and Hutchinson continued to travel from commune to commune with much the same findings. At Kutter-Russian, a commune of slightly more than 3,000 "souls" (Goodrich noted that the local authorities always referred to the inhabitants as "souls"), there were 622 children under the age of fifteen as of January 1921. By October, 400 of the children had died of cholera, typhus, or starvation.[40] At Dehaus, the commune had only a thousand bushels of grain to feed the

39. Ibid., chap. F, p. 7.
40. Ibid., chap. G, p. 3.

more than 6,000 peasants through the winter. This, of course, was impossible to do, and the commune leaders knew that death was a certainty for many.[41]

In Norga, a commune of 8,561, Goodrich found the majority of peasants to be satisfactorily nourished. It puzzled him, then, when the local officials predicted that half of the population would be wiped out by the end of the winter if foreign relief was not forthcoming. "Why is it," Goodrich asked the farmers at Norga, "that when so many of you have plenty of bread and meat for the present you permit others at your doors to starve to death?"[42]

> They were silent for quite a bit and then one strong faced man said slowly and gravely: "You Americans do not understand. It cannot be helped. It is necessary that some must die in order that others may live, otherwise, if help did not come we would all die. It was so in the great drought of 1891. America helped us then. We hope that she will be able to save many of us again."
>
> And I concluded that I indeed did not understand. For it seemed to me that I would share my last crust of bread with another who was hungry and both of us live or die together. But that Volga peasant had expressed the sentiment that I heard everywhere. It is not easy for us who have not been imbued with that something we call oriental fatalism, and which I found expressed in every phase of life in Russia, to understand that indifference with which they look upon death from cholera, typhus or starvation, or at the hands of the government. They seemed to place little value on human life. To them it was the case of "Kismet, it is fate."[43]

Goodrich subsequently visited several other communes before returning to Moscow by train on Monday, October 24. On the return trip to Russia's capital city, his assigned interpreter again missed the train, which says much about Soviet promptness. The following night, Goodrich left for Kazan, the capital of the Tatar Republic. For the first time

41. Ibid., p. 4.
42. Ibid., p. 5.
43. Ibid., p. 5 1/2.

since he arrived in the Soviet Union, he dared to sleep in pajamas. He had been assured by the train authorities that his compartment had been properly deloused; therefore, he deemed that it was worth taking a chance to slip out of his clothes for the night.[44]

The following day, Goodrich rode the train westward, seeing the same dreary, monotonous landscape for hours. To pass the time, he talked with Sir Phillip Gibbs, a well-known British newspaper reporter, and typed about ten thousand words of his diary on his portable typewriter. That evening, Goodrich and Gibbs were dragged into a session of the great American indoor sport—poker. Goodrich won 180,000 rubles from his more experienced card-playing colleagues before retiring to the luxury of sleeping in his pajamas.

On his way to Kazan, Goodrich noted the tremendous natural resources that the new Soviet Union was blessed with. "Unless I am much mistaken," Goodrich wrote, "there will develop in this Russian timberland within the next fifty years a great people and a great country."[45]

The various religions practiced by the Tatars impressed Goodrich. Although more than 60 percent of the people in Kazan were Muslim, intermixed with the mosques were synagogues and Orthodox Greek, Roman Catholic, and Lutheran churches. At the time Goodrich visited Kazan, it served as the capital city for the newly formed Tatar Autonomous Soviet Socialist Republic. By October 1921, more than three hundred thousand Tatars had emigrated to other parts of the Soviet Union or abroad in an attempt to escape the famine.[46]

The desperation of the times is illustrated by an incident that occurred just a week before Goodrich arrived in Kazan. A peasant man with three small children tried to board the last boat bound for the Caspian Sea, where there was a chance for survival. He was denied admission to the boat, however, because a rule existed that an adult could go with only two children. Without hesitation, the man threw the

44. Ibid., pp. 5–10.
45. Ibid., chap. H, p. 3.
46. Ibid., pp. 3–4.

youngest child into the Volga River and got on the boat with the other two children. When briefly stopped by the Cheka officer, the man exclaimed: "They would not permit all of us to go. If I remained here with them we would all die. Is it not better that one should die in order that three may live?" After hearing that explanation, the Cheka officer permitted the man to leave.[47]

As Goodrich noted, there were five hundred thousand Tatar children between the ages of five and fifteen and another four hundred thousand under the age of four who were receiving no help whatsoever. This knowledge brought Goodrich much sadness:

> It would be impossible, I found, with the limited means of the American Relief Administration to give anything like adequate relief to all of the children of this Tatar republic in the Volga valley. The only thing to be done was to select the worst districts and do the best that could be done with the relatively small amount of food stuffs at the disposal of the administration.
>
> Unless Uncle Sam himself came to the relief of these distressed people I felt that hundreds of thousands of them, many helpless children, were doomed.[48]

On November 1, Goodrich wrote a fourteen-page typewritten report to Hoover detailing the seriousness of the famine. The following day, he wrote a similarly lengthy report to Charles Hughes.[49]

> To Hughes, whom Goodrich classified as a doctrinaire opponent of everything Red, the governor stressed themes of Soviet moderation and pragmatism. "On every hand," he stated, "I see the most conclusive evidence of the return of the Government to a capitalistic basis . . . and there is a feeling everywhere I have gone that the Government has turned the

47. Ibid., p. 10.

48. Ibid., p. 6.

49. Letter from James Goodrich to Herbert Hoover, November 1, 1921; letter from James Goodrich to Charles Hughes, November 2, 1921. James P. Goodrich Papers, box 24.

corner and that every step from this time on will be a return to the capitalistic . . . form of government."[50]

That same day, Goodrich met with the president and the prime minister of the Tatar Republic before returning to Moscow on Sunday, November 3. The following night, he watched a performance of *The Doll Maker* at the famous Bolshoi Ballet. The following day, he traveled to Petrograd (now St. Petersburg), four hundred miles northwest of Moscow, to visit homes where abandoned children were being taken care of. He happened to be there on Monday, November 7, the fourth anniversary of the Russian Revolution, which had started in St. Petersburg. The population of the city had dwindled from 2,400,000 to only 600,000 since the revolution. Conditions were only slightly better than what he had found in the Volga communes.[51]

On November 10, Goodrich returned to Moscow in a snowstorm; the temperature was fifteen degrees below zero. He again visited the orphanages where the ARA had already established assistance programs and met with several top banking officials and the secretary of agriculture. Goodrich expressed concern that Soviet authorities could easily confiscate wealth, just as they had done before. In response, the Russian officials all tried to convince the former governor that the Soviet Union was deserving of foreign capital. "'The changes now going on in our government are fundamental. Mr. Lenin has had a real change of heart,' they [Soviet banking officials] answered. 'It is not a mere strategic move on the part of the communists. It is not temporary. The retreat toward capitalism has actually set in. It will continue until capitalism is established and full assurance given to everyone that the right of contract and private property in Russia will be respected.'"[52]

Goodrich himself had seen measures taken by the Bolsheviks that lent

50. Rhodes, *James P. Goodrich, Indiana's "Governor Strangelove,"* p. 74, quoting in part from Goodrich's letter to Hughes, November 2, 1921, James P. Goodrich Papers, box 24.

51. Goodrich, "Russia Manuscript," chap. J, p. 3.

52. Ibid., chap. J, p. 8.

some credibility to these opinions. Yet he was far from convinced that the Soviet Union was worth investing in at that point.

After his meetings, Goodrich returned to the ARA headquarters in Moscow and summarized these conversations and his famine investigations in a report to Hoover.

> His four weeks in Russia left Goodrich with two dominant impressions: that Communism had failed miserably, and that the people of Russia were coping courageously with the catastrophe. . . . [Thus, while at] the same time that he held Communism in utter disdain, he had nothing but admiration for the good-natured, industrious Russian population. As he wrote Hoover, "I am very impressed by the ability of the people to adapt themselves to the very trying situation that confronts them."[53]

On receiving Goodrich's account, Hoover cabled Goodrich, requesting him to return to the United States to report personally on his investigations. On his return, Goodrich retraced his steps from Moscow, passing through Latvia, Lithuania, Poland, Germany, Belgium, and finally England. He boarded the steamship *George Washington* on November 20 to return to the United States. Goodrich arrived in New York City on December 3 and went immediately to Washington, D.C., to meet with Hoover.[54]

The initial groundwork of the investigation was now completed, but what lay ahead was an even more daunting task for Hoover and Goodrich: to convince a skeptical, Red-fearing United States Congress that the starving Russian peasants were deserving of immediate American aid.

53. Rhodes, *James P. Goodrich, Indiana's "Governor Strangelove,"* pp. 75–76, quoting in part from "Governor Goodrich's Preliminary Report on Russia," November 1, 1921, in *Documents of the ARA,* vol. 3, pp. 398–410, Hoover Institution.

54. A brief account of Goodrich's return is contained in an Associated Press article dated November 16, 1921, "Hoover Recalls Gov. Goodrich to Report on Russian Famine" (with no newspaper reference), James P. Goodrich Papers, box 15.

Chapter 13

Emissary to Russia

Dec. 10, 1921, Winchester, Ind.

Hon. James P. Goodrich,
Think it would be desirable for you to be here as soon as possible. The House is not very favorable and best we can probably get at the moment is a hearing before the Ways and Means Committee.
Herbert Hoover, Washington, D.C.

In his last report to Herbert Hoover before he left the Soviet Union in November 1921, James Goodrich outlined the terrible suffering he had seen. He also wrote at length about the political turn of events he had discovered. Goodrich stressed to Hoover that the Russian peasant still had a friendliness toward the American people that had changed little from before the Russian civil war. He also offered an opinion that Lenin's Bolshevik government was evolving into a regime that was less antagonistic to capitalism than had been previously thought. Moreover, Goodrich noted that he had talked to men of political affairs in the country and "found not one particle of sentiment for the old order (under the Czars) and the Russian people will have none of it." He continued, "If Lenin can hold the majority of his party with him, and especially Trotsky and the army, this government will stand."[1]

After learning about Goodrich's account, President Warren G. Harding was convinced that direct aid from the United States government was the only way that relief could reach Russia in time to prevent

1. Letter from James P. Goodrich to Herbert Hoover, n.d., Frank A. Golder Papers, box 31, ARA Personnel Records, Hoover Institution.

the famine from becoming horrific in scope. Hoover encouraged this thinking. The ARA director was against the alternative, an appeal to the American public, for several reasons: First, it would take a relatively long time to mount because of the difficult logistics of such a campaign and because public sentiment was generally not in favor of helping the Bolsheviks; second, there would be private fund-raising groups that the ARA simply could not control; and third, a direct appeal to Congress had the best chance of maximizing a large return.

On December 6, President Harding made his first state of the union address to Congress. In that address, the president requested that Congress appropriate for Russian famine relief $10 million. This would be enough to purchase ten million bushels of corn and one million bushels of seed corn.[2] On December 10, United States congressman Joseph W. Fordney of Michigan introduced legislation in the House of Representatives that would appropriate the $10 million that Harding was seeking. Meanwhile, the urgency of the situation was growing. On December 8, Colonel Haskell, director of ARA Russian operations, sent Hoover a sober forecast of what would occur if aid did not come immediately: "Somewhere between five million and seven million people in this area must die unless relieved from outside Russia. . . . As a Christian nation we must make greater effort to prevent this tragedy. Can you not ask those who have already assisted this organization to carry over eight million children through famine in other parts of Europe to again respond to the utmost of their ability?"[3]

By December 5, Goodrich had already returned to Indiana. Just five days later, he received Hoover's telegram, summoning him back to Washington to appear before Congress. Instead of having hearings held before the Ways and Means Committee, Hoover had managed to have testimony heard before a more influential body, the House Foreign Af-

2. *Public Papers of the Presidents of the United States, Warren G. Harding* (Washington, D.C.: Federal Register Division, National Archives and Records Service), 19: 2626–27.

3. Letter from Colonel Haskell to ARA, December 8, 1921, ARA Personnel Records, box 81–2, Hoover Institution.

fairs Committee. The hearings lasted two days, December 13 and 14. The first day was devoted entirely to the issue of famine relief. The second day's testimony, about recent Soviet political developments, was offered in a closed executive session by Goodrich, Hoover, and others.

At the December 13 hearing, Goodrich was the first to testify. His testimony was the longest and most complete of any of the witnesses. Others who testified included Hoover; Samuel Gompers, president of the American Federation of Labor (AFL); Dr. Vernon Kellogg, secretary of the National Research Council; Carl Vroonman, former assistant secretary of the Department of Agriculture; and Ralph Snyder, executive board member of the American Farm Bureau Federation.[4]

In his opening statement, Goodrich first explained the conditions that led up to the great Soviet famine: the seven years of foreign and civil war that had disrupted normal agricultural cycles in the Volga region; the subsequent reduction in the amount of crops that had been planted; and the terrible drought of the preceding summer and the partial drought of 1920. Goodrich next recounted his nearly two-month tour of sixteen different communes in the famine regions.[5]

On reading Goodrich's report and the exchange that took place between him and members of the committee, one is immediately struck by Goodrich's decisiveness. When the former governor was asked during the hearing whether the proposed $10 million in relief was adequate, he answered unequivocally that it would take twice that—$20 million but no more—to successfully address the famine. He also attempted to allay any fear by the committee that American relief would not go directly to the starving peasants, but would be confiscated by authorities or pocketed by Communist bureaucrats. "I heard of one man caught stealing American food who was . . . shot by order of the Soviet authorities," Goodrich said. Goodrich interspersed his very thorough sta-

4. See *For the Relief of the Distressed and Starving People of Russia,* 67th Cong., 2d sess., H.R. 9458 and H.R. 9459. The bill was introduced by Joseph W. Fordney, a representative from Michigan.

5. U.S. Congress, House, 67th Cong., 2d sess., *Russian Relief Hearings,* December 13, 1921, pp. 3–5.

tistical summary with sympathetic anecdotes: finding the two orphan girls in Markstadt half-naked and sobbing; meeting the distraught hospital administrator at Kazan; hearing the disturbing news from the farmers at Norga, who predicted that one-half of the commune's population would be dead by the end of winter if foreign relief was not forthcoming.[6]

Hoover's testimony primarily dealt with the anticipated criticisms of providing relief to a nonrecognized government that America feared. He emphasized the humanitarian nature of the undertaking. He also informed the committee that relief had been offered only after negotiations had resulted in the release of all American prisoners of war in Russia. The future president further made the observation that United States famine relief would not have the unintended result of propping up the Communist regime. This was so, Hoover argued, because the aid would be going to a region of Russia primarily outside the scope of socialist (communist) influence:

> The problem that we are confronting is not a problem of general relief to Russia, for which there can be some criticism, but is a problem of relief to an area suffering from an acute drought. In other words, we are making a distinction here between the situation created by the hand of man as distinguished from the situation that might be called an act of God. This Volga area, as has been stated, is practically altogether an agricultural region. It has not been the scene of any extended socialist organization, as that is a city phenomena. It comprises a population of farmers, of which apparently one-third are of German extraction. . . . I think you will find in Nebraska alone many thousands of farmers who migrated from the Volga Valley. You will find many thousands of farmers in the Northwest of the same population.[7]

By these last remarks, it is obvious Hoover was trying to sensitize the committee into believing that the Volgarian peasants were really just

6. See "Finds View Supported by Report of Goodrich," *Indianapolis News,* Dec. 16, 1921, p. 1, col. 3.

7. U.S. Congress, *Russian Relief Hearings,* December 13, 1921, p. 38.

destitute "blood cousins" who deserved American generosity. Hoover went on to explain that it would be impossible to provide sufficient relief funds privately, since the ARA had been able to raise from a skeptical American public only approximately $500,000 in contributions since August. Finally, Hoover appealed to the economics of the relief. He attempted to persuade the committee that famine aid through the direct provision of agricultural products would relieve a glutted American commodities market: "We are today feeding milk to our hogs; burning corn under our boilers. From an economic point of view there is no loss to America in exporting those foodstuffs for relief purposes. If it is undertaken by the Government it means, it is true, that we transfer the burden of the loss from the farmers to the taxpayer, but there is no economic loss to us as a Nation, and the farmer also bears part of the burden."[8]

During the second day of testimony, held in closed session, Goodrich noted the concessions to capitalism that the Communist regime had sanctioned: farmers were now able to keep and sell for personal profit surplus crops; retail shops and banks were beginning to reappear; serious discussions regarding the role of private property and contracts were under way. All of this was very important to members of the committee because of the desire, on the part of many in Congress, to investigate whether recognition of Russia and the establishment of diplomatic relations could or should be pursued.

After the day's hearing, United States senator Joseph I. France of Maryland announced to the press that Goodrich's testimony would go far toward bringing about a marked alteration in American policy toward the Soviet Union. Senator France had initiated legislation that would create a seven-person commission to investigate the resumption of trade relations between the two countries as well as the issue of diplomatic recognition by the United States of the Soviet republic.[9]

A spirited debate about the proposed famine relief occurred on the

8. Ibid., p. 39. See also "Congress Asked for 20 Million to Help Russia," *Indianapolis News,* December 14, 1921, p. 1, col. 3.

9. See "Finds View Supported by Report of Goodrich," *Indianapolis News,* December 16, 1921, p. 1, col. 3.

House floor, during which time Goodrich's testimony was often used as the reference point. Despite this rhetorical tussle, the House of Representatives passed the relief legislation by a vote of 181 to 71. In the Senate, however, approval was less trouble-free. Senator Tom Watson of Georgia made a number of arguments against the bill, including the fact that the Soviet Union still owed the United States nearly $200 million, as well as the spurious argument that "the Russians do not even know how to mill corn; they don't like it, won't eat it."[10]

Despite these objections, the Senate passed the legislation in a very short time. By December 22 President Harding signed the relief measure into legislation. From the time of the relief bill's introduction to its passage, exactly twelve days had passed. Considering the normally slow, grinding process of legislation, the quick passage was a miracle. Clearly Goodrich's and Hoover's testimonies had confirmed the seriousness of the famine and the urgency to act. By Christmas, news had reached the Russian peasants that America had come to their rescue.[11]

Goodrich's knowledge of the situation was truly convincing. One Soviet expert claimed that Goodrich possessed "more intelligence of real human sympathy or understanding about Russia" than almost anyone he had ever met.[12] The crucial role that Goodrich's testimony played before Congress is perhaps best summarized in a letter that Edgar Rickard, director-general of the ARA, wrote to Walter L. Brown, ARA's European director, shortly after enactment of the famine legislation:

> We have had many examples in this Russian job of his [Hoover's] uncanny ability to anticipate events of the future. As a remarkable instance is his choice of Governor Goodrich to prepare himself on Russian first-hand information for the efforts on Congress. While, of course, the Chief

10. U.S. Congress, Senate, 67th Cong., 2d sess., December 21, 1921, p. 62.

11. See "Goodrich Plea Wins America's Aid for Russia," *Indianapolis Star,* December 14, 1921, p. 1, col. 3.

12. These remarks are attributed to Alexander Gumberg, a native Russian who met Goodrich at this time. Gumberg worked in the United States in furthering Soviet-American relations after the Bolsheviks took power. See James K. Libbey, *Alexander Gumberg and Soviet-American Relations, 1917–1933* (Lexington: University Press of Kentucky, 1977), p. 80.

> applied the method of attack, Goodrich was responsible for the personal work which carried the Bill through despite the opposition of the Leader of the House, the Speaker of the House, the Chairman of the Appropriations Committee and the Chairman of the Foreign Relations Committee, an array of opposition which is considered to be impregnable and able to definitely block legislation. Hence, we have Goodrich to thank for the chief work in securing this money.[13]

When James Goodrich appeared before the House Foreign Affairs Committee in December 1921, he held no official position with the ARA. His earlier investigation in the Soviet Union had been simply as a private citizen, and only his travel expenses had been covered by the relief organization. On Christmas Eve, however, President Harding signed an executive order that appointed Hoover and Goodrich to the five-member Purchasing Commission for Russian Relief as chairman and vice-chairman, respectively.[14] Just days before, Hoover had appointed Goodrich to the ARA Executive Committee. From January 4 to March 22, 1922, the Purchasing Committee met at least once a week to review bids by various agribusinesses. The committee reviewed hundreds of bids. When Hoover was unavailable to attend, Goodrich chaired the meetings until his second departure for the Soviet Union in mid February.[15]

By the end of January 1922, only one month after Congress had passed the legislation, $12 million had been spent for the following pur-

13. Letter from Edgar Rickard to Walter Brown, December 30, 1921, ARA Personnel Records, box 1A/236, Hoover Institution. See also Rhodes, *James P. Goodrich, Indiana's "Governor Strangelove,"* p. 87.

14. See *Public Papers of the Presidents of the United States, Warren G. Harding* (Washington, D.C.: Federal Register Division, National Archives and Records Service, 1922), 18:9033. Other members of the five-member Purchasing Commission included Edgar Rickard, Edward Flesh, and Donald Livingston. Rickard served as executive director of the American Relief Administration.

15. "Minutes of the Meetings of the Purchasing Commission for Russian Relief" (appointed under Congressional Act 117, 67th Congress, H.R. 9458), Warren G. Harding Papers, box 568, file 156, folder 7, Manuscript Division, Ohio Historical Society, Columbus, and Warren G. Harding Papers, roll 181, Manuscript Division, U.S. Library of Congress.

chases: 6,945,000 bushels of corn, 1,370,652 bushels of seed wheat, 9,800 tons of corn grits, and 340,000 cases of condensed milk. By the end of January, three million bushels of grain had already been sent to the Soviet Union by thirteen steamships. Additional ships were in port loading in New York, Baltimore, Philadelphia, and New Orleans. By May 22, 1922, fifty-eight steamships had transported cargo to meet the needs of the starving Russians.[16] It was perhaps the largest relief effort ever undertaken by the United States government.

Ironically, no sooner had Goodrich received his appointment to the ARA Executive Committee than it was decided that he should return to Russia, but, strangely enough, not under the official auspices of the ARA. Rather, President Harding had decided that Goodrich should serve as an unofficial emissary. Since Goodrich could not become involved in political matters and still be officially associated with the ARA, he wore a different hat when he returned to Russia in February 1922. An article by the Associated Press briefly described the former governor's new position:

> Goodrich will return to Russia in charge of the governmental end of the relief, it was learned today [Dec. 22, 1921], with his connections to the American relief administration severed. This will permit him to become an advance agent of American relations.
>
> It will be remembered that the American relief administration, when it entered Russia, agreed to avoid all political activities. Goodrich, when he returns to Russia, will be ostensibly an American commissioner, much as Dresel was at Berlin, although his mission will not be the subject of public announcement by the administration.
>
> This solves the administration's main difficulty in dealing with Russian

16. These figures were given by Goodrich in late January 1922 and reported in the *New York Sun*. See "Relief for the Starving Millions of Russia Near: Transportation Problem Settled, Says Ex-Gov. Goodrich, Back from Three Months Sojourn in Famine Districts," January 28, 1922 (article in James P. Goodrich Papers, box 15). For a list of dates, port of debarkation, name of steamship, port of delivery, and tonnage transported, see Warren G. Harding Papers, box 568, file 156, folder 6, Manuscript Division, Ohio Historical Society, Columbus, Ohio, and Warren G. Harding Papers, roll 181, Manuscript Division, U.S. Library of Congress.

> questions. The President and his close advisers have felt that they lacked information upon which they could rely. Most of the reports from Russia they took with a grain of doubt, as inspired by propagandists.[17]

The United States and Russia had had no formal diplomatic relations since the Bolshevik revolution in October 1917. Thus, the Harding administration believed that Goodrich's second trip could serve as an excellent opportunity for an unofficial representative to share America's concerns over Soviet domestic and foreign policies. Also, since Goodrich had the ear of President Harding, Secretary of State Charles E. Hughes, and Hoover, Communist leaders could be assured that their views, conveyed to Goodrich, would be relayed in confidence to the highest United States political authorities.

On February 12, 1922, Goodrich left on his second tour. It was during this trip that he met with the Soviet president, Vladimir Lenin. Goodrich arrived in Moscow on March 9. In his manuscript about his trips to Russia, Goodrich describes the Moscow of March 1922 as totally different from the one he had left the preceding November: The streets were filled with activity, the people had a sense of cheerfulness, more stores were open, and people could purchase more than the necessities of life.[18]

At Tsaritsin, Goodrich learned that American corn had recently arrived and that some twenty thousand peasants from the region had come on sledges in one day to carry it away. By mid March, 135 trains were carrying fifty thousand tons of American corn to the furthermost corners of the famine region. Men were working around the clock to unload the grain.[19]

17. See Frank J. Taylor, "U.S. and Russia May Resume Relations Soon," *The Globe*, December 21, 1921 (article in James P. Goodrich Papers, box 15); "Russia Looks to America (Not Food, but Resumptions of Relations, Is Big Desire)," *Indianapolis Star*, December 22, 1921, p. 5, col. 2.

18. Goodrich, "Russia Manuscript," chap. K, p. 1.

19. Ibid., pp. 1–2. Goodrich's report on the success of famine relief is also contained in two unidentified newspaper articles, "Millions Fed Daily and Panic Has Disappeared, Hoover Reports to Harding," and "Goodrich is Optimistic: Returning from Russia Today to Report to Harding," April 19, 1922, James P. Goodrich Papers, box 15.

Goodrich was forced to spend his first week in Moscow dealing with ARA personnel problems that were embarrassing to the relief organization: drunkenness by members of the local (Moscow) team, and an ARA officer in Petrograd who blatantly hired prostitutes.[20] Moreover, Goodrich had hand-carried a letter from Hoover to Colonel Haskell that contained Hoover's concern that most of the Russian ARA staff were Catholic. "I haven't any prejudice in any religious matter as you know," wrote Hoover to Haskell, "but if we are going to have peace in the United States we need to have a sprinkling of Protestants on the job somehow."[21]

On March 18, Goodrich traveled to Samara to find further troubles: The Cheka had recently made two hundred arrests for illegal political activity. Five Russian ARA officials were on the list. In an unrelated matter, forty-nine members of an organization of bandits were on trial in Samara. They had killed about a dozen people in carrying out their thievery. Goodrich attended the last evening of the trial with the chief of the new Department of Justice of Samara, a Monsieur Zgakanoff. Nine of the bandits were sentenced to death, and the rest were sent off to serve sentences varying from three years to life imprisonment in Siberia.[22]

If the activities of the local ARA teams were not exactly encouraging, the success of food distribution was. Heavy snows and below freezing temperatures had allowed peasants from long distances, up to three days away, to travel by sledges to the distribution centers. They hauled away several hundred pounds of corn each. Still, death had been a common visitor in many of the communes. On March 19, Goodrich attempted to travel by train to Orenburg, only to have the train stopped: first, to avoid a gang of bandits, and, later, by a terrific snowstorm that blocked the tracks for several days. When it was learned how long it

20. Goodrich recounts his efforts to get these personnel problems under control in two letters to Walter L. Brown, director of the London ARA office, dated March 6, 1922, and March 10, 1922, James P. Goodrich Papers, box 16.

21. Letter from Herbert Hoover to Colonel Haskell, February 16, 1922, James P. Goodrich Papers, box 19.

22. Goodrich, "Russia Manuscript," chap. K, pp. 7–9.

would take for the tracks to become cleared, Goodrich had his car attached to a freight train and attempted to return to Samara. The freight train became lodged in an "insurmountable snowdrift," and Goodrich was stuck for another five days near the town of Bogotae. The misfortune did allow Goodrich to discuss with several local peasants the conditions that existed. What he learned was not pleasant:

> It was here that I received a direct report of cannibalism. The drivers told me that in the commune of Yerasinoffskoya a woman ate the body of her little daughter who had died and then committed suicide. In the commune of Alexaiefstoya, I was told, a woman by the name of Theodosia Astankovo had exposed for sale in the bazaar, human flesh taken from the body of a person who had died. She was arrested, tried and executed by the Cheka for the offense.
>
> . . . I saw one peasant in the group of visitors from the distant communes eating a dark greenish sort of bread. I asked him what it was made of and he told me that the ingredients were camel's dung and grass. The other peasants in the group nodded their heads in confirmation and approval of the statement.[23]

The misery caused by the famine was not limited to within Russia's borders. Rats and mice from the famine region were migrating by the hundreds of millions to Hungary, overrunning Budapest. In the Hungarian capital, market halls, food stores, and warehouses were swarming with the rodents. In some Hungarian villages, farmers gave up raising poultry and began breeding cats to try and stop the rat and mice plague.[24]

Meanwhile, Goodrich became livid because of the inefficiency of the Russian train system. He claimed that a good American worker could do the work of ten Soviet railroaders. Despite repeated delays on the return trip to Moscow, the common response of both railroad worker and passenger alike was "Nitchevo," meaning "it doesn't mat-

23. Ibid., chap. L, p. 4.

24. "Rats from Russia Overrun Budapest," *New York Times,* January 29, 1922, p. 3, col. 4.

ter."[25] While Goodrich was delayed in returning to Moscow, he took the opportunity to write a lengthy letter to President Harding. The report dealt only briefly with the immense gratitude that the Russian people felt toward America for coming to their rescue. The remainder of Goodrich's letter was concerned with Russia's political conditions. Goodrich lobbied forcefully for recognition of the Bolshevik regime. In his opinion, whether the American public and officials liked it or not, the Bolsheviks were the only power in Russia capable of running the government.

> I do not look for this Government to fall, but believe it will stand whether we recognize it or not. . . . What would happen if the present Government should fall? No outstanding figure, no group of men, so far as I can see, exists in Russia to take its place. It is my opinion that there would be anarchy; that the Russia which America has constantly tried to preserve would fly to pieces and be broken into numerous little, petty states, a prey to the designs of every other country in Europe which might be interested in the breaking up of this vast empire. . . .
>
> It may be a poor Government Russia now has. It is not all we would want. It is contrary to American ideals, and I believe the principles upon which the Russian Government is founded are destructive of orderly progress, and under it the people cannot prosper as they should. But whatever we may think about it, it is respected. It means law and order everywhere in Russia. Under the new system of justice, under the new economic policy, I believe it will give to the Russian people the opportunity to work out their own salvation, and through a somewhat rapid progress, as we measure progress in the life of nations, there will finally evolve in Russia a sound system of Government very much like our own.[26]

The fervor with which Goodrich believed in United States recognition of the Bolshevik regime is easily seen in the concluding paragraphs of his letter to President Harding:

25. Ibid., pp. 5–6.

26. Letter from James Goodrich to Warren Harding, March 24, 1922, pp. 7–8, Frank A. Golder Papers, box 31, Hoover Institution.

I believe that the continued policy of isolation and non-recognition of our Government is only delaying the economic reconstruction and the political development of this country. Whatever may have been the wisdom of the attitude of America in the past, I believe the time is near at hand when we should recognize the Revolution as an accomplished fact, resume relations with Russia, and give American capital a free opportunity to enter in and assist in her economic development.

Our Government and its people are opposed to communism. Is not the surest way to destroy the present Communist Government to bring it into contact with the outside world?[27]

Goodrich arrived back in Moscow on Thursday morning, March 30. In the Russian capital, he was invited on April 1 to a formal dinner with the president of the Russian banking system and the director of forestry. He discovered later that the two men's interest in dining with him was to learn Washington's attitude toward Russian recognition. Without United States diplomatic recognition, Russian businesses could not deal directly with their American counterparts. The terribly anemic performance of the post–civil war Russian economy was at least partially a result of the policy of the Harding administration. The high-level Russian officials could not understand why America, on the one hand, was willing to provide tremendous famine relief, but, on the other, refused to recognize the Communist government. Goodrich writes of the conundrum:

When I told him [Scheineman, president of the Russian banking system] that America was in Russia spending $50,000,000 dollars solely because the people believed it a Christian duty to feed the starving million[s] in Russia, with no ulterior purpose, and no hope of receiving anything in return, the expression on Scheineman's face indicated that he wondered if I thought he was foolish enough to believe that sort of thing.

In closing the interview I told him I was only a private citizen but I was quite certain it was useless to talk to American business men and bankers about coming into Russia until Russia by the clearest and most

27. Ibid., p. 8.

> unmistakable acts, both by law and administration, gave assurance that private property and contract, freedom of trade, free speech, and free press were guaranteed, not only to the nationals of other countries but to the Russian people as well. I assured him that in America we did not believe any sound, prosperous, economic order could be established upon any other foundation.[28]

Goodrich subsequently met with the Russian commissar of railroads and the commissar of foreign affairs (comparable to the United States secretary of state). The latter also confronted Goodrich about recognition. That same week, Goodrich attended a meeting of the Communist Party held in the Imperial Theatre in Moscow and heard an address by Leon Trotsky, who then served as secretary of the Soviet army. Although Trotsky's speech was generally well received by an audience that was "intensely patriotic and nationalistic in spirit," he was openly criticized by one Russian. Goodrich believed that the fact that the dissenter was able to openly criticize one of the highest-ranking Soviet leaders was significant because it indicated a growing sense of freedom of speech.[29]

Goodrich left Moscow on April 4, 1922. He arrived in New York on April 18, having traveled from England on the ocean liner *Olympic.* Goodrich's return, replete with a message purported to be direct from Lenin, prompted the *Detroit Free Press* to predict that the reestablishment of United States–Russian relations was just around the corner.

> Washington, April 17 [1922]—A message that is expected to be an important factor in shaping the administration's policy toward Soviet Russia is now en route from Nicolai Lenine to President Harding. It is being brought to the United States, it was learned Monday on good authority, by ex-Gov. James P. Goodrich of Indiana, who has been in Russia for some weeks in connection with the administration of American relief distribution.
>
> . . . In Moscow, it is understood, Governor Goodrich saw Lenine a number of times and fully acquainted the soviet chieftain with the views

28. Goodrich, "Russia Manuscript," chap. M, p. 5.
29. Ibid., chap. N, pp. 9–11.

> of President Harding, with the result that Lenine was glad to take the opportunity to send a message to Washington.
>
> The nature of the Russian communication, of course, is not officially known here, but Governor Goodrich's arrival in Washington is being eagerly awaited.
>
> Some new and concrete developments in Russian-American relations are expected in the very near future. It is confidently believed in many quarters that some form of American recognition for the Lenine-Trotzky regime is not far distant.[30]

Goodrich had, in fact, met with Lenin only once during his second trip.[31] On his return, Goodrich denied publicly that he carried any message from the Soviet leader to Harding. It is unlikely, however, that his meetings with Lenin, the Soviet foreign minister George Chitcherin, and other Russian leaders were limited to discussing the success of the relief work, as Goodrich claimed.[32]

At a breakfast meeting with Hoover in Washington on the morning of April 20, Goodrich reported on the success of the relief effort. Goodrich and Hoover then proceeded to discuss Russian developments at a luncheon that same day with President Harding at the White House.[33] At these meetings, Goodrich's reports tended to take on a po-

30. "Lenine Note on Way to U.S.," *Detroit Free Press,* April 17, 1922 (article located in James P. Goodrich Papers, box 15). See also "Goodrich Leaves Moscow for America to Report to Sec. Hoover on Famine Conditions in Russia," *New York Times,* April 5, 1922, p. 31, col. 3; "Goodrich Arrives in London; Is Optimistic as to Famine Conditions," *New York Times,* April 12, 1922, p. 4, col. 3; "Goodrich Is Returning to U.S. to Report to Pres. Harding on Famine Conditions," *New York Times,* April 19, 1922, p. 21, col. 7; "Goodrich Arrives in U.S.," *New York Times,* April 20, 1922, p. 17, col. 3; and "Goodrich Reports to Harding and Hoover, Gives Formal Statement," *New York Times,* April 21, 1922, p. 3, col. 1.

31. J. C. Young, "Goodrich Discusses N. Lenin," *New York Times,* May 21, 1922, sec. 7, p. 11, col. 1.

32. "Goodrich Depicts Russia to Harding," *New York Times,* April 21, 1922, p. 3, col. 1.

33. Goodrich mentions his breakfast meeting with Hoover and his luncheon with Harding at the White House in a letter to Colonel Haskell, April 20, 1922, James P. Goodrich Papers, box 19.

litical tone. Privately, Goodrich continued to press the issue of recognition to Harding, Secretary of State Hughes, and Hoover. It would be a matter that would preoccupy and frustrate the former governor for the next decade. Publicly, he still limited his discussion to the famine and the tremendous success the ARA had had in overcoming great obstacles to provide humanitarian relief.

On May 16, 1922, Goodrich met again with Hughes and Hoover in Washington, D.C., before embarking on his third tour of Russia on May 18. He stopped in both London and Paris to meet with top-level officials about the political situation in Russia. In London, Goodrich met on the morning of May 28 with the controversial United States ambassador to Great Britain, George Harvey. Harvey told Goodrich that the Soviets would soon meet the conditions set down by the American government in order to obtain recognition.[34]

Goodrich arrived in Moscow on June 7. A week later, he was invited to view some property in the government's possession. Believing the property to be simply some furs, Goodrich was not particularly excited about the invitation. When he arrived at the storehouse, however, his attitude changed. Three large sealed chests were brought out and their locks were broken. There in front of him were the Russian Crown jewels in all their brilliance. Goodrich wrote: "The old Czar's crown, the crown of the Czarina, and the various members of the royal family were there, brilliant with diamonds, varying from one to two hundred carats, all of purest water, and of wonderful color. There were crowns of diamonds,

34. In Paris, Goodrich met with a Mr. Logan, who was present at the Genoa conference at the invitation of the British prime minister Lloyd George. From Logan, Goodrich learned that a clear division existed between the pragmatic Communists, who were willing to accede to the capitalist countries' demands, and the more ideological Communists, who were unwilling to move from their original position. Goodrich's views of political events in Russia are summarized in two letters to Hoover: May 28, 1922; and June 2, 1922, Frank A. Golder Papers, box 31. See also "Goodrich Leaves London for Moscow to Investigate Harvest Prospects," *New York Times*, May 30, 1922, p. 20, col. 3; "Goodrich Arrives in Moscow," *New York Times*, June 7, 1922, p. 8, col. 2.

and pearls of emeralds, rubies, and amethysts; collars, bracelets, and necklaces of the precious stones. The scene beggared description."[35]

Goodrich was shown the collection, purportedly worth $500 million at the time, for two reasons: first, to dispel the rumors that the crown jewels had been broken up and sold; and second, to inquire whether the jewels could be used as the basis for a loan in America to purchase agricultural implements and supplies.[36] The first goal was accomplished, since Goodrich's account of the incident was carried in newspapers by the Associated Press across the United States and Europe. Without formal recognition by the United States government, however, loans to the Soviet Republic, with or without the crown jewels as collateral, were out of the question.

It was during Goodrich's third trip that he held a conference with Monsieur Rakovsky, the president of the Ukraine, whom Goodrich called "the clearest headed man I had met in Russia." Rakovsky praised the work of the ARA. He also expressed his hope that it would continue its efforts in the Soviet Republic long after the immediate crisis had ended. The Ukrainian leader also pressed Goodrich on the issue of Soviet recognition. He probed Goodrich regarding whether America would take concessions for private property that had been confiscated by the national government after the civil war. Goodrich's answer was much the same as before: Without a change in Soviet policy allowing for the private ownership of property and permitting American businesses to operate in Russia with limited governmental intrusion, the United States would not recognize or invest in the Soviet Republic.[37] To be safe, Goodrich always combined this response with the caveat that he was speaking only as a private citizen. It was clear, however, that he was espousing the Harding administration's views. Privately, Goodrich was much more sympathetic to Russia's plea for recognition than he ever let on to the Russian leaders.

35. Goodrich, "Russia Manuscript," chap. O, p. 1. Goodrich describes the incident in a letter to Hoover, June 19, 1922, James P. Goodrich Papers, box 24.

36. Goodrich, "Russia Manuscript," chap. O, p. 2.

37. Ibid., pp. 5–7.

After Goodrich's meetings, he cabled a brief report to Secretary Hughes. The matter that Goodrich spent the most time discussing was Lenin's health. If news reports were accurate, Lenin's death was imminent. Who would succeed him, whether there would be an attempt by other factions to overthrow the Bolsheviks from power, and other related questions were of critical importance to the United States. Goodrich wrote to Hughes:

> The most definite and best authenticated report is that while he [Lenin] has had a very light stroke of apoplexy and some mental disturbance his affliction is really due to an acquired or inherited syphilitic infection and that it will yield to a well known specific. . . . The executive committee of five of the communist party whom Lenine consulted on all important matters, consisting of Lenine, Trotsky, Kamenev, president of the Moscow commune and brother in law of Trotsky, Zenovev, president of the Petrograde commune and Stalin, a Georgian prince who is very much trusted by Lenin has just been increased by the addition of Tomsky and Rakow, very close friends of Lenine. Rykov and a prominent communist by the name of Zurupa have been designated by Lenine to preside in his absence and are so acting.
>
> It was determined yesterday to select a committee of three to act for and have full power of Lenine in his absence. There is evidence on every hand that the communist party is preparing to meet the situation should Lenine die. My judgment is that the death of Lenine will not mean the downfall of Bolshevik government or even its serious embarrassment but that it will stand and continue to function.[38]

In the meantime, Goodrich resumed his investigations of famine conditions by traveling through the various provinces. In the Tatar village of Tahtalla, he met with the president of the commune and learned that conditions had improved only marginally since the autumn of 1921. "'In last September we had 1177 souls in this commune,' he said. 'There are 522 people left. Nearly 300 starved and the rest emigrated or died of

38. Telegram from Goodrich to Hughes, June 12, 1922, Frank A. Golder Papers, box 31.

typhus. Only about 12 percent of our livestock is left. If it were not for America we would all be dead. We raised very little last year and are now getting 250 adult and 250 child rations for relief, so you see the Americans are practically feeding the whole commune.' "[39]

Lawlessness continued to be a problem as well. Bands of marauders who had previously fought with the anti-Communist White Army continued to raid the communes and steal from and kill the Communist leaders. The problem was that most of the peasants were sympathetic to and befriended these soldiers, hating the Communists also. As one commune leader told Goodrich, only about 5 percent of the peasants were Communists themselves.[40]

Despite these political problems, Goodrich noted on his return to Moscow from Samara that, as far as the eye could see, "the fields bore evidence of good husbandry." The weather had been excellent, and all indications were that the countryside east of Moscow would bear a bumper crop of rye, wheat, and other grain. "It seemed [to me] that in a few short weeks the work of American relief in Russia would be over."[41]

During Goodrich's second week in Moscow, he received separate invitations to meet with Leon Trotsky, head of the Russian army; Lev B. Kamenev, chairman of the Soviet Relief Commission; Maxim Litvinoff, acting secretary of state in Chitcherin's absence; and Leonid Krassin, commissar of foreign trade, to discuss political relations between the United States and Russia. President Harding and Secretary Hughes had suggested that Goodrich meet with the highest leaders of the Soviet Union in order that they might better understand America's attitude toward Russia, but Goodrich was reluctant to show his eagerness to meet. Goodrich intentionally waited to receive these invitations, and then he turned down the separate invitations, agreeing to meet with the Soviet leaders only collectively. Kamenev arranged the meeting while

39. Goodrich, "Russia Manuscript," chap. P, pp. 6–7.
40. Ibid., chap. Q, pp. 1–3.
41. Ibid., p. 4.

Goodrich was away from Moscow surveying the success of famine relief in several of the outlying provinces.[42]

On Sunday, June 18, Goodrich returned to Moscow. On the following day, the meeting with the Soviet leaders was held at the Kremlin office of Kamenev. Present were Kamenev, Litvinoff, Krassin, and Grigori Sokolnikoff, commissar of finance. Also present was Aleksei Rykov, acting president of the Soviet Republic and president of the Soviet Council. Rykov held these positions because of Lenin's stroke of May 26, which had left the Soviet premier paralyzed over a good part of his body. Trotsky missed the meeting. Dr. Golder served as Goodrich's interpreter. The points that Goodrich raised were contained in a note that Secretary Hughes had sent on March 25 to Litvinoff, listing specific conditions that had to be met prior to recognition.[43]

42. Goodrich details his strategy in arranging the meeting with the Soviet leaders in his letters to Hoover dated June 10 and June 15, 1922, James P. Goodrich Papers, box 2. In the latter letter, Goodrich wrote to Hoover:

> I have not seen any of the men of the "higher-ups" as yet. I have been getting all the information I could from the outside and will send you additional memoranda by the next courier covering a great deal of information I have received. Mr. Kamenev and Mr. Rakow by messenger indicated a desire to talk matters of a political nature. I have declined to do so. Mr. Sakaloff, counsel for the commissariat of concessions asked me yesterday if I would accept an invitation to discuss matters with the central executive committee including Trotsky and others. I told him that I would give serious consideration to an invitation of that kind. I am rather expecting it. I have been standing rather stiff on this matter because I felt that if any discussion of America's attitude toward Russia was to be had at all it only should be with those men in authority.

43. Goodrich details the events leading up to the meeting and summarizes the meeting itself in a memorandum (pp. 14–19) attached to his letter to Hughes dated June 19, 1922, James P. Goodrich Papers, box 2. The relevant part of Hughes's note to Litvinoff states:

> It is only in the productivity of Russia that there is any hope for the Russian people and it is idle to expect resumptions of trade until the economic bases of production are securely established. Production is conditioned upon the safety of life, the recognition by firm guarantees of private property, the sanctity of contract, and the rights of free labor. If fundamental changes are contemplated, involving due regard for the protection of persons and property and the establishment of conditions essential to the maintenance of commerce, this Government will be glad to have

What ensued for the next three hours was a discussion covering the broadest range of issues integral to American-Russian relations. Time and again, Goodrich raised issues that concerned the Harding administration with regard to Soviet political, economic, and legal affairs: the lack of procedural due process in Russia, the lack of separation between the executive and judicial departments, the restrictions on the ownership of private property, the setting aside of contracts, the power and manipulation of labor unions, the Russian debt owed to the United States, the compensation due American companies that had been nationalized or whose property had been otherwise expropriated, and the reluctance of the United States to lend money to the Soviet Republic. On each issue, one or more of the five Soviet leaders—Rykov, Kamenev, Krassin, Litvinoff, and Sokolnikoff—responded to rebut or diffuse Goodrich's arguments.[44]

With regard to the issue of debts owed to the United States, the Russian political leaders stood in unison in refusing to recognize and pay the foreign debts that had been incurred during the deposed czar's reign. Rykov added: "You know that Russia cannot pay. It seems foolish to ask Russia to issue her obligations to pay when she knows that without financial help she cannot pay." To this, Goodrich rejoined with his typical American "can do" attitude: "'The difficulty with you gentlemen is that you yourselves have no faith in Russia,' I replied. 'Russia can pay, once her industrial and economic system is restored. You ought to show your faith in Russia by frankly saying that you recognize your

---

> convincing evidence of the consummation of such changes, and until this evidence is supplied this Government is unable to perceive that there is any proper basis for considering trade relations. . . .

The foregoing is contained in a letter from Evan E. Young, American commissioner at Riga, to United States secretary of state Charles E. Hughes, September 29, 1922, Warren G. Harding Papers, box 567, file 156, folder 2, p. 13, Manuscript Division, Ohio Historical Society, and Warren G. Harding Papers, roll 181, Manuscript Division, U.S. Library of Congress.

44. See Goodrich, "Russia Manuscript," chap. R. The meeting between Goodrich and the Soviet leaders lasted three hours, according to Goodrich's letter to Charles E. Hughes, June 20, 1922, Frank A. Golder Papers, box 31.

debts, that they are valid obligations; that you will give us your undertaking to pay these debts, and will fix a definite time when interest and principal will be paid.'"[45]

Goodrich subsequently drafted a summary of the meeting and forwarded it to Hughes and Hoover. In Goodrich's letter to Hughes, the former governor painted a gloomy picture of the deteriorating conditions in Russia:

> It is difficult to picture the terrific economic collapse of Russia and the frightful waste of Russia's depleted resources that is going on at the present moment. . . . If no substantial results follow the Hague conference and I presume little will be accomplished there, I am convinced that the best thing to do with the Russian situation is to appoint an international commission of experts to examine the whole economic condition of Russia, in Russia, and make a report.[46]

On the next day, June 20, Goodrich attended a trial of the Socialist revolutionaries, this time with Dr. Sokolnikoff, minister of finance. Thirty-four prisoners who had denounced and killed many Communists were being tried for their political beliefs and activities. Goodrich left the trial in the late afternoon to attend a Moscow parade celebrating the Third Internationale. The day marked the anniversary of the slaughter of thousands of Communists by the "Whites," and the Communist Party was attempting to make the most of it. All factories and offices had been closed, and tens of thousands of workers—not very enthusiastically, Goodrich noted—marched in step and weakly cried out "Comrades all together!" Goodrich observed that many banners denounced the political prisoners whose trial he had just left. By the end of the three-hour parade, a curious thing happened. Large crowds of marchers gathered before the Great Hall of the Nobles, demanding to be admitted to the trial of the revolutionaries. Against the defense's objection, the court admitted the workers and permitted them to read a petition condemning the prisoners for "inciting a revolution in Russia,

45. Goodrich, "Russia Manuscript," chap. R, p. 7.

46. Letter from Goodrich to Hughes, June 20, 1922, Frank A. Golder Papers, box 31.

holding them responsible for the death of millions of Russian workers and peasants, and demanding the infliction of the death penalty."[47]

The following day, Goodrich returned to the Volga valley to continue his inspection of ARA famine relief operations. On his return to Moscow, he began inquiring into the state of American business interests in Russia. He met with the managers of the Westinghouse Corporation, International Harvester, and the chairmen of the Soviet State Bank and the Commission on Concessions. From these meetings, Goodrich learned that the Soviet government rejected private ownership of property but was willing to enter into long lease agreements with foreign corporations. The major problem that plagued businesses was not the lack of private ownership or the lack of access to natural resources; rather, the major impediment was the liberal labor laws that at the time excessively burdened foreign businesses. It was far cheaper for American and German companies to manufacture goods in their own countries and ship them to Russia than it was to produce goods in the Soviet Union. For instance, under Soviet law, women workers who became pregnant were entitled to a full salary for seven months while on maternity leave. The managers of International Harvester told Goodrich that benefits of this kind made up nearly 25 percent of the company's entire payroll.[48]

Goodrich next spent an afternoon touring the Kremlin, whose name means "fortress" in Russian. In his manuscript, he describes in detail the various historical sights he visited: the sixty-foot-high wall surrounding the towers, minarets, and gilded domes that adorn the churches and monasteries within the Kremlin; the twenty-six-foot-high, 185-ton bell that Empress Anna had cast in 1733; and the huge, elaborately decorated palaces of the czars. The Kremlin tour made quite an impression on him.[49]

On June 30, 1922, Goodrich left Moscow, completing his third trip to the Soviet Union. On his return train trip from Berlin to Riga, he found

47. Goodrich, "Russia Manuscript," chap. S, pp. 5–6.
48. Ibid., chap. T, pp. 1–4.
49. See Goodrich, "Russia Manuscript," chap. U, pp. 1–7.

that Leonid Krassin, the Russian secretary of foreign trade, was a fellow passenger. The two spoke for several hours, with Krassin trying to convince Goodrich that American financial assistance and resumption of trade were justified. Goodrich told Krassin that before the United States would consider resuming trade relations with Russia, it would first want to know whether Russia was capable of succeeding in its own internal affairs: Could it balance its budget? Could its railroads make money? Could the natural resource trusts be operated efficiently? and so on. Goodrich further reminded Krassin that the Russian government had promised to submit a comprehensive plan of reconstruction at the Genoa, Italy, international economic conference in March 1922, but had failed to do so. Goodrich wanted to know what the plan was. He writes of Krassin's response: "M. Krassin then proceeded for half an hour to talk about a perfectly foolish, impractical scheme involving railroad building, electrification, restoration of agriculture, purchase of thousands of tractors—all to be done by the Bolshevik government. Had this statement come from some young, enthusiastic communist I would not have been surprised, but coming from Krassin I was astounded."[50]

On July 21, Goodrich returned from the trip along with Cora on the ocean liner *Mauritania.* Marie Moorman, the daughter of Goodrich's business partner, Jesse Moorman of Winchester, had accompanied the Goodriches. After his third trip, Goodrich had intervened to arrange for four young Europeans to immigrate to the United States to begin new lives: Josephine Friedrich and Marie Kohlman from Bavaria, Peter Stuer from Latvia, and Hans Fredrichson from Denmark. Friedrich, who spoke no English and only a little French when she first arrived in Boston in September 1923, lived with the Goodriches as a companion to Cora from October 1923 to 1928, when she married.[51]

Upon Goodrich's return in July 1922, he participated in a conference for officers of the ARA in New York. At this conference, the leadership

50. Ibid., p. 5.

51. "Refugees from Chaos: The German-Americans," *Winchester (Ind.) News-Gazette,* n.d.

of the ARA decided to cease feeding adults in Russia. They concluded, however, that they would continue feeding about one million children for another year.[52] Goodrich and Hoover traveled to the White House on September 6, at which time Goodrich updated President Harding on the famine and the political discussions he had held with the Soviet leaders. Goodrich started to press privately for at least an open consideration of Russian recognition by the Harding administration. A brief newspaper excerpt captures the essence of Goodrich's thinking:

> Formal expression by former Governor Goodrich of Russian views attributed to him in private conversation in Washington was regarded tonight as likely to lead to interesting developments in the Administration situation growing out of Secretary Hughes' determined stand against recognition of the Soviet regime.
>
> Although Mr. Goodrich is essentially an administrative agent of the American Relief Administration, his reports on economic and political conditions are said to have been submitted to President Harding and Secretary Hughes no less than to Mr. Hoover. Mr. Goodrich is not, however, in any sense an agent of the Administration to negotiate terms of recognition with the Moscow leaders, it was said.
>
> It has been an open secret that Mr. Goodrich was convinced that whatever contrary views might be held as to the wisdom of communist political theories, that regime was the de facto government of Russia and the greater good was to be derived from recognition of it as such.[53]

Clearly, Secretary Hughes had a different opinion, and his strong will would not submit to Goodrich's powers of persuasion. Hughes was a former governor of New York, an associate justice of the Supreme Court, and the Republican candidate for president in 1916, when he narrowly lost to Woodrow Wilson. He would also become the eleventh

52. "Phone Association to Hold Annual Meeting" (Goodrich reports on Russia "As I See Her"), *Indianapolis News,* September 19, 1922, p. 9, col. 1; see also "Goodrich Praised by Russian Newspapers for His Relief Efforts," *Indianapolis News,* July 27, 1922, p. 22, col. 4.

53. Contained in a clipping dated July 7, 1922, Public Ledger Bureau, James P. Goodrich Papers, box 18. See also "Goodrich Tells of Report on Russia," *Indianapolis News,* n.d. (found in James P. Goodrich Papers, box 15).

chief justice of the Supreme Court in 1930. The secretary of state believed that he should be the one sitting in the White House. At the very least, he was convinced that directing America's foreign policy was his job. Hughes was adamantly opposed to any consideration of recognition without the radical changes dictated in his March 25 letter to Litvinoff.

Unable to shake Hughes from his position, Goodrich returned, discouraged, to Indiana and his neglected business interests. By mid September, negotiations to reestablish relations between the two countries had come to a complete halt. The Harding administration had decided, following Goodrich's recommendation in June, to appoint a commission to examine the economic conditions in Russia. The Soviets refused to allow an American investigation team to enter Russia, however, unless the United States reciprocated by allowing a Soviet team to visit and examine America's economic conditions. The demand by Moscow infuriated Hughes. It essentially ended communications between the two countries for a considerable time. In early September, the *Times* of London reported that it had recently learned that more than 1.7 million Russians had been executed by the Cheka during the Soviet civil war, more than had been killed during all of World War I. The horrific news, reported in United States newspapers, solidified America's impression that the Communists were a brutal lot and were not to be trusted.[54]

Privately, Goodrich remained very interested in the reestablishment of United States–Russian relations. Haskell kept Goodrich informed of ongoing ARA activities as well as of political matters by writing him periodically from Moscow. Goodrich also kept a close eye on political developments in the Soviet Union through newspaper accounts and correspondence with Hoover and other ARA officials.[55] In late Novem-

54. See "Washington Ends Negotiations for Inquiry in Russia," *Baltimore Sun*, September 19, 1922; "1,766,118 Executed by Russian Cheka," *New York Times*, n.d. (reporting article from *Times* of London dated September 2, 1922, James P. Goodrich Papers, box 15).

55. See memorandum from J. A. Lehrs to Colonel William N. Haskell (copy to James P. Goodrich), September 9, 1922, regarding interview between Haskell and Kamenev. Letters from Haskell to Goodrich, October 9, 1922, and October 11, 1922,

ber 1922, Goodrich tried to resurrect the idea of an American commission's visiting the Soviet Union with the understanding that a Russian commission would be permitted to come to the United States at an undesignated later date. He floated the idea past Haskell in Moscow, who in turn discussed it with Karl Radek (chief of the Russian Propaganda Bureau), but apparently nothing came of the proposal.[56]

Back in Indiana, Goodrich attempted to stay involved in the Russian recognition issue. He had given up on converting Secretary Hughes to his way of thinking; instead, he focused on gaining the support of Hoover. "I would rather have them in the family circle where we can talk things over with them," Goodrich wrote to Hoover. He added, "With the departure of the A.R.A. the last point of contact with Russia will be severed."[57] Goodrich was far from alone in seeking the establishment of diplomatic relations with the Soviets. On March 15, 1923, the Women's Committee for Recognition of Russia met for its second annual conference in Washington, D.C. In a telegram to President Harding, the delegation demanded a change in United States policy, mentioning Goodrich's position in the bargain:

> As American women gathered in [the] Capital of the United States to confer upon this vital phase of our foreign policy, we protest against the worn out excuses offered by our government against reestablishment of diplomatic relations with present government of Russia. We stand unreservedly for full and immediate recognition of Russia realizing that this is a moral necessity and is fundamental to the economic stability of

---

James P. Goodrich Papers, box 19; letter from Haskell to Walter Lyman Brown (copy to James P. Goodrich), February 20, 1923, James P. Goodrich Papers, box 20. Dozens of articles about the Soviet Union and famine relief are contained in Goodrich's collected papers, which indicates that Goodrich stayed abreast of events in Russia after his third trip. See James P. Goodrich Papers, box 15.

56. This is mentioned in a letter from Colonel Haskell to Christian A. Herter of the Department of Commerce, December 2, 1922, Frank A. Golder Papers, box 31.

57. Letter from Goodrich to Hoover, January 30, 1923, Commerce Papers, box 240, Herbert Hoover Presidential Library, West Branch, Iowa; see also Rhodes, *James P. Goodrich, Indiana's "Governor Strangelove,"* p. 131.

> Europe since our delegation visited Secretary Hughes a year ago. Many Americans have advocated a change in our Russian policy, including Bishop Nuelson of the Methodist Church, Mr. Malcolm Sumner of the New York Bar, and ex-Governor Goodrich, President of National City Bank of Indianapolis, all of whom have been to Russia.[58]

Nonetheless, Hughes clearly had the upper hand in influencing Harding's views. He periodically sent to the president letters from Americans who had lived in the Soviet Union and who supported the administration's position of nonrecognition. Harding seemed content to believe that he and Hughes were right, despite protests to the contrary.[59]

Meanwhile, on June 16, 1923, a dinner was held in Moscow informally concluding the ARA's work in Russia. Almost all of the top Soviet leaders were present, including Kamanev, who was now acting head of the Russian government as a result of Lenin's medical relapse in March. In addition to Kamanev, Chitcherin, Litvinoff, Radek, and Sokolnikoff were there. Trotsky, absent from Moscow, wrote a glowing letter thanking the ARA for its relief efforts. He let it be known "that both people and the Government of Russia are ready to make every effort to reestablish normal relations with the great American people."[60]

58. Warren G. Harding Papers, box 567, file 156, folder 3, Ohio State Historical Society, Columbus, Ohio, and Warren G. Harding Papers, roll 181, Manuscript Division, U.S. Library of Congress.

59. See letter from Evan E. Young to Hughes, September 29, 1922; letter from Hughes to Harding, October 24, 1922, which includes Young's letter; letter from J. O. J. Taylor, superintendent of Siberia Mission, M. E. Church, South, to Hughes, June 8, 1923; and letter from Hughes to Harding, June 12, 1923. Harding's letter of June 15, 1923, to Hughes states: "It is very gratifying to have these expressions of approval from one [Taylor] who is in a position to properly appraise the situation in Russia." Warren G. Harding Papers, box 856, file 156, folder 4, Manuscript Division, Ohio State Historical Society, and Warren G. Harding Papers, roll 181, Manuscript Division, U.S. Library of Congress.

60. Goodrich was not present for this dinner. A list of the Russian leaders and ARA officials in attendance and a digest of the speeches given at the occasion can be found in James P. Goodrich Papers, box 16. See also Walter Duranty, "Soviet Heads Thank America for Relief," *New York Times,* June 17, 1923.

Frustrated at the pace of negotiations, Goodrich attempted in June 1923 to press his views about recognition directly with President Harding. He wrote to Harding seeking an opportunity to meet with the president; however, before the meeting ever came about, Harding became ill and died in San Francisco on August 2.[61] Harding's death made it necessary for Goodrich to start all over, promoting a more moderate American policy toward Russia with Calvin Coolidge, Harding's successor. Goodrich was totally discouraged by the attitude of Hughes and the lack of any interest on the part of the State Department to reexamine the situation. In an August 1923 letter to Edgar Rickard, the ARA's executive director, Goodrich wrote:

> I am becoming so thoroughly disgusted with the conduct of our State Department with respect to the whole foreign situation that I don't know what to do. I don't even want to talk about it. We are in the world, yet not out of the world. We have set ourselves on a little pedestal apart from all the rest of the world and are assuming the position of the world's schoolmaster, undertaking to tell them all what to do. Occupying the most important position in the world, we are not able to make it effective for bringing about industrial peace and stability. . . . The Democrats might not do better. I doubt they would do much worse.[62]

Shortly afterward, Hoover tried to arrange a fourth trip for Goodrich, in which he would establish "at least a temporary contact in Russia." The commerce secretary also suggested Goodrich's name to the Rockefeller Foundation as a possible representative of the foundation in the Soviet Union. Goodrich had a "very pleasant" talk with the Rockefeller Foundation, but nothing came of this meeting or of Hoover's hopes to use Goodrich to further United States trade possibilities with the Krem-

61. Letter from Goodrich to Harding, June 5, 1923, Frank A. Golder Papers, box 32; Rhodes, *James P. Goodrich, Indiana's "Governor Strangelove,"* p. 134.

62. Letter from Goodrich to Rickard, August 9, 1923, ARA Personnel Records, box 288, Hoover Institution; see also Rhodes, *James P. Goodrich, Indiana's "Governor Strangelove,"* p. 135.

lin.[63] Goodrich would wait for two more years before he would again visit the Soviet Union and attempt to influence Washington to view Russia differently.

63. Letter from Hoover to Goodrich, September 12, 1923; letter from Goodrich to Hoover, September 17, 1923, ARA Personnel Records, box 261 Hoover Institution; Rhodes, *James P. Goodrich, Indiana's "Governor Strangelove,"* pp. 135–36.

Chapter 14
Return to Russia, 1925

[My presence] was a touch of the outside life at this Commune [Schilling]. They all seemed glad to see an American. They welcomed me with a heartiness that left no doubt as to its sincerity and bid me Godspeed with a regret that plainly was stamped upon their faces.

JAMES P. GOODRICH, "Russia Diary"

AT THE END of August 1925, James Goodrich embarked upon his fourth and final trip to the Soviet Union.[1] For five weeks, Goodrich and his wife Cora, Colonel William Haskell, and Frank Golder toured the Volga region and the cities that the former governor had first visited in 1921. What he found was "remarkable progress" in agriculture, railroads, banking, and manufacturing. At a personal level, the fourth trip was an opportunity for Goodrich to renew his own fondness for the Russian people. When he visited the commune of Schilling, Goodrich met a peasant woman who was selling vegetables and fruit. He told her who he was in his broken Russian, and the woman

> cried and threw her arms around my neck and kissed me on either cheek and told me that I saved her children from starvation. Soon a crowd of people were gathered around me and I saw several faces whom I recognized among those I met three years ago. It was a wholesome looking lot of folks gathered around here, ignorant as far as the ordinary education

1. For a thorough examination of Goodrich's fourth and final trip to the Soviet Union, see Benjamin D. Rhodes, *James P. Goodrich, Indiana's "Governor Strangelove,"* pp. 140–55.

> goes, but with a world of good hard common sense and of great industry; educated and given a fair chance in life they will give a good account of themselves.[2]

Goodrich had returned with Golder to the Soviet Union at the invitation of the Russian Academy of Science, which was celebrating its twentieth anniversary. He held no official position and was simply attending as a representative of Indiana University. Golder represented Stanford University. The academy was holding an international conference for delegates from Europe as well as from the United States, China, India, and other countries. It was the first formal opportunity Russian intellectuals had had since 1914 to meet with their foreign counterparts. Goodrich and Golder were the only delegates from the United States.

Goodrich took every opportunity to learn about the progress the Soviet people had achieved since he had last visited in 1922. He met with a vast array of officials, both public and private. One of his first meetings was in Leningrad with Dr. Ivan Pavlov, the Nobel Prize–winning physiologist, who is perhaps best known in the West for his conditioned reflex experiments involving dogs. Pavlov was an outspoken critic of Communism. He constantly denounced Lenin to Goodrich and refused in 1922 to receive any special treatment during the famine. "These fellows have learned they cannot run a government according to their Marxian philosophy," Pavlov told his visitor.[3]

On September 5, Goodrich met with Dr. Oldenburg, secretary of the Russian Academy of Science. Goodrich had first met Oldenburg in 1921. At that time, Goodrich and Golder had offered the eminent professor of modern Oriental languages, on behalf of the Rockefeller Foundation, $500,000 for the purpose of maintaining the operations of the Russian Academy of Science. Oldenburg had refused the generous offer because he was attempting to force the Russian government to support the academy. The maneuver had apparently worked, since the Communist government had contributed two million rubles (at that time about

2. Goodrich, "Russia Diary," September 20, 1925, p. 85.

3. Ibid., p. 9.

$1 million) in 1925 toward sustaining the academy. Oldenburg praised the Communist regime, and especially Lenin. He believed that the moderate faction of the Communist Party was gaining control and that the government would continue to move toward a fuller embrace of capitalism.[4]

Back in Moscow on September 7, Goodrich found the Russian capital abuzz with activity. Everywhere he went, Russians repeatedly asked him about the "Scopes Monkey Trial," which was going on in Dayton, Tennessee, and about who or what was a "Ford"? Goodrich held two meetings with Maxim Litvinoff, who was still acting commissar of foreign affairs in the absence of Chitcherin. In a series of meetings with private citizens, Goodrich learned that there was a tremendous shortage of housing. Families of several members were forced to live in apartments of only two or three rooms. Because housing was first offered to workers at an artificially low rent (as little as three dollars a month) there was no incentive for investors to build any additional housing. The low rent was subsidized by the rest of the taxpayers.[5] Goodrich subsequently met with the commissar of transportation, the head of the Textile Trust, and the assistant commissar of agriculture. From the latter, he learned that in 1925 Russia would have in excess of one billion poods (1.8 million tons) of foodstuffs, quite a different situation from the one that had existed in 1922.[6]

On the evening of Monday, September 14, Goodrich and Golder attended a meeting of the Moscow Soviet in the famous Bolshoi Theatre. While he claimed the meeting was pure "propaganda from start to finish," he could not help but mention with pride the reception that the delegates attending the Academy of Science anniversary received from the thousands who attended the meeting. "When the names of the two American delegates [Goodrich and Golder] were read and we arose, the entire theatre stood up as one person and cheered again and again until

4. Ibid., pp. 17–20.
5. Ibid., pp. 51–52, 62.
6. Ibid., pp. 40–50.

we too were compelled to go to the front and cries of 'America' arose from all over the great building."[7]

The following day, Goodrich attended a meeting of the economic research section of the Academy of Science, accompanied by the Soviet minister of finance Grigori Sokolnikoff. The featured speaker was the noted British economist John Maynard Keynes. According to Goodrich, Keynes's address was not well received. It is little wonder, given that throughout the talk Keynes criticized Lenin and Leninism, attacked the gold standard, and advocated instead a monetary standard based upon the average value of certain basic products.[8]

A meeting the next day with a young Russian reinforced Goodrich's belief that the Soviet Union under the Communists was on its way to economic prosperity.

> He was enthusiastic over the great improvement of the condition of the Russian worker as compared to Czarist times. I asked him to put in writing the various advantages the Russian worker now possesses that he did not have under the Czar and he gave me a list of fifty-one different benefits that flowed from the Revolution. . . . Among the many things he recited were an eight-hour day, the right to organize in Unions, the right of free assembly and free speech, the benefits of school system for his children. The right where married to have a single room for himself and family. He admitted that the condition of the Russian worker and his standard of life was very much lower than an American worker, but he said: "We are just getting started. We expect some day to build our country to the same condition that now obtains in America."[9]

On Friday, September 18, Goodrich, with a young interpreter, left for Saratov to retrace his previous journeys while on the famine relief missions in 1921 and 1922. Although the crop conditions were generally much improved, Goodrich found the appearance and plight of the Russian peasants little different. As he stated, "Men and women while

7. Ibid., p. 69.
8. Ibid., p. 74.
9. Ibid., p. 78.

strong and rugged physically are miserably dressed and have a pathetic, sad appearance as they stand along the railway in the little Communes through which we passed."[10] On September 20, Goodrich took the steamboat *Leon Trotsky* down the Volga River. He and his interpreter traveled to Tsaritzin, whose name had recently been changed to Stalingrad in honor of Joseph Stalin.[11]

While in the Ukraine, Goodrich met with President Petrofsky of the Ukraine Republic, who was one of six chairmen of the Central Executive Committee of the Soviet of Russian Republics. Petrofsky also asked about the Scopes trial and the question of recognition. Goodrich recounted again the conditions necessary for the Communist government to be recognized by America: recognition and payment of the debts contracted by the Kerensky government; restoration of American property in Russia nationalized by the Soviet government; and cessation of propaganda by sympathizers associated with the Third International Communist Party.[12]

On his return to Moscow, Goodrich met with the general manager of Amtorg, the Russian agency that conducted export and import business in America. Goodrich also had a lengthy discussion with Litvinoff on the afternoon of September 25 about Russian-American relations.[13] Two days later, Litvinoff invited Goodrich to dinner to continue the discussions. Present at Litvinoff's home opposite the Kremlin, besides Litvinoff, were Nikolay Bukharin, the editor of *Pravda,* and Karl Radek, director of propaganda. During the two-hour discussion, Litvinoff, Radek, and Bukharin emphatically denied that the government had any connection with the Third Internationale. On the issue of recognition, the Soviet leaders conveyed a sense of befuddlement. It was well known that the Weimar Republic of Germany had extended diplomatic recognition in April 1922 and Great Britain had in 1924. By 1925, the United States remained the major holdout.

10. Ibid., p. 80.
11. Ibid., pp. 91–92.
12. Ibid., pp. 102–3.
13. Ibid., pp. 106–7.

On the afternoon of Tuesday, September 29, Goodrich met with Joseph Stalin. At the time, Stalin held the positions of secretary of the Politburo as well as secretary of the Communist Party. During a two-hour meeting, Stalin, who would become the most important and powerful figure in modern Russian history, covered much of the same ground with Goodrich as had been covered by Litvinoff, Radek, Krassin, Kamenev, and other Soviet leaders. Goodrich raised with Stalin the matter of the inflammatory anti-American speech he had heard Kamenev give before the Moscow Soviet on September 14. Stalin expressed disappointment over Kamenev's remarks as well as those of Zinoviev, who espoused support for the Third Internationale. Stalin concluded the meeting by repeating "what was so often said to me in Russia," wrote Goodrich, "that the Russian people liked the Americans and preferred closer cooperation with them than to any other country in the world."[14] Goodrich's brief appraisal of the stolid Georgian was that he was "a man of rare good common sense, sound judgment, and in my opinion is easily the most powerful factor in Russia."[15]

The following day, Goodrich met with Leon Trotsky in Trotsky's Kremlin office. Trotsky tried to convince Goodrich that the Soviet Union deserved recognition. He detailed the government's plan to attract foreign capital, reduce the costs of production in agriculture, and be competitive in the world markets. As for Trotsky's proposal to continue the heavy subsidizing of workers' rents, Goodrich called the plan "rotten economics."[16]

When Goodrich departed Russia on October 7, his work was not finished. In Berlin, he met with Chitcherin, the Soviet foreign minister, at the Russian embassy. Chitcherin expressed outrage over the note he had received from the United States secretary of state C. E. Hughes in December 1923. Hughes's note had followed President Coolidge's speech to Congress, in which Coolidge had given a strong indication that

14. Ibid., pp. 120–22.
15. Ibid., p. 120.
16. Ibid., pp. 123–24.

American policy toward the Communists was softening. Given the capacity in which he was visiting the Soviet Union, Goodrich was clearly not in the position to speak for either Hughes or the president.[17]

Goodrich's impressions on his fourth trip confirmed what he had begun to believe when he had visited in 1922: that Russia under the Communists was making great progress and that conditions, despite severe internal problems, were generally much better than they had been under the czars. The items he specifically mentioned in support of this assessment included the extension of voting rights to intellectuals, scientists, and technicians; the decentralization of power from Moscow in favor of local governments; the amendment of marriage laws to recognize church marriages and of the inheritance laws to remove the prohibition against inheritances of more than five thousand dollars; the reinstatement of private traders; the defeat of Zinoviev, Kamenev, and Sokolnikoff, who opposed addressing the issue of international debts on any terms; and the rise in power of Stalin and the movement toward the right. From his perspective, the government's adoption of "State capitalism" was a step in the right direction, a step that would ultimately lead to the eradication of the last vestiges of Communism.[18]

When Goodrich returned to the United States in October 1925, he was more certain than ever that Russian recognition would be of benefit to both countries. In an attempt to convince President Coolidge of the changes he had seen, he traveled to Washington and met with both the secretary of state, Frank B. Kellogg, and Coolidge. Hoover had arranged the meetings. Kellogg was even more dogmatic than his predecessor had been in opposing recognition, while Coolidge, true to his cautious nature, "made no commitments and urged Goodrich to summarize his views on paper."[19]

Disheartened by the tepid response, Goodrich nonetheless returned to Winchester and wrote to the president in November 1925: "It is safe to say today that the working classes of Russia are in better condition

17. Ibid., pp. 126–27.

18. Ibid., pp. 128–32.

19. Rhodes, *James P. Goodrich, Indiana's "Governor Strangelove,"* pp. 153–54.

and better satisfied than they were under the Tsar." He went on to state that recognition would promote world stability, renew American business ties with Russia, and "accelerate rather than retard the march now going on from communism to capitalism."[20]

After spending five years stewing about the problem, Goodrich finally gave up lobbying for United States recognition of the Communists. It was not until eight years later, on November 16, 1933, that President Franklin D. Roosevelt finally granted recognition to the Soviet Union through an exchange of letters with Litvinoff.[21] Goodrich believed that the many years of nonrecognition not only hurt the Soviet people but delayed a grand opportunity for American businesses to prosper in a vast country that could have benefited from American goods.

Goodrich's opportunity to participate in the ARA famine-relief efforts in Russia is significant for several reasons. First, his investigations into the famine and his subsequent testimony before Congress gave credibility to earlier reports of the famine that the media had tended to sensationalize. Goodrich was a highly respected former governor. He had long served as a member of the Republican National Committee and was generally well known and highly regarded in Washington's political circles. His firsthand experience of the famine, coupled with his business and political background, gave credibility to his testimony. In fact, during debate about famine-relief legislation on the House and Senate floors, members of Congress made repeated references to Goodrich's testimony before the House Foreign Affairs Committee. Their faith in Goodrich's views was summarized in an Associated Press article written in February 1922: "Goodrich is a man known to be, as one commentator expressed it, 'a hard-boiled Republican, who thinks as the President does.' Goodrich is a wealthy Indiana public utilities owner, long in poli-

20. Letter from Goodrich to Coolidge, November 23, 1925, James P. Goodrich Papers, box 3.

21. See Franklin D. Roosevelt Papers, vol. 2, pp. 471, 474–75; *The Annals of America: 1929–1939*, vol. 15 (Chicago: Encyclopaedia Britannica, 1976), pp. 219–20.

tics, and high in his party's counsel. When he came back from Russia, and made his report on Russia, the President believed it. The same was true of senators and representatives with whom the former governor has spoken."[22]

Second, James Goodrich's testimony made it clear that only immediate relief would prevent one of the worst famines in history. The ARA was not in a position to raise funds privately because of the general skepticism among the American people toward Communist Russia. Goodrich and Hoover, however, convinced Congress that public relief would not result in propping up the Bolshevik government. It would merely address starvation among the peasant class.

Third, Goodrich told the story of Communist Russia and, in a very real way, assisted in providing a more realistic perception of the Soviet Republic and its people to the American public. Goodrich addressed groups in large and small cities alike and gave interviews to many national newspapers.[23] Major articles about his various trips were reported by the *Independent,* the *New York Times,* the *New York Sun,* the *New York Herald,* the *Detroit Free Press,* the *Pittsburgh Times,* the *St. Louis Post-Dispatch,* the *Indianapolis Star,* and other leading papers in the United States. Even the *China Press* of Shanghai reported on Goodrich's investigation.[24] Goodrich himself wrote articles in *Outlook* and *Century*

22. Undated and unattributed article contained in James P. Goodrich Papers, box 15.

23. Goodrich addressed the Foreign Policy Association at the Hotel Astor in New York City on January 26, 1922 (see "Goodrich Addresses Foreign Policy Association," *New York Times,* January 27, 1922, sec. 2, p. 1, col. 7; "Former Governor of Indiana Tells of Conditions in Russia," *St. Louis Post-Dispatch,* January 27, 1922) and the Brooklyn, New York, Chamber of Commerce on February 18, 1922 (see "Tells Brooklyn Chamber Country Requires Huge Loans to Restore Economic Conditions," *New York Times,* February 19, 1922, p. 20, col. 8). Goodrich also spoke before several other groups. See "Ex-Governor Will Address Columbia Club on Sovietism," *Indianapolis Star,* January 16, 1922, p. 1, col. 4; "Phone Association to Hold Annual Meeting," *Indianapolis News,* September 19, 1922, p. 9, col. 1.

24. Sidney Brooks, "Russia as a Hoosier Banker Sees Her," *The Independent,* November 21, 1925, p. 583; "Soviet's Fall Unlikely: Ex-Gov. Goodrich Tells Why He Thinks Russian Government Will Continue," *New York Times,* January 29, 1922, sec. 7, p. 9, col. 1; "Tells President and Hoover of Economic Conditions and Result of Relief Work,"

magazines as well as a major article, "The True Communists of Russia," for *Current History.*[25]

Fourth, Goodrich served as an important conduit for initiating relations between the United States and the new Soviet government. Formal diplomatic relations between the two countries had come to an abrupt halt in 1917 when the Bolsheviks took control of the government. Between 1917 and 1933, Goodrich was probably the highest-ranking American emissary to have direct and repeated contact with the Soviet leadership.

Goodrich's analysis of the causes of Russia's pathetic conditions and what it would take for Russia to become a self-sufficient and profitable nation were right on the mark. He correctly attributed Russia's decline during the post–civil war era of the early 1920s to a totally inexperienced and idealistic group of radicals, among whom were Lenin, Trotsky, Rykov, and Krassin. He wrote in the last chapter of his manuscript about his trips to Russia:

> Individuals of no experience in the practical affairs of life, idealistic dreamers and radical socialists under the old order: who had been in prison, banished and driven from the country, obsessed by the theories which had never been put to the practical test in a large way: as indiffer-

New York Times, April 21, 1922, p. 3, col. 1; "Relief for the Starving Millions of Russia Near," *New York Sun,* January 28, 1922; Charles G. Ross, "Outlook for Recognition of Russia More Hopeful, U.S. Authorities Believe," *St. Louis Post-Dispatch,* May 3, 1922; "Russians Weary of War and Revolution, but Better Off Than Under Czars, Says Hoover's Emissary After Tour of Country," *St. Louis Post-Dispatch,* May 6, 1922; "Lenin Dolls Up His Government," *Salem (Ore.) Statesman,* March 24, 1922; "American Relief Memorial," *(San Antonio) Texas Express,* April 24, 1922; "Goodrich Heads Mission," *China Press,* August 23, 1922; "Goodrich Optimistic as to Russian Famine," *New York Times,* April 12, 1922; "Lenine Note on Way to U.S.: Message Being Brought by Goodrich Expected to Help Shape Soviet Policy," *Detroit Free Press,* April 17, 1922; "Relief for the Starving Millions of Russia Near," *New York Sun,* January 28, 1922.

25. J. P. Goodrich, "The True Communists of Russia," *Current History,* September 1922, reviewed in *The Freeman,* October 18, 1922; James P. Goodrich, "Can Russia Come Back?" *Outlook* 130 (March 1, 1922): 341–44; James P. Goodrich, "Impressions of the Bolshevik Regime," *Century* 104 (May 1922): 55–65; "As Goodrich Sees Russia" (review of Goodrich's article in *Century*), *Pittsburgh Times,* May 14, 1922.

> ent to the hard facts and realities of life as were the scholastics of the middle ages, composed the major part of the government. They placed in positions of trust, dealing with large affairs of vital importance, persons of no experience, largely drawn from the workers and peasants of Russia. Filled with class hatred, possessing remarkable energy and thirst for power, they destroyed everything that stood in their way.[26]

Despite these pitfalls, Goodrich was optimistic that Russia's leadership was gradually recognizing the foolishness of its earlier policies and would successfully transform modern Russia into greatness. He wrote:

> Russia is a great country, the population of which, by unheard of distress, slowly is learning the value of freedom, individual initiative and private property. Thru the establishment of these principles, and no other way, will the country be restored and an opportunity afforded this really great people to work out their own future according to the possibilities that lie within them. The question naturally arises. Has the Bolshevist government reached a situation where it is prepared to and will give the guarantees essential to the resumption of normal business in Russia? It is my judgment that it will soon reach that point.[27]

If Goodrich was on target in diagnosing Russia's illness and cure, he was significantly off the mark in predicting the timing of recovery and health. Not even to this day, more than seventy years after Goodrich's last visit, can Russia lay claim to being the economic and world power that the former Indiana governor predicted it would become. In defense of Goodrich's optimism, it must be remembered that when he completed his fourth and final trip, the Soviet government's adoption of a new comprehensive economic-political policy had been in effect for more than four years. The New Economic Policy (NEP) was announced in March 1921 by Lenin. Its purpose was to retreat temporarily from the unattainable goal of Communism to state capitalism. Under the NEP, the monetary system and the market economy were restored. Peasants were allowed to dispose of their products for personal gain after meet-

26. Goodrich, "Russia Manuscript," chap. Y, pp. 2–3.
27. Ibid., p. 21.

ing their tax obligations; most small-scale industries were denationalized to allow the rise of a new class of small-business owners. Many outside and inexperienced followers of Soviet policy, such as Goodrich, believed that the NEP was a sign of a broader acceptance of capitalism and not simply the aberration from Communism that it turned out to be.[28]

Part of Goodrich's miscalculations may be explained by his understandable fondness for the Russian people and his deep desire to see the Soviet nation prosper. Goodrich knew the Russian people and their leaders personally. They were not faceless bureaucrats uniformly and fervently devoted to full-fledged Marxist Communism. They convinced him that they generally liked Americans and simply wanted to be treated as equals, which necessitated mutual recognition. Furthermore, unlike Washington's "three H's" (Harding, Hughes, and Hoover), who knew the Russian political leadership only by reputation, Goodrich had met with the highest echelon of the Communist leadership: Lenin, Stalin, Trotsky, Rykov, Kamenev, Chitcherin, Bukharin, Litvinoff, Radek, Sokolnikoff, and Krassin. He believed that he understood the fractious elements in the Communist Party, and he was convinced that the moderate-conservative wing would ultimately prevail. He believed that this powerful faction would be concerned with improving living conditions and would toss aside the leftists' utopian dream of Marxist Communism.

In hindsight, however, it is clear that Goodrich did not fully appreciate the zealotry and ruthlessness that many of these same leaders would adopt in creating a totalitarian communist organization. Contrary to Goodrich's appraisal, communist political ideology, not prag-

28. Goodrich writes about the NEP in "Russia Manuscript," chap. Y, pp. 14–23. For more thorough discussions of the NEP, see Warren B. Walsh, *Russia and the Soviet Union* (Ann Arbor: University of Michigan Press, 1958), pp. 423–33; Edward Hallett Carr, *The Bolshevik Revolution, 1917–1923*, vol. 2 of *A History of Soviet Russia* (New York: Macmillan, 1951), pp. 280–383; George von Rauch, *A History of Soviet Russia* (New York: F. A. Praeger, 1967), pp. 124–31; and Adam B. Ulam, *A History of Soviet Russia* (New York: Praeger, 1976), pp. 59–87.

matism, prevailed in the next several decades. The NEP, which was in full force when Goodrich visited the Soviet Union, was an aberrational concession. It was viewed by Lenin and later by Trotsky and Stalin as necessary to prevent a complete overthrow of the Bolsheviks, not as a long-term policy goal. Moreover, Stalin's own calculating mind and personal ambitions caused him in 1928 to move away from the NEP in order to rid himself of rivals such as Kamenev, Trotsky, Zinoviev, and Bukharin. In a series of adroit political maneuvers, Stalin shifted to leftist policies that these rivals opposed. He, thus, was able to condemn them for creating factionalism and deviation from the Communist line. Stalin then either demoted them or eliminated them altogether. The playing out of this sort of personal ambition would have been nearly impossible for Goodrich to forecast.

Despite the political turn of events that Goodrich failed to foresee accurately, the first and primary purpose of his travels to Russia—to assist in famine relief—was a complete success. A total of 381 Americans served with the ARA in Russia at one time or other during the twenty-two months that the relief organization had a presence in the Soviet Union. A handful of this number were regular army officers; the majority were volunteers, like Goodrich, who saw an opportunity to play an important role in relieving suffering.[29] Despite its small numbers, this group was responsible for feeding as many as ten million starving Russians. The ARA efforts undoubtedly prevented millions from dying. The ARA's campaign is considered one of the greatest humanitarian undertakings in history. It is little wonder that James Goodrich considered it his greatest personal adventure.

29. See "American Relief Memorial," *(San Antonio) Texas Express,* April 24, 1922.

Pierre Goodrich with his fraternity brothers at Phi Gamma Delta fraternity, Wabash College, circa 1915. Pierre is in the second row, third from right. (Courtesy Philip Magner, Wabash, Ind.)

Pierre Goodrich, *left,* and James P. Goodrich, *center,* circa 1918. (James P. Goodrich Collection, Herbert Hoover Presidential Library-Museum, West Branch, Iowa)

Men's Bible class, Easter Sunday, April 12, 1914. Even while governor, James P. Goodrich, seventh from right in front row, returned to Winchester to teach the class. (First Presbyterian Church, Winchester, Ind.)

Graduation ceremonies at Indiana University, Bloomington, June 12, 1918. Standing is William Lowe Bryan, president of the university; seated directly behind him is James P. Goodrich, and to Bryan's right is Theodore Roosevelt, the commencement speaker. (Courtesy: Indiana University Archives)

Governor Goodrich and W. E. Stalnaker leaving the Pathfinder Company, Indianapolis, after a flag-raising ceremony. (Courtesy Auburn-Cord-Duesenberg Museum, Auburn, Ind.)

Theodore Roosevelt and Governor Goodrich rode through the streets of Indianapolis when Roosevelt opened the War Stamps drive there, circa 1918. (James P. Goodrich Collection, Herbert Hoover Presidential Library-Museum, West Branch, Iowa)

1917
1919

At a small ceremony in the Indiana State House, Governor James P. Goodrich signs the document ratifying Indiana's passage of the Nineteenth Amendment to the United States Constitution, extending the franchise to women, January 16, 1920. (Indiana Historical Society)

Facing page: top, a parade at Monument Circle, downtown Indianapolis, celebrated the return of 130,000 soldiers who fought in World War I (Bass Photo Co. Collection, Indiana Historical Society Library, negative no. 66384F); *bottom,* May 7, 1919, Governor Goodrich; Will Hays, National Republican Party chairman; and United States Senator James E. Watson on the reviewing stand at the parade celebrating the return of Hoosier soldiers from World War I. Cora Goodrich is farthest left, Hays is third from left, Goodrich is fifth from left, and Watson is farthest right. (Indiana Historical Society)

James Goodrich, as Special Investigator for the American Relief Administration, Russian Unit, meets with Russian peasants, February 1922. (American Relief Administration Collection—Russian Unit, Hoover Institution Archives)

Facing page: top, June 18, 1939, on the steps of James and Cora Goodrich's home in Winchester. *Front row,* Pierre Goodrich, Lou (Mrs. Herbert) Hoover, Herbert Hoover, and James P. Goodrich. Behind the Hoovers are their son Allan and daughter-in-law Margaret and Cora Goodrich. (*Winchester Journal-Herald*); *bottom,* James P. Goodrich, Indiana delegate to the Republican National Convention in Philadelphia, with Indiana's favorite son and Republican presidential nominee, Wendell Willkie, June 25, 1940. (AP/ Wide World Photos)

For thirty-three years Percy E. Goodrich was a director of the Grain Dealers National Mutual Fire Insurance Company in Indianapolis, also serving as vice-president and chairman of the board. Goodrich is standing, second from left, circa 1935. (Grain Dealers National Mutual Fire Insurance Company, Indianapolis, Ind.)

Eugene C. Pulliam, the publisher of the *Indianapolis Star* and *News.* The Goodrich family became the second-largest stockholders in Central Newspapers in the late 1930s. Pierre Goodrich served on the board of Central Newspapers with Pulliam for almost thirty-five years. (Robert T. Ramsay, Jr., Archival Center, Wabash College, Crawfordsville, Ind.)

III

Businessmen with the Midas Touch

Chapter 15

The 1920s

The business of America *is* business.

CALVIN COOLIDGE, Speech to the Society of American Newspaper Editors, January 17, 1925

THE 1920s marked both the best and worst of times in Indiana. On the one hand, soldiers from the war had returned to their families, the nonfarm economy was booming, and prosperity and "speakeasies" reigned, prompting the decade to become popularly known as the "Roaring Twenties." On the other hand, the same type of intolerance that had resulted in blatant discrimination against Americans of German heritage during the "European War" once again returned, clad in white hoods and sheets, to menace Catholics, Jews, and African Americans. By 1923, the Ku Klux Klan (KKK), which had originated in the South, took hold in a serious way in Indiana. By that year, the KKK claimed a membership of three hundred thousand in Indiana, and the Hoosier state was the home of the Grand Dragon of the Klan, David Curtis Stephenson. Many municipal, county, state, and federal politicians were members. Klan endorsement was seen by many as a necessary prerequisite for public office. The Klan allegedly helped to elect two Indiana governors and two senators, including Edward L. Jackson, who was governor from 1925 to 1929. In his reelection bid for the Senate in 1926, James Watson was even accused of seeking Klan endorsement.[1]

1. For Klan activity in Indiana, see M. William Lutholtz, *Grand Dragon: D. C. Stephenson and the Ku Klux Klan in Indiana* (West Lafayette, Ind.: Purdue University

Shortly after leaving office as governor in January 1921, James Goodrich was appointed president of the National City Bank of Indianapolis. He had been associated with the bank as a client since his early days in the statehouse. Because of the bank's poor financial health, which made either reorganization or merger inevitable, the directors sought out Goodrich for his managerial abilities, and he became a major stockholder. In 1923, Goodrich arranged for the National City Bank to be merged with another longtime Indianapolis financial institution, American Fletcher Bank.[2] In the early 1920s, the former governor also managed to purchase a controlling interest in the Aetna Trust and Savings Company in Indianapolis. These commercial ties would continue to keep him and his family involved with Indianapolis businesses. They would lead to larger commercial opportunities in the 1930s.

By the early 1920s, Indianapolis had become an important midwestern business and cultural center. Several publishing houses had located in Indianapolis, and some important authors, most notably James Whitcomb Riley and Booth Tarkington, did their best work there. The city, which was the state's capital, had grown to a population of 320,000 residents. At the same time, Indianapolis retained a certain small-town atmosphere, no doubt in part because so many of its inhabitants were, in fact, recent migrants from Hoosier farms and small towns in search of opportunity.

By 1923, Pierre and Dorothy had made the move from Winchester to an affluent and scenic neighborhood in Indianapolis at 1529 Park Avenue.[3] In Indianapolis, Pierre practiced law as a junior partner with the firm of Haynes, Mote and Goodrich in the Hume-Mansur Building. Pierre knew both Haynes and Mote because they had served in his fa-

---

Press, 1993); Kathleen M. Thee, *Women of the Klan: Racism and Gender in the 1920s* (Berkeley: University of California Press, 1992); and Virginia Black, "Behind the Hood," *Fort Wayne (Ind.) News-Sentinel,* January 25, 1992, summit sec., pp. 6–8. Regarding the KKK's alleged support of James Watson, see "Watson Declares Klan Indorsement Work of Enemies," *Indianapolis Star,* June 10, 1924, p. 1, col. 5; "Watson Denies Deals for Support of Klan," *Indianapolis Star,* October 23, 1926, p. 3, col. 2.

2. See "J. P. Goodrich, Former Governor of Indiana, Dead at 76 Years," *Indianapolis News,* August 18, 1940, p. 1, col. 6.

3. 1924 *Indianapolis (City) Directory,* roll 17, Indiana State Library, Indiana Division.

ther's administration. Paul H. Haynes died shortly after Pierre joined the firm. Mote was a Randolph County native and had been a top campaign adviser to James Goodrich in his 1916 race for governor. For Mote's efforts, in 1917 James Goodrich appointed him secretary of the Indiana Public Service Commission, chairman of the governor's Legislative Council, and chief oil inspector until the position was abolished in 1920. Mote later became president of the Northern Indiana Telephone Company and ran unsuccessfully for the United States Senate in 1944. Pierre and Mote, who advertised themselves as public utility counselors, severed their partnership in the fall of 1926 after a falling out.[4]

Pierre practiced alone for the next year and a half, taking offices on the seventh floor of the Continental Bank Building. In 1928, he and John Raab Emison formed a partnership. James Goodrich served in the position of counsel to the firm. Emison, a native of Vincennes, Indiana, was a graduate of DePauw University (1919) and Harvard Law School (1922), where he and Goodrich first met in 1920. Before going into partnership with Pierre, Emison had served as assistant United States attorney for the Southern District of Indiana and as judge of the Superior Court of Knox County.[5]

The two attorneys, under the firm name of Goodrich and Emison, remained in Goodrich's Continental Bank Building offices. The building, now called the Electric Building, faced Indianapolis's Monument Circle. Both Pierre and Emison had a penchant for corporate law and seldom took on legal work that involved the writing of briefs or practice before courts. In 1929, Goodrich and Emison hired a young associate lawyer, Albert Campbell. Campbell, also a DePauw and Harvard Law graduate, became a partner in the 1930s. His professional relationship with Pierre was one of the longest Goodrich ever had.[6]

4. Mote grew up in Spartansburg, Indiana. He was superintendent of the Parker City school system and principal of the Union City High School before leaving Randolph County and getting involved in politics with James Goodrich in Indianapolis. See "Carl H. Mote, Head of Farm Group, Dies," *Indianapolis Star,* April 30, 1946, p. 4, col. 2. Pierre and Mote practiced at 1109–10 Hume-Mansur Building, Indianapolis.

5. Mrs. John Raab (Kathryn) Emison, interview, November 24, 1992.

6. Ibid.

At the same time that Pierre was developing a successful corporate practice with his small law firm, he was also seizing upon business opportunities with his father through Engineers Incorporated, the family investment company. Engineers Incorporated was originally organized as a company that owned gas, water, and electric companies and provided financial, and some managerial, services for them.[7] Formed on November 20, 1925, Engineers Incorporated purchased a number of struggling companies in the 1930s. Pierre later (with the aid of family members) turned these companies into highly profitable business operations and sold them at huge profits in the 1960s and 1970s. Over the years, a number of close family members or friends were made directors of Engineers Incorporated: Perce G. Goodrich (1952); Russell Martin of Tipton, Indiana (1953); Benjamin Rogge (1960); and J. Dwight Peterson (1961).[8] Even before the Depression, Pierre had established himself as a leading corporate lawyer. Until 1927, he was president of the Indiana-Ohio and the Western Ohio Public Services companies, and by 1929, at the age of thirty-five, he was the president of Engineers Incorporated, the Interstate Telephone and Telegraph Company, and the P. F. Goodrich Corporation (a personal holding-investment company).

Pierre was also a director of the Union Insurance Company, the Continental National Bank of Indianapolis, the Aetna Trust and Savings Company, the Equitable Securities Company of Indianapolis, the Peoples Loan and Trust Company, and the Peoples Investment Com-

7. P. F. Goodrich to E. Victor Willetts, Jr., December 27, 1972. The articles of incorporation of Engineers Incorporated were filed with the Indiana secretary of state's office on November 20, 1925. The incorporators were James, William Wallace ("W. W."), and Pierre Goodrich. Pierre was president and W. W. was secretary. The five directors were James, Pierre, W. W., Percy, and John B. Goodrich. Engineers Incorporated was reorganized on September 19, 1938. Its office was always that of Pierre's law practice. It was dissolved as of December 29, 1969. See "Engineers Incorporated," Closed Corporations, State Archives, Indiana Commission on Public Records, AR 17-650.

8. See the annual reports for these years for the additions of directors to the board of Engineers Incorporated. In 1960, Helen Schultz was made secretary and treasurer of Engineers Incorporated. "Engineers Incorporated," Closed Corporations, State Archives, Indiana Commission on Public Records, AR 17-650.

pany of Winchester.[9] In addition, he was secretary, treasurer, and a director of the Patoka Coal Company, located near Winslow, Indiana.[10] Over the course of his lifetime, the number of companies Pierre would control through his family's fortune expanded even more, numbering in the dozens.

If the natural gas boom marked the decade of the 1890s, the 1920s can be most closely identified with the automobile revolution. Almost overnight, the horse and buggy disappeared. In 1910, there were only a few hundred cars in east-central Indiana, but by 1923, several thousand loud and strange-looking motorized vehicles could be seen scurrying about, operated by inexperienced and erratic drivers. Driving standards were lax at the time. There was no driver's training, licensing of drivers involved no test of skill or equipment, and traffic was largely unregulated. This resulted in a high rate of accidents, as James Goodrich could attest. Those who were not affluent enough to travel in their own vehicles hitched rides or used another growing type of transportation—the interurban.[11]

At the end of his term as governor, James Goodrich vowed that he would never seek elective office again. While he remained true to this personal pledge, he did not quit undertaking acts of public service. His most noteworthy work, documented in the preceding chapters, was in the former Soviet Union on behalf of the American Relief Administration and the Warren G. Harding administration. Over the course of the next two decades, however, James Goodrich held several other important positions in the administration of public and private affairs.

In 1923, James Goodrich was appointed to the Indiana Deep Waterways Commission to investigate the possibility of securing a deep-water channel between the Great Lakes and the Atlantic Ocean via the St. Law-

9. *Book of Indiana* (Indianapolis: James O. Jones, 1929), p. 326.

10. See William H. Andrews, "Ayrshire Collieries Corporation—Profit with Ecology" (research paper, Indiana University, n.d.).

11. Dwight W. Hoover, *Magic Middletown* (Bloomington: Indiana University Press, 1986), pp. 48–51.

rence River. At the same time, the former governor was also appointed to the Great Lakes–St. Lawrence Tide Water Commission. This latter commission was established by eighteen states that combined their efforts to investigate the opening of the Great Lakes to oceangoing vessels through the St. Lawrence River. The commission found that deepening the St. Lawrence Seaway to thirty feet would allow up to 88 percent of all ships entering American ports to travel, through a series of locks, nearly the complete distance of the Great Lakes.

Ultimately, the need to take action was seen as so great as to compel the creation of a commission at the federal level. Therefore, on March 14, 1924, President Coolidge established the International St. Lawrence Waterways Commission, and Coolidge appointed James Goodrich to serve on this commission. Herbert Hoover, still United States secretary of commerce, chaired the commission. The commission was charged to advise the president on the development of shipping from the Great Lakes to the Atlantic Ocean. The commission was established because of the need for a number of upper-Midwest and Northeast states—Ohio, Indiana, Kentucky, Illinois, Iowa, Missouri, Kansas, Nebraska, North and South Dakota, Wisconsin, Minnesota, Pennsylvania, and New York—to have a natural transportation link to the rest of the trading world. The completion of the Panama Canal in 1914 had put these states—which collectively had more than forty million inhabitants who gained their livelihood from basic industries—at a distinct economic disadvantage to other regions of the country when it came to the transportation of goods.[12]

From the summer of 1924 until December 1926, the commission studied the benefits and costs of making the St. Lawrence Seaway navi-

12. See U.S. Congress, Senate, *St. Lawrence Waterway Project,* 69th Cong., 2d sess., 1927, S. Rept. 183, pp. 2–10. In 1924, ten years after the completion of the Panama Canal, shipping a ton of staple goods by sea from New York City to San Francisco cost approximately half of what it cost to ship the same goods from Chicago to San Francisco by rail. Similar discrepancies existed with regard to the transportation of goods from the Midwest to ports in South America and overseas. As a result, the cost of transporting one bushel of grain, for example, from the Midwest had increased six to eighteen cents.

gable for oceangoing vessels.[13] On December 27, 1926, the commission issued its report to President Coolidge.[14] After James Goodrich's work on the commission was completed, the issue had a long debate before resolution occurred. The Senate in 1932 rejected the proposed seaway treaty between the United States and Canada; a second treaty, signed by President Franklin D. Roosevelt in 1941, remained unratified by the Senate for the next eight years. Finally, the Senate approved a treaty with Canada in 1954 when it became apparent that Canada would proceed on its own with the seaway project if the United States did not cooperate.[15]

Although it was nearly thirty years after the St. Lawrence Seaway Commission's report was completed that the project was finally attempted, the commission's study laid the groundwork for the ultimate success of the seaway. When the project was finally begun in May 1954, it followed many of the recommendations that were contained in the Hoover Commission's report of December 1926. More than twenty-two

13. The commission also examined two other routes: an "all-American" route that did not cross Canada's southern border and therefore did not require the complications of treaty negotiations with Canada, and the Lake Ontario–Hudson River route that passed through New York state. The commission found that there would be a tremendous savings in adopting the St. Lawrence Seaway route. The commission cited the following reasons for adopting the St. Lawrence Seaway route: there would be fewer navigable miles through canals—137 miles on the All-American route, 128 miles on the Ontario-Hudson route, 21 to 25 miles on the St. Lawrence route; there would be fewer locks—nine locks compared with twenty locks on the Ontario-Hudson route; the number of obstructed bridges would be substantially smaller—eight bridges compared with fifty-four on the Ontario-Hudson route; and, finally, the distance via the St. Lawrence from Great Lake ports to northern European ports would be shorter than the Ontario-Hudson route by 625 miles. Completion of the St. Lawrence Seaway had other economic advantages beyond lower transportation costs. For example, the development of the St. Lawrence waterway could result in harnessing huge hydroelectric power from the great rapids which then obstructed navigation on the river (ibid.).

14. The commission's report was referred to the U.S. Senate Committee on Commerce on January 3, 1927, and a number of hearings and follow-up studies were held on the report.

15. See "St. Lawrence Seaway," in *The New Encyclopaedia Britannica,* 15th ed., vol. 24 (Chicago: Encyclopaedia Britannica, 1992), pp. 1073–76, particularly p. 1075.

thousand workers were employed on the project over the next five years. They deepened channels, constructed locks and channels, and created a thirty-mile-long Lake St. Lawrence. When the project was completed in April 1959, the St. Lawrence Seaway provided 9,500 miles of navigable waterways, allowing some forty million tons of cargo to move through the system annually. It was one of the largest civil engineering feats ever undertaken.[16]

Another event occurred in 1923 that preoccupied Goodrich for several months. Warren T. McCray, who had succeeded Goodrich as governor, became embroiled in a personal financial crisis and had to plead for relief from creditors. McCray and Goodrich, who had previously run against each other for governor in the Republican primary of 1916, were not friends. Thus, when Goodrich came to McCray's rescue, it was not out of any sense of fondness or loyalty he had for McCray, but an attempt to mitigate the embarrassment that disclosure of McCray's financial situation would bring to the Republican Party. Goodrich claimed that he helped raise $350,000 to save McCray. Apparently, the effort was all for naught, because shortly thereafter the Bank of Kentland, to which McCray owed the money, failed. McCray was subsequently charged with and convicted of mail fraud. He resigned the governorship in April 1924 and received a ten-year prison sentence.[17]

At about this time, Goodrich began to raise money for a more worthwhile cause. In 1924, at the age of sixty, Goodrich became chairman of the board of trustees at Wabash College.

> In this position Goodrich provided frequent investment advice to the college treasurer and solicited money for the endowment fund. Seeking

16. Ibid.

17. "M'Cray Not to Resign; Sees Politicians' Hand," *Indianapolis News,* October 1, 1923, p. 1, col. 1; "Indiana in Turmoil over M'Cray's Case: Goodrich Denies Charge," *New York Times,* October 3, 1923, p. 1, col. 5; "M'Cray Bank Shuts; Asserts Solvency," *New York Times,* October 14, 1923, p. 1, col. 4; "Gov. McCray Guilty of Attempted Fraud; He Goes to Jail and Is Not Likely to Appeal," *New York Times,* April 29, 1924, p. 1, col. 4; "Indiana" (editorial on McCray), *New York Times*, April 30, 1924, p. 18, col. 1; Benjamin D. Rhodes, *James P. Goodrich, Indiana's "Governor Strangelove"* (London: Associated University Presses, 1996), pp. 136–37.

> a contribution from John D. Rockefeller, Goodrich wrote that Wabash College sought to achieve, in the midwest, a position comparable to that of Amherst, Bowdoin, and Williams colleges in the east. Increasingly it was Goodrich who became the financial guardian angel of the college. He personally assumed the cost of remodelling the president's home and repairing its furnace, and in 1919 he pledged the substantial sum of $50,000 to the Wabash College endowment fund.[18]

The 1928 presidential election was another event that greatly preoccupied James Goodrich during the 1920s. While Goodrich himself was no longer considered for the top national post, he was a close friend to the two Republican candidates who were: Herbert Hoover and James Watson. Watson had been a leading candidate for vice-president in the 1924 election before Calvin Coolidge selected a little-known Chicago banker, Charles Gates Dawes, as his running mate. Watson, who had allowed the 1920 Republican presidential nomination to slip through his fingers, was determined to garner the 1928 nomination. On February 8, 1928, he announced his intention to run for the office he had desired from the time he and James Goodrich were high school classmates in the 1870s. On April 14, Watson returned to Winchester to proclaim his candidacy before his hometown well-wishers.[19] A packed crowd of two thousand attended the ceremony at the new Winchester High School gymnasium. A parade made up of marching bands, local Girl Scout and Boy Scout troops, and others marched from downtown under a large banner that crossed South Street and which read "Our Jim for President." The south pole anchoring the banner was planted in James Goodrich's front yard.[20]

18. Rhodes, *James P. Goodrich, Indiana's "Governor Strangelove,"* p. 138. See also *Wabash Bulletin* 39 (October 1940), supplement, pp. 11–12; letter from Goodrich to Treasurer O. E. Gregg, June 30, 1920, James P. Goodrich Papers, box 3; letter from Goodrich to John D. Rockefeller, June 21, 1920, James P. Goodrich Papers, box 2; letter from Goodrich to Dr. George L. McIntosh, September 16, 1919, James P. Goodrich Papers, box 2.

19. "Watson Announces Candidacy for President; Selects M. Bert Thurman for Campaign Manager," *Indianapolis News,* February 9, 1928, p. 1, col. 4; Maurice Early, "Watson Defines Policies in Talk at Native Town," *Indianapolis Star,* April 15, 1928, p. 1, col. 3.

20. Marianna Reed, interview, July 20, 1992. Ms. Reed, a Girl Scout at the time, participated in the parade and ceremony.

Ironically, Goodrich did not support his childhood friend. He opposed Watson's entry into the presidential race, believing it would destroy party unity, and supported Hoover. Goodrich's disappointment in Watson's candidacy is evident in a letter he wrote to the United States congressman Will Wood:

> I have known [Watson] all his life [and] you are perfectly at liberty to tell him all I have said in this letter. There has never been a time and I can cite you to numerous occasions where the interest of the party conflicted with Jim's desires, when he didn't sacrifice the party. . . . I only have sympathy and pity for him. It is discouraging to see him with his really unusual ability betraying the great trust the people have committed into his hands, for the simple reason that he has no moral foundation on which to build. I say this not in anger but rather in sorrow.[21]

Watson ended up defeating Hoover by twenty-five thousand votes in the Indiana primary election, but Hoover captured all other states and easily won the presidential nomination at the Kansas City national convention. Much to the chagrin of Goodrich, he was asked by Hoover's Indiana state campaign manager to remain in the background and not to publicly support Hoover during the national campaign.[22]

On November 4, Hoover defeated Democratic candidate Alfred E. Smith of New York, receiving the electoral-college vote of forty of the forty-eight states. With the conservative Hoover in the White House, most Americans were convinced that prosperous times would continue. Indeed, the "Great Engineer" and humanitarian, as Hoover was known, had repeatedly pronounced that an indefinite continuation of a businessman's government would result in unfettered growth. Only months before his overwhelming victory over Smith, Hoover proclaimed, "We in America today are nearer to the final triumph over poverty than ever before in the history of any land."[23] Of course, less than fourteen

21. Letter from Goodrich to Wood, March 13, 1928, James P. Goodrich Papers, box 13.

22. See Rhodes, *James P. Goodrich, Indiana's "Governor Strangelove,"* pp. 157–58.

23. Williams, Current, and Freidel, *A History of the United States: Since 1865*, p. 456.

months later, with the occurrence of "Black Friday" in October 1929, all such rosy projections changed.

While James Watson would never realize his dream of being president, he would be almost as near in power to the top position as any elected official could be. In January 1929, Watson was elected majority leader of the United States Senate, a position he would hold throughout the duration of the Hoover administration. James Goodrich would often travel to Washington to see Watson, now an important spoke in the inner circle of Washington power. Will Hays, Goodrich's other longtime political colleague who had Washington connections, had resigned his position as President Harding's postmaster general in 1922 to become the first president of the Motion Picture Producers and Distributors of America, at the princely salary of $100,000 a year.[24]

Goodrich's other close friends in the nation's capital included President and Mrs. Hoover. If anything, the friendship between the Hoovers and the Goodriches grew closer while Hoover occupied the presidency. At the age of sixty-five, Goodrich was not interested in obtaining a post in Hoover's administration, but he regularly offered advice to the president. For instance, while staying at the White House (in the Lincoln suite) in February 1932, Goodrich again approached Hoover about recognizing the Soviet Union. Preoccupied with the prolongation of the Depression and only months away from undertaking a presidential campaign, Hoover had no interest in taking on the thorny issue. "No occasion to recognize Russia, no sentiment in [the] country for it," he told his good friend.[25]

The Goodriches also arranged for several groups of Indiana friends to be received by the Hoovers.[26] One such occasion was described by

24. See Will H. Hays, *The Memoirs of Will H. Hays,* pp. 323–63; Raymond Moley, *The Hays Office* (Indianapolis: Bobbs-Merrill, 1945), pp. 32–67.

25. James Goodrich, "Diary," February 2, 1932, James P. Goodrich Papers, box 3; see also Rhodes, *James P. Goodrich, Indiana's "Governor Strangelove,"* pp. 156–57.

26. Mary Johnson, formerly Mary Miller and a Girl Scout, recalls that Cora Goodrich arranged for the Girl Scouts of Winchester to visit the White House and have tea with Mrs. Hoover. At the time, Mrs. Hoover was president of the Girl Scouts of America (interview, January 1, 1992).

Emma Lieber in a humorous vignette about Cora Goodrich that was recorded in Lieber's biography about her husband, Richard Lieber. Mrs. Lieber wrote:

> Though Governor Goodrich never was President of these United States, he and his wife frequently were house guests in the White House. I want to tell you of an amusing instance. The Goodriches happened to be guests of the President on one occasion when Richard and I (and of course many others) were invited to be in the receiving line at one of the receptions that President and Mrs. Hoover were giving. . . .
>
> That evening we all were invited to a dinner at the home of Senator and Mrs. James Davis [of Pennsylvania]. Again a White House automobile was sent to the hotel to take us and Governor and Mrs. Goodrich to the home of Senator Davis and then after the dinner return us to the White House for the reception. . . . [Later], Mrs. Goodrich, who noticed how tired we were, thought we ought to go back to our hotel and to bed. She beckoned to a very fine looking gold-braided man, believing him to be a servant in livery, and said, "Please call one of the White House automobiles and see that Colonel Lieber and his ladies are taken to their hotel."
>
> Mrs. Goodrich did not realize it, but poor Richard did, and for once he was embarrassed, that she had made this request to an—Admiral! The Admiral had a sense of humor and merely winked an eye at Richard, then personally saw to it that a chauffeur was notified and we were taken to our hotel in grand style.[27]

At a professional level, James Goodrich only once served as a formal adviser to Hoover. On October 18, 1929, the president appointed Goodrich to an important commission on conservation. Hoover did this at a news conference at the White House in which he announced the formation of the Commission on the Conservation and Administration of Public Domain (commonly known as the Public Lands Commission).[28] The commission was composed of one representative from each of the eleven western states in which public land existed. J. R. Garfield, secretary of the interior under President Theodore Roosevelt,

27. Emma Lieber, *Richard Lieber,* pp. 96–97.

28. See Herbert Hoover Papers, pp. 330–31, 333–34. The Public Lands Commission was formally created by an Act of Congress dated April 10, 1930.

chaired the committee. Hoover appointed James Goodrich as a general representative. Hoover's previous work with Goodrich, as well as the former governor's own reputation in establishing Indiana's conservation program and state park system, were factors that led to Goodrich's appointment.[29]

The commission first met in June 1930. During that summer, members traveled approximately nine thousand miles by automobile throughout the western states, gathering data. At that time, approximately 179 million acres of land remained in public domain (owned neither by states nor by individuals). The commission was charged with evaluating how best to preserve and make use of the land. The commission initially examined how to dispose of the surface rights of the land; at that time up to 50 percent of all sheep and 15 percent of all cattle in the United States grazed on public land. The commission later investigated a host of ancillary issues: land reclamation; national forests; flood control; power sites; reservations for Native Americans; the extraction of minerals, including oil and gas; national parks; bird refuges; and game reserves.[30] Finally, on January 16, 1931, the commission issued its final report to President Hoover.[31]

The commission's far-ranging report has implications even to this day. For instance, the commission's recommendations for water conser-

29. Ibid.

30. These issues had become critical for analysis because of prior federal legislation and the overuse of some resources. Since 1785, Congress had enacted legislation that encouraged settlement on federal lands. That culminated in the Homestead Act of 1862, which provided 160 acres of public land free of charge to anyone over the age of twenty-one who would settle it for five years. The idea was that, once the land was settled and communities had been established, the territories could be converted into states. Much of this settled public land, however, was eventually abandoned and became wild again. Still other public land was never settled. As a result, overgrazing and erosion depleted the value of the nearly worthless land even more. See *Report of the Committee on the Conservation and Administration of the Public Domain* (Washington, D.C.: Government Printing Office, January 16, 1931), pp. 11–17.

31. In November 1930, the commission held hearings in Washington, D.C., and studied the material which it had collected in the preceding months. Numerous conservation and wildlife organizations appeared before the commission, presenting evidence and making recommendations.

vation and flood control led to the building of hundreds of dams and irrigation projects that made millions of acres tillable and suitable for grazing. The commission's recommendations with regard to the appropriation of public lands to the states caused many states to create and develop conservation programs, nature preserves, and state parks.[32]

Goodrich disagreed with much of the report and signed it reluctantly. He insisted that the states could administer public lands better than Washington could and that the commission had recommended the relinquishment of too little federal control. "My position is so diametrically opposite to that of the rest of the Commission that I wonder why I was put on it," he wrote to Garfield. "I should have resigned when the report first came in."[33]

Previously, in March 1927, James Goodrich had begun serving on the board of directors of the American-Russian Chamber of Commerce, located on West Fifty-seventh Street in New York City. In this capacity, he was able to renew his acquaintance with Maxim Litvinoff, the Soviet foreign minister, with whom he worked closely. Most of the American directors were heads of large corporations doing business in the Soviet Union, such as the Westinghouse Corporation, United States Steel, Chase National Bank, General Electric, and the Remington Typewriter Company. The Chamber of Commerce published a series of reports promoting a "how-to" guide for companies trading in the Soviet Union and sponsored informal trade delegations between the two countries. Goodrich's inability to influence American foreign policy toward Russia through the Harding and Coolidge administrations was apparently why he sought to encourage trade between the two powers through private channels.[34]

32. See *Report of the Committee on the Conservation and Administration of the Public Domain,* pp. 17–37.

33. Letter from Goodrich to Garfield, January 25, 1931, James P. Goodrich Papers, box 3; see also Rhodes, *James P. Goodrich, Indiana's "Governor Strangelove,"* p. 159.

34. The first mention of James Goodrich's serving as a director of the American-Russian Chamber of Commerce is in a March 1927 quarterly publication (Rept. 7) found in the Library of Congress under the American-Russian Chamber of Commerce, HC 331.A8.

Because of his close affiliation with Teddy Roosevelt, Goodrich was appointed in 1920 as a member of the Theodore Roosevelt Memorial Trust, a commission charged with honoring the twenty-sixth president of the United States. In the private sphere, Goodrich, in addition to being chairman of the Wabash College Board of Trustees, also served as a trustee of the Presbyterian Theological Seminary in Chicago (from 1919 to 1940), as a trustee of the American Child Welfare Association, and as vice-president and member of the executive committee of the Civil Legion of America.[35] Occasionally, he spoke at such occasions as the dedication of the World War I monument in his hometown of Winchester on November 11, 1928. The monument, the statue of a doughboy, had been donated by the Goodrich family in recognition of the thirty-six men from Randolph County who died during the war.[36] And although he would not seek elective office again, James Goodrich was still sought by the Republican Party for his leadership. From the time he stepped down as governor in 1920, he attended until his death nearly every Republican national and state convention as a delegate from Indiana.

During the 1920s, Pierre was enjoying great success in the business world. In his private life, however, the situation was not the same, at least in the latter half of the decade. On September 16, 1926, his boyhood friend and the best man at his wedding, Carl McCamish, traveled to Cincinnati and committed suicide by shooting himself through the chest. In the early 1920s, after the death of his sister, Carl McCamish had moved back to Winchester from Indianapolis to work in the family business, a highly successful burial-supply company. Carl had given up being a doctor to assist his parents with the family company. He also served on the town council. According to newspaper accounts, poor

35. "James Putnam Goodrich," *Who's Who in America,* vol. 1 (Chicago: A. N. Marquis, 1943), p. 468.

36. "War Memorial: Dedicated on Armistice Day," *Winchester (Ind.) Journal-Herald,* November 12, 1928, p. 1, col. 2.

health and overcommitment both at work and in the community led McCamish to take his own life.[37]

In 1927, Pierre began experiencing excruciating back pain. The condition worsened to the point that in late September he sought medical attention at the Mayo Clinic in Rochester, Minnesota. He had back surgery in Indianapolis the following year. Another blow, emotionally more agonizing than any physical pain he would suffer, struck Pierre shortly after.[38] In August 1928, after eight years of marriage, Dorothy divorced him. Their only child, Frances (whom they called "Nancy"), was not quite seven years old.[39]

Family members and close friends suggested a number of reasons for the marriage's breakup. First, Dorothy was a socialite and conversationalist who enjoyed parties and outings with friends. She was also a consummate storyteller who needed a willing audience of listeners.[40] As for Pierre, cocktail parties and social gatherings completely bored him. To his way of thinking, these occasions provided little opportunity to engage in meaningful (philosophical) conversations. Moreover, they

37. Carl McCamish, Pierre's best man, was the son of James McCamish and Ida Kitselman McCamish, members of what probably were the two most prominent families in Randolph County after the Goodriches. The McCamishes operated a large burial-supply company, and the Kitselmans became wealthy making roller skates and fencing, later moving their operations to Muncie, Indiana. See obituary, *Winchester (Ind.) Journal-Herald,* September 17, 1926, p. 1, col. 8; "Kills Himself at Cincinnati: Winchester Man Ends His Life with Shotgun, While in Automobile," Associated Press story (publication unknown), September 16, 1926; "M'Camish Funeral," *Winchester (Ind.) Journal-Herald,* September 23, 1926, p. 1, col. 8.

38. We know that Pierre was at the Mayo Clinic from a telegram that was sent there to James Goodrich by James Watson on September 29, 1927, in which Watson refers to Pierre's condition. Watson also refers to Pierre's recovery in a letter to James Goodrich dated October 3, 1927, James P. Goodrich Papers, box 28.

39. August 11, 1928, Dorothy Goodrich (Plaintiff), Pierre Goodrich (Defendant), Divorce Index, Marion County, Indiana, Plaintiff, Case A-45384.

40. Margaret Morton Kimball (niece of Dorothy Dugan), interview, October 25, 1992. According to Rosanna Amos, "She [Dorothy] always wanted to be the social butterfly, and even though Pierre Goodrich came from a very well known family, that was never his interest. I don't think he was ever interested in socializing at all. Being known was not important to him" (interview, December 10, 1991).

kept him away from his business and intellectual pursuits.[41] Pierre was known to work extremely long hours, which did not accommodate Dorothy's desire to be more social.

Second, during the early years of his marriage, Pierre was quite frugal. Despite enjoying early financial success from his legal practice and businesses, he was ever mindful, almost as if he were still at college, of unnecessary expenditures. His parsimony did not suit Dorothy, who had grown up in comfortable environs as the daughter of a wealthy Indiana banker.[42] Finally, there may have been another love interest. Pierre's parents were heartbroken over the divorce.

Pierre remained single for the next twelve years, while Dorothy, on Christmas Day in 1933, married Louis Haerle, an Indianapolis businessman.[43] Dorothy's second marriage appeared to be a happy one. She became active in Indianapolis social circles and, for a time, worked as an occupational therapist for the Riley Hospital for Children.[44] In 1965, she and Haerle moved to La Jolla, California, to retire. Dorothy passed away in February 1987.[45]

For many years after their divorce, Pierre and Dorothy remained in contact over the upbringing of their daughter. Nancy had gone to school at Shortridge High School in Indianapolis but graduated from

41. Gilbert Snider, interview, December 23, 1991.

42. Mary Simpson, interview, April 19, 1992; Elizabeth Goodrich Terry, interview, November 16, 1991.

43. Marriage Records, Marion County, Indiana, Louis Haerle and Dorothy Goodrich, December 25, 1933, bk. 140, p. 425. Haerle worked for the Hibben-Hollweg Company in Indianapolis, a dry-goods establishment that sold textiles, linens, and other cloth products. Dorothy and her new husband lived on an estate in Zionsville, which they called Pinegate Farm.

44. Margaret Kimball, interview, October 25, 1992. According to Mrs. Kimball, Dorothy participated in the Indianapolis Women's Club (a literary group), the Junior League, the Indiana Vassar Club, and the Indianapolis Dramatics Club (a theater group). She even wrote a cookbook. Dorothy's involvement in the Indianapolis Literary Club was so well remembered that the club honored her with the dedication of a book in 1987. That was shortly after Dorothy's death (she died on February 14, 1987) and twenty years after she had resigned from the club to move to California.

45. Obituary, *Decatur Democrat,* February 23, 1987, p. 4, col. 2.

Tudor Hall School in 1939. She then matriculated at Vassar College in Poughkeepsie, New York, her mother's alma mater. After only two years, however, she ran away from the campus, causing substantial distress to both of her parents. She later traveled extensively in Europe, and she enrolled at Oxford and the Sorbonne but failed to earn a degree.[46]

James Goodrich's work on various federal and state commissions enabled him to continue his long-term interest in public affairs. Financially secure, James was able to devote much time to serving on these commissions and on the boards of several private organizations. The bulk of his time, however, was still spent in increasing his own and his family's fortunes.

President Coolidge's philosophy that "the business of America is business" was taken to heart by the Goodriches: In June 1920, while James was still governor, his family founded the Railway Service and Supply Company in Indianapolis, which primarily repaired freight cars and constructed or repaired railway equipment.[47] In 1923, James became a major investor in and treasurer of the Patoka Coal Company, a strip mine in Pike County, Indiana.[48] In November 1925, James established Engineers Incorporated, and in April 1926, the Goodriches formed the Interstate Telephone and Telegraph Company, which provided tele-

46. Ibid. For a brief account of Nancy Goodrich Poniatowski, see Margaret Moore Post, "Cora J. Frist Goodrich," in *First Ladies of Indiana and the Governors, 1816–1984* (Indianapolis: Pierson Printing, 1984), p. 134.

47. See "The Railway Service Corporation," Dissolved Corporations, State Archives, Indiana Commission on Public Records, AR-1988. The Railway Service Corporation was founded on June 26, 1920, by Claude Barnes and Merl Chenoweth, both employees of Goodrich companies. On November 19, 1921, a petition to change the name to the Railway Service and Supply Corporation was filed and granted. On February 1922, Edward Goodrich was elected chairman. According to the March 13, 1922, report, the company had capital stock of $500,000.

48. Patoka Coal Company was formed on July 8, 1919, having previously operated as the Globe Coal Company. There is no indication in the corporate records that the Goodrich family had an interest in Patoka Coal until 1923. At that time, Jesse Moorman was president and James Goodrich was treasurer. See "Patoka Coal Company," Dissolved Corporations, State Archives, Indiana Commission on Public Records, AR 17-890 and 3055-107.

phone service to communities in both Indiana and Ohio.[49] In May 1926, Pierre was one of three incorporators who founded the Muncie Theatre Realty Company, a holding company for movie theaters in Muncie, Indiana.[50]

Despite forming and acquiring interests in these companies in the mid 1920s, James Goodrich detected something wrong in the economy. The former Indiana governor was a master at seeing a business opportunity and capitalizing on it. He was especially keen when it came to anticipating economic cycles and the profitability of various enterprises. His most far-reaching and important business decision came approximately two years before the Great Depression. James Goodrich's nephew and cousin to Pierre, Perce "Bud" Goodrich, tells the story:

> The Goodrich brothers had family meetings often and Uncle Jim came into a family meeting and just told his brothers, "We're going to get out of the utility business." He sensed something was wrong with the economy and that things were going to happen that he didn't like. Uncle James told his brothers, "We're going to pool our money and form a corporation so if, down the road, we see something we want to buy or something we want to invest in, we'll have the cash to do it. In the meantime we'll invest the money in short term securities."[51]

49. The articles of incorporation were filed for Engineers Incorporated on November 20, 1925. The Interstate Telephone and Telegraph Company was formed on April 7, 1926, by Pierre F. Goodrich. Pierre had to clear the usage of the name "Interstate Telephone Company," because a company by that name had been founded on December 24, 1910. It was no longer in operation, however, having failed to file annual reports for three consecutive years with the secretary of state's office. See "Interstate Telephone and Telegraph Company," Dissolved Corporations, State Archives, Indiana Commission on Public Records, 2547-6.

50. The articles of association of Muncie Theatre Realty Company were filed with the Indiana secretary of state's office on May 5, 1926. The incorporators were Leslie Colvin, Pierre F. Goodrich, and J. J. Kiser, all of Indianapolis. The capital stock of the corporation was $425,000. The company reincorporated on July 7, 1933. At its height, it owned approximately eight movie theaters in the Muncie, Indiana, area. Its office address was that of Pierre's law office, 712 Continental Bank Building. See "Muncie Theatre Realty Company," Dissolved Corporations, State Archives, Indiana Commission on Public Records, AR 2438-9.

51. Perce Goodrich, interview, November 9, 1992.

Obviously, James Goodrich's experience as governor and in banking gave him a certain advantage in foretelling the onset of the Great Depression. It is equally evident, however, that thousands of other politicians, businessmen, and bankers either totally misread or disregarded the signs that foretold the horrific economic times to come. James's brothers followed the former governor's directions precisely. The five businessmen soon liquidated their interests in most of the small-town utility companies, such as Citizens Heat, Power and Light Company in Winchester; Washington Heat, Light and Power Company in Daviess County; Jeffersonville Water, Light and Power Company in Clark County; Union Power, Heat and Light Company of Union City, Indiana; and the Indiana-Ohio and the Western Ohio Public Services companies. The sales generated huge profits for the family. For instance, the sales of the Washington Heat, Light and Power Company and the Jeffersonville Water, Light and Power Company, according to James Goodrich, amounted to half a million dollars.[52]

The brothers continued to maintain controlling ownership or a large interest, however, in the Goodrich Brothers Hay and Grain Company, Peoples Loan and Trust Company, Patoka Coal, and a handful of utilities, such as the Eastern Indiana Telephone Company. As Percy recalled years later, the grain and feed business was "recession proof," whereas

52. The Jeffersonville Water and Gas Company (which became the Jeffersonville Water, Light and Power Company) was sold to the Interstate Public Service Company on February 1, 1927. The Interstate Public Service Company, based in Indianapolis, had purchased dozens of city electric, water, and gas companies throughout Indiana in the 1920s. See *Moody's Public Utilities* (New York City, 1927), p. 366. In 1927, the Goodriches and Jesse Moorman and Carl Semans also sold the Washington Water, Light and Power Company to a group of investors from New York City. The Indiana-Ohio and Western Ohio public services companies were also liquidated in 1927. See annual report, Washington Water, Light and Power Company, 1927, Dissolved Corporations, State Archives, Indiana Commission on Public Records. The annual reports for Citizens Heat, Light and Power of Winchester and Union Heat, Light and Power of Union City show that after 1927 the Goodriches, with one exception, were no longer officers or directors of these companies. The exception is William Wallace Goodrich, who was a director of Citizens Heat, Light and Power until approximately 1930.

many of the family's other holdings were not.[53] The money they received from selling their interests in the utilities was invested in short-term certificates of deposit by Engineers Incorporated. The year was 1927. That move would make it possible for the family to increase its fortune tenfold in the 1930s and 1940s.

53. Percy Goodrich told this to Ivan Barr in the late 1940s. Ivan Barr, telephone interview, March 27, 1993.

Chapter 16

The 1930s

Dear Pierre,

. . . I am very happy over the way the telephone companies are coming out. They are bound to be very profitable in the long run . . . I think you ought to keep after Frazier about the sales of Peru plants. Also call up Thompson, of the Milan Furniture Company at Milan, Indiana, and see if he has made any progress in that direction. I suggest that you do not liquidate any more of No. 3 until you come on [to Baltimore], unless conditions out there make it necessary. I think it was a good idea to liquidate Ohio Telephone Service 101. It will convince the bank department that bonds of that character are not affected by market conditions. This market is going to touch bottom before a great length of time, and when it does it will be a good time to begin to buy some stocks. . . . I think you are doing a splendid job on things, Pierre, and I heartily approve [of] everything you have done.

James Goodrich, September 27, 1937

In September 1937, James Goodrich lay in a Baltimore bed at Johns Hopkins Hospital suffering from an irregular heartbeat. The condition was so serious that he would be bedridden for the next several weeks. He had suffered a heart attack in June, causing him to cancel a planned extensive tour of the Soviet Union that summer. He had hoped to study the industrial progress the Great Bear had made under Stalin since his last trip in 1925. After his release, he began giving more time to his philanthropic interests, particularly educational and religious institutions. Two of his larger gifts were to Wabash College: $150,000 for the construction of a much-needed science hall and

$113,000 to establish scholarships for advanced studies in honor of a former president of the college. He also contributed more than $90,000 to Hanover College, part of which was to help endow a chair in musical education.[1]

Goodrich's illness brought him face-to-face with his own mortality and also resulted in a de facto change in the chain of command. Pierre was now in control of the family's financial empire. Pierre did, however, receive weekly letters from his father while James was recuperating at Johns Hopkins. The letters offered Pierre advice and encouragement regarding many of the decisions he had to make: when to sell what stocks, what loans should be made and for how much and under what conditions, recommendations on how to cut operating expenses, and so forth.[2]

At the time, there were many successful family-run businesses in central Indiana: the five Ball brothers (glass) and the Kitselmans (wire and steel) in Muncie; the Irwin and Miller families (diesel engines and banking) of Columbus; and, of course, the Lilly family of Indianapolis (pharmaceuticals). But Pierre Goodrich had no need to look beyond the mentoring of his own father and four uncles to obtain most of the knowledge and cunning that would make him a highly successful businessman. Other family-run companies might have been larger, but few, if any, families in the Midwest had their fingers in so many corporate pies. By the late 1930s, the Goodriches had already established themselves as a financial powerhouse in banking and securities, commodities, newspapers, transportation, and public utilities. They would add others.

1. See "Former Governor Goodrich Gives $150,000 Donation to Wabash College for Building," *Winchester (Ind.) Journal-Herald,* November 8, 1937, p. 1, col. 7; O. P. Welborn, secretary-treasurer, the Board of Trustees, "A Statement of the Gifts of James P. Goodrich to Wabash College," *Wabash Bulletin* 39 (October 1940), supplement; "Goodrich Grants Hanover $50,000," *Indianapolis Star,* December 9, 1937, p. 1, col. 4. In April 1938, the former governor returned to Johns Hopkins Hospital. See "Out of Politics, Goodrich Avers," *Indianapolis Star,* April 11, 1938, p. 2, col. 3.

2. Letters between James P. Goodrich and Pierre F. Goodrich, James P. Goodrich Papers, Pierre F. Goodrich folder.

Everyone in the family was a partner in the dynasty. William Wallace, the youngest Goodrich brother, graduated from Winchester High School in 1889. He then attended Wabash College briefly before studying electrical engineering at the Armour Institute in Chicago. In the early 1890s, he returned to Indiana and got his start in the hay and grain business in New Castle, where he stayed and operated a gas company. He returned to Winchester and operated the Rock Oil Company and, for a time, the Union Heat, Light and Power Company, the utility that provided Union City and Portland with natural gas. When Union Heat was sold in the 1920s, William became the manager of the Indiana-Ohio Public Service Company, an electric utility, until it was sold in 1927. He then became associated with the Peoples Loan and Trust Company in Winchester, where he remained until he retired. William passed away in November 1948.[3]

With his second wife, Louise Gordon, William Wallace had two children: Elizabeth and Perce. Elizabeth "Betty" Goodrich Terry was born in 1906. She married Phillip Terry in September 1939. The couple lived in Indianapolis for twenty-five years until Phillip's death in 1967, at which time Elizabeth returned to her hometown. Elizabeth had no children. She continues to reside in Winchester.

Perce Gordon "Bud" Goodrich grew up in Winchester and graduated from Wabash College in 1930. He was successful in the business world in his own right, serving as president and director of the Indiana Telephone Corporation; the Public Telephone Corporation in Greensburg, Indiana; and the Peoples Loan and Trust Company. Perce would serve as an officer and director of several of the Goodrich company boards over the years, including that of Engineers Incorporated. Perce was also president of his own companies in Portland, Indiana—the Portland Service Company, Inc., and the Portland Insurance Company—as well as a co-owner of several other businesses.

From his first marriage to Gaynel Graber, Perce had a daughter, Eliza-

3. "W. W. Goodrich Funeral Services Wednesday at 2," *Winchester (Ind.) News,* November 23, 1948, p. 1, col. 7; Richard Wise, "Goodrich Father Was a Public Spirited Citizen," *Winchester (Ind.) News-Gazette,* February 19, 1984, p. 1, col. 2.

beth Putnam Orrill, who lives in Madison, Indiana. From his second marriage to Frances Ann Hawkins in December 1939, Perce had two other children: Janice Gordon Goodrich Gerson, who resides in Zionsville, Indiana, and John Baldwin Goodrich, who owns and manages a plating company in Portland, Indiana. John Baldwin also serves as a director of the Peoples Loan and Trust Bank and is on the Portland school board. Perce Goodrich passed away in September 1996.[4]

John "Jay" Goodrich, the middle brother, oversaw the operation of seven large farms in Randolph and Jay counties. He had started out in 1884 buying and shipping hay, but in 1888 he went into partnership with Percy in the hardware and furniture business. In 1891, he sold his interest in the business to his brother Ed and again became involved in the hay business. He became president of the Goodrich Brothers Hay and Grain Company in January 1898, when the company was formed. By the time of Jay's death, Goodrich Brothers owned approximately twenty-four grain elevators throughout central and northern Indiana. At times, there were as many as 150 railroad cars waiting to be loaded at the Goodrich Brothers' huge grain elevator on the north edge of Winchester. Although he was a very successful farmer, a costly hobby nearly caused Jay to be alienated from the family. Shortly after the turn of the century, Jay became active breeding, training, and racing trotting and pacing horses. He eventually became destitute from the wealthy-man's sport, since his horses were perennial bridesmaids. Finally, the other four Goodrich brothers paid off Jay's debts on the condition that he forgo any further association with the sport.[5]

Jay's marriage to Charlotte Martin resulted in the birth of two sons:

4. See "Goodrich Dies at 88," *Winchester (Ind.) News,* September 4, 1996, p. 1, col. 1; and "'Bud' Goodrich, 88, Jay Businessman" (obituary), *Muncie (Ind.) Star Press,* September 4, 1996, p. 5A, col. 3. Elizabeth Goodrich Terry was born on January 1, 1906. Perce Goodrich was born on August 21, 1908. Perce Goodrich's holdings and achievements, while not as great as those of his first cousin Pierre, were certainly noteworthy: He was co-owner of the Ramsey Men's Shop, Portland Office Supply, Quaker Trace Inn, Wayside Furniture Company, and Gulley Ford; director of PLatCo Realty Corporation; and a cofounder of Steed Field Airport in Portland, Indiana.

5. "John B. Goodrich" (obituary), *Winchester (Ind.) Journal-Herald,* November 8, 1937, p. 1, col. 3; Perce G. Goodrich, interview, November 9, 1992.

John Baldwin, who was born in the same year as Pierre, 1894; and James, who was born in 1897 but died four years later. After attending Wabash College for one year (1912), John Baldwin worked for Peoples Loan and Trust Company. He then served in the United States military, fighting in France during World War I. On his return, he became secretary and later manager of the insurance department of the Peoples Investment and Guaranty Company. He later obtained the sole interest in the Peoples Investment and Guaranty Company and changed its name to Standard Securities. John's only marriage was to Helen C. Cummins in 1964, when he was nearly seventy years old. The couple had no children together. John B. Goodrich is perhaps best remembered as a generous benefactor to Wabash College, the First Presbyterian Church of Winchester, Goodrich Park, and the American Legion Post in Winchester.[6]

Edward Goodrich, the second-youngest of the original five Goodrich brothers, was born the day that Ulysses Grant was elected president for the second time in 1871. In January 1911, he became a director of the Randolph County Bank, the local competitor of his brother James's Peoples Loan and Trust Company. Two years later, he was named vice-president, and in 1918 he ascended to the presidency of the financial institution. Ed would remain president of the Randolph County Bank until his death in 1953. Beginning in 1912, he also managed the local electrical and water company, Citizens Heat, Light and Power. Ed Goodrich held this position until 1926, when Citizens was sold. In 1922, Ed became chairman of the board of the Railway Service and Supply Company in Indianapolis. Ed was perhaps the most competitive of all the Goodrich brothers. Moreover, he was the one most likely to disagree with James on business decisions.

If James was impulsive and quick to react, Ed was just the opposite—cautious, guarded, refusing to make a decision until he absolutely had to. Handsome and big, Ed was known as "King Ed" because of his im-

6. "John Goodrich Dead at 76," *Winchester (Ind.) News-Gazette,* January 7, 1971, p. 2, col. 1.

posing presence. He was so conservative that legend has it that he would refuse to tell someone the time when asked for fear of getting it wrong.[7] Ed's marriage to Elizabeth Neff resulted in one child, Florence, who was born on May 12, 1897. She married Francis Dunn, originally from Marion, Indiana, in November 1921. Florence and Francis Dunn had two sons: Wesley, a retired psychologist, lives in Florida; Edward, once a jewelry manufacturer in Elwood, Indiana, is now retired and resides in Indianapolis. Before her death in 1994, Florence contributed approximately $1 million to the Indianapolis Symphony Orchestra and another $1 million to Butler University in Indianapolis.[8]

Percy, the oldest brother, was born in 1861. He operated the coal business in Winchester and worked as secretary and manager of the Goodrich Brothers Hay and Grain Company. The power for the electric company was generated locally by burning coal and fuel oil. Percy had been president of the National Hay and Grain Association in the 1920s and 1930s; vice-president and director of the family investment company, Engineers Incorporated; and a founding investor of the Eastern Indiana Telephone Company, the Rock Oil Company, and several other early family businesses. Percy was also a director of the Grain Dealers National Mutual Fire Insurance Company in Indianapolis for thirty-three years, serving as vice-president of the company from 1929 to 1935 and chairman of the board from 1947 to 1951. During the early years of the twentieth century, operators of country grain elevators had difficulty obtaining insurance coverage, because of the high incidence of explosions caused by grain dust. The only insurance they were able to obtain was from East Coast insurers at extremely high premiums. Therefore, a group of Hoosier grain owners formed the Grain Dealers National Mutual Fire Insurance Company. The company eventually wrote policies

7. As his brother Percy remembered, Ed would take out his pocket watch, "turn the face toward you so he [wouldn't] have to make a declaration of time, [and] you [could] look for yourself." Percy Goodrich, "Ed Goodrich," *Down in Indiana* 84 (November 5, 1949), Archives, Indiana Historical Society Library, Indianapolis; Wise, "Goodrich Father Was a Public Spirited Citizen."

8. Edward Dunn, telephone interview, December 29, 1996.

in states throughout the country.[9] Despite two marriages, Percy had no children.

Thus, by the 1930s the family held a substantial interest in many of the core businesses in east-central Indiana:

Banking	Peoples Loan and Trust Company; Randolph County Bank; and several smaller banks, including those in Eaton, Farmland, Modoc, Redkey, Ridgeville, and Tipton. James Goodrich's own banking interests extended to Indianapolis and included the National City Bank and Aetna Trust and Savings Company.
Agriculture	Twenty-four hay, grain, and seed elevators in central and northern Indiana and seven local farms.
Telephones	Eastern Indiana Telephone Company, Interstate Telephone and Telegraph Company, Investors Telephone Company, and others.
Other public utilities	Citizens Heat, Light and Power Company in Winchester; Union Heat, Light and Power Company in Union City; Portland Gas Company; Indiana-Ohio Public Service Company; and light and power companies in Washington and Jeffersonville, Indiana.

James Goodrich's business interests extended into coal, railroads, and oil refining. The family also owned a water company and an ice-delivery

9. William J. Wood (attorney for the Grain Dealers National Mutual Insurance Company), interview, November 4, 1996.

business, and sold farm machinery.[10] Thus, it is evident that the Goodrich financial dynasty was truly a family empire, built by the hard work of all five original brothers.

Besides their varied business interests, the Goodriches were active in other endeavors throughout the community. They seemed to be omnipresent in their hometown. Ed served as president of the Winchester school board, and James had been a board member in the 1890s and early 1900s. Ed was also a leader and benefactor of the local Masonic lodge. John and William Wallace took on leadership positions in the Presbyterian Church, and William was a charter and lifelong member of the Elks Lodge of New Castle, Indiana. Cora and the brothers' mother, Elizabeth, were active in the local library association and stalwart members of the Presbyterian Church. Percy and James were charter members of the Winchester Rotary Club in 1919, and James was a founding library board member. It seemed to some people that there was not much that went on in the local community that the Goodriches were not involved with in some way.

Their influence also extended beyond their local community. Percy Goodrich, for instance, was a family historian and a generous philanthropist. Percy's foremost interest, like James's, was education. What James Goodrich was to Wabash College as a valued trustee and benefactor, Percy was to Hanover College of Indiana. Although he never attended college, Percy was a member of the Hanover College Board of Trustees from 1921 until his death in 1951. During that time, he served for eighteen years as president of the board (1930 to 1948). When he passed away, his widow, Ethyl, served on the board of trustees until her retirement in 1967. The beautiful southern Indiana campus, nestled on a mountainside overlooking the Ohio River, held a certain charm for Percy. Percy's first wife, Susan, died in 1932. In February 1940, when he married Ethyl Jones Kuhner, he insisted that the small, simple ceremony be held in the Hanover chapel, officiated by Hanover's president. Percy devoted much of his free time and most of his resources to Han-

10. Ivan Barr, telephone interview, March 27, 1993.

over: He endowed chairs in speech and business administration (the Elizabeth Edger Goodrich Chair of Public Speaking and the Goodrich Professorship of Business Administration) and four student scholarships. The Goodrich Science Building on campus is named for Percy. He contributed nearly $500,000 to Hanover during his lifetime, and on the death of Ethyl in 1970, the remainder of his estate, in excess of $1,500,000, devolved to Hanover.[11]

From 1947 to 1950, Percy wrote a weekly newsletter entitled *Down in Indiana.* Mailed to a select group of thirty members of the National Grain Dealers Association, the newsletter contained ramblings and reminiscences about family, friends, and events that Percy had experienced during his nearly ninety years of life.[12] A year before Percy's death, Percy and Calvin Goodrich, a first cousin to the five Goodrich brothers, wrote a history of the Goodrich family's early years.[13] James had traveled with Percy to Virginia in the late 1930s to complete some of the research for the family history. Percy, like his brother James, was an ardent Republican. He greatly admired Abraham Lincoln, cofounding and serving as president of the Randolph County Lincoln Club in 1932. For the next twenty-five years, the Lincoln Club held annual meetings in Winchester, where speakers included United States senators and representatives, governors, and other political and military

11. See "P. E. Goodrich—A Good Trustee," *Bulletin of Hanover College* 43 (September 1951), p. 6; Mrs. Albert G. Parker, Jr., "Percy Goodrich Was Our Friend," *Hanover Alumni News* 5 (October 1951), p. 3; Katharine McAfee Parker, "In Gratitude for P. E. and Ethyl L. Goodrich," *The Hanoverian* 2 (August 1970), pp. 3–7; and "Percy E. Goodrich Leaves Large Trust Fund to Hanover College," *Indianapolis Star,* August 24, 1951, p. 14, col. 2. The four student scholarships were the Belle Edger Fund, the Elizabeth Edger Scholarship Fund, the Percy E. Goodrich Fund, and the Susie Engle Goodrich Fund. The science hall at Hanover is named for Percy Goodrich.

12. These "letters" included stories of Percy's past experiences and short biographies of people Percy knew during his long life. He sent the newsletters to a group of thirty dealers in the National Grain Dealers Association called "The Circle" and to other friends and family members. One collection of the letters is located at the Hanover College Archives, Hanover, Indiana, and another can be found in the library of the Indiana Historical Society, Indianapolis.

13. *A Great-Grandmother and Her People* (Winchester, Ind.: privately printed, 1950).

leaders. Percy also gathered an impressive collection of books and articles about Lincoln during his lifetime, which was donated to the Winchester Public Library at his death.[14]

In temperament and personality, Pierre was probably more like his uncles Percy and Ed than like his own father. Percy and Ed were also shrewd businessmen, not least because they had ability to keep their employees' noses to the grindstone. Gene Comer, a Winchester resident, worked for Percy Goodrich as a young man fresh out of high school. His employer's attitude prompted Comer to write the following poem when he was just eighteen years old and give it to his boss:

> *ELEVATOR*
>
> *I remember the times that we have sat*
> *And listened to the boss.*
> *About the ways of management,*
> *About profit and loss.*
> *"And if you want your bonus,"*
> *He would always say,*
> *"See that the lights above your desk*
> *Are off throughout the day."*
>
> *We come to work at half-past seven,*
> *So early in the morn.*
> *We work and slave throughout the day*
> *Hauling in the corn.*
> *He says, "Do this," he says, "Do that,"*
> *At least nine hours a day.*
> *And we pray for five o'clock,*
> *For then he goes away.*

14. See "Twenty-second Annual Banquet of the Randolph County Lincoln Club" (program in author's possession), Thursday, February 11, 1954. The function was held at Beeson Clubhouse in Winchester, Indiana. Some of the better-known speakers to address the Lincoln Club were the United States senators William E. Jenner and Homer Capehart of Indiana, Indiana governors Ralph Gates and George N. Craig, and United States congressmen Charles Halleck of Indiana and William Henry Harrison of Wyoming.

They tell us life is pleasant.
They tell us life is great.
Some day perhaps we'll find this out,
But how long do we have to wait?
Down with the tyrant, down with the boss,
Down with the Goodrich Feed,
And to hell with his "Profit and Loss."
I hope it goes to seed.[15]

"A lot of people were down on the Goodriches as businessmen," said Ivan Barr, who worked for the Goodrich Brothers Company and its successor from 1946 to 1968. "I think a lot of it was because of their success. They were considered crooked. That's very unfair and very unjust, because they were honest," Barr stated. "If you were found as an employee cheating on the scales [weighing grain or coal] in the Goodriches' favor, you were fired immediately," Barr stated. "They wouldn't tolerate that. So I found they were criticized very unjustly because of the fact, I think, that they were so successful."[16]

Not every local resident that remembers the Goodrich family in the 1930s and 1940s is as charitable as Barr. In east-central Indiana, the Goodrich brothers were often viewed as predators, ravenous in seizing every opportunity to gobble up utilities, banks, grain elevators, and farms whenever such businesses became available at low prices. Moreover, many disgruntled workers complained about the low wages the Goodriches paid.[17] It was well and good, many complained, that the Goodriches gave away tremendous sums to educational institutions such as Wabash and Hanover. If you were the breadwinner responsible for raising a family, however, that knowledge little compensated for low pay.

Another reason for grumblings about the Goodrich brothers' business prowess was the *timing* of their success. Their prosperity as a family

15. "Elevator," *Poems and Short Stories of Gene Comer* (privately printed, 1992), p. 9.
16. Ivan Barr, telephone interview, March 27, 1993.
17. Ibid.

became particularly conspicuous during the late 1920s and 1930s, when other families were struggling for their very survival. The Great Depression was especially tough on the farm community. Many farm families were losing their properties and their way of living. From 1921 to 1928, the United States agricultural population decreased by three million farmers. Nearly every family had to contend with unemployment and meager times. In 1927, the annual income of all 6.3 million farmers in the country averaged only $548. It only became worse when the Great Depression hit two years later. By 1932, twelve million Americans were unemployed and five thousand banks had failed.[18]

Moreover, the perception (and to a large degree the reality) was that the Goodrich family had a monopoly in many area businesses. Winchester resident Ralph Owens rented a farm from John "Jay" Goodrich in the 1920s. He believes that the Goodrich brothers could drive a hard bargain with the local farmers because they owned all the grain elevators within the geographical area. They were by far the largest grain dealers in Indiana. "You were forced to buy and sell from the Goodrich brothers," said Owens. "There were no other elevators [under different ownership] doing business."[19]

But some stories about the Goodrich brothers' supposed exploitations bordered on the ridiculous. For instance, one longtime Winchester attorney remembers a childhood rumor about James Goodrich's alleged exploitation of the Russian famine relief effort for his own private gain. The story held that the former governor successfully raised $10 million from private sources, contributed only $2 million to the starving Russian children, and pocketed the rest.[20] Another rumor was that the Goodrich brothers had intentionally decreased the gas pressure on a wellhead. They then allegedly bought the gas well for a pittance when the owner believed it was going dry.[21] It is true that the Goodrich brothers bought almost all their businesses at extremely depressed prices, but there is no

18. Williams, Current, and Freidel, *A History of the United States: Since 1865*, pp. 443–45.

19. Ralph Owens, interview, July 7, 1992.

20. John T. Cook, interview, November 9, 1995.

21. George Daly, interview, October 25, 1995.

evidence that they did anything illegal. The Depression had brought about many bankruptcies and receiverships. Invariably, almost every corporation the Goodriches took over in the 1930s, as will be seen, was bought for well below previous market prices.[22]

During the 1930s, James Goodrich strongly opposed President Franklin Delano Roosevelt's economic remedies for the sorry state of the country. He believed that Roosevelt's New Deal programs of intervention in business would make matters only worse. In 1936, Goodrich wrote to Frank Litschert, his longtime secretary: "This whole New Deal is about to go to smash. . . . Roosevelt and the whole outfit are mad, charging everyone who fails to agree with them, with bad faith."[23]

Goodrich especially ridiculed the high salaries that he saw postal workers receive and the subsidies extended to the farm community. He believed that cutting federal spending, not increasing it, was the only way to restore the nation to prosperity. He had written in 1933 to Herbert Hoover, who had been out of the White House for nine months: "Had we been permitted to go on without Government interference, while we might have had the wage increase that follows every recovery, yet with increasing employment and accelerated demand for goods and a gradual improvement in farm prices already under way, our situation would have been vastly better, in my opinion, than it is at this time."[24]

22. In 1933, for instance, James Goodrich was able to secure a 51 percent interest in City Securities when Dwight Peterson came to him in hopes of avoiding bankruptcy; similarly, the Indiana Telephone Corporation was in bankruptcy when the Goodrich brothers bought it for pennies per share in 1934. Pierre gained a controlling interest in the Ayrshire Collieries when Margaret Mellon had to sell shares in order to pay death taxes as a result of her husband's death in World War II. The Goodrich family received a 20 percent interest in Central Newspapers when Eugene Pulliam needed capital to buy an Indianapolis radio station. In each situation, James and Pierre Goodrich bought at low prices the interests the Goodrich family gained in each of these companies, but there is no evidence that they obtained the interests through illegal measures. See also chapter 17.

23. Letter from Goodrich to Litschert, January 17, 1936, James P. Goodrich Papers, box 13.

24. Letter from Goodrich to Hoover, September 9, 1933, James P. Goodrich Papers, box 23. See also Rhodes, *James P. Goodrich, Indiana's "Governor Strangelove,"* p. 162.

Interestingly, less than two months after he had written to Hoover condemning Roosevelt's domestic policies, Goodrich wrote to Roosevelt, praising him for his foreign policy in granting recognition to the Soviet Union:

> Although I am not of your political faith, as you know, I want to congratulate you upon the invitation extended to Russia to send someone here to discuss the matter of the resumption of relations between America and Russia.
>
> I am glad to know Mr. Litvinov is coming over. I got quite well acquainted with him on my four trips to Russia. He is a man of undoubted ability, sensible and realistic in his dealings.
>
> I trust that you will see your way clear to extend recognition without any strings tied to it and then sit down as equals and discuss the question of just how the situation is to be handled.
>
> Experience and observation have taught me that Russia can be depended upon to meet her obligations, her record in that respect is at least as good as that of any of our "associates" in the World War.
>
> I shall not hesitate publicly and otherwise to support you in this matter.

Roosevelt acknowledged Goodrich's letter, thanking him for his support and advice. It would seem that that was the only issue on which Goodrich ever agreed with the longtime president.[25]

In June 1936, Goodrich attended the Republican National Convention in Cleveland, Ohio, serving as a member of the platform committee. At the time, he still had hopes of drafting Hoover for the party nomination. When Hoover refused to seek the position, Goodrich willingly endorsed Governor Alf Landon of Kansas for the nomination. Goodrich was not surprised, however, by Roosevelt's landslide victory over Landon in November.[26] The times were desperate, and the American people had little interest in changing the path toward recovery that the charismatic incumbent promised.

25. Letter from Goodrich to Roosevelt, November 6, 1933, James P. Goodrich Papers, box 23; Rhodes, *James P. Goodrich, Indiana's "Governor Strangelove,"* p. 162.

26. Rhodes, *James P. Goodrich, Indiana's "Governor Strangelove,"* pp. 163–64.

In the spring of 1940, James Goodrich contracted pneumonia and was briefly hospitalized in March and April. He had remained intermittently ill since his hospitalization in Baltimore in the fall of 1937 and had been hospitalized several times since, including a stint at a well-known Battle Creek, Michigan, sanitarium in the spring of 1938.[27] Since then, he and Cora had spent the winters in Fort Lauderdale, Florida. Finally, in May 1940, Goodrich recovered sufficiently to attend the Republican State Convention, where presidential hopeful Wendell Willkie spoke. In June, James Goodrich felt well enough to attend the Republican National Convention in Philadelphia. He went to the convention as a delegate from Indiana's Tenth Congressional District. Goodrich had hoped to see the New York district attorney Thomas E. Dewey (who was just thirty-eight years old) or Ohio Senator Robert Taft receive the Republican presidential nomination. Instead, Willkie won the race.

Goodrich, James Watson, and other Hoosiers were Willkie's breakfast guests on the day that Willkie garnered the nomination. Watson was also an Indiana delegate to the convention, as he had been to every Republican National Convention since 1912. Willkie and Watson had made up after Watson had criticized Willkie for his previous Democratic Party membership. As Watson had told Willkie when he first learned that Willkie was seeking the Republican presidential nomination, he was glad to have a reformed prostitute (Willkie) in his church (the Republican Party), but he didn't want him leading the choir the next Sunday.[28]

The meeting of Watson and Goodrich in Philadelphia marked the last time the two longtime chums and politicians would be together. Although marked by jealousy and often strained, the friendship of these two men had endured a lifetime, no doubt largely because of their mutual passion for Republican politics, conservative values, and public ser-

27. See "Out of Politics, Goodrich Avers," *Indianapolis Star,* April 11, 1938, p. 2, col. 3 (reports about Goodrich's hospital stay at the Battle Creek, Michigan, sanitarium).

28. Willkie's national campaign headquarters was located in Watson's adopted hometown of Rushville, Indiana. See "Goodbye to Old Jim" (obituary of James E. Watson), *Passing Parade,* August 4, 1948, pp. 47–49.

vice. Together, Goodrich and Watson had dominated Indiana Republican politics during the first thirty years of the century. "Sunny Jim" Watson, the humorous, backslapping, and scandal-ridden politician, had lost his United States Senate seat in the 1932 Democratic landslide after being considered one of the most powerful and colorful figures on the national political scene. He remained in Washington, D.C., and practiced law until his death in 1948.[29]

When James Goodrich returned to his hometown after the 1940 Republican National Convention, he experienced a recurrence of "nervous heart." In late July, he suffered a stroke and became bedridden again. His last political act was to write Willkie on August 10 to offer him encouragement in his national race against Roosevelt. "I do not believe any President has ever, on his inauguration, faced as serious a situation as you will confront next January."[30] On the following day, Goodrich suffered another stroke. Four days later, James Goodrich died, at the age of seventy-six, at the Randolph County Hospital in Winchester, of a cerebral hemorrhage. Cora and Pierre, as well as other family members, were at the former governor's bedside at the time of his death.

On August 18, James Goodrich's funeral was held in Winchester. The

29. Watson's career in politics rivaled that of Goodrich in every way. Until Lee Hamilton, former United States congressman from Indiana's Ninth Congressional District, surpassed Watson's record, Watson had served longer in Congress (thirty years and under eight presidents) than any other representative from Indiana. In addition, he was chairman of the Republican State Convention in 1904, 1912, 1918, 1922, and 1924, and had attended every national Republican convention from 1876, when he was twelve years old, to 1948. In 1943, Watson was honored on his eightieth birthday in Rushville, Indiana, for his years of public service (see "Tribute to the Honorable James E. Watson," brochure in the author's possession). A feature article in *Atlantic Monthly* delivers an excellent portrayal of Watson. See "Senator James E. Watson: The Professional Public Servant," *Atlantic Monthly,* February 1932, pp. 183–90. Watson died at the age of eighty-three in Washington, D.C., on July 29, 1948. He was buried at Cedar Hill Cemetery in the nation's capital.

30. Letter from Goodrich to Willkie, August 10, 1940, James P. Goodrich Papers, box 28; see also Rhodes, *James P. Goodrich, Indiana's "Governor Strangelove,"* pp. 166–67.

service was marred by a torrential rainstorm that had traffic in a logjam throughout the streets of the small community. Several hundred people came to pay their final respects: politicians, businessmen, religious leaders, and townspeople who had been the governor's longtime friends. Some of the most noteworthy were James Watson; Will Hays; the Reverend John F. O'Hara from New York; Will Irwin from Columbus, Indiana; Glen R. Hillis, the 1940 Republican nominee for governor; Archibald Bobbitt, Republican state chairman; and the presidents of Wabash and Hanover colleges. Herbert Hoover and Thomas Dewey sent telegrams conveying their condolences. The Reverend Gustav Papperman, the former minister of the Winchester Presbyterian Church who then served as pastor of the Irving Park Presbyterian Church in Chicago, performed the services. The statehouse flags were lowered to half-staff in remembrance of the state's twenty-eighth governor.[31]

With the death of James Goodrich, Pierre lost the most significant person in his life, a father and mentor of exceptional influence. James Goodrich was one of the most accomplished men in modern Indiana history. In public life, his contributions and range of interests are both numerous and laudable: He was Indiana's highly successful World War I governor (1917–21); Indiana state Republican chairman for nearly a decade (1901–10); Republican national committeeman (1912–16); chairman and member, respectively, of the Indiana and International St. Lawrence Waterways commissions, appointed by President Coolidge (1923–27); lead American Relief Administration investigator of the Soviet Union Famine Relief Commission and special United States envoy to Russia (1921–23), appointed by President Harding; member of the National Public Lands Committee, appointed by President Hoover (1929–30); and trustee of the Theodore Roosevelt Memorial Committee.

His civic, educational, and religious contributions were nearly as impressive: trustee of Wabash College (1904–40) and board chairman

31. "State, National Dignitaries Hear Goodrich Eulogized at Final Rites," *Indianapolis Star,* August 19, 1940, p. 3, col. 6; "Tribute Is Paid to J. P. Goodrich," *Indianapolis Star,* August 16, 1940, p. 5, col. 3; "J. P. Goodrich, Former Governor of Indiana, Dead at 76 Years," *Indianapolis News,* August 18, 1940, p. 1, col. 6.

for sixteen years (1924–40); leadership positions in the Knights of Pythias (a fraternal and charitable society), Knights of Labor, and the National Grange; founding member of the Winchester Volunteer Fire Department (1897) and Winchester Rotary Club (1919);[32] trustee of the McCormick Theological Seminary and the Presbyterian Theological Seminary in Chicago; Winchester School Board member for fourteen years and founding member of the Winchester Library Board; elder and Sunday school teacher of the Winchester Presbyterian Church for twenty-five years; a thirty-second-degree Mason; and member of numerous other organizations.

As a philanthropist, he had contributed approximately $1 million to charitable causes, particularly favoring private higher education: nearly $400,000 to Wabash College, where he received an honorary master's degree in 1915 and an honorary doctorate in 1917; large sums to Oakland City College, the Presbyterian Theological Seminary in Chicago, Hanover College, where he was awarded an honorary Doctor of Science degree in 1938, and the University of Notre Dame, where he received an honorary LL.D. in 1917 (he had been a very close friend of Notre Dame's eighth president, Father John W. Cavanaugh). In June 1937, James Goodrich gave twenty-eight acres of parkland to the town of Winchester. This acreage was added to eighty acres that the Goodrich family had previously donated to their hometown. Also in June 1937, James gave $50,000 to beautify the park.[33]

It was in the business arena that James Goodrich left his greatest legacy to his family. Jim Goodrich's life was one which Horatio Alger himself would have admired. James and his four brothers had started as

32. For a reference to Goodrich as a founding member of the Winchester Volunteer Fire Department, see Winchester City Council Records, bk. 1, ordinance 217. Each volunteer of the department was paid one dollar for each run he made. For a reference to James Goodrich as a founding member of the Winchester Rotary Club, see "Winchester Rotary Club Celebrates 75th Anniversary" (special edition), *Winchester (Ind.) News-Gazette,* December 2, 1994, p. 6.

33. The sum of $1 million that Goodrich gave away is mentioned in Charles F. Remy's "Governor Goodrich and Indiana Tax Legislation," *Indiana Magazine of History* 43 (March 1947): 41–56, at p. 44.

youths with little, working as farmhands for pennies an hour. By the end of his life, James had amassed millions and had laid the groundwork for his son to achieve far greater wealth. Pierre would be the biggest beneficiary of his father's amazing entrepreneurship. He would step into the leadership position of several companies left to him at his father's death.

The deaths of the original five Goodrich brothers happened over a period of sixteen years: John on November 7, 1937; James on August 15, 1940; William Wallace on November 22, 1948; Percy on August 11, 1951; and Ed on November 21, 1953. The remaining family members—the wives and children of the original five Goodrich brothers—subsequently pooled their individual shares of the various family businesses into a voting trust. They allowed Pierre to exercise virtual control over the trust, delegating to him the authority to make the day-to-day corporate decisions.[34] The family members were content to allow Pierre to

34. The lives of the Goodrich brothers deserve much more elaboration than space will allow here. For the curious reader, a longer account of each brother can be found in the front-page obituaries of the Winchester newspapers (*Journal-Herald* and *News*): Jay, November 6, 1937; James, August 16, 1940; William Wallace, November 23, 1948; Percy, August 12, 1951; and Edward, November 22, 1953. The remaining family members included the surviving wives of the original five Goodrich brothers and their children: James's wife, Cora (Frist), died on October 30, 1941; Jay's wife, Charlotte (Martin), died on August 12, 1941; Edward's wife, Elizabeth (Neff), died on November 3, 1958; William Wallace's first wife, Charlotte (Moore), died in approximately 1899 in childbirth, and his second wife, Louise, passed away on December 21, 1964; Percy's first wife, Susie (Engle), died in 1934, and his second wife, Ethyl (Jones Kuhner), passed away on November 12, 1973.

The five original Goodrich brothers and their wives had five surviving children (the five cousins): Jay and Charlotte's first son, John, was born on March 10, 1894, and passed away on January 6, 1971. He married Helen C. Cummins in 1964, and they had no children, although Helen had a daughter, Suzan Shilling, from an earlier marriage. Jay and Charlotte's second son, James, was born on September 6, 1897, and passed away on September 10, 1901. James and Cora's son Pierre was born on September 10, 1894, and passed away on October 25, 1973. Pierre and his first wife, Dorothy Dugan, had one child, Frances, born on October 10, 1921; she resides in Indianapolis. Pierre had no children from his second marriage with Enid Smith (born May 17, 1903; died Novem-

have such discretionary control because he and his father had a tremendous record of making the right corporate decisions. Moreover, Pierre's two male cousins—John and Perce—were engaged in successful businesses of their own. They had little time to contribute to the daily decisions of the Indianapolis-based corporations, although they served as board members of many of the companies.

How Pierre operated as a businessman is illuminated by an account given by E. F. Gallahue in his autobiography, *Edward's Odyssey.*[35] Gallahue became a highly successful entrepreneur in his own right as president of American States Insurance, based in Indianapolis. He shared with Pierre not only the ability to build a business, but also a great yearning to understand human nature. A reader of Sigmund Freud and the Swiss psychiatrist Carl Jung, Gallahue had a lifelong interest in literature, religion, and, especially, matters involving mental health. No doubt this background prevented Gallahue from becoming discouraged when negotiations between Goodrich and him for the sale of the Union Insurance Company continued without result for several months in 1941. Even after several meetings between the two men, a deal had not been struck. Gallahue's attorneys told their boss that it was foolish for him to pursue the matter with Goodrich any further. But Gallahue did not give up.[36] Gallahue recalled how his patience paid off:

---

ber 26, 1996). Edward and Elizabeth Neff Goodrich had a daughter, Florence, who was born on May 12, 1897, and passed away on July 15, 1994. Florence married Francis Dunn (born on January 23, 1896; died on February 13, 1976) in 1921, and they had two sons: Wesley, born on December 20, 1922; and Edward, born on October 31, 1925. William Wallace and his second wife, Louise, had two children. Elizabeth ("Betty"), who was born on January 1, 1906, still lives in Winchester. Elizabeth married Phillip Terry (born on January 18, 1896; died in 1967) on September 2, 1939, and they had no children. William Wallace and Louise's second child, Perce "Bud" Gordon, was born on August 21, 1908, and died on September 3, 1996.

35. *Edward's Odyssey: An Autobiography of Edward Gallahue* (New York: Doubleday, 1970), p. 88.

36. Ibid. According to Gallahue, his patience in dealing with Goodrich was partly a result of his realization that it was a good deal for both himself and Pierre, partly a result of his understanding how Goodrich operated, and partly purely sentimental. Gallahue's

> Pierre was a very gracious person, and if he wanted to take up part of our meeting talking about Greek philosophy and Asiatic mysticism, it was all right with me; for I had some knowledge of these subjects and would at least find them interesting. He was a highly intelligent person who simply approached matters differently from most businessmen. Instead of moving directly from "A" to "B," he chose to surround a subject in concentric circles. While his method took longer, it was effective in covering every item. Finally, after several months, Pierre and I arrived at the basis for a sale.[37]

Pierre's methodical, painstaking style of negotiation was totally unlike his father's. Despite its nontraditional nature, it was a style that almost always proved financially fruitful. The sale of the Union Insurance Company was the first of many successful business deals that Pierre would execute on his own.

---

first job in the insurance business was with the Union Insurance Company, which paid him fifty dollars a month. It would bring Gallahue great satisfaction if he could now own the company that had given him his first job.

37. Ibid.

Chapter 17

Companies! Companies! Companies!

A well-run company is not accidental. . . . Our company must be well-run from every aspect, with prompt and reliable accounting, highly intelligent engineering, the development of very superior personnel in every department and effective public relations. . . . If you will study all I have said, I think you will see what it is we need during the next 7–10 years. We cannot do it overnight. We can only do it by being prompt in our own action; and that means we must have intelligent information promptly.

PIERRE F. GOODRICH, Memorandum, Indiana Telephone Corp., May 30, 1973

THE GOODRICH brothers' decision in 1927 to sell their interests in several public utilities was the genesis of bigger things to come. With the premium prices they were able to command for the companies, they deposited the profits and waited for even better business opportunities.

What came first would shock and alarm the nation. On what would become known as Black Friday (October 29, 1929), the stock market crashed. In that one day, an unprecedented sixteen million stocks were sold. Over the next two weeks, stocks lost more than 40 percent of their value. The slide continued until 1932, when stocks were worth barely one-fourth what they had been worth before the crash. Employment was slashed. By 1933, more than 25 percent of able-bodied workers were out of jobs. Factory jobs were extremely scarce, because companies were pouring out more goods than consumers could purchase. Those who were fortunate enough to have work toiled for meager pay.

Thirty percent of Americans still made their living on farms. Commodity prices collapsed to such an extent that a farmer was able to sell a bushel of corn, on average, for only 31¢ in 1932, whereas he had received $1.51 a bushel in 1919. Wheat had gone from $2.16 per bushel in 1919 to 38¢ per bushel in 1933. Prices became so depressed that many farmers started burning corn in their homes for heat. It was cheaper than burning coal. It took ten bushels of wheat to buy a cheap pair of shoes. Banks folded, securities crashed, relief lines grew longer, and the nation's confidence in itself dived to unprecedented depths. The worst possible combination of economic factors produced the deepest and longest depression in America's history.[1]

Ironically, the five Goodrich brothers prospered during this period, because they had what few others did: hundreds of thousands, perhaps even millions, of dollars deposited in banks that *they* controlled. They were not immune, however, to anxious customers who rushed to financial institutions throughout the country seeking a return of their deposits. They were, however, in a position to control their own destiny in a way that the overwhelming majority of others could not. By February 1933, five thousand banks had failed across the country. During the bank holidays from February to March 1933, Peoples Loan and Trust Company was one of the few banks in Indiana (perhaps in the nation) that never closed. When depositors lined up to withdraw their deposits at the bank in Farmland, Indiana, James Goodrich (who owned a large share of the bank) purportedly took a couple of suitcases of money to the bank and handed out withdrawals to any depositor who demanded one. Within hours, the run on the bank had stopped.[2]

The Great Depression of the 1930s gave the Goodrich family the opportunity to enter the big leagues of corporate owners. One of their first buys would be in a business in which the family was already well established—the telephone industry. The industry was still in its infancy when the Goodriches began to invest in it heavily. In 1929, only one in

1. See Williams, Current, and Freidel, *A History of the United States: Since 1865*, pp. 463–73.

2. Perce G. Goodrich, interview, November 9, 1992.

every ten families had a telephone.[3] Thus, the potential for growth was tremendous. By 1929, Pierre was already president of the Interstate Telephone and Telegraph Company and vice-president of the Investors Telephone Company. Moreover, he was a director of the Batesville (Indiana) Telephone Company; the Public Telephone Company at Greensburg, Indiana; and the United Telephone Company, which served Portland and Union City, Indiana, and Greenville, Ohio. His family still retained a large interest in the Eastern Indiana Telephone Company, which served their home county. Pierre was also a director of telephone companies in Iowa, Arkansas, and North Carolina. His expertise and his ability to invest in the industry made him a much-sought-after director.[4]

The family's largest investment in the telephone industry, however, would be the purchase of what would become the Indiana Telephone Corporation (ITC). Based in Seymour, Indiana, ITC served a large geographical area across south-central Indiana. At the time it was sold in 1978, ITC had grown to be the fourteenth largest of approximately sixteen hundred independently owned telephone companies in the country. It served 122,000 households.[5]

In October 1934, Engineers Incorporated (the Goodrich family) purchased the Southern Indiana Telephone and Telegraph Company when the business was in receivership.[6] The Goodriches had the name of the company changed to the Indiana Telephone Corporation. Pierre served as president and chairman of the board of ITC from October 18, 1934, until his death in October 1973. It is interesting to note that the stock-

3. Williams, Current, and Freidel, *A History of the United States: Since 1865*, p. 464.

4. "Pierre F. Goodrich, Indianapolis," *Association Book of Indiana* (Indianapolis: James O. Jones, 1929), p. 326.

5. "Want Phone Company? Give Board a Ring," *Indianapolis Star*, August 25, 1977, p. 62, col. 3.

6. The Indiana Telephone Corporation was incorporated in Indiana on October 18, 1934, as successor in the reorganization of the Southern Indiana Telephone and Telegraph Company. The latter company was originally incorporated in Indiana on December 30, 1919. At one time, ITC operated forty-one exchanges in southern Indiana and had 1,917 miles of pole lines. See *Moody's Public Utility Manual* (1960), p. 1717.

holders of the bankrupt Southern Indiana Telephone and Telegraph Company had been offered a substantially higher price from other wooers. These other potential purchasers wanted to buy on credit, but the Goodriches offered cash.

"No one had cash during the Depression. They merely had paper which was worthless in the eyes of creditors and stockholders," said Gilbert Snider. "Thus, Engineers Incorporated was able to pay a pittance for the business," added Snider.[7] Indeed, stock in the bankrupt Southern Indiana Telephone and Telegraph Company was purchased for a few cents a share in 1934. When the company was sold in 1978, the per-share sale price was one hundred seven dollars.[8]

Over the next forty years, Pierre Goodrich took tremendous pride in reorganizing and controlling the operations of the newly formed ITC. True to his management style, he personally visited with employees, often spending hours observing operations and asking technical questions. Although the region that ITC serviced included mostly rural areas, ITC had some of the most up-to-date technology available in the telephone industry. Goodrich was especially excited about the future use of fiber optics, which at the time of his death was just developing. He took every opportunity he could to remain informed about new equipment. In September 1960, in conjunction with a trip to Germany to attend a Mont Pelerin Society meeting, Pierre visited the giant high-tech company Siemens at Lengerich, Germany. He went to learn about the latest European communications developments.[9]

7. Gilbert Snider, interview, December 23, 1991. In a company memorandum, Goodrich makes a brief reference to the financial condition of the old Southern Indiana Telephone and Telegraph Company when it was purchased in 1934. See "ITC Memorandum No. 1—Re: Employees; Good Citizens; Good Supervisors; Good Customers," March 5, 1970 (rev. May 30, 1973), exhibit 3, p. 3 (in the possession of T. Alan Russell, Paris, Ill.).

8. T. Alan Russell, interview, July 2, 1994. As controller of the Indiana Telephone Corporation when ITC was sold in 1978 to the Continental Telephone Corporation, Russell was involved in the valuation of the shares.

9. Goodrich visited the Siemens plant in conjunction with attending a Mont Pelerin Society annual meeting at Kassel, Germany, from September 5 to September 10,

In the 1940s, Goodrich became convinced that the United States would experience a period of substantial inflation in the 1950s, 1960s, and 1970s. At the time, that was not an uncommon projection among many economists. It was a result of the perception that the United States was going to suffer hyperinflation, just as South American countries had, because of governmental deficit spending and devaluation of the currency. Goodrich acted on his hunch. As early as 1947, he began refinancing ITC's debt on a long-term basis at very low fixed interest rates. This astute business decision was a major contribution to the company's subsequent profitability when it was sold in 1978.[10]

After Goodrich's death, his former secretary, Helen Schultz, was

---

1960. Ruth Connolly, interview, October 25, 1991. Alan Russell also recalled the time in the early 1970s when he and Goodrich "crashed" a local exchanging station owned and operated by the Bell Corporation near where Goodrich lived in northern Indianapolis. Goodrich wanted to learn as much as he could about the competition. The employees recognized Goodrich and invited Russell and him in and showed them around. T. Alan Russell, interview, July 2, 1994.

10. Economist Milton Friedman remembers talking to Goodrich about his decision to refinance the telephone company. Letter from Milton Friedman to author, December 19, 1991. A summary of Goodrich's refinancing of the ITC's long-term debt is located in "ITC Memorandum No. 1," pp. 9–10. Goodrich writes:

> *Our bond financing is the result of a very long series of negotiations going back as far as 1947.*
>
> Our conviction that monetary inflation is likely to continue and that this will be reflected in higher interest rates, plus greater governmental interference with the market, have caused us to refinance our Series 1, 2 and 3 bonds which would have matured in 1977, our Series 4 bonds which would have matured in 1984, and Series 5 bonds which would have matured in 1986, as part of the Series 10 bonds which will mature in 2008. The refinancing accounted for $3,375,000 of the total $4,875,000 borrowing. This gives us additional options and hopefully may keep us from having to go to the money market before 1991. . . .

In addition to refinancing ITC's long-term debt at low fixed interest rates, Goodrich made other innovative business decisions that led to the company's profitability. For example, he negotiated contracts with equipment providers requiring them to guarantee replacement parts for up to twenty years (an exceptionally long time); he also depreciated equipment over a period as short as nine years. T. Alan Russell, interview, July 2, 1994. Goodrich speaks about both the twenty-year provision for parts replacement and the nine-year depreciation of equipment in "ITC Memorandum No. 1," p. 12.

named president of ITC. She had previously served as ITC's secretary-treasurer as well as Goodrich's secretary. William Fletcher, an accountant, and Goodrich's friend and adviser, was selected as executive vice-president.[11] Fletcher had worked for the accountancy firm Arthur Andersen and Company.

In 1977, Lovett C. Peters, whom Goodrich had previously employed to arrange the sale of the Ayrshire Collieries Corporation in 1969, was again hired. This time he oversaw the sale of ITC. A merger was struck in January 1978 whereby ITC shareholders received stock in Continental Telephone Corporation. Continental was then the third-largest independent telephone company in the country. The sale was valuated at approximately $52 million. The Goodrich family owned approximately 46 percent of ITC's stock, making their share of the sale worth approximately $24 million.[12] In 1989, GTE purchased Continental Telephone, and the original ITC shareholders received GTE stock in exchange.

Eugene C. Pulliam and Pierre F. Goodrich came from very different backgrounds, but the two men shared many of the same conservative values and deep convictions. Pulliam, the grandfather of the former vice-president Dan Quayle and the son of a poor Methodist minister,

11. See "Notable Career of ITC President Goodrich Ends, Helen E. Schultz Advanced to Top Office," *ITC Highlights,* November–December 1973, pp. 1 and 3. Although the Indiana Telephone Corporation had approximately three hundred shareholders, the Goodrich family was by far the largest owner, holding, in August 1977, 237,066 of the company's 512,000 shares of common stock (approximately 46 percent). See "Want Phone Company? Give Board a Ring," *Indianapolis Star,* August 25, 1977, p. 62, col. 3.

12. See "Merger with Continental," *Indianapolis Star,* June(?) 1978. (A copy of the article is located in the Business and Technology section of the Marion County Public Library, "Indiana Corporations," general files section.) Continental Telephone acquired the Indiana Telephone Corporation in June 1978 for 3,456,115 common shares. Under the terms of the merger, Indiana Telephone shareholders traded one common share of that stock for approximately 6.75 shares of Continental. The price range of Continental stock per share in 1978 was between $14.16 and $16.83. See *Moody's Public Utility Manual* (1979), p. 586.

was a self-made newspaper titan.[13] His career spanned sixty-five years in journalism. During that time, he bought and sold some fifty newspapers in thirteen states, still controlling at the time of his death in 1975 the *Indianapolis Star,* the *Indianapolis News,* the *Muncie Star,* the *Arizona Republic,* the *Phoenix Gazette,* and several smaller city dailies in Indiana.[14]

In the early 1930s, the Depression hit Pulliam particularly hard. He had overextended himself financially by buying a chain of newspapers, particularly a number of smaller papers in Oklahoma. In March 1934, Pulliam established Central Newspapers, a holding company for his newspapers in Oklahoma and Indiana.[15] A short time later, he sold several of these papers to the managers who were running them at the time.[16]

Pulliam also wanted to own an Indianapolis radio station and Indianapolis newspapers. This desire eventually brought him together with James and Pierre Goodrich, who, at the time, were directors of City Securities, the securities firm that Pulliam went to for financing. Pulliam saw the tremendous potential that radio offered as a news medium. In 1936, he became interested in purchasing radio station WIRE in Indianapolis. The station was owned by a Chicago businessman who sold it to Pulliam for $340,000. Pulliam raised the capital for the purchase

13. Pulliam's grandson Russell Pulliam wrote *Publisher Gene Pulliam, Last of the Newspaper Titans* (Ottawa, Ill.: Jameson Books, 1984).

14. The other Pulliam family newspapers include the *Vincennes Sun-Commercial,* Topics Newspapers, and the *Arizona Business Gazette.* The *Muncie Star* and *Muncie Press* merged in 1996 to become the *Star-Press.*

15. Central Newspapers was formed on March 30, 1934. See "Central Newspapers, Inc.," Office of the Indiana Secretary of State, Corporation Division, packet 193037-082. See also Pulliam, *Publisher Gene Pulliam, Last of the Newspaper Titans,* p. 76. The newspapers that made up Central Newspapers in 1934 were seven Oklahoma daily papers (*El Reno Tribune, Hobart Democrat-Chief, Elk City Daily News, Mangum Daily Star, Clinton Daily News, Altus Times-Democrat,* and *Alva Review-Courier*) and four Indiana newspapers (*Lebanon Reporter, Linton Citizen, Vincennes Sun-Commercial,* and *Huntington Herald-Press*).

16. Pulliam, *Publisher Gene Pulliam, Last of the Newspaper Titans,* pp. 84–85.

by selling his Oklahoma newspapers and borrowing the rest.[17] Hard currency was especially difficult to come by, and thus James and Pierre Goodrich entered the picture. They were in the position to invest in Central Newspapers with cash they had on hand from the sale of the Goodrich public utility companies in the 1920s.

In exchange for the cash investment by the Goodriches, through Engineers Incorporated, James and Pierre negotiated with Pulliam a business arrangement that gave the Goodrich family a slightly less than 20 percent interest in Central Newspapers. The deal was struck on the condition that Central Newspapers shares were not to be sold publicly or passed on to nonfamily members. Purportedly, another agreement between the Goodrich and Pulliam families was that nothing was to appear on the editorial pages of any of Central Newspapers' papers that would conflict with the ideas of free enterprise and individual freedom.[18]

As long as Eugene C. Pulliam and Pierre Goodrich were alive, there was little chance that this agreement would be breached. Although later in life Pulliam enjoyed hobnobbing with the likes of Lyndon B. Johnson, Hubert Humphrey, and lesser-known liberals, he was more comfortable with such conservatives as Barry Goldwater and Richard Nixon.[19] Pierre, always looking ahead, was concerned with what would

17. Ibid., p. 95. At one time, Pulliam went to City Securities to arrange for the underwriting of a corporate bond to purchase one of the Indianapolis newspapers. The Goodrich-Pulliam connection may have been made at that time, since both James and Pierre were affiliated with City Securities. Pierre was a vice-president and board member of City Securities.

18. Ruth Connolly, interview, October 25, 1991; Rosanna Amos, interview, December 10, 1991.

19. Pulliam, *Publisher Gene Pulliam, Last of the Newspaper Titans,* p. 83. Russ Pulliam quotes Paul Porter, a New Deal Democrat, who began working for Eugene Pulliam in 1929 on one of his papers. Porter later became chairman of the Federal Communications Commission. Porter states, "[Pulliam] was suspicious of power in government and overconcentration of industrial or economic power and had an almost religious faith in individualism."

happen after he and Pulliam were gone from the scene. In a section in the *Liberty Fund Basic Memorandum* on the free press, Goodrich stipulated that the directors of Central Shares and Liberty Fund have an obligation to use their minority ownership in Central Newspapers to help keep the newspapers true to the ideals of Eugene C. Pulliam.[20]

The contractual provision that restricted shareholders from liquidating their Central Shares stock proved to be a formidable obstacle. The fewer than two hundred stockholders in Central Newspapers were unable to sell their shares in Central Newspapers on the open market. As a result, it was impossible for Pulliam and Goodrich family members to realize the substantial increased value that was created by the quickly growing newspaper company. Finally, as a result of a "restructuring" that was worked out in 1989, Central Newspapers became publicly traded on the New York Stock Exchange. This listing on a publicly traded stock market allowed family members to sell their shares.[21]

In 1940, Pierre formed a holding company called Central Shares. Central Shares' sole function was to hold the stock the Goodrich family owned in Central Newspapers. Central Shares was dissolved in 1989, and its stock was dispersed to the individual shareholders (all Goodrich family members).[22] Clearly, the investment in Central Newspapers was one of the best business deals the Goodrich family ever made. The four major newspapers that Pulliam purchased in the 1940s came to dominate the print markets in Indianapolis and Phoenix when these capital cities experienced explosive growth. Phoenix has grown from just

20. Pierre F. Goodrich, *Liberty Fund Basic Memorandum*, p. 93.

21. See Kevin A. Drawbaugh, "Shareholders OK Stock Changes: News and Star Parent Firm Prepares Class A Public Offering," *Indianapolis News*, July 28, 1989, sec. C, p. 2, col. 2; Kathy Barks Hoffman, "Quayle Newspaper Going Public," *U.S.A. Today*, June 15, 1989, sec. B., p. 2, col. 2.

22. Perce G. Goodrich, interview, May 2, 1993. According to Perce Goodrich, for some unknown reason Engineers Incorporated could not continue to be the holding company for Central Newspapers' stock. Therefore, in 1940, Pierre Goodrich formed Central Shares for that purpose.

seventy-five thousand residents shortly after World War II to in excess of one million people in the 1990s.[23]

This increased circulation, combined with Pulliam's hard-hitting news style and sophisticated marketing, increased Central Newspapers' value from a few million dollars in the late 1940s to well in excess of $500 million by the 1990s. Central Shares was the third-largest shareholder of Central Newspapers stock when it was dissolved in 1989. In exchange for Central Shares stock, Central Shares shareholders received Central Newspapers nonvoting stock. In 1996, the shares owned by the estate of Enid Goodrich and Liberty Fund still accounted for approximately an 16.6 percent interest in Central Newspapers.[24]

23. Pulliam bought the *Indianapolis Star* in 1944 for $2.35 million and paid $4 million to obtain both the *Arizona Republic* and the *Phoenix Gazette* in 1946. In 1948, he bought the *Indianapolis News* for $4 million. Pulliam, *Publisher Gene Pulliam, Last of the Newspaper Titans,* pp. 111–12.

24. The swap amounted to a restructuring because voting-rights stock was exchanged for nonvoting-rights stock. The approximate worth of Central Newspapers is not known, but it has been appraised at between $450 million and $1.5 billion. See "Who Owns Central Newspapers?" *Indianapolis Business Journal,* October 24–30, 1988, p. 1, col. 1. According to a news article in 1990, Mrs. Pierre F. (Enid) Goodrich and Liberty Fund owned a combined total of 4,314,600 of 23,245,750 shares of class A common stock, which amounted to approximately 18.56 percent of all shares. The stock is now traded on the New York Stock Exchange (NYSE symbol ECP). See "Central Newspapers, Inc.," *Indianapolis Business Journal,* May 7–13, 1990, p. 25, col. 2. See also "Central Newspapers, Inc. (Earnings and Dividends)," *Indianapolis Business Journal,* January 29, 1990, sec. A, p. 26, col. 1; Kathy Barks Hoffman, "Quayle Newspapers Going Public," *U.S.A. Today,* June 15, 1989, sec. B, p. 2, col. 2; Kevin A. Drawbaugh, "Shareholders OK Stock Changes: News and Star Parent Firm Prepares Class A Public Offering," *Indianapolis News,* June 28, 1989, sec. C, p. 2, col. 2; Julia Flynn Siler and Richard Fly, "The Quayle Family Newspapers: Black, White—and Green All Over," *Business Week,* August 28, 1989, pp. 28–29; "Quayle Papers' Stock Plan," *New York Times,* August 14, 1989, sec. C, p. 6, col. 6; and "Prospectus," *Central Newspapers and Subsidiaries* (1992), Marion County Public Library, Central Newspapers files.

The greatest benefit in the 1989 swap of Central Shares stock for Central Newspapers stock was the avoidance of capital-gains tax. The amendments to the 1986 tax code supposedly eliminated this tax advantage. Because the swap was deemed a "restructuring" by the IRS (the Goodrich family giving up voting stock for nonvoting stock), however, no capital gain was recognized. That meant that approximately $130 million in

City Securities Corporation is the oldest and largest investment banking company in Indiana and one of the largest in the Midwest. It is responsible for underwriting many of the largest municipal and corporate capital projects that have taken place in Indiana. For instance, it took the lead in 1953 in structuring revenue bonds for the building of the $280 million Indiana Toll Road that crosses the northern border of Indiana.

City Securities also became a leader in underwriting university and college building projects. It has handled the financing for the construction of such projects as Indiana University's Memorial Stadium (football), Assembly Hall (basketball), and dozens of other building projects on the campuses of Indiana, Purdue, Ball State, and Indiana State universities. At the municipal level, it has been the underwriter for hundreds of municipal securities projects; for new sewage, water, and electric utility facilities; roads; and public buildings (such as the RCA Dome in Indianapolis).

At the corporate level, City Securities assisted in the financing of major corporations.[25] From 1945 to 1960, a time when Pierre Goodrich was very much involved as vice-president and a director on the board, City Securities underwrote commitments to 160 separate corporate finance offerings totaling more than $67 million.[26]

Despite these later successes, City Securities nearly folded during the early years of the Great Depression. In 1930, its parent holding company, City Shareholders, and two sister subsidiaries failed and were placed into receivership by Indiana's banking department.[27] J. Dwight

---

Central Shares stock was allowed to be exchanged for Central Newspapers stock without tax consequences (W. W. Hill, interview, May 25, 1993).

25. Examples include the Marsh supermarket chain (the largest grocery chain in Indiana), Central Newspapers, the Indiana Insurance Corporation, American States Insurance Corporation, and the Hamilton Manufacturing Company.

26. E. Bruce Geelhoed, *Indiana's Investment Banker: The Story of City Securities Corporation* (Muncie, Ind.: Ball State University, 1985), p. 88.

27. Ibid., p. 33. The two sister subsidiaries that folded were the City Trust Company and the City Trading Company.

Peterson, who later became president and chairman of the board, saved City Securities from a similar plight. He convinced Indiana's banking authorities of the company's solvency. He accomplished this difficult task by obtaining financial backing from James Goodrich, whom Peterson had first met in the late 1920s.

"In the late 1920s, dad called on Governor Goodrich in Winchester for investments," said John Peterson, son of J. Dwight. "Governor Goodrich liked my father and they became very close friends."[28] A few years later, James Goodrich provided the capital support needed to keep City Securities' doors open. A summary of minutes from a City Securities board meeting records how the Goodrich-Peterson agreement proceeded:

> On May 1, 1931, Peterson explained to the corporation's Board of Directors that he and the Goodrich family proposed to purchase the outstanding shares . . . held by its receiver (. . . a 1930s version of a leveraged buy-out) and take any other measures necessary to maintain the firm's activity. The directors approved the plan and, over the course of the next seven months, Peterson subsequently gained the approval of Indiana's banking authorities for the reorganization of City Securities Corporation under the ownership of the Peterson and Goodrich families.[29]

Peterson's ability to obtain the financial backing of a former governor would have helped persuade Indiana's banking authorities to approve the deal. As a result, the Goodrich family negotiated a 51 percent interest in City Securities.[30] Pierre became a member of the board and vice-president in 1934. Because the securities that City Securities held were worth only a portion of their pre-Depression value, the company had to look for alternative sources of income to keep the doors open. With

28. John Peterson, interview, January 15, 1992.

29. Ibid., p. 36. Geelhoed obtained this information from "Minutes of the Board of Directors Meetings," May 6, 1931, and December 31, 1931, City Securities Corporation records.

30. Cecil Fritz, telephone interview, November 25, 1992.

James Goodrich's assistance, Peterson purchased the Aetna Trust and Savings Company in 1933 for only five thousand dollars.[31] James was a former president of Aetna Trust and Savings Company, and in 1933, Pierre served as one of its directors.[32] Thus, it was apparently the Goodrich father-son connection that enabled the financial deal to be struck. The new insurance division of City Securities proved to be immediately profitable. The premiums generated from insurance sales helped to keep City Securities solvent until municipal and corporate bond underwriting recovered in 1935.[33]

After World War II, City Securities Corporation grew at a rapid rate. It arranged financial deals for such construction projects as bridges, courthouses, public schools, college dormitories, athletic facilities, and university buildings.[34] It established itself as the number-one banking investor in municipal, school, and corporate bonds in Indiana. As the oldest and largest independently owned broker-dealer in Indiana, City Securities owed much of its success to the connections that its board of directors and management personnel had established. In 1954, when City Securities was growing at a phenomenal rate, J. Dwight Peterson served on the boards of directors of twenty-one companies, and Pierre Goodrich served on the boards of thirteen others.[35]

31. Geelhoed, *Indiana's Investment Banker*, p. 38; John L. O'Donnell, "The Financial Operations of a Regional Investment Bank" (Ph.D. diss., School of Business, Indiana University, 1954), p. 103.

32. "Pierre F. Goodrich, Indianapolis," *Association Book of Indiana*, p. 326.

33. Geelhoed, *Indiana's Investment Banker*, pp. 38–41. In 1930, City Securities underwrote only $75,000 of municipal and corporate securities business. It incurred losses during the next three years through the liquidation of securities of doubtful value. In 1935, however, City Securities underwrote $1,800,000 in municipal and corporate securities and had survived the worst of the Depression years.

34. Ibid., p. 64. According to Geelhoed, between 1949 and 1984, Indiana's public school corporations issued 773 separate bond issues, with a face value of more than $2 billion. City Securities functioned as manager or joint manager of 390 of those 773 issues, or slightly more than 50 percent of the total.

35. See John L. O'Donnell, "The Financial Operations of a Regional Investment Bank," p. 81. During his lifetime, Peterson served on the boards of directors of more than fifty-five companies. See Edward Wills, Jr., "City Securities Leader Who Helped

During the first half of Goodrich's long tenure as a director (1935–53), City Securities was the sole underwriter for sixty-two corporate securities ventures,[36] which meant that fledgling companies wanting to attract outside investment would hire City Securities to underwrite a corporate bond. During that time, for every company City Securities took on as a client, five more were knocking on its door. The board reviewed these proposals, often in a painstaking way, before voting on whether to accept underwriting responsibility. The proposals, reviewed quarterly, numbered in the hundreds. Corporate proposals came from all types of businesses: automobile parts, meat-packing, electronics, banking, home appliances, mining, insurance, textiles, jewelry, and soft-drinks, just to name a few.[37]

Goodrich's experience—derived from decades of decision making—taught him what worked and what did not. It was experience that Pierre could translate into other aspects of life. One would be hard-pressed to find in academia anything closely resembling that type of exposure.

In 1889, John B. Goodrich, one of the five original Goodrich brothers, started a hay-baling and -buying business in Winchester at the same location where the brothers' father, John B. Goodrich, and maternal grandfather, Edward Edger, had begun a grain business in 1860.[38] Later, on January 5, 1898, the five brothers—Percy, James, John, Ed, and William Wallace—incorporated the business, naming it the Goodrich Brothers Hay and Grain Company.

Shape Indiana's Future Is Honored," *Indianapolis Star* (republished in Geelhoed, *Indiana's Investment Banker,* p. 20).

36. See John L. O'Donnell, "The Financial Operations of a Regional Bank," p. 81 and table 21.

37. Ibid.

38. Perce G. Goodrich, interview, November 9, 1992. See also "The 90th Anniversary of the Goodrich Brothers' Company," County Elevators, Shippers, and Feeddealers' Luncheon, January 23, 1950, Columbia Club Ballroom. Guests at the function were Percy E. Goodrich, chairman of the board of Goodrich Brothers, and Henry F. Schricker, governor of Indiana. See also "Indiana Grain Dealers Honor P. E. Goodrich," *Muncie (Ind.) Star,* January 24, 1950, p. 14, col. 2.

Percy Goodrich took over the management of the hay and grain company. Early on, the five brothers and their wives were the sole stockholders of the company, which bought grain and shipped it by train primarily to East Coast markets. It also sold feed for stock, seed, and farm machinery, and, before refrigeration, operated an ice company.

By the late 1920s, Goodrich Brothers had acquired twenty-four grain elevators in central and northern Indiana, becoming Indiana's largest grain business. In the mid 1940s, Percy Goodrich, who was then well into his eighties and had no children, approached his nephew Perce about taking over the management of the company. Perce did manage Goodrich Brothers for about a year but was also actively engaged in overseeing his own companies in Portland, Indiana. He soon resigned from the position. At that time, in 1947, Percy turned to a young acquaintance by the name of Samuel R. Harrell, seeking a friendly merger.

Percy Goodrich had become friends with Sam Harrell in the mid 1940s while on vacation in Fort Lauderdale, Florida.[39] At the time, Harrell was already chairman of the board of Acme-Evans, an Indianapolis milling company that owned several large city elevators. Percy and Harrell reached an amicable agreement for a merger. A fairly complex deal was struck. Harrell did not have the cash to buy out the Goodrich family stockholders. Therefore, in exchange for relinquishing its common stock in the twenty-four elevators, the Goodrich family received preferred shares in the company that was formed from the merger, Acme-Goodrich. Harrell was named president and Percy Goodrich was elected chairman of the board. Another five grain elevators already owned by Acme-Evans were added to the twenty-four owned by the Goodrich family, so, after the merger, Acme-Goodrich controlled twenty-nine grain elevators. The deal at the time (December 12, 1947) was valued at $1.8 million. Pierre and his law partner Claude Warren did the legal work for the Goodrich side of the merger.[40]

39. See Percy E. Goodrich, "Sam Harrell," *Down in Indiana* 78 (August 27, 1949), Indiana Historical Society Library, Indianapolis, Indiana.

40. Roger Budrow, "S. R. Harrell Group Buys Goodrich Grain Firm," *Indianapolis News,* December 12, 1947, p. 1, col. 1; p. 17, col. 8; "The 90th Anniversary of the Goodrich

Acme-Goodrich eventually operated some thirty-seven grain elevators in Indiana, and Percy Goodrich remained chairman of the board until his death in 1951. On January 23, 1950, a special luncheon was held at the Columbia Club in Indianapolis in recognition of ninety years of operation of the Goodrich family grain company (1860–1950). Indiana's governor, Henry F. Schricker, was the guest speaker at the luncheon.[41] Unfortunately for the Goodrich family, the occasion was one of the last things to celebrate about the grain company. Troubled times lay ahead for Acme-Goodrich.[42]

It is a fact of United States westward expansion that whenever a community was established, three buildings would almost invariably appear first: a church, a tavern, and a bank. Almost every small town had its own locally operated lending institution. James Goodrich capitalized on small-town banking, making it the linchpin of all his other highly successful business operations. In addition to Peoples Loan and Trust Company, the Goodriches owned substantial interests in nearly a dozen other small-town Indiana banks at one time or another.[43]

When James Goodrich died in August 1940, Pierre became president of Peoples and remained chief executive until his death. After Pierre passed away, he was succeeded by his cousin, Perce G. Goodrich. In 1984, Pierre's widow, Enid, sold her controlling interest in the bank. At that time, the assets of the bank totaled more than $50

Brothers' Company"; Donald F. Elliott, telephone interview, April 15, 1993. Elliott knows the history of the Goodrich-Harrell merger, having been one of the lead attorneys for the Goodrich stockholders in the litigation battle between Pierre Goodrich and Samuel Harrell in the mid 1960s.

41. See "Goodrich Brothers' Company," County Elevators, Shippers, and Feed-dealers' Luncheon, January 23, 1950.

42. Donald F. Elliott, telephone interview, April 15, 1993.

43. Perce G. Goodrich, interview, May 2, 1993; Rodney Medler, interview, June 9, 1993. These included banks in Tipton, Modoc, Redkey, Ridgeville, La Crosse, Eaton, Saratoga, Farmland, and Lynn. James and Pierre also owned interests in the National City Bank (which James became president of in the early 1920s) and the Continental National Bank in Indianapolis.

million.[44] Begun at the turn of the century, the Peoples Loan and Trust Company was the start of much of the Goodrich family's success. It provided not only necessary capital, but also many of the personal contacts that resulted in investments in the other family business holdings.

The smaller companies that Pierre Goodrich controlled or on whose boards of directors he served numbered in the dozens. In addition to those already mentioned, they included the Continental National Bank of Indianapolis; the Union Insurance Company; Equitable Securities Company of Indianapolis; Muncie Theatre Realty Corporation (which owned and operated eight movie theaters in the Muncie, Indiana, area); Indiana Produce (a commodities company based in Huntingburg, Indiana); PLatCo Realty Corporation (which owned and leased real estate, primarily bank property); the Peoples Investment Company of Winchester; the Calumet Refining Company; the Bankers Trust Company in Gary, Indiana; Gary First National Corporation; Equitable Securities Company; Cumberland Quarries; Indianapolis Broadcasting; High Vacuum Processes; the Kingston Oil Company; Indianapolis Railways; and the Railroad Service and Supply Company in Indianapolis. In the 1920s and 1930s, Goodrich was also involved in companies that his father and uncles had invested in, including the Wasmuth-Goodrich Company and the Indianapolis Transit Company. The latter operated interurban trains in central Indiana and later ran streetcars and buses in Indianapolis. At one time, Pierre even owned a small railroad called the Algers, Winslow and Western Railway Company. The railroad operated along a twenty-two mile stretch of track in southern Indiana and hauled coal from the Ayrshire and Patoka coalfields to the main rail lines. Thus, by the 1940s, the Goodrich financial empire was in place. But there was one more large corporation that would play an extremely important role in Pierre Goodrich's future plans.

44. For a brief history of the bank, see "Peoples Loan and Trust Company Sold: Bank Will Remain in Local Hands," *Winchester (Ind.) News-Gazette,* February 15, 1984, p. 1, col. 6; and "General Operation Will Continue as in the Past," *Winchester (Ind.) News-Gazette,* February 15, 1984, p. 1, col. 2.

Chapter 18
Ayrshire Collieries Corporation

> Responsibilities of management in a country, the expressed policy of which is to maintain a free competitive economy, are weighty. We must constantly endeavor to produce coal at low prices to assure continuity of sales and to protect our markets from competitive sources of energy. . . . It is paramount that the coal industry adopt a progressive and enlightened policy in respect to wages and hours, safety, working conditions and other related problems. Finally, we must strive to obtain a fair return to our stockholders and thus make it possible to obtain capital for future needs of the industry.
>
> ROBERT P. KOENIG, foreword to "The Ayrshire Story"

IN 1923, James Goodrich obtained a large interest in a small coal company named Patoka Coal in southwestern Indiana. Within twenty-five years, Pierre Goodrich went on to become chairman of the board of a company that merged with Patoka Coal, the Ayrshire Collieries Corporation. It became the Goodrich family's largest business holding. Interestingly, two other extremely important entities spun off from the coal company: first, Meadowlark Farms, a subsidiary company dealing with land reclamation and ecology; and, second, Liberty Fund, Inc., whose primary endowment devolved from the personal proceeds Pierre Goodrich realized when he sold Ayrshire in 1969 (see chapter 29).

The coal mines that made up the Ayrshire Collieries Corporation are located in Illinois, southwestern Indiana, Kentucky, and Wyoming. They are now owned by the Cyprus-Amax Minerals Company, a large conglomerate. Pierre's association with Ayrshire went all the way back to his father's business dealings immediately after James Goodrich had served as governor.

James Goodrich became treasurer of the Patoka Coal Company in 1923 through association with Jesse Moorman of Winchester, Indiana, then president of Patoka Coal.[1] Moorman and James Goodrich were longtime friends and business partners. (In 1912, for instance, James Goodrich had assisted Moorman in obtaining the contract for citywide garbage disposal in Indianapolis.)[2] At the time, Patoka Coal was a small colliery that operated from a single strip mine in Pike County, Indiana.[3] James Goodrich had gained considerable knowledge about the coal industry from attempting to manage a coal crisis during his time as governor.[4]

Pierre Goodrich became secretary and treasurer of Patoka Coal in 1929. In 1937, he was appointed executive vice-president. After this time, another coal company, the Electric Shovel Coal Corporation, had gone

1. The first annual report of the Patoka Coal Company, filed with the secretary of state on October 1, 1920, showed an Indianapolis address and listed only two officers, one being J. T. Moorman of Winchester. James Goodrich had apparently become associated with the Patoka Coal Company through a friendship and business affiliation with Moorman. Moorman, like James Goodrich, was one of Winchester's wealthiest citizens. James Goodrich continued as secretary and treasurer until 1929 and as a director until his death in 1940. From 1937 to 1940, James Goodrich was president of Patoka Coal. See William H. Andrews, "Ayrshire Collieries Corporation—Profit with Ecology" (research paper, Indiana University, n.d.), pp. 5–6. Andrews based most of his paper on an interview with Albert Campbell in the late 1970s or early 1980s.

2. Rodney Medler, interview, April 28, 1993. See also "Moorman Forms Company," *Winchester (Ind.) Democrat,* January 11, 1912, p. 1, col. 2. (The article refers to Moorman's obtaining the garbage collection contract. With capitalization of $200,000, Moorman also formed a reduction company to turn the garbage into fertilizer and tankage.) Marie Moorman, Jesse's daughter, accompanied James and Cora Goodrich as a companion to Mrs. Goodrich on the Goodriches' ARA trip to the Soviet Union in 1922.

3. Patoka Coal was located near Winslow. It had been organized in 1918 to take over a partly equipped mine that had belonged to the Globe Coal Mining Company. See "Early History of Ayrshire," in "Handbook" (Ayshire Coal Company), pt. 1, p. 4 (in Cyprus-AMAX Coal Archives).

4. James P. Goodrich, *Autobiography,* pp. 131–33.

into receivership. At the public hearing in Chicago, Pierre Goodrich had become acquainted with Electric Shovel's top management: Tommy Hitchcock, Jr., Robert P. Koenig, and James Melville. Subsequently, Patoka Coal Company transferred its operating properties to Patoka Coal Company of Delaware, which was then merged with Electric Shovel Coal Corporation in 1939. The original name of the resulting company was Ayrshire Patoka Collieries Corporation, later to become simply Ayrshire Collieries Corporation. The consolidated company had eight directors. Pierre and his law partner at the time, Albert M. Campbell, represented Patoka Coal's interests on the board. Even after the merger, Patoka Coal continued to exist as a separate legal entity, as a holding company for stock in the Ayrshire Patoka Collieries Corporation.[5]

On the board of directors, Goodrich was outnumbered by the five Ayrshire directors, based in New York, who held all the major offices of the company.[6] Over the next seven years, however, Goodrich managed to increase his family's interest in the consolidated company so that by 1946 he was elected chairman of the board of directors. How did he do it? Apparently, the major cause was beyond Goodrich's control—the onset of World War II. In the early 1940s, Hitchcock and Koenig were

5. Andrews, "Ayrshire Collieries Corporation—Profit with Ecology," pp. 6–7. Beyond Andrews's paper on Ayrshire, several histories of the Ayrshire Coal Company have been written, including Clayton G. Ball, "The Ayrshire Story," *Mechanization,* March 1947, pp. 57–66; "Early History of Ayrshire," pt. 1 (in Cyprus-AMAX Coal Company Archives); and "The Ayrshire Story," *Mechanization,* July 1959. See also "Amax Today: How It Came to Be," *Engineering and Mining Journal,* September 1972, and letter from Pierre F. Goodrich to E. Victor Willetts, Jr., December 27, 1972 (in the possession of Liberty Fund, Inc.).

6. The five New York board members were Thomas Hitchcock, chairman of the board; Robert P. Koenig, president; William P. McCool, a New York lawyer, secretary; Howard E. Lowman, treasurer and assistant secretary; and Charles Greeff, a Wall Street stockbroker. See Andrews, "Ayrshire Collieries Corporation—Profit with Ecology," p. 10. According to Pierre Goodrich's longtime administrative assistant, Helen (Schultz) Fletcher, Goodrich had spent considerable time with Greeff and his wife Adele in the 1930s at their home on Long Island, New York. In fact, Greeff had counseled Goodrich on many of Pierre's successful investments during this time. Letter from Helen Fletcher to author, June 18, 1996.

chairman of the board and president of Ayrshire, respectively. Hitchcock was also a partner in Lehman Brothers, an investment company in New York. He had married Margaret Mellon of the extremely wealthy Pittsburgh banking family. Koenig, a brilliant corporate strategist, was a mining engineer by training and had served as president of the Electric Shovel Coal Corporation before it merged with Ayrshire and Patoka. Both Hitchcock and Koenig served in World War II, leaving Ayrshire.[7]

In addition to being a successful banker, Hitchcock may well have been the greatest polo player that the United States has ever produced. In April 1944, Hitchcock was killed in England while flying a training mission, ending what the *New York Times* called "one of the most gallant and one of the most spectacular careers in modern American life."[8] His death left his widow, Margaret, with large estate taxes. She decided to sell Hitchcock's shares to help pay off the death taxes, and Goodrich bought a large percentage of the available stock.[9]

Koenig, who had been gone from Ayrshire for nearly three and a half years while serving in Europe, did not return to his position until

7. In addition to being president of Ayrshire, Koenig was president of Fairview Collieries Corporation and Delta Collieries Corporation at the time he left in April 1942 to serve in Europe. Koenig returned from World War II, resumed his former positions, and later became Meadowlark Farms' first president. Both Delta Collieries and Meadowlark Farms were subsidiaries of Ayrshire Collieries. See Ball, "The Ayrshire Story," *Mechanization,* March 1947, p. 63.

8. "Hitchcock Killed in Crash in Britain," *New York Times,* April 20, 1944, p. 1, col. 3. According to the obituary, in addition to being a successful banker, Hitchcock, an alumnus of Harvard and Oxford universities, was a colorful military hero (a flyer in both wars).

9. Richard H. Swallow, telephone interview, December 20, 1992. Swallow was chief engineer of Ayrshire (he later became vice-president and chief engineer) at the time Goodrich bought the additional stock from Mrs. Hitchcock and was able to replace the board with his own people. He claimed intimate knowledge of the details. In fact, he stated that he and a group of Ayrshire management personnel had discussed trying to buy the shares themselves in order to take control of the company. According to William Nordhorn, a longtime Ayrshire employee, Goodrich had, in fact, encouraged five or six other investors to purchase some of Hitchcock's shares. William Nordhorn, telephone interview, January 16, 1993.

October 1945.[10] During that time, Goodrich had purchased enough stock so that by 1946 he had a controlling interest in the company. He subsequently replaced a sufficient number of directors to be elected chairman.[11] By 1949, only two New York directors remained on the Ayrshire board, neither of whom was an original member.[12]

During the years of Goodrich's management, Ayrshire's growth, both in terms of coal production and in terms of sales, increased at an impressive rate. In 1940, Ayrshire's sales had been $2.27 million; by 1968, the company's sales had climbed to almost $60 million, some twenty-six times 1940 sales. Also, by 1968, income had increased to a lofty $5.45 per share from just 15¢ per share in 1940. Moreover, the number of Ayrshire employees had grown from 484 in 1940 to 1,064 in 1968. This increase had occurred in spite of advanced technology that had eliminated hundreds of positions.[13]

By the time Goodrich sought to sell Ayrshire in 1968, the company was the eleventh-largest producer of bituminous coal in the country. Ayrshire had some of its strongest years just before Goodrich sought a merger with potential purchasers. At the age of seventy-four, however, Goodrich recognized that his own mortality would not allow him and the company's other aging managers (Ayrshire's president, Norman

10. See Ball, "The Ayrshire Story," p. 63.

11. Robert Koenig, who had been president of Ayrshire, went on leave from 1942 to 1945 and served on the staff of General Dwight D. Eisenhower in Europe. During that time, Goodrich placed his law partner Albert Campbell in the position of executive vice-president of Ayrshire. After Koenig returned in 1945, he remained with Ayrshire for only five years. According to Richard Swallow, Koenig eventually left because he was disappointed that Goodrich did not want to make the changes necessary to make Ayrshire grow even faster than it did. Koenig moved in 1950 to the presidency of the Cerro de Pasco Copper Corporation, later the Cerro Corporation. There, he had a successful career as an industrialist and financier. Richard H. Swallow, telephone interview, December 20, 1992. See also Charles J. Endicott, *Historical Information and Data: Ayrshire Coal Corporation, Now Amax Coal Company, Division of Amax Inc.*, p. 5; Andrews, "The Ayrshire Collieries Corporation," p. 32.

12. Ayrshire "Handbook," pt. 2, p. 1 (directory of personnel, March 1, 1949).

13. See Andrews, "The Ayrshire Collieries Corporation," p. 11, table 2.

Kelb, was seventy-five years old) to continue Ayrshire's growth without the infusion of new management and additional capital.

Goodrich was forced to either bring in younger management or sell Ayrshire outright. In the company's *1968 Annual Report,* Goodrich reported that Lovett C. Peters had been hired "as agent of the company, looking toward the sale of the company's assets or merger into another company."[14] Pierre had first become acquainted with Peters in 1955 when they both served on the board of the Foundation for Economic Education in Irvington-on-Hudson, New York. In 1968, Peters had left top-level management at the Continental Oil Company, and Goodrich offered him the position of president at Ayrshire. Although Peters turned down the position, he did suggest to Goodrich that an added incentive made the timing right for the sale of Ayrshire.[15]

Peters and others in the oil and coal industries had successfully lobbied Congress to adopt legislation that had the net effect of increasing the worth of oil and coal companies by as much as 50 percent. The legislation, known as Reserve Production Payment, allowed a purchasing company to borrow money on the basis of the value of the reserves of an oil or coal company and then pay off the loan with pretax, instead of aftertax, dollars.[16]

Goodrich took Peters's advice and invited five companies to discuss the possibility of a sale or merger.[17] The two leading contenders were the Ashland Oil and Refining Company of Ashland, Kentucky, and

14. Ibid., pp. 23–24 and note 17. Peters had previously been executive vice-president of the Cabot Corporation, a large Boston concern in chemicals, oil, and gas, and before that financial vice-president and treasurer of Continental Oil Company. Peters is now president of the Pioneer Institute for Public Policy in Boston, Massachusetts.

15. Lovett C. Peters, telephone interview, June 25, 1994.

16. Ibid.

17. According to William Stimart, who was a personal assistant to Ayrshire president Norman Kelb and intimately involved in the negotiations for the sale of Ayrshire, the five companies invited to bid for Ayrshire were Ashland Oil and Refining Company of Ashland, Kentucky; American Metal Climax (AMAX) of Greenwich, Connecticut; Kerr-McGee of Oklahoma City, Oklahoma; Sun Oil of Philadelphia, Pennsylvania, and Dallas, Texas; and FMC of Chicago (telephone interview, January 21, 1993).

American Metal Climax (AMAX) of Greenwich, Connecticut. A deal was struck between Ashland and Ayrshire in January 1969. At that time, Goodrich and the president of Ashland made a joint announcement that both boards of directors had approved the purchase of Ayrshire. In a complex financial arrangement, Ayrshire stockholders were to receive approximately $125 million.[18]

The deal between Ayrshire and Ashland fell through in early April 1969, however, because of an escape clause in the agreement of which Ashland was able to take advantage.[19] The winter of 1968 had been particularly harsh in the Midwest. The amount of coal that was mined was subsequently reduced, and Ayrshire's profits plummeted. This prompted Ashland's management to exercise its escape clause.[20] Kerr-McGee, an oil exploration company out of Oklahoma, tried to take over Ayrshire by offering less than half what Ashland did. Goodrich became extremely upset with Kerr-McGee's proposed takeover plan and immediately contacted AMAX to arrange a sale.[21]

18. The *Wall Street Journal* quoted from a joint announcement between Goodrich and the president of the Ashland Oil Company to the effect that both boards of directors had approved the purchase of Ayrshire by Ashland. See "Ashland Oil Plans to Buy or Lease Ayrshire Assets," *Wall Street Journal,* January 22, 1969, p. 34, col. 1. The deal with Ashland was apparently as complete as possible. Peter M. Garson, who later became president of Amax Coal Sales but who at the time worked for Ayrshire's subsidiary, Republic Coal and Coke Company in Chicago, remembers that Ashland had purchased draglines and trucks from Ayrshire in anticipation that the deal would be completed. Moreover, the Ayrshire employees had a party to celebrate the company's new Ashland ownership (telephone interview, December 30, 1992). The announcement of the proposed sale in *Forbes* magazine made Goodrich extremely upset. See "Going, Going, . . . Gone," *Forbes,* February 15, 1969, p. 55, col. 1.

19. According to William Stimart, Ashland placed several escape clauses in the original agreement between Ayrshire and Ashland. Stimart said that Ashland was known in the industry to do this in other merger situations in order to escape from bad deals (telephone interview, January 21, 1993).

20. Ibid.

21. William Stimart said that Ayrshire's stock got as high as $135 per share when it began to search for a buyer and that Ashland and Ayrshire had agreed on $125 a share in reaching terms on January 22, 1969. When the deal between Ayrshire and Ashland fell through on April 3, however, Kerr-McGee attempted to take Ayrshire over by offering only approximately $50 a share (telephone interview, January 21, 1993).

In less than three weeks from the time that the Ayrshire-Ashland deal fell through, Goodrich had reached a tentative agreement with American Metal Climax, subject to approval by the directors and stockholders of both companies.[22] This agreement culminated with the sale of Ayrshire to American Metal Climax in October 1969. At the time, American Metal Climax owned no coal mines. Although it was a large minerals conglomerate, its primary business operations involved mining molybdenum, lead, and copper in the upper Midwest.[23]

Goodrich and his family were by far the largest owners of Ayrshire, controlling 334,000 of the total 790,891 shares in the company, or about 44 percent. The second-largest owner of Ayrshire stock was Henry Crown of Chicago, who held a 17.7 percent interest. Crown was also the major stockholder in General Dynamics, one of the largest military defense companies in the world. For some reason, Goodrich would not talk to Crown. As a result, Lovett Peters had to serve as the negotiator between the two men, shuttling back and forth between Indianapolis and Chicago in an attempt to strike a deal that was acceptable to both

22. According to William Stimart and Peter M. Garson, the deal between Ayrshire and Ashland fell through because of tax uncertainty about the way Ashland proposed to finance the merger. Also, in the first quarter of 1969, Ayrshire showed a loss for the first time in its history (William Stimart, telephone interview, January 21, 1993; Peter M. Garson, telephone interview, December 30, 1992). William H. Andrews's assessment is essentially the same. See also Andrews, "The Ayrshire Collieries Corporation," p. 26. For an announcement of the deal, see "Ayrshire Has Merger Offer," *Indianapolis News,* April 24, 1969, p. 43, col. 6. AMAX subsequently merged with Cyprus Minerals on November 15, 1993, and the surviving corporation became known as Cyprus-Amax Minerals Company.

23. Final stockholder approval for the merger between Ayrshire and American Metal Climax came on October 31, 1969. In addition to the Ayrshire Coal Company, the sale included two subsidiaries: Republic Carbon Products, a marketing company; and Dayton Fly Ash, an Ohio-based firm that collected and sold fly ash to the cement industry. See "Amax Today: How It Came to Be," *Engineering and Mining Journal,* September 1972. On July 18, 1969, the *Indianapolis Star* initially reported that the deal between Ayrshire and AMAX was to have a value of approximately $63 million, less than 60 percent of the original Ashland offer ("Ayrshire, AMAX Boards Approve Merger Terms," p. 32, col. 1). Only two months later, however, the *Wall Street Journal* estimated the deal to be worth more than $100 million ("Ayrshire Metal Climax and Ayrshire Collieries Tie Backed by Holders," September 22, 1969, p. 14, col. 2).

men. Finally, in October 1969, Crown was satisfied that Goodrich had obtained what was believed at the time to be top dollar for the coal company.[24] The sale of Ayrshire was reported in the *Wall Street Journal* to be valued in excess of $100 million.[25] The actual amount of Goodrich's personal interest in the sale is purported to have been between $25 and $30 million.[26] Lovett Peters received a handsome fee for negotiating the deal, purportedly $750,000.[27]

Much of the constant profitability of Ayrshire under Goodrich's control can be attributed to his ability to capitalize on emerging markets and to hire extremely capable personnel. When it came to selling Ayrshire, however, Goodrich and Peters may well have underestimated the company's true worth because of their inability to foresee the future desirability of low-sulfur coal, the growing political hostility toward nuclear generated power, and the Arab oil embargo of 1973.

During Pierre Goodrich's forty years of association with the coal industry, a dramatic shift had occurred in markets. When James and Pierre first began with Patoka Coal in the 1920s, the demand for coal came primarily from railroads and domestic consumers. By the 1960s, most of Ayrshire's sales were to electric utility companies and industrial customers. Ayrshire weathered the transitional period of the 1950s extremely well, whereas other coal companies underwent considerable retrenchment in both production and employment. Ayrshire accom-

24. Lovett C. Peters, telephone interview, June 25, 1994. Peters explained that there were approximately three hundred stockholders of Ayrshire stock. The stock was sold openly on the American Stock Exchange.

25. "American Metal Climax and Ayrshire Collieries Tie Backed by Holders," *Wall Street Journal,* September 22, 1969, p. 14, col. 2. See also "Stockholders OK Ayrshire, Amax Merger," *Indianapolis Star,* September 20, 1969, p. 30, col. 7; "Amax-Ayrshire Merger Completed," *Black Diamond* (coal publication), November 1969, p. 6, col. 1.

26. Andrews, "The Ayrshire Collieries Corporation," p. 28; see also Byron K. Trippet, "Pierre F. Goodrich," *Wabash on My Mind,* pp. 182–83 (Trippet wrote that Goodrich's personal gain from the sale was in the range of $40 million).

27. Andrews, "The Ayrshire Collieries Corporation," p. 27. According to Andrews, Peters received $250,000 from Ayrshire and an additional $500,000 payable by AMAX subject to the completion of the merger for a total of $750,000.

plished this through the efforts of its sales subsidiary, Republic Coal and Coke Company. Goodrich had purchased the Chicago-based coal sales company in 1944. Republic Coal and Coke Company achieved growth for Ayrshire primarily by developing long-term contracts with utility companies.[28]

According to Richard H. Swallow, who worked for Ayrshire and its predecessors for thirty-seven years, Goodrich's most important decision was to have Ayrshire obtain as many options for coal reserves as possible.[29] Goodrich had as many as nine drill crews exploring potential coal reserves throughout a large portion of the country, including Tennessee, Pennsylvania, Kentucky, Alabama, and Wyoming. Through aggressive leasing practices, Ayrshire's coal reserves had increased from 52 million tons in 1940 to 2.35 billion tons in 1968. At its peak, Ayrshire owned outright more than 165,000 acres, 50,000 of them in Wyoming alone.[30]

Therefore, when Ayrshire was purchased in 1969, the real benefit that

28. Ibid., p. 23. Andrews also attributes Ayrshire's ability to succeed during the difficulties of the 1950s to the increase in industrial and electrical power production in the Midwest and the technological progress of strip mining, which increased productivity at the same time that it was able to cut costs. Goodrich himself makes essentially these same observations in a letter to Dr. Solomon Fabricant, Department of Economics, New York University, January 3, 1972, Pierre F. Goodrich Collection, Archives, Wabash College, Crawfordsville, Indiana.

29. Richard H. Swallow, telephone interview, December 20, 1992. Swallow was vice-president and chief engineer when he retired in 1965. Swallow said that after Robert Koenig returned to Ayrshire from World War II, he wanted Ayrshire to be more aggressive in terms of seeking growth opportunities than Goodrich did. Swallow said that Koenig convinced Goodrich of the importance of expanding coal reserve options and that Goodrich was willing to spend a large amount in research and development to accomplish this end (hiring numerous geologists, land agents, attorneys, and so forth). Goodrich refused, however, to take the steps necessary to make Ayrshire expand faster, which frustrated Koenig, prompting him to leave in 1950. Much of what Swallow remembers is substantiated by Joseph Andrews's paper on Ayrshire. Andrews also reported that as much as $85 million of the $125 million that Ashland Oil offered Ayrshire in January 1969 was in exchange for coal-reserve leases that Ayrshire owned. See also Andrews, "The Ayrshire Collieries Corporation," p. 25.

30. Irwin H. Reiss, interview, January 11, 1994.

the Indiana-based company offered was the ownership of huge coal reserves. It was estimated that Ayrshire (or its successor) had enough reserves to sustain production rates at its 1969 levels for two hundred years.[31] With AMAX aggressively pumping in millions of dollars in new capital investment into the former Ayrshire holdings, Ayrshire was able to increase production and market share dramatically. AMAX became the third-largest coal company in the United States by 1975 (Ayrshire was the eleventh-largest when Goodrich sold Ayrshire in 1969).

Goodrich and his advisers may have miscalculated in selling Ayrshire by underestimating the worth of the coal-lease reserves Ayrshire had obtained in the Gillette, Wyoming, area (later the Belle Ayr mine). Before the sale to AMAX, Ayrshire put a very low value on these reserves of low-sulfur coal, but they alone are probably worth in excess of $1 billion.[32] Coal output from the Belle Ayr mine went from 900,000 tons in 1973 to well over 7 million tons by 1976. By the early 1980s, the combined capacity of the Belle Ayr and Eagle Butte mines (Eagle Butte is north of Belle Ayr in Wyoming) exceeded 30 million tons annually.[33]

In addition to the size of the Wyoming mines was an additional attraction—they contained low-sulfur coal. Although burning low-sulfur coal produces less energy than does high-sulfur coal, it also produces less air pollution. With the added attention that acid rain and other pollution problems received in the 1970s and 1980s, low-sulfur coal became increasingly more valuable. Therefore, the worth of the Wyoming mines substantially increased.

"There was a lot of doubt whether the western mines were going to amount to much," said George Martin, retired manager of Ayrshire's Sun Spot Mine in Illinois. "But these mines became a major factor and carried AMAX coal economically through the late seventies and early eighties."[34]

31. See "Going, Going, . . . Gone," *Forbes*, February 15, 1969, p. 55, col. 1.

32. William Stimart, telephone interview, January 21, 1993.

33. See "Welcome to the Mother Lode of Western Energy" (brochure published by AMAX Coal), located at the Indianapolis–Marion County Public Library, Business and Technology Department, Indiana Businesses File, AMAX Company.

34. George Martin, telephone interview, April 27, 1993.

The reasons Goodrich was not more aggressive in the 1950s and 1960s in having Ayrshire exploit its vast coal reserves appear to be twofold: first, to have exercised the coal-field options would have required a considerable infusion of capital. Goodrich was not interested in having the company go into any further debt in order to achieve this large and immediate expansion. At the time of the merger in October 1969, American Metal Climax assumed $40 million of Ayrshire debt as part of the $100 million transaction.[35]

Goodrich also purportedly thought that atomic energy was eventually going to put the coal industry out of business. Thus, Goodrich's overestimation of the technical capability and political acceptance of nuclear energy may have prompted him to believe that he had received top dollar for Ayrshire's holdings.[36] Apparently, Goodrich even believed that the use of nuclear "fusion" (as opposed to nuclear "fission") might be-

35. Richard H. Swallow, telephone interview, December 20, 1992. When the deal between Ayrshire and Ashland was struck in January 1969, an article in *Coal Age* reported that with the proceeds from the $125 million sale Ayrshire was going to liquidate approximately $20 million in debt. See *Coal Age* 75 (February 1969), p. 28. It is believed, however, that a more accurate debt figure is $40 million, as reported in the *Wall Street Journal*. See "American Metal Climax and Ayrshire Collieries Tie Backed by Holders," *Wall Street Journal*, September 22, 1969, p. 14, col. 2.

36. Richard Swallow provided this information and assessment; namely, that Goodrich believed that nuclear energy was going to become much more widely accepted and that the days of burning coal as a primary energy source were numbered. Richard Swallow, telephone interview, December 20, 1992. William Stimart refuted that assessment. He said that Goodrich did not believe that. Stimart said that he was intimately involved in the negotiations, and he would have had better knowledge than Swallow, who had retired four years earlier (in 1965), regarding what Goodrich thought. William Stimart, telephone interview, January 21, 1993. Swallow said, however, that he had had conversations with Goodrich later that led him to believe that Goodrich thought that the coal industry would eventually be harmed by the ready availability of nuclear energy. Apparently, others also thought nuclear energy was a threat to the coal industry. See Brice O'Brien, "Coal Industry: Atomic Power," *Vital Speeches* 35 (April 1, 1969): 379–84. While nuclear power is not popular in the United States, its use has increased tremendously worldwide. Today, nuclear power generates more electricity than the world used from all sources of power in 1958. It is estimated that nuclear energy provides 17 percent of the world's electricity. See "Earth Diary," *The Rotarian*, December 1996, p. 14, col. 3.

come feasible in the near future, so that there would be an overabundance of cheap energy.[37]

Goodrich's concern about the widespread use of atomic energy was not unique. Many in the coal industry had been led to believe that atomic energy might produce up to 50 percent of the electric-utility market by the end of the twentieth century.[38] Finally, Goodrich and Peters could not have foreseen the 1973 Arab oil crisis and how that would increase the value of energy companies, especially domestic ones.

Goodrich was extremely pleased when a Chicago financial analyst told him, unaware of his Ayrshire connections, that he (the analyst) believed that American Metal Climax (AMAX) had paid too much for Ayrshire in 1969.[39] With the benefit of more than twenty-five

37. Swallow said that after he retired in 1965 from Ayrshire, Goodrich wrote to him and asked him how soon he (Swallow) thought it would be until nuclear fusion became a reality. Swallow wrote Goodrich and said that he had no idea, but he enclosed an article about fusion from one of the energy magazines he had subscribed to (telephone interview, December 20, 1992).

38. See Brice O'Brien, "Coal Industry: Atomic Power," pp. 379–84. O'Brien was general counsel of the National Coal Association when he delivered this speech to the San Diego chapter of the American Nuclear Society. O'Brien mentions several times in his address the "oversell" and "propaganda" of atomic energy that has "scared our people to death." It is interesting that only once in a speech of approximately eight thousand words did O'Brien mention the safety concerns that have subsequently plagued the nuclear energy industry. He believed that coal had a much brighter future than most energy experts forecast. That was true, O'Brien asserted, not because of the political and safety problems that atomic energy would subsequently experience, but because experts concluded that there would not be enough uranium to fuel the large nuclear power plants. O'Brien's speech says much about man's ability to forecast the future accurately.

39. Fred Young, interview, September 30, 1992. Young said that Goodrich had visited Harris Bank shortly after selling the Ayrshire Coal Company to American Metal Climax. According to Young, "Pierre Goodrich asked Fred Wightman (a financial analyst working for Harris Bank at the time), 'What do you think of American Metal Climax?' Wightman responded, 'Well, we have a lot of that stock here in the bank and we think a lot of it. But we think they paid too high a price for the coal mines, Ayrshire Collieries.'" Goodrich smiled and was obviously very pleased with what he had heard, said Young.

years of hindsight, it is clear that AMAX received the better end of the deal.[40]

40. William Stimart admits that AMAX probably got the better of the deal, although he believed that that was solely because of Ayrshire's undervaluation of the worth of the Belle Ayr mine in Gillette, Wyoming. It was not, according to Stimart, because Goodrich believed that the coal industry's days were numbered because of the increasing use of nuclear energy (telephone interview, January 21, 1993). It seems to the author that another reason that AMAX may have been able to make a good purchase was that Goodrich was in a hurry to make a deal to keep Kerr-McGee of Oklahoma from achieving a hostile takeover.

Chapter 19
The Ecologist

To waste, to destroy, our natural resources, to skin and exhaust the land instead of using it so as to increase its usefulness, will result in undermining in the days of our children the very prosperity which we ought by right to hand down to them amplified and developed.

PRESIDENT THEODORE ROOSEVELT, Message to Congress, December 3, 1907

. . . What we need is a good biography of Pierre Goodrich, the pioneer, that can be made required reading in all high school and college courses on ecology.

JOHN CHAMBERLAIN, "Strip Mining: Can It Unlock Fertile Land?"

DURING the first twenty years of the twentieth century, many Americans began to be aware of ecology. President Theodore Roosevelt was one of the first national leaders to take an interest in preserving much of America's most scenic and pristine lands. Local chapters of such conservation organizations as the Sierra Club were also being established across the country, furthering environmental awareness. At the state level, in 1917, James P. Goodrich had been instrumental in creating the Indiana Department of Conservation, which greatly expanded the fledgling Indiana state parks system. At the federal level, in 1930, the former governor served on the Public Lands Commission, which examined land reclamation, wildlife reserves, and other environmental issues. Generally, ecological and wildlife practices became popular and were used as themes in books and movies. One of the best-known naturalist authors in the country was Indiana's own Geneva "Gene" Stratton-Porter, from nearby Geneva, Indiana. During the early part of the century, Stratton-Porter's books, such as *Freckles* (1904), *A Girl of the Limberlost* (1909), *The Harvester* (1911), and *A Daughter of the Land* (1918) were very well received. At the height of Stratton-Porter's popularity, publishers estimated that she had a following of fifty million readers, making her one of the five most popular American authors of the 1920s. Several of her books were made into popular movies. Pierre Goodrich was related to Stratton-Porter through his first wife, Dorothy Dugan.[1]

As previously noted, Pierre's values regarding personal, business, and public conservation can be at least partially attributed to his upbringing. His mother went to extremes to economize. Moreover, James Goodrich was ever watchful as well, constantly questioning how business and government could be conducted more efficiently. For example, in early 1920, while James Goodrich was still governor, he traveled to New York by railcar. When he disembarked at one large train depot, he noticed that railroad workers were extracting used wool packing from casings that covered the old passenger and freight-car axles. James observed that the men were simply throwing the used wool away. He realized that there was a market for recycling the wool. In June 1920, James Goodrich had two employees of the Goodrich Brothers Hay and Grain Company, Claude Barnes and Merl Chenoweth, form the Railway Service and Supply Corporation. Goodrich money was used to finance the new company, which became quite profitable. This episode demonstrates James Goodrich's shrewd business eye.[2]

Pierre hated waste of any kind and thought that it was one of man's

1. See Barbara Olenyik Morrow, *From "Ben-Hur" to "Sister Carrie": Remembering the Lives and Works of Five Indiana Authors* (Indianapolis: Guild Press of Indiana, 1995), p. 96. Stratton-Porter was married to Charles D. Porter, pharmacist, banker, and great-uncle to Dorothy Dugan.

2. Perce G. Goodrich, interview, November 9, 1991. See also "Railway Service Corporation," Dissolved Corporations, State Archives, Indiana Commission on Public Records, AR-1988. On November 19, 1921, a petition to change the name of the company to the Railway Service and Supply Corporation was filed and granted. On February 14, 1922, Edward Goodrich was elected chairman. The company had capital stock of $500,000 as of March 13, 1922.

greatest sins.[3] As a businessman, he took extraordinary measures to preserve his family's assets, increasing the worth of existing capital through steady, often innovative practices. Pierre Goodrich was not prone to go after quick profits, especially if extravagant expenditures or exploitation of natural resources was involved. He took a tight-fisted approach to investment and relished squeezing more out of less. It was that philosophy that made him, in every sense, a true ecologist.[4]

Goodrich detested public waste. During World War I, he had served in the Quartermaster Corps, that branch of the army concerned with furnishing war supplies. He often related to employees and friends the story of how the government took over the railroads for the purpose of shipping supplies. The custom at the time was to "featherbed," a union practice that demanded extra workers by contract in order to provide more jobs and prevent unemployment. Goodrich denounced the practice, especially during a period of national crisis.[5]

From a business perspective, the operations of the Ayrshire and Patoka collieries provided Pierre Goodrich with one of his greatest challenges: to practice savings and ecology simultaneously. At their height, the collieries owned or leased more than 165,000 acres of land in Kentucky, Illinois, southwestern Indiana, West Virginia, and Wyoming.[6] Strip mining had occurred both in the United States and abroad for hundreds

3. Roy Barnes, interview, February 8, 1992.

4. Pierre Goodrich's abhorrence of waste can be seen in the way he conducted his private life. Time, not money, was his most precious possession, and he safeguarded it prudently—to his way of thinking. He avoided most social or fraternal organizations because he believed them to be time-consuming and nonproductive. For the same reasons, he did not watch television. "I've always felt that there are a lot of things to do and learn about in life, and a person can waste a great deal of time on things that don't matter," Goodrich once told an interviewer. Thomas R. Keating, "He's Unknown—and Remarkable," *Indianapolis Star,* April 12, 1973, p. 21, col. 1.

5. Rosanna Amos, interview, December 12, 1991.

6. Goodrich wrote to the Wabash College president Paul W. Cook in December 1966 that Meadowlark Farms at the time held between 25,000 and 26,000 acres of land in various states of cultivation. Moreover, "there is in this land relationship to the coal

of years, and the mined lands often resembled moon craters. At the time, strip-mine operators took the view that there was little or no economic reason to reclaim land. The free market simply did not factor into the cost of mining coal any negative effect on the environment. Pierre Goodrich challenged this view, not only because of potential profits but also because of his belief in responsible land husbandry.[7]

A singular event occurred in the early 1940s that was a significant factor in Goodrich's deepening interest in conservation. In the summer of 1942, Richard Lieber, longtime chairman of the Indiana Commission on Conservation, found himself without a job or office. Lieber had previously resigned as chairman of the commission in 1933 after having served under three governors (James P. Goodrich, Warren T. McCray, and Edward L. Jackson). Lieber then served for the next nine years as a paid consultant to the National Park Service. He had an office in Washington, D.C., to which he would commute regularly from Indianapolis. When appropriations for the National Park Service were cut, Lieber had nothing to do.

At that time, in August 1942, Pierre provided Lieber an office, free of charge, in his legal suite on the seventh floor of the Electric Building in downtown Indianapolis. Lieber was very grateful for Goodrich's generosity. The two, despite a significant age difference, became exceptionally close friends. In December 1942, Lieber's book *America's Natural Wealth* was published by Harper and Brothers in New York. Lieber dedicated the book to James P. Goodrich, who had given him the opportunity to apply his love of nature to the preservation of Indiana's most pristine land. When Lieber died in April 1944, the normally reserved Pierre took

---

business, around 60,000 acres." Letter from Goodrich to Paul W. Cook, December 2, 1966, Pierre F. Goodrich Papers, Archives, Wabash College, Crawfordsville, Indiana. Irwin H. Reiss stated that at one time the Ayrshire Collieries Corporation owned as much as 165,000 acres outright. Reiss said that Goodrich never wanted to buy the land on a lease or royalty basis, but to own it outright (interview by William C. Dennis, February 11, 1994).

7. Chamberlain, "Strip Mining: Can It Unlock Fertile Land?" *Roanoke (Va.) Times,* July 31, 1974.

the conservationist's death extremely hard, telling Lieber's wife that he felt as though he had lost a second father.[8]

After Lieber's death but on his recommendation, Pierre Goodrich established in November 1945 a subsidiary corporation of the Ayrshire Collieries that he called Meadowlark Farms.[9] Earlier, Goodrich had contacted the College of Agriculture at the University of Illinois and met with Charles Stewart and Laurence Norton, both professors of agricultural economics. Goodrich explained to the two professors his desire to reclaim the mined coal lands owned by Ayrshire. Professor Stewart initially did not believe Goodrich. He thought that the coal executive was simply attempting to promote public relations in order to improve the bad image that strip-mine operators had because of the way they stripped coal fields. Ultimately, however, Goodrich was able to convince the two academics of his sincerity. Stewart and Norton ultimately put Goodrich in touch with Irwin H. Reiss. Reiss did not immediately take a position with Goodrich. He first served in Burma during World War II and then worked in an avocado business in southern California. In November 1948, Reiss finally returned to Indiana to manage Meadowlark Farms. Goodrich placed the subsidiary's headquarters in Sullivan, Indiana, which was in proximity to Ayrshire's coal fields in the southwestern part of the state.[10]

According to Reiss, who served as general manager and later as presi-

8. Emma Lieber, *Richard Lieber,* pp. 160–61; Roy Barnes, interview, February 8, 1992. See also William H. Andrews, "Ayrshire Collieries Corporation—Profit with Ecology" (research paper, Indiana University, n.d.), p. 17 and footnote 15. Andrews briefly describes the relationship between Pierre Goodrich and Lieber based on an interview with Goodrich's law partner Albert Campbell.

9. William H. Andrews, "The Ayrshire Collieries Corporation—Profit with Ecology," p. 17 and n. 15. Andrews obtained this information in an interview with Albert M. Campbell, who served as vice-president of the Ayrshire Coal Company and was Goodrich's law partner beginning in the 1930s. See also *Strip Mine Farming* (Sullivan, Ind.: Meadowlark Farms, 1952).

10. Irwin H. Reiss, interview, June 29, 1996. Another reason that Sullivan may have been chosen as the headquarters site for Meadowlark Farms, according to Reiss, was that it was the home of Will H. Hays, Sr., a longtime friend of James and Pierre Goodrich.

dent of Meadowlark Farms (1948–83), "[In the mid 1940s], the college courses or even the reference books on reclamation were not available, but Mr. Goodrich felt that with a commonsense application of technology, management and capital, something constructive could be done with surface-mined coal lands."[11]

Owners were reluctant to take any measures to restore the land to its prestripped appearance because the cost of reclamation was generally greater than the land's profitable use; that is, the land could not be easily converted into valuable farm or commercial ground. For ecological reasons, that was especially unfortunate, because stripped land created vast scenic and soil erosion problems.[12] As chairman of the Ayrshire Collieries, Goodrich could not tolerate seeing thousands of acres, stripped of coal, lying ruined and useless. The purposes of Meadowlark Farms were twofold: first, to make productive use of the land before strip mining; and, second, after the coal had been removed, to make the stripped land suitable for some profitable use, preferably agricultural or recreational. Today, this is common practice and is, in fact, mandated by federal and state laws. When Goodrich began the reclamation process in the 1940s, however, he was one of the first in the nation to practice reclamation on a large scale. The problem was not that there was insufficient technology available to reclaim the land, but that the job had to be accomplished on the basis of very thin profit margins.

Meadowlark Farms also came about because of the demands of the coal industry. To be in the coal business, a colliery had to enter into long-term contracts (twenty to thirty years). To have sufficient reserves to deliver on those long-term contracts, coal companies had to buy the

11. Ibid. Reiss not only became general manager and later president and CEO of Meadowlark Farms, but in 1960 Goodrich appointed Reiss to the board of the Ayrshire Collieries Company and, in 1961, to the board of the Republic Coal and Coke Company. Reiss was also a founding member of Liberty Fund, Inc., in 1960 (Irwin H. Reiss, interview, June 29, 1996).

12. Irwin H. Reiss, "We Are Farmers, Not Miners," *Coal Mining and Processing,* May 1974; Carol L. Cornforth, "Reclamation Commitment Proves Rewarding," *Coal Mining and Processing,* March 1973; Irwin H. Reiss, interview, June 29, 1996.

reserves and the surface land rights to guarantee delivery. Thus, farming Ayrshire's land was natural, both before and after mining.[13]

To accomplish reclamation successfully, Goodrich sought out soil specialists and applied practical business methods. "He would buy grass seed by the truck loads," said Roy Barnes, who worked at the Goodrich Brothers Hay and Grain Company in Winchester.[14] Goodrich had soil specialists analyze the soil to see what would be the best use of the land once the coal had been removed. Options included agricultural use, such as the planting of crops or the grazing of livestock; reforestation; and recreational use. In the 1960s, after Ayrshire strip mined forty acres near Fairview, Illinois, Meadowlark Farms created a lake on the land on the town's outskirts.[15] By the early 1970s, a million bushels of corn a year were being grown on land controlled by Meadowlark Farms, and five hundred head of cattle and two thousand hogs per year were being produced on Meadowlark land.[16] At its height, Meadowlark Farms was farming and managing approximately fifty thousand acres of land owned by Ayrshire Collieries.[17]

For the first three years of Meadowlark's existence (1945–48), it became involved in farming by establishing six corporate farms. A resident manager supervised the farm and the farmhands who lived there. All the livestock and farm machinery were owned by Ayrshire. Goodrich and Reiss soon realized that that type of operation was not necessary. In fact, they found that the practice was counterproductive in that the employees had no vested interest in what was being produced or in turning a profit. Soon after, an arrangement was instituted whereby farmers could stay on their land. Leases were adopted that encouraged farming both before and after coal was removed. Approximately two hundred tenant farmers were cultivating Meadowlark land by the early 1980s.[18]

13. Irwin H. Reiss, interview by William C. Dennis, February 11, 1991 (tape and transcript of interview are in the possession of Liberty Fund).

14. Roy Barnes, interview, February 8, 1992.

15. Reiss, "We Are Farmers, Not Miners."

16. Irwin H. Reiss, interview, June 29, 1996.

17. Irwin H. Reiss, interview by William C. Dennis, February 11, 1991.

18. Ibid.; Irwin H. Reiss, interview, June 29, 1996.

By the early 1970s, AMAX (the successor to Ayrshire) owned land and held options to mine coal in twenty counties in Illinois, Indiana, Kentucky, Wyoming, and Montana. At that time in Indiana alone, Meadowlark Farms had leased approximately twenty-five hundred acres to the Department of Conservation for public fishing, camping, boating, swimming, and hiking. Other lands were resown with clover and other seed, which turned wasteland into valuable farm ground. Ayrshire and AMAX, through Meadowlark Farms, were able to accomplish this while turning a profit.

When Goodrich sold the Ayrshire Collieries Corporation to American Metal Climax (AMAX) in 1969, part of the agreement was that American Metal Climax had to maintain Meadowlark Farms' reclamation operations. So successful were Meadowlark Farms' practices that they were adopted by AMAX and other strip-mining operations throughout the country. As a result, wheat, corn, and other crops are now raised over played-out coal seams. Other uses of the land, such as the grazing of livestock, continue to this day.[19]

Another reason for Goodrich's concern about reclamation came from L. E. "Buck" Sawyer. Sawyer served as director of forestry and reclamation for the Indiana Coal Producers from 1944 to 1969. In that position, Sawyer encouraged corporate owners such as Goodrich to practice sound reclamation and assisted them in doing so, especially with the planting of trees.[20] Thus, the efforts of Goodrich, Lieber, Reiss, and Sawyer had a significant influence in making Indiana a state leader in reclamation practices long before state and federal governments passed legislation mandating such actions. Probably the most important and comprehensive federal legislation regulating reclamation did not occur until 1977, when Congress passed the Surface Mining and Control Reclamation Act. That was more than thirty years after Goodrich had established Meadowlark Farms.

19. Irwin H. Reiss, interview, June 29, 1996. According to Reiss, when Cyprus Minerals Company purchased AMAX Coal in December 1993, the operations of Meadowlark Farms were ended. As a result, the farms that were once operated by Meadowlark were sold to farmers and other investors.

20. Andrews, "The Ayrshire Collieries Corporation—Profit with Ecology," p. 17.

Anne C. Lawrason, who worked for Goodrich, recalls how important the work of Meadowlark Farms was to her employer: "I believe [Mr. Goodrich's] greatest accomplishment, in his own eyes, was creating the beautiful Meadowlark Farms out of an ugly, scarred former strip-mining project. He never tired of telling how he used the same machinery that did the mining to renovate the land and make it productive."[21]

Goodrich's ecological efforts have not gone unnoticed. Over the past fifteen years, John A. Baden, chairman of the Foundation for Research on Economics and the Environment (FREE) in Bozeman, Montana, has conducted more than two dozen Liberty Fund conferences linking the ideas of liberty and ecology. In the early 1980s, Baden established the Pierre F. Goodrich Conservation Award. To date, two individuals have received the honor: Arthur Temple, Jr., of Diboll and Lufkin, Texas; and David True of Casper, Wyoming. Temple, a third-generation owner of a large east Texas timber company, has been instrumental in reintroducing nearly extinct native species into more than twenty thousand acres of woodland in Texas and Louisiana. True, formerly an independent oil driller and chairman of the board of regents at the University of Wyoming, has managed and cared for indigenous wildlife on two large ranches in Wyoming.[22]

21. Letter from Anne C. Lawrason to author, December 11, 1995.

22. John Baden, telephone interview, December 30, 1996. Baden wrote in a letter to the author: "I believe Mr. Goodrich could be noted as the businessman who has done the most to create the field of restoration ecology" (January 10, 1996).

Chapter 20

The Later Years, 1940–1960

The liberal party is a party which believes that, as new conditions and problems arise beyond the power of men and women to meet as individuals, it becomes the duty of the Government itself to find new remedies with which to meet them. The liberal party insists that the Government has the definite duty to use all its power and resources to meet new social problems with new social controls. . . .

FRANKLIN DELANO ROOSEVELT,

The Public Papers and Addresses of Franklin D. Roosevelt

As the rumblings of World War II began in the late 1930s, Pierre Goodrich opposed the United States' entering into another European conflict just as he had opposed America's "unnecessary" involvement in World War I. He supported the isolationist views espoused by the America First campaign and conservatives such as Senator Robert Taft of Ohio.[1] Goodrich also opposed conscription. He

1. Henry Regnery said that Goodrich's opposition to the United States' getting involved in World War II was well known (interview, October 3, 1992). Stephen Tonsor believed that Goodrich might have belonged to the America First campaign in the late 1930s and early 1940s. If Goodrich was not a member, then at least he appeared to be in sympathy with its tenets. The organization, whose most famous member was Charles Lindbergh, opposed the United States' entry into World War II. It claimed a membership of some 800,000 in 1941 before the Japanese invasion of Pearl Harbor. America First was based in Chicago. Henry Regnery's father and Robert Hutchins, both of whom Goodrich knew personally, were leaders of the organization. Stephen Tonsor, interview, December 5, 1992. Goodrich's opposition to "Wilson's War" (World War I) is summarized in exhibit 5 of his "Memorandum No. 1" to employees of the Indiana Telephone Company.

believed that mandating the draft should never precede a large-scale voluntary appeal to participate in armed conflict.[2]

Moreover, Pierre, like his father, was no friend of Franklin Roosevelt's New Deal policies, which, among other things, promoted governmental expansion into business and individual affairs. The acts of Congress and the regulations of agencies and commissions in the 1930s added a new federal level to what had been previously governed by state law. One day in the late 1930s, Pierre attended a weekly roundtable luncheon of local Harvard Law School graduates at the Athenaeum Club in Indianapolis. During the luncheon, Goodrich blasted President Roosevelt. He stated that the New Deal "was destroying the country in general and lawyers in particular."[3] It was a belief he would hold for the rest of his life. At a more personal level, Goodrich passionately opposed Roosevelt's decision to intern American citizens of Japanese descent during World War II. He hired several persons of Japanese heritage to work for him during the war, a practice that was apparently not well received in his northern Indianapolis neighborhood.[4]

At about this time, Goodrich became interested in a small newsletter known as *Human Events.* Frank Hanighen and Felix Morley were the two founders of *Human Events.* Early on in the newsletter's formation, Henry Regnery, a young and upcoming Chicago publisher, was a financial backer of the enterprise, along with Joseph N. Pew, Jr., the vice-president of Sun Oil Company. Morley, a former Rhodes Scholar and Pulitzer Prize–winning newspaper columnist, had been editor of the *Washington Post* in the 1930s and early 1940s. He was president of

2. W. W. Hill, interview, May 5, 1993. According to Hill, Goodrich argued that a few should not have the power to risk others' lives and fortunes. Goodrich believed that a true patriot will risk his life for his country because of his desire to defend it, not because he is compelled to do so. Goodrich's views regarding the draft seem very similar to Leonard Read's, whose views on conscription can be found in *Government—An Ideal Concept* (Foundation for Economic Education: Irvington-on-Hudson, N.Y., 1954), p. 62.

3. Harry T. Ice, *History of a Hoosier Law Firm* (Indianapolis: privately printed, 1980), p. 143.

4. Letter from Anne C. Lawrason to author, September 20, 1996.

Haverford College when Hanighen approached him in 1944 about beginning the publishing venture. The purpose of *Human Events,* according to Morley, was to promote ideas that advocated means to a "durable peace" and involved "the reporting of facts which newspapers overlook."[5]

Though the magazine's circulation amounted to only a few thousand in the months immediately after World War II, its influence was far greater than its numbers would indicate.[6] Goodrich met Morley in the early years of Morley's involvement with *Human Events.* Pierre thought highly of the conservative publication and its attempt to deal with the problems that the end of World War II brought to the world. Morley aptly described the magazine's approach of addressing the centralization of power, a concern Goodrich obviously shared:

> Get the journalists, the professors, the clergy and the women's leadership on your side, I argued, and the masses will in time follow automatically. . . . those who formulated public opinion must first be shown that it was contrary to their personal interests [to have the centralization of power in government]. . . . Therefore the contrary appeal, as old as that of Cicero, should be clearly and unemotionally made to Reason, on the perhaps optimistic assumption that this would in time trickle down to lower levels.[7]

Goodrich often sent subscriptions to *Human Events* to family members, employees, and acquaintances.[8] In May 1947, Goodrich invited Morley to lecture at Wabash College. Morley's three lectures at Wabash were later published as part of a book, *The Power in the People.* In 1981,

5. Felix Morley, *For the Record* (South Bend, Ind.: Regnery/Gateway, 1979), p. 401.

6. Articles in *Human Events* in many ways anticipated and advanced ideas that were later developed and adopted in both the Marshall Plan and the European Common Market. Such essays included Edmund H. Stinnes's "The Unification of Europe," May 31, 1944. See Morley, *For the Record,* p. 401.

7. Morley, For the Record, p. 422.

8. A number of acquaintances and family members, including Dale Braun, Rodney Medler, Don Welch, and Elizabeth Terry, recall being sent free issues of *Human Events* by Goodrich.

Liberty Fund republished Morley's *Freedom and Federalism.*[9] Goodrich and Morley's friendship deepened through meetings of the Mont Pelerin Society and personal visits.[10] Goodrich also funded scholarships through the Winchester Foundation for an elementary school that Morley was associated with in Gibson Island, Maryland, Morley's retirement home.[11]

In the spring of 1949, Goodrich became interested in another publishing venture. While on a trip to New York City, he visited the Liberal Arts Press, located on Seventy-second Street. Goodrich took an immediate interest in the small publishing company and its owner, Oskar Piest. Piest was a German native and a former economics adviser to a large Berlin bank. In 1935, he fled Germany because of the political turmoil that existed during Hitler's rise to power. Once in the United States, Piest became involved in publishing, serving as editor in chief to the Hafner Press and publisher of the Library of Liberal Arts.[12]

The Library of Liberal Arts published a series of inexpensive, paperbound reprints of shorter classics in the fields of philosophy, religion, political science, education, and literature. Among the authors published by the press were Plato, Aristotle, Augustine, Thomas Aquinas,

9. Morley's book, which was partially funded by Goodrich, was *The Power in the People* (New York: D. Van Nostrand, 1949). Morley edited Liberty Fund's *Essays on Individuality* (1977), a collection of essays by such well-known contributors as Milton Friedman, Friedrich A. Hayek, and John Dos Passos.

10. Morley was a founding member of the Mont Pelerin Society. Several letters between Morley and Goodrich are located in the Felix Morley Collection, Archives, Herbert Hoover Presidential Library, West Branch, Iowa.

11. Gibson Island Country School in Gibson Island, Maryland. See letter from Goodrich to Morley, May 1, 1959; letter from Morley to Goodrich, May 7, 1959; and letter from Morley to Goodrich, July 26, 1955. Felix Morley Collection, Archives, Herbert Hoover Presidential Library.

12. Once Goodrich met Piest in the spring of 1949, he wrote to Roscoe Pound, inquiring about Piest's background and qualifications, especially Piest's intellectual capabilities and integrity. Goodrich wrote to Pound because he learned that Pound was an adviser to the Hafner Press. Pound responded with a recommendation of Piest. See letter from Goodrich to Pound, May 6, 1949, and letter from Pound to Goodrich, May 9, 1949, Roscoe Pound Collection, Pierre F. Goodrich file, Archives, Harvard University Law School. The subsidiary of the Library of Liberal Arts that actually published the books was the Little Library of Liberal Arts.

and Thomas Hobbes. Goodrich entered into what eventually became a twenty-thousand-dollar loan agreement with Piest, which enabled Piest to expand the offerings of inexpensive classic texts. As a result, between 1950 and 1960, the Library of Liberal Arts was able to increase publication from a few titles to hundreds. At the publishing company's height, its books were used in approximately eight hundred colleges and universities. Goodrich was so pleased with the outcome of this loan to Piest that he wrote about the transaction in Liberty Fund's *Basic Memorandum*. Goodrich used the success story as an example of a time when the Liberty Fund directors should be willing to consider extending loans to further a cause consistent with the foundation's philosophy.[13]

In 1939, James and Cora Goodrich donated $11,000 to Cora's hometown of Lynn, Indiana, for the construction of a community library in memory of her parents.[14] The donation was matched by $11,800 from the Federal Work Projects Administration (WPA). On July 4, 1941, 150 Lynn citizens began razing an old building on the site where the new Frist Memorial Library would be built.[15] Cora did not live to see the completion of the library named in her family's honor. She passed away on October 31, 1941, slightly more than a year after her husband's death.[16] While most of Cora's life had been spent as a supporter of James Good-

13. *Liberty Fund Basic Memorandum*, exhibit II-f, pp. 53–55. Piest makes reference to the first loan that Goodrich agreed to extend to him in a letter to Goodrich dated August 12, 1950. Piest went on to sell the Liberal Arts Press to the Bobbs-Merrill Publishing Company in 1961. He went to work for Bobbs-Merrill before becoming employed by the American Fletcher National Bank and Trust Company in Indianapolis. Piest later returned to Europe and worked as a representative out of American Fletcher's Brussels, Belgium, office. See file of Oskar Piest, Liberty Fund, Inc., Indianapolis.

14. See "Jonas L. P. Frist Estate Makes Contribution to Town of Lynn Which Will Enable Town to Complete Construction of Library with No Expense to Local Taxpayers," *Lynn (Ind.) Herald*, December 22, 1939, p. 1, col. 6; "History of the Lynn Library," on file at Washington Township Public Library, 106 North Main Street, Lynn, Indiana.

15. "Lynn Residents Celebrate 4th by Working for Community," *Richmond (Ind.) Palladium-Item and Sun-Telegram*, July 5, 1941, p. 1, col. 4.

16. "Mrs. James P. Goodrich, Widow of State's World War Governor, Dies," *Indianapolis Star*, November 1, 1941, p. 12, col. 4.

rich's amazing range of accomplishments, she had assumed leadership positions in her own right in a number of state and local organizations: In 1909, she became district president of the Indiana Federation of Clubs; in 1914, she began the Madonna Class, a women's Bible study at the Presbyterian Church; from 1925 to 1926, she served as local chapter president of the Daughters of the American Revolution.[17] Moreover, in rearing Pierre, the diminutive woman had perhaps as much influence on him as his powerful father.

Pierre and his second wife, Enid, attended the library's dedication on Sunday, June 13, 1943.[18] The ceremony included the unveiling of a large portrait of Cora's family, the Frists, which still hangs in the library.[19] Also in 1943, the unveiling of another portrait of interest to Pierre took place. Goodrich had hired Wayman Adams, one of America's great portrait painters, to rework a portrait of his father. Adams had originally begun the portrait of James P. Goodrich when the latter was still in the governor's office, in December 1920. The portrait was hung in the Indiana statehouse, where it remains to this day.[20]

17. "Services for Mrs. Goodrich to Be Sunday," *Indianapolis News,* November 1, 1941, p. 4, col. 2. Cora Goodrich was responsible for the establishment in Winchester of the Caroline A. Palmer chapter of the Indiana Federation of Clubs. She was also a charter member of the Woman's Club of Indiana.

18. See "Frist Memorial Library Building" (program for the building's dedication, located at Washington Township Public Library, Lynn, Indiana), Lynn, Indiana, Sunday, June 13, 1943, 2:00 P.M. Goodrich's attendance at the dedication was mentioned in a letter from Merl Chenoweth, then Lynn clerk and treasurer, to Goodrich dated June 9, 1943, in which Chenoweth specifies when Goodrich is to transport the speaker to the dedication. An article in the *Lynn Herald* also mentions the presence of Pierre and Enid Goodrich at the dedication. See "Dedication Successful," *Lynn (Ind.) Herald,* June 18, 1943, p. 1, col. 4.

19. The dedication speaker was William Hough of Greenfield, Indiana, a longtime friend of James Whitcomb Riley. Hough reminisced about the poet and read from Riley's writings. He also spoke about the war and the needs of the new library. "Dedication Successful," *Lynn Herald,* June 18, 1943, p. 1, col. 4.

20. During his lifetime, James Goodrich refused to allow the portrait to be hung. See Wilbur D. Peat, *Portraits and Painters of the Governors of Indiana, 1800–1978* (Indianapolis: Indiana Historical Society, 1978), pp. 70–71; "Portrait of James P. Goodrich by Wayman Adams," *Indianapolis News,* December 25, 1920, p. 1. col. 2; "Portrait by Wayman Adams Bought for Statehouse," *Indianapolis Star,* October 25, 1941, p. 4, col. 5.

On February 3, 1941, in Chicago, between the deaths of his parents, Pierre had married Enid Smith of Indianapolis. Pierre had first become acquainted with Enid in 1928, when she was his nurse at St. Vincent Hospital in Indianapolis, where he had back surgery. Enid was born in Enid, Oklahoma, on May 17, 1903. Her family moved to Indianapolis shortly after her birth. She attended Shortridge High School and received a resident nursing degree from St. Vincent Hospital and a bachelor's degree from Case Western Reserve University in Cleveland, Ohio.

Enid was one of six children. She did not come from a wealthy, well-known family, as had Pierre's first wife. The couple's long courtship was strained by circumstances largely beyond their control. James and Cora Goodrich had never totally understood or gotten over their son's divorce. As a result, Pierre was placed in a delicate position: He wanted very much to remain on good terms with his parents yet retain the close relationship he had developed with Enid. It was a troubled situation that only partially resolved itself in the autumn of 1941, after the passing of both of his parents.[21]

Throughout her life with Pierre, Enid showed great tolerance and understanding of her husband's time-consuming interests. As for Pierre, he had considerable confidence in Enid and valued her advice. Although Enid never had the scholarly interests that her husband had, she possessed a great deal of common sense. When Pierre established Liberty Fund in 1960, he kept Enid well advised of the details, and she was made a founding lifetime board member. Enid attended Liberty Fund board meetings regularly for more than twenty-five years. She was also a director of Pierre's other foundations: Thirty Five Twenty, Inc., based in Indianapolis, and the Winchester Foundation. After Pierre's death, Enid continued to be active in philanthropic circles in the Indianapolis area: she was a trustee of the Indianapolis Museum of Art; a member of the President's Council at Conner Prairie, a restored pioneer village; and a 1994 recipient of the Individual Philanthropist Award by the Indiana chapter of the National Society of Fund Raising Executives. In 1994 she

21. Elizabeth Terry, interview, November 16, 1991; Florence Dunn, interview, July 18, 1992; and Kathryn Emison, interview, November 24, 1992.

was named by Indiana's former governor Evan Bayh as a Sagamore of the Wabash, the state's highest civilian honor. Enid passed away in November 1996 at the age of ninety-three.[22]

After they were married, Pierre and Enid went to Hawaii on their honeymoon. While in Hawaii, the newlyweds visited Admiral Husband Kimmel, the officer in charge of the soon to be infamous naval base at Pearl Harbor.[23] Pierre took along on his honeymoon a suitcase full of books. Albert Campbell, Pierre's longtime law partner, joked that one of the first things Enid would have to get used to in married life was Pierre's preoccupation with reading. Goodrich could become so immersed in a book that he became oblivious to anything else going on around him, even a honeymoon.[24]

Several years later, another marriage took place in Goodrich's immediate family. In May 1952, his daughter, Nancy, married a Polish prince, Edmond Poniatowski, at the Vincent Astor estate in Rhinebeck, New York. Pierre was concerned that whoever married his daughter might find his wealth the primary attraction. The couple later lived in Paris for several years, during which time father and daughter seldom saw each other. It was the beginning of a strained relationship.[25]

In May 1946, Pierre and Enid moved to 4220 Central Avenue in northern Indianapolis, where they would live during the remainder of Pierre's life. Set in a lovely neighborhood across from the St. Joan of Arc

22. Gilbert Snider, interview, December 23, 1991. For more information about Enid Smith Goodrich, see her obituary, "Civic Leader Enid Smith Goodrich Was Fund Director, Museum Trustee," *Indianapolis Star/Indianapolis News,* November 28, 1996, sec. D, p. 7, col. 1; *Muncie (Ind.) Star Press,* November 28, 1996, p. 12A, col. 1; *Winchester (Ind.) News-Gazette,* November 27, 1996, p. 2, col. 1.

23. "When [Mr. Goodrich] decided he wanted to talk with someone about something, he didn't give up," said Ruth Connolly. "He always had great connections" (interview, October 25, 1991). Goodrich's connections were indeed strong. For instance, twice he met with the West German chancellor Konrad Adenauer (Rodney Medler, interview, June 9, 1993).

24. Henry Regnery (as told to him by Albert Campbell), interview, October 3, 1992.

25. "Anne D. Goodrich, Polish Prince Wed," *Indianapolis Star,* May 3, 1952, p. 6, col. 1. Rosanna Amos, interview, December 10, 1991.

Catholic Church, the home is a beautiful example of Georgian architecture. In the late 1960s, Goodrich had extensive renovation done to the home, including surrounding it with an iron fence and building a carriage house.[26]

Despite his father's longtime involvement in politics, particularly partisan Republican politics, Pierre himself was pretty much a bystander in the political arena. During his fifty years of residence in Indianapolis, however, many a Republican candidate came knocking at Goodrich's door seeking his support. In February 1972, Dr. Otis Bowen, then a Republican candidate for governor, visited Goodrich, looking for a campaign contribution and endorsement. Bowen was treated no differently from any other visitor. Goodrich proceeded to engage Bowen in a lengthy discussion, challenging Bowen on what he believed were the candidate's less than conservative beliefs. After a fairly virulent exchange, Bowen left, disgruntled. The future two-time Indiana governor was not the first candidate who left Goodrich's office shaking his head. Bowen left with empty hands, not receiving the campaign contribution he had sought. Instead, Goodrich sent him literature, including Lord Acton's letter containing the admonition that "power tends to corrupt and absolute power corrupts absolutely." As Bowen recalls, "Those who knew of my appointment were very interested in the outcome. [My campaign manager] asked if I thought a follow-up appointment would be productive. I advised that I had no desire to face [Mr. Goodrich] again."[27]

26. Letter from Dr. Marvin Vollmer to author, August 5, 1996. Marvin Vollmer and Alicia Byers are the current owners and occupants of the home. The house was built in approximately 1905 by Robert and Alta Hawkins. In 1946, it was sold by Iris T. and Jack Adams to the P. F. Goodrich Corporation, which owned the home from May 1, 1946, to May 4, 1965, when Goodrich liquidated the holding company. The holding company sold the house directly to Pierre and Enid Goodrich. For a chronological history of the ownership of the house, see memo attached to letter of August 5, 1996, from Dr. Marvin Vollmer to author (in author's possession).

27. Bowen visited Goodrich on February 24, 1972. Just as he did with all his guests, Goodrich sent to Bowen Lord Acton's letter and the *Federalist*, nos. 6 and 51. See "Memorandum to Staff, Liberty Fund, Inc.," from R. Amos, December 1, 1982.

The 1952 Republican National Convention in Chicago marked an exception to Pierre Goodrich's tendency not to become directly involved in politics. In this contest, the stakes were high. Goodrich had been a longtime supporter of the United States senator Robert Taft, who was challenging Dwight D. Eisenhower for the Republican presidential nomination. Goodrich, like most supporters of the conservative wing of the Republican Party, was suspicious of Eisenhower's "internationalist" views and believed that he would do little to roll back Franklin Roosevelt's New Deal policies. Almost all political insiders and columnists believed that the race between Taft and Eisenhower would be extremely close. Therefore, every delegate was deemed critical. A hotly contested battle for control of Indiana's delegates to the convention ensued. What added fuel to the controversy was the power play that had developed between Goodrich's business partner Eugene C. Pulliam, an Eisenhower backer, and Indiana's two Republican United States senators, Homer Capehart and William Jenner, both strong Taft supporters.

As publisher of Indiana's two largest newspapers, Pulliam was not content to report on the bruising tug of war in Chicago. He had finagled

---

Dr. Bowen, who later served as secretary of health and human services in the Ronald Reagan administration, wrote:

> The appointment with Mr. Goodrich was arranged by my campaign manager J. B. King. I was warned that the interview might be difficult but was not quite prepared for the ordeal. I don't recall all the conversation but do remember that the conversation was one-sided and dwelt mainly on trying to convert me to his views.
>
> I thought I was quite conservative but left with the idea that he thought I was a "wild-eyed liberal." He did give me literature to read and either sent or gave to me Lord Acton's letter and other papers. . . . (Letter from Bowen to author, September 3, 1996)

Edgar Whitcomb said that to the best of his recollection Pierre never contributed to his campaigns for secretary of state or governor (interview, April 18, 1992). Richard O. Ristine said that Goodrich did not support him in his bid for governor in 1964 (interview, February 15, 1993). W. W. Hill, who ran for the state senate and United States Congress, also said that Goodrich did not contribute to any of his campaigns (interview, July 9, 1993).

to get himself "elected" as a delegate to the convention in a deal with Senator Jenner that many considered highly suspicious. "We decided it'd be better to make him a delegate than have him hounding us all the time," explained Lisle Wallace, chairman of the Taft campaign in Indiana.[28] Nonetheless, Jenner and the other Taft supporters wanted a delegation that was 100 percent loyal to Taft. This is where Goodrich came in.

The controversy began with the issue of whether the Indiana state Republican convention could force Pulliam or any other delegate to vote for Taft. Pulliam took his fight straight to the readers of his newspapers, threatening to sue the Republican Party if he was not allowed to vote as a delegate for Eisenhower.[29] After Pulliam won a minor victory that allowed him free rein to vote for whomever he wanted, the challenge was to hold onto Indiana's other delegates who had earlier committed to Taft.[30] Goodrich, in an uncharacteristic role, worked the Indiana delegation both on and off the convention floor. He tried to persuade them not to defect to Pulliam's (and therefore Eisenhower's) camp.[31]

As an interesting side note, at the July convention, Goodrich was introduced to William Casey by Henry Regnery. At the time, Casey was

28. Quoted from Russell Pulliam, *Publisher Gene Pulliam, Last of the Newspaper Titans,* p. 158. Technically, Pulliam was elected from the Eleventh Congressional District to the national convention, not at the state Republican convention.

29. At the state convention on June 7, 1952, Homer Capehart was able to get passed a voice-vote resolution that purportedly bound all Indiana delegates to vote for Senator Taft. Pulliam threatened legal action if the Taft forces insisted upon controlling all delegates. See Farwell Rhodes, Jr., "Fight to Keep Muzzle off Indiana Delegates Taken to National GOP," *Indianapolis Star,* July 2, 1952, p. 1, col. 4; see also Ben Hibbs, "Will GOP Commit Suicide at Chicago?" *Indianapolis Star,* July 3, 1952, p. 1, col. 1. Hibbs's editorial supports Pulliam's views.

30. Ibid. The next day, Pulliam and the Republican state chairman and senator Homer Capehart reached an agreement that the delegates would not be bound. See "Anti-Ike Yoke Lifted for State Delegates," *Indianapolis Star,* July 3, 1952, p. 1, col. 2.

31. Henry Regnery remembers that Goodrich was one of the leaders in successfully holding the Indiana delegation to support Taft (interview, October 3, 1992).

a New York City tax attorney and a strong Taft supporter.[32] While Goodrich met with most of Indiana's thirty-two delegates to the convention privately, Casey campaigned for Taft in a tenacious manner similar to Pulliam's. Casey had set up an underground newspaper. Each morning on the doorstep of every delegate and alternate, a paper appeared with headlines that read, "We All Like Ike, but Ike Can't Win" and "Ike's a Me-Too Republican—Let's Nominate a Real Republican."[33]

The significance of Goodrich's meeting with Casey is not that the two men ultimately succeeded in helping Taft garner the nomination. They did not. Eisenhower won on the first ballot in an unexpected landslide. The important thing about their meeting is that Goodrich had made contact with a man who would later play a very important role in Goodrich's establishment of Liberty Fund. Casey did much of the legal and tax preparation work involved in forming the foundation between 1960 and 1962. He would later hold high public office, becoming chairman of the United States Securities and Exchange Commission (SEC), director of the Central Intelligence Agency (CIA), and chairman of Ronald Reagan's 1980 presidential campaign.

As Goodrich came to know Casey, he saw a man much like himself: unflappable and impatient, a voracious reader and lover of ideas, a lawyer with such tremendous energy that he often kept three secretaries busy at once. Casey's shambling manner totally belied his considerable intellect and scholarly erudition. Moreover, like Goodrich, Casey possessed the ability to absorb new information and new ideas like a sponge yet relentlessly held to the moral traditions of his middle-class Catholic upbringing in Queens.[34] Because he met Casey there, Goodrich's work

32. Ibid. Regnery said that he introduced Casey to Goodrich on the floor of the convention. At the time of the 1952 convention, Casey served as a director on the board of Henry Regnery's publishing house. See also Joseph E. Persico, *Casey* (New York: Viking, 1990), p. 93.

33. Persico, *Casey,* p. 92.

34. This attribution of characteristics to Casey is detailed in Joseph Persico's biography *Casey,* pp. 41–42. A closer examination of Casey reveals an extraordinary number of traits that he shared with Goodrich. See Persico, *Casey,* p. 45.

at the Chicago convention proved to be not totally fruitless, despite Taft's landslide defeat.

Goodrich's numerous businesses generally enjoyed a string of years of strong success. In the late 1950s, however, his fortune turned when a business deal went sour. In December 1947, Pierre's uncle, Percy Goodrich, had struck a deal with Indianapolis businessman and attorney Samuel Harrell. The purchase arrangement involved the sale of the Goodrich family's twenty-four grain elevators in central and northern Indiana to Acme-Evans, a large grain and milling company in Indianapolis. The resulting company became known as Acme-Goodrich. Harrell took over the presidency of Acme-Goodrich while Percy Goodrich, at the age of eighty-six, became chairman of the board. The Goodrich family received $1.8 million plus preferred stock in Acme-Goodrich. Moreover, approximately one hundred other stockholders received preferred stock in Acme-Goodrich.

After Percy Goodrich died in 1951, Pierre was the largest minority shareholder and the second major force, behind Harrell, in the company. By that time, the company was the dominant grain business in Indiana, owning thirty-seven grain elevators across the state.

In Harrell, a hard-nosed and successful businessman, Goodrich had met his match. Harrell was a large, imposing man who was also bright, ambitious, and polished. He had grown up in Noblesville, Indiana, and had served as a World War I navy pilot before graduating from the University of Pennsylvania and Yale Law School. In the mid 1920s, Harrell returned to practice law in Indianapolis and became involved in the grain and milling business. He later served as chairman of the board of directors of the Indianapolis Board of Trade, founded Indiana's honorary order the Sagamore of the Wabash, and ran unsuccessfully for governor in 1952 and lieutenant governor in 1956.[35]

35. Goodrich and Harrell also served together as trustees of the National Foundation for Education for American Citizenship. For a summary of Harrell's life, see "Samuel R. Harrell, President, Acme-Evans Company, Inc." (unpublished typescript, Citizens Historical Association, Indianapolis, November 20, 1948), Indiana Division, Indiana State Library. See also Noble Reed, "Harrell Seeks GOP Gubernatorial Nomi-

In the mid 1950s, Harrell had the idea of creating a grain company that would be structurally similar to General Motors, having five independent divisions, and he established General Grain. In 1958, Harrell's plan was to make General Grain the umbrella company for the five divisions, which were Acme-Goodrich (rural Indiana grain elevators), Acme-Evans (a milling company based in Indianapolis), Early and Daniels (Cincinnati), Cleveland Grain (Cleveland, Ohio), and the Tidewater Grain Company (a Philadelphia grain export company).[36]

From the start, Goodrich and the other minority stockholders in Acme-Goodrich were against the merger. They believed that the preferred shares, which they owned, were considerably undervalued by Harrell. At the August 10, 1958, stockholders' meeting, the minority shareholders formally voted against the consolidation plan.[37] Under Indiana law, any stockholder who opposes a merger has the right to have his or her shares purchased by the new or surviving company at the price of the shares on the effective date of the merger. Harrell proposed such a purchase price and the Indiana Securities Exchange Commission found the merger fair and equitable, but the minority stockholders objected to the appraised value of the stock. Goodrich and a Winchester dentist by the name of John Beals (Pierre's second cousin) subsequently brought a legal action on behalf of all 104 minority stockholders.[38]

At a lengthy trial before the Boone Circuit Court in Lebanon, Indiana, in July 1962, Beals and Goodrich succeeded in winning a jury verdict for the minority shareholders that increased their preferred stock value almost twenty dollars per share. Harrell appealed the verdict. Finally, in December 1966, the Indiana Court of Appeals ruled in *General*

---

nation," *Indianapolis Times,* January 25, 1952, p. 8, col. 1; "Lieutenant Governor Job Sought by Harrell," *Indianapolis Star,* June 17, 1956, sec. B, p. 4; "Samuel Harrell Was Grain Broker, Lawyer," *Indianapolis News,* August 6, 1986, p. 51, cols. 1–2.

36. Ivan Barr, telephone interview, March 27, 1993.

37. See *General Grain, Inc. v. Pierre F. Goodrich,* 221 N.E. 2d 696, 698 (Ind. Ct. App. 1966).

38. See *John Beals et al. v. General Grain, Inc., and Acme Goodrich, Inc.* (filed in Marion County Superior Court and venued to Boone Circuit Court, decision July 18, 1962; *General Grain, Inc. v. Pierre F. Goodrich et al.,* 221 N.E. 2d 696 (December 7, 1966).

Grain, Inc. v. Pierre F. Goodrich in favor of Harrell.[39] Goodrich appealed the decision to the Indiana Supreme Court. In June 1967, the state's highest court affirmed the decision of the court of appeals in favor of Harrell.[40]

The lengthy legal contest between Goodrich and Harrell is interesting for two reasons. First, it was probably the first large dissenting shareholder case in Indiana, therefore setting an important precedent for later case law.[41] Second, it is an instance in which a conflict of personalities came back to haunt Pierre. Goodrich was accustomed to being able to control events that involved his business interests. In this situation, however, he did not have the votes to control the direction of Acme-Goodrich, and he could not move Harrell to oppose the consolidation plan. As a result, the two men had a falling out, and the legal battle that ensued was inevitable.[42]

39. At the trial of *John Beals v. General Grain, Inc., and Acme Goodrich, Inc.,* in the Boone Circuit Court, the jurors found in favor of Beals, Goodrich, and the other minority shareholders on July 18, 1962. The jury awarded the total sum of $585,180.19 to the minority shareholders, which included costs plus interest from August 12, 1958. The Indiana Court of Appeals, however, reversed the trial jury's award. Reversal was based on the grounds that the jury instructions were improper because they stressed that the jury should apply the book value of liquidating value of the stock instead of the fair-market value (221 N.E. 2d 696, 702–03 [Ind. Ct. App. 1966]; rehearing denied January 3, 1967).

40. See *General Grain, Inc. v. Pierre F. Goodrich et al.,* 227 N.E. 2d 445 (Ind. Sup. Ct. 1967).

41. Alan H. Lobley, telephone interview, April 16, 1993. Lobley was one of three attorneys from the Indianapolis law firm of Ice, Miller, Donadio and Ryan who represented Goodrich and other minority shareholders in the appeal.

42. Goodrich may have suffered from another relationship that had gone sour. Donald R. Mote was an associate judge sitting on the Court of Appeals in 1966 that reversed the jury verdict in favor of Goodrich. Mote's brother, Carl H. Mote, had been a top adviser to James Goodrich in the governor's administration and Pierre's law partner from 1923 to 1926. Donald Mote not only sat on the court of appeals that heard Harrell's appeal, but was also elevated to Indiana's supreme court just before Goodrich appealed the decision of the court of appeals. Donald F. Elliott, Jr., an Indianapolis attorney who represented the minority shareholders before both Indiana's court of appeals and supreme court, believes that a longtime grudge between Goodrich and Judge Mote may have influenced Mote's Appellate Court and Supreme Court decisions.

After the Indiana Supreme Court decision, settlement negotiations resulted in Harrell's returning six elevators to the preferred (minority) stockholders in exchange for their releasing all claims against General Grain. With six elevators, the minority stockholders formed a company called Indiana Elevators. The company was based in Winchester, the original location of the Goodrich Hay and Grain Company seventy years before. Unfortunately, the lengthy legal battle had taken its toll on the grain elevators' business. The substantial legal costs, combined with Harrell's failure to maintain the grain operations, resulted in a substantial loss of business for Indiana Elevator. It folded in 1968, less than a year from start-up. It was one of the few business deals in which the Goodrich family came out on the losing end.[43]

"[Donald] Mote had an animus against Pierre that went way back and he carried it onto the court's decision," claims Elliott (telephone interview, April 15, 1993).

43. Ivan Barr, telephone interview, March 27, 1993. Joe Ebert, who had been a sales representative for Acme-Goodrich, headed up operations of Indiana Elevators. Most of the other grain elevators originally owned by the Goodrich family were eventually sold by General Grain, many of them to the operators who had run them for Acme-Goodrich. Once Harrell won and Goodrich exhausted all appeal rights, Harrell sought costs involved in the appeal against the minority stockholders. The Indiana Court of Appeals awarded Harrell $17,439.20. See *General Grain, Inc. v. Pierre F. Goodrich et al.*, 233 N.E. 2d 187 (Ind. Ct. of App. 1968).

Richard Hilts, an Acme-Evans employee since 1951 who held the position of president after Harrell, remembers that Harrell did not spend any money to maintain the grain elevators. That, coupled with the loss of business to larger grain elevators, the elimination of many railroad lines to the small grain elevators, and the increased grain storage capacity that farmers had on their own farms, resulted in the small elevator's becoming a thing of the past (telephone interview, May 13, 1993).

Chapter 21

The Later Years, 1960–1973

It is inconceivable to me that businessmen generally, and utility managers almost consistently, think that by ignoring the effects of monetary inflation, they are somehow going to avoid the problem. If they did not ignore the subject but made an attempt to report it publicly—which they can do if their auditors, lawyers, and economists are willing to inform themselves—I am quite sure that they would be much farther along than they are now.

PIERRE F. GOODRICH, "Monetary Inflation, Growth and Accounting"

IN THE EARLY 1960s, Goodrich decided that he had outgrown his office space on the seventh floor of the Electric Building, where he had been since 1935. He began to examine other business offices in downtown Indianapolis. Not finding any office quarters suitable, he decided to build his own office building. He purchased property at 3520 Washington Boulevard, which was owned and occupied by Mrs. Bertha Caldwell, Richard Lugar's mother, and had been the United States senator's childhood home.[1] In 1962, Goodrich had the house demolished and the land rezoned, and replaced the home with a modern office building. The building, which still stands, is now occupied by an architectural firm.

The building served as the nerve center for Goodrich's many corporate operations. But probably more important to Pierre, it was also the location for the early work of Liberty Fund. The care with which

1. Goodrich purchased the property from Bertha Caldwell in 1962. Richard Lugar, interview, October 29, 1992.

Goodrich oversaw the building's construction is indicative of the time and thought he could put into a project once he became interested in it. Goodrich spared no expense. In landscaping the grounds, he had shrubs and trees transported from southern Indiana at a cost of thirty-five thousand dollars.[2] Moreover, he duplexed the utilities of the building so that it could function in times of emergency. In addition to having the building connected to city water, he had a deep well dug. He also had both gas and oil boiler systems put in place for heat. An air-handling system regulated the air moisture content so that the office always had fifty percent humidity, and an electric generator was installed to serve in case of a power outage. Goodrich even had double ceilings and extra-thick walls constructed to add to the building's sturdiness and soundproofing. He had a large oval conference table designed for Liberty Fund conferences and special chairs made to order.[3]

"He was a man of great thought," said Robert Longardner, who purchased the building in the mid 1970s and still occupies it today. Goodrich obviously believed "the work of the [Liberty Fund] was very important and it had to be physically protected in case there was ever a catastrophe," added Longardner.[4]

Goodrich's partnership with John Raab Emison terminated in 1939. Emison returned to his hometown of Vincennes to practice with his fam-

2. Robert Longardner, interview, December 28, 1992. The trees and shrubs were purportedly moved from a garden near or in Tell City, Indiana. Longardner was told this by William H. Fletcher, who worked with Goodrich at the time as the Indianapolis manager of Arthur Andersen and Company.

3. Robert Longardner, interview, December 28, 1992; William H. Fletcher, interview by William C. Dennis, January 25, 1991. According to Fletcher, Goodrich had the large oval conference table, which Liberty Fund still uses, designed for twenty-two people to sit around. Goodrich believed that no more than twenty-two people could converse at one time and expect to learn anything of substance. Goodrich wanted the chairs to be ones that participants could sit in comfortably for a long time and still be attentive. He called them his "Du Pont" chairs, for the large chemical company where he got the idea for them.

4. Robert Longardner, interview, December 28, 1992.

ily's law firm, the oldest firm west of the Allegheny Mountains.[5] Goodrich's partnership with Albert Campbell continued intact, however, and in 1941 a young attorney by the name of Claude Warren joined the firm of Goodrich and Campbell. This relationship proved very fruitful, and the three attorneys practiced law together for the next twenty-one years. After Campbell left in 1962, Warren remained with Goodrich as a partner until Pierre passed away.

By the early 1960s, the Goodrich family companies were enjoying tremendous success. The country's economy had flourished during the decades of the 1940s and 1950s, and so had Ayrshire Collieries Corporation, the Indiana Telephone Corporation, City Securities, Central Newspapers, and the many other smaller companies in which the Goodrich family held a large interest. Most of Goodrich's legal work involved companies in which he had a financial stake, but the firm of Goodrich, Campbell, and Warren also took on a few outside clients, such as public utility companies. Warren became an expert in public utility law and was sought after for his expertise. While Albert Campbell and Claude Warren practiced with Goodrich at different times for the better part of three decades, a number of younger attorneys also practiced with the firm as associates, including John M. Kitchen, Carter W. Eltzroth, and Gilbert Snider.[6]

In March 1957, Goodrich hired a young woman by the name of Helen Schultz. Miss Schultz, as Pierre would always refer to her, became his top assistant. She had graduated from Culver-Stockton College in Missouri and had worked for Illinois Bell before beginning her apprenticeship under Goodrich. Schultz was an extremely capable person, and over the course of several years, her boss and mentor began to trust her

5. Mrs. John Raab (Kathryn) Emison, interview, November 24, 1992. Raab Emison (nephew of John Raab), telephone interview, April 12, 1993. The law firm was founded in 1819 and is now called Emison, Doolittle, Kalb and Roellgen. According to Kathryn Emison and John Raab's son, James, another reason for Emison's leaving the partnership was that the relationship between John Raab and Goodrich had soured because of Goodrich's demands for perfection. "My dad could damn near get along with anyone, but he and Pierre just didn't hit it off," said James Emison (telephone interview, April 16, 1993).

6. Gilbert Snider, interview, December 23, 1991.

more and more with the handling of top administrative duties. Schultz's competency was evident to others as well. Martha Wharton, who met Goodrich and Helen Schultz only once, in 1966 for a job interview, recalled thirty years later that "Miss Helen Schultz ran that [office] and, indeed, gave orders to Mr. Goodrich! I may not have been in awe of HIM, but I was agape at HER competence and commanding presence!"[7] Indeed, after Goodrich's death in 1973, Schultz replaced him as president of both the Indiana Telephone Corporation and Liberty Fund.

The 1960s marked a relatively stable period in Goodrich's life. With the exception of the Acme-Goodrich failure, his businesses were doing well, and he enjoyed considerable satisfaction in his involvement with several educational organizations. Goodrich initiated a number of policy changes for his companies that only years later would be adopted by competing businesses. Because of his concern over inflation, he restricted the Peoples Loan and Trust Company's ability to lend money at a fixed interest rate to five years. Goodrich believed that to predict what interest rates would be beyond that would be pure speculation. In essence, that had the effect of creating variable-rate mortgages, because borrowers had to renegotiate the interest rate of their mortgages every five years or seek financing elsewhere. Although variable-rate mortgages are now extremely common, they were unheard of in the 1960s. Of course, that conservative decision put Peoples Loan and Trust Company at a distinct disadvantage in competition with other banks, which made fixed-rate home loans for periods as long as thirty years. But the policy helped to save Peoples from the dire situation that many banks found themselves in during the late 1970s and early 1980s, when banks were holding long-term loans that yielded 6 to 8 percent interest but had to

7. Letter from Martha Wharton to author, December 14, 1995. Schultz, now Helen E. Fletcher, lives in Jacksonville, Florida. She denies she ever gave orders to Pierre. She wrote to the author: "I appreciate the compliments which Martha Wharton paid to me but no one (except possibly Mrs. Goodrich) gave orders to Mr. Goodrich—suggestions or reminders, yes; orders, no" (letter, June 18, 1996).

pay depositors interest at 15 to 16 percent.[8] Goodrich also initiated fee-based services long before they became common in other banks. This reflected his belief, which he stated often in his memorandums to employees, that those who benefit from a service should pay for it, and that costs should not be passed on to all ratepayers or depositors.[9]

In the telephone industry, Goodrich advanced policies that reflected his awareness of how quickly the industry was changing. For example, he depreciated the expense of new equipment at a far faster rate than was allowed under the depreciation schedules of state and federal tax laws. This had the effect of enabling his telephone companies to deduct the expense of the new equipment from income sooner rather than later, therefore reducing annual corporate income and dividends to shareholders. Goodrich's belief in the faster depreciation rates reflected his views about the true rate at which new equipment would become obsolete and need replacing. He used this logic (along with the argument about how inflation increased the expense of new equipment at a cost higher than was generally calculated) to justify higher rate increases before the Indiana Public Service Commission.[10]

At the same time, Goodrich also negotiated long-term contracts with telephone-equipment suppliers. Most generally, he required from these suppliers contractual commitments of up to twenty years. The normal commitment was less than half that time. In other words, if a company wanted to sell telephone equipment to the Indiana Telephone Corporation or the Public Telephone Corporation at Greensburg, then that supplier would have to agree to provide parts for that equipment for up to twenty years after the sale. Goodrich justified this "apparent conflict between our twenty year provision for parts and a nine year obsolescence plan" based on the ability of larger telephone companies (such as AT&T and Western Electric) to have "captive manufacturing compa-

8. Chris Talley, interview, March 20, 1995.
9. Ibid.
10. T. Alan Russell, interview, July 2, 1994.

nies" (meaning they, not the suppliers, could dictate the terms and price of new and repaired equipment).[11]

Throughout the 1950s and 1960s, the issue of labor unions continually was one that Goodrich had to confront. Goodrich strongly opposed unions: He believed that they protect poor employees at the expense of good employees and unnecessarily handcuff management in adopting work changes. He further believed that the call to unionize would succeed only if employees were not being treated right by the employing company. The Ayrshire Collieries Corporation was unionized by one or more of the miners' unions, and the Indiana Telephone Corporation (ITC) was temporarily unionized for about two years before Goodrich's death. The ITC employees later decertified the union. The existence and the threat of organized labor forced the boards of the various Goodrich companies to change their compensation packages. In the 1950s, ITC employees started to receive pension benefits after the threat of unionization was repeatedly made. Generally, Goodrich saw to it that his employees received a compensation package, complete with benefits as good as those of competing companies that were unionized. He believed that if he did that, there would be little chance for union efforts to succeed.[12]

The business practice that Goodrich took the greatest long-term interest in was the accounting of inflation. As a business executive overseeing companies that were constantly replacing expensive equipment, Goodrich was greatly concerned about inflation. He took on the analysis of the problem much as he took on anything that had stirred his curiosity, with almost obsessive attention. Goodrich recognized that inflation erodes profits because the replacement rate of equipment in today's dollars does not accurately reflect the true cost when inflation is factored in.[13] Goodrich was greatly concerned about the practical ef-

11. Ibid.

12. Ibid.; Walter "Guido" Seaton, interview, January 16, 1993; letter from Helen Fletcher to author, June 18, 1996.

13. Gilbert Snider, interview, December 23, 1991; Don Welch, interview, December 16, 1991; William Fitts, interview, December 28, 1991.

fects of inflation. In the late 1960s and early 1970s, inflation was high. On the basis of what he had observed in several South American countries, he knew that inflation could wreak havoc, not only on individual businesses, but on whole economies as well.[14] Goodrich was so convinced in the 1940s that the United States was going to experience a period of substantial inflation that he refinanced the whole of the Indiana Telephone Corporation's debt on a long-term basis at low fixed interest rates.[15]

In support of his warnings about inflation, Goodrich hosted Ludwig Erhard, chancellor of West Germany from 1963 to 1966, in Indianapolis on February 19, 1968. Erhard is credited with performing the "German economic miracle" when he was the German minister of economics. In that position, on Sunday, June 20, 1948, he abolished all wage and price controls and introduced a new German currency, the deutsche mark. These bold initiatives resulted in Germany's having one of the strongest economies in Europe within a decade. Erhard and Goodrich had become friends through their mutual association with the Mont Pelerin Society. The former chancellor spoke at the Columbia Club about the evils of inflation and countries' engaging in deficit financing to support ballooning budgets.[16]

Goodrich became an expert on inflation and spoke often about the need to control and properly account for it to anyone who would listen.

14. Don Welch, interview, December 16, 1991.

15. Letter from Milton Friedman to author, December 19, 1991.

16. Harrison J. Ullman, "Erhard Stresses Dangers of Deficit Financing," *Indianapolis Star,* February 20, 1968, p. 2, col. 4; "Erhard Warns of World Inflation," *Indianapolis News,* February 20, 1968, p. 2, col. 6; *Columbian,* April 1968, p. 2. See also "Erhard, Ludwig," *The New Encyclopaedia Britannica,* vol. 4 (Chicago: Encyclopaedia Britannica, 1992), p. 540. For a brief discussion of Erhard's "economic miracle," see Milton and Rose Friedman, *Free to Choose* (New York: Harcourt Brace Jovanovich, 1979), p. 56. Erhard's trip to speak in Indianapolis on February 19, 1968, was his lone appearance in the United States at that time. Goodrich had Erhard and three of Erhard's assistants flown to Indianapolis from Bonn, Germany, for the speaking engagement. The total cost of the engagement was $7,000, including a speaking fee for Erhard of $1,500. The expenses were paid by Liberty Fund. See "Minutes of the Board of Directors of the Liberty Fund, Inc.," November 10, 1967, p. 139 (in the possession of Liberty Fund).

He believed that most people (including many economists) simply did not understand how inflation could lead to political and social upheaval. Goodrich often discussed, with an economic historian's knowledge, how past national crises such as the French Revolution and the rise in power of Napoleon in France and of Hitler in Germany had been brought about by the manipulation of money.[17] A 1979 article in the *Indianapolis Star* paid a late tribute to Pierre for his recognition of the importance of accounting for the effect of inflation in a business context:[18]

> Goodrich, noted for his financial genius and wide-ranging scholarship, urged other companies to [account for inflation], observing that people and firms might do well to chart financial progress two ways: In the common arithmetic language of current dollars that everyone uses and in constant dollars which have been adjusted for inflation.
>
> . . . With double-digit inflation jolting the nation in the early 1970s, Goodrich began to get some attention for his theory. Nobel Laureate Milton Friedman, the University of Chicago economist who had long been acquainted with Goodrich's work, began suggesting in national speeches that corporations might do well to follow the lead of Indiana Telephone in accounting for inflation.[19]

Goodrich knew that there is a built-in pressure for company officials not to report the effects of inflation: inflated figures look good to shareholders and mitigate the chance that financial analysts will spot a firm's poor performance.[20] Goodrich's method of accounting (price-level accounting) eventually attracted national and even international attention. He corresponded with businessmen and academics from all over

17. See "Pierre F. Goodrich Tours Company," *ITC Highlights,* July 1971, pp. 1–2; "Indiana Telephone Corporation Annual Report," December 31, 1972, pp. 3–5.

18. John H. Lyst, "'Real Dollar' Statements Gain New Attention," *Indianapolis Star,* September 12, 1979, p. 31, col. 1.

19. Ibid.

20. Ibid.

the country.[21] Stanford University, the University of Pittsburgh, and the University of Michigan used Indiana Telephone Corporation's annual reports in their graduate business courses. England's largest news magazine, *The Economist,* favorably discussed ITC's accounting methods in a January 1971 article. In 1978, the Shell Oil Company, a Dutch corporation, became the first major company to record inflationary dollars in its annual reports.[22]

In support of his theories, Goodrich employed top accountants and economists to appear before the Indiana Public Service Commission on behalf of the ITC. Experts such as Dr. William A. Paton, a professor of accounting at the University of Michigan; Dr. John K. Langum, former vice-president of the Federal Reserve Bank of Chicago; and Dr. Benjamin A. Rogge, Distinguished Professor of Political Economy from Wabash College, often represented Goodrich before rate hearings. Of course, Goodrich was attempting to justify rate increases. But it was just as important to him to enlist the testimony of these experts to educate the commission and orient them to his way of thinking.

"One of [Goodrich's] pet projects was to devise an accounting system

21. Letter from Goodrich to Dr. Solomon Fabricant, Department of Economics, New York University, January 3, 1972, Pierre F. Goodrich Collection, Solomon Fabricant file, Archives, Wabash College, Crawfordsville, Indiana.

22. See "How Inflation Warps Accounts," *The Economist,* January 16, 1971, pp. 58–59. For a good discussion of Goodrich's views on inflation, see Pierre F. Goodrich, "Monetary Inflation, Growth, and Accounting," *Public Utilities Fortnightly,* October 28, 1971, pp. 79–81. In a 1973 letter to Indiana Telephone Corporation stockholders, Goodrich explained why not reporting the effects of inflation actually undermines many of the reasons that accounting practices are undertaken in the first place:

> It seems reasonable to state that the first and basic reason for accounting is to ascertain useful information for the management concerning the business and its operation, and that such information being available for management is then also available for shareholders, other security holders and regulatory bodies—tax authorities included.
>
> It is important that [businessmen] know the truth concerning the return of the purchasing power of the dollars their shareholders have invested in the business which they manage for the purpose of providing a product for a profit. . . . (John H. Lyst, "'Real Dollar' Statements Gain New Attention")

that would prevent the government from taxing away the so-called capital gains of business through the ravages of inflation," wrote Paul L. Poirot, who knew Goodrich from their mutual involvement with the Foundation for Economic Education. "What [Goodrich] did not seem to realize is that there is no way to prevent inflation if the government is in charge of the monetary system," Poirot added.[23]

It would seem inconceivable that Goodrich was not aware of the Federal Reserve's role in controlling inflation through monetary policy, especially given Goodrich's familiarity with the writings of Milton Friedman and other monetarists. Goodrich probably believed that it was only by educating others regarding the havoc that inflation could create that monetary policy would eventually be reviewed. Goodrich did not believe that a person had to be an elected official, a Washington, D.C., lobbyist, or an academic to influence governmental decisions. Ultimately, Goodrich's unwavering attack against inflationary policies may have had a significant influence. On his periodic trips to Chicago in the late 1960s and early 1970s, Goodrich often visited Harris Bank and talked with the bank's top economist, Dr. Beryl Sprinkel. The two men discussed a wide range of issues, and especially the pitfalls of inflation. Some years later, Sprinkel became a high-level official at the United States Treasury Department. Toward the end of Ronald Reagan's first term, Sprinkel was named chairman of the Council of Economic Advisers. In this role, he had considerable influence in helping further anti-inflationary policies both with the administration and through discussions with Federal Reserve officials.

"Mr. Goodrich believed that preaching the correct doctrine about inflation might well have an effect on policy," said Sprinkel. "He saw in me a kindred soul. We might each learn something from a discussion of these issues," Sprinkel added.[24]

23. Letter from Paul L. Poirot to author, November 8, 1992.

24. Beryl Sprinkel, telephone interview, January 22, 1993. Despite Goodrich's desire to have inflation recognized from an accountancy perspective, the government's objection to doing that seems to have some validity, at least from a practical perspective. Traditionally, the government has been opposed to recognizing inflation for fear of building it into people's expectations and thereby accelerating it.

Pierre Goodrich was as much interested in the capital growth of the companies he and his family held controlling interests in as he was in their dividend income. One reason was that he hated paying taxes. He loathed the thought that the government would profit from his and his employees' hard work, only to spend the money on boondoggles of one kind or another. Under United States tax law, the paying of corporate dividends amounts to double taxation. First, the company pays tax on the income as corporate tax. Second, whenever there is a distribution of dividends, the individual shareholder must report the dividend as personal income and pay tax on it. The top accounting firm of Arthur Andersen and Company, based in Chicago, established a branch office in Indianapolis in 1960, at first to advise Goodrich's companies. William Fletcher, the managing partner of Arthur Andersen's branch office, became a close adviser to Goodrich, spending hundreds of hours annually consulting him on business matters. Fletcher later served on the board of the Indiana Telephone Corporation and as an executive with the Peoples Loan and Trust Company. Goodrich went to extraordinary efforts to see that Uncle Sam's share was as minuscule as possible, all within the confines of the law.[25]

Toward the end of each fiscal year, Goodrich would hire extra accountants and require existing employees to work overtime figuring out the maximum amount of charitable deduction vis-à-vis dividends that would result in the least tax liability.[26] Goodrich would often contribute stock in one of his companies to Wabash College or to other charitable institutions. By contributing stock rather than cash, Goodrich was able to deduct the market value of the stock at the time it was given, not when it was purchased. By doing this, he avoided any capital gains taxes and was able to deduct the value of the stock from current income. At the same time, the educational institutions enjoyed the appreciated value of the stock. Goodrich used this to tremendous advantage in both

25. Gilbert Snider, interview, December 23, 1991; William H. Fletcher, interview by William C. Dennis, January 25, 1991.

26. Gilbert Snider, interview, December 23, 1991.

reducing his tax liability and benefiting the charitable organizations he supported.[27]

Goodrich's insistence on paying low dividends and investing profits back into his companies was not popular. Other directors in his companies were constantly informing Goodrich that shareholder interest would diminish if the policy of paying low dividends continued; moreover, those investors who needed the income from the shares in order to live were also extremely upset. Despite this opposition, Goodrich generally prevailed in maintaining the paying out of low dividends. Of course, those investors who did hold on to the stock until the time the company was sold enjoyed extremely handsome profits as a result of the huge capital appreciation of the stock.[28]

Toward the end of his life, the central and overriding business concern that Goodrich confronted was liquidating his many corporate interests and laying the foundation for the work of Liberty Fund, Inc. In 1968, Indiana Elevators, the successor to the Goodrich Brothers Hay and Grain Company, went into bankruptcy. On May 8 and May 9, 1969, respectively, Goodrich held shareholders meetings in Indianapolis to dissolve the holding companies of Engineers Incorporated and the Patoka Coal Company. Engineers Incorporated was the family company that was responsible for most of the corporate purchases in the 1930s and 1940s. Patoka Coal had merged with Ayrshire Collieries in 1939 but had technically remained a holding company of Ayrshire stock until its liquidation. Another holding company, the P. F. Goodrich Corporation, was also dissolved in the mid 1960s, dispensing the stock it held directly to investors, who were mostly Goodrich family members.[29] In October 1969, Goodrich sold Ayrshire Collieries to American Metal Climax. Less than a year later, in August 1970, he sold the Goodrich family's 51 percent ownership in City Securities to Dwight Peterson, who was

27. Ibid.
28. Ibid.
29. Don Welch, interview, April 29, 1996.

already president.[30] The Goodrich family, under Pierre's management, continued to hold either a controlling or a large interest in the Indiana Telephone Corporation, Central Shares (the holding company for Central Newspapers stock), the Peoples Loan and Trust Company, and the Eastern Indiana Telephone Company in Winchester.

To what degree Goodrich had plans of selling off these other corporate interests before his death is unknown, but he acknowledged in Liberty Fund's *Basic Memorandum* that the securities of a utility company (undoubtedly his own) would be one of the main assets of the foundation.[31] He had hoped that Liberty Fund might be able to operate the businesses he still owned and apply the profits toward the purposes of the Liberty Fund.[32] The tax problems that arose from this plan proved formidable, however, and were not totally resolved even at the time of his death (see chapter 29).[33] Nonetheless, Goodrich's desire to see Liberty Fund come to fruition under his guidance became an overriding concern.

In addition to liquidating the Goodrich holding companies, Goodrich stepped down from a number of foundation boards: the Great Books Foundation (1957), the Indianapolis Symphony Orchestra (late 1950s), the China Institute of America (1965), the Intercollegiate Studies Institute (1965), the Institute for Humane Studies (1963), and Wabash College (1969). Although only a handful of Liberty Fund conferences had been held by the early 1970s, Goodrich had laid the groundwork for his greatest contribution to society.

30. When Goodrich sold his family's interest in City Securities to the Dwight Peterson family, they obtained an 84 percent share of the corporation's ownership, and the remaining 16 percent was owned by other employees of City Securities Corporation. See E. Bruce Geelhoed, *Indiana's Investment Banker: The Story of City Securities Corporation* (Muncie, Ind.: Ball State University, 1985), p. 117.

31. Pierre F. Goodrich, *Basic Memorandum,* p. 91.

32. Don Welch, interview, December 16, 1991.

33. See Paul M. Doherty, "Foundations' Status Scrutinized Closer," *Indianapolis Star,* n.d. (copy in author's possession).

Pierre Goodrich at approximately forty-five years old. (Courtesy Mrs. Perce G. Goodrich, Portland, Ind.)

Pierre Goodrich, chairman of the board, examines one of the Ayrshire Collieries Corporation's many coal operations, circa 1945. Goodrich is on the left. (Courtesy Mrs. Perce G. Goodrich, Portland, Ind.)

Directors of the Ayrshire Collieries Corporation, circa 1960. *Left to right:* J. Dwight Peterson, Albert M. Campbell, Harold D. Wright, J. B. F. Melville, Pierre F. Goodrich, Norman E. Kelb, E. S. Pearce, and Irwin H. Reiss. (Ayrshire Collieries Corporation)

James and Pierre Goodrich served on the Wabash College Board of Trustees for a combined total of sixty-five years. Pierre is in the front row, farthest right; Byron K. Trippet, the president of Wabash College, is farthest left, second row. (Robert T. Ramsay, Jr., Archival Center, Wabash College, Crawfordsville, Ind.)

The dedication of the Lilly Library containing the Goodrich Seminar Room at Wabash College, April 11, 1959. *Left to right:* Byron K. Trippet, president of the college, and Ivan L. Wiles, Norman E. Treves, Eli Lilly, and Pierre F. Goodrich, trustees. (Robert T. Ramsay, Jr., Archival Center, Wabash College, Crawfordsville, Ind.)

Facing page: top, an early meeting of the Mont Pelerin Society. Pierre Goodrich is sixth from right; to his right and in front is Enid Goodrich. (Mont Pelerin Society Collection, Hoover Institution Archives, Stanford, Calif.)

At Wabash College 1951 graduation ceremonies, Dr. Y. P. Mei received an honorary doctorate. A professor of philosophy at the college during the 1950–51 school year, Mei was on leave from Yenching University in Peking. *Left to right:* Dr. Mei, Pierre F. Goodrich, and Frank Sparks, president of Wabash. (Robert T. Ramsay, Jr., Archival Center, Wabash College)

Pierre Goodrich became a trustee of the China Institute in America in 1949 and served on the board until the mid 1960s. At the institute's Christmas party in New York City, December 1, 1949, *left to right:* Mrs. Huan-shou Meng, Pierre F. Goodrich, Enid Goodrich, an unidentified person, and Dr. Chih Meng, director of the institute from 1930 to 1967. (Mansfield Freeman Center for East Asian Studies, Wesleyan University, Middletown, Conn.)

Leonard Read, founder of the Foundation for Economic Education, was a dynamic speaker, prolific writer, and champion of liberty. He and Pierre Goodrich enjoyed a close friendship during Goodrich's more than twenty years as a FEE trustee. (Foundation for Economic Education, Irvington-on-Hudson, N.Y.; photo by Bachrach)

Pierre Goodrich established a long-time friendship with the Austrian economist Friedrich von Hayek (1899–1992) through their membership in the Mont Pelerin Society. Hayek was the 1974 recipient of the Nobel Prize in Economics. (Mont Pelerin Society Collection, Hoover Institution Archives, Stanford, Calif.)

Harvard Law School class of 1920. Pierre Goodrich is in the third row, third from left (wearing glasses); Roscoe Pound is in the middle of the front row, seated. (Art Collection, Harvard Law School)

Roscoe Pound, a former dean and professor at Harvard Law School, is regarded as perhaps the greatest jurisprudential scholar of the twentieth century. Pierre Goodrich was instrumental in having two of Pound's important works published: *The Constitutional Guarantees of Liberty* (1956) and *Jurisprudence* (1959). (Library of Congress)

Ludwig von Mises. Goodrich's firm friendship with the economist grew out of their mutual involvement with the Foundation for Economic Education and the Mont Pelerin Society. (Courtesy Bettina Bien Greaves, Irvington-on-Hudson, N.Y.)

Benjamin Rogge (1920–80), a former dean and Distinguished Professor of Political Economy at Wabash College, was probably Pierre Goodrich's closest friend and intellectual confidant. (Robert T. Ramsay, Jr., Archival Center, Wabash College, Crawfordsville, Ind.)

Pierre Goodrich, 1894–1973. (Courtesy Mrs. Perce G. Goodrich, Portland, Ind.)

The Goodrich homestead, Winchester, Ind. (Courtesy Mrs. Perce G. Goodrich, Portland, Ind.)

IV

Pierre F. Goodrich

Crusader and Philosopher

Chapter 22

Associations and Causes

Americans of all ages, all stations in life, and all types of disposition are forever forming associations. There are not only commercial and industrial associations in which all take part, but others of a thousand different types—religious, moral, serious, futile, very general and very limited, immensely large and very minute. . . . In every case, at the head of any undertaking, where in France you would find the government or in England some territorial magnate, in the United States you are sure to find an association.

ALEXIS DE TOCQUEVILLE, *Democracy in America*

THE SWISS psychiatrist Carl Jung observed that most people experience two halves of life. The first half, ending sometime near middle age, is when an individual is concerned with choosing a career, finding a mate, establishing a family, and becoming financially secure. The second half is when a person begins to grow more aware of his or her own mortality. Later life is often occupied in the pursuit of previously undeveloped interests in religion, relationships, social causes, and matters beyond strictly self-interested concerns.[1]

It appears that Pierre Goodrich experienced such a transformation in middle age. Up until that time, Goodrich had been focused on his numerous business interests, working hard to build his family's companies into profitable enterprises. Work was his consuming passion, and he worked with an emotional drive that far exceeded what was necessary to obtain any personal comforts.

1. Jolande Jacobi, *The Psychology of C. G. Jung* (New Haven, Conn.: Yale University Press, 1973), pp. 148–49.

Sometime in the mid 1940s (and after the death of his father), Pierre's interests turned decidedly intellectual and associational. While he had always been an avid reader and discussant of ideas, he began to devote large blocks of time to probing those ideas that are at the heart of a society. Thus, the years after James Goodrich's death marked a definite turning point in Pierre's priorities. Pierre was still a force to be reckoned with when any major decision was made pertaining to his family's business empire. Yet, beginning in the mid 1940s, he had the luxury of spending hours reading and thinking about intellectual matters.

From a practical perspective, he was able to devote so much time and energy to these interests because he had surrounded himself with extremely capable business partners and operating lieutenants: Robert Koenig and, later, Norman Kelb at the Ayrshire Collieries Corporation; Irwin H. Reiss at Meadowlark Farms; E. S. Welch and William Scheidler at the Indiana Telephone Corporation; Dwight Peterson and Noble Biddinger at City Securities; Eugene C. Pulliam and his son Eugene S. Pulliam, at Central Newspapers; Don Welch at Peoples Loan and Trust Company; William H. Fletcher of Arthur Andersen and Company; and Albert Campbell, Claude Warren, and, in later life, Helen Schultz at his law offices.

While Goodrich was not a typical businessman-Rotarian type, he did not oppose membership in organizations altogether. Over the course of his life he took on the quiet support and occasional leadership of many organizations, associations whose missions he supported through substantial contributions of time and money. Membership in these associations were deep and lasting commitments for Goodrich. They also provided him with a forum in which to vent his strong opinions and to communicate with others who had basically the same ideological beliefs.

As Tocqueville would have agreed, the idea of "getting involved" is a "peculiarly American notion of the relationship between self and society."[2] It was one that Goodrich took a much greater interest in as he

2. Quote from Robert N. Bellah, ed., *Habits of the Heart: Individualism and Commitment in American Life* (Berkeley: University of California Press, 1985), p. 167.

sought to look outside himself, to have a greater understanding of the public good, and to influence others' understanding of the freedoms and obligations of responsible citizenship.

One of the first educational organizations that Goodrich became active with was the Great Books Foundation, based in Chicago, Illinois. Pierre served on its national board from the time of its founding in April 1947 until November 1955.[3] The Great Books Foundation is an independent, nonprofit educational corporation whose stated mission is to provide people of all ages with the opportunity to read, discuss, and learn from outstanding works of literature.[4]

The Great Books Foundation was established in 1947 by Dr. Robert M. Hutchins, then chancellor of the University of Chicago and previously the university's president, and Mortimer Adler, at the time a professor of philosophy of law at the University of Chicago. The original board of directors was made up of a blue-ribbon panel of national educators, librarians, publishers, and businessmen such as Pierre Goodrich and Lynn A. Williams. Williams was a friend of Goodrich and had been vice-president of Stewart-Warner Corporation in Chicago. In the early years, Henry Regnery's publishing company published the shortened paperback editions of classics of which the Great Books reading list was composed. These works included Plato's *Republic,* Sophocles' *Antigone,* Marx's *Communist Manifesto,* Adam Smith's *Wealth of Nations,* and dozens of other classic works.[5] By mid 1948, the Great Books Founda-

3. The minutes of the directors' meeting of the Great Books Foundation reveal that Goodrich was elected unanimously to the board of directors on April 3, 1947. The foundation met at its headquarters on 20 North Wacker Drive, Chicago, Illinois. Letter from Leslie A. Simmer, editorial assistant, the Great Books Foundation, to author, December 12, 1991; letter from Sharon Crowley, assistant to the president, the Great Books Foundation, to author, May 23, 1996.

4. Fact Sheet, Great Books Foundation, 35 East Wacker Drive, Suite 2300, Chicago, IL 60601-2298.

5. Because of the controversy that surrounded Regnery's publication of William Buckley's *God and Man at Yale,* Regnery lost the contract to publish the Great Books works. See Henry Regnery, *Life of a Dissident Publisher* (New York: Harcourt Brace Jovanovich, 1979), pp. 170–73.

tion had thirty thousand readers in two hundred American cities. Today, its basic program still consists of twice-monthly meetings at which participants discuss the works of Plato, Aristophanes, Aristotle, Marx, Kant, Freud, Shakespeare, and dozens of other influential writers and thinkers of Western culture.

Goodrich took a special interest in promoting the Great Books Foundation in Indiana. In 1947, he formed the Indiana State Temporary Committee of the Great Books Foundation in which he served as chairman.[6] The presidents or deans of several Indiana colleges, including Butler, Wabash, Earlham, Hanover, DePauw, and Notre Dame, served on the committee. Before Goodrich established the temporary committee, only Indianapolis, South Bend, and Goodrich's hometown of Winchester had Great Books programs in the state,[7] but Goodrich undertook to establish dozens of chapters in Indiana. There may have been more than thirty such chapters established throughout the state at Goodrich's instigation.[8] He advertised in newspapers throughout Indiana seeking qualified Great Books leaders to head chapters in small towns. He also contacted friends and acquaintances, especially friends in smaller communities such as Anderson, Crawfordsville, Columbus, Huntington, Liberty, Lawrenceville, Lynn, Richmond, and Sullivan. Goodrich apparently thought that citizens from these smaller towns might benefit most by having a forum to discuss great literary works.[9]

6. Formal members of the committee were Dr. M. O. Ross of Butler University, Lynn A. Williams, Jr., and Frank Sparks, then president of Wabash College.

7. See Lowell Parker, "Winchester, Indiana: Literary Guinea Pig," *Indianapolis Star Magazine,* September 28, 1947, pp. 16–17.

8. The author was unable to determine precisely how many Great Books discussion chapters were established as a result of Goodrich's initiation; however, according to material at Wabash College, participants from as many as thirty-five Indiana towns and cities attended the three-day training sessions for discussion leaders. Presumably, most of these towns and cities had Great Books chapters. See letter from Robert S. Harvey, Wabash College registrar, to Pierre F. Goodrich, August 31, 1948, Great Books Collection, Archives, Wabash College.

9. For instance, Goodrich contacted Will Hays, Jr., and Norman and Mary Johnson to start Great Books chapters in their towns of Sullivan and Liberty, respectively. Both chapters met for a while (Hays claims that the one at Sullivan was quite successful)

Moreover, Goodrich partially underwrote the cost of training conferences for discussion leaders—at Wabash College in August 1948 and September 1949, and one at Earlham College in Richmond, Indiana.[10]

During the summer of 1947, Goodrich hired Dale Braun, then principal of Winchester High School and later superintendent of schools, to meet with community and business leaders. Braun's task was to attempt to create an interest in establishing Great Books chapters in other towns and cities throughout the state.[11] "Pierre saw in the Great Books program and the Socratic method the opportunity to get people to think," said Braun. Goodrich also employed Professor Jack Charles of Wabash College to lead discussion groups.[12]

Another friend of Goodrich's, D. Elton Trueblood, also helped Pierre start several chapters. Dr. Trueblood was then professor of religion at Earlham College and a nationally known speaker and author. He had become acquainted with Goodrich when Trueblood had taught briefly at Wabash College in 1946.[13]

One of the most successful, if short-lived, Indiana Great Books chapters was in Goodrich's hometown of Winchester. It was funded anonymously by Goodrich through the Winchester Foundation, which Good-

---

before interest finally waned. Will Hays, interview, May 8, 1992; Norman and Mary Johnson, interview, January 1, 1992.

10. The 1948 seminar was held in August. The 1949 seminar was held from August 31 to September 3. Information about Goodrich's advertising in small-town newspapers to locate chapters and leaders was contained in a letter from Roy Schukman to William C. Dennis, Liberty Fund, April 29, 1996 (copy in author's possession).

11. Dale Braun, interview, July 17, 1992. Braun recalled visiting and even hosting dinners in several Indiana towns, including Fort Wayne, Columbus, and Columbia City.

12. Letter from Jack Charles to author, January 28, 1993.

13. According to Dale Braun, the Great Books program in Indiana cities and towns never did catch on as Goodrich had hoped. Only a handful of communities had chapters that lasted more than a year. Dale Braun, interview, July 17, 1992. Elton Trueblood's memories of the success of Great Books were different: "You can quote me as saying that the program was a tremendous success, made so partly by the influence of Mr. Goodrich. . . . We met because of the close connection with Wabash College to which he was devoted. I often visited him in his office in Indianapolis" (letter to author, December 3, 1991).

rich had established in 1945. The foundation purchased the books for the chapter. At the chapter's height, approximately fifty adults and two dozen teenagers met in three subgroups every Monday night at the old Winchester High School gymnasium. Goodrich would often attend, driving from Indianapolis especially for the meetings or extending one of his frequent weekend visits to Winchester.

Elton Trueblood often led the discussions, and John Barden, an assistant dean at the University of Chicago, was also an invited discussion leader. Later, members of the Winchester group led their own discussions. The success of the chapter, in a small blue-collar midwestern town reminiscent of communities in Sinclair Lewis's and Sherwood Anderson's novels, was featured in the *Indianapolis Star Magazine* in 1947. In August 1948, it even caught the attention of *Parade* magazine, meriting a feature article in the national publication.[14]

By the mid 1950s, Goodrich had become somewhat impatient with the Great Books program. He also questioned the convictions of many of his fellow promoters of the Great Books concept. Goodrich saw in the Great Books program the thinking that "[a]ny idea is as good as another," said William C. Dennis, a senior program officer of Liberty Fund. "That wasn't Goodrich's way of looking at the world. He thought some ideas were better than others and [he thought] he understood why."[15]

Goodrich finally resigned from the Great Books national board in November 1955; he did, however, continue to support the foundation through gifts from the Winchester Foundation and Liberty Fund. Although Goodrich ceased to be a board member, he did take from the

14. See Lowell Parker, "Winchester, Indiana: Literary Guinea Pig," pp. 16–17; Ernest La France, "Winchester and the Great Books: Indiana Town Reads the Classics for Recreation and Self-improvement," *Parade,* August 1, 1948, pp. 5–7. By 1949, there had been some loss of enthusiasm for Great Books discussions in Winchester, but the death knell came to the local chapter with the polio epidemic. Voluntary public meetings were avoided for good reason. Harry Fraze, interview, October 26, 1991. Fraze was co-leader of the Winchester chapter (along with Anna Marie Gibbons). Fraze, a mortician by profession, was the town's mayor at the time, and Gibbons was a reporter for the local newspaper.

15. William C. Dennis, interview, October 25, 1991.

Great Books Foundation two important concepts he would later incorporate into his establishment of Liberty Fund seminars: readings from original texts and the Socratic discussion seminar.

No other organization that Goodrich was affiliated with was as closely aligned with his philosophical beliefs about individual liberty as the Foundation for Economic Education (FEE). FEE, based in Irvington-on-Hudson, New York, about thirty miles north of New York City, was established in 1946 by Leonard E. Read, who had the idea of an organization set up to proclaim the ideals of liberty. Read had been employed in city chamber of commerce work for most of his working life before establishing FEE. In 1939, he was appointed director of the Los Angeles Chamber of Commerce. Both before and during his tenure there, he traveled widely around the country speaking passionately about the virtues of liberty, free enterprise, and entrepreneurship.

Read eventually tired of chamber of commerce work because he was always at the beck and call of its business members.[16] He decided to begin a small organization that would research and discuss the ideals of liberty, one that would be beholden to no other individual institution or interest group.[17]

Read bought the building that FEE still occupies for forty thousand dollars in 1946 and sought out several scholars to read, research, write, and speak.[18] An amazing range of talent passed through FEE's doors during its early years of existence: Fred Fairchild, former economist at Yale University, and economist Henry Hazlitt served as founding trustees; Ludwig von Mises was on FEE's payroll as an adviser; Friedrich Hayek lectured on occasion; and F. A. "Baldy" Harper, who would later

16. Edmund Opitz, telephone interview, October 10, 1992.

17. Ibid. Opitz, a minister, served as a senior staff member, editor of *The Freeman* (a monthly magazine produced by FEE), and "resident theologian" for FEE from 1955 until 1992. For a more complete examination of Read and FEE, see Mary Sennholz, *Leonard Read: Philosopher of Liberty* (Irvington-on-Hudson, N.Y.: Foundation for Economic Education, 1993).

18. Sennholz, *Leonard Read: Philosopher of Liberty,* p. 72.

establish and serve as president of the Institute for Humane Studies, served on FEE's staff.

FEE's early success in publishing also helped establish it as an institution of far-ranging influence. FEE promoted and later republished Hazlitt's *Economics in One Lesson,* subsidized the first printing of Mises's *Human Action,* republished a new translation of Frederic Bastiat's *The Law,* and published a revised edition of Henry Grady Weaver's *The Mainspring of Human Progress.* The three books by Hazlitt, Bastiat, and Weaver have, together, sold more than two million copies.[19]

Read, like Goodrich, possessed an incredible breadth of interests and talents. He wrote twenty-seven books during his life, lectured to thousands of audiences, corresponded widely, and was a lifetime learner.[20] Goodrich was on FEE's board of trustees for more than twenty years (1952–73). As a trustee, he served with dozens of other distinguished businessmen and academics.[21] Goodrich would often bring to FEE board meetings an array of gourmet cheeses and a selection of fine wines.[22] In addition to making direct financial contributions to FEE, Goodrich sent dozens of employees from his coal company, farming operations, bank, and other businesses to various FEE seminars.[23]

19. Telephone interview, Bettina Bien Greaves, Foundation for Economic Education, December 5, 1997.

20. "The Foundation: Yesterday, Today, and Tomorrow" (pamphlet prepared for the new chairman of FEE's board of trustees), FEE's offices, Irvington-on-Hudson, New York. Read had hoped that Rogge would be his successor, and Rogge had even been added to FEE's payroll before he decided to remain at Wabash College. For more about Read, see Mary Sennholz, *Leonard E. Read: Philosopher of Liberty*.

21. These men included B. E. Hutchinson, vice-president and treasurer of Chrysler Corporation; Ben Moreell, president of Jones and Laughlin Steel Company in Pittsburgh and a former United States Navy admiral; J. Howard Pew, chairman of Sun Oil Company; Jasper Crane, vice-president of DuPont Corporation; Leo Wolman, a professor of economics at Columbia University; and Goodrich's close friend Dr. Benjamin Rogge.

22. Edmund Opitz, telephone interview, October 10, 1992. Goodrich also arranged for the accounting firm of Arthur Andersen to conduct an annual independent audit of FEE (Hans Sennholz, interview, October 16, 1992).

23. Paul L. Poirot, emeritus editor of *The Freeman,* letter to author, November 8, 1992.

In Leonard Read, Goodrich found a man who was as devoted to the causes of liberty and free enterprise as he was. Read's book, *Government—An Ideal Concept,* made a tremendous impression on Pierre. The two men would often talk for hours about ideas, and Read was the recipient of many of Goodrich's infamous late-night telephone calls.[24] Goodrich had a great fondness for Read and hosted a dinner in Read's honor in Indianapolis at the Woodstock Country Club. Goodrich was also responsible for Read's speaking at Wabash College and in Winchester. Next to Benjamin Rogge, Leonard Read probably had the greatest intellectual influence on Goodrich of any contemporary mind. Goodrich remained a lifelong supporter of FEE initiatives. Even today, the Winchester Foundation and Liberty Fund, established by Goodrich, contribute financially to FEE operations.[25]

From 1949 until the mid 1960s, Goodrich served as a trustee of the China Institute of America in New York City.[26] The China Institute, whose predecessor was the China Foundation, was founded in 1926 by American educators John Dewey and Paul Monroe of Columbia University. The China Foundation's primary objective had been to dispense monies that had been set aside for the United States out of the Boxer Indemnity Fund as a result of the Boxer Rebellion.[27]

The China Institute's purposes were primarily fourfold: to disseminate information concerning Chinese and American education, to promote a closer relationship between Chinese and American educational institutions through the exchange of professors and students, to assist

24. Edmund Opitz said that Leonard Read would often come into work and report that Goodrich had called him the night before as late as 2:00 A.M. Read said that the conversations were more like monologues by Goodrich than discussions, since Goodrich often called to share whatever was bothering him (telephone interview, October 10, 1992).

25. Ruth Connolly, interview, October 25, 1991.

26. The China Institute of America, 125 E. 65 Street, New York, N.Y.

27. See Chih Meng, *Chinese American Understanding: A Sixty-Year Search* (New York: China Institute of America, 1967), p. 121.

Chinese students in America in their education, and to stimulate interest in America in the study of Chinese culture.[28]

Goodrich first became involved with the China Institute in 1948 as a contributor.[29] The following year, he was not only elected as a trustee but served as one of three vice-presidents of the China Institute. Another of the vice-presidents was Thomas J. Watson, Jr., then president of International Business Machines (IBM). Henry R. Luce, founder of *Time, Life,* and *Fortune* magazines, served as president during that time. Children of Christian missionaries, Luce and his sister, Elisabeth Luce Moore, were reared in China, and Moore remains a trustee even today.[30]

Beginning in 1949, Goodrich served on the institute's finance committee. Charles Edison—son of the inventor Thomas A. Edison and former secretary of the navy and governor of New Jersey—was chairman of the committee in the late 1940s and early 1950s. The years from 1949 to 1953 were critical for the very survival of the China Institute. Chinese-American relations had deteriorated during the late 1940s. Until 1945, the Chinese government, banks, and private Chinese individuals had contributed substantial sums toward educating Chinese students in America. The political upheaval in China after 1945, however, culminating in the Communist Revolution in 1949, cut off practically all funds from China. Soon after that, the Korean War complicated and strained relations between America and China even more.

28. Ibid., p. 142. In pursuit of this last goal, an Indiana project affiliated with the China Institute was initiated by Floy Hurlbut, who was a professor of science at Ball State College in Muncie. It is not known if Goodrich was involved, although his participation in some form is highly likely. In 1950, Hurlbut persuaded Ball State president John R. Emens to invite China Institute director Chih Meng and other Chinese scholars to Ball State to form a China Institute of the Midwest. The resulting workshop inspired a number of Indiana colleges to introduce their own courses or workshops on China.

29. According to China Institute records, the first mention of Goodrich was in 1948 as an "associate," meaning a benefactor. See "Annual Report of the Director for 1948," China Institute of America, Mansfield Freeman Center for East Asian Studies, Wesleyan University, Middletown, Conn.

30. Although Henry R. Luce died in 1973, his son Henry Luce III serves as a trustee. Elisabeth Luce Moore, although well into her nineties, continues to serve as a trustee and has done so for nearly fifty years.

By the end of 1949, more than 12,000 Chinese academics, scientists, and writers had managed to escape to the United States. As of October 1952, 5,406 Chinese students or teachers were stranded in America. The United States Congress had passed legislation prohibiting from leaving America any Chinese who had scientific or technical skills that could be useful to an enemy of the United Nations. This was meant to apply to Communist China, which was then not a member of the United Nations. Therefore, many recent Chinese graduates with M.D.'s and Ph.D.'s were forced to take unsuitable positions merely to survive. They became perfect targets for Communist promises of utopia in Red China.[31]

At that time, the China Institute, and specifically the Finance Committee on which Goodrich served, took on the monumental task of raising money to help these Chinese students and recent graduates find employment. By the end of 1949, some 1,500 Chinese had registered with the China Institute's job placement bureau. Within a few months, some 2,000 had been referred to employers and 250 had received jobs.[32]

During the years in which Goodrich served as trustee, the institute played host to dozens of American and foreign dignitaries, including Eleanor Roosevelt, Nobel Prize–winning novelist Pearl Buck (author of *The Good Earth*), Mrs. Wendell Willkie, former United States secretary of state George C. Marshall, and Chinese Nationalist leader Chiang Kai-shek. In the mid 1950s, Pierre arranged for Roscoe Pound, his former law professor at Harvard, to address the institute. Pound had become an expert in Chinese constitutional law after spending three years as an adviser both on the Mainland before the 1949 revolution and in Formosa (Taiwan) after the revolution.

31. These observations were made by Elisabeth Luce Moore and Chih Meng. See speech by Elisabeth Luce Moore, vice-president of China Institute, "China Institute's 'Double Ten' Dinner," held in the Grand Ballroom, Waldorf-Astoria, October 9, 1952; see also memorandum from Chih Meng, director of China Institute, to General Edwin N. Clark, president of the China Institute, December 29, 1952. Both documents are located in "Miscellaneous Documents Related to China Institute" (1991.3.45), Mansfield Freeman Center for East Asian Studies, Wesleyan University, Middletown, Conn.

32. Address by Elisabeth Luce Moore, October 9, 1952.

Goodrich was known as a generous contributor to the institute, full of ideas and an innovative thinker.[33] "There are so many members on boards who don't want to rock the boat," said Mrs. Elisabeth Luce Moore, "but Pierre rocked!"[34]

Goodrich and Chih Meng, China Institute director from 1927 to 1967, corresponded and talked regularly. They were both stubborn men and often strongly disagreed about institute policy.[35] Shortly before Meng retired as director, he and Goodrich apparently had a falling out that resulted in Pierre's resignation from the board in the mid 1960s. But he did not leave before he had contributed significantly to the institute's mission.[36]

Goodrich passionately loved music, as both an amateur violinist and a listener. He had been exposed to church and choir music as a boy in the Presbyterian Church and played in community orchestras as a youth. His father had supported the talents of young Winchester musicians by providing scholarship money and loans for college music instruction.

Pierre also financially supported young musicians, especially at Wabash College. No doubt Goodrich's intense feeling for music was encouraged by his parents at a very early age. He began playing the violin as a youth. When he was a young man, his mother bought him a Stradivarius violin, which was valued at forty thousand dollars at the time of Pierre's death.[37] Goodrich loved opera, and most business trips to New

33. Goodrich's generosity was noted by Mrs. Elisabeth Luce Moore, telephone interview, October 9, 1992.

34. Ibid.

35. Ibid.

36. Ibid.; Rosanna Amos, interview, December 10, 1991. The falling out between Goodrich and Meng must not have been too great, since Goodrich and his wife attended Meng's retirement dinner in 1967 in New York City. See "Minutes of the Board of Directors of the Liberty Fund, Inc.," April 24, 1967, p. 119 (in the possession of Liberty Fund).

37. Roy Barnes said that Cora Goodrich had paid thirty-five thousand dollars for the violin (interview, February 8, 1992); see also "Goodrich Property Sale to Be Private,"

York were not complete unless Goodrich and his guests went to the Metropolitan Opera.[38] In Indianapolis, he faithfully attended the Starlight Musical programs on Butler University's campus and was a leading supporter of the Indianapolis Symphony Orchestra and of the Indianapolis Choral Society.[39]

Goodrich served on the board of directors of the Indiana State Symphony Society from 1939 to 1954. The society was the organization responsible for establishing and maintaining the operations of the Indianapolis Symphony Orchestra (ISO).[40] These were fifteen critical years in the life of the young Indianapolis Symphony. From 1940 to 1951, the violin virtuoso Jascha Heifetz performed with the ISO on five occasions.[41] On at least one of these visits to Indianapolis, Heifetz visited Goodrich's home at 4220 Central Avenue to play Pierre's Stradivarius.[42]

The institutions and causes that Goodrich was involved with numbered in the dozens. Some of the more important ones were the Intercollegiate Studies Institute, now based in Wilmington, Delaware; the Institute for Humane Studies, formerly located at Menlo Park, California (now located at George Mason University in Fairfax, Virginia); the Committee for Monetary Research and Education at Harriman, New York; the Philadelphia Society; the Foundation for Foreign Affairs; the National Foundation for Education in American Citizenship; the Institute of Paper Chemistry at Appleton, Wisconsin; and Phi Beta Kappa and Phi

---

Indianapolis Star, December 3, 1975, p. 43, col. 7 (reports the sale of a Stradivarius violin appraised at forty thousand dollars and a Vangelisti violin appraised at three thousand dollars).

38. Don Welch, interview, December 16, 1991.

39. Ibid. A number of Goodrich's friends said that Goodrich often invited them to Indianapolis to attend Starlight Musical productions.

40. This information was provided to the author by Lorri Church, Public Relations Office, Indianapolis Symphony Orchestra, December 7, 1992.

41. Ibid. The occasions when Heifetz performed with ISO were January 5 and 6, 1940; January 31 and February 1, 1941; December 16 and 17, 1944; February 26 and 27, 1949; and January 27 and 28, 1951.

42. Roy Barnes, interview, February 8, 1992.

Gamma Delta, educational honor and fraternal societies, respectively. Goodrich either served as a trustee of or was a contributor to each of these organizations. His scholarship contributions to the Institute for Humane Studies, for example, made it possible for several students to work toward graduate degrees.[43]

Goodrich created educational and grant-making organizations of his own. The first was the Winchester Foundation, established in 1945 for "the encouragement and stimulation of interest in and study of the arts, music, philosophy and religion." Another was a foundation he named simply Thirty Five Twenty (now the Pierre and Enid Goodrich Foundation), which was the street address of his business offices on Washington Boulevard in Indianapolis. The most important institutions to Goodrich, however, were Wabash College, the Mont Pelerin Society, and his own foundation, Liberty Fund.

43. Letter from B. A. Rogge to Kenneth S. Templeton, Jr., regarding a Special Loan and Scholarship grant from the Winchester Foundation to Gary North for graduate study, May 6, 1969; letter from Kenneth S. Templeton, Jr., to Don E. Welch, secretary, the Winchester Foundation, acknowledging grants of fifteen hundred dollars for graduate students Arthur N. Chamberlain III and Gus diZerega, July 18, 1967, Benjamin Rogge Collection, Institute for Humane Studies file, Archives, Wabash College.

Chapter 23
Wabash College

What does a liberal education, such as a college like Wabash professes to give, do for a young man? It places before him materials, which are studied in a scientific manner and by the experimental method, that his mind may rediscover and grasp for itself the principles that underlie human existence. The mind is disciplined and given breadth, scope, reach. . . . It awakens a genuine intellectual interest and imparts the social point of view. A truly "liberal culture" is thus a genuine and serious preparation for a life of service in a thoroughly socialized world. It is essential to good citizenship.

CHARLES A. TUTTLE, "A Liberal Education"

A SMALL COLLEGE in west-central Indiana has played an extremely important role in the lives of the Goodrich family since their first association with the institution nearly one hundred years ago. Wabash College is located in Crawfordsville, Indiana, a conservative small town of about fifteen thousand, approximately forty-five miles northwest of Indianapolis. Crawfordsville is perhaps best known for being the home of Lew Wallace, a Wabash alumnus who was a Civil War general, United States ambassador to Turkey, and author of the novel *Ben Hur,* the most popular novel of the nineteenth century, which was later made into one of the most popular movies of all time.

Although it views itself as a private independent college, Wabash has ties with the Presbyterian Church: It was founded by five Presbyterian ministers in 1832, and its first six presidents were ordained Presbyterian clergymen. It is a top-notch academic institution that achieved in the

1950s the academic reputation that James Goodrich had hoped for when he was one of the college's most enthusiastic supporters as chairman of the board of trustees in the 1920s and 1930s. Wabash has served as the undergraduate college of several Rhodes scholars, and many of its graduates have achieved considerable success in business, law, politics, medicine, academia, and the arts.[1] Since its establishment, Wabash has been an all-male college. No doubt that fact is indicative of the college's inclination to maintain traditions and loyalty to the institution. An interesting story that reveals Wabash's conservative nature involves an incident that occurred just a few years after James Goodrich first became a member of the board of trustees in 1904.

The young Ezra Pound, America's enigmatic poet of the early and mid twentieth century, had been hired to teach modern foreign languages at Wabash in the fall of 1907. From the beginning, Pound was obviously less than enamored of his new provincial midwestern home. After only six weeks at the college, Pound wrote to his parents, mocking his adopted state and the popular verse style of Indiana's poet laureate, James Whitcomb Riley: "There seems to be plenty to be done here. Of course if you can find . . . as good a job for me somewhere in the effete

1. Wabash's academic excellence is apparent in many ways. It has had seven students selected as Rhodes scholars and has had several former Rhodes scholars on its faculty, a truly large number given its small size (fewer than one thousand students annually). In a 1985 study on graduate education in the United States from 1951 to 1980, Wabash ranked sixteenth out of fifteen hundred colleges and universities in the percentage (12.9 percent) of its graduates who went on to receive doctorate degrees. Susan Cantrell, Wabash College News Bureau, telephone interview, April 7, 1993. Its list of alumni is truly impressive, including Lew Wallace; Will Hays, Sr., former Republican national chairman, postmaster general, and first president of the Motion Picture Producers Association; Thomas Marshall, vice-president of the United States under Woodrow Wilson (1912–20); and Robert Allen, former chairman and CEO of AT&T and a current member of the Wabash College Board of Trustees. In 1924, eight years after Goodrich graduated, of the then living Wabash alumni, 1,489 were in business, 505 were lawyers, 501 were professors or teachers, 425 were ministers, 259 were physicians or surgeons, 209 were agriculturalists, 148 were journalists, 98 were bankers, 92 were scientists, and 57 were engineers. See *Wabash—A Record of Honor* (Crawfordsville, Ind.: Wabash College, 1924).

east I would be very likely to abandon my 'igh callin' and skidoo to paats more plush-lined than Hoosier."[2]

Pound did not have to wait long to move on, although it was the decision of the Wabash College administration rather than his own. He had been at the college less than six months when a cleaning lady disclosed to Wabash's president that she had found a young woman in Pound's bed one morning. According to Pound, he had met the penniless young girl the night before. She had been stranded in a blizzard after a burlesque show, and he had offered her his accommodations while he slept in his study. Once the "affair" had become known, the trustees were contacted and only one outcome was possible.[3]

The Goodrich family's experiences with the small college proved to be far more successful and long-standing. At the May 1915 graduation ceremony, James Goodrich received an honorary master of arts degree from Wabash for his tireless work on the board of trustees. Two years later, during his first year as governor, he had bestowed upon him an honorary doctorate of laws. Pierre graduated from Wabash in 1916 and in 1940 assumed his father's position on the board of trustees, a position he held until 1969.[4] At the 1949 commencement, Pierre, too, was awarded—along with Goodrich's business associate Eugene Pulliam, Sr.—the special degree of Doctor of Laws.[5] In 1955, Pierre received the college's Alumni Award of Merit. From 1959 to 1969, Pierre served as vice-chairman of the board.[6] After Pierre stepped down from the board, he

2. C. David Heyman, *Ezra Pound: The Last Rower* (New York: Viking, 1975), p. 11.

3. Ibid. A fuller and even more sympathetic account of Pound's short tenure at Wabash can be found in James Insley Osborne and Theodore Gregory Gronert, *Wabash College: The First Hundred Years, 1832–1932* (Crawfordsville, Ind.: R. E. Banta, 1932), pp. 291–92.

4. Pierre assumed the position of trustee on the board almost immediately after his father's death. Moreover, a memorial service for James Goodrich was held at the Wabash chapel on October 6, 1940. See letter from G. V. Kendall, acting president, to Pierre F. Goodrich, September 23, 1940, Pierre F. Goodrich files, Archives, Wabash College.

5. See *Wabash Bulletin* 45 (September 1949): 4–5.

6. All documentation in the files on Goodrich at Wabash College's archives indicate that he served as vice-president of the board of trustees from 1958 to 1969. Records

was designated trustee emeritus, the first such honor bestowed on a former trustee in the college's history.

Throughout most of the twentieth century, the Goodrich family has supported Wabash College. For instance, John Goodrich, Pierre's first cousin, established a trust fund that has contributed several million dollars to the college since his death in 1971.[7] In addition to being chairman of the board of trustees for sixteen years (1924–40), James Goodrich often came personally to the financial rescue of Wabash.[8] In December 1918, he pledged to give up to one-tenth of any sum raised up to $500,000 to increase the college's endowment. In 1927, the former governor contributed toward the building of a new chapel and gave the dedication speech at that facility on January 10, 1929. In 1928, he contributed $50,000, making it possible for the college to build its first gymnasium. In November 1937, he contributed $150,000, completely financing the building of the college's science hall, now called Goodrich Hall. The significance of these contributions may be better appreciated when it is considered that in 1927 a semester's tuition at Wabash was eighty-five dollars per student.[9]

Pierre, too, contributed much financially to Wabash, but his greatest contribution was his role in furthering the school's academic programs.

---

also show, however, that Eugene N. Beesley served as vice-president from 1965 to 1975. The board may have had two vice-presidents from 1965 to 1969.

7. By the terms of the John B. Goodrich trust fund, monies from the fund can be allocated to three entities: Wabash College, the Winchester Presbyterian Church, and the Winchester Park Department for the John B. Goodrich Park (Terri Matchett, vice-president and trust officer, American National Bank Trust Department, interview, January 17, 1996).

8. See "Goodrich Leaves Wabash $100,000," *Indianapolis News,* October 9, 1940, p. 15, col. 6. The article states that James Goodrich's financial contributions to Wabash started in 1909, three years before Pierre matriculated at the school.

9. See James Insley Osborne and Theodore Gregory Gronert, *Wabash College: The First Hundred Years, 1832–1932,* pp. 335, 337, 385; "A Statement of the Gifts of James P. Goodrich to Wabash College," by O. P. Welborn, secretary-treasurer, the Board of Trustees, Wabash College. Nobel Prize–winning physicist Arthur Holly Compton of the University of Chicago gave the dedication speech at the Goodrich Science Building. A tribute to James P. Goodrich by the Wabash College Board of Trustees is found in the *Wabash Bulletin* 39 (October 1940), supplement.

According to the former Wabash president Byron Trippet, Goodrich "exerted a profound influence on the intellectual life of Wabash in the post–World War II era."[10] At the time, Pierre was very involved in the Great Books movement. In the mid 1940s, he worked closely with Wabash president Frank Sparks and with Byron Trippet, who then served as dean of the college. He and Trippet traveled to the University of Chicago and later to St. John's College in Annapolis, Maryland, to investigate the Great Books programs at both schools. At Chicago, they met with Robert Hutchins and Mortimer Adler, and at St. John's they met with the school's president, the poet Stringfellow Barr. They analyzed the success of St. John's decision to adopt the Great Books program as its total curriculum.

As a result of these and other inquiries, the Colloquium on Important Books for juniors and seniors at Wabash in 1946 was born. The colloquium stressed the Socratic method of book discussion and deemphasized the use and importance of textbooks and professorial lectures. Trippet recounts that being around Pierre during these years was an important chapter in his own education.[11]

> In 1946–47, I found myself drawn into numerous and lengthy conversations with Pierre about education. After overcoming whatever initial reservations and suspicions he may have had about me, he drew me increasingly into his interests. For the better part of the next ten years, we worked closely together. Despite the endless, lengthy long-distance telephone calls at all hours of the day and night, despite the frequent interminable conferences, despite the rigors of travelling with Pierre, I acknowledge that I learned a great deal from this man, and in the process I learned to respect and admire much of what he stood for.[12]

10. Byron Trippet, *Wabash on My Mind,* p. 185.

11. Ibid.

12. Ibid. Trippet gave a short speech in April or May 1946 at a dinner for alumni, trustees, and friends of Wabash College at the Columbia Club in Indianapolis. Trippet states in *Wabash on My Mind,* "Pierre Goodrich, who I am sure prior to that evening had been distrustful of me because of a pro-Roosevelt speech I had made in 1937 that annoyed his father, Governor Goodrich, sought me out afterwards to get better acquainted. This was the beginning of a close relationship with Pierre . . ." (pp. 53–54).

Pierre also furthered the college's intellectual life by bringing to campus such prominent scholars as Russell Kirk, the Austrian intellectual Erik von Kuehnelt-Leddihn, and Roscoe Pound, former dean of Harvard Law School. During the fall semester of 1962, Goodrich underwrote the costs of having F. A. "Baldy" Harper from the Institute of Humane Studies teach at Wabash.[13] In the late 1950s and 1960s, Goodrich also funded lectures by William Buckley, newspaper columnist and founder of the *National Review;*[14] Friedrich Hayek, internationally known economist; Felix Morley, former president of Haverford College and former editor of the *Washington Post;* Dr. Bruno Suviranta of Finland; Archduke Otto von Hapsburg, heir to the Hapsburg throne; B. R. Shenoy, director of economics of the Research Center, New Delhi, India; and Ludwig Erhard, chancellor of West Germany from 1963 to 1966.[15] The lectures by Pound and Morley were published in

13. Harper's semester was paid for out of the Wabash College Unallocated Fund contributed to by Goodrich's companies. Goodrich makes reference to it during an October 1962 Liberty Fund board meeting. See "Minutes of the Meeting of the Board of Directors of the Liberty Fund, Inc.," October 1, 1962, p. 27 (in the possession of Liberty Fund).

14. *God and Man at Yale: The Superstitions of Academic Freedom* (Chicago: Regnery, 1951).

15. Hayek spoke to the Wabash Conservative Economics Club on May 12, 1960; Suviranta's lectures at Wabash on September 23 and 25, 1958, were entitled "Finland and Russia" and "Finland and the Middle Way," respectively; Archduke Otto spent three days on the Wabash campus during the last week of October 1961; Shenoy spoke at Wabash on April 6, 1964, on foreign aid and the economic development of India, and on April 7, 1964, to two classes at the college on planning, development, and inflation in India. Dr. Ludwig Erhard gave the commencement address at Wabash in May 1959 and addressed approximately one thousand members and guests of the Indiana Academy of Arts and Sciences that evening. Erhard also spoke as a guest of Wabash and Goodrich at the Columbia Club in Indianapolis, where Goodrich was a member, on February 19, 1968. According to the April 1968 issue of *The Columbian* (vol. 59, no. 4, p. 2), Erhard's lectures were sponsored by Wabash College, the Indianapolis Chamber of Commerce, and Liberty Fund. In essence, Goodrich brought Erhard to Indianapolis and financed the speaking engagement. See also "Erhard Warns of World Inflation," *Indianapolis News,* February 20, 1968, p. 2, col. 6.

book form.[16] All the lectures were financed by gifts to Wabash from Goodrich.

In March 1957, Pierre undertook a major project at Wabash, seeing to the design and completion of the Goodrich Seminar Room in the Lilly Library. The Goodrich Room is a large conference room (approximately sixty feet long, forty feet wide, and twenty feet high) located in the center of the school's library. The library was named for Eli Lilly, whose contributions were mostly responsible for its construction.

The concept behind the layout of the room is a chronology of the great civilizations of mankind. The names of the great writings and thinkers of each epoch are carved into the room's limestone walls, from the ancient cultures of Egypt, Babylon, China, Greece, and the Roman Empire to the expression of civilization by northern European powers, the Renaissance and the Reformation. The chronological carvings end with the Declaration of Independence, encompassing the tremendous outpouring of thought and development of individual liberty.

Pierre wanted the seminar room to serve as the location for Socratic discussions on the ideals written about by the great thinkers whose names are on the surrounding walls. At the time, some Wabash faculty members called the seminar room Goodrich's Folly, but Byron Trippet, who had worked hard with Pierre to see to the room's completion, defended its worth. The seminar room was dedicated on June 4, 1959.[17] Goodrich donated two thousand books from his own library to be placed in the room, many by authors whose names are carved on

16. Roscoe Pound's lectures on February 26, 27, and 28 and May 1, 1945, were later published as *The Development of Constitutional Guarantees of Liberty* (New Haven: Yale University Press for Wabash College, 1957). Felix Morley's lectures were given in May 1947 under the sponsorship of the Pierre F. Goodrich Seminars program. His three lectures provided the first three chapters of his book *Power in the People* (New York: D. Van Nostrand, 1949).

17. Byron Trippet, "Dedication Remarks," June 4, 1959 (found in the pamphlet "Goodrich Seminar Room," Lilly Library, Wabash College).

the walls, such as Homer, Hesiod, Socrates, Virgil, Paul the Apostle, Thomas Aquinas, Chaucer, Martin Luther, John Locke, David Hume, and Immanuel Kant. The books encompass a variety of fields: music, poetry, science, history, drama, philosophy, theology, and political theory.[18] True to his independent streak and much to the chagrin of the college's librarian, Goodrich devised his own catalogue identification system for the donated books.[19]

Goodrich made many other contributions to his alma mater, but seldom without strings attached. The tight control Goodrich held over his gifts was explained by Richard O. Ristine, who served on the board of trustees with Goodrich and is a former Indiana lieutenant governor. "If [Pierre] was going to spend money on the college, he saw no reason why there shouldn't be strings attached to it as if he was investing in the capital of the Greensburg Telephone Company," said Ristine.[20]

Therefore, Goodrich gave blocks of stock and monetary gifts to the school, but usually with the proviso that the money could not be used or the stocks sold without his approval.[21] Between 1941 and 1962, Goodrich made a total of 133 individual contributions (generally stock in one of his corporations) totaling nearly $333,000.[22] Pierre was particularly

18. Pat Redmond, "Pierre Goodrich Puts Rare Books on Wabash Shelves," *Indianapolis Star,* March 27, 1959, p. 19, col. 3. Attached to each book's inside cover is a label that lists what Goodrich believed were three fundamental questions that each person must confront: "What am I?" "Can I?" and "Ought I?" Goodrich himself told an interviewer a few days before the room's dedication his answer to the third question, "We have to be free to make this choice."

19. For a more thorough discussion of the Goodrich Room and the authors whose names occupy its walls, see *The Goodrich Seminar Room of Wabash College: An Explication* (Indianapolis: Liberty Fund, 2000).

20. Richard O. Ristine, interview, February 15, 1993. Ristine served on the board with Goodrich from 1958 to 1969, when Goodrich resigned. Apparently, the men were on good terms. Ristine said that Goodrich had even invited him over to his house in Indianapolis after Trippet resigned in 1965 to tell Ristine that if he would seek to become president of Wabash Goodrich would support him.

21. Trippet, *Wabash on My Mind,* p. 184.

22. This information is garnered from a letter that William B. Degitz, Wabash's former business manager, sent to Goodrich at Pierre's request, detailing all the gifts he

generous in his support of music programs. His contributions brought to the campus several outstanding musicians and choirs such as the Westminster Choir of England. Furthermore, his gifts allowed the Wabash Glee Club (thirty-five male students) to travel and perform in Europe during the summer of 1967, and the choir's director, R. Robert Mitchum, to study choir music in Europe in 1965.[23]

Despite these contributions, many at Wabash thought Pierre Goodrich to be a stingy giver when they took into account his vast financial holdings. This is especially so because of the difference between Pierre and his father, who was the college's financial guardian angel during the 1920s and 1930s. An even more frequent comparison was made of Pierre and fellow Wabash trustee Eli Lilly. A nonalumnus, Lilly served on the board from 1946 until his death in 1977 and is Wabash's largest single benefactor. Throughout his lifetime, Lilly contributed stock to the college worth nearly $40 million.[24] Goodrich was not inclined to be so generous. He doubted that a liberal arts college, even his dear alma mater, could responsibly spend his hard-earned money. On his death, Goodrich left $155,000 to Wabash College. College officials had hoped for much more.

Although for most of his life Goodrich was extremely proud of Wabash, in his later years he was disappointed that the college had not differentiated itself more from other small liberal arts institutions.[25]

---

had made since Frank Sparks became president of Wabash in 1941. The gifts did not all come personally from Goodrich but included gifts from entities that Goodrich controlled, such as the Winchester Foundation and the Muncie Realty Corporation. See letter from William B. Degitz to Pierre F. Goodrich, January 8, 1962, Pierre F. Goodrich Collection, Archives, Wabash College.

23. Rosanna Amos, interview, December 10, 1991. See "Minutes of the Board of Directors of the Liberty Fund, Inc.," March 17, 1967, p. 115 (for grant to the Wabash Glee Club), and April 22, 1965, p. 71 (for grant to Mitchum to study the music of Christianity in Europe). For his contributions to music on campus, Goodrich was honored by the Wabash Glee Club with a special merit award.

24. Richard O. Ristine, interview, February 15, 1993.

25. Henry Regnery, longtime friend of Goodrich's, recounted that Pierre often invited his friends to the Wabash campus for lectures (interview, October 3, 1992).

"Mr. Goodrich thought that Wabash College might become his ideal college institution and he was always interested in eventually giving it a lot of money," said Stephen J. Tonsor, emeritus professor at the University of Michigan. "But Wabash didn't pan out and Pierre found more and more things that were unsatisfactory about Wabash."[26]

As will be seen, Goodrich's notion of the "ideal college" was clearly radical. It is little wonder that Wabash did not uniformly embrace Pierre's beliefs. Nonetheless, it is true that Goodrich had a significant influence in the direction the college did pursue.

If anyone understood the mind and had the ear of Pierre F. Goodrich, it was Benjamin Arnold Rogge. Through their mutual attachments to Wabash College, Rogge and Goodrich established a close intellectual and personal friendship that lasted nearly thirty years. Rogge was a Nebraska farm boy who had taken economics degrees from Hastings College (A.B., 1940), the University of Nebraska (M.A., 1946), and Northwestern University (Ph.D., 1953). In the late 1940s, Rogge was one of more than a dozen sterling academics that Wabash president Frank Sparks enticed to Wabash from other top colleges and universities. This was part of an effort to upgrade both the prestige and the true academic caliber of the college.[27]

Rogge and Goodrich became particularly close after Rogge was ap-

26. Stephen J. Tonsor, interview, December 5, 1992.

27. Rogge joined Wabash's faculty in 1949 after having taught briefly at the University of Minnesota and Northwestern University. A number of other top academics were attracted to the school, including Elton Trueblood, who left Stanford, and John Van Sickle, who left Vanderbilt (Trueblood stayed only a semester before moving on to Earlham). Rogge was part of the "second echelon" of young academic talent that included Lewis Salter (physics), Philip Wilder (political science), John Forbes (history and art), and Theodore Bedrick (math and Latin). Sparks managed to procure such top professorial talent by means of accomplished salesmanship and high salaries. See *Wabash on My Mind,* p. 60. See also "Free-enterprise Champion Dr. Benjamin A. Rogge Dies," *Crawfordsville (Ind.) Journal-Review,* Nov. 17, 1980; and "Benjamin Arnold Rogge (1920–80)," in *Ideas on Liberty: Essays in Honor of Paul L. Poirot* (Irvington-on-Hudson, N.Y.: Foundation for Economic Education, 1987), pp. 39–41.

pointed academic dean in 1956.[28] Despite a twenty-six-year age difference between them (Rogge was born in 1920), Rogge became Goodrich's closest intellectual colleague and perhaps his closest personal friend as well. In some ways, however, the two were qualified to be free enterprise's "odd couple," so different were they in temperament and demeanor. Goodrich was reserved, Victorian, private, and even stoic, whereas Rogge had an outgoing, gregarious, and jovial personality. The thread that tied them together was the passion they shared for free-market ideas and their desire to see those ideas spread at Wabash and beyond.

Goodrich funded many of Rogge's trips to Mont Pelerin Society meetings and to other conferences. The two men often traveled together and engaged in long and heated exchanges about economics, education, human nature, and almost everything else. In September 1964, Rogge stepped down as dean and was appointed Distinguished Professor of Political Economy by an agreement among Rogge, Trippet (then Wabash's president), and Goodrich. Under the arrangement, Goodrich's contributions to Wabash partially paid Rogge's salary and travel expenses. This provided Rogge with the opportunity to accept off-campus speaking and teaching invitations.[29]

28. Rogge became dean of the college when Byron Trippet left that position to assume the presidency of Wabash. Sparks resigned as president in 1956 to run for governor of Indiana, but he stayed on as chairman of the board of trustees. When Sparks became president of Wabash in 1941, perhaps his most successful undertaking was to gather a powerful, affluent, and influential board of trustees that included men such as Eli Lilly; Eugene Beesley, CEO of the Lilly Corporation; Edmund Ball, president of Ball Brothers Corporation of Muncie; and Goodrich. Dr. Philip Wilder, telephone interview, February 19, 1992.

29. See letter and memorandum from Byron Trippet to Pierre F. Goodrich and Dean Ben A. Rogge, June 15, 1964, files of Byron Trippet, Archives, Wabash College. The memorandum states in part:

> I am summarizing in this memorandum my own understanding of the several points of agreement the three of us have reached concerning an important portion of Ben Rogge's new role at Wabash College beginning September 1 of this year. . . .
>
> 4. One of Ben's important reasons in resigning as dean of Wabash is his desire to be freer than he has been to accept off-campus assignments and opportunities which would be compatible with his teaching obligations at Wabash and his special

As a consequence, Rogge began to accept speaking engagements throughout the Midwest and beyond. He became the darling of businessmen's groups and was a much-sought-after speaker before utility, banking, and other professional organizations. Moreover, he became widely known by lecturing at summer business conferences at the universities of Michigan and Wisconsin. Beginning in 1966 and until his death in 1980, Rogge also successfully directed the Wabash Institute for Personal Development, a summer program for business executives.[30] In 1960, Rogge had been named a founding board member of Liberty Fund. In 1971, Goodrich had Rogge appointed as a director of the Indiana Telephone Corporation.[31]

Rogge was popular among business executives because he was able to articulate and confirm their existing beliefs in the free enterprise system. Rogge did not, however, feign support to attract an audience; he be-

---

role referred to in the above paragraph. Mr. Goodrich and I agree to remember this special interest of Ben's and agree that what he accepts and what he does not accept in the way of such outside invitations is left to his sole discretion. . . .

7. With the above points of agreement in mind, it is my further understanding that we can use for the year 1964–65 income from the Goodrich Seminar Fund and the Goodrich Unallocated Fund to cover the following items:

$5,000 to Rogge's salary
$2,000 for Rogge's travel
$1,500 for visiting speakers

Further documentation of the agreement is reflected in the "Minutes of the Board of Directors of the Liberty Fund," June 25, 1964, p. 58.

30. The programs at Michigan and Wisconsin were the Public Utility Executive Program (Michigan) and the American Bankers Association's School of Banking (Wisconsin). Wabash's liberal arts program for businessmen has had a number of titles, including the Wabash Executive Program and the Wabash Institute for Personal Development. Rogge made the program highly successful. It is a three-year summer program in which corporate executives come to campus for several weeks each during three summers to discuss philosophical, political, ethical, and business issues after reading from a prepared list of books. For a historical summary of the program, see George D. Lovell, "The Wabash Institute for Personal Development," in *These Fleeting Years: Wabash College, 1832–1982* (Crawfordsville, Ind.: Wabash College, 1982), pp. 120–25.

31. See "College Professor New Board Member," *ITC Highlights,* June–August 1971, p. 2.

lieved as deeply as any free-marketeer in the virtues of a market economy and shared these convictions with great persuasion, wit, and enthusiasm. His was a friendship that Goodrich greatly cherished.

In the last decade of his life, Pierre Goodrich's disappointment in his alma mater became widely known among Wabash's administration and trustees. He began to attend campus events less frequently and said little at board meetings.[32] Apparently, Goodrich had hoped that Rogge would become president in 1965, succeeding Trippet as Trippet had succeeded Frank Sparks in 1956.[33] But it is probable that Rogge did not want to return to administration, having just left the position of dean so that he could teach and lecture more freely. Moreover, Rogge's fundamental economic and philosophical beliefs were no doubt incongruous with the times. Thus, it is questionable whether he would have been appointed to the presidency even if he had sought the position.

Goodrich was displeased with both the manner in which the college was being run and the liberal beliefs that he believed many of the faculty members and administrators held.[34] Finally, in the spring of 1969, Goodrich resigned from the board of trustees. Ironically, Byron Trippet, who had left as president of Wabash four years earlier and was then

32. Richard Ristine, interview, February 15, 1993.

33. Stephen Tonsor, interview, December 5, 1992. Tonsor said that Goodrich had told him once that he had hoped Rogge would eventually become president of Wabash. If that had happened, it is possible that Goodrich would have contributed much of his wealth to the college in furtherance of his and Rogge's beliefs, which they expressed in the jointly written paper "Education in a Free Society."

34. Apparently, Goodrich's unhappiness with the direction in which Wabash was heading had been long-standing. In a letter written as early as June 1960, he expressed these sentiments to Trippet.

> Dear Byron,
>
> . . . I also, on further reflection, believe the College is not headed in the direction of further individual freedom and perhaps my views would not accomplish much. I am very busy and it is likely that I would also waste my time. . . . (Letter from Goodrich to Trippet, June 25, 1960, Pierre F. Goodrich Collection, Archives, Wabash College)

serving as vice-president of La Universidad de Las Americas in Mexico City, was appointed to complete Pierre's term.[35]

The 1960s presented difficult and disturbing times for many college trustees and administrators. Not even a small conservative college like Wabash was immune to the radical influences and troubled times that were sweeping over the nation's campuses: the Vietnam War was raging; long hair, experimentation with drugs, demonstrations, and faddish music and dress had become common; and respect for and adherence to authority and tradition were at their lowest ebb.[36] What probably galled Goodrich most was his belief that what was being taught at Wabash was openly hostile to free enterprise and other fundamental principles in which he believed so fervently. Also, the faculty was continually pressing to have Wabash become coeducational, despite the fact that almost all of the alumni and a large percentage of the student body wanted the college to remain an all-male institution.[37]

35. See *Wabash on My Mind,* pp. 190–91, n. 23. The reason Goodrich gave for resigning in 1969 was pressing business matters. No doubt this was partially true, because he was attempting to sell off many of his business holdings, such as the Ayrshire Collieries Corporation. Moreover, he was putting a tremendous amount of time into establishing Liberty Fund. It was also true, however, that he had lost much of his enthusiasm for his alma mater and felt more and more that the time and energy he expended on it was not fruitful. Richard Ristine said that Goodrich seemed increasingly uncomfortable and aloof at board meetings. Finally, the Goodrich Seminar Room was not being used as Goodrich had intended. There had been some grumblings from professors and students about the restricted use of the room. With all of this happening at once, Goodrich did not feel appreciated; even more important, he did not believe that his efforts were bearing fruit, and he came to believe that his time was being wasted (interview, February 15, 1993).

36. Although Goodrich allegedly did not watch television, he no doubt was very much aware of campus uprisings and was concerned about the vehemence and fervor of the demonstrations. He sent a copy of a newsletter produced by the leftist Students for a Democratic Society (SDS) to Wabash president Paul W. Cook in March 1968. The newsletter described classes run by SDS members in which students were taught to disrupt city college campuses and city political offices. See "Subcellar Student Subversion," *U.S.A.* 15 (March 1, 1968), Pierre F. Goodrich files, Archives, Wabash College.

37. Rem Johnston, interview, July 30, 1993. Johnston, a 1955 graduate of Wabash, is now a trustee and is intimately familiar with what was happening at Wabash in the late 1960s and the early 1970s.

Still another factor in Goodrich's general disenchantment with Wabash was that important personalities had changed at the college. The two presidents whose ideas most closely resembled his own—Frank Sparks and Byron Trippet—were now gone. Pierre's association with Sparks developed during the first fifteen years that he served on the board (1940–55). Sparks's association with the Goodrich family and his tremendous rags-to-riches story, however, dated back to the 1920s. At that time, James Goodrich had come to Sparks's financial rescue by providing a business loan that enabled Sparks to fulfill a major contract as a supplier to the Ford Motor Company. Sparks went on to become a millionaire before he was forty, then went to college at Butler University, obtained his Ph.D. at the University of Southern California, and became Wabash's eighth president.[38] During his long tenure as president (1941–56), Sparks had been extremely supportive of Pierre, especially in terms of trying to accommodate Goodrich's intellectual interests in the college.[39]

38. Frank Sparks was an amazing man about whom Byron Trippet had hoped someone would write a biography. Sparks grew up on a farm near Culver, Indiana, but early on engaged in business with definite plans to become a millionaire by the time he was forty years old. He began a company in the early 1920s known as the Indianapolis Tire and Pump Company. Sparks was a great salesman and a hard worker. His company floundered, however, until he landed a contract with Ford to produce a hundred thousand tire pumps. James Goodrich provided a line-of-credit for Sparks, and overnight the company (then known as Noblitt-Sparks Industries) flourished. Sparks later moved the company to Columbus, Indiana, changed its name to Arvin Industries, and went on to produce heaters, radios, and other automotive products. He soon became extremely rich. Sparks was not content with his wealth, however, and he decided he wanted to become a college president. He allowed himself ten years to achieve his plans, and he proceeded to earn a bachelor of arts degree from Butler University and a doctorate in economics from the University of Southern California. In 1941, he was appointed president of Wabash College. Sparks remained in that position until 1956, when he resigned to run for governor of Indiana. He lost at the Republican convention to Harold Handley, who went on to become governor from 1957 to 1961. For a more detailed account of Sparks's life, see Trippet, *Wabash on My Mind,* pp. 40–80, and Patrick J. Furlong, *Indiana: An Illustrated History* (Northridge, Calif.: Windsor Publications, 1986), pp. 204–5.

39. Sparks was very supportive of Goodrich's efforts in establishing the Indiana State Temporary Committee of the Great Books Program. Sparks served on the com-

Byron Trippet, the next president, was a close friend of Goodrich's. He had shown Pierre great patience, respect, and deference for some twenty-five years. Trippet presided over Wabash during what has become known as the Golden Age in the college's history. It was during these years (1956–65) that Wabash enjoyed its strongest academic reputation. Goodrich had great affection for Trippet not only because of his self-effacing attitude, but also because Trippet was a very admirable man and had an excellent mind. Trippet had been a Rhodes scholar after graduating from Wabash in the 1930s.[40]

Into Trippet's place stepped Paul W. Cook, a former Harvard Business School professor. Cook and Goodrich did not see eye-to-eye philosophically. The strained relations that developed between Goodrich and Cook (and thus Wabash) can be seen clearly in one of Cook's letters to Goodrich: "Possibly you had forgotten that the principal purpose of our meeting was to enable you to inform me of the fact that you disavowed your college and had disinherited it. Since I had just made a commitment to it as the best hope for the attainment of ideals which I am sure we share, I suppose our views on almost any issue were bound to appear

---

mittee and donated much time to it. Trippet describes in his recollection of Goodrich the relationship that Goodrich and Sparks enjoyed: "Pierre served as a Wabash trustee from 1940 to 1969. During much of that time he was a vice-president of the board. He was always a trustee who had to be reckoned with in major decisions and the reckoning had to be done before formal meetings. He [Goodrich] was quite fond of Frank Sparks and Frank 'handled' Pierre well . . ." (*Wabash on My Mind,* p. 183).

40. According to Hall Peebles, a professor of religion at Wabash who knew both Goodrich and Trippet, Trippet had a mind like that of Edmund Burke, possessing extreme clarity of thought and articulate expression. Trippet's insightful remembrances of Goodrich in *Wabash on My Mind* (pp. 182–87) confirm this view. Trippet was a native of Princeton, Indiana. He graduated from Wabash in 1930 and then studied in Switzerland for a year before spending two years as a Rhodes scholar from 1930 to 1932. He went on to devote almost all of his adult life to Wabash College, serving as an assistant professor of history in 1935, as dean from 1939 to 1955, and finally as president from 1956 to 1965. According to Peebles, Trippet got tired of the endless fund-raising and traveling that went along with being president of a private institution and retired in 1965 (interview, February 15, 1993).

to be in conflict. If nothing else, conflict confirms for you the wisdom of a decision you have already made."[41]

As Richard Ristine distinctly remembers, Goodrich was not particularly appreciated on the board during the 1960s. "Pierre always wanted to interfere with the academic life of the college," said Ristine. It was mainly because of this that other trustees did not want Goodrich to become chairman of the board.[42] Steps were taken to ensure that that did not happen. In the mid 1960s, Ivan Wiles, the Wabash board chairman as well as president of General Motors' Buick Division, was compelled to resign because of the ill health of his wife. Goodrich was vice-chairman at the time. In anticipation of Wiles's resignation, several members of the board nominated a co–vice-chairman, John Collett, thus preventing Goodrich from automatically ascending to the top position. Collett went on to succeed Wiles in 1965 and remained chairman until 1975.[43]

Goodrich attempted to influence what was taught on campus by endowing a chair in free-market economics. Ben Rogge drafted an extensive proposal for the establishment of the P. F. Goodrich Chair in Political Economy. Rogge's proposal provided that the occupant of the endowed chair would be allowed to hold the position only if his thinking was consistent with the principles set forth in the *Liberty Fund Basic Memorandum* and his reappointment was satisfactory to Liberty Fund.[44]

41. Letter from Paul Cook to Goodrich, December 12, 1966, Pierre F. Goodrich files, Archives, Wabash College.

42. As to the involvement in college matters of the Wabash board, apparently the prevailing attitude was (and still is) that trustees are to assist primarily in fund-raising. Their delving deeply into academic matters was not appreciated. Tradition has been, according to Ristine, that a trustee comes on the board knowing that he or she is to "give, get, or get off." Goodrich's long-term commitment to become intimately involved in academic issues was apparently not appreciated by other board members, who apparently either did not think it proper or did not want to devote that much time to micromanaging the college's academic affairs (interview, February 15, 1993).

43. Ibid.

44. See B. A. Rogge, "Memorandum Concerning Possible Uses of Funds Coming to the College Under the Terms of the Recent Agreement with P. F. Goodrich" (espe-

In 1964 Rogge stepped down as dean of the college to become Distinguished Professor of Political Economy. There were no official strings attached to the endowed professorship, and Goodrich's name was not formally associated with the position. Goodrich's preference for anonymity may well partially explain the distancing that took place. Another likely reason, however, is that Rogge's intellectual credibility had been called into question by some of his fellow faculty members. Ristine remembers the minor controversy that arose: "Rogge was resented on the faculty somewhat, because he was the only person getting funds from Goodrich," recalled Ristine, adding, "People thought that he had changed his own economic philosophy to accommodate Pierre. Of course, he hadn't. Total belief in the free-enterprise system was Rogge."[45]

Ristine's memory is supported by a reference in a letter that Wabash president Paul Cook wrote to Goodrich in January 1967:

> Since I believe the lack of candor between us serves no useful purpose, let me go further along this line and say that I think you have to some extent harmed Ben, and in so doing harmed Wabash, since he is an invaluable resource. The quasi-restricted support given him has tended to undermine his credibility with the faculty, in the same way that would undermine the credibility of a witness who had the same relationship to you. This is completely without regard to the merits, of course; as you

---

cially section II—The P. F. Goodrich Chair in Political Economy), Benjamin Rogge files, Archives, Wabash College. Ristine claims that Rogge told him that he (Rogge) didn't believe that a chair should be endowed just for the purpose of teaching free-market economics; accepting Ristine's memory, it seems strange that Rogge would draft such a proposal unless it was simply to appease Goodrich. After reading Rogge's memorandum and learning how devoted Rogge was to free-market principles, such a comment by Rogge seems peculiar. Ristine went on to say, "Milton Friedman said to me once, 'Don't ever have a chair of free enterprise.' He said if you teach economics correctly and expose bright students to all facets, they'll come to the conclusion that there should be a free market. But don't ram it down their throats. Pierre really didn't believe that" (interview, February 15, 1993). Rogge's proposal was not the first that Goodrich had expressed an interest in. In 1957, there had been some discussion among Goodrich, Sparks, and Rogge about the possibility of a visiting professorship's being funded by Goodrich. See "Memorandum, to Dr. Sparks, Mr. Goodrich," April 13, 1957, Pierre F. Goodrich Collection, Wabash College.

45. Richard Ristine, interview, February 15, 1993.

know, however, a witness that is on permanent retainer to a defendant cannot command the credibility of a truly independent expert.[46]

Cook's tenure as president was brief, lasting only two years (1966–68), but Goodrich was not impressed by Cook's successor, Thaddeus Seymour. Goodrich had lobbied for Dick Ristine to succeed Cook. The board, however, although divided, finally supported in 1968 the selection of Seymour, who came to Wabash having just served as dean of Dartmouth College.[47] Goodrich believed that Seymour was much too cavalier in demeanor to do honor to the position that Sparks and Trippet had occupied with considerable grace and distinction.[48] Ben Rogge tried to encourage closer relations between the two men, but there is no evidence that it worked.[49]

Although in his later years Goodrich lost some of the strong positive feelings he had held for Wabash, he still continued to support his alma mater, at least nominally. Goodrich continued to contribute to the John Van Sickle Club, a conservative campus organization named for a free-market economics professor. Van Sickle was partially responsible for introducing Goodrich to the Mont Pelerin Society. He had also co-

46. Letter from Paul W. Cook, Jr., president, Wabash College, to Pierre F. Goodrich, January 7, 1967, p. 2, Pierre F. Goodrich files, Archives, Wabash College.

47. Frank W. Misch served as acting president in the interim. Ristine recalls that Goodrich did not support him (Ristine) for governor in 1964, but that he did support him strongly to succeed Cook in 1968 as Wabash's president. In fact, Goodrich had Ristine over to his house in Indianapolis to discuss the possibility of Ristine's appointment. Byron Trippet discusses briefly the friction that existed on the board and among the alumni between the Ristine supporters and the Seymour supporters. Trippet contends that one reason he was asked to fill Goodrich's position on the board when Pierre resigned in 1969 was to help Seymour. See *Wabash on My Mind,* pp. 190–91 and n. 23.

48. According to Edward McLean, professor of politics at Wabash, Goodrich did not think highly of either Seymour's informal dress or his showmanship (Seymour was an amateur magician who often performed on and off campus) (interview, May 8, 1992).

49. Rogge wrote Seymour a memorandum in November 1969 about a testimonial dinner that was held for Goodrich on Pierre's seventy-fifth birthday. Rogge attached a flattering letter that Frank R. Barnett, a Wabash alumnus, had written to honor Goodrich (see chapter 33 for the publication of the letter). It is evident that Rogge wanted Seymour to know Goodrich's virtues. See Ben Rogge, "Memorandum," November 17, 1969, Benjamin A. Rogge files, Archives, Wabash College.

written a college economics textbook with Rogge.[50] Moreover, Goodrich established a competition named in honor of his father in which any member of Phi Kappa Psi Fraternity at Wabash or DePauw University could take part. (James P. Goodrich was a Phi Kappa Psi member as a student at DePauw in addition to being a long-standing trustee of Wabash.) The competition entailed the writing and submission of an essay "concerning a society of free individuals."[51]

After Ben Rogge's death, the remaining Goodrich monies designated for Rogge's salary were funneled into Goodrich funds that support music programs and a lecture series. The lecture series continues today, bringing many prominent academics to Wabash each year. These lecturers have included William B. Allen, former dean of James Madison College at Michigan State University; Alasdair MacIntyre of the University of Notre Dame; J. Rufus Fears, academic chair at the University of Oklahoma; George B. Martin, formerly of Wofford College and now president of Liberty Fund; John Gray, chair at the University of London; Tim Fuller, dean of Colorado College; and George Carey, professor of government at Georgetown University.[52] Many of the lectures of these scholars are being published by the Intercollegiate Studies Institute in a multivolume series. The first volume, *Derailing the Constitution: The Undermining of American Federalism,* was published in 1995.[53]

50. John Van Sickle was a prominent free-market economics professor at Wabash along with Rogge from 1946 to 1961. Van Sickle was an early Mont Pelerin Society member. The campus journal of the John Van Sickle Club was the *Wabash Journal of Economic, Social, and Political Opinion,* a libertarian publication that Ben Rogge nominally oversaw as a faculty member in the 1960s and 1970s.

51. The essay had to be based either on the *Liberty Fund Basic Memorandum* or on other books located in the Goodrich Seminar Room. The first-place winner was to receive up to half of the income from a fund that Goodrich had established, and the second-place finisher was to receive no more than half the amount that the first-place winner had received. See letter from Pierre F. Goodrich to William Degitz, business manager, December 31, 1968, Pierre F. Goodrich files, Archives, Wabash College.

52. Edward McLean, interview, May 8, 1992. McLean is the Wabash professor who has been most closely involved in administering the Goodrich Lecture Series since Benjamin Rogge's death in 1980.

53. Edward B. McLean, ed. (Bryn Mawr, Pa.: Intercollegiate Studies Institute, 1995). The second volume in this series is tentatively titled *A History of the Concept of Liberty.*

Chapter 24

The Mont Pelerin Society

> It is important to look in a little detail at the failure of intellectual leadership in the twentieth century, or rather at its apparent inability to offer clear and firm guidance to a perplexed humanity, because this failure or inability lay at the root of the tragedies of the age. . . .
>
> PAUL JOHNSON, *Modern Times: The World from the Twenties to the Nineties*

COMMUNISM and fascism in general, and the writings of Marxists, Leninists, and Hitlerites in particular, formed the intellectual foundation for much of the greatest suffering that mankind has ever known. Yet it was not just the idealism of communism and fascism that attracted their widespread adoption in the first half of the twentieth century. As Paul Johnson suggests in his book *Modern Times*, the failure of Western intellectual leaders to argue persuasively that democratic-capitalist principles are worth defending allowed both left-wing and right-wing authoritarian ideologies to be uncritically accepted.

In the spring of 1947, a group of classical liberal scholars came together at Mont Pelerin, Switzerland, to address this failure. They met at a time when the fascist Axis powers had just been defeated in a cataclysmic world war and the sphere of influence (political, military, and intellectual) of the communist Soviet state was rapidly expanding.

These liberal scholars, political leaders, and journalists recognized that unless a proper intellectual framework could be established in support of the "free society," including the virtues of the market economy, there was no reason that totalitarian ideologies such as fascism and communism could not continue to prosper. Moreover, this group of thinkers also realized that another threat—not as violent as that of authoritarian regimes but potentially as oppressive of individual liberty—existed in the false doctrines taught by proponents of the socialist (welfare) state. This made even democratically elected governments, classical liberal scholars warned, the breeding ground for "collectivist ideas" that would result in the denial of individual freedom.

Pierre Goodrich considered the Mont Pelerin Society one of the most important associations to which he ever belonged. The society is not noteworthy because of Goodrich's influence on it (Goodrich was more a student than a teacher at the conferences and meetings he attended). Rather, the significance of the Mont Pelerin Society lies in the way this relatively small group of thinkers influenced Goodrich and reinforced his own beliefs that ideas could have a transforming effect on individual behavior as well as on public policies.

From April 1 to April 10, 1947, thirty-nine participants from ten countries met at the Hotel du Parc on Mont Pelerin sur Vevey, in Switzerland, to discuss classical "liberalism and its decline, the possibility of a liberal revival, and the desirability of forming an association of people who held certain common convictions about the nature of a free society."[1] The conference was the brainchild of the eminent Austrian economist Friedrich A. Hayek, who was then teaching at the London School of Economics, but other leading liberal scholars, such as Wilhelm Röpke, Albert Hunold, John Jewkes, Karl Popper, Walter Eucken, Ludwig von Mises, Frank Knight, Aaron Director, Milton Friedman, and Fritz Machlup, were also important in sustaining the society in its early years.[2]

The group of thinkers who attended the founding meeting of the

1. R. M. Hartwell, *A History of the Mont Pelerin Society* (Indianapolis: Liberty Fund, 1995), p. 26. For a thorough account of the establishment of the Mont Pelerin Society, see chapters 1 and 2 of Hartwell's work. For a briefer account of the early history of the Mont Pelerin Society, see Dr. Albert Hunold, "The Mont Pelerin Society," *World Liberalism,* spring 1955. *World Liberalism* is a publication of the Liberal International.

2. A complete list of the thirty-nine participants can be found in Hartwell's *History of the Mont Pelerin Society,* pp. 45–46.

Mont Pelerin Society realized that the war of recent ideas had been dictated by a long series of distinguished intellectuals dating back at least one hundred years to the time and writings of Marx and Engels. Among these thinkers were such notable scholars as John Maynard Keynes, Arnold Toynbee, Bertrand Russell, Oswald Spengler, T. S. Eliot, and J. A. Schumpeter. They argued collectively that capitalism was a flawed economic and social system for several reasons: It was immoral because it allowed a great inequality of incomes between rich and poor; because its short-sighted principles had led to two great depressions (beginning in 1894 and 1929); and because capitalism contained a corrupting influence and could be blamed for everything from environmental pollution to disregard for human dignity in search of profits.[3]

Coupled with the widespread criticism of capitalism was the equally broad belief that governmental intervention could serve to mitigate the pitfalls of capitalist principles. It was these beliefs, combined with a defeated Europe that was still smoldering after World War II, that confronted the founding members. The members of the society

> concluded that the threat to freedom had its origins in theories about society [socialist interventionist ideas] that were demonstrably false but widely accepted almost unquestioningly; they agreed, therefore, that "the battle for ideas" had to be won before there could be a substantial reversal of political trends towards *dirigisme.* In forming a Society to combat intellectual error and doctrinal absolutism, the members also sought strength, courage, friendship, information, and ideas from each other, and they sought an institutional means of continuous association and of spreading their ideas widely.[4]

In furthering their objectives, this small group of a few dozen leading scholars set out to discuss what they believed were the critical questions that challenged the "free society":

> What are the essential characteristics of the competitive order, and how can competition be maintained? What should be done, therefore, about

3. Hartwell, *A History of the Mont Pelerin Society,* pp. 10–12.
4. Ibid., preface, p. xii.

> monopolies, both labor and industrial? . . . What, in particular, is the liberal response to the problems of inequality and poverty? How important are order, security, and solidarity compared with competition and increasing wealth? . . . How can the world be reeducated so that people understand liberal principles and their functions in a free society? Two other questions, of direct political relevance, were also asked. What should be the appropriate policy for the rehabilitation of Germany? What are the chances of achieving European federation?[5]

The Mont Pelerin Society is not a think tank in the traditional sense in which that term is understood in the United States, because it has no permanent headquarters or staff. More important, it has no unified policy objectives. As R. M. Hartwell, author of *A History of the Mont Pelerin Society,* states, by holding regular conferences and meetings, the society "sets out to educate the intellectuals, . . . and to lay the intellectual foundation of a liberal society and economy. This is not to say it has not influenced governments, only that it has not tried to do so directly, and that any influence it has had has been through the ideas it generated, not through political action."[6]

Pierre Goodrich's first contact with the Mont Pelerin Society occurred in September 1951, when he attended the fourth annual conference in Beauvallon, France, as a guest.[7] Goodrich's trip to the southern

5. Ibid., pp. 34–35. For the proceedings of the first Mont Pelerin Society meeting, including subjects discussed and speakers, see Hartwell's *History of the Mont Pelerin Society,* pp. 47–49.

6. Ibid., preface, p. xvi. Hartwell's observation is supported by the concluding paragraph of the society's statement of aims:

> The group does not aspire to conduct propaganda. It seeks to establish no meticulous and hampering orthodoxy. It aligns itself with no particular party. Its object is solely, by facilitating the exchange of views among minds inspired by certain ideals and broad conceptions held in common, to contribute to the preservation and improvement of the free society. (Hartwell, *A History of the Mont Pelerin Society,* p. 42. For the complete statement of aims, see pp. 41–42.)

7. Goodrich was one of six guests who attended the Beauvallon conference. A total of fifty-three members attended. For a more thorough treatment of the conference, see Hartwell, *A History of the Mont Pelerin Society,* pp. 92–94; and *Swiss Review of World Affairs,* November 1951.

French coastal city started a close association with the society that lasted the rest of his life. The 1951 invitation had been extended by Friedrich Hayek and Albert Hunold, Mont Pelerin Society president and secretary, respectively, through John Van Sickle, a conservative economics professor at Wabash College.[8] Goodrich had first become acquainted with Van Sickle when Pierre began serving as a trustee of the college. In fact, it was Goodrich who had provided funds enabling Van Sickle to attend, besides the Beauvallon conference, earlier Mont Pelerin Society meetings at Seelisberg, Switzerland (1949), and Bloemendaal, The Netherlands (1950).[9]

The meeting at Beauvallon brought together a truly impressive list of thinkers, including Ludwig von Mises and Frank Knight, with both of whom Goodrich later established friendships. It was at Beauvallon that Rebecca West presented a detailed discussion of the source of the pro-Soviet bias outside Russia. The topic that captured the most interest among the participants, however, was the treatment of capitalism by the historians. The resulting series of papers was later published in book form as *Capitalism and the Historians.*[10]

By the time Goodrich was invited to join the society, its membership had grown from the original 39 participants in 1947 to 167 members in 1951. The early members were an imposing group that included three future Nobel Prize winners in economics (Hayek, Friedman, and George Stigler); prominent businessmen such as Jasper E. Crane of the DuPont Corporation; politicians such as Ludwig Erhard (the future chancellor of West Germany), Luigi Einaudi (president of the Italian Republic), and the prime minister of Morocco; and top economic advisers from most western European countries. Also among the members were well-known American journalists such as Walter Lippmann,

8. Goodrich mentions this in his paper "Why Liberty?" which he read at the Princeton, New Jersey, conference in 1958.

9. See letter from John V. Van Sickle to Pierre F. Goodrich, July 24, 1951, Pierre F. Goodrich Collection, John Van Sickle folder, Archives, Hoover Institution.

10. Hartwell, *A History of the Mont Pelerin Society,* pp. 93–94; Friedrich A. Hayek, ed., *Capitalism and the Historians* (Chicago: University of Chicago Press, 1954).

Max Eastman (*Reader's Digest*), Henry Hazlitt (*Newsweek*), and Felix Morley (editor of the *Washington Post*).[11]

In the following years, Goodrich attended many of the Mont Pelerin Society's annual conferences: Seelisberg, Switzerland, 1953; Berlin, Germany, 1956; St. Moritz, Switzerland, 1957; Princeton, New Jersey, 1958; Kassel, Germany, 1960; and Aviemore, Scotland, 1968. To those that Goodrich could not attend, he sent his dutiful secretary Helen Schultz. After each conference, she wrote lengthy summary reports for Goodrich on the papers and discussions held. Nominated by Goodrich, Schultz became a member of the society in 1970.[12]

In an embarrassing situation, Goodrich was indirectly (and apparently unwittingly) involved in an incident that threatened the society's very existence. It is an example of how individuals, even highly intelligent and distinguished persons, can jeopardize a larger cause in pursuit of their own personal agendas. The gravity of the incident is suggested by the fact that Hartwell, in his history of the Mont Pelerin Society, devotes an entire chapter to the matter.[13]

In April 1959, society secretary Albert Hunold used the small surplus of funds from the 1958 Princeton, New Jersey, meeting of the society to publish the first issue of the *Mont Pelerin Quarterly*. This was followed by publication of the journal in July and October 1959. Hunold then secured funding for the quarterly for another year by obtaining a grant

11. See Hartwell, "The Founding of the Society," chap. 2 in *A History of the Mont Pelerin Society*. Hartwell's work also contains a list of participants at the first conference (pp. 45–46) and a list of members of the society (p. 51).

12. Schultz attended several Mont Pelerin meetings during Goodrich's lifetime, including Semmering, Austria, 1964; Stresa, Italy, 1965; Vichy, France, 1967; Aviemore, Scotland, 1968; Caracas, Venezuela, 1969; Munich, Germany, 1970; and Mont Pelerin, Switzerland, 1972. After Pierre Goodrich's death, Schultz attended meetings of the Mont Pelerin Society with Enid Goodrich in Brussels, Belgium, in 1974, and Saint Andrews, Scotland, in 1976. Letter from Helen E. Schultz Fletcher to author, April 21, 1995. Schultz was nominated by Goodrich and accepted into the society in 1970. See various folders under the names of conferences, Pierre F. Goodrich Collection, box 1, Hoover Institution.

13. See Hartwell, "The Hunold Affair," chap. 5 in *A History of the Mont Pelerin Society*.

from the Winchester Foundation through Goodrich (a Hunold admirer). Goodrich served as president and sole benefactor of the small foundation.[14]

Problems arose because Hunold had failed to obtain the approval of the society president, Wilhelm Röpke, before continuing the publication of the quarterly. Hunold, who despite contributing a large amount of time, energy, and funds in service to the society, had become a very unpopular figure in the society because of his dictatorial manner and his desire to see the society become more politically active. There were several members who defended Hunold, however, and Goodrich was foremost among them. During the controversy, Goodrich wrote Hunold such a gushing letter of support that the Swiss economist sought Pierre's permission to publish the letter openly in the *Mont Pelerin Quarterly.*[15]

The crisis came to a head in August 1962, when Hunold released the quarterly's last publication, "How the Mont Pelerin Society Lost Its Soul." The sixty-page journal was little more than a propaganda piece designed to inflate the importance of Hunold's work to the society and to publicize the "vendetta" that Hunold claimed Hayek and Machlup were conducting against him. Earlier, in April 1962, Goodrich received a tersely worded letter from the normally urbane Hayek castigating him for providing funds for the quarterly.

> Dear Mr. Goodrich,
>
> . . . I do not know precisely what promises you have made to Dr. Hunold but I cannot believe that they can be of a nature which bind you to finance an illegal publication. Dr. Hunold is certainly not entitled to receive any funds on behalf of the Society.

14. Ibid., p. 70.

15. See letter from Pierre F. Goodrich to Hunold, June 16, 1961; letter from Hunold to Goodrich, January 9, 1962, Pierre F. Goodrich Collection, Hunold file, Archives, Hoover Institution. Goodrich refused Hunold's request to publish his (Goodrich's) letter of June 16, 1961. See letter from Goodrich to Hunold, January 22, 1962, Pierre F. Goodrich Collection, Hunold file, Archives, Hoover Institution.

For your personal information I will add that I have now formally moved that Dr. Hunold be expelled from the Society.

Sincerely yours,
F. A. Hayek[16]

The real issue was not so much the "illegal" publication, but the matter of who had ultimate control over the operations and direction of the society. A perusal of the letters that circulated among Goodrich, Hayek, Van Sickle, F. A. Harper, and Röpke over the Hunold affair makes it evident that Goodrich gained firsthand knowledge about the ruinous aspects of power. The bitter tone of Röpke's letter to Goodrich captures the disappointment that the scuffle for domination created:

> To me, there is something so regrettable that it verges on the crudely humorous, that a Society organized to further the search for principles of a voluntary society of free men, should become rocked to its very roots by a contest for or of power. That such a thing could happen suggests that perhaps we should be ready to start all over again in whatever way may be required to avoid such an occurrence. And this is not a thought to be ignored, for any society devoted to liberty in any real sense of hope.[17]

The society survived the struggle between the pro- and anti-Hunold forces. It was not, however, without casualties: Röpke resigned in December 1961, and Hunold resigned nine months later, taking several members with him.[18] Goodrich withstood the ordeal and kept his mem-

16. Letter from F. A. Hayek to Goodrich, April 15, 1962, F. A. Hayek Collection, box 34, folder 17, Archives, Hoover Institution.

17. Letter from Wilhelm Röpke to Goodrich, July 1, 1961, Pierre F. Goodrich Collection, Röpke folder, Archives, Hoover Institution. See also Hartwell, *A History of the Mont Pelerin Society*, p. 123; John V. Van Sickle's letter to Goodrich, November 10, 1961, Pierre F. Goodrich Collection, Van Sickle folder; letter from F. A. Harper to Goodrich, May 16, 1960; and Goodrich's rejoinder letter to Harper, May 20, 1960, Pierre F. Goodrich Collection, Harper folder, Archives, Hoover Institution.

18. Hartwell, *A History of the Mont Pelerin Society*, p. 124 and note 80. Hunold's letter of resignation, dated August 2, 1962, was sent to members along with the last publication of the *Mont Pelerin Society Quarterly*.

bership intact. Moreover, he continued to attend conferences and meetings when his business commitments allowed him to do so. Goodrich, true to his nature, kept up a regular correspondence with many of the members, especially foreign scholars.[19]

The significance of Goodrich's association with the Mont Pelerin Society is twofold: first, association with like-minded thinkers reinforced his own belief that without a proper intellectual understanding of the dynamics that sustain a society, any society will be continually susceptible to the promises of false ideologies, to the detriment of individual liberty. Goodrich undoubtedly saw how important it was to have a proper setting in which this understanding could be pursued.

Second, the Mont Pelerin Society provided Goodrich with the opportunity to associate with leading scholars, statesmen, and journalists to the extent that his own learning and breadth of experience were greatly enlarged. The importance of many of these intellectual friendships will be discussed in chapter 25. Goodrich's long association with the Mont Pelerin Society clearly provided him with an education of the first rank and helped him to formulate his plan to establish Liberty Fund.

19. Goodrich's correspondence with members of the Mont Pelerin Society was prolific and included more than twenty scholars throughout the world, including B. R. Shenoy, director of economics, Research Center, New Delhi, India; Enoch Powell, member of the British Parliament; Wilhelm Röpke, German scholar and successor to F. A. Hayek as president of the Mont Pelerin Society; and Manuel F. Ayau, the president of the board of the Universidad Francisco Marroquin in Guatemala City, Guatemala. See Pierre F. Goodrich Collection, box 2, Archives, Hoover Institution.

Chapter 25
A Scholar's Life

. . . intellectual curiosity is the lifeblood of real civilization.
GEORGE MACAULAY TREVELYAN, *English Social History*

AS A RESULT of his friendships with Friedrich Hayek, Roscoe Pound, Ludwig von Mises, Milton Friedman, and other great modern-day thinkers, Pierre Goodrich was influenced by some of the greatest scholars of the twentieth century. Although Hayek was slightly younger than Goodrich, the Austrian economist served as an important mentor to the Hoosier businessman. Pound had been one of Goodrich's professors at Harvard. Their earlier student-teacher relationship developed into a personal friendship. The many other influential scholars that befriended Goodrich numbered in the dozens.

Friedrich A. Hayek was probably the most prodigious classical liberal scholar of the twentieth century. Hayek's writings were overwhelming not only in sheer number (he published some 18 books, 15 pamphlets, and 142 articles), but in breadth of subject matter as well. Although he began his career as a technical economist, his lectures and writings in later life extended to political philosophy, legal anthropology, the philosophy of science, and the history of ideas. Hayek was clearly one of the greatest and most wide-ranging scholars of the human sciences in modern times. For his considerable contributions, Hayek was awarded the Nobel Prize for Economics in 1974.[1]

1. See Peter J. Boettke, "Friedrich A. Hayek (1899–1992)," *The Freeman* (August 1992), pp. 300–303. Hayek was born in Vienna in 1899 and earned doctorates from the

Hayek had a tremendous influence on Goodrich, and Goodrich highly valued their intellectual exchanges and friendship. Hayek also respected Goodrich's erudition. Pierre not only showed a deep interest in the Austrian's ideas, but also provided Hayek with both an American's and a businessman's perspective that grew out of a long working familiarity with economic, business, and political concerns from a nonacademic background.

The two men first met when Goodrich was invited to attend the September 1951 meeting of the Mont Pelerin Society at Beauvallon, France.[2] At that time, Hayek had left the London School of Economics to teach at the University of Chicago's Committee on Social Thought. By the late 1950s, Goodrich had become an important member of the Mont Pelerin Society. Goodrich also knew Hayek from their mutual association with the Foundation for Economic Education (FEE). Goodrich had become a trustee in 1952, and Hayek lectured occasionally at trustee meetings. Also, in 1955 and 1960, Hayek lectured at Wabash College on the relationship of economic institutions to the problem of

---

University of Vienna in law (1921) and in economics (1923). One of his early mentors was Ludwig von Mises. Hayek briefly attended Mises's lectures at the University of Vienna and worked closely with Mises in the late 1920s and early 1930s at the Institute for Business Cycle Research in Vienna. Building on Mises's work, Hayek published two important books, *Monetary Theory and the Trade Cycle* (1929) and *Prices and Production* (1931). These works, combined with an invitation to serve as guest lecturer at the London School of Economics in 1930, caused Hayek to be named Tooke Professor of Economic Science and Statistics at the University of London.

Hayek became a British citizen in 1938, although he later took up academic posts in the United States and Germany, in which countries he lived during most of the last forty years of his life. Through a lifetime of teaching and writing, Hayek and Mises championed the Austrian School of economics in the twentieth century, providing the main challenge, especially in the 1930s and 1940s, to the growing acceptance of Keynesian governmental and socialist economic philosophy. See also Sylvia Nasar, "Friedrich von Hayek Dies at 92; an Early Free-Market Economist," *New York Times,* March 24, 1992, sec. D, p. 22, col. 1.

2. Goodrich was invited by John Van Sickle of Wabash College through Hayek and Albert Hunold, founding members of the Mont Pelerin Society. See Pierre F. Goodrich, "Why Liberty?" p. 5. Goodrich had paid for Van Sickle to attend both the 1950 Mont Pelerin Society meeting at Bloemendaal, Holland, and the 1951 Beauvallon meeting.

human freedom. Another personal meeting of note occurred when Hayek attended a March 1968 meeting of Liberty Fund, where he addressed the board on the concept of power. Goodrich also funded Hayek's lecture before the Philadelphia Society later that month.[3]

Goodrich and Hayek met occasionally in the 1950s and 1960s in Chicago and at Mont Pelerin Society meetings, but Goodrich's intellectual exchange with the noted scholar developed primarily through frequent correspondence that took place between them during a span of twenty years. Goodrich's letters to Hayek tended to be lengthy, rambling, and didactic. But Hayek seemed favorably inclined toward Goodrich's thoughts and historical discussions about law, business practices, politics, ethics, and other subjects. The Austrian also shared with Goodrich some of his writings at the draft stage, encouraging and appreciating Goodrich's observations.[4]

Before the publication of Hayek's *The Constitution of Liberty* in 1960, Goodrich read the entire manuscript, took voluminous notes, and responded to particular draft chapters by writing several lengthy letters to Hayek. *The Constitution of Liberty* is considered to be one of Hayek's two masterpieces, along with his better-known book *The Road to Serfdom.*[5] Milton Friedman's observation that Goodrich "loved to get into

3. Hayek spoke in 1955 at a conference sponsored by the Volker Fund. Two other well-known speakers gave addresses at the week-long conference: Professor Bertil Ohlin, economist and then official leader of the Liberal Party of Sweden; and John Jewkes, professor of economics at Merton College, Oxford. The conference ran from June 22 to June 30, 1955. See *Wabash Bulletin* 51 (May 1955): 17. Hayek spoke on May 12, 1960, before the Wabash Conservative Economics Club (for which Goodrich provided financial support). Hayek attended the March 27, 1968, meeting of the Liberty Fund board and the Philadelphia Society's national meeting in Chicago on March 28, 1968. Liberty Fund contributed $650 to have Hayek deliver his lecture before the Philadelphia Society meeting in Chicago. See "Minutes of the Meeting of the Board of Directors of the Liberty Fund, Inc.," January 24, 1968, p. 149, and March 27, 1968, p. 153 (in the possession of Liberty Fund).

4. Hayek's collected papers are located at the Hoover Institution Archives. Correspondence between Hayek and Goodrich is found in box 22, folder 6; box 34, folder 17 (Liberty Fund); and box 43, folder 22 (Philadelphia Society).

5. Nasar, "Friedrich von Hayek Dies at 92; an Early Free-Market Economist."

a vigorous intellectual argument, especially with people who were fundamentally in agreement with his basic philosophy," seems especially accurate with regard to Goodrich's communications with Hayek.[6] Clearly, Goodrich and Hayek were kindred spirits in terms of philosophical outlook, yet Pierre seemed to relish the opportunity to analyze, dispute, and embellish Hayek's ideas. In response to Hayek's draft of *The Constitution of Liberty,* Goodrich made the following comments:

On preserving and expanding freedom—

> I think that if you really wish to preserve freedom and to see more of it rather than less of it, convincing thought and determination must develop in churches, schools, and public concern and conversation. . . . Some of the things we have accomplished by the power of the state could have been accomplished, and still [can] be if the people had the fortitude that goes with determined ideals, without state intervention if the state would just keep out of it and if the community would assume its local responsibility.

About the misdirected efforts of churches and clergy—

> The social gospel of American Protestantism was so exciting a thing to most ministers in their churches as it developed into a program of state action that perhaps they ceased to perform any service with individuals. Had they, however, performed their proper example and teaching to individuals, they might have given some hope of a responsible community *through individuals and not through the state.*

About the proper assumption of responsibility by corporate boards—

> I have had years of experience on corporate boards. One of the most difficult things to achieve is a corporate board that works and assumes its responsibility. . . . One important thing to notice is that the board and management in a great many cases are not risking their own capital.
>
> Whether the capital be large or small, if that capital is proportionately a substantial amount of the individual's assets he operates differently as

6. Letter from Milton Friedman to author, December 19, 1991.

an individual than if he had no capital. His mind functions differently and his actions are different. (Would this also be true of the employee?)[7]

Hayek's importance to the classical liberal cause and to the American conservative movement can hardly be overestimated. George Nash, in his book *The Conservative Intellectual Movement: Since 1945*, credits Hayek's *The Road to Serfdom* (1944) with being the single most important factor in furthering conservatism after World War II.[8] *The Road to Serfdom* and Hayek's other writings provided the intellectual arsenal to combat the still-popular appeal of central planning that academics, particularly American ones, had adopted. The intellectual currency that the book generated for the conservative cause, along with Hayek's own stature on the world intellectual scene, gave great impetus to the conservative movement.

Subsequently, a number of conservative organizations and magazines appeared that classical liberal thinkers such as Goodrich supported: *Human Events* (1944), the Foundation for Economic Education (1946), *The Freeman* (1950), the Intercollegiate Studies Institute (1953), William Buckley's *National Review* (1955), and the Institute for Humane Studies (1960). These organizations and periodicals gave conservatives intellec-

7. These quotations all come from the same letter from Goodrich to Hayek, March 31, 1959, F. A. Hayek Collection, box 43, folder ID 22, Archives, Hoover Institution.

8. *The Road to Serfdom* (New York: Basic Books, 1979), p. 5. Originally published, with a foreword by John Chamberlain, by the University of Chicago Press, 1944, *The Road to Serfdom* was extremely significant because it challenged with clarity and brilliance John Maynard Keynes's popular views about the alleged necessary intervention of the state in economic and social affairs; moreover, unlike other treatises that warned of the dangers of a growing state (such as Mises's *Socialism*), *The Road to Serfdom* reached a wide audience. In the United States, it obtained great recognition primarily as a result of Henry Hazlitt's review of the book in the *New York Times* literary supplement and an extract published in the April 1945 *Reader's Digest*. See Henry Hazlitt, "An Economist's View of 'Planning,'" *New York Times Book Review*, September 24, 1944, p. 1, col. 1; see also Hans Kohn, "World Challenge," *Saturday Review of Literature*, October 21, 1944, pp. 26–27; "Freedom and Planning: Case for the Individualist," *Times (London) Literary Supplement*, April 1, 1944, p. 165, col. 1. *The Road to Serfdom* soon became a best-seller and was one of the most widely read and debated books in the postwar era.

tual respectability and affirmed that their beliefs could withstand the criticisms of modern liberal and socialist attacks.[9] Thus, it is understandable, given Goodrich's growing preoccupation with the idea of liberty, that he sought out Hayek more than any other leading thinker with whom to exchange ideas and to further his own education.

Goodrich's associations with eminent scholars spanned at least the last three decades of his life. In his desire to have a greater understanding of myriad subjects, he sought these intellectual trysts and nurtured the resulting relationships with great care. His friendship with Roscoe Pound, America's most prominent modern legal scholar, is one example.

Pound's importance as a legal scholar has long been recognized. His Harvard colleague, Samuel Williston, remarked that Pound's proposition that law should be treated as a social science was "probably the greatest contribution that has been made in the twentieth century to American legal thought."[10] Pound taught law for fifty-four years (mostly at Harvard), wrote dozens of books and articles on jurisprudence, and became a scholar of Chinese law. Moreover, Pound also had a distinguished career as a botanist, holding a Ph.D. in botany and publishing widely on botanical subjects.[11]

9. During World War II and immediately afterward, Hayek was the main advocate of that view. Other spokesmen who were able to make cogent and sustained arguments for conservative values were Richard Weaver (*Ideas Have Consequences,* 1948), Russell Kirk (*The Conservative Mind,* 1953), and William Buckley (*God and Man at Yale,* 1951). Still, it was Hayek who was most articulate in explaining the important role that freedom—in all its facets—played in saving the world from even greater destruction.

10. Quote taken from Samuel Williston's book review of J. H. Landman's *The Case Method of Studying Law* (1930), in *Harvard Law Review* 43 (April 1930): 972. For a comprehensive analysis of Pound's legal thought and contributions, see Edward B. McLean, *Law and Civilization: The Legal Thought of Roscoe Pound* (Lanham, Md.: University Press of America, 1992).

11. Pound also taught law at the University of Nebraska, Northwestern University, the University of Chicago, and UCLA, as well as at schools in China and India. Two full-scale biographies of Pound have been written: Paul Sayre, *The Life of Roscoe Pound* (Iowa City: College of Law Committee, 1948); and David Wigdor, *Roscoe Pound: Philosopher of Law* (Westport, Conn.: Greenwood Press, 1974). See also Edward B. McLean, *Law and Civilization: The Legal Thought of Roscoe Pound.*

Goodrich was Pound's student at Harvard during the 1916–17 school year. Pound had been on the Harvard faculty for six years, but 1916 marked the first year that he also served as dean of the law school, an influential position that he would hold for the next twenty years. His appointment gave him a preeminence unrivaled in American legal education at the time. During Pound's brilliant career, he was a Nebraska appellate court judge at the age of thirty, dean of the Nebraska College of Law at the age of thirty-three, and president of the Académie Internationale de Droit Comparé (International Academy of Comparative Law).[12]

There is no indication that Goodrich and Pound crossed paths from the time Pierre graduated from Harvard in 1920 until the mid 1940s, when both men attended a breakfast meeting at Indianapolis attorney Clair McTurnan's residence on North Meridian Street.[13] McTurnan, also a Wabash and Harvard Law School graduate, had been a longtime trustee of Wabash College. At that meeting, Pound discussed with Goodrich an interest he had in exploring the history of the legal and constitutional guarantees of freedom. Goodrich immediately proposed that his former law school professor give a series of lectures on the topic at Wabash College.[14] Pound subsequently delivered four extensive lectures at Wabash, on February 26, 27, and 28, and March 1, 1945.

Pound's lectures traced the history of the protection of individual liberty from the time of medieval England, through the era of the Tudors and Stuarts (1485–1714), up to the time of the founding of the American colonies and the adoption of the United States Constitution and the Bill of Rights.[15] Goodrich maintained regular contact with Pound after Pound spoke at Wabash. In fact, in the fall of 1945, Good-

12. See Wigdor, *Roscoe Pound: Philosopher of Law,* pp. 49–131.

13. Sometime in 1944, both Pound and Goodrich attended a breakfast at Clair and Inez McTurnan's house, located at the intersection of Fifty-second and North Meridian streets. McTurnan was a sought-after litigator. Lawrence McTurnan (nephew to Clair), telephone interview, May 17, 1993. See letter from Goodrich to Pound (referring to the meeting), January 7, 1955, Roscoe Pound Papers, Archives, Harvard Law School.

14. Ibid.

15. Pound had intended to return to Wabash to complete a set of lectures detailing the constitutional guarantees of freedom up to modern times, but his commitment to

rich, Frank Sparks (then Wabash College's president), and several other Wabash graduates unsuccessfully tried to persuade Pound to come to Wabash to head the proposed Roscoe Pound Institute of Government.[16] Moreover, from 1946 to 1956, Goodrich and Pound exchanged more than thirty letters, and Goodrich visited Pound on at least three occasions in Boston and Cambridge, Massachusetts.[17] During this extended time, Goodrich sought Pound's insights on a variety of topics.[18]

In 1946, the Chinese Ministry of Justice and several of Pound's former Chinese students at Harvard sought Pound's input as an adviser on drafting a new Chinese constitution.[19] In the summer of 1946, Pound traveled to China for that purpose, and within a short time he learned the rudiments of the Chinese language. Pound returned to Harvard

---

completing his five-volume collection *Jurisprudence* and the fact that he was in his mid eighties at the time prevented him from undertaking the arduous task. See letter from Goodrich to Pound, November 9, 1955, Roscoe Pound Papers, Archives, Harvard Law School.

16. See letter from J. W. Fesler to Pierre F. Goodrich, September 1, 1945; letter from J. W. Fesler to Roscoe Pound, September 4, 1945; and letter from Roscoe Pound to J. W. Fesler, September 8, 1945. Roscoe Pound Collection, Archives, Wabash College.

17. Goodrich visited Pound in January 1947, in May 1955, and again in 1956. The letters that were exchanged between the two men, from June 5, 1946, to April 13, 1956, are located in the Roscoe Pound Collection, Archives, Harvard Law School. References to the three meetings of Goodrich and Pound can be found in Goodrich's letter to Pound, February 3, 1947; Pound's letter to Goodrich, May 3, 1955; and Goodrich's letter to Pound, November 9, 1956.

18. In the spring of 1946, for instance, Goodrich read Pound's *An Introduction to the Philosophy of Law,* which was published in 1921. Goodrich, in typical fashion, wrote to Pound and inquired whether Pound had changed his views about whether law was a mechanism much like government, which continually tried to recognize and satisfy a person's "wants or claims or desires through social control." Goodrich believed that any such legal recognition resulted in the "corresponding loss of [man's] own control of his individual actions and destiny." Goodrich to Pound, June 5, 1946, Roscoe Pound Papers, Archives, Harvard Law School. The two men also exchanged lengthy letters on the importance of Luther, Calvin, Hus, and Wycliffe on the Puritan revolution and the importance of the Puritan revolution in influencing American political and constitutional history. Letter from Pound to Goodrich, May 9, 1949; letter from Goodrich to Pound, April 7, 1952. Roscoe Pound Papers, Archives, Harvard Law School.

19. Pound's experiences in China are briefly described in Wigdor's *Roscoe Pound: Philosopher of Law,* pp. 276–78.

in the fall of 1946. In January 1947, Goodrich met with Pound in Boston. Goodrich had already expressed a deep interest in Chinese philosophy. Apparently, the meeting between the two men sparked in Goodrich an interest in Chinese law. Goodrich subsequently obtained an English translation of the newly adopted Chinese constitution. In February 1947, Goodrich wrote to Pound offering unsolicited and detailed comments on what he believed were the strengths and weaknesses of the new Constitution and how it might be improved.[20]

It is pure speculation that Goodrich's interest in serving as a trustee of the China Institute of America may have derived from his association with Pound, but it was in 1948 that Pierre first contributed financially to the China Institute. One year later, Goodrich became a trustee. In May 1949, Goodrich made arrangements for Pound to address members of the China Institute.[21]

After Pound retired from Harvard in 1947, he spent the next three years in China as an adviser to the Ministry of Justice. In that position, Pound helped establish a court system and reestablish law schools that had been disbanded as a result of eight years of Japanese occupation. When the Communists took over the Chinese government in 1949, Pound returned to the United States to teach and to help establish the law school at the University of California at Los Angeles. He remained there until 1953, when he left to teach in India.[22]

20. Letter from Goodrich to Pound, February 3, 1947, Roscoe Pound Papers, Archives, Harvard Law School. The Chinese constitution was adopted by the National People's Congress in the fall of 1946 and became effective on December 25, 1946. Pound's response to Goodrich explained how difficult it had been to draft a constitution that all would be satisfied with given the diverse cultural and legal backgrounds of the advisers—British, French, American, and, of course, Chinese. Letter from Pound to Goodrich, February 14, 1947, Roscoe Pound Papers, Archives, Harvard Law School; see also Roscoe Pound, "The Chinese Constitution," *New York University Law Quarterly Review* 22 (April 1947), p. 194.

21. Letter from Pound to Goodrich, April 12, 1949; letter from Goodrich to Pound, May 1, 1949; letter from Pound to Goodrich, May 9, 1949. Roscoe Pound Papers, Archives, Harvard Law School.

22. Pound explains his activities from 1947 to 1955, when he had reached the age of eighty-five, in a letter to Goodrich dated November 22, 1955, Roscoe Pound Papers, Archives, Harvard Law School.

In 1954, at the age of eighty-four, Pound returned to Boston, where he worked for the West Publishing Company as an editor until June 1955. As Pound explained to Goodrich in a letter, he was forced to take teaching and editing positions because it was impossible for him to live on a retired Harvard professor's salary.[23] Goodrich visited Pound in May 1955 during the thirty-fifth reunion of Goodrich's graduating class. At that time, Goodrich proposed that the four lectures that Pound had given more than a decade earlier at Wabash be published. Pound eagerly accepted the offer. Goodrich subsequently arranged for the Yale University Press to publish the lectures in book form on behalf of Wabash College.

Goodrich took a tremendous interest in arranging the publication of *The Development of Constitutional Guarantees of Liberty.* He did everything from commenting on the galley proofs to handling the negotiations between Pound and the Yale University Press for the publication. Goodrich even traveled to Boston in 1956 to meet with Pound to ensure that his former professor was pleased with the final product.[24] The book was successfully received in academic circles. By 1979, *The Development of Constitutional Guarantees of Liberty* had been translated into several foreign languages, including Portuguese, Vietnamese, Arabic, Spanish, and Hindi.[25]

Despite Pound's international prominence as a legal scholar and teacher, he was forced to work at editing.[26] In certain academic circles,

23. Ibid.

24. Goodrich spent an extraordinary amount of time working on the publication of Pound's lectures. Approximately twenty-five pieces of correspondence were sent between Goodrich, Pound, and the Yale University Press in 1956 in regard to the preparation and publishing of the lectures. See letters between Goodrich and Pound, Roscoe Pound Collection, Archives, Harvard Law School.

25. See letter from Ann S. Bujalsk, Rights Department, Yale University Press, to President, Wabash College, Roscoe Pound Collection, Archives, Wabash College, October 2, 1979.

26. Apparently, Pound's political views were one reason that his meager pension was never increased by Harvard in his retirement years. (Hayek was treated in much the same way, being forced to leave the University of Chicago in 1962 for Freiburg University in Germany because Chicago refused to pay him a pension.) See Murray N. Rothbard, *Ludwig von Mises: Scholar, Creator, Hero* (Ludwig von Mises Institute: Auburn University, 1988), p. 81, n. 54.

his reputation had been slightly tarnished because of his outspoken support for the Nationalist Party in China. It was a political view that was not widely shared by his Harvard faculty colleagues.[27] Although the Harvard Law School provided Pound with an office when he returned to Cambridge in June 1955, the arrangement did not provide any extra stipend.

Goodrich saw that Pound was well compensated for the publication of the *Constitutional Guarantees of Liberty.*[28] Moreover, Goodrich helped support Pound financially in the mid and late 1950s so that Pound was able to finish in 1959 his long-awaited work *Jurisprudence.* Pound had be-

27. "[Pound] found Chiang Kaie-shek an exceptional leader—wise, tenacious, and democratic. He insisted that there was little corruption and no censorship in China, and he compared the exclusion of liberal political parties to the fate of Republicanism during the New Deal." Wigdor, *Roscoe Pound: Philosopher of Law,* p. 277. See also Roscoe Pound, "Other News of China," *American Affairs* 10 (July 1948); letter from Pound to Goodrich, April 12, 1949, Roscoe Pound Papers, Archives, Harvard Law School; "Roscoe Pound's Analysis of Chinese-American Affairs—Hits United States Aims for Compromise, Misconception of Red Role," 81st Cong., 1st sess., *Congressional Record* (April 2, 1949), 95, pt. 3:3765–67. According to Edward McLean, a professor at Wabash College and the author of a book on Pound, Pound was not appreciated by the Harvard faculty or administration, because of his strong political support of the Nationalist government in China. Subsequently, Pound's retirement emolument was never increased from the time he retired in 1947. Consequently, Pound had to teach and take on other jobs, such as the editing position with West Publishing, until Goodrich's financial support in 1955 enabled Pound to return to legal scholarship. Edward McLean, interview, May 8, 1992. Pound alludes to this as well in the preface to *The Development of Constitutional Guarantees of Liberty* (p. vi) and in his preface to *Jurisprudence.*

28. At Yale University Press's request, Goodrich helped to subsidize the book's publishing, because Goodrich was convinced that the source materials on which Pound's lectures were based should be included in the book. See letter from Eugene Davidson, Editor, Yale University Press, to Goodrich, February 28, 1956; letter from Goodrich to Davidson, March 3, 1956. Roscoe Pound Collection, Archives, Harvard Law School. Pound asked for no financial compensation for the book, because he said he had been paid well (five hundred dollars) for the lectures he gave at Wabash College in 1945. Goodrich, however, saw that Pound was paid fifteen hundred dollars for an advance on the book. See letter from B. K. Trippet to Pound, April 3, 1957; Pound to Goodrich, April 8, 1957. Roscoe Pound Collection, Archives, Harvard Law School. While these amounts may seem paltry by today's standards, Pound's response indicates that he was pleased by the payment for such a scholarly book.

gun the monumental five-volume treatise nearly a half century before. Characteristically, all this was done by Goodrich anonymously.[29]

Throughout his lifetime, Goodrich established friendships with many other great scholars. He was a great admirer of Ludwig von Mises, the Austrian economist who spent the last thirty years of his long and productive life in the United States, much of it teaching at New York University. Mises and Hayek were integral proponents of the Austrian School of economics. The Austrian School is composed of economists who believe that individual behavior in a free market, not class interest or governmental monetary policy, is the appropriate baseline for economic analysis.[30] Goodrich became familiar with Mises through the Foundation for Economic Education and the Mont Pelerin Society. From 1946 to 1973, Mises was closely associated with FEE as an adviser and gave regular seminars to the trustees.

After Mises's magnum opus *Human Action* was published in 1949, Goodrich attempted several times to read this monumental work. He became bogged down, however, because of Mises's eclectic vocabulary. After a dictionary of Mises's terminology was produced, one autumn in the mid 1960s Goodrich traveled with his wife Enid and his top assistant Helen Schultz to Montauk, Long Island. There, the three spent nearly a month reading the book in an apartment overlooking the Atlantic Ocean.[31] Goodrich was extremely impressed with *Human Action,* gave it as a gift, and quoted from it widely both in everyday conversation and in letters and other writings. The 890-page book attempts to explain economic and social processes and the need for reform.[32] At a time

29. Roscoe Pound, *Jurisprudence* (St. Paul, Minn.: West Publishing, 1959). Goodrich subsidized Pound's writing of his treatise through grants from the Winchester Foundation.

30. For an excellent overview of Austrian economics, see *The Foundations of Modern Austrian Economics,* ed. Edwin G. Dolan (Kansas City: Sheed and Ward, 1976).

31. Letter from Helen Fletcher to author, June 18, 1996; Ruth Connolly, interview, October 25, 1991.

32. William F. Campbell, now professor of economics at Louisiana State University, wrote: "I thank [Pierre Goodrich] most for my high school graduation gift which was a

when economic analysis was becoming increasingly fragmented, analyzing only one aspect of economic life at a time (business cycles, role of inflation, monetary policy, and so forth), *Human Action* was a serious attempt to provide a general praxeology of human behavior from an economic perspective.[33]

In June 1954, Wabash College hosted Mises for a conference on economics and freedom at French Lick, Indiana.[34] Moreover, on March 7, 1956, and October 17, 1961, Goodrich attended dinners in New York City honoring Mises for, respectively, the fiftieth anniversary of Mises's earning his doctorate degree and his eightieth birthday.[35] Pierre and Enid developed a personal friendship with Mises and his wife Margit. In the late 1950s, Goodrich also briefly employed Mises to advise the board of directors of the Ayrshire Collieries Corporation on the dangers of inflation to the coal industry.[36] Goodrich and Mises corresponded sporadi-

---

select library of books including von Mises's *Human Action* which more than any other book interested me in economics and rational thought" (letter to author, May 15, 1993). *Human Action* was originally published by Yale University Press in 1949. Yale published a second edition in 1963 in which many mistakes were made. As a result, the rights to the book were reassigned, and the work was published by Henry Regnery in 1966.

33. No doubt Goodrich thought so highly of Mises and of *Human Action* in particular because in the book Mises attempts to give a complete theory of how economics interacts with the individual as he makes choices in the real world. See Murray N. Rothbard, *The Essential von Mises* (Lansing, Mich.: Bramble Minibooks, 1973), pp. 35–47.

34. John Van Sickle, a Wabash economics professor and a former student of Mises's, arranged the conference. The conference was held on June 15, 1954, and was partially sponsored by the Volker Foundation. Mises's topic was "The Market and the Role of Saving." Other presenters were Professor Friedrich August Lutz of the University of Zurich and Professor George William Keeton of the University of London. See *Wabash Bulletin* 51 (May 1955): 17; Margit von Mises, *My Years with Ludwig von Mises* (New Rochelle, N.Y.: Arlington House, 1976), p. 152.

35. Both dinners honoring Mises were held at the New York University Club. Enid Goodrich accompanied Pierre at the dinner honoring Mises on his eightieth birthday.

36. Evidence of Goodrich's friendship with the Miseses can be found in a letter from Margit von Mises to Pierre and Enid, inviting them to dinner one Friday in November 1963. Margit prepared Wiener schnitzel for the Goodriches. See letter from Margit von Mises to Pierre F. Goodrich, October 25, 1963, Pierre F. Goodrich Collection, box 1, Ludwig von Mises folder, Archives, Hoover Institution. Mises's eleven-page memorandum on inflation was given to the Ayrshire Board of Directors on February 21, 1958.

cally because Mises was much less charitable with his time than Hayek was. Nonetheless, Goodrich was a willing devotee of Mises, constantly championing the great scholar's views.[37]

Another great German-speaking thinker that Goodrich admired was Ludwig Erhard. In general, Goodrich loved everything German, from philosophy and economics to wines, colognes, and automobiles (he often drove a Mercedes-Benz). Goodrich also believed that German technology was superior to any other.[38] No doubt his great admiration for Germany made Pierre especially proud to host Ludwig Erhard, a former West German chancellor, on two separate occasions in Indiana. Goodrich had become acquainted with Erhard at an annual Mont Pelerin Society meeting in St. Moritz, Switzerland, in September 1957. Shortly afterward, he invited the then German vice-chancellor and minister of economic affairs to speak at Wabash College.[39] After more than a year of negotiating a date and a topic, Erhard traveled to the United States and gave two lectures at Wabash on the European Common Market.[40]

37. According to Bettina Bien Greaves, a friend of Mises who has made the study of his writings and teachings her life's work, Mises was neither so cordial as Hayek nor so willing to spend time with students. "He often would say to a question asked by someone, go read it in my book on page so and so." Hayek, on the other hand, was not only a brilliant thinker but also a very gracious and accommodating person. Bettina Bien Greaves, interview, October 19, 1992. An example of Goodrich's admiration for Mises is the fact that Pierre was one of only two people who purchased a bronze bust of Mises (for $175). The bust was made shortly after the dinner honoring Mises on the fiftieth anniversary of his earning his doctorate. See letters between Goodrich and George Koether (automotive editor of *Look* magazine): Koether to Goodrich, December 7, 1956; Goodrich to Koether, February 15, 1957; Koether to Goodrich, April 9, 1957. Pierre F. Goodrich Collection, box 1, Ludwig von Mises folder, Archives, Hoover Institution.

38. Ruth Connolly, interview, October 25, 1991.

39. Ludwig Erhard (1897–1977) was the West German minister of economic affairs from 1949 to 1963, when he succeeded Konrad Adenauer as chancellor of the Federal Republic.

40. Erhard had been West Germany's top economic minister after World War II. He served as West Germany's chancellor from 1963 to 1966. Erhard is credited with being the father of West Germany's "economic miracle," that period of time after World War II when West Germany's economy strongly recovered because of Erhard's bold decision to eliminate wage and price controls. For a brief account of this episode and

Erhard attended Wabash's 1959 commencement, at which time he received his first honorary degree from an American college or university.[41] During the same visit, Erhard addressed more than a thousand members of the Indiana Academy of Social Sciences at Wabash. He stressed, at the height of the Cold War, the importance of a free economy in establishing and maintaining a free society.[42] At Goodrich's invitation and expense, Erhard returned nine years later, in 1968, to speak at the Columbia Club in Indianapolis on the evils of inflation.[43]

Goodrich established friendships with other scholars. These included Bertrand de Jouvenel of France and Henry Hazlitt, a former *New York Times* and *Newsweek* economics reporter and a founding member of FEE, as well as other top minds already mentioned: Milton Friedman,

---

its importance, see Peter G. Klein, ed., *The Collected Works of F. A. Hayek: The Fortunes of Liberalism* (Chicago: University of Chicago Press, 1992), pp. 13–14, 193–94; "Ludwig Erhard," *New Encyclopaedia Britannica,* vol. 6 (Chicago: Encyclopaedia Britannica, 1991), p. 540.

41. See "Wabash to Hear Top Adenauer Aide," *Indianapolis News,* May 25, 1959, p. 11, col. 2; "Erhard Hopes Progress by His Germany Justifies Aid," *Crawfordsville (Ind.) Journal and Review,* June 8, 1959, p. 1, col. 1; Lester M. Hunt, "Visiting German Stakes Peace on West's Willingness to Fight," June 8, 1959, p. 1, col. 3; Pat Redmond, "Erhard Warns of World Inflation," *Indianapolis News,* June 8, 1959, p. 17, col. 2 (picture on p. 14); "Ludwig Erhard Spoke at Wabash in 1959," *Indianapolis Star,* October 16, 1963, p. 3, col. 1. Although Wabash College was the first American college or university to award Erhard an honorary degree, both Columbia and Harvard universities later proclaimed that they were first. See "Wabash First to Award Erhard Honor," *Indianapolis News,* June 3, 1965, p. 19, col. 1.

42. Erhard said:

> You can't take two systems exactly opposite in nature and try to strike an average. You can't combine a collectivized, compulsory economy with a free market economy. You can't combine dictatorship with democracy or slavery with human dignity and somehow try to reconcile them and find a combination. . . . The whole free world must be interested [in the unification of Germany] on the basis of freedom. (Lester M. Hunt, "Visiting German Stakes Peace on West's Willingness to Fight," *Indianapolis Star,* June 8, 1959, p. 1, col. 3)

43. The former West German chancellor spoke about another economic evil that both he and Goodrich believed threatened any free society: inflation. See "Erhard Warns of World Inflation," *Indianapolis News,* February 20, 1968, p. 2, col. 6; *Columbian,* April 1968, p. 2.

Russell Kirk, Leonard Read, D. Elton Trueblood, Benjamin Rogge, and F. A. Harper of the Institute for Humane Studies. A younger group of academics also established friendships with Goodrich, including Stephen Tonsor, an emeritus professor of history at the University of Michigan; George Roche, former staff member of FEE and a longtime president of Hillsdale College; Henry Manne, former dean of the George Mason University School of Law in Virginia; and Gottfried Dietze, an emeritus professor of political science at Johns Hopkins University. In 1968, Dietze dedicated his book *America's Political Dilemma* to Goodrich.[44] Pierre Goodrich continued to learn by exchanging ideas with these top minds.

44. The full title of Dietze's book is *America's Political Dilemma: From Limited to Unlimited Democracy* (Baltimore: Johns Hopkins University Press, 1968).

Chapter 26

Education in a Free Society

Tenure is not needed by the competent and, hence, shields only the incompetent. We are not dissuaded from this position by any arguments with reference to so-called academic freedom. *We simply do not believe in academic freedom.* We do believe in the idea that each man should be free to say what he will; but we don't believe that any one has the right to say what he will and be paid for the saying of it by someone else who doesn't wish to so pay him! In this sense, academic freedom is, in fact, a denial of freedom—the freedom of each man to expend his resources on only those uses that he sees fit—including the choice of sources of learning.

BENJAMIN A. ROGGE AND PIERRE F. GOODRICH, "Education in a Free Society"

If a nation expects to be ignorant and free, in a state of civilization, it expects what never was and never will be.

Letter from Thomas Jefferson to Colonel Charles Yancey, January 6, 1816

IN RECENT years, no topic, with the possible exception of health care, has been discussed in the United States with greater interest and intensity than educational reform. City and community school boards are hotbeds of virulent debates about educational change; politicians at the local, state, and national levels have joined the fray in suggesting various policy changes. Few proposals, however, have seriously challenged the radical vision of Pierre Goodrich, the recommendations he began making more than forty years ago. Probably Goodrich's most important contribution in this area is his understanding of the important role that education plays in shaping character and citizenship.

Goodrich's private passion for learning evolved into a public involvement with the educational process beginning in the mid 1940s. By that time, he had already served as a trustee of Wabash College for several years. These years of experience had convinced him that the traditional liberal arts college was sorely in need of a deeper understanding of its role in influencing society. Moreover, Goodrich recognized the necessity for greater participation and direction on the part of the college's governing body, a direction he was eager to provide.

Goodrich also saw the need to create greater adult educational opportunities. He believed that education must extend beyond the classroom and into the homes of average citizens. Because of that belief, he took on the quiet leadership of such organizations as the Great Books Foundation, the China Institute of America, the Foundation for Economic Education, and the Institute for Humane Studies, which have been discussed in earlier chapters. His association with these organizations, as well as his friendships with scholars, reactivated his own education.

During the last thirty years of his life, Goodrich gave substantial thought to educational questions. From a philosophical perspective, his thinking culminated into the drafts of two documents: the "Education Memorandum," and a paper he wrote jointly with Benjamin A. Rogge, "Education in a Free Society."[1]

If it is true that human liberty is becoming more encroached upon by government, Goodrich asserted, then "it is worth looking at what

1. Pierre F. Goodrich, "Education Memorandum" (May 12, 1969); Anne Husted Burleigh, ed., *Education in a Free Society* (Indianapolis: Liberty Fund, 1973). Goodrich and Rogge's paper was published in a collection of essays with the same title. It served as the position paper for a Liberty Fund seminar attended by leading scholars, educators, and business people. The seminar was held at Liberty Fund headquarters in Indianapolis from March 28 to March 31, 1971. Besides "Education in a Free Society," other essays presented by scholars included "Reason of University" (Gottfried Dietze); "The Revitalized College: A Model" (Russell Kirk); "The Political Economy of Modern Universities" (Henry G. Manne); and "Authority, Power, and the University" (Stephen J. Tonsor). A fifth essay, "The Lost Tools of Learning," by British writer Dorothy L. Sayers, was included in the published collection.

part education may or may not play" in this process.[2] Goodrich saw education as part of a broader political, economic, philosophical, and religious framework. According to Goodrich, understanding education's proper role in this overarching framework is imperative in achieving and maintaining a society of free individuals. In his writings, he attempted to prove his point through a series of propositions about human nature that were, in his mind at least, indisputable.

First, because human society is made up of ignorant and imperfect individuals, man is prevented from fully understanding the universe or the "infinite creator." Since man possesses powers of observation and reason, however, he can assume that there is order in the universe and an infinite creator. Using these limited attributes, man is able to discern other human qualities, such as the capacity to reason, the ability to learn through the senses, and the possession of emotions and will.[3]

Second, man must accept that he was created fallible and with limitations. Such fallibility and shortcomings tend to mitigate the good and accentuate the bad; at the very least, imperfect man is incapable of creating a perfect society, "and the choice is not between good and bad, or perfect and imperfect, . . . but between two or more imperfections."[4]

Goodrich next explains that, given man's imperfections, it would be oppressive, "utterly illogical," and sheer folly to believe that giving even the most able men power over less able men would produce a better situation.[5] All men are ignorant, proclaimed Goodrich. The fact that some are marginally less ignorant than others does not mean that they should decide for others. Rather, each man can be educated to decide for himself what is best for him, given his own knowledge of his desires and corresponding obligations.

Therefore, education is essential in eliminating the need to have some make decisions for others. It plays the important role of helping "the individual develop the capacity to think in the realm of ideals and make

2. "Education Memorandum," p. 7.
3. Ibid., pp. 8–10.
4. Ibid., p. 11.
5. Ibid.

choices of imperfections with relation to [these] ideals."[6] In short, education should make man more adept at reasoning about the imperfect choices he has. In this sense, man is more free because he is basing decisions more on reason and less on ignorance and emotion.[7]

Goodrich proceeds to state what he believes are the limitations of education: "Even the best of all possible [educational] arrangements cannot make man into God or into a saint—or even into a good, decent human being. To be educated in the sense we have in mind here is something, perhaps a very important something, but it is not the alpha and the omega of human existence."[8]

Thus, instead of elevating education as the be all and end all of humanity, Goodrich believed that the purpose of education is much less lofty. In fact, he did not believe education has any one purpose. The state's attempt to impose one on the individual negates the very freedoms that proper education should embrace: "Whether the individual pursues an education for the sheer delight in learning or to acquire knowledge for personal decision-making and action or to better serve his God—or even to do no more than flaunt his learning before others—the choice of purpose (as well as means) is *his* and not society's."[9]

Goodrich recognized that the importance of knowledge in making decisions about the desirability of freedom creates an apparent paradox: "How will a citizenry not deliberately educated in the ways of freedom be able to withstand the constant temptations and pressures to abandon freedom in the hope of some transient advantage? In other words, does

6. Ibid., p. 6.

7. Goodrich acknowledges, however, that even this proposition has its pitfalls and provides an incomplete explanation for man's often errant behavior. Goodrich recognizes the challenge of the so-called Faust myth: "we cannot be comfortable with the assumption that the knowledgeable man will also be the noble or virtuous man. In fact, in the Faust myth, it is precisely the most learned who is most susceptible to the temptations of the Devil, to the lure of temporal power over others. (It is tempting to explain the behavior of many modern intellectuals in somewhat this way.)" (*Education in a Free Society*, p. 59)

8. Ibid., pp. 59–60.

9. Ibid., p. 62.

the survival of the free society require that its citizens be unfree in at least one area, the area of education?"[10]

To these questions, Goodrich and Rogge's answer is that the best way to ensure that the student is educated in the virtues of freedom is to have society as a political unit have nothing to do with education: society should not provide education with subsidies (including tax relief), or operate any education programs, or coerce participation in such programs. Agents paid by the state are least likely to promote individual freedom, because of the "temptation to turn education to the purposes of expanding state power (and, hence, their own power), rather than of restricting and limiting that power."[11]

Critique of the Modern Educational Institution

Goodrich often spoke and wrote about the limits of formal education. Because he viewed education in its broadest sense—something beyond the validation of college degrees and the certification of specialties—he knew that obtaining the imprint of higher education's approval did not automatically produce intelligence, skill, or wisdom. Moreover, he believed that literacy alone (that is, the mere technical ability to read) was as likely to be used to manipulate people's thinking as to promote independent thought; this is especially so when propaganda is the primary source material available to the reader or listener.[12]

10. Ibid., p. 63.

11. Ibid., pp. 64–65. Who then is to decide? Clearly, an adult student should be able to decide what kind of educational arrangement he or she will pursue and for what purpose. Although he recognized the problems that could arise, Goodrich believed that the parents of minor students, not the "all-wise agents of the state," should make those decisions for their children. This belief flies in the face of well-known utopian schemes advanced by the likes of Plato, Fourier, Robert Owen, B. F. Skinner, and Mao. They all advocated that children should be taken from their parents at an early age so that their upbringing could be controlled by the state, not the foolish and primitive family circle (ibid., p. 67).

12. See Goodrich, "Education Memorandum," p. 21; see also Goodrich's memorandum regarding his discussion with F. A. Hayek, dated May 13, 1960. Goodrich writes:

> We discussed the question of whether there was any explanation why people could not by their intellect achieve a vicarious understanding of these problems

Goodrich was especially critical of the lecture format used in most high schools and colleges, and the reliance upon textbooks. He believed that both the lecture system and textbooks created a "false sense of infallibility." For that reason, Goodrich believed that primarily students should use original texts such as those used by the Great Books Foundation. Moreover, Goodrich believed that, under the existing system of grades and degrees, the professor is part of "the corrupting tendency inherent in the relationship between himself, as the expounder, and the student who seeks credit and advancement under the bureaucratic power of which the professor is an official."[13]

Furthermore, Goodrich believed that insufficient weight is given to the student's ability to educate himself with the help of others, while excessive concern is given to techniques, bureaucratic departmentalization, and formalities. He stated that focusing on the latter has handicapped the student's ability to think cogently and independently. He also believed that they have made the education process more inefficient and irresponsible.[14] "'Education' is something that happens within an individual. No matter how formally educational the setting or the process, if nothing happens to the supposed learner, nothing educational has taken place."[15]

Goodrich and Rogge were also critical of the public financing of education. They specifically challenged the alleged spillover of benefits coming from the supposed advantage of a better-educated citizenry and the importance of education in developing equal opportunity. They be-

---

through reading and thinking. He had no explanation of it except he thought it generally was true. The fact is he really does not have much confidence in general education as such in the sense that he thinks the American people expect far too much of it.

He arrives, apparently partly by experience as well as reason, at the view I have held for some time, that mere literacy is a very efficient tool for dictatorship control. . . . (Pierre F. Goodrich Collection, box 1, F. A. Hayek folder, Archives, Hoover Institution)

13. Goodrich, "Education Memorandum," p. 26.

14. Ibid., p. 24.

15. Burleigh, *Education in a Free Society,* p. 57.

lieved that a coerced system of funding accomplished neither of these "benefits."[16]

Moreover, Goodrich believed that many of the true impediments to equality of opportunity, especially as they relate to career opportunities, are false in nature or created, ironically, by the state itself by the imposition of credentialism. He and Rogge write: "Much of the apparent relationship between schooling and income either does not establish causation or reflects state action that has required degrees and diplomas as cards of admission to various careers."[17]

Furthermore, the very importance of education in shaping an individual's understanding is exactly why Goodrich adamantly opposed government involvement with education, including financing it. Goodrich and Rogge argued, "To the collectivist we say, if you insist on controlling something, make it the peanut-butter or hula-hoop industries, but for God's sake don't mess with our young people's minds!"[18]

16. Ibid., p. 73. Specifically, Goodrich and Rogge refuted the contention that the Cs should be forced to pay for the education of the Bs because, otherwise, the Bs would not have an equal chance in the race of life. Goodrich's response to this argument was that because individual abilities are so variable it is impossible for individuals to start as equals, let alone end up as equals. To guarantee equality of opportunity would require the state to intervene on a continual basis to ensure a level playing field. This assurance of equality, from both a philosophical and a practical viewpoint, could be accomplished only through continuous state intervention that coerced compliance and would negate, not further, freedom. "The only equality that is consistent with freedom is equality before the law" (ibid., p. 74).

Goodrich and Rogge insisted that instead of promoting freedom, public financing in fact negated individual freedom by allowing the As of this world (state) to decide that the Cs (taxpayers) should pay some part or all of the cost of educating the Bs (students). In this sense, Goodrich did not believe that educating the Bs necessarily benefited the Cs (spillover of benefits argument): "As two of the C's in modern America [Goodrich and Rogge], we deny that we have gained from the schooling provided the B's; in fact, inasmuch as most of that schooling, as it relates to citizenship, has been antifreedom, we believe that we have been *damaged* by the schooling of the B's. For the state to tax us to support the teaching of collectivist ideas is a real violation of our freedom" (p. 76).

17. Ibid., p. 75.

18. Ibid., p. 83. Goodrich believed that hypocrisy prevails in our state-supported education system. If government were to tax people so that Catholic or Lutheran teach-

Goodrich also recognized that the state's encroachment into educational matters significantly impedes the teaching of the most important elements of a child's life—virtue and character. These aspects are intimately related to moral and religious values that generally cannot be taught under our current system, which demands a rigid separation of church and state. Writing, in the late 1960s, at a time of great political and social turbulence on America's campuses, Goodrich was especially critical of the way institutions of higher learning intentionally hide the social and political philosophies of their faculties:

> Most college administrations have found it desirable . . . not to emphasize the fact that on their campuses the students will be confronted by faculties far more liberal or left-wing than the prevailing point of view among parents, trustees, taxpayers, and donors. In how many college catalogs do you find prospective students and their parents given any information on the social philosophies to which the student is exposed on that campus? Do they say, "Send your son to College X and he will be taught by 5 Marxist, burn-down-the-buildings activists, 15 non-Marxist, just-seize-the-buildings activists, 100 left-of-center modern liberals, 10 Ripon Society Republicans, and 2 eccentric conservatives just reaching retirement age"? As Professor George Stigler of the University of Chicago has said, " . . . the typical university catalogue would never stop Diogenes in his search for an honest man."[19]

Goodrich was also critical of how the academic system of job protection, embodied in the concepts of tenure and academic freedom, pro-

---

ings must (or even could) be taught in the churches and the schools (as is the case in many western European nations), the average American would be up in arms. This is so because the idea of the separation of religion and state is ingrained in our minds and is believed to be memorialized in our Constitution. Regarding education, Goodrich could not understand why taxpayers were required to finance teachers and professors who teach Marxism, socialism, or other creeds condemning free society. To Goodrich, this distinction made little sense, and he thought the best solution was to eliminate public education subsidies.

19. Ibid., p. 79 (quoting, in part, George Stigler, "The Intellectual and the Market Place," *Selected Paper*, No. 3, Graduate School of Business, University of Chicago, February 1967, p. 7).

mulgates questionable integrity and mediocrity. He believed that these protections allow academics to teach and publish freely without being accountable for the consequences of their ideas. He debunks the idea of academic freedom. Goodrich and Rogge claimed that the very notion has developed out of a confusion between natural rights (individual liberties such as private property and freedom of speech and religion) and man-made rights (for example, a "right" to health care or education).[20]

Thus, to Goodrich, the guise of academic freedom has allowed nondisclosure by colleges about what they are doing. Moreover, it has allowed faculties to insulate themselves from the discipline and harsh realities of the marketplace. In his general criticisms of the modern university, Goodrich would have agreed very much with Martin Anderson, a Hoover Institution Fellow, who wrote in his 1992 book *Impostors in the Temple:*

> The academic intellectuals enjoy most of the material dreams of any socialist—a guaranteed job for life (tenure), excellent working conditions, recreation facilities, subsidized housing, and generous pensions. Professors do not have to worry about the whims of a tyrannical boss who might fire them. The only people to whom they answer, the only ones who effectively judge them are—other professors. Through the custom of "peer review," they have evolved a unique system in which they essentially judge themselves.[21]

20. Goodrich wrote:

> To impose on the individual entering the relationship of teaching through being hired by any given college, restrictions and responsibilities, including the right to dismiss him, is an entirely different matter from restrictions on individual liberty apart from such employment. . . .
>
> "This confusion between individual freedom and academic freedom—the success with which teachers and their power-seeking organizations have confused the human liberty of the individual to seek truth and exercise free will—especially freedom from the state—has been the cloak behind which individuals have indulged in irresponsibility, undeveloped reason, insufficient education, irrational activity, the arrogance of infallibility, and personal and collective power." ("Education Memorandum," pp. 32–33)

21. *Impostors in the Temple* (New York: Simon and Schuster, 1992), p. 14.

Moreover, Goodrich was critical about the *in loco parentis* role that many colleges assume. As a partial result, colleges perform poorly their true mission—educating minds.[22] He also believed that too much importance on the part of trustees and administrators is given to fund raising, buildings, athletics, and the sponsoring of other noneducational functions, such as college fraternities and dances. Correspondingly, Goodrich believed that too little attention is given to assessing "professors, their standing, integrity, the beliefs they hold and on an honest disclosure of these things."[23]

Goodrich believed that a "free educational society contemplates a multiplicity of educational institutions."[24] Therefore, although he had in mind what he believed would be an ideal college (one in which individuals would come to be committed to a free society), he recognized that in a free educational marketplace, consumers might or might not select his ideal as their ideal.[25]

Goodrich's ideal college would be private and for-profit. "School departments which have become bureaus and power-seeking devices" would be eliminated, as well as courses and divisions.[26] He would also do away with grades and degrees.[27] The educational format would be composed of three main elements: (1) individual study by students, (2) seminars on assigned readings, and (3) lectures delivered by the faculty or visiting lecturers.[28] Students could study for as long as they chose, so long as they did not disrupt the studies of others.

Faculty members would serve at the pleasure of the administration (as at-will employees), and their income would be directly related to

22. Burleigh, *Education in a Free Society,* pp. 91–92.

23. Ibid., p. 40.

24. "Education Memorandum," p. 21.

25. Burleigh, *Education in a Free Society,* pp. 82–83.

26. "Education Memorandum," p. 24.

27. Burleigh, *Education in a Free Society,* pp. 90–91. Goodrich believed that the opportunity for students who were inclined to be evaluated could be provided by having them pay extra to write papers and take exams and have them evaluated.

28. Ibid., p. 88.

their effectiveness in teaching (although worthwhile research activities could add to their remuneration). Thus, if professors were not successful in attracting students to their seminars or were not otherwise contributing to the stated goals of the college, they could be fired, could have their salaries decreased, and so forth.[29] Finally, in Goodrich's ideal college, trustees would have a much greater degree of control in directing school policy than they do in the traditional liberal arts college. One of Goodrich's strongest criticisms about existing institutions of higher learning is that power is too diffusely spread among such various factions as administrators, alumni, donors, faculty, state regulators, student government, and trustees. As a result, it is difficult to know who is the real decision maker and is therefore accountable.[30]

Goodrich's examination of the pitfalls of higher education came from an interesting perspective, that of a free-market businessman and a trustee of a small, all-male liberal arts college. Such a perspective offered a unique opportunity for insight, but no doubt it also limited his appreciation for the multiplicity of backgrounds and perspectives that exist at large state-supported universities.

Goodrich had served as a trustee for thirty years, during the full tenures of three Wabash College presidents and the partial terms of two others.[31] He had seen many educational fads come and go. His criticisms were not aimed at superficial academic matters, nor were they even aimed at weightier ones such as whether a curriculum should center on the literature of primarily Western culture (selections from Goodrich's *Basic Memorandum* reading list strongly suggest that he thought they should). Rather, his criticisms went to the very core of institutional and noninstitutional learning.

To Goodrich's credit, he recognized that the blame for the fundamen-

29. Ibid.

30. Ibid., pp. 86–87.

31. The three college presidents during whose tenures Goodrich served as a trustee were Frank Sparks (1941–56), Byron Trippet (1956–65), and Paul Cook (1966–68). Goodrich also served as a trustee when George Kendall was acting president (1940–41) and during the first year of Thaddeus Seymour's tenure as president (1968–69).

tal problems plaguing colleges and universities cannot be placed solely on the backs of professors. As Martin Anderson observes, between 1960 and 1975, an additional eight million students poured into American colleges and universities. This caused the hiring of 352,000 new faculty members and led to a predictable watering down of standards. Relatively easy access to tenure during that period accelerated the teaching profession's alienation from the marketplace and severed any tie between power and accountability. As a result, professors have had to answer little to parents, alumni, and regents.[32]

Anderson further observes (a point Goodrich made more than forty years before in the earliest version of the "Education Memorandum")[33] that the group that bears most responsibility for the current sorry state of higher education is that of the men and women who constitute the governing boards of colleges and universities, the trustees and regents. Goodrich noted that "college trustees, as the product of present day education, are not prepared to consider these problems with a critical educational background and to assume the responsibility which is their responsibility."[34]

Goodrich believed that education should be treated no differently from any other business endeavor for which a natural market exists (note that he titled his earliest writing about education a memorandum,

32. Anderson, *Impostors in the Temple,* pp. 34–35; see also Richard Armey, "Socialism on Campus" (review of *Impostors in the Temple*), *Wall Street Journal,* August 19, 1992, sec. A, p. 10, col. 1.

33. Goodrich's earliest draft of the "Education Memorandum" was written in 1951. In a May 1952 draft, Goodrich emphasized the importance of leadership by trustees. At that time, he had already lamented the lack of preparedness of most trustees in assuming their rightful responsibility. See May 26, 1952, draft of "Education Memorandum," chap. 7, p. 7 (Pierre F. Goodrich file, Foundation for Economic Education, Irvington-on-Hudson, N.Y.).

34. "Education Memorandum," p. 35. With trustees and regents unwilling to assume their proper roles of authority, current congressman Richard Armey argues that "faculty and administrators are instead left to regulate themselves, with the outcome similar to what one might expect if a parent allows a child to run free in a candy store. Mr. Anderson's point is that universities are big business and must have a similar command structure." Armey, "Socialism on Campus."

a business document used to convey internal communication). He wanted to eliminate educational subsidies (today, many state institutions receive as much as 60 percent of their budget from government) and the protection of tenure. As to so-called academic freedom, Goodrich thought it an ill-founded right. He fervently embraced the idea that the Constitution protects every person's right to free speech, but, just as deeply, believed it does not protect a person's right to an occupation.[35]

In many ways, Goodrich's views on education were the most important of all his philosophical beliefs. He believed that only if the critical role of education in society is properly understood could education help to produce a liberated and responsible citizenry. Without this proper understanding, man was doomed to dependency and unsound decision making.

It is doubtful, however, that Goodrich's model would do anything but allow limited groups (those who already value education) to thrive. If state educational subsidies were totally removed, especially at the primary level, could children from poor areas ever hope to have an opportunity to enter into mainstream society? Proponents of school choice argue that the only sector of society that has a full choice of educational options today is the affluent. Giving rich and poor the same subsidy (for example, through a voucher system), advocates argue, would make it possible for parents and students to choose their own schools. Goodrich, however, apparently opposed *any* state subsidy, no matter how it was distributed. If that is the case, then, given Goodrich's own observations about man's weak and fallible nature, would individuals voluntarily, without state financial incentives, assist those who are most in need of quality instruction? This is a difficult question that neither Goodrich nor Rogge seems to address.

35. Goodrich shared this view with former Supreme Court justice Oliver Wendell Holmes, who observed when sitting on the highest court of Massachusetts, "[A policeman] may have a constitutional right to talk politics, but he has no constitutional right to be a policeman." *McAuliffe v. Mayor of New Bedford,* 155 Mass. 216, 29 N.E. 517 (1892).

Chapter 27

Moral, Political, and Metaphysical Beliefs

> The ideas of economists and political philosophers, both when they are right and when they are wrong, are more powerful than is commonly understood. Indeed, the world is ruled by little else. Practical men, who believe themselves to be quite exempt from any intellectual influences, are usually the slaves of some defunct economist. . . . soon or late, it is ideas, not vested interests, which are dangerous for good or evil.
>
> JOHN MAYNARD KEYNES, *The General Theory of Employment, Interest and Money*

WHILE Pierre Goodrich was no friend of John Maynard Keynes's economic or political views, he no doubt embraced the British economist's insight that ideas ultimately control much of human behavior. Thus, the ideas that a person studies and discusses are critical. As former Wabash president Byron Trippet recalls, Goodrich "saw no reason why a college needed a library of more than about 5,000 books, provided they were the *right books,*" meaning that they contain the right ideas.[1]

Goodrich's own thought, as reflected in such writings as the *Basic*

1. Byron K. Trippet, *Wabash on My Mind* (Crawfordsville, Ind.: Wabash College, 1982), p. 185 (emphasis added); see also Plato, *Republic,* trans. H. D. P. Lee (Middlesex, England: Penguin Classics, 1972). Plato states: "Then it seems that our first business is to supervise the production of stories, and choose only those we think suitable, and reject the rest. We shall persuade mothers and nurses to tell our chosen stories to their children and so mould their minds and characters rather than their bodies. The greater part of the stories current to-day we shall have to reject" (p. 115).

Memorandum, "Education Memorandum," "Why Liberty?" and his letters, is not particularly noteworthy for its originality or cogent expression. His thinking is important, however, in its attempt to examine critically both human understanding and the forces that compel human action; moreover, his philosophical perspective also reveals a strong influence by many great thinkers of Western civilization. Goodrich's voracious appetite for books enabled him to become extremely knowledgeable about both the literature of his time and, more important, works that have influenced ideas for centuries.[2] While it is not possible to trace Goodrich's thinking to any particular writer, it is clear that many of his beliefs were shaped by classical thinkers. The core ideas of these scholars of ethics, political theory, epistemology, and metaphysics deserve a brief exploration.

Early on in the *Basic Memorandum,* Goodrich takes up a philosophical matter that the Greek moralist and political philosopher Plato (427–347 B.C.) is particularly known for—the nature, origin, scope, and limits of human knowledge (epistemology). Plato believed that man often goes astray because he is ignorant of what the right action is. Therefore, doing right is a matter of proper education and, ultimately, knowledge. Similarly, Goodrich recognized that "all individuals have an imperfect knowledge of man, his origin and his destiny, and the universe in which he exists."[3]

Man's imperfection, his imperfectibility, and his inability to obtain perfect knowledge are common themes that run throughout Goodrich's writings. This is why proper education is so important to Goodrich's worldview. Goodrich believed that whenever man becomes unshackled from perceiving the world primarily through sense experience and be-

2. A number of people I interviewed mentioned how well read Goodrich was. Russell Kirk wrote: "He subscribed to, and read, a wide—very wide—variety of periodicals. I was surprised that he had encountered an essay of mine in the pages of *The Monist,* the Jesuit magazine published in London." Letter to author, February 8, 1992.

3. Pierre F. Goodrich, "Why Liberty?" p. 10; *Basic Memorandum,* pp. 13, 21–22 (exhibit I-a).

gins the difficult journey toward using reason to apprehend reality, it is possible for him to acquire at least a partial understanding of the world. He denies, however, the possibility that man can ever obtain perfect knowledge or escape the influence of sense experiences. Furthermore, Goodrich recognized that doing wrong may not be merely a matter of lack of knowledge, but also a result of "weakness of the will" (lacking the fortitude to do what one already knows is the right thing) or even of heredity.[4]

Goodrich departs from Platonic thinking regarding who should ex-

4. Goodrich states that man "as we know him . . . has some *imperfect* capacity for reason and for communicating his ideas, past and present, by means of words." Goodrich also believed, however, that man "learns through his senses, and through a conception we hardly know how to describe except through the term mysticism." Moreover, man "acts in response to love, compassion, and fortitude"; "acts in response also to envy, hate, and jealousy" ("Why Liberty?" p. 6). Here, Goodrich describes man as "he is." It seems that Goodrich is not always consistent in his views about whether man is that way (that is, governed primarily by the senses) and cannot change or whether man is capable of apprehending knowledge by a more reasoned way.

Another related Platonic idea that Goodrich loosely adopts is distinguishing between the ideal and the real. Goodrich maintains that even if the ideal he has sketched—for example, the ideal college—cannot be realized in every detail, it is still worth describing as a standard to aim for. Moreover, the only hope of realizing the ideal (or a close approximation of it) requires political power to be placed in the hands of philosophers. The philosopher has a passion for truth that is related not to expedient short-term solutions, but to the unchanging reality which is the object of knowledge. This idea is also explored in Plato's *Republic,* pp. 231–44; see also "Why Liberty?" p. 5.

Goodrich believed that "genetics" explained some aspects of human behavior and should be investigated further. He wrote in a company memorandum:

> There always have been bad people (especially in the Lockeian sense of the word) who gain important celebrity, but some of the best research which has been permitted to become public (we are now so near dictatorship that we are unable to permit research to be free and become public, especially if it doesn't suit the prevailing power trend) indicates that there are such things as genes. . . . The matter of heredity is very important. The heredity factor is something we have known for a long time but we have decided not to apply it to human beings, and uncontrolled romanticism, emotionalism and lack of responsibility has been the "in" thing. ("Indiana Telephone Corporation Memorandum, No. 5—The Union Idea," March 20, 1973, revised May 30 and July 5, 1973, p. 2 [in the possession of T. Alan Russell])

ercise decision-making powers. He denies outright Plato's notion of the philosopher-king as the proper decision-maker for a society. Plato believed that those who have the greatest aptitude for ruling should be placed in absolute authority. Goodrich refutes the whole notion of Plato's philosopher-king by means of a two-pronged attack. First, "the very nature of a society of imperfect human beings excludes the possibility of a perfect choice";[5] therefore, it is not necessarily true that the philosopher-king is capable of making better decisions for others than those others, who have greater knowledge of their own abilities and desires, can make for themselves.

Second, "it is self evident that man's faculties (for example, physical, reason, integrity . . .) decline or improve by lack of use or use thereof, and the nature of that use."[6] In other words, the individual loses something important if he continually delegates the responsibility for making decisions in his life to a ruler. Soon, he will not be able to make the critical decisions nor undertake the actions necessary to keep himself free and able to make use of his potential. If this continues, man will ultimately degenerate, becoming dependent upon others for his welfare. According to Goodrich, a society preferable to Plato's would allow all men sufficient freedom that "some men, less fallible than others, may move closer to man's ultimate destiny than other men, and in so doing help all men."[7]

British empirical thinker John Locke (1632–1704) is probably the theoretical architect most responsible for democracy as it exists in the Western world today. Locke's *Treatise of Civil Government* contains many of

5. Goodrich, *Liberty Fund Basic Memorandum,* p. 15.

6. Ibid., p. 17.

7. Goodrich, "Why Liberty?" p. 11. This idea is also contained in the *Liberty Fund Basic Memorandum* (p. 17). Goodrich's thought appears very similar to one expressed by F. A. Hayek in *The Counter-Revolution of Science: Studies on the Abuse of Reason* (Glencoe, Ill.: Free Press, 1952; Indianapolis: Liberty Fund, 1979): "Many of the greatest things man has achieved are the result not of consciously directed thought, and still less the product of a deliberately coordinated effort of many individuals, but of a process in which the individual plays a part which he can never fully understand . . ." (p. 150).

the ideas that formed the basis for the political philosophy of the founders of the American and French republics. Moreover, the *Treatise* also contains the primary framework for many of Goodrich's own beliefs about the nature of private property, the existence of natural rights, the origins and scope of government, and the separation of governmental powers.[8]

Goodrich believed that the primary purpose of government is to ensure that no person or group can coerce another into doing something he or she does not want to do. This belief in minimal government is grounded in Lockean theory. Locke's "law of nature" espouses that "no one ought to harm another in his life, health, liberty or possessions." Moreover, Goodrich, like Locke, believed that the state exists to prevent coercion at the hands of others and to address disputes that arise when individuals form organized societies for mutual benefit under a social contract. Obviously, then, a mechanism must be established to resolve these disputes in an efficient, orderly, and fair way. Such a mechanism is a judiciary system based upon integrity and law.[9]

Goodrich believed that law, not force, should be the basis upon which government operates to prevent coercion of the individual by others. Moreover, perhaps even more important to Goodrich, adherence to law is necessary to prevent those cloaked with governmental power from ruling tyrannically. Adherence to the rule of law, then, by elected officials as well as by the populace is absolutely necessary in an orderly society where free and voluntary exchanges are possible.

Locke opposed monarchy and dictatorship for the very reason that a true monarch or dictator is above the law; in fact, a monarch or dictator

8. John Locke, *Treatise of Civil Government and A Letter Concerning Toleration* (New York: Appleton-Century Co., 1937). One of Goodrich's favorite modern thinkers was Gottfried Dietze, an emeritus professor at Johns Hopkins University. Goodrich thought highly of and was influenced by Dietze's book, which discussed the potential tyranny of majoritarian rule (*American Political Dilemma*, Johns Hopkins University Press, 1968). Stephen Tonsor, interview, December 5, 1992.

9. Locke, *Treatise of Civil Government*, pp. 5–12 ("Of the State of Nature"), pp. 13–15 ("Of the State of War"), and pp. 63–81 ("Of the Beginning of Political Societies").

is the law. Such a government operates solely at the caprice of the authoritarian ruler, and the society he or she controls is correspondingly unstable.[10] Locke's rationale for opposing a monarchy is logically consistent with the reasons Goodrich opposed absolute power held by any one person or group: (1) as a practical matter, no correctional force exists to curb the power monger's abuses; and (2) morally, absolute power is opposed to the idea of the "rule of law" and the universality of action (for example, Kant's categorical imperative). Goodrich's constant warning about the abuses of power is evident in his repeated references to Lord Acton's admonition that "power tends to corrupt and absolute power corrupts absolutely."

Locke's theory of rights was important to Goodrich as well. As to property rights, Goodrich believed deeply in the Lockean notion that such rights arise from man's "mixing his labor" with things originally given to mankind in common.[11] An example of how seriously Goodrich believed in property rights occurred in the early 1970s. The incident arose when a presenter at an early Liberty Fund seminar on education gave a paper that had actually been written by Dorothy L. Sayers. Sayers, a distinguished English writer, had been deceased for more than a decade at the time. The presenter gave the paper without making any reference to the true author of the work. It was two weeks later that the plagiarism incident became known. Goodrich was livid that such a violation had occurred at a Liberty Fund seminar where the primary purpose of bringing the conferees together was to examine education's role in furthering freedom and virtue.[12]

Locke's other views about individual rights also heavily influenced

10. Ibid., pp. 115–18 ("Of Paternal, Political, and Despotical Power Considered Together"), pp. 134–41 ("Of Tyranny").

11. Ibid., pp. 18–33 ("Of Property").

12. Stephen J. Tonsor, interview, December 5, 1992. The paper, "The Lost Tools of Learning," was written by Sayers, a British academic and novelist, but delivered, unacknowledged, by a presenter. Sayers's paper was eventually published under her name in *Education in a Free Society,* ed. Anne Husted Burleigh (Indianapolis: Liberty Fund, 1973), pp. 231–63.

Goodrich. For instance, Goodrich embraced Locke's theory about when and to what extent governmental intervention is appropriate in curbing such rights. Goodrich, like Locke, believed that all men are equal in the sense that they have rights that are *anterior* to those given them by society. Since these natural rights are not given to them by society, society cannot take them away.[13] There is no definitive list of these natural rights, but Goodrich no doubt believed that they include at least the rights recognized in the United States Constitution; for example, private property, free speech, freedom of assembly, and freedom of association and religious expression.

What Locke and Goodrich did not believe is that somehow government could create rights; Goodrich did not believe, for instance, that there is such a thing as a right to housing, to an education, to a job, or to health care. These may be benefits, but they are not rights. Thus, they are not entitled to the same protections as, for example, the rights to property and freedom of speech. Therefore, Goodrich would have been totally opposed to a 1970 United States Supreme Court decision that held that "welfare entitlements [are] more like 'property' than a 'gratuity.' Much of the existing wealth in this country takes the form of rights that do not fall within traditional common-law concepts of property. It has been aptly noted that '[s]ociety today is built around entitlement.'"[14]

Goodrich believed that the confusion in distinguishing between rights and benefits (so-called entitlements) actually results in the violation of others' rights. That is why he was so adamantly opposed to what he considered were simply the "man made rights" (and therefore not really rights at all) of academic freedom and tenured faculty protection. Also, Goodrich did not believe that any definition of equality should extend beyond "equality before the law." The principle that "all men are created equal" is only applicable to this limited meaning, Goodrich contended. Otherwise, it is silly to suggest that individuals are born equal

13. Locke, *Treatise of Civil Government,* pp. 5–12 ("Of the State of Nature").

14. *Goldberg v. Kelly,* 397 U.S. 254, 295 (1970).

in terms of talent, intelligence, family wealth, physical appearance, prowess, and so forth. Any attempt to extend equality to these other areas means that government must constantly intervene to remake a level playing field.

Goodrich departed from Locke's thinking concerning the virtues of majoritarian government (democracy). Locke believed that authority lies with the people who elect government. Government is merely the means of carrying out the people's will. But Locke did not seem to realize or appreciate, Goodrich would contend, that the majority can become a tyranny; the majority, like any monarch, can become a despot by suppressing the desires of the minority. Therefore, Goodrich was very skeptical of trusting the will of a majority: "In a large corporation the stockholders, who operate as a majority, are a kind of democracy (I am afraid of democracies; for example, I cannot select the necessary element of a good common law judge by a majority vote . . .) and they have no right to dispose of the assets of the minority stockholders."[15]

The German philosopher Immanuel Kant (1724–1805) was an original thinker who had a tremendous influence on shaping Goodrich's views of ethics and morality. In Kant, Goodrich found a philosopher who had systematically examined the ethical underpinnings of a morally responsible society. Kant's categorical imperative was the center of Goodrich's ethical life.[16] Kant's appeal to Goodrich lay primarily in three fundamental premises upon which the philosopher built his overarching moral framework: rationality, universality, and freedom of will.

Kant contended that, to the degree we are rational, morality is simply the expression of our own free will. We can establish a moral law of conduct simply by being obedient to our conscience. Therefore, our behavior is guided by both reference to and reverence for our "higher selves." The need for an external influence such as government to co-

15. Letter from Goodrich to Friedrich A. Hayek, December 24, 1970. F. A. Hayek Collection, box 22, folder 6, Archives, Hoover Institution.

16. Stephen J. Tonsor made this observation in a December 5, 1992, interview.

erce us to do the right thing should be unnecessary or, at the very least, minimal. Goodrich believed that Kant's maxim of the categorical imperative, if strictly followed, rendered government largely superfluous. Goodrich writes in the *Basic Memorandum:*

> The Will to Liberty as referred to in the *Liberty Fund Basic Memorandum* is of a higher order than, for example, the will to satisfy one's own liberty only.
>
> It is a will which recognizes as a practical necessity a concern about the liberty of others.[17]

Thus, how do we know whether our conduct is ethical or not? Like Kant, Goodrich believed that if a person can will an act that should be "universalized" (meaning that the act should be permissible for everyone to do), then that act is morally allowable. Therefore, lying is not an act that is ethically permissible, because it would be disastrous if falsehoods were universalized (it would destroy the important institution of trust).[18] Nonetheless, in Kantian thinking, the intent, not the utility, of a law or principle is what creates moral worth. Similarly, the actor's intent, not the result of the act, is what gives an act its ethical character. For instance, a passerby who attempts to save a drowning person but who ends up drowning himself is a morally good person despite the fact that the result is disastrous.

According to Kant, the principle's intent should be based on a sense of duty. Duty is to be performed entirely for its own sake, not in order to promote human happiness or fulfillment.[19] Goodrich suggested, however, that ethical behavior produces both of these human qualities, although they are not the overriding reasons why a person should be ethical. Goodrich wrote: "It seems observable that the nature of ethical capacity is such that it has its own reward. The greater an individual

17. "The Will to Liberty," *Basic Memorandum*, p. 28.

18. See *The Moral Law: Kant's Groundwork of the Metaphysics of Morals,* translated and analyzed by H. J. Paton (London: Hutchinson Publishing Group, 1948), pp. 24–38.

19. Ibid.; see also Richard Norman, *The Moral Philosophers* (Oxford: Clarendon Press, 1983), p. 95.

exercises his ethical capacity the greater is his self and the greater are the happiness and health of the inner peace which exists."[20]

The German theologian Martin Luther (1483–1546) and the French Protestant reformer John Calvin (1509–64) also significantly influenced Goodrich's moral, ethical, and political beliefs. Pierre was raised in the Presbyterian Church, in which Calvin is historically considered the single most important figure. Luther and John Knox (1505–72), the latter of whom led the Protestant Reformation movement in Scotland, closely followed. Goodrich knew these theologians' teachings intimately. In the *Basic Memorandum,* both Luther's and Calvin's writings are prominently listed, and the *Basic Memorandum* has a strong Calvinist strain.

Luther's and Calvin's writings are responsible for much of modern society's conceptions of sin and salvation as well as for the virtues of capitalism, political liberty, and obedience to state authority. Their writings also helped to form common spiritual, social, political, and cultural beliefs that we have failed to associate with these two towering sixteenth-century figures simply out of ignorance of their historical importance. Goodrich knew that as founders of the Reformation, Luther and Calvin were so powerful that even popes and emperors were intimidated by them. Why? The two theologians were not supported by great armies; on the contrary, both men were opposed to force and violence. Their power lay in the widespread acceptance of their teachings. These teachings boldly challenged the authority of the Catholic Church and, to a lesser degree, the political hierarchy of the time.

Luther struggled with the amount of legitimacy to give to secular government. He recognized that the state played an important role in maintaining minimal order in a violent, sinful (non-Christian) world. But he also believed that such authority was limited, did not extend into matters of faith, and must be exercised justly.[21] Luther's teachings about

20. *Basic Memorandum,* p. 79.

21. See "Temporal Authority: To What Extent It Should Be Obeyed," in *Martin Luther's Basic Theological Writings,* ed. Timothy F. Lull (Minneapolis: Fortress Press, 1989), pp. 655–703.

freedom in an ethical and spiritual context were more edifying to Goodrich.[22]

Politically, Calvin is a more important historic figure than Luther. "Calvin rendered incalculable service to modern liberty by showing how political tyranny could be constitutionally checked, and by cultivating the qualities necessary to revolution and self-government."[23] Before Luther and Calvin, Christians were generally not involved in the affairs of state, for two reasons: First, the devout follower believed that his business did not involve the material world, but God's Kingdom; and second, the feudal subject had been raised to believe that kings and feudal lords were the natural holders of authority, sanctioned by God, and the caretakers of the peasant and his family. But Luther and Calvin, especially Calvin, helped to change these beliefs.[24]

Luther's and Calvin's teachings formed the basis for protest (the root of the word *Protestant*) against what they believed to be abuses by the established Church. Moreover, this protest grew to include political protest. It was based on the idea that every person—including ordinary men and women—had a duty to be politically active in order to realize a God-fearing world here on earth. Thus, the idea of the citizen came to the fore. The Christian was not to divorce himself from this

22. For instance, Luther taught that true Christian freedom rests in faith, accepting Jesus Christ as lord and savior, not in strict adherence to the Old Testament's commandments or in the belief in the sanctity of good works. Moreover, Luther taught the importance of the priesthood of all believers. He wrote: "The woman or man who knows the grace of God in Jesus Christ is set free to act on the basis of responding love and the real needs of the neighbor. This action need not be contaminated by the continual pressure of the self wanting justification, praise, or credit for whatever is done" (*Martin Luther's Basic Theological Writings,* p. 578). See also Martin Luther's treatise *On Christian Liberty,* in *Martin Luther's Basic Theological Writings,* pp. 595–629 ("The Freedom of a Christian").

23. Georgia Hardness, *John Calvin: The Man and His Ethics* (New York: Henry Holt, 1931), p. 221.

24. For an excellent discussion of the political, social, and spiritual environment leading up to the Reformation, see Michael Walzer, *The Revolution of the Saints: A Study in the Origins of Radical Politics* (Cambridge, Mass.: Harvard University Press, 1965), pp. 4–20.

world in anticipation of a greater and holier life to come. This "Calvinist conscience" formed the basis for an "extraordinary view of politics as work and of work as a permanent effort and an endless struggle with the devil."[25] The roots of James Goodrich's political and business prowess may be partially explained by these prevailing Protestant beliefs.

Pierre was fascinated with the ways in which Luther's and Calvin's teachings influenced the English and American Puritans. Calvin's political theory, with its clear democratic tendencies, helped to pave the way for the American Revolution and the United States Constitution.[26] Both Luther's and Calvin's teachings, therefore, commanded political participation by the believer. Their teachings also emphasized the importance of work, revolution, and warfare as means of resisting temptation, instilling discipline, and overcoming misguided, concentrated, or tyrannical forces.[27]

Goodrich's beliefs were also shaped by dozens, perhaps hundreds, of other great scholars and theologians. Many of them and their works are memorialized in the *Liberty Fund Basic Memorandum* book list (see appendix B). These great thinkers were included in the list because Goodrich believed that their works had helped to lay the cultural and intellectual foundation for Western democratic society in general and the beliefs of the Founding Fathers in particular.[28] Some of the most important thinkers, in addition to those discussed above, were Aristotle, Edmund Burke, David Hume, Adam Smith, William Black-

25. Ibid., p. 21.

26. For more information regarding Calvin's influence on English Puritans, see Hardness, *John Calvin: The Man and His Ethic,* pp. 237–57.

27. See the following chapters in Walker, *The Revolution of the Saints: A Study in the Origins of Radical Politics:* "The Attack upon the Traditional Political World," pp. 148–98; "The New World of Discipline and Work," pp. 199–231; "Politics and War," pp. 268–99. Goodrich's interest in Luther and Calvin as spokesmen against concentrated religious powers can be seen in a series of letters between him and Roscoe Pound. See Goodrich to Pound, May 6, 1949; Pound to Goodrich, May 9, 1949; Goodrich to Pound, April 7, 1952. Roscoe Pound Papers, Archives, Harvard Law School.

28. See *Basic Memorandum,* pp. 111–14.

stone, Alexander Hamilton, James Madison, John Jay, John Stuart Mill, and Lord Acton.[29]

Because this chapter began by mentioning the British economist John Maynard Keynes, perhaps it is fitting to close with a brief comparison of Goodrich's and Keynes's beliefs. The two men had similar backgrounds: They lived during approximately the same period, they were the offspring of upper-middle-class parents who were raised during Victorian times, and they shared similar educational and religious upbringings. There, however, the similarity ends.

John Maynard Keynes (1883–1946) is one of the most significant economists of the twentieth century because his views on state planning have been so broadly adopted by Western democratic governments. Keynes believed that inequality came about because of "risk, uncertainty, and ignorance" and that society could be advanced by the elimination, or at least a considerable reduction, of all three.[30] His prognosis for the problem, as far as this goes, is not unlike Goodrich's.

29. The influences of these great philosophers and political scientists were not merely meaningless abstractions to Goodrich. He incorporated many of their ideas into his own belief system and applied them to contemporary problems that confronted him in his pursuit of a truly free society. For instance, Goodrich discusses in the *Basic Memorandum* the problem of governmental intervention in regulating utilities whose stock is owned by Liberty Fund. Goodrich asks: In light of the fact that Liberty Fund opposes governmental regulation, would it be better to get out of the utility business altogether or to remain in the utility business and fight against state intervention? Goodrich mentions the different approaches of Erasmus, who fought against the oppressiveness of the Catholic Church while remaining within its fold, and Luther, who attacked the Church from outside (*Basic Memorandum,* pp. 91–92). Goodrich readily admits that both men accomplished much. Goodrich finally acknowledges that which example the board should follow (Erasmus's or Luther's) may have something to do with the timing of other events. Since Goodrich drafted the *Basic Memorandum,* the issue has become moot, since federal and state law forbid a not-for-profit and tax-exempt organization to own more than a small percentage of a company's stock.

30. Keynes gave a lecture at Oxford in 1924 entitled "The End of Laissez-Faire" in which he stated: "Many of the greatest economic evils of our time are the *fruits of risk, uncertainty, and ignorance*. It is because particular individuals . . . are able to take advantage of uncertainty and ignorance, and also because for the same reason big *business*

Keynes's prescription for removing these obstacles, however, was for "the state to act as the director of investment to smooth the flow of investment so as to reduce uncertainty and increase the capital stock and the level of output."[31] How exactly does the state act, and at whose direction? Keynes believed that the state should be guided by an intellectual elite that would place social progress ahead of its own class interests. In short, an intellectual elite acting under the notion of "noblesse oblige" (privilege entails responsibility) should properly make the choices in a democratic society.[32] The principal challenge was to make the intellectual elite understand and accept its responsibility. In responding to Friedrich Hayek's *The Road to Serfdom,* Keynes wrote to Hayek, summarizing his views on this point:

> Moderate planning will be safe if those carrying it out are rightly oriented in their own minds and hearts to the moral issue. This is already true of some of them. But the curse is that there is also an important section who could almost be said to want planning not in order to enjoy its fruits but because morally they hold ideas exactly the opposite of yours, and wish to serve not God but the devil. . . .
>
> What we need is the restoration of right moral thinking—a return to proper moral values in our social philosophy.[33]

Keynes rejected Adam Smith's theory of the "invisible hand," and he wrote in 1938 "that self-reliant individuals acting in their own interest cannot reach a maximum for society." Therefore, what self-interest cannot achieve, Keynes argued, an intellectual elite could—namely, an optimum society—by directing society toward worthy ends.[34]

---

is often a lottery, that great inequalities of wealth come about . . ." (*The Collected Writings of John Maynard Keynes,* vol. 9, p. 291).

31. Allan H. Meltzer, *Keynes's Monetary Theory: A Different Interpretation* (Cambridge: Cambridge University Press, 1988), pp. 304–5.

32. These observations were made by Allan H. Meltzer at a talk he gave about his book on Keynes (*Keynes's Monetary Theory*) at the American Enterprise Institute, Washington, D.C., on November 14, 1989.

33. *The Collected Writings of John Maynard Keynes,* vol. 27, p. 387.

34. Meltzer, lecture, American Enterprise Institute, November 14, 1989.

Goodrich rejected the very heart of Keynes's philosophy. He did not believe that the intellectual elite for which Keynes had such high hopes could carry out the task that Keynes expected it to accomplish. Goodrich believed that ignorance was far too pervasive to enable even an elite body to make decisions in the best interests of others. Moreover, Goodrich believed that Keynes failed to "ponder why society would delegate so much authority to a small, non-elected group."[35] In Goodrich's judgment, Keynes's proposal would sacrifice specific individual freedoms in order to obtain a higher social standard. As will be seen in the next chapter, this was a notion that Pierre Goodrich was unwilling to accept.

35. Meltzer, *Keynes's Monetary Theory: A Different Interpretation,* p. 317.

Chapter 28

Why Liberty?

A Democracy cannot exist as a permanent form of government. It can only exist until the voters discover that they can vote themselves largesse from the public treasury. From that moment on the majority always votes for the candidates promising the most benefits from the public treasury, with the result that a Democracy always collapses over loose fiscal policy, always followed by dictatorship. The average age of the world's greatest civilizations has been two hundred years. These nations have progressed through this sequence: From bondage to spiritual faith; from spiritual faith to great courage; from courage to liberty; from liberty to abundance; from abundance to selfishness; from selfishness to complacency; from complacency to apathy; from apathy to dependency; from dependency back again to bondage.

ALEXANDER FRASER TYLER

The people never give up their liberties but under some delusion.

EDMUND BURKE, Speech at County Meeting of Buckinghamshire, 1784

At the invitation of Friedrich Hayek, Pierre Goodrich delivered his paper "Why Liberty?" at the September 1958 annual meeting of the Mont Pelerin Society at Princeton University.[1] Why, of all the ideals, problems, and issues that confront mankind, was liberty

1. Hayek wrote to Goodrich in March 1958, suggesting that on the first day of the upcoming annual meeting Goodrich deliver a "brief statement of what you consider the basic philosophy of a free enterprise society [is], including, if you so wish, a criticism of what I know you consider as the persistent failure of the Mont Pelerin Society to get down to fundamentals." See letter from Hayek to Goodrich, March 23, 1958, Pierre F. Goodrich Collection, box 1, F. A. Hayek folder, Archives, Hoover Institution. Hayek

Goodrich's lifelong preoccupation? There were times during his life when he seemed to think about little else.[2] An examination of the im-

---

had previously written to John Van Sickle, professor of economics at Wabash College, asking if he believed Goodrich would deliver the paper. Hayek wrote:

> Dear John:
>
> I am exceedingly grateful to you for letting me see Pierre Goodrich's most sensible comments on the Mont Pelerin Society. I wish he knew how much I agree with him and how disappointed I am that all my attempts to get a good discussion of the general principles have never succeeded. My only complaint is that he does not speak up at the Conferences, for he has evidently a great deal to say—and I should very much wish that somebody should once frankly criticize our activities on these lines.
>
> I am now writing mainly to ask whether you think that in the special circumstances which I shall explain there might be a chance of prevailing upon him to speak. . . .
>
> Sincerely yours,
>
> F. A. Hayek
>
> (Hayek to Van Sickle, March 8, 1958, F. A. Hayek Collection, box 74, folder 8 [correspondence with Pierre F. Goodrich], Hoover Institution)

Goodrich delivered his paper "Why Liberty?" on the evening of September 8, 1958. Two other papers were delivered that evening, one by Ludwig von Mises ("Liberty and Property") and the other by Felix Morley ("The Meaning of Freedom"). See "Program of the Meeting of the Society at Princeton Graduate College, Princeton, New Jersey, U.S.A., September 8–13, 1958," Pierre F. Goodrich Collection, folder 4 (Mont Pelerin Society), Archives, Hoover Institution.

"Why Liberty?" was subsequently published in pamphlet form and distributed by Eugene C. Pulliam, Sr., the Indianapolis publisher who was also Goodrich's business partner. Pulliam sent one thousand copies of the pamphlet to Goodrich and five hundred to the Foundation for Economic Education. See copy of Leonard Read's letter to Pulliam, March 13, 1959, Pierre F. Goodrich Collection, box 1, "Why Liberty?" folder, Archives, Hoover Institution. Goodrich also discussed the paper in a seminar at Wabash College on October 15, 1958. The pamphlet also contained the statement of aims of the Mont Pelerin Society, established at the society's first meeting in April 1947.

2. Walter "Guido" Seaton, a retired employee of the Indiana Telephone Corporation, was called to a meeting in Indianapolis in the late 1950s in which Goodrich participated. At dinner later that evening, he sat next to Goodrich. Seaton said that he and Goodrich had talked little throughout the meal, exchanging nothing more than pleasantries. Suddenly, Goodrich asked Seaton, "Do you think power corrupts?" Seaton responded, "Well, I guess it could." Seaton said that he and Goodrich did not say another word to each other during the rest of the evening (interview, January 16, 1993).

portance liberty had for Goodrich will serve to render a greater understanding of his overall philosophical beliefs.

In the September 1958 paper, Goodrich quoted two very different views about both the nature and efficacy of power:

> And *Power,* as the biographies of so many statesmen reveal (for example, that of Sir Thomas More), heightens sensitiveness, stimulates the imagination of purposes and expedients, generates invention, develops *compassion* when it places men where they confront the sorrows which *government* exists to assuage and the trials which must be visited on some in order that others may have a more abundant life; and *power* develops *humility* and fortitude. These are precious qualities in the service of mankind, and inseverable from power. (Herman Finer, foreword to *Essays on Freedom and Power* by Lord Acton)

> Power tends to corrupt and absolute power corrupts absolutely. (Letter from Lord Acton to Bishop Creighton, April 5, 1887)

Goodrich thought that the view of power one accepts must be determined by one's belief about the nature of man. He explained why he believed Lord Acton's observation is clearly the more accurate one. As a basic premise, Goodrich submits—and it would seem foolhardy to suggest otherwise—man is imperfect and therefore fallible. Man has some capacity to reason, however, and some persons have a greater facility for rational thought than others. It is partially under this pretext that some claim the authority to determine what is best for others.[3] Goodrich believed, however, that human impulses other than reason often guide and influence decision making: love, compassion, fortitude, envy, hate, fear, lust, greed, and so forth. Goodrich was convinced that imperfect man is often led astray in his exercise of power by these other impulses and by his proclivity, once he gains power, to believe in his own infallibility.

3. Goodrich writes, "It follows that power, *however* obtained, be it by force of arms or by a proclamation with a gold seal affixed to it, transforms the holder of that power into a more *imperfect* man, in fact a dangerous man—he has force over the destinies of other men" ("Why Liberty?" p. 14).

Goodrich believed that even if the occasional wise and benevolent dictator appears (such as Plato's philosopher-king), it is highly improvident for any person to be given power over others. Why? Because the state is no better than the imperfect human beings who hold the power of the state. When a man is elevated to a higher position of power, his imperfections become magnified, and he is more likely to make errors in judgment about what is in others' best interests.[4] One man simply cannot make better decisions for others than they can make for themselves, for every man has a greater knowledge of his own individual needs and desires than anyone else can possibly have. Any argument to the contrary, Goodrich believed, was merely based on expediency; for example, to enable officeholders to do the popular thing at the moment to gain votes rather than to allow individuals to work out their own destinies.

Moreover, Goodrich believed that those who occupy a seat of governmental power often become corrupted, seeking more and more power. The examples in history that support Goodrich's position are so numerous that only some of the most egregious need be mentioned: from the Egyptian pharaohs to Roman emperors such as Caligula ("Would that the Roman people had a single neck [to cut off their head]");[5] from Cesare Borgia and Robespierre to modern dictators such as Stalin, Hitler, and Mao.

Goodrich was convinced that even democratically elected officeholders are prone to succumb to the lure of power. Thus, Goodrich did not

4. Goodrich states:

Is not a perfect state inconceivable unless one assumes perfection within mankind? If power tends to corrupt then the power of the state inevitably increases and implements man's imperfections.

If you accept the Acton principle, as I do, that "Power tends to corrupt and absolute power corrupts absolutely," then it seems to me that you must conclude that the essential nature of that corruption is imperfect man's deification of his ends and his tendency to justify the use of any means he may possess, including force, to accomplish his ends. *He becomes the superman beyond good and evil.* ("Why Liberty?" p. 13)

5. From Suetonius, "Gaius Caligula," *De viris illustribus,* sec. 30.

think that to be dangerous a person with power had to have a sinister side; rather, he believed that the possession of authority was a corrupting influence to the powerholder and would result in the negation of freedom to individuals over whom authority is employed. Power exercised for the general good was the most dangerous because it was disarming and, therefore, least resisted.[6]

Furthermore, while Goodrich believed that the most dangerous power was that of government, his suspicions about powerholders extended well beyond those who exercise it by the authority of the state; he believed that power was dangerous wherever there was a consolidation of authority with the sanction of force.[7] Lord Acton's admonition to Bishop Creighton was, after all, directly in response to what Acton perceived as the corruption of the papacy of the late nineteenth century.[8]

6. Goodrich wrote in the *Basic Memorandum:* "It is observable that the most dangerous of those powers is the power of government, especially when it is combined with unlimited authority accepted by the people generally and when it purports to be for a *general good.* Where the alleged *general good* is concerned with securing man's eternity by governmental force applied to him, such a *general good* is probably the most dangerous of all exercise of governmental powers" (p. 23, exhibit I-b).

7. Goodrich was especially interested in the common-law offense of assault, in how the mere threat to inflict injury, combined with the apparent ability to carry the threat out, constituted an actionable crime and an abuse of power. Russell Kirk recounted a conversation he had with Goodrich about the offense. "In the last conversation we had together at his office, Pierre told me about English common-law decisions concerning assault. That offense did not necessarily go so far as physical attack: he cited a case in which a man stood silent, a drawn sword in his hand, obstructing a public pathway; and he subsequently was found guilty of assault, even though he struck no one and did not threaten aloud persons who approached him" (letter from Russell Kirk to author, February 8, 1992).

8. Thus, Goodrich applied Acton's caveat in other contexts, "It is desirable to have a free society and that means neither business nor labor organizations must be given the force of government to achieve their ends and they must not abuse their power by exercising force."

Goodrich acknowledged that there is always the attempt to justify the exercise of power as a means to achieve an end objective.

> I believe that Lord Acton's statement . . . can be observed in all sorts of human affairs and every person should be able to judge that for himself if he will be honest. I would clearly say that that power which is for the greatest good of the greatest

Goodrich's perceptive observations about the potential abuses associated with power are not merely abstract insights. They are supported by studies that have noted the change in behavior experienced by persons who obtain power.

> The acquisition of power and the pleasure it gives become ends in themselves, unattached to such worthwhile goals as improved policy, a more human workplace, or a more efficiently run organization. Great amounts of time and energy are then invested in power acquisition so that the person has more and more control, influence, and corresponding pleasure. The same time and energy become unavailable for other activities in life, such as love, achievement, ethical concerns, or education.
>
> From the intoxication due to power, and from the fact that other activities become less important, people's judgments become cloudy. They become tempted to use power for their own benefit, and the resulting actions are often illegal or enter very gray areas of the law or of the commonly accepted ethical standards.[9]

> number [utilitarianism], especially for the good of your eternity, has to be the most dangerous of all powers. Even in the business world you have, in the first place, a suspect mission because you cannot properly state your purpose to be for any proper good except that of the business being operated at a profit. (Letter to F. A. Hayek, December 24, 1970, F. A. Hayek Collection, Hoover Institution)

In operating his businesses, Goodrich did not openly oppose unionization, but neither would he do anything that would assist collective representation. For instance, in the late 1950s, when a handful of employees (including Walter Seaton) attempted to form a union at the Indiana Telephone Corporation, Goodrich did not fight their attempts. He neither sanctioned their efforts nor, presumably, favored laws that forced unionization. According to Seaton, there were at least two reasons the union did not succeed. First, Goodrich refused to withhold union dues from individual employees' paychecks, thus compelling the union to try to extract dues individually from employees. That effort proved to be a failure. Second, employees, especially linemen, were spread out over a large area in south-central Indiana, thus making it very difficult to get employees together for union meetings. Seaton stated that eventually the reason to unionize—to obtain certain benefits, and especially a retirement plan—no longer existed, because Goodrich agreed to set up a retirement plan for the employees (interview, January 16, 1993).

9. Richard W. Brislin, *The Art of Getting Things Done: A Practical Guide to the Use of Power* (New York: Praeger, 1991), p. 45. Brislin bases his writing on research by David

Moreover, Goodrich identified a specific characteristic of the person in a position of power—the reluctance to accept negative feedback, because such criticism interferes with the pleasure associated with "calling the shots." Subordinates soon realize that flattery serves them better than constructive criticism.[10] Since the powerholder receives no negative information, he or she believes that there are no problems and comes to feel infallible.

Goodrich did his best to avoid falling into that trap. He often circumvented his field managers at both the Ayrshire Collieries Corporation and the Indiana Telephone Corporation. Goodrich would visit miners in the coalfields and telephone operators at their work stations. He questioned workers about improvements, cost reductions, production, and customer satisfaction. He knew from experience and common sense that managers are tempted to tell the boss what they believe he wants to hear.[11]

Kipnis, who wrote *The Powerholders* (Chicago: University of Chicago Press, 1976). Kipnis's research findings can be summarized by the following eight potential cumulative metamorphic effects on a holder of power:

1. The use of power is pleasurable and intoxicating.
2. The powerholder puts efforts into achieving more power.
3. The judgment of the powerful person becomes cloudy due to a preoccupation with gaining influence and control.
4. The powerholder uses the resources for self-benefit.
5. Negative feedback is no longer available from subordinates and instead the powerholder is the beneficiary of flattery.
6. The powerholder develops a lofty view of his or her own self-worth.
7. The worth of subordinates is devalued by the powerholder.
8. The powerholder takes too much credit for the accomplishments of subordinates. (*The Powerholders,* p. 47)

10. In a letter to F. A. Hayek, Goodrich wrote: "Several years ago we hired a county agent for important land work who had 15 years allegedly successful experience. It did not work out and I suspect one of the reasons was that he had been adjusted to sensing what the people wanted to be told as a part of his success as county agent. In working for us his mental ability was partly blocked by his constant sensitiveness to what we wished to be told. This was not good" (February 18, 1959, p. 3, F. A. Hayek Collection, box 34, folder 17, Archives, Hoover Institution).

11. William Nordhorn, interview, January 16, 1993.

Goodrich's remedy for the consolidation of power was to decentralize decision making, holding each individual responsible for his or her success or failure:

> The most helpful choice of imperfections is a free society which *men must maintain* in all its *inseparable* parts:
>
> The *inseparable* freedom, responsibility for and *hazards* of a decentralized free and competitive market economy (both in things and labor), a *decentralized* free and competitive educational society, a *decentralized* free and competitive church and religious society, and a *decentralized* free, competitive and representative political society limited to preventing or discouraging force by man over man.[12]

Goodrich believed that education alone could enlighten individuals and persuade them to take correct action and accept moral responsibility. Therefore, coercion by the state is not only unnecessary but counterproductive. "Pierre believed that the scholar or great teacher would have influence over the person but would not have power over him," said the Reverend Edmund Opitz, a staff member at the Foundation for Economic Education who knew Goodrich for the better part of twenty years.[13]

Therefore, Goodrich believed that there are many ways to influence

12. "Why Liberty?" p. 6.

13. Edmund Opitz, telephone interview, October 10, 1992. Goodrich was, however, leery of the educated person's being given power solely on the theory that because the individual was well trained, he would exercise power prudently and wisely. He thought that the temptations of power were too great.

> It might be possible to argue that the extensive knowledge of consequences of human actions which would come from being truly educated would lead a man to choose virtuous behavior, if on no other grounds than that of efficiency; i.e., the knowledge that right action succeeds while wrong action fails. But the Faust myth still rises to challenge us, and we cannot be comfortable with the assumption that the knowledgeable man will also be the noble or virtuous man. In fact, in the Faust myth, it is precisely the most learned who is most susceptible to the temptations of the Devil, to the lure of temporal power over others. (It is tempting to explain the behavior of many modern intellectuals in somewhat this way.) (*Education in a Free Society*, p. 59)

properly individuals, but all these methods entail moral persuasion through some form of educational process (for example, pamphlets, books, debates, individual study, and discussion). Power by the state, to the degree it need exist at all, should be limited to ensuring that no person's freedom is infringed upon by others.

Liberty as a Prerequisite of Moral Value

Goodrich believed that there could be little, if any, moral value in a person's actions if that individual was acting under compulsion. If a person gives to the poor or aids another in any way solely because he is forced to by, for example, a tax or a mandate enforced by the police powers of the state, then the moral value of the act is destroyed. If a person cannot do otherwise, then his actions possess no moral worth; that is, there is no exercise of the human will. The influence of Kant's thinking on Goodrich is apparent here.

Therefore, Goodrich believed that moral conduct (consisting of respectful behavior toward others and the world at large according to some universal law, such as natural law) is less prevalent where freedom is lacking. For instance, in any society where the state, church, corporation, or another person has power over others, one is likely to find intolerance, brutal treatment of people, and a general disregard for individual rights. Historical examples abound: the Crusades of the eleventh to thirteenth centuries, Robespierre's "Reign of Terror," institutional slavery, the early Industrial Age's exploitation of workers, the purges of Stalin, and Hitler's Holocaust.

Thus, to Goodrich's way of thinking, individual freedom is a prerequisite not only for moral value but also for moral behavior. A critical caveat to Goodrich's moral view of freedom is his belief that the existence of individual freedom has to be exercised in tandem with individual responsibility. To Goodrich, the concepts of freedom and responsibility were inseparable. Goodrich exemplified this belief in his business practices. For example, he strove to make a profit from his coal-mining operations, but he did not believe that his property right gave him the freedom to plunder the land. He believed that his coal company held the land, and other resources, in trust for future generations.[14]

Goodrich also believed that another prerequisite to a free society is the acceptance of mistakes in the exercise of freedom.[15] A free society is subject to the whims of individual decision makers and the values that free individuals pursue. Therefore, any particular individual or group that believes itself to be enlightened about cultural, economic, political, or spiritual matters may well disagree with the values that others, exercising their own freedom, choose to embrace. Leaders of a free society must refrain, however, regardless of how foolish or wrong they believe others' values to be, from exercising the power to compel "right" action in others.[16] Similarly, if a society becomes morally reckless in the exer-

14. Goodrich's philosophy and its practice are well summarized in the Ayrshire Collieries annual report that Goodrich issued in 1946, the year after he established Meadowlark Farms. "Your company has recognized that coal operators have certain community obligations, and should demonstrate their willingness to conduct their affairs so far as possible without giving cause for public criticism, which leads to governmental interference, with its tendency to unrealistic approach[es]. The problems involve the field of land use, conservation, and rehabilitation, and can be solved, and operations administered, only by specialists" (William H. Andrews, "Ayrshire Collieries Corporation—Profit with Ecology" [Research paper, Indiana University, n.d.], p. 19).

15. Goodrich wrote, "It also seems evident that it is necessary, as a part of this discipline that he must be free to make choices which appear to be good or bad, fortunate or unfortunate. The freedom to do this, coupled with the responsibility of abiding by the results of that choice, is a necessary part of maintaining liberty" (*Basic Memorandum,* p. 17).

16. There are other ways to influence "bad" behavior. Ludwig von Mises offers insights that Goodrich would endorse.

> Freedom really means *the freedom to make mistakes.* This we have to realize. We may be highly critical with regard to the way in which our fellow citizens are spending their money and living their lives. We may believe that what they are doing is absolutely foolish and bad, but in a free society, there are many ways for people to air their opinions on how their fellow citizens should change their ways of life. They can write books, they can write articles; they can make speeches; they can even preach at street corners if they want—and they do this in many countries. But they must *not* try to police other people in order to prevent them from doing certain things simply because they themselves do not want these other people to have the freedom to do it. ("Socialism," chap. 6 in *The Morality of Capitalism* [Irvington-on-Hudson, N.Y.: Freeman Classics, 1992], p. 49)

cise of its freedoms and refuses to exercise its corresponding responsibilities, that society may end up sowing the seeds of its own destruction. That is why a free society must be based on strong moral convictions and moral values of a particular kind.

Goodrich believed that maximum liberty is important not only because it eliminates the control that some would otherwise have over others, but also because it liberates the potential in individuals and therefore the energy and potential of a community and nation.[17] He further held that when the state or other power assumes responsibility over others, it hinders individual initiative. Thus, statist societies deny individuals the opportunity to achieve their potential and therefore deny society the contributions of enterprising people.

Clearly, one of the main reasons that the United States became such a strong economic and moral power is that its citizens have had the freedom to exercise and benefit from their own talents. Goodrich believed that the main reason that statist societies are generally anemic in comparison is that the state either smothers individual initiative or intervenes to choose winners and losers in advance of individual achievement. Goodrich also believed that it was impossible for the state to justly or wisely make such assessments. He wrote, "Anything we know of man's history would indicate that such men can not be identified prior to their achievement. Verdi was refused admission for a scholarship at the Conservatory in Milan as lacking *aptitude* in music. He stayed in Milan and studied privately. Verdi developed his *aptitude* without benefit of the Conservatory."[18]

By comparison, the strength of free enterprise is the mobility that individuals possess in the economic system. In schemes of central planning (for example, socialism) and precapitalist societies (for example,

17. John Quincy Adams summarizes this idea quite well in a letter to James Lloyd (October 1, 1822). "Individual liberty is individual power, and as the power of a community is a mass compounded of individual powers, the nation which enjoys the most freedom must necessarily be in proportion to its numbers the most powerful nation" (John Bartlett, *Familiar Quotations,* 15th ed., ed. Emily Morison Beck [Boston: Little Brown, 1980], p. 418).

18. "Why Liberty?" p. 11.

aristocracy), economic and social positions are rigid. The opportunity to do what one desires or to move upward economically or socially is often limited. In these systems, the state (central planners) or the station of one's birth significantly determines the course of a person's life. The free enterprise system, however, allows the individual greater opportunity to choose the way in which he or she wants to operate in society. This freedom includes the freedom to make unwise decisions. Less dogmatic supporters of the capitalist system will find fault with this premise, but Goodrich believed that history supported his contentions.

One of the most famous and brilliant passages in all literature is Fyodor Dostoyevsky's narrative of "The Grand Inquisitor" in *The Brothers Karamazov.* It presents a disturbing view of man's inability to accept the freedom that he has been given by Christ's former presence on earth. The novella within the novel is about the return of Christ in fifteenth-century Spain. There, Christ encounters "The Grand Inquisitor," the oldest and most powerful Cardinal in the Catholic Church.

The Grand Inquisitor denies Christ because Christ has asked too much in asking man to believe in Him without the evidence of miracles. The Grand Inquisitor accepts man as he is—weak, slavish, ignoble—incapable of living up to the ideals that Christ had taught in his earthly message. Thus, the Grand Inquisitor concludes that Christianity has become merely a utopian dream. The Grand Inquisitor chastises Christ and claims that if the Son of God really loved mankind, he would not have asked so much of human beings. The Grand Inquisitor concludes that most men are incapable of freedom and have instead chosen happiness ("the bread of earth"). As one critic wrote, "Never has the problem of freedom been raised with such vehemence as in 'The Legend of the Grand Inquisitor.'"[19]

> The craving for community of worship is the chief misery of every man individually and of all humanity from the beginning of time. For the sake of common worship they've slain each other with the sword. . . . Thou

19. Geir Kjetsaa, *Fyodor Dostoyevsky: A Writer's Life,* trans. Siri Hustvedt and David McDuff (New York: Fawcett Columbine, 1987), pp. 337–43; ibid., p. 341.

> [Christ] didst know, Thou couldst not but have known, this fundamental secret of human nature, but Thou didst reject the one infallible banner which was offered Thee to make all men bow down to Thee alone—the banner of earthly bread; and Thou has rejected it for the sake of freedom and the reach of Heaven.[20]

Goodrich often referred to the dilemma of "The Grand Inquisitor" in letters and other writings. For instance, in a letter to F. A. Hayek he wrote, "I certainly do not wish to join the Grand Inquisitor in my concept of human beings, but, on the other hand, my experience and observations would be that we can put up with a great deal of hardship and a great deal on things we would like to see better than they are in the interest of *freedom* and *inequality*."[21] He debated in his own mind whether man is capable of accepting freedom. Goodrich's fundamental question was: Is man so weak that he is incapable of accepting a free and responsible world, complete with all the obligations, hardships, and inequalities that freedom entails?

Goodrich was very much aware of atheistic socialism's contempt for Christianity and the minimalist state. The atheist-socialist condemns modern Christianity and capitalism because neither guarantees man happiness, peace, or food. Rather, they leave it to free individuals to embrace or reject the ideals of charity, sacrifice, and the market to satisfy human need. This difference between the two ideologies begs the question why the modern welfare state, not the minimalist state that Goodrich advocated, has evolved in nearly every industrialized nation. Is this because of the recognition of the "man on the street" that he cannot meet the ideals (freedom and its requisite responsibilities) of Christianity and the minimalist state? Or is it merely because man has been hoodwinked by statists into giving up his liberties? Perhaps the answer is both.

In any event, Goodrich constantly asked himself and others a very

20. Fyodor Dostoyevsky, "The Grand Inquisitor," *The Brothers Karamazov*, book 5, part 5.

21. February 18, 1959; see letters from Goodrich to F. A. Hayek, February 18, 1959, p. 5, box 22, folder 6, and December 24, 1970, p. 6, box 43, folder 22, F. A. Hayek Papers, Hoover Institution; "Why Liberty?" p. 12.

straightforward question: What does a society do about those who do not want to be free and who want the state to take care of them? Goodrich's good friend Benjamin Rogge believed that left to their own devices many people who are dependent on the welfare state would in fact take care of themselves, leading to smaller government. Goodrich was less certain of this outcome. He believed, along with Hayek, that a free society contains in itself the seeds of its own destruction.[22] This conviction prompted Goodrich to believe also that proper education and perpetual vigilance are needed to guard against the erosion of individual freedoms.

One criticism of Goodrich's vision of liberty is that he focused too much attention on what Isaiah Berlin, in his celebrated essay "Two Concepts of Liberty," calls "negative freedom." Negative freedom, according to Berlin, is the absence of coercion by others. Simply put, the belief is that the individual is free if he is not compelled by some outside force to do other than what he wills to do.[23] This conception of liberty overlooks the forces within man that may make him unfree.

What Berlin describes as "positive freedom" focuses attention on

22. Ruth Connolly, one of Goodrich's former secretaries, often heard Goodrich and Rogge discuss this problem. She said that Rogge believed that many people who are now wards of the state had enough initiative to take responsibility for their lives if they could no longer depend on the state for their survival. Goodrich apparently was somewhat less optimistic. He wrote F. A. Hayek the following:

> This, of course, leaves the problem of what on earth you do with those who are enemies of a free society or those who do not wish to be free (I suppose this refers to those who cannot see that their responsibility temporarily passed to government will in the end leave them completely un-free) and with those who are unable to be free. Unless the concept of one vote to each individual is reasonably exploded and unless it is realized that the important thing is not the vote but the freedom of the individual who wishes to be free and responsible, adequately protected from intimidation in his own society and defended from external enemies, then your concept that a free society contains in it its own destruction may be definitive. I think it is coupled with a franchise which can be purchased by the method of taxation, that has to be so. (December 24, 1970, p. 6, F. A. Hayek Papers, box 43, folder 22, Hoover Institution)

23. Berlin's essay "Two Concepts of Liberty" is contained in his *Four Essays on Liberty* (Oxford: Oxford University Press, 1969), pp. 118–72.

what the individual could become if he were free from inherent limitations: passions, penury, psychological hang-ups, and so forth.[24] If the individual can overcome these personal obstacles, he or she is much more apt to achieve self-realization. Goodrich's writings support the view that most people if freed from outside influences do possess the capability and will to become self-directed. A philosopher with a less-hopeful view of human nature might argue that most individuals if left to their own devices will remain slaves to their passions or environment. The difference in emphasis between the two views demonstrates, as Berlin observes, "that conceptions of freedom directly derive from views of what constitutes a self, a person, a man."[25]

A second and perhaps more substantive criticism of Goodrich is the preeminence he ascribes to liberty in all situations, seemingly neglecting other values and qualities, such as justice, happiness, security, and abject poverty. As Berlin notes: "Without adequate conditions for the use of freedom, what is the value of freedom? First things come first: there are situations, as a nineteenth-century Russian radical writer declared, in which boots are superior to the works of Shakespeare; individual freedom is not everyone's primary need. . . . The Egyptian peasant needs clothes or medicine before, and more than, personal liberty."[26]

In defense of Goodrich, no doubt he would argue that even the Egyptian peasant needs a minimal amount of liberty to enjoy his meager life; moreover, in theory, at least, the possibility of enjoying greater material comforts and self-esteem will depend upon the individual's receiving and being responsible for greater amounts of personal freedom.

In sum, Goodrich believed that liberty is the prerequisite for man's achieving his greatest expression of personhood and the enjoyment of a prosperous society. The exercise of talents and abilities, the moral value of human behavior, the working out of personal destiny—all of these are possible only in a state of freedom from statist or other forms of external control.

24. Ibid., p. 131.
25. Ibid., p. 134.
26. Ibid., p. 124.

Goodrich knew that liberty is not something that, once obtained, need no longer be sought. Life is a continual process of securing and maintaining freedoms. Therefore, liberty must be continually taught, like English, mathematics, and history. If it is not, there are many forces in human nature that will induce humanity to abandon liberty in pursuit of easier and seemingly more expedient solutions to social, political, and economic problems.[27]

27. The desire for freedom is the driving force behind most revolutions, but, ironically, once obtained it is also easily taken for granted. In George Orwell's *Animal Farm,* after revolting against the humans, most of the animals forget why the revolution took place; thus the animals leave themselves open for oppression by the pigs. Unfortunately, such behavior is not uncommon in the human world.

Chapter 29

Liberty Fund, Inc.

What spectacle can be more edifying or more seasonable, than that of liberty and learning, each leaning on the other for their mutual and surest support?

JAMES MADISON

It is intended to use this Fund to the end that some hopeful contribution may be made to the preservation, restoration, and development of individual liberty through investigation, research, and educational activity.

PIERRE F. GOODRICH, *Liberty Fund Basic Memorandum*

WHAT do men and women who have much more money than they could possibly ever spend on themselves do? They form a foundation. Where a man's treasure is, there is also his heart.[1] Through the Lilly Endowment, Pierre Goodrich's contemporary Eli Lilly made tremendous contributions to historical research, education, and other causes throughout the state of Indiana and beyond; Harrison Eiteljorg, another Indianapolis businessman who made his fortune in the coal industry, built a fabulous museum of original American Indian and western art; Hoosier industrialist Irwin Miller's love of architecture has resulted in prize-winning and aesthetically beautiful churches, libraries, and schools in his hometown of Columbus, Indiana.

Pierre F. Goodrich wanted to be an architect of the mind. His vision was Liberty Fund, Inc. He left his fortune—an endowment now valued

1. Matt. 6:21.

well in excess of $360 million—to encourage a deeper understanding of what it takes to achieve and maintain a free society.[2] He did not want his money to be spent for the construction of a football stadium or a gymnasium. In fact, the only capital building project to which he is known to have contributed was the Goodrich Seminar Room at Wabash College's Lilly Library. He gave money for that undertaking only because he hoped the seminar room would serve as the venue for frequent philosophical discussions. Goodrich thought money should be spent on developing minds and culture, not on "things."[3] He felt appreciated most not when he received honorary degrees or certificates of merit, but when people accepted his ideas.

Irwin H. Reiss, a founding board member of Liberty Fund, believes he has at least a partial understanding of why Goodrich established this unique foundation. "Mr. Goodrich saw liberty and freedom for the individual slipping through our hands and if he could leave a legacy to future generations and halt that loss of freedom, I think he, in his own

2. As of April 1996, Liberty Fund had total net assets of $129,745,645, with a fair-market value of $161,358,195. See annual report of Liberty Fund, Inc., available at Liberty Fund offices, 8335 Allison Pointe Trail, Suite 300, Indianapolis, Indiana, pursuant to Section 6104(d) of the Internal Revenue Code. In June 1997, it was announced that the estate of Enid Smith Goodrich had left approximately $80 million to Liberty Fund, bringing the total endowment to more than $200 million. Enid Goodrich also left large gifts to other cultural institutions, including approximately $40 million to the Indianapolis Museum of Art and $40 million to the Children's Museum of Indianapolis. Smaller amounts were left to the Indianapolis Symphony Orchestra, Conner Prairie, and other Indianapolis institutions. See Steve Mannheimer, "A $160 Million Windfall," *Indianapolis Star and News,* June 20, 1997, p. 1, col. 1. Most of the assets held by Liberty Fund are invested in stocks and bonds through Harris Bank of Chicago, Illinois; the U.S. Trust Company of New York, New York; and Peoples Loan and Trust Bank of Winchester, Indiana.

3. When his uncle Percy sought Pierre's advice about building a band shell in Winchester, Indiana, Pierre responded that Percy's money could be better spent in fostering an excellent band. If that could be successfully achieved, Pierre reasoned, the local townspeople might build a band shell themselves. See letter from Pierre F. Goodrich to P. E. Goodrich, October 4, 1948 (the letters of Percy Goodrich are held by the family of Perce G. Goodrich, Portland, Indiana).

opinion, would feel like he was really accomplishing something. And he surrounded himself with people who felt like that and could help him implement this concept."[4]

One reason Goodrich formed Liberty Fund is that he did not think that the kind of continual learning he believed was important could be facilitated by donations to an existing college, university, or foundation.[5] Goodrich believed that the traditional liberal arts college, let alone the large university or technical school, was sorely in need of reform. Rather than risk contributing his millions to a particular educational institution in hopes that it might embrace his vision (his years of association with Wabash College made him highly doubtful that such an institution existed), Goodrich decided to create his own foundation. Goodrich's establishment of Liberty Fund can be seen as the culmination, the magnum opus, of his life.

Liberty Fund was incorporated in the state of Indiana on August 18, 1960. It was also on that date that the founding board of directors first met.[6] Goodrich's vision for Liberty Fund existed for several years before 1960, however, as is evident from his years of writing the *Basic Memorandum,* the document that is the foundation's bible. The first board of directors of Liberty Fund included Goodrich and his wife Enid (who were elected lifetime directors), Benjamin A. Rogge (then dean of Wabash College), Irwin H. Reiss (then president of Meadowlark Farms in Sullivan, Indiana), and Don E. Welch (then vice-president of Peoples Loan and Trust Company in Winchester, Indiana). Helen Schultz

4. Irwin H. Reiss, interview by William C. Dennis, February 11, 1991.

5. J. Charles King, interview, December 10, 1993; Donald Welch, interview, November 23, 1991.

6. The articles of incorporation of Liberty Fund are located at the Indiana secretary of state's office, 302 W. Washington Street, Room E018, Indianapolis, Indiana. The incorporators included Pierre F. Goodrich, Enid Goodrich, John B. Goodrich (Pierre's first cousin), Lucy Ann Elliott (a longtime secretary and administrative assistant to both Pierre and his father), and Helen E. Schultz (secretary to Pierre and later the second president of Liberty Fund).

served as secretary and treasurer (she was named a Founder Member in June 1967).[7]

In his creation of Liberty Fund, Goodrich was assisted by the late William Casey, as well as by Goodrich's personal attorney, William Hunter. Casey was a top-notch tax lawyer who later became director of the Securities and Exchange Commission, director of the Central Intelligence Agency, and chairman of Ronald Reagan's 1980 presidential campaign. Another individual who assisted in the early formation of Liberty Fund is William Fletcher, who at the time was a partner with Arthur Andersen, the large accounting firm based in Chicago. Fletcher was managing partner of Arthur Andersen's Indianapolis office from 1960 to 1972. Goodrich consulted with these men extensively about the establishment of Liberty Fund and the need to have it exist as a tax-exempt private foundation.

In August 1962, the Internal Revenue Service (IRS) denied Liberty Fund's initial application for tax-exempt status. The formal basis for the denial was that Liberty Fund was "not organized exclusively for educational purposes within the intention of section 501(c)(3)."[8] Appar-

7. "Minutes of the Organizational Meeting of the Board of Directors of Liberty Fund, Inc.," August 18, 1960. Helen Schultz became a Founder Member of the Liberty Fund board of directors on June 14, 1967 (for the term of her natural life). See "Minutes of the Board of Directors of the Liberty Fund, Inc.," June 14, 1967, p. 128 (in possession of Liberty Fund, 8335 Allison Pointe Trail, Suite 300, Indianapolis, Indiana). Schultz resigned as president and member of the board of directors in April 1978.

8. Letter from J. F. Worley, Chief, Exempt Organization Branch, Internal Revenue Service, Washington, D.C., to Liberty Fund, 100 S. Meridian Street, Winchester, Indiana, August 10, 1960 (in the possession of Liberty Fund). Apparently, Liberty Fund's application was originally denied because of the concern that the IRS had about its activities being not purely educational, but somewhat political. This concern apparently arose as a result of the contents of the *Basic Memorandum,* which was attached to Liberty Fund's application for 501(c)(3) status. The view was that the *Basic Memorandum* had a strong libertarian tone to it. The IRS was concerned that for Liberty Fund to achieve its objectives (a free society), it would have to advocate legislation, since that was the only means to reverse or overturn the existing political structure. See correspondence between Goodrich, Casey, and William Hunter, August–September 1962, tax-exempt-status file, Liberty Fund.

ently, the real basis of the IRS's denial was that it believed that the goal of the foundation was to promote political (legislative) change. After Casey, Fletcher, Hunter, and Goodrich redrafted the articles of incorporation, however, the IRS granted Liberty Fund tax-exempt status in December 1962.[9]

An indicator that Goodrich had designs for establishing Liberty Fund in the 1950s is his plan for endowing the foundation. In 1945, Goodrich had formed the Winchester Foundation. Goodrich made monetary contributions to the Winchester Foundation in the 1950s with the intent that those funds would spill over into his education foundation (then unnamed) when it became operable as a nontaxable private foundation.[10] In May 1962, Liberty Fund held only a minuscule endowment of slightly more than $4,000. By June 1963, however, after Liberty Fund's tax-exempt status had been achieved, Goodrich transferred funds from the Winchester Foundation to Liberty Fund. Those funds, which were in the form of cash, stock, and real estate, amounted to nearly $670,000. Almost all the contributions were made from five

9. Letter from J. F. Worley, Chief, Exempt Organizations Branch, Internal Revenue Service, Washington, D.C., to Liberty Fund, 100 S. Meridian Street, Winchester, Indiana, December 4, 1962 (in the possession of Liberty Fund). Goodrich, Casey, Hunter, Fletcher, Reiss, and Welch met on August 23 and 24, 1962, and redrafted the articles of incorporation to respond to the IRS's denial. See "Minutes of the Meeting of the Board of Directors of the Liberty Fund, Inc.," October 1, 1962, p. 27, and memorandum to file of Helen Schultz detailing the reasons for the denial.

10. Don E. Welch, interview, December 16, 1991. Goodrich contributed $1,000 to Liberty Fund on August 18, 1960. According to the board minutes, this was the first money funding the foundation. See "Minutes," Liberty Fund, August 18, 1960. Board meetings of Liberty Fund were held in Goodrich's law offices at 711 Electric Building, Indianapolis, until mid 1962. Thereafter, they were held at 3520 Washington Boulevard, Indianapolis, until after Goodrich's death, when Liberty Fund moved to 7440 N. Shadeland Avenue, Indianapolis. According to William Fletcher, the reasons for moving the headquarters were twofold: first, Liberty Fund (and the other Goodrich companies) had grown too large for the building; second, the location on Washington Boulevard was in a marginal neighborhood, and Fletcher and the board believed that it was not prudent to maintain offices there. William Fletcher, interview by William C. Dennis, January 25, 1991 (recording in the possession of Liberty Fund).

holding companies controlled by Goodrich himself: Engineers Incorporated; the P. F. Goodrich Corporation; Central Shares, Inc.; Muncie Theatre Realty; and Patoka Coal Company (a holding company that owned shares in the Ayrshire Collieries Corporation).[11]

In the 1960s and 1970s, Liberty Fund was primarily a grant-making foundation. Gottfried Dietze, professor of political science at the Johns Hopkins University, served as a paid consultant to the board during that time. At board meetings conducted by Goodrich and attended by Enid Goodrich, Rogge, Reiss, and Welch, the board would consider grant requests from several institutional and individual applicants. The board would then contribute amounts as small as fifty dollars to assist, for instance, with a professor's traveling expenses to attend a conference. Many of the early awards included grants to the Foundation for Economic Education (FEE), the Foundation for Foreign Affairs, the Great Books Foundation, Wabash College, the China Institute of America, and other institutions in which Goodrich took a long-term interest. Each grant request was measured against whether its purpose was consistent with the criteria contained in the *Basic Memorandum.*[12]

At the time of his death, Goodrich was fighting for Liberty Fund to exist as an operating foundation. He was still working with tax advisers and the Internal Revenue Service to see that his personal profit from the sale of the Ayrshire Collieries Corporation was transferred to Liberty Fund with no, or minimal, tax. As Goodrich wrote to his tax attorney, E. Victor Willetts, he saw that how the taxation issue was finally resolved would have major implications, beyond the viability of the foundation

11. In the spring of 1962, the Winchester Foundation contributed five thousand dollars to Liberty Fund. This was the single largest gift to Liberty Fund until after it received tax-exempt status in December 1962. After that, in 1963, thousands of shares and tens of thousands of dollars were transferred from the Winchester Foundation to Liberty Fund. The shares were of Engineers Incorporated, the P. F. Goodrich Corporation, Central Newspapers, Ayrshire Collieries Corporation, Central Shares, Inc., and the Peoples Loan and Trust Company. See "Minutes of Meeting of the Board of Directors of Liberty Fund, Inc.," January 21, 1963, pp. 36–38.

12. See "Board Minutes" of Liberty Fund, January 25, 1961.

itself. "We are hopeful that we can be declared an operating foundation which will have a chance to survive, and survival may be worthwhile not only to us and to the people working with Liberty Fund, but to society itself (usually, however, prophets prophesy too late—wasn't Jewish society all through after Solomon, really, and the great prophets, Amos, Hosea and Micah came along 200–300 years later)."[13]

Goodrich left two trust funds with combined assets in excess of $26 million. This formed the foundation's initial substantial endowment. Most of this money came from Goodrich's sale of the Ayrshire Collieries Corporation in 1969. Other money that was funneled into the Liberty Fund's endowment came from the liquidation of holding companies (for example, Engineers Incorporated and the P. F. Goodrich Corporation), the sale of City Securities in 1970, and the 1978 sale of the Indiana Telephone Corporation. Well into the 1990s, approximately one-fourth of Liberty Fund's endowment was held in stock in Central Newspapers.[14] Tax-free transfers of stock were especially important because of the steep capital-gains tax that Goodrich (and later his estate) would otherwise have had to pay.[15]

Still, other tax obstacles plagued Liberty Fund during its early years. For instance, Goodrich had initially planned for Liberty Fund to manage the companies that the Goodrich family controlled even after his death. Goodrich had hoped this could be achieved, because it would have provided the board of directors with a unique opportunity to apply to practical, day-to-day business operations the classical liberal eco-

13. Letter from Pierre F. Goodrich to E. Victor Willetts, December 27, 1972 (in the possession of Liberty Fund).

14. As of November 1996, the value of Central Newspapers stock that Liberty Fund owned was in excess of $37 million. Still, this represents less than 5 percent of the total stock ownership of Central Newspapers (Liberty Fund archives).

15. Don E. Welch, interviews, November 23, 1991, and December 16, 1991. The Internal Revenue Service sought capital-gains tax on two trusts Goodrich had established valued at $26.1 million. The IRS alleged that the total capital gains tax on this amount was $6.8 million. Goodrich's estate lawyers fought the levy and ended up settling with the IRS for $1 million. See "IRS Settles Estate Claim for 1 Million," *Indianapolis Star,* July 24, 1975, p. 30, col. 1.

nomic theories that underlie Liberty Fund's philosophy. Such an arrangement, Goodrich thought, would provide the additional benefit of allowing the income generated from his businesses to be transferred tax-free to the operation of Liberty Fund. That would have provided Liberty Fund with ongoing operating capital to carry on its research and grant-making activities.[16] Both federal and state laws, however, essentially precluded such a plan. The Tax Reform Act of 1969 held that a foundation could not retain its tax-exempt status and hold more than a nominal percentage of stock in any one company. Therefore, Goodrich and the subsequent directors of his businesses had to sell off companies such as the Indiana Telephone Corporation. After they were sold, the proceeds could be transferred to Liberty Fund without incurring capital-gains taxes.[17]

In 1973, after Goodrich's death, Helen Schultz was elected president of the foundation. Neil McLeod, who had served as economist and director of the Institute of Paper Chemistry in Appleton, Wisconsin, was hired as executive director. Benjamin Rogge served as a paid consultant, spending two to three days each week working on Liberty Fund affairs. William Fletcher was financial vice-president and treasurer.

By the mid 1970s, Schultz, McLeod, Rogge, Fletcher, and the board of directors reached a decision that was extremely critical to the viability and success of Liberty Fund.[18] Beginning in May 1975, Liberty Fund entered into, in essence, a probationary period of three years during which it made the transition from a grant-making to an operating foundation, what Goodrich had desired himself. During that time, the general So-

16. Don E. Welch, interviews, November 23, 1991, and December 16, 1991.

17. Don E. Welch, interview, December 16, 1991.

18. According to Henry Manne, former dean of the George Mason University School of Law in Fairfax, Virginia, shortly after Pierre's death there had been considerable discussion among the directors regarding whether to become an operating foundation or remain a grant-making foundation. Manne had written to either Helen Schultz or Neil McLeod suggesting that the outside controls surrounding an operating foundation were really not much greater than those surrounding a grant-making foundation. He suggested that Liberty Fund become an operating foundation by contracting with people to develop seminars for the foundation (telephone interview, May 2, 1995).

cratic seminar format, which is now the core of Liberty Fund's program structure, was fully developed.

From 1975 to 1978, Liberty Fund contracted with both the Institute for Humane Studies (IHS) and individual scholars to hold conferences and seminars. Moreover, a senior-scholars program was established in conjunction with IHS in which prominent scholars such as Friedrich Hayek were invited to conduct seminars.[19] Henry Manne, a longtime director of the Center for Law and Economics and formerly associated with George Mason University in Virginia, coordinated approximately a dozen conferences during those three years and many other conferences in later years. Many of the early seminars dealt with practical topics such as planning and the American constitutional legal system, advertising and free speech, deregulation, bankruptcy, and private alternatives to the judicial process.[20]

According to Manne, "Liberty Fund is generally credited today by the most senior and outstanding scholars in the field of law and economics with having created that whole field. Almost every one of those conferences resulted in either a book or a symposium issue of a law review. Many of them were cited in United States Supreme Court cases. They were absolutely cutting-edge stuff on mundane topics that, nonetheless, philosophically could be always pushed to the issues of a free society."[21]

After its three-year probationary period, in March 1979 Liberty Fund received a determination by the Internal Revenue Service granting it operating-foundation status.[22] Under its new operating arrangement, Liberty Fund has gone on to sponsor more than sixteen hundred conferences, with more being added each year. Subsequent seminars have included such diverse topics as the "Christian Idea in a Secular Culture:

19. "Liberty Fund, Inc., Operating Program 5/1/75 through 4/30/78" (a compilation of activities from May 1975 to April 1978 in the possession of Liberty Fund).

20. Henry Manne, telephone interview, May 2, 1995.

21. Ibid.

22. Letter from Jeanne S. Gessay, Chief, Rulings Section 1, Internal Revenue Service, to Liberty Fund, March 29, 1979 (in the possession of Liberty Fund).

C. S. Lewis and T. S. Eliot," "Economic Calculation Under Inflation," "Business and Liberty," "Freedom and Responsibility in Plato's *Laws,*" "The Influence of Foreign Affairs on the American Founding," and "The Rise of Capitalism in the West."

Beginning in 1976, Liberty Fund initiated a film series. Four films were produced: *Adam Smith and the Wealth of Nations, The Industrial Revolution, Hong Kong: A Story of Human Freedom and Progress,* and *A Design for Liberty: The American Constitution.* From 1976 to 1982, the first three films reached a broad audience, being viewed by more than a hundred thousand high school and college classes, service organizations, and other groups. It is estimated that nearly four million people viewed the films in person and another eleven million viewed them on television.[23]

Also in 1976, Liberty Fund contracted with IHS, the Reason Foundation, and the Center for Libertarian Studies to organize summer seminars for young scholars (graduate students and new professors). The Liberty Fund Research Seminars were conducted in New York, Chicago, and California until 1980.[24] In recent years, Liberty Fund has employed resident scholars to perform research at its Indianapolis offices.

Liberty Fund, as a private, operating foundation, must meet several Internal Revenue Code spending requirements. When the earnings of the endowment exceed this required expenditure, which has generally been true during the last twenty years, then the corpus increases.[25]

23. A fifth film, about zoning in Houston, Texas, was stopped in production and was never completed or released for viewing. The total production costs of the first three films were $734,828.40: (*Adam Smith,* $136,731.68; *The Industrial Revolution,* $310,668.72; *Hong Kong,* $287,428.00). For a while Modern Talking Picture Service distributed the four films, which are now distributed by Liberty Fund. For additional information about the film series, see "Liberty Fund Films" (in the possession of Liberty Fund).

24. For information about the Liberty Fund Research Seminar series, see copies of memorandums of the projects located in Liberty Fund files, Indianapolis, Indiana.

25. Internal Revenue Code spending requirements result in Liberty Fund spending between 66% and 85% of the minimum investment return, which is 5% of the average market value of the endowment during the year.

Goodrich's vision for Liberty Fund can be at least partially attributed to his years of serving on other educational boards. In the 1940s, 1950s, and 1960s, Goodrich served as a director of the Great Books Foundation, the Foundation for Economic Education, the China Institute, the Institute for Humane Studies, and Wabash College. Moreover, his membership in the Mont Pelerin Society enabled him to benefit from the experiences he had gained during his long association with this education-oriented body.

Liberty Fund seminars are a major activity of the foundation, and they originate from Goodrich's own vision. From the Great Books Foundation, Goodrich adopted the following ideas: the small Socratic seminar that has one or two moderators who encourage discussion among participants on a particular topic (seminars usually have sixteen participants); the importance of discussion rather than lecture; the idea that great texts should form the core of discussion; and the belief that the great conversations worth pursuing were begun in the ancient past, have continued into the present, and will continue in the future.

From Leonard Read of FEE, now a cooperating institution with goals similar to those of Liberty Fund, Goodrich learned the importance of involving people of myriad backgrounds. Goodrich also took from FEE the ideas that political and intellectual liberty are closely linked with economic freedom and that economic freedom has its responsibilities beyond maximizing the greatest profit.

From his association with the Mont Pelerin Society, Goodrich realized the importance of reaching out to scholars and intellectuals who have common regard for individual liberty. This is true for several reasons. First, Goodrich and his associates knew that even with the help of resources as great as those held by Liberty Fund only a small percentage of the total population can ever directly participate in a sponsored seminar. Therefore, in order to maximize the resources of Liberty Fund, it is important to attract participants who are in a position to affect the thinking of others. It is not by accident that the majority of Liberty Fund participants are academics. Others in positions of intellectual influence, however, are also invited to attend conferences, including individuals in business, the media, government, and the learned professions, including law, medicine, and the ministry. Second, many participants are repeatedly invited to attend seminars; this practice is based upon the belief that thinking about the ideal of a society of free and responsible individuals is a continuous and evolving experience that is best achieved through repeated conversations with other learned individuals.[26]

The central tenets of Liberty Fund can be summarized briefly. First, education is a lifelong process; Goodrich sought people who recognized that their education was not yet complete. Second, Liberty Fund seminars are generally built around works and ideas of the past. Goodrich valued learning that accumulates throughout the ages, based on the experiences of preceding generations. He recognized that human nature does not change greatly but is not immutable. Man is capable of raising himself to a higher plane of thought and behavior by studying and reflecting upon the great thinkers of the past.[27]

Third, Liberty Fund seminars are based on a theory of action that focuses on the future. Goodrich believed that the opportunity to engage in discussion about important issues and ideas was worthwhile. Inherent in the seminar format is the belief that man is a truth-seeking being, able to gain insights into complex matters and to test hypotheses, capable of reaching virtually unconditional judgments on the basis of reasoned discourse. These qualities make it possible to improve the lot of both individuals and society. Without this underlying belief, seminar discussions would have little value.[28]

The ground rules of Liberty Fund seminars are extremely important:

26. William C. Dennis, senior program officer, Liberty Fund, interview, October 31, 1996.

27. This observation about Goodrich is based on knowledge gained from many interviews. I also noticed several similarities between Goodrich's thought and that of one of the great theologians and philosophers of the Middle Ages, Thomas Aquinas. An excellent lecture about Aquinas that summarizes many of the views of this great theologian was given by Michael Novak of the American Enterprise Institute on December 19, 1989. These observations by Novak seem especially appropriate to Goodrich and are summarized as such.

28. Observations made by Michael Novak about Thomas Aquinas's thought, lecture, American Enterprise Institute, December 19, 1989.

No one participant is able to dominate a discussion, and the role of the moderator is to ensure that the true exchange of ideas (a sort of cross-pollination) occurs. Moreover, in an attempt to build a sense of community, participants dine together for all meals and stay for the entire conference, which is usually held at a hotel. Speakers are not sought to address the seminar participants; everyone participates in formal and informal discussions. Liberty Fund seminars have been held in locations as diverse as Australia, South America, and Europe, as well as in hundreds of cities in North America. Participants are given an honorarium.

As a tax-exempt, private operating foundation, Liberty Fund is purely an educational foundation and is unique for what it is not. For instance, it does not (and cannot by law) engage in politics or political action of any kind. It does not, as do such traditional think tanks as the Heritage Foundation, the Brookings Institution, and the American Enterprise Institute, concern itself with influencing topical political debate. It does not attempt to reach the largest number of people. It seldom seeks publicity, and it is hardly known, even in Indianapolis, the location of its headquarters.

Liberty Fund's charter, known as the *Basic Memorandum,* was written by Goodrich in the late 1950s and early 1960s with the consultation of a number of broadly educated people he knew from the business and scholastic world.[29] The *Basic Memorandum* is a detailed 129-page blueprint of Goodrich's "means of relating and combining ideals, experience and business practice." The manual is primarily composed of Goodrich's views about how Liberty Fund should operate: everything from how new board members should be selected to what should hap-

29. For instance, in the 1950s, Goodrich had used month-long stays at an apartment in Montauk, Long Island, to write much of both the *Basic Memorandum* and the "Education Memorandum." Letter from Helen Fletcher to author, June 18, 1996. In the foreword, Goodrich lists the people who assisted him with the ideas for the *Basic Memorandum:* Frank R. Barnett; William H. Brady, Jr.; Richard C. Cornuelle; James L. Doenges, M.D.; F. A. Harper; F. A. Hayek; Ralph Husted; William A. Jahn; Felix Morley; Oskar Piest; Paul L. Poirot; Eugene C. Pulliam, Sr.; Leonard E. Read; Henry Regnery; Irwin H. Reiss; Wilhelm Röpke; B. A. Rogge; John V. Van Sickle; Ludwig von Mises; and David McCord Wright.

pen to Liberty Fund in the event that it becomes impossible for it to carry out its stated purpose.[30] The *Basic Memorandum* also contains Goodrich's views—as they were expressed in letters and other works he authored—on such subjects as man's ignorance and imperfect nature, the desire of men to govern others, and the problems of power.

The *Basic Memorandum* also contains selections from John Mill's *On Liberty* and the Statement of Aims of the Mont Pelerin Society. At the end of the *Basic Memorandum* is a book list containing seventy-six great literary works: from the Old and New Testaments to books by more than thirty thinkers, including Aristotle, Luther, Goethe, Lord Acton, F. A. Hayek, and Ludwig von Mises. Goodrich recommended that board members and anyone interested in enduring ideas should read liberally from this list. The list of books is reproduced in appendix B.

In years to come, the *Basic Memorandum* will no doubt take on even greater significance as a guide to Goodrich's desires for the foundation. While almost all current board directors knew Goodrich personally, many future directors, who will not have had the benefit of knowing Goodrich, will have to rely even more on the tenets found in the *Basic Memorandum* if they are to maintain the foundation's integrity.[31] Still, the memorandum is vague; it is not an explicit guidebook, but a reflective document about Goodrich's personal concerns. As Liberty Fund senior fellow William C. Dennis states, "The *Basic Memorandum* doesn't tell us what to do; it tells us how to *think* about what we should do."[32]

The publishing arm of Liberty Fund is another important aspect of the foundation. In 1971 Liberty Fund published in book form the papers

30. According to Don E. Welch, a founding board member, Goodrich was very concerned that the forces opposing individual liberty might become so strong in the United States that Liberty Fund might have to move to another country to remain operational (interview, December 16, 1991). See also *Basic Memorandum*, pt. 3 (Board of Directors—Qualifications, Selection, and Overall Consist, including exhibits III-a and III-b), pp. 59–71.

31. J. Charles King, interview, December 10, 1993.

32. William C. Dennis, interview, October 31, 1996.

presented at the seminar "Education in a Free Society."[33] Since that time, Liberty Fund has published more than one hundred titles, many of them reprints of such classical texts as Adam Smith's *Wealth of Nations, The Selected Writings of Lord Acton,* Ludwig von Mises's *Socialism,* and F. A. Hayek's *The Counter-Revolution of Science.* A cuneiform inscription, the earliest-known appearance of the word "freedom" (*amagi*), or "liberty," is imprinted in each book.[34]

In April 1978, Helen Schultz stepped down as president of Liberty Fund. Neil McLeod succeeded her, serving until May 1986 in that position. After McLeod's retirement, Dr. W. W. "Dub" Hill, a former Indiana state senator, headed Liberty Fund until 1992. Hill was succeeded by T. Alan Russell as chairman and chief executive officer and by J. Charles King, a former philosophy professor, as president. King, in turn, turned over the presidency in November 1995 to George B. Martin, formerly a professor of literature at Wofford College in South Carolina.

The board of directors is composed of men and women who take Goodrich's mission seriously. They bring to their positions diverse and valuable experiences from their own occupational backgrounds: Among them are a former president of a large Illinois milling company, a bank president, a founder of the Universidad Francisco Marroquin in Guatemala, a former president of the Indianapolis Power and Light Company, a lawyer and current college professor of political science, a former president of Meadowlark Farms, and a former undersecretary of defense during the Nixon administration. Pierre's wife Enid served as vice-chairman of the board until her death in November 1996.[35]

33. Letter from Anne C. Lawrason to author, September 20, 1996.

34. See Jeff Swiatek, "Liberty Fund Carries on Founder's Dream," *Indianapolis Star,* May 1, 1988, sec. B, p. 19, col. 3.

35. Directors of the Liberty Fund board in 2000 included T. Alan Russell, chairman, former president of Illinois Cereal Mills, Inc., in Paris, Illinois; Chris L. Talley, treasurer, current president of Peoples Loan and Trust Bank; Manuel F. Ayau, a founder and former rector of the Universidad Francisco Marroquin in Guatemala; Ralph W. Husted, former president of the Indianapolis Power and Light Company and former president of the Indianapolis Public School Board of Education; George B. Martin, president, former chairman of the English department and professor at Wofford College; Roseda

Was Pierre Goodrich's decision to establish Liberty Fund a wise one, especially in light of the huge sum of money that he left to the foundation? Would it have been better for Goodrich to have applied his wealth to more practical ends? With so many needs and problems in the world—humanitarian, educational, social—could not the assets have been used to support more beneficent, humane, and practical endeavors? Moreover, if Goodrich truly wanted to influence people's thinking, would it not have been better for him to establish a more traditional think tank whose results could have been more readily seen and evaluated? These questions are invariably raised whenever the work of Liberty Fund is closely examined.

To see the intrinsic worth of Liberty Fund takes a certain kind of long-term vision. Changing people's perceptions of themselves and how they are governed and behave in society is an ongoing endeavor. Yet the foundation has the luxury of taking a long-term approach: It does not have shareholders or employees to appease; it is not beholden to anyone or anything except the tenets that Goodrich set out in the *Basic Memorandum.* There is no reason that the foundation should not continue to exist in perpetuity.

It is interesting to observe how unusual an institution Liberty Fund is. In many ways, it is a modern replica of the ancient Greek academy: While it invites participants to address searching questions, it is not interested in obtaining specific answers or in applying the information that is shared toward a specific purpose; it has a permanent staff and board of directors, but no permanent group of students. It does have disciples, however: participants who have noted the influence that

---

Doenges Decker, family friend to Pierre and Enid Goodrich, who was closely involved, with her husband James Doenges, in many aspects of a free society; Edward B. McLean, an attorney and professor of political science at Wabash College; Irwin H. Reiss, former president of Meadowlark Farms; Richard A. Ware, former president of the Earhart Foundation and undersecretary of defense in the Nixon administration; George W. Carey, professor of government, Georgetown University; and Richard W. Duesenberg, visiting professor at St. Louis University Law School and former general counsel of Monsanto Corporation.

the foundation has had through its extensive seminar and publishing endeavors.

"There's a totally different set of ideas being discussed in what you call political philosophy," said James M. Buchanan, a 1986 winner of the Nobel Prize in economics who is general director of the Center for Study of Public Choice at Virginia's George Mason University. "Surely it [the Fund] has been in part a contributor to that."[36]

"It has made a tremendous difference in seeing that the predicate questions of a society are discussed," said Stephen J. Tonsor, an emeritus professor at the University of Michigan who has attended dozens of Liberty Fund seminars.[37] That is indeed the mission of Liberty Fund: to see that the larger questions about man and individual freedom are continually asked and examined. That momentous task and responsibility are commensurate with the desires and the inquiring mind of Liberty Fund's founder.

36. Quote taken from article by Jeff Swiatek, "Liberty Fund Carries on Founder's Dream."

37. Stephen J. Tonsor, interview, December 5, 1992.

V

The Goodriches Assayed

Chapter 30

Who Was Pierre F. Goodrich?

Pierre Goodrich was the most complicated man I have ever known. I could write a book about this man, but I despair of doing justice to his multisided personality and his amazing range of interests.

BYRON K. TRIPPET, *Wabash on My Mind*

ONE DAY in late April 1971, Pierre F. Goodrich, president for thirty-five years of the Indiana Telephone Corporation, decided to visit the corporate headquarters in Seymour, Indiana. He did not come to the offices to meet with upper-level management or to discuss the company's performance in the last business quarter. Rather, he came to see the recently installed telephone equipment, the women who responded to customer complaints (the so-called 114 girls), Marcella Patton, Mary McCallum, Jean Thomson, and the other operators and secretaries.

At seventy-six, an age when many multimillionaires have been retired for a decade, the crusty but soft-spoken CEO began asking questions of the operators: How did the new electronic switching stations work? How did the operators keep them clean? Did they like automation better than the old manual system? The operators grew weary of Mr. Goodrich's intense curiosity. They simply wanted to get on with their work, but they were too intimidated by the austere and elderly president to seek leave from his seemingly endless questions.[1]

For Pierre Goodrich, the occasion was bittersweet. It was a day of

1. Doris Lewis, telephone interview, March 1, 1993.

nostalgia. He was old enough to remember when the mainstay of the company was the magneto-crank telephone, when telephone operators were called upon to contact the local doctor to notify him that a baby was on its way. He further recalled that the local operators in Seymour, Greensburg, and Winchester had been the hub of a great deal of information. The passing of that day was rather sad. He realized that the operators no longer knew the customers; they had become mere button pushers. Moreover, he knew that recently invented fiber optics and microwave transmission would transform modern communications even further. All these changes marked the end of an era.[2]

But the company president had another agenda that day. He came to discuss ideas he believed had great relevancy for years to come. Dressed in his conservative dark coat and top hat and perceived as eccentric by his employees, he wanted to discuss matters that were meaningful to him throughout his lifetime of accomplishment: a love of freedom, responsibility, personal commitment, tenacity, and other virtues he extolled and embodied.

On that day, the employees gathered into small groups to meet Mr. Goodrich, a man whom they knew more by reputation than through personal contact. He did not come to make a speech; Pierre F. Goodrich

2. Rosanna Amos, longtime secretary for Goodrich, told me how Goodrich felt after he had gone to the Indiana Telephone Corporation and seen all the technological changes that were being made. She explained that he told her what it was like in the 1930s when he first became involved with the company. She said that he was very sad about the elimination of the operators' function as the source of information for the community (interview, December 10, 1991).

The accuracy of Amos's memory is confirmed by a passage contained in the last memorandum that Pierre Goodrich wrote to the employees of the Indiana Telephone Corporation, approximately five months before his death. The memorandum states in part: "From the viewpoint of local neighborliness, there is nothing better than an old-fashion manual board with a knowledgeable operator who is humanly interested in the community. We know this from experience. It has always been important to people to be in contact with their doctor when they needed him and the old manual system made this possible . . ." (memorandum, May 30, 1973, p. 4 [in the possession of T. Alan Russell, Paris, Ill.]).

seldom made a speech. He came, in essence, to conduct a symposium, to converse about his greatest concerns and deepest beliefs: man's ignorance and imperfection, the existence of laws not created by man, and the courage of the Founding Fathers.

The employees listened politely. Few of them had ever read, or even heard of, the *Federalist* or the work of the Austrian economist Ludwig von Mises, both of which Goodrich spoke about in detail and with passion. The informal discussions went on all afternoon and into the evening, when a company dinner was held. Goodrich later wrote a letter thanking the employees for their thought-provoking conversations, though, in fact, they had said little. Combining business with intellectual discussions was Goodrich's lifelong habit. For Pierre Goodrich, it was difficult to say where business ended and scholarly discourse began.[3]

Pierre F. Goodrich was a remarkable man: unconventional, enigmatic, demanding, elusive, inquisitive, skeptical, impassioned, private, and perceptive, with nearly inexhaustive energy. "Mr. Goodrich was way before his time," said Ruth Connolly, one of his secretaries at Liberty Fund.[4]

Indeed, the Indianapolis-based businessman was a visionary. As chairman of the board of Ayrshire Collieries Corporation, Goodrich began the reclamation of stripped coalfields thirty years before federal and state regulators forced such action upon coal operators. In banking and the telephone industry, he advocated changes that only in the past ten

3. What Goodrich discussed at his meetings with the employees and his follow-up thank-you letter is contained in the July 1971 *ITC Highlights,* a newsletter published by the Indiana Telephone Corporation. It contains more than a dozen pictures of Goodrich meeting with employees or touring the facility. Shortly after visiting the Seymour offices, Goodrich went to the ITC offices at Jasper, Indiana, and conducted a similar tour and meetings with the employees. Walter Seaton said that Goodrich talked a great deal about the *Federalist* papers, but apparently at the time none of the employees had any idea what they were (interview, January 16, 1993).

4. Ruth Connolly, interview, October 25, 1991.

years have been fully adopted by others. His own companies bought the latest technology. He was constantly trying to find out what the competition was doing. He was keenly interested in the latest gadgets.[5]

Although Pierre Goodrich was visionary in his business practices, he was often anachronistic in his personal life. He did not own a television, because he believed that television would disrupt his passion for books and ideas.[6] Although he could afford the best clothes, his abhorrence of waste prompted him to continue to wear suits that were badly worn and dated. In the 1960s, when smoking at work was commonplace, he demanded that his offices be nonsmoking. His demeanor was often that of the stereotypical absent-minded professor; although worth millions, he could be so deep in thought that he would forget to take pocket change for lunch.[7]

Defining his life presents many problems. His friends and acquaintances disagreed about Goodrich's personality and beliefs. To some, Goodrich was gracious, hospitable, and refined;[8] to others, he was irascible, suspicious, and unkempt.[9] One theology professor who attended an early Liberty Fund seminar on religion left the conference convinced

5. Alan Russell said that once, in the early 1970s, when he drove Goodrich home after a board meeting, Goodrich decided he wanted to go to a competing telephone company's switching station. He and Russell "crashed" the place, arriving unannounced, and were given a tour by the men who were on duty at the time (interview, July 2, 1994). When Goodrich attended a meeting of the Mont Pelerin Society in Kassel, Germany, in early September 1960, he visited the giant communications company Siemens and learned all he could about the latest telephone technology that the company had (Ruth Connolly, interview, October 25, 1991).

6. Ruth Connolly did remember providing Goodrich and his wife Enid with a television on which to watch Neil Armstrong's July 1969 moon landing. Shortly after that historic event, Goodrich also watched with considerable interest and apparently some satisfaction the critical scrutiny given to Senator Edward Kennedy as a result of the Chappaquiddick incident (interview, October 25, 1991).

7. Rodney Medler, interview, June 9, 1993.

8. Frank Jessup, telephone interview, February 27, 1993.

9. Telephone interviews: William Stimart, January 21, 1993; William Waldbeiser, January 15, 1993.

that his host was an atheist.[10] Yet Pierre Goodrich's discussions and writings repeatedly refer to an "infinite creator." Moreover, his vast knowledge of Scripture was well known.[11] He was convinced that the pursuit of ideas about liberty was of the utmost importance to a society, yet he did not choose to champion those ideas by the traditional means of holding a political office or an academic position. Moreover, Goodrich avoided socializing, because he believed that membership in most social organizations was a waste of time. Yet he would take any time necessary to examine some small, obscure point if he believed it would enable him to make a better business decision or if it furthered a philosophical insight.

"Hours did not mean anything to Pierre," said Will Hays, Jr., who served with Goodrich on the Wabash College Board of Trustees. "Pierre would be so intense about something that was interesting to him, that it just consumed him. He could not understand that the person he was talking to would not be as interested in it as he was."[12]

Goodrich was a voracious reader. Moreover, he constantly challenged others to read, especially material that reinforced his own strong convictions about liberty, the virtues of the free market, and the evils of governmental power. When employees and acquaintances said that they did not have time to read as broadly as Goodrich had hoped because of work or family commitments, his common response (and he meant it quite seriously) was, "What are you doing between midnight

10. Letter from Gerhart Niemeyer to author, November 10, 1992. ("It is a great pleasure that I think back to my association with Pierre Goodrich. I believe the pleasure was mutual. That could not be expected, for while Pierre Goodrich was an atheist, I was deeply committed to belief in Jesus Christ and his salvation. . . .")

11. In his paper "Why Liberty?" and in his letters and the *Basic Memorandum,* Goodrich constantly refers to an "infinite being." As to his knowledge of Scripture, many people remember that Goodrich could quote chapter and verse. Gerhart Niemeyer, too, recalls that Goodrich was proud of his knowledge of Scripture (letter, November 10, 1992).

12. Will Hays, Jr., interview, May 8, 1992.

and 2:00 A.M.?" (he often stayed up that late reading himself).[13] It was not uncommon for Goodrich to start business meetings with book discussions, and he often had magazine and journal subscriptions sent to friends and acquaintances.[14] For instance, after Goodrich met the young Richard Lugar, a former Indianapolis mayor and currently Indiana's senior United States senator, Goodrich sent Lugar letters containing titles of books by conservative philosophers and legal scholars. "Pierre knew that I had studied politics, philosophy, and economics at Oxford," said Lugar. "He thought I should be aware of these writers if I hadn't already been exposed to them."[15]

Goodrich also challenged Eli Lilly, another prominent Indianapolis figure and fellow Wabash College trustee, to take up the classics.[16] Anyone who visited Goodrich at his Indianapolis office, whether on a business or a personal call, was likely to leave with a book in hand or to be mailed a packet of selected readings. The material would almost always include numbers 10 and 51 of the *Federalist.* Also included would be a copy of the letter of the British historian Lord Acton containing the well-known admonition that "power tends to corrupt and absolute power corrupts absolutely" and Rudyard Kipling's poem "The Gods of

13. Interviews: Rosanna Amos, December 10, 1991; Irwin H. Reiss, June 26, 1996.

14. Peter Garson, telephone interview, December 30, 1992. Dale Braun recalled that for years Goodrich had the periodical *Human Events* sent to him (interview, July 17, 1992). Paul Poirot wrote (letter, November 8, 1992) that Goodrich had literature from the Foundation for Economic Education, notably *The Freeman,* sent to several people.

15. Richard Lugar, interview, October 29, 1992.

16. Lilly admitted to Goodrich that he had had such mixed success confronting "the uncertain seas of philosophy" that "biography and history and some of the lesser humanities will, I am afraid, have to be my joy and solace." Letter from Lilly to Goodrich, January 8, 1951, Frank Sparks Papers, Eli Lilly folder, Archives, Wabash College. Lilly wrote:

> Dear Mr. Goodrich:
>
> Thank you very much for your interesting list of great books and your questions about them. Your work in this field has borne important results and you have again been a public benefactor. Your service entitles you to every co-operation and as you will find enclosed the poor record of my cruises into the uncertain seas of philosophy. . . .

the Copybook Headings" (see appendix C).[17] A list was kept of the people who visited Goodrich in the early 1970s and who were sent the above readings. The list, several pages in length, includes national political insiders, former Indiana governors, congressmen, leading national journalists, academics, and businessmen.[18] It was as if Pierre Goodrich's office was a stopping-off place for prominent figures who were on a pilgrimage to greater understanding. Goodrich was just as apt to have the same literature sent to the plumber who had fixed his sink the day before or the janitor whom he had recently engaged in vigorous debate.[19]

Former Indiana governor Edgar D. Whitcomb remembers when he first met Goodrich, in 1958. Whitcomb was attempting to get a manuscript that he had written published. "Once I was advised that he might be of help, I went directly to Pierre's office and the receptionist showed me in," said Whitcomb. "Mr. Goodrich was sitting in the corner reading a book." Whitcomb discussed with Goodrich his manuscript, *Escape from Corregidor.* It was about Whitcomb's experiences in a Japanese prisoner-of-war camp during World War II. "After I introduced myself and my purpose for visiting," added Whitcomb, "Pierre pulled a watch out of his pocket and said to me, 'It is a quarter till twelve. I can give you fifteen minutes.'"

17. Letter from Lord Acton to Bishop Creighton, dated April 5, 1887, *Essays on Freedom and Power* (Boston: Beacon Press, 1948), p. 364. Goodrich often repeated this sentence both in conversation and in his writings.

18. Rosanna Amos kept a copy of the list. Visitors of Goodrich between 1970 and 1973 included William Casey, the former CIA director and campaign chairman to Ronald Reagan; former Indiana governor Edgar D. Whitcomb; former Indiana governor and United States secretary of health and human services Otis Bowen; congressmen Richard Roudebush and William Bray; columnists and academics Jeffrey Hart, Thomas Sowell, George Roche, Russell Kirk, John Chamberlain, and Karl Brandt (of Stanford University); publishers Henry Regnery and Eugene Pulliam, Sr. and Jr.; economist Milton Friedman; Leonard Read of the Foundation for Economic Education; and Charles Stabler of the *Wall Street Journal.*

19. "When Mr. Goodrich returned from the hospital one time, he had me send letters and books to the nurses, because he had gotten into lengthy discussions with them about political philosophy," said Rosanna Amos (interview, December 10, 1991).

Two and a half hours later, after lunch and a lengthy philosophical discussion, Whitcomb emerged from Goodrich's office with at least eight books in hand; Goodrich had also called Henry Regnery on the spot, and Regnery published Whitcomb's manuscript soon afterward.[20]

William Campbell, now a professor of economics at Louisiana State University, appreciated Goodrich for giving him a copy of Ludwig von Mises's *Human Action,* which introduced him to economics and rational thought. Campbell credits this small gesture as having a major influence on the direction of his intellectual interests. Campbell also remembers the influence that Goodrich had on his father, Albert, a longtime law partner and business associate of Pierre's: "My father felt personally indebted to Pierre for interesting him in the cause of human liberty. I think it is safe to say that my father would not have dedicated himself to Wabash, Hillsdale, [and] Rockford College without the personal influence of Pierre Goodrich."[21]

Victor Milione, former president of the Intercollegiate Studies Institute, had similar praise for Goodrich. "What I admired about Pierre most was here was a man that had tremendous wealth and could have sat on his backside and played golf whenever he wanted to, but instead he got involved in issues and ideas. Pierre spent a great deal of time thinking about the future. He wasn't simply doing these things for his own material benefit."[22]

Pierre Goodrich's strengths and foibles say much about him. He had a prodigious memory, especially for details. In both business and foundation meetings, Goodrich often prevailed in his arguments because of his ability to quote verbatim from some relatively obscure source.[23]

20. Edgar D. Whitcomb, interview, April 18, 1992. Whitcomb calls Goodrich's telephone call to Regnery the major reason that Whitcomb's manuscript was published.

21. Letter from William Campbell to author, May 15, 1993.

22. Victor Milione, telephone interview, October 19, 1992.

23. Telephone interviews: Edmund Opitz, October 10, 1992; Elisabeth Luce Moore, October 9, 1992.

"He would call me on the telephone and we would talk for an hour," said Dale Braun, who worked for Goodrich briefly to establish Indiana chapters of the Great Books Foundation. "We'd then talk again six months later and Pierre would quote me word for word what I had told him during our earlier conversation. I remember I had to be careful what I told him for fear he'd hold me to the letter of it months later."[24]

John Kidder remembers when he was manager of the Ford dealership shortly after World War II in Goodrich's hometown of Winchester. Because the war had consumed most of the country's steel, cars for private use were extremely difficult to come by. One Monday morning, on Goodrich's return to Indianapolis, he drove into the Ford dealership to purchase gasoline. He was driving a 1941 Lincoln Continental. "I told Pierre at the time that if he was ever interested in selling the car, I'd like to purchase it for the dealership," said Kidder. "He didn't say anything, just nodded his head. Six years later I got a letter from Pierre asking if I was still interested in buying the Lincoln."[25]

Goodrich often addressed his employees by their last names. He believed that casual familiarity (referring to one another by first names) could result in the degeneration of a relationship.[26] Nonetheless, he did not put himself on any pedestal. While he could dominate a conversation, he was generally a good listener and took an interest in most of his employees' suggestions and opinions. Apparently, Goodrich's intense curiosity was partially natural, but no doubt much of it was also deliberate. The reason for his inquisitiveness could be to gain the knowledge necessary for a more intelligent business decision or to explore the depth of thinking of the examinee, or possibly both.

"One day we were in Indianapolis at a meeting for the purpose of buying telephone equipment and Pierre had hired an expert to give us advice," said Perce Goodrich, adding parenthetically, "If you were in

24. Dale Braun, telephone interview, December 2, 1991. Goodrich's extraordinary memory was mentioned by several persons interviewed.

25. John Kidder, interview, October 10, 1993.

26. Ruth Connolly, interview, October 25, 1991.

a meeting with Pierre, something that would normally take an hour, might take half or even a full day. Finally, I said, 'Pierre, you hire an expert to tell you what to do and then you second guess 'em and don't take their advice.' He said, 'Let me tell you something, Perce, when you hire an expert you gotta check on them to see if they know what they're talking about.' "[27]

No one impressed Pierre Goodrich on the basis of a job title or degrees. Goodrich had to be convinced that the person actually had the knowledge that he or she professed to have. Goodrich's inquisitiveness became infectious. People who were around him would start to ask, "Is there another way?" and, "Would it be better to attempt it in this manner?"[28] Goodrich would propose even more difficult and searching questions that had little to do with the business arena directly: Are human beings perfectible? Are they empty vessels? Are there moral absolutes or are morals relative? Who determines what is morally right? How is economic prosperity achieved and maintained? These questions were anxiety-producing to some because they challenged their belief systems and their very comfortable way of living. Moreover, Goodrich's questions were not simply abstractions. He wanted to know why a person did something and why some other course of action was not preferable. That attitude led him to challenge the modern welfare state at a

27. Perce Goodrich, interview, November 9, 1992. Ralph Husted, a member of the Liberty Fund board of directors, had similar memories of Goodrich's long-windedness at board meetings.

> Board meetings were called by Pierre Goodrich whenever he thought there was something to talk about. The meeting would start at about nine o'clock in the morning and would start by Pierre talking about the subject for which he had called the meeting. . . . So he would start talking. We would sit there and listen all morning. We would adjourn for lunch and Pierre would resume his discussion. It was a one-man discussion. About four o'clock in the evening, Helen Schultz would say, "Mr. Goodrich, we have an agenda." Pierre would continue with his discussion. About five o'clock, Helen would say again, "Mr. Goodrich, we have an agenda," and between Helen sitting on one side of him and Mrs. Goodrich sitting on the other, holding a watch, he finally yielded to the agenda and we would get through it in about five minutes. (Interview by William C. Dennis, June 12, 1990)

28. Rosanna Amos, interview, December 10, 1991.

time (the 1950s, 1960s, and early 1970s) when belief in its virtues was at its zenith.

His probing nature extended into the process by which he hired employees. "Before Pierre Goodrich would hire a new person—and it didn't make any difference what type of job—he would interview them personally and sometimes the interview would go on for hours," said Rosanna Amos.[29]

When Goodrich interviewed an applicant for a top management position, the interview could last up to three successive days. Moreover, it was the exception, not the rule, that the questions had anything to do with the position that the applicant was seeking.

"I was interviewing for the chief financial officer's position of the Indiana Telephone Corporation in August 1971," said Alan Russell, now chairman of Liberty Fund. "I expected my first question to be on budgets or closings. But that wasn't the first question. The first question from Pierre was what is the difference between a paramecium and an amoeba? I was able to tell him that they were both one cell animals and that they reproduced differently, but that was probably the closest I came in two days of answering any one of his questions." Goodrich was trying to find out if the candidate had an inquiring mind and whether the candidate had a desire to learn or believed he already knew everything there was to know.[30]

The one encounter Martha Wharton of Indianapolis had with Goodrich in 1966 left an indelible impression upon her. She had come to his

29. Ibid. Professor Edward McLean mentioned that when he first met Goodrich, their meeting lasted for a couple of hours. Goodrich wanted to know what books McLean read, his personal philosophy, and so forth (interview, May 8, 1992). In considering new employees, one approach that Goodrich employed was to hire individuals on a part-time basis. "He was always curious to see if [a part-time employee] was someone he'd like to have in the office as a permanent employee," said Rosanna Amos. "Mr. Goodrich would find an excuse to have this person do something especially for him, and then he'd sit and talk with them and ask them all kinds of questions. He wanted to know what you read, and why you read it, and what you thought about it" (interview, December 10, 1991).

30. T. Alan Russell, interview, July 2, 1994.

offices at 3520 Washington Boulevard to interview for what she had been initially told was a legal secretary's position. For Wharton, the meeting was unforgettable.

> As the interview unfolded, it became apparent that Mr. Goodrich was not really looking for a *legal* secretary after all, but rather for a more well-rounded generalist. I liked that, and warmed to the idea of working for such a fascinating personality. He rambled at length about all the different enterprises he was involved in, and I recall he seemed to be especially fond of discussing his coal mining interests. I grew up in the coal area of Southern Illinois, so was able to respond well enough to avoid looking like a dummy. I felt we were developing a good rapport.[31]

The rapport quickly deteriorated, however, when Wharton corrected Goodrich in his use of a word during a trial run at dictation. Convinced she had "cooked her goose," she left the interview, not in intimidation or awe of the man, but "with a keen awareness that I had been in the presence of greatness." (Much to her surprise, Wharton was offered the job by Goodrich, but she turned it down because it was below her salary expectations.)[32]

There was no doubt about it: Goodrich could be tough on employees. "He might accept a mistake once," said Gilbert Snider, "but if you failed a second time that indicated a pattern to Mr. Goodrich. He couldn't tolerate laziness. Human frailties were only accepted by Pierre in very limited amounts. He just overestimated his employees' capabilities in relation to his own."[33] Rosanna Amos echoed Snider's opinion: "Mr. Goodrich could lose interest in someone real fast if they did one thing that was stupid."[34]

Thus, personal contact with Pierre Goodrich was often not pleasant. He could be demanding, self-centered, and pedantic to the point of boredom. It was not unusual for him to conduct his business activities

31. Letter from Martha Wharton to author, December 14, 1995.
32. Ibid.
33. Gilbert Snider, interview, December 23, 1991.
34. Rosanna Amos, interview, December 10, 1991.

without apparently thinking about the inconvenience that it might place on others who had to deal with him. For instance, monthly board meetings for the Eastern Indiana Telephone Company and Peoples Loan and Trust Company were held in Winchester on Friday and Saturday nights, respectively, to accommodate Goodrich's Indianapolis work schedule, not anyone else's.[35] The meetings could go on into all hours of the night and start again early the next morning. He would often have food brought into the meetings so that the flow of the discussion would not be interrupted. One Christmas Eve, Goodrich continued a meeting well into the evening and apparently never gave any thought to the difficult position in which it placed employees with children.[36] Goodrich simply did not place the same value on family and social activities as others did: He didn't have a particularly close relationship with his only child, and he viewed most social gatherings as worthless because they were nonproductive.

In terms of demeanor, Goodrich was often dogmatic in expressing his point of view and unrelenting in prosecuting his case. He also possessed conflicting traits in temperament: a subtle shyness and a strong (at times, dominating) personality. In terms of self-reflection, neither James Goodrich nor Pierre Goodrich seemed to express inner feelings or motives. Seldom in the hundreds of letters of Pierre Goodrich's I read or the numerous discussions I had with Pierre's associates did I learn of any sharing of inner thoughts or feelings. Pierre Goodrich may have been a philosopher, but he was not a poet.

Moreover, Goodrich had an abiding, often unrealistic belief that reason either does or should control people's behavior. He had difficulty

35. Interviews: Ralph Litschert, November 10, 1991; Don Welch, December 16, 1991. Anne C. Lawrason, a former Goodrich employee, wrote: "He [Goodrich] was just impossible at times, and we all felt like tearing our hair out. The infuriating part was that he never even realized how demanding and ridiculous he seemed to us. He could be extremely kind and caring, and I know he thought of his employees (at least, some of us) as his family" (letter to author, December 11, 1995).

36. This point was mentioned to me three times in interviews: William Stimart, January 21, 1993; Arlene Metz, November 10, 1992; and Kenneth Sullivan, February 19, 1996.

appreciating that individuals often make decisions on the basis of emotional, and not purely rational, motives. For instance, he was convinced that customers of his Indiana bank, the Peoples Loan and Trust Company, did business with it because Peoples was one of the soundest and best-run small banks in the state. Yet former bank employee Rodney Medler insists that it was excellent service that attracted customers to the bank. Goodrich too often undervalued the human touch. "One thing I could never get Pierre to understand," said Medler, "was the importance of customer service. Most customers don't know who owns a bank or how well capitalized it is. But Pierre believed that people stayed at home and studied these things before they deposited their money. He didn't appreciate how much service and a familiar face meant to keeping customers satisfied."[37]

Goodrich also did not seem to appreciate fully how wealth and higher education offered opportunities that not everyone had access to. He sometimes attributed a person's lack of success to weakness of will. He did not seem to realize that many individuals are not in a position to change their fortunes dramatically.[38] Because of his brilliance and his advantages, Pierre Goodrich could at times overestimate the degree to which people are captains of their fate.[39]

37. Rodney Medler, interview, June 9, 1993. That the financial operations of the bank were sound is apparently true, because Peoples never closed during the Depression and has had a good business record ever since. Goodrich saw to it that the bank had a loan-to-deposit ratio of about 25 percent, whereas most other banks had a loan-to-deposit ratio of 50 to 60 percent. Goodrich intentionally did this, according to Chris Talley, president of Peoples Loan and Trust Bank, because it ensured that the bank had adequate liquidity in case there was ever a run on the bank (interview, March 20, 1995).

38. For instance, Rodney Medler said that Goodrich once remarked to him that he (Goodrich) couldn't understand why a particular farmer didn't invest more of his income back into his farm. Medler says that caused him to think that Goodrich didn't realize how difficult it was for a working man to raise a family and pay a mortgage off on just one income (interview, June 9, 1993).

39. Anne C. Lawrason, who worked with Goodrich daily as a secretary from 1970 to 1973, stated that Goodrich once remarked to her that he was a "self-made man." He was apparently blind to many of the advantages (such as education, business knowledge, and financial inheritance) that he had received from his parents (inter-

Yet despite these shortcomings, according to dozens of people, Pierre Goodrich was the most remarkable person they had ever met. "I would describe Pierre Goodrich as a man who actually had 'the vision of greatness,'" said Elton Trueblood, a well-known theologian who became a close friend of Goodrich's through their work with the Great Books Foundation.[40] Few that I interviewed would disagree with Trueblood's assessment.

One evening in the early 1920s, Alice Miller Bly accidentally crossed paths with Pierre Goodrich, the town's young new attorney, across from the old Winchester High School. Alice's family was waiting for her to come home for dinner and had nearly given up. There was a thunderstorm, and it had been raining for quite some time when Alice finally trudged through the door, bedraggled. "Alice said that she and Pierre Goodrich had been out talking in the rain about literature and she couldn't get away from him," said Mary Johnson, Alice's sister. "She had an umbrella and Pierre didn't."[41]

This seemingly trivial incident is indicative of the intense feeling that Goodrich had for ideas. He could become consumed with the need to share his insights and bring illumination to a conversation. In his desire

---

view, September 15, 1996). Goodrich often advised his employees to buy the best, whatever the product, because in the long run buying the best was the most cost-efficient. But, says Rosanna Amos, he did not seem to appreciate that not everyone could always afford to buy the best (interview, December 10, 1991). Goodrich was also strongly opposed to the extension of consumer credit. Generally speaking, a disdain for credit is laudable, even more so today than during Goodrich's life. But Goodrich appeared not to understand that a young couple, for example, might need to purchase some goods on time. Rodney Medler, interview, June 9, 1993.

40. Trueblood said this about Goodrich in both the telephone interview I had with him on December 12, 1991, and in a letter I received from him dated December 3, 1991. Trueblood wrote in part: "We both became involved in the *Great Books Program* because we were both convinced of the importance of what Professor [Alfred North] Whitehead called 'the habitual vision of greatness.' . . . I would describe Pierre Goodrich as a man who actually had 'the vision of greatness.'" Whitehead's complete statement is, "Moral education is impossible apart from the habitual vision of greatness."

41. Mary Johnson, interview, January 1, 1992.

to record ideas that he believed were important, Goodrich, in the late 1960s, hired a person to establish an "ideas file." The duties were to read newspapers, magazines, and journals such as the *New York Times, Barrons,* the *Chicago Tribune, Human Events,* the *Indianapolis Star,* and the *Indianapolis Press.* The task was to clip any article found on such subjects as inflation, war, the Middle East, Lord Acton, gold and the gold standard, United States Supreme Court decisions, Social Security, espionage, legislating morality and its futility, Japanese internees, Calvin, Locke, Luther, Hegel, Plato, the virtues, and anything to do with Germany. Pierre Goodrich would often sit down with the person responsible for the ideas file along with several others to discuss for hours these ideas and the publications from which they came. The ideas files filled several large upright cabinets in Goodrich's offices. Goodrich's preoccupation with ideas knew no time limitations. Several persons I interviewed remarked, often with humor and sometimes with irritation, that he would call them in the middle of the night or would interrupt their dinner, seemingly oblivious of the time or the disruption.[42]

Goodrich was a classic perfectionist. He had an extremely difficult time reaching closure in almost everything he ever attempted—be it a conversation, a personal letter, a business meeting, writing a business document, or anything else (he made and remade his will eleven times between 1949 and 1969).[43] He regarded almost each endeavor as unfinished, incomplete, and capable of being improved upon; many things he wrote were stamped "Draft Only."

42. While Ben Rogge was on vacation playing golf in Alabama one summer day, Goodrich called Rogge off the course to discuss a matter that Pierre believed was of the utmost urgency, but they ended up discussing some philosophical point. This, unfortunately for business colleagues and friends alike, was not an isolated incident. Interviews with Edward McLean, May 8, 1992, and Perce G. Goodrich, November 9, 1992. Many interviewees, perhaps more than a dozen, recalled Goodrich's lengthy late-night telephone calls.

43. See Lou Hiner, "IRS Reviews Goodrich Tax," *Indianapolis News,* May 18, 1978, p. 40, col. 1. According to the article, Goodrich prepared eleven wills between 1949 and his last one on March 3, 1969.

His painstaking manner exasperated almost everyone who had to work with him.[44] "I think there was a driving force within him to seek the unobtainable," said Arlene Metz, who sat through many lengthy meetings in the early 1960s taking dictation from Goodrich. "I don't think he left one stone unturned. Regular hours didn't mean anything to him. You worked until you got something done."[45]

Goodrich's drive for perfection carried over into his need to master his varied interests. When something piqued his curiosity, he would learn all about it. He was not content to dabble in something or simply become acquainted with its rudimentary elements. Rather, Pierre Goodrich would research his interests, consult experts about them, and discuss them in depth. He would not let go of an interest until he had mastered it. It did not matter whether the interest involved understanding the evils of inflation, the inner workings of telephone equipment, cooking, the origins and qualities of gemstones, Eastern mysticism, agriculture, or distinguishing the bouquets of fine German wines.[46]

44. Goodrich believed that sufficient reflection on problems could result in choosing the least imperfect option. This attitude can be readily seen in Goodrich's behavior as a businessman and intellectual. The longevity of Goodrich's business meetings is legendary; it was not uncommon for them to last an entire day or even longer. He would probe and explore nearly every conceivable avenue to ensure that he had as firm a grasp of the particulars as possible in order to make a wise business decision or to analyze the work of an employee or specialist. "He wanted all the details and you had [better] be well prepared," said Richard H. Swallow, chief engineer of the Ayrshire Collieries Corporation for three decades (telephone interview, December 20, 1992).

45. Arlene Metz, interview, November 10, 1992.

46. Goodrich's preoccupation with German wines is a good example of his tremendous curiosity. Helen Fletcher wrote:

> Mr. Goodrich may have been a teetotaler in his younger years, but, by the time I came to work with him in 1957, he had developed an appreciation of fine wines and had several loose-leaf notebooks (which continued to grow in size) that contained the labels of wine bottles along with comments about where and with whom he had drunk each particular bottle of wine. I believe it was Henry Regnery who introduced Mr. Goodrich to the vineyards and some of the vintners along the Moselle River at the time of one of the early Mont Pelerin meetings. Mr. Goodrich revisited this area and other wine-producing areas during his various trips to

Although he did not embrace organized religion to any great degree as an adult, he was a student of most of the great world religions. Many acquaintances commented on Goodrich's vast knowledge of Greek Orthodoxy and Eastern mysticism, but he was equally knowledgeable about mainstream Christian faiths. When Goodrich arranged in 1972 to meet with John Waltz, a new Winchester town councilman at the time, one of the first things he wanted to know was Waltz's church affiliation.

"When I told him I belonged to the Disciples of Christ Church," said Waltz, "Pierre told me all about the history of the denomination, how the Disciples had evolved from earlier Christian denominations. His knowledge was amazing."[47]

One year before Christmas in the 1930s, Goodrich studied the motions of galaxies and calculated what the sky must have looked like in the year of Christ's birth. He then had Roy Barnes, a local Winchester artist and Goodrich company employee, design a Christmas card with the stars' configuration on the cover. Goodrich had the card printed and sent to family members and friends.[48] This is just one example of

---

> Europe. Mr. Goodrich was fortunate that the original owner of his home on Central Avenue was a wine lover and had a wine cellar built into his house. Therefore, Mr. Goodrich was able to store the wines which he liked. These were not necessarily well-known or expensive wines—they were wines he liked. Wine was a special part of good meals, and was drunk as an accompaniment to the meal as it is in Europe. I never saw Mr. Goodrich overindulge. I don't recall seeing Mr. Goodrich drink a mixed-drink at any occasion. . . . (Letter to author, June 18, 1996)

William H. Fletcher also recalled Goodrich's incredible array of interests. "He was intensely interested in everything that went on around him, and business was part of that. It was not a separate part of life, but it was part of the whole thing . . ." (interview by William C. Dennis, January 25, 1991).

47. John Waltz, interview, March 6, 1993. Goodrich's detailed knowledge of the Bible went all the way back to childhood. His mother taught a boys' Sunday school class when Pierre was a youth, and he would spend hours studying the Bible in preparation for one of her lessons (Rodney Medler, interview, June 9, 1993).

48. Roy Barnes, interview, February 8, 1992; James Emison, telephone interview, April 16, 1993. Emison, whose father was a law partner of Goodrich at the time, remembers receiving the card and hearing his father telling him how Pierre had designed its front.

how fascinated he could become with an idea or concept once it piqued his curiosity.[49]

49. Another example of this behavior is when Goodrich became extremely interested in cooking during one European trip in the late 1950s. He subsequently returned to his Indianapolis home and filled his kitchen with expensive copper cooking pots and learned as much about the preparation of fine cuisine as he could (Rodney Medler, interview, June 9, 1993).

Chapter 31

Defining Influences

> The little world of childhood with its familiar surroundings is a model of the greater world. The more intensively the family has stamped its character upon the child, the more it will tend to feel and see its earlier miniature world again in the bigger world of adult life. Naturally this is not a conscious, intellectual process.
>
> CARL JUNG, *The Theory of Psychoanalysis*

IF, AS SOCIOLOGISTS and psychologists tell us, individual character and values are formed at an early age, what does Pierre Goodrich's upbringing reveal about him? Was there anything unique about his childhood and adolescent years that could explain his deep convictions and strong personality, or were these qualities achieved through experiences in later life?

Pierre F. Goodrich grew up in Winchester, Indiana, at the turn of the twentieth century and lived there until he was eighteen. He returned home at the age of twenty-five to practice law for the next three years of his life (1920–23). For Pierre, growing up in a small Hoosier town was nearly idyllic. His adolescence was filled with Tom Sawyer–like experiences, complete with opportunities for youthful adventure: fishing, sports and games, family outings, travel, and challenging intellectual pleasures.

Winchester was an incredibly homogeneous community and part of an almost equally homogeneous state. The town is located ten miles west of Ohio, near the beginning of what the Delaware Indians called the Wapahani (White River). At the time, Winchester was populated almost entirely by people of German, Irish, and English descent—no Jewish families and few blacks or Catholics.[1] It was a world where a young boy had a great sense of security and support, crime was rare, people left their front doors unlocked, and distinctions between right and wrong were made early and often. Moreover, northern European cultural, social, and religious influences, especially Germanic notions of strict discipline, duty, and obedience to authority, were significant.[2]

The institutions that became an integral part of the Goodrich family's lives—church, family, government, finance, and business—were all within a short distance of their homes. They were constant physical reminders of turn-of-the-century midwestern values. For instance, Pierre's elementary and high schools were literally just down the street; in them, he gained an exceptionally fine early education.[3] His grandmother, Elizabeth Goodrich; his kindergarten teacher and great aunt, Belle Edger; all four of his uncles and their families; and friends such as the Millers, the McCamishes, the Moormans, and the Jaquas lived within two blocks of his home. The Presbyterian church he attended was located across the street; the county courthouse and jail were two blocks west; the town library was two blocks north.

Moreover, Pierre's father and his uncle Edward were presidents of

1. In the 1990 United States Census Bureau survey, residents of Randolph County listed their ancestry as German, 35.8 percent; Irish, 18.5 percent; English, 17.3 percent; American, 10.2 percent; Dutch, 4.3 percent. See *Muncie (Ind.) Star*, December 21, 1996, p. 1, col. 8.

2. The strong German influence can be seen in an account in James Watson's *As I Knew Them*. According to Watson, when he first ran for the United States House of Representatives in 1894 (the year Pierre was born), he was successful in defeating an incumbent of thirty years' standing because he gave many of his speeches in German, the native language of many of his constituents. Watson had learned German from a boyhood friend (p. 6). Winchester's midwestern value system is even more obvious when it is recalled that it is less than twenty-five miles east of Muncie, Indiana, the town that was chosen for a decade-long sociology study in the 1920s and 1930s by Robert S. and Helen Merrell Lynd because it represented "Middletown, U.S.A."

3. At Winchester High School, Goodrich's curriculum included chemistry, geometry, United States and world history, Latin, philosophy, astronomy, calculus, trigonometry, English literature, and music, among other subjects.

two of the town's most prominent banks. As to the spiritual life of the town, the Society of Friends meetinghouse, the Congregational church, the Disciples of Christ church, the Methodist church, and, of course, the Presbyterian church were all part of the neighborhood where Pierre grew up. Finally, there were the important institutions of politics and the military. Winchester and Randolph County, probably even more than most small rural American communities of the time, were deeply patriotic and political around the turn of the century. It was a community that had produced five Civil War generals.[4] Nearly twenty-four hundred men (approximately one of every twelve residents) from the county had fought for the Union cause; despite deep opposition to violence, Quaker parents who were fervent abolitionists sent their sons off to fight against slavery. As a boy, Pierre would have known Civil War veterans such as John Macy, Sr., and Charles Jaqua, who shared

4. Four of the five men who became Union generals from Randolph County went on to have outstanding political careers. They were all living when James Goodrich was a young man, and they would have been well known to him, if not personally, then by reputation. Isaac P. Gray was a state senator for Randolph County (1869–73), governor of Indiana (1884–88), and United States ambassador to Mexico (1893–95); Thomas M. Browne served as chief clerk of the State Senate (1861), state senator (1863–65), Republican candidate for governor (1872), prosecuting attorney, and United States representative from the Sixth Congressional District (1876–90). Browne gave James Goodrich an appointment to the United States Naval Academy in 1881. Silas Colgrove, a colonel in the Twenty-seventh Indiana Cavalry, passed a stolen copy of General Robert E. Lee's orders to General George McClellan, which resulted in the bloody battle at Antietam in September 1862. He later became a brigadier general but gained national prominence as the president of the military commission that tried the celebrated case of Horsey, Milligan, and Bowles, three Hoosier Knights of the Golden Circle who were accused of treason. He also served as state representative from Randolph County (1857–61) and Randolph County circuit judge (1873–79). Asahel Stone served as state representative (1848–49 and 1871–73) and state senator of Randolph County (1861–63) and was president of the Randolph County Bank in Winchester for more than twenty-five years; Jonathan Cranor, the least distinguished of Randolph County's five generals, later moved to Ohio, where he was elected to the Ohio state legislature in 1868. He moved back to Randolph County in 1872, where he operated a hardware store and served as a state deputy marshal. See "General Cranor" (summarizes the careers of all five men), *Randolph County History: 1818–1990*, pp. 211–12.

wondrous stories about the battles at Chickamauga, Gettysburg, and Antietam.

This spirit and pride in military service spilled over into community celebrations. The two largest community events each year were Decoration Day (now Memorial Day) and the Fourth of July. On these important public holidays, thousands of townspeople gathered along Winchester's broad streets. The main event was a jubilant parade in which bands played and regiments of the Grand Army of the Republic (Civil War veterans) marched from villages all over the county to the Winchester town square. On July 21, 1892, for instance, at the ceremony marking the dedication of the county's Civil War Soldiers and Sailors Monument, an estimated fifteen thousand people appeared, including Oliver P. Morton, Indiana's Civil War governor, who grew up in nearby Centerville, Indiana. On October 11, 1900, an estimated ten thousand people welcomed Teddy Roosevelt to Winchester. Such patriotic gatherings—complete with windy speeches made with great spirit and love of country—continued well into the twentieth century.

Furthermore, politics was a religion in the small community, celebrated with as much enthusiasm and reverence as a country church's gospel revival. At least four men who had formerly held the office of president (Benjamin Harrison, Theodore Roosevelt, William Howard Taft, and Herbert Hoover) visited Winchester during Pierre's lifetime. The county had produced two governors (including James Goodrich) and a powerful United States congressman and senator (James Watson). Two men from the county also ran for president of the United States (Watson, in 1928; and Isaac Gray, who lost Democratic nominations to Grover Cleveland, in 1892, and to William Jennings Bryan, in 1896). Most of the time, Pierre's father held leadership positions in the Republican Party at the county, state, or national level. Moreover, dozens of other men from Winchester held federal or state office positions, men such as Thomas Browne, John Macy, Sr., Enos Watson, Leander Monks, and Union B. Hunt, mentors of James Goodrich's and names with whom Pierre would be very familiar.

I offer this brief local history to show the reader the rich environment in which the Goodriches grew up. The town's institutions provided them with structure and support. I believe that these institutions emotionally and psychologically reinforced a value system that remained with Pierre into adulthood, but which he saw during his own lifetime severely strained and weakened. Times and conditions are so different today that it is difficult for most of us to appreciate the spirit, stability, and fraternity of community, family, church, and political involvement that existed during Goodrich's formative years.

Pierre Goodrich grew up in a town where, if you were from a prominent family like his, almost everyone knew you. They knew your parents and probably your extended family. There were considerable societal pressures to conform to widely accepted customs; moreover, virtues such as honesty, integrity in business, and responsibility to one's family and friends were also of serious import. How one was perceived and how one behaved were indivisible. The following excerpt about James Goodrich from a local history book published in 1914 tells us much:

> Personally, James P. Goodrich is a gentleman of the strictest integrity, and his private character and important trusts have always been above reproach. . . . He has so impressed his individuality upon his county and state as to win the confidence and esteem of his fellow-citizens and has become a strong and influential power in leading them to high and noble things. Measured by the accepted standard of excellence, his career, though strenuous, has been eminently honorable and useful, and his life fraught with great good to his fellows and to the world. Unpretending as to piety, yet few men more dutifully fulfill the Master's command to care for the needy—to minister unto the sick, clothe the naked, feed the hungry and speak cheer to those in prison. Many the circumstances in which his left hand knoweth not the generosity of his right. In fact, Mr. Goodrich is a well-rounded man in all directions, keen in business, forceful in public counsel, decisive in action, faithful to confidences reposed in him, a friend and well-wisher of all human kind.[5]

5. John L. Smith and Lee L. Driver, *Past and Present of Randolph County, Indiana* (Indianapolis: A. W. Bowen, 1914), pp. 1523–24.

One's first reaction, of course, is "what tripe!" No one could be that virtuous, and clearly whoever wrote this biography (probably Lee L. Driver, former superintendent of schools in Winchester) should have his head examined. One's second reaction, upon slight reflection, is that the passage simply reflects the oratory of the time, the tendency toward flowery, exaggerated language. But let me suggest a third interpretation that does not necessarily contradict either of the first two observations. Who one was and how one was perceived were extremely important. If one did not live up to the esteem that one had in the community, he could lose face. The anonymity of contemporary life clearly mitigates this pressure.

Late in life, Pierre Goodrich recalled what it meant to be a small-town lawyer. In such a position, an attorney served as "an officer of the Court," morally an agent of the judicial system, responsible for furthering truth and not obscuring it.[6] Again, I believe the cynicism of modern society, in which to many the idea of lawyering and justice appear to be incompatible, hinders our understanding. Perhaps the atmosphere of the time was best captured in a letter written by a townswoman, Ella Clark. In November 1920, she wrote a young Winchester man, William Bales, who was then a student at the University of Michigan School of Law:

> My Dear Bill,
>
> There was much said about the dignity of the Randolph County Court and how it stood in the eyes of the state. I was glad to hear it and when I thought of the young lawyers at the bar and soon-to-be, John Macy, Pierre Goodrich, and yourself, with your father as judge of the Court[, it] makes me feel that as good as it may have been, the dignity will not only be maintained but the standard raised.[7]

6. Letter from Goodrich to F. A. Hayek, December 24, 1970. F. A. Hayek Collection, box 43, folder 22, Archives, Hoover Institution, Stanford, California.

7. See Miriam Halbert Bales, *We Pass the Words Along: A 300-Year Chronicle of the Bales Family* (Muncie, Ind.: privately printed, 1984), p. 166. Ella Clark wrote the letter on November 16, 1920, to William Bales, who was engaged to Mrs. Clark's adopted daughter, Jenny Jessup.

I believe that Winchester—like most small towns of turn-of-the-century America—was a bastion of moral rectitude. Practicing attorneys with no formal legal education and law school graduates alike did not take classes or bar examinations in ethics. (Now, it seems that every profession from accountancy to real estate requires courses and seminars on morals and civility.)[8] At the turn of the century, people were brought up in an atmosphere of religious and societal commitments, and they were expected to observe high standards of personal and professional moral conduct. I do not suggest that scandal and exploitation did not take place, but merely observe that they were rare. The scandalous and the exploitative risked being ostracized by the community, and the community was their world. Standards of responsibility were inculcated into an individual by family (nuclear and extended), church, neighbors, and business mentors. The idea that laws or a watchdog agency was necessary to coerce compliance with professional standards seemed alien to many businessmen of that day. It is clear that many people, including Pierre Goodrich, never accepted that such things were necessary, despite recognizing the abuses that brought such laws and agencies into existence.

Pierre's view of personal responsibility is perhaps best reflected by the "gentlemen's rule" that exists even today at Wabash College. Wabash does not have elaborate rules of conduct, as do many—perhaps most—institutions of higher learning. Rather than specifying what is appropriate student behavior, Wabash's code simply states: "The student is expected to conduct himself, at all times, both on and off the campus, as

8. See Richard B. Schmitt, "Ethics Courses for Lawyers Draw Comers," *Wall Street Journal,* July 8, 1993, sec. B, p. 2, col. 2. At least one professional has realized the futility of teaching ethics as a series of "rules": "For an ethics specialist, Mr. [Michael] Daigneault has surprisingly little use for the traditional rules of the game governing attorney conduct. Most of the rules, he says, are useless or ambiguous in guiding attorneys through the ethical minefields they face on a daily basis. Instead, he teaches virtues, and his lectures tend to be sprinkled with Kant, Confucius, and the Bible, rather than black-letter law" (ibid.).

a gentleman and a responsible citizen."[9] I think that Pierre Goodrich believed that any further elaboration or coercion of conduct (prior to a wrong being done) was unnecessary.

But the institutions that helped shape James and Pierre Goodrich's beliefs and personalities have been severely eroded. Societal changes that took place during Pierre's lifetime (and to a much lesser degree during his father's) have dramatically decreased the influence of family, the church, the community, and the sense of patriotism and moral certitude that helped form people's professional and personal behaviors. As a result, government has been viewed by those in political power—who are forced to deal with problems when others in society cannot or will not—as the remaining vehicle that can shore up the gaps that have developed as a result of the erosion of other character-forming institutions.

The erosion of family, church, and community can be readily seen. In James's and Pierre's young lives, family members and friends lived in proximity to one another. But today, family members and "close friends" (emotionally and psychologically speaking) are apt to live thousands of miles away. Neighbors, who are apt to be strangers, often have little to do with meeting emotional and psychological needs. Moreover, the increased acceptance of mobility and moral relativity has made it much easier for individuals to avoid family and community responsibilities. In a less mobile and more closed society, individuals accepted (or at least tolerated) those responsibilities.

Therefore, I believe the role of the extended family in the lives of James and Pierre Goodrich was extremely important, as the role that John Macy, Sr., had in serving as a mentor to James Goodrich, both as a young lawyer and politician, indicates. And even though James Goodrich was gone from home during a considerable period of Pierre's adolescence, Pierre had the constant support of his uncles and aunts,

9. As quoted in Suzanne McBride, "Incoming Wabash Chief Plans Healing," *Indianapolis News,* June 14, 1993, sec. A, p. 10, col. 3.

his grandmother, his great-aunts, his cousins, and his friends. They all lived a few houses away. Is it any wonder that Pierre felt such a strong bond with and commitment to his family when he was placed in charge of the Goodrich financial empire in the 1940s?

In contrast to the community in which James and Pierre Goodrich grew up is modern society. In the latter, there is a tendency for the individual to draw inward, not to see himself or herself as part of a larger community. The individual, sensing isolation and the relativity of all judgment, is no longer guided by community and religious standards, but makes himself or herself the measure of all things. As a result, personal gratification and narcissistic pleasure become the primary pursuit of the individual.[10] Is it any wonder that drug and alcohol addiction, divorce, crime, greed, and a sense of isolation and loneliness have come to be identified with modern times?

The decreasing significance and changing role of the church in people's lives is another contributing factor. Quite simply, the church today does not function as it did in earlier generations. Society is suffering from the loss of commitment both to the institution and to the Christian ethic it extolled.

> A review of the history of Protestantism in the Western world indicates that most new religious bodies originally were organized around a call to a high level of religious commitment. . . . As the decades roll past, the natural institutional tendency is to drift away from that call to high commitment. Gradually the focus shifts from Christian commitment to "taking care of the members." Kinship and friendship ties, local traditions, institutional survival goals, real estate concerns and seniority replace Christian commitment as the guiding force in making decisions.[11]

All one has to do is look at Pierre Goodrich and his ancestry to see how true this observation is. Pierre's grandmother, Elizabeth Goodrich,

10. See Joseph Beroff, Elizabeth Douvan, and Richard Kulka, *The Inner American: A Self-Portrait from 1957 to 1976* (New York: Basic Books, 1981), pp. 14–25.

11. Lyle E. Schaller, *Twenty-one Bridges to the Twenty-first Century* (Nashville: Abingdon Press, 1994), p. 25.

was a founding member of Pierre's home church. James and Cora Goodrich were Sunday school teachers in that church for more than twenty-five years. The First Presbyterian Church of Winchester was a focal point of spiritual and social engagements for the entire Goodrich family. Yet the church's significance faded during Pierre's own lifetime. He himself admitted that he was a "backslid Presbyterian." Pierre spoke and wrote in euphemistic terms about the "infinite creator," but nowhere in his writings or during discussions I had with his associates and family did I learn that Pierre had deep spiritual convictions. He was a scholar of the Bible and extremely knowledgeable about world religions, but his pursuit of the spiritual always seemed to be scholastic, detached, and unemotional. Goodrich lamented that the modern clergy spent much of its time preaching the social (political) gospel of the times (civil rights and equality), yet there is no indication that he thought that the preaching of the traditional gospel would have a transforming effect as powerful as that of an understanding based on a study of secular thinkers such as Kant, Locke, and Lord Acton.

The above observations are not meant to criticize the Goodrich family, but to show how growing secularization drastically changed people's beliefs and deeply altered society during Pierre Goodrich's lifetime. Society's problems are so widespread that even small-town America is not exempt from them.[12] Moreover, in the past fifty years, government has

12. The Goodriches' hometown of Winchester, Indiana, I believe, represents what has happened culturally, economically, and socially throughout America in the past seventy years. Whereas the physical appearance of Winchester has changed little from the time Pierre Goodrich was a boy, if one digs beyond the veneer of the town, the community is vastly different from the one Pierre left in the mid 1920s. At that time, in Pierre's home county, single-parenting as a result of never being married or divorced was extremely rare. In 1990, however, although there was essentially no change in population since 1900, there were 882 single mothers in Randolph County; there were also 234 single fathers raising children. Crime in Randolph County has exploded. Not long ago the Randolph County circuit and superior courts had approximately fifteen hundred pending misdemeanor and felony cases. Randolph County is not unique. I would suggest that if you look at nearly any other community in America you will find similar statistics. The number of people who live together, drift apart, marry, divorce, live to-

allocated vast resources in an attempt to deal with the social crises society now faces, often with negligible results.[13]

---

gether with another, marry again, move to another city or town, get another job, and have several live-in relationships is staggering.

Economically, the figures are telling as well. In Winchester in 1945, there were 152 retail stores and other business establishments within a one-block radius of the county courthouse. Today, there are fewer than 45. A Wal-Mart and other smaller discount stores in a strip mall east of town have put dozens of stores out of business. There were at least thirty "mom and pop" corner groceries in 1945; today, there are three convenience stores owned by out-of-town business chains.

The change in the town's makeup is even more dramatic. Just across the street from the courthouse is a Chinese restaurant where the owners and employees speak Mandarin. A Mexican restaurant is located down the street. Three computer businesses exist in town. Whereas the town square was once filled on Friday and Saturday nights with farmers and others who had come to town to do their trading and gossiping, now the streets on weekends are empty, and the stores close on Friday afternoon and do not reopen until the following Monday. Even the television antennas that dotted the airspace in the 1960s are gone, replaced by cable and satellite dishes.

Randolph County has consistently had the highest unemployment rate of any county in the state over the past several years. Whereas the Industrial Revolution did not come to the county until well into the twentieth century, within the past twenty years, the county has lost more than five thousand relatively high-paying blue-collar jobs. The four largest employers are owned by companies out of state, one a French corporation (a glass company), another a South African one (Union City Body Company). Men and women who had high-paying jobs have either had to move to the larger cities or accept minimum-wage service jobs. Alcoholism, divorce, children born out of wedlock, drugs, and crime have come to be a way of life for many small-town and rural people. What was once seen as the bedrock of America, this country's small towns, complete with their Judeo-Christian belief system, has eroded to such an extent that the moral, and oftentimes physical, landscape of small-town America is little different from that of Detroit, Chicago, Los Angeles, or New York.

13. In Randolph County, Indiana, the following social and economic agencies providing human services exist today (remember that this is a county of only twenty-seven thousand people): the Randolph County Division of Family and Children (food stamps, Aid for Dependent Children, juvenile and family services); the Randolph County Literacy Coalition; the Jay County–Randolph County Developmental Council (workshops for adults with mental disabilities); Randolph County Services, Inc. (agency for the handicapped and aging); Women, Infants and Children, Inc.; the Randolph County Extension Office; Randolph County Homemaker Services; the Randolph County Community and Economic Development Foundation; the Randolph County Home (for the

Pierre Goodrich strongly challenged the trend against the growing statism that he saw. An examination of his heritage holds, I believe, at least a partial explanation. The idea of commitment to something outside oneself (family, community, neighbors, objective truth, and so forth) was inculcated in Goodrich and his family. What frustrated Goodrich was that he saw the power of the state over individuals' lives growing in an attempt to shore up ideals and institutions. The state behaves in this way in order to provide at least some nominal guidance in people's lives. Goodrich recognized, however, that the state merely compels people to act in a certain way without requiring the individual to understand why. The state does this almost solely by sanctions (for example, laws, taxes, and police) or by incentives (for example, social services and subsidies). It does little to educate people about citizenship. Goodrich believed that the use of coercion is in direct opposition to the exercise of individual understanding and will.[14]

---

elderly); the Randolph County Health Department; the Randolph County Step Ahead program; Headstart; Jobs Training Partnership Agency; Vocational Rehabilitation; the Dunn Mental Health Clinic; the Division of Disability, Aging and Rehabilitative Services; the Social Security Office; Area Six Community and Senior Services, Inc. (providing Meals on Wheels and nutrition sites for elderly); the Veterans Services Office; the Randolph County Weatherization Project; and the Victims Assistance Program. All of these organizations are either totally funded or receive some funding from federal, state, or local tax sources. The number of private social service agencies for drug and alcohol addiction, marriage and family counseling, and financial consultation is nearly as large. For a more thorough discussion of these services, see "Step Ahead Invites Community Interest," *Winchester (Ind.) News-Gazette,* November 27, 1996, p. 1, col. 3.

14. I believe that Pierre Goodrich was fully aware of the causes of the growth of the state. I also believe, however, that he may have overestimated the ability of the average individual to comprehend and withstand the incredible changes, complexities, and isolation produced by our modern technology-driven society. To his credit, I think Goodrich realized that ideas about liberty and our nation's heritage have to be kept alive if our society is not to lapse into a kind of modern Dark Ages.

Chapter 32

Why Did They Work So Hard? Work, Ideas, Citizenship, and Virtue

The following statements are therefore true: "Good works do not make a good man, but a good man does good works; evil works do not make a wicked man, but a wicked man does evil works." Consequently it is always necessary that the substance or person himself be good before there can be any good works, and that good works follow and proceed from the good person, as Christ also says, "A good tree cannot bear evil fruit, nor can a bad tree bear good fruit" [Matt. 7:18].

MARTIN LUTHER, "The Freedom of a Christian"

[As a result of the Reformation and Luther] one thing was unquestionably new: the valuation of the fulfillment of duty in worldly affairs as the highest form which the moral activity of the individual could assume. This it was which inevitably gave every-day worldly activity a religious significance. . . . That was [man's] calling.

MAX WEBER, *The Protestant Ethic and the Spirit of Capitalism*

LIFE GRANTS nothing to us mortals without hard work," wrote Horace, the Latin lyric poet, more than two thousand years ago.[1] But why was work so important to the Goodrich family? What did it give them besides material comforts?

With all the political expertise possessed by his father, why did Pierre not become directly involved in politics? He had the money, the poten-

1. Horace, *Satires,* 1.9, 59.

tial for name recognition, and the intelligence. Perhaps most important, he wanted to be influential.

A political life was never in the cards for Pierre. First, he simply would not have been any good at it. He was much too shy and private to subject himself to the public spotlight. Pierre was not the hand-grabbing, back-slapping type. Second, politics is a means of compelling people to act in accord with some collective decision. While Pierre was intensely interested in changing human behavior, he wanted people to change as a result of their own volition, through a proper understanding of the rights and duties of citizenship. He thought he could best accomplish this end through education. Third, politics involves compromise, and Pierre Goodrich was uncompromising. "Mr. Goodrich would often say," recalled Rosanna Amos, "be reasonable—do it my way."[2] Before Goodrich reached a decision, he gave most matters such tremendous thought that he would have been frustrated with constituents or politicians who did not. Finally, Goodrich would not have tolerated politics' most evident pitfall—its lack of candor. While he could be diplomatic, he was just as apt to be blunt. Pierre was not one to shrink from stating what he believed to be the truth, even if the listener was not prepared to hear it.[3]

If a political career was not right for Pierre, why did he become a businessman? Why did he not pursue a career as an economics professor or a big-city lawyer or a stockbroker? Why did he not just forgo a professional life altogether and sip gin-and-tonics at some Mediterranean villa? He certainly did not have to work. Why, then, did achieving success as a businessman become his consuming passion? Why did he, his father, and the Goodrich family in general "devote their best energies for long hours day after day to this driving activity [work] seem-

2. Rosanna Amos, interview, December 10, 1993.

3. William H. Fletcher told William C. Dennis, "[Pierre Goodrich] had reservations about all of us. I don't think there were absolutely any exceptions and, fortunately or unfortunately, he would talk about you face to face and not always in the absence of the individual . . ." (interview, January 25, 1991).

ingly so foreign to many of the most powerful impulses of human beings"?[4]

Pierre Goodrich's occupational choice had much to do with following in his father's footsteps. The Goodrich family had controlling interests in several companies long before Pierre came on the scene; someone had to be James Goodrich's successor if the family financial empire was to endure. Pierre was the best person to step into his father's shoes. He had served as his father's business disciple for nearly twenty years and was a direct beneficiary of his father's (and to a lesser extent his uncles') hard work and tremendous foresight. After James Goodrich died in 1940, running the family financial empire was Pierre's life's work. To succeed his father as head of the Goodrich companies or on the board of Wabash College was an honor and a great responsibility.

But more important, Pierre's occupation and ambitions gave expression to his enculturation. The manner in which he approached business and life suggests that a distinct belief system, instilled in him at a young age, dominated his thinking and actions. This enculturation may be only partially explained by John Maynard Keynes's observation in 1925 that "our age is concerned with the Love of Money, with the habitual appeal to the Money Motive [being] nine-tenths of the activities of life, with the universal striving after individual economic security as the prime object of endeavor, with the social approbation of money as the measure of constructive success, and with the social appeal to the hoarding instinct as the foundation of the necessary provision for the family and for the future."[5]

Money, as Keynes observes, means security to the individual; it also produces a sense of power and well-being, and is an indicator of success. Perhaps the most stimulating emotion it creates is simply the thrill of making it. I believe, however, that, for the Goodrich family, wealth possessed another significance that equaled or exceeded all the others combined.

4. Quote taken from Robert S. Lynd and Helen Merrell Lynd, *Middletown: A Study in Contemporary American Culture* (New York: Harcourt, Brace, 1929), p. 73.

5. "Soviet Russia—III," *New Republic,* November 11, 1925, pp. 301–2.

How this yet-to-be fully described belief system was instilled in Pierre might be best seen in the wedding gift his parents gave him in July 1920. Whereas many wealthy parents might give their newlywed son an expensive new car or pay for a lavish honeymoon, James and Cora Goodrich gave Pierre an investment—ten thousand dollars in stock in a coal company.[6] Although later in life Pierre stayed at expensive hotels when he traveled, in general, his lifestyle was simple and frugal. His Indianapolis home was one of the finest examples of classical Georgian design anywhere, yet for a man of his considerable wealth it was rather modest.[7] To Pierre, the most valuable items in his home were his Stradivarius violin and a first edition of Adam Smith's *Wealth of Nations.*[8] Goodrich drove expensive cars (Lincolns and Mercedes-Benzes), but he could have had a fleet of cars. Former Wabash president Byron Trippet recalls:

> In fairness to Pierre, it should be remembered that he was a prudent, almost puritanical steward of his money. There was nothing religious or sanctimonious about his puritanism. It reflected simply his own notion of how wealth should be conserved and used. There was nothing ostentatious or frivolous about his life style. He dressed carelessly and casually in conservative taste. . . . [His home] had an austere kind of beauty about it, but nothing lavish was displayed. . . . From [his] life style . . . , no one would guess that Pierre was a multimillionaire.[9]

6. See "Cravens Accepts Coal Challenge," *Indianapolis Star,* July 20, 1920, p. 1, col. 3. In the article, James Goodrich admits that he had bought ten thousand dollars' worth of stock in the LeNoir Coal Company (owned by Jesse Moorman) and had given it to his son as a wedding present.

7. See "Indianapolis Architecture" (and accompanying picture), *Indianapolis Star,* July 18, 1976, p. 15, col. 1.

8. Bettina Bien Greaves, telephone interview, October 16, 1992. Greaves said that when she and Leonard Read visited Pierre at his home on Central Avenue, the first edition of Adam Smith's *Wealth of Nations* (1776) was the thing Goodrich was most proud to show them.

9. Byron Trippet, "Pierre F. Goodrich," in *Wabash on My Mind,* p. 184. Pierre's parents' house and lifestyle were much the same. In a 1976 article, Josephine Friedrich, a German-born woman James and Cora Goodrich brought back with them from their trip to Russia in 1923, recalled the couple's "plain" living. Friedrich lived with James and

To have enjoyed an indulgent, ostentatious life would have been completely against Goodrich's moral and religious upbringing. To that extent, I disagree with Trippet's appraisal that there was "nothing religious or sanctimonious about [Pierre's] puritanism." James, Pierre, and the Goodrich family in general did not work to gain greater wealth for personal consumption; their passion for work (and Pierre's passion for ideas) had religious roots. In large measure, the Goodriches' outward demeanor fit closely with the German sociologist Max Weber's "ideal-type" of the capitalist entrepreneur:

> He avoids ostentation and unnecessary expenditure, as well as conscious enjoyment of his power, and is embarrassed by the outward signs of the social recognition which he receives. His manner of life is . . . distinguished by a certain ascetic tendency. . . . It is, namely, by no means exceptional, but rather the rule, for him to have a sort of modesty. . . . He gets nothing out of his wealth for himself, except the irrational sense of having done his job well.[10]

I believe that work and the wealth that it produced was a form of worldly asceticism for James, Pierre, and, in large measure, the entire Goodrich family. Work was a virtuous activity, but the Protestant notion of ascetic propriety "acted powerfully against the spontaneous enjoyment of possessions, it restricted consumption, especially of luxuries."[11] Max Weber's major thesis is that the Reformation (including Luther's and Calvin's radical teachings, which largely brought it about) made the accumulation of wealth not only acceptable, but a sign of godly approval.[12] But wealth is not primarily, as the Protestant reform-

---

Cora Goodrich from 1923 to 1928 as a companion to Mrs. Goodrich. She recalled that the Goodriches remained nonaristocrats who mostly spent their time reading and studying, and who were unaffected by their possessions and powerful friends. See R. Alan Rice, "The Governor James P. Goodrich Home—Its Past, Present, Future," *Winchester (Ind.) News-Gazette,* October 13, 1976, p. 8.

10. Weber, *The Protestant Ethic and the Spirit of Capitalism,* p. 71.

11. Ibid., pp. 170–71.

12. In a letter that James Goodrich wrote to Cora from New Orleans in March 1895, he speaks disapprovingly of the southern city, which was very "worldly" in his eyes:

ers argued, for personal consumption and pleasure. As Pierre's longtime assistant Helen Schultz Fletcher stated, "Mr. Goodrich believed that we hold our assets in trust to our Creator, and that idea was a very important part of the philosophy back of his actions."[13] The Reverend Gustav Papperman, delivering the eulogy at James Goodrich's funeral in 1940, said much the same thing: "The Governor felt that he had been given talents that were a trust, that he was to administer them faithfully. . . . There was a firm religious basis on which his life was built."[14]

I think that there was an intimate correlation between James's and Pierre's religious and moral upbringings and their choice of professions and ambitions. I believe that this is true even though in later life Pierre did not embrace organized religion to any great degree. The Goodriches were stalwart members of their church dating back to at least Pierre's grandfather, John Baldwin Goodrich, who was superintendent of the Congregational church in Winchester. Pierre's paternal grandfather and grandmother attended school at the Winchester Seminary in the 1850s. There, devotions were as much a part of the curriculum as mathematics and spelling. Elizabeth Edger Goodrich also attended Liber College in the late 1850s, where moral teachings were the core of instruction, and was a founding member of the First Presbyterian Church of Winchester in 1882. As Liber College's president, Ebenezer Tucker, recalled in 1873, "The school has been noted for studiousness, integrity, love of freedom, absence of pride and naughtiness, unity of feeling."[15] Pierre's uncle Percy was a longtime superintendent of the Sunday school; James

"But finally believing as a Frenchman always does that happiness, and not 'serving God,' is the 'Chief End of Man' they [the founders of New Orleans] named one street 'Felicity,'" he wrote. Letter from James P. Goodrich to Cora Goodrich, March 13, 1895 (in the possession of Priscilla Klosterman, R.R. 2, Ridgeville, Ind.).

13. Letter from Helen Schultz Fletcher to author, June 18, 1996.

14. See "State, National Dignitaries Hear Goodrich Eulogized at Final Rites," *Indianapolis Star,* August 19, 1940, p. 3, col. 6. Papperman also said of the former governor: "He is a notable example of what a man can achieve in our country with hard work and ambition to succeed."

15. As quoted in Michael McBride, "College Long Gone, but History Still Strong," *Muncie (Ind.) Star Press,* January 3, 1997, sec. D, pp. 1–2.

Goodrich was an elder of the church and taught a men's Sunday school class for more than twenty-five years. Cora Goodrich was a Sunday school teacher and oversaw a boys' Bible study group of which Pierre was a member. Both she and Pierre were extremely knowledgeable about the Bible.[16] Pierre taught a young men's Sunday school class from 1920 to 1922. Pierre's other uncles and aunts also held leadership positions in the local Presbyterian church.[17]

As did other small midwestern towns of the late nineteenth and early twentieth centuries, Winchester, Indiana, reflected the religious values of the time. The separations between church, state, business, and family life simply were not as distinct or as great as they are today. The overwhelming majority of Protestant denominations, including the Goodrich family's Presbyterian church, embraced a strongly Calvinistic Christianity. It was an ethos that had originated in America with New England Puritans more than two centuries earlier and had been transported to the Midwest (via the Carolinas and Virginia) by pioneering families such as the Goodriches. For Pierre, that belief system was reinforced at Wabash College, where campus life for an ambitious student involved hard work, discipline, exposure to serious works, and mandatory daily chapel.[18]

The Goodriches' religious ethos was mixed with a Benjamin Franklin

16. In a letter from Calvin Goodrich to Pierre, it is evident that Pierre's knowledge of the Bible was substantial. Calvin writes: "Through Peckham, an old-time university associate, I learn that you are an authority on the Bible. I judge from his remark that you had cast something of awe upon him in this matter . . ." (letter, August 30, 1947, Black Mountain, N.C., in the possession of Perce G. Goodrich, Portland, Ind.).

17. A question that is probably unanswerable but would be worth examining is: What specific doctrines did James Goodrich teach Sunday after Sunday for twenty-five years to his men's Bible class at the Presbyterian church?

18. Up until World War I, and during the four years that Pierre was an undergraduate student (1912 to 1916), daily chapel was a mandatory morning activity Monday through Friday. See "Required Chapel," in *These Fleeting Years, 1832 to 1982* (Crawfordsville, Ind.: Wabash College, 1982), p. 168. The role of Presbyterian pioneer settlers and ministers in the early years of Indiana's formation is excellently presented in a book by L. C. Rudolph, *Hoosier Zion* (New Haven, Conn.: Yale University Press, 1963).

worldview that associated prosperity with the Victorian virtues—self-reliance, hard work, patriotism, frugality, cleanliness, and so on. In James Goodrich's "Russia Manuscript," he describes a simple but revealing encounter that occurred during his third visit to the Soviet Union. In May 1922, he had just entered the small village of Bezdona, which, he had been informed by everybody, was "the worst place in all famine-stricken Russia."

> Just before we arrived there we saw three peasant girls pulling weeds in a field and asked them how the crops were.
>
> "All right" was the reply.
>
> "Will you have enough food to go through the next year?" I inquired.
>
> "We have planted and cared for our crops," one of them answered. "The result is now in the hands of God."
>
> From the appearance of the crops and the number of people at work in the fields pulling weeds and hoeing I felt sure that God's answer would be an abundant crop and that no one would starve in this little commune. For God still helps those who help themselves.[19]

James Goodrich's last words are not biblical; they come straight from Benjamin Franklin's *Poor Richard's Almanack.*[20] This view of the world combines spiritual worthiness with worldly prosperity achieved by planning, hard work, thrift, and diligence. James Goodrich's view of governing was no different. During his four-year term as governor, he made "economy and efficiency" the overriding concerns of his administration.[21] Before the Reformation, the accumulation of wealth was

19. Goodrich, "Russia Manuscript," chap. P, pp. 5–6, James P. Goodrich Papers, box 16, Herbert Hoover Presidential Library, West Branch, Iowa.

20. "God helps them that help themselves" (Franklin, *Poor Richard's Almanack*).

21. James Goodrich's almost total preoccupation with this aspect of governing could also be seen in a negative light. In a 1919 history about the first century of Indiana statehood, the following statement was included in an otherwise positive account of his years as governor. "Perhaps the most common criticism of his (Goodrich's) administration thus far is of a lack of what may go to make a State worthy of admiration outside of success in a business way . . ." (Jacob Piatt Dunn, *Indiana and Indianans* [Chicago: American Historical Society, 1919], p. 785).

viewed as evil, but post-Reformation teachings gradually sanctioned such accumulation so long as it was not done dishonestly or with avarice. What was condemned was the "pursuit of riches for their own sake": "For wealth in itself was a temptation . . . , [but] the religious valuation of restless, continuous, systematic work in a worldly calling, as the highest means to asceticism, and at the same time the surest and most evident proof of rebirth and genuine faith, must have been the most powerful conceivable lever for the expansion of that attitude toward life which we have here called the spirit of capitalism."[22]

One need only reflect upon the Goodriches' various business operations to reach the conclusion that they had a passion for accumulation almost religious in its intensity. They did not pay high salaries to their employees, pay large dividends to their shareholders, or take large profits for themselves. They continually invested back into their companies a large percentage of the income the companies generated. This constant reinvestment, combined with their skillful management, made the Goodrich companies extremely valuable when they were ultimately sold.[23]

Moreover, from a practical perspective, the large capital growth of the companies was another reason Pierre was so concerned about inflationary policies. Much of the worth of the Goodrich companies (and of hard-earned wealth in general) would have been eroded if inflation had gotten out of hand, because capital gains were taxed at a very high rate. Pierre realized that inflation allows a taxing authority to drain resources from the private sector while not appearing to be confiscatory. In James Goodrich's "Russia Manuscript," he describes repeatedly the devastating effects that inflation had on the economy in post–civil war Russia,

22. Weber, *The Protestant Ethic and the Spirit of Capitalism*, pp. 171–72.

23. The author was told repeatedly by former employees that the Goodrich family paid low wages at their various companies. Indeed, as mentioned in chapter 16, I believe it was one reason why they were not held in high esteem by some people in the communities where they did their business. Howard Melander, comptroller of Indiana Telephone Corporation, 1967 to 1971, interview, December 12, 1995; letter from Martha Wharton to author, December 14, 1995.

where inflation wreaked havoc by making the ruble nearly worthless. Pierre would have known about this directly from his father. He also knew about the ruinous effects of inflation in revolutionary France in the 1780s and in pre–World War II Germany.

The spirit of capitalism is not unique to the Goodrich family. The Protestant aesthetic that favored investment and accumulation over consumption and dissipation is what made America a great economic power in the nineteenth and twentieth centuries. But the Goodrich family is a particularly interesting case.

Education was a large part of the Goodriches' work ethos. Almost all of the Goodrich money ended up supporting education in one form or another: Wabash College, Hanover College, Butler University, Oakland City University, the University of Notre Dame, the Presbyterian Seminary of Chicago, Liberty Fund, the Great Books Foundation, the Foundation for Economic Education, the Institute for Intercollegiate Studies, the China Institute of America, and on and on. The family viewed education as a process by virtue of which the individual remained informed, made better business decisions, learned the importance of citizenship, and was given an opportunity for individual self-improvement. Therefore, work and education became the centerpieces of the Goodrich family's ethical and practical life. An examination of Pierre's customary twelve- to fourteen-hour business day reveals that he made little, if any, distinction between work and avocational interests.[24] He was almost always engaged in a process of understanding, whether it was about squeezing greater profits from his coal operations, studying some classic text, or clarifying and refining his thinking by writing lengthy letters. I think that is why making a decision was such an arduous task for Pierre—he seldom thought he understood something well enough to reach a conclusion about it. Moreover, I cannot recall study-

24. William H. Fletcher, who worked closely with Goodrich from 1960 to 1972, stated: "[Pierre Goodrich] was intensely interested in everything that went on around him, and business was part of that. It was not a separate part of life, but it was part of the whole thing . . ." (interview by William C. Dennis, January 25, 1991).

ing another individual whose thoughts and actions were so intimately fused. It was not simply that Pierre Goodrich had a tendency to think or speak in a stream-of-consciousness manner; to a large degree, his life was lived in that manner.

Goodrich's preoccupation with ideas is very interesting. He applied his ideas while making practical business decisions in a complex, highly developed way, which was not always true of his father. Although James Goodrich was a highly intelligent and savvy businessman and politician, he was not an intellectual, as Pierre was. James was a technician. As Richard Hofstadter writes in his Pulitzer Prize–winning book *Anti-intellectualism in American Life,* the successful professional man must have a substantial store of knowledge and an acquired stock of mental skills, but he exercises his knowledge and skills primarily for the "pursuit of externally determined ends." That was James Goodrich: businessman, politician, community leader. He applied information and knowledge to address practical external problems.[25]

Pierre also had a practical side, as his highly successful years as president, CEO, director, and significant stockholder of dozens of companies indicate. At the same time, however, Pierre's pursuit of ideas took on a character and meaning of its own; the ideas had a significance that went beyond their practical application. Hofstadter offers an insight that enables us to understand Pierre Goodrich as an intellectual:

> The difference is not in the character of the ideas with which he works but in his attitude toward them. I have suggested that in some sense he [the intellectual] lives for ideas—which means that he has a sense of dedication to the life of the mind which is very much like a religious commitment. This is not surprising, for in a very important way the role of the intellectual is inherited from the office of the cleric: it implies a special sense of the ultimate value in existence of the act of comprehension. Socrates, when he said that the unexamined life is not worth living, struck the essence of it. We can hear the voices of various intellectuals in

25. Richard Hofstadter, *Anti-intellectualism in American Life* (New York: Alfred A. Knopf, 1963), p. 27.

history repeating their awareness of this feeling, in accents suitable to time, place, and culture. . . . The noblest thing, and the closest possible to divinity, is thus the act of knowing.[26]

For Pierre, meaning and virtue were in the activity or idea that engaged him at the time. As for James, he fits squarely into the Benjamin Franklin mold, in which the constant application of intellect toward practical ends became a method of achieving growth.[27] Through work, "a person achieves virtue in much the [same] way he or she attains wealth, position, or learning—by ceaseless productive activity."[28]

To confirm this contention, one need only examine James Goodrich's life. When one does so, the first question that comes to mind is: How could one person possibly have done so many things so well? Both James and Pierre led extremely active lives, lives in which activity of a certain kind had special significance. It was performing the activity well, not the recognition that it produced, that was the primary motivation for both father and son. I believe that Percy Goodrich's remembrance of his younger brother, quoted in chapter 1, supports this observation, as does a letter that James Watson wrote to James Goodrich in April 1930: "I remember how you used to 'slip about' over the State going everywhere and getting the organization into shape without anybody knowing anything about it and I always regarded that as about the high water mark in our organization politics."[29]

Pierre had the same sort of reluctance about appearing in the lime-

26. Ibid., pp. 28–29.

27. *Individualism and Commitment in American Life,* p. 20.

28. Ibid.

29. Letter from Watson to Goodrich, April 9, 1930, James P. Goodrich Papers, box 28. Percy Goodrich observed: "[James] was an indefatigable worker and very earnest in everything he did and was one of the three greatest Governors the State ever had. . . . It is strange when there are so many school houses, roads, parks, etc. that nothing was ever named in his honor and I am not desiring to blame anyone for it. I believe it was his reticence to appear in the limelight. . . . He would organize a crowd to go someplace to have a political rally and then at the last minute would slip out to do some obscure work elsewhere." P. E. Goodrich, "Governor Jim," *Down in Indiana* 61 (December 4, 1948).

light. It is, however, the idea of work that is of primary importance in the makeup of both father and son. Their tendency to avoid recognition for their achievements is important in that it indicates that they did not need (or at least did not seek) attention to reinforce their sense of identity or self-worth.

I believe it is obvious that, for Pierre, work was much more than the pursuit of position and wealth; work as a businessman and the pursuit of ideas as an intellectual were for him a way of life, a calling. I further believe that in James's and Pierre's minds there was a close relationship between work and citizenship. Both men were strongly influenced by a Calvinist worldview in which work was a means of creating God's kingdom on earth. I am not suggesting that this was the result of conscious thinking, but their lifestyle was based on the belief that an active earthly life devoted to meeting practical needs is superior to a life of denial and contemplation. Pierre also believed, as Hofstadter poignantly writes, that striving for comprehension was in a way an act of piety.

The religious beliefs held by James and Pierre dictated how wealth was to be accumulated and, to a lesser extent, how it was to be spent. The Goodriches' ethical philosophy was totally different from that held by the robber barons of the late nineteenth century, such as J. P. Morgan, Cornelius Vanderbilt, and James Fisk. Those men acquired vast wealth by means of exploitation and ruthlessness, and then spent much of their money by living indulgent lives.

Pierre demanded that his companies operate within the law, despite the fact that he often disagreed with the law. Achieving wealth by dishonest means was not ethically acceptable to him. Moreover, aware that some of his father's early deals had been called into question, Pierre desired above all else that his own business reputation remain above reproach.[30] At the same time, however, Pierre had little regard for the

30. Another reason that Pierre was so determined to stay within the laws was the rumors that some of the early business ventures of his father and Jesse Moorman were less than ethical. Rodney Medler, interview, April 27, 1993. It would be nearly impossible to substantiate any alleged improprieties several decades later, but it is known that Pierre could not tolerate having his own integrity called into question. It may well be

opinions of others regarding his personal appearance or his eccentric habits.[31]

Although the Protestant ethic viewed properly obtained wealth as a sign of virtue ("You shall know a tree by its fruit"), it did not specify what should be done with that wealth. That fact was especially troubling to Pierre. James and Percy Goodrich gave away much of their personal wealth to educational institutions such as Wabash and Hanover colleges, but Pierre had a much more difficult time dispersing his own fortune. The virtues of accumulation are not necessarily those of distri-

---

that James Goodrich did not engage in any "shady" deals. Is buying a company out of bankruptcy and paying only a few cents on the dollar it had been worth a few months before a "shady deal"? That is how the Goodrich family acquired most of its later wealth—that and working extremely long hours. See also "[James P.] Goodrich Sued for Accounting by Agnes M. Todd of Bluffton," *Winchester Journal-Herald,* June 13, 1939, p. 1, col. 2.

31. Rodney Medler, interview, June 9, 1993. Apparently, one reason James Goodrich was subject to persistent rumors about the ethical aspects of his business dealings was that he continued to have vast holdings in many businesses at the same time he held the positions of chairman of the state Republican Committee (1901–10), Republican national committeeman (1912–20), and governor (1917–21). For instance, James Goodrich purportedly helped Jesse Moorman obtain the garbage collection contract for Indianapolis in May 1912 and subsequently obtained stock in it. Moreover, he and his family owned the Union Heat, Light and Power Company, which furnished gas to Winchester, Union City, and Portland under a monopoly arrangement. For a discussion of some charges of impropriety, see "'Jim' Goodrich County Boss for Twenty Years," *Winchester (Ind.) Democrat,* October 5, 1916, p. 1, col. 6; "Cravens Accepts Coal Challenge," *Indianapolis Star,* July 20, 1920, p. 1, col. 3 (James Goodrich was charged by a state Democratic senator with improper business relations with coal and railroad companies). In 1913, James Goodrich was also implicated in a fund-raising scam that involved his friend James Watson and the National Association of Manufacturers. Purportedly, a Colonel Martin M. Mulhall went to members of the National Association of Manufacturers and raised approximately twenty-three thousand dollars for Watson and sent it to the Republican state committee. The money was never accounted for, but several officials, including James Goodrich, who was Republican chairman, were implicated. The author could not find any further articles implicating Goodrich, although the Mulhall Affair became the source of a major congressional investigation in Washington, D.C. See Louis Ludlow, "Where Did Fund Go? Is Mystery Up to Mulhall," *Indianapolis Star,* July 28, 1913, p. 1, col. 1.

bution.[32] Pierre did not believe that the causes that most philanthropists contribute to were worthy of his money. Liberty Fund received most of his fortune after Pierre had, no doubt, examined and rejected every other option.[33]

32. This observation about Goodrich was made by Stephen J. Tonsor (interview, December 5, 1992).

33. Ibid. William Fletcher makes this observation (interview by William C. Dennis, January 25, 1991). From the author's understanding, Liberty Fund was neither very active nor did it come into most of Goodrich's wealth until after Pierre had passed away in 1973. Apparently, that was partly because of the difficulty Pierre had getting the IRS to allow a tax-free transfer to Liberty Fund of his personal proceeds from the sale of his companies. Another possible reason was that Pierre thought he might find some other better use for his money. That suggestion was made by Stephen Tonsor (interview, December 5, 1992).

Chapter 33

Epilogue

Biographies are but the clothes and buttons of the man—the biography of the man himself cannot be written.

MARK TWAIN, *Autobiography*

BY THE LATE 1960s, the world had changed, and Pierre Goodrich had a difficult time changing with it. Society and business had become increasingly more complex and resistant to straightforward analysis. In Goodrich's business dealings, long gone were the days when he could attend City Securities board meetings and read thoroughly every company prospectus presented for board action; such proposals had grown from a few pages in the 1930s to dozens, sometimes hundreds, of pages full of legal and technical jargon. (When he served as president of the National City Bank in the 1920s, James Goodrich oversaw the construction of the Railway Exchange Building on Washington Street in Indianapolis. The former governor purportedly had the building erected on the basis of a written contract that amounted to a single page.) Corporate boards increasingly had to rely on hordes of attorneys, accountants, and other advisers just to understand and consummate "simple" transactions. As early as the late 1930s, Pierre had lamented the demise of the general legal practitioner, who was no longer able to function in a society that required more and more specialists.[1]

1. See Harry T. Ice, *History of a Hoosier Law Firm* (Indianapolis: privately printed, 1980), pp. 143–44.

Moreover, Goodrich's coal, telephone, and banking businesses had become increasingly inundated with demands from federal and state regulatory entities—rate commissions and oversight, health, safety, environmental, and labor agencies—for detailed information about everything imaginable that had to do with business operations. Coupled with these demands was the ever-growing attention paid by the media to business practices. Goodrich loathed snooping reporters who wanted to delve into the details of his financial empire. When the sale of the Ayrshire Collieries Corporation occurred in February 1969, the deal, along with a picture of a grinning Pierre F. Goodrich, was reported in *Forbes* magazine. The article gave the details of the merger, including Pierre's personal profit. The publicity infuriated him.[2]

In his later years, Goodrich was described as a "discontented man." Things had not worked out as he had hoped. First, there were the personal disappointments and tribulations, such as his estrangement from his daughter, Nancy, who lived in Paris until after his death. (She proceeded to hire a string of attorneys, including a former Indiana governor, Matthew Welsh, to contest her father's will. While her paternal grandparents, James and Cora, had established trust funds that would provide for her comfortably for the rest of her life, she deeply believed that she was entitled to an inheritance larger than the $150,000 her father had left her).[3] There was also the death in January 1971 of John Goodrich, a cousin only six months older than Pierre.[4] Pierre and John

2. Gilbert Snider, interview, December 23, 1991. The magazine erroneously reported that Goodrich's share of the sale would amount to a personal take of $44.5 million. See "Going, Going, . . . Gone!" *Forbes,* February 15, 1969, p. 55.

3. Goodrich's daughter brought suit in Marion County Probate Court, Indianapolis, contesting her father's will. See "Pierre Goodrich Will Contested by His Daughter," *Indianapolis News,* December 6, 1973, p. 34, col. 6; "Goodrich Daughter to Contest His Will," *Indianapolis Star,* December 7, 1973, p. 37, col. 6; "Goodrich Estate More Than $2 Million," *Muncie (Ind.) Star,* January 3, 1974, p. 19, col. 5; "$2,179,368 Listed in Goodrich Estate," *Indianapolis News,* January 4, 1974, p. 23, col. 3; "Goodrich Property Sale to Be Private," *Indianapolis Star,* December 3, 1975, p. 43, col. 7 (reported the sale of a Stradivarius violin appraised at forty thousand dollars and a Vangelisti violin appraised at three thousand dollars).

4. See "John B. Goodrich" (obituary), *Winchester (Ind.) News-Gazette,* January 7, 1971, p. 4, col. 1.

had been very close in childhood, almost like brothers. Moreover, the periodic tax obstacles that impeded Goodrich's designs for Liberty Fund added to his discontent.[5]

Second, the situation at his alma mater, Wabash College, continued to deteriorate, at least in Goodrich's eyes. Beginning in 1970, a number of policy decisions were made on the campus that reaffirmed the wisdom of his decision the previous year to resign as an active trustee: After 137 years of having mandatory chapel, Wabash's faculty and administration voted to discontinue the twice-weekly service on the grounds that it no longer served as an "education phenomenon" to the students.[6] Furthermore, in order to appease black students who were outraged by the firing of a black professor, the college agreed to establish the Malcolm X Institute of Black Studies.[7] In May 1970, students met in the Goodrich Seminar Room of the Lilly Library to discuss whether to strike against United States action in Southeast Asia and the "political repression of Bobby Seale, Chairman of the Black Panther Party." The students believed that both acts demonstrated the "callous disregard of the American government for rights." Within twenty-four hours of the first student meeting, a vast majority of professors supported the protests. Classes at Wabash were suspended for several days.[8] It is not known with certainty what Goodrich thought about these incidents, but

5. After Pierre's death in October 1973, several tax problems developed with regard to income and estate taxes. The Internal Revenue Service initially sought capital-gains taxes of $6.8 million on two trusts valued at $26.1 million owned by Goodrich. As part of those trusts, the IRS disallowed more than $19.5 million in charitable deductions to four foundations that Goodrich had set up and to Wabash College. The IRS finally settled for roughly $1 million. Claude Warren, Jr., interview, July 5, 1993 (Warren, along with his father and several other lawyers, performed the financial work on Pierre's income and estate tax filings). See also "IRS Settles Estate Claim for 1 Million," *Indianapolis Star,* July 24, 1975, p. 30, col. 1; Lou Hiner, "IRS Reviews Goodrich Tax," *Indianapolis News,* May 18, 1978, p. 40, col. 1.

6. See Robert S. Harvey, ed., *These Fleeting Years: Wabash College, 1832–1982* (Crawfordsville, Ind.: Wabash College, 1982), pp. 169–71.

7. "The Malcolm X Institute of Black Studies," ibid., pp. 162–63; Edward B. McLean, interview, February 15, 1997.

8. See "Students Strike to Protest Cambodian Invasion," in *These Fleeting Years: Wabash College, 1832–1982,* pp. 157–59.

it is safe to say that they convinced him that the board of trustees had become a weak, ineffective body, with little input into or control over the college's activities.

Third, on the public front, Goodrich was disappointed about the direction in which he saw the country moving, away from what he believed were the virtues of the free society and toward a growing acceptance of statism, collectivism, and mediocrity. Despite the nation's temporary alarm over conformity and dependency, memorialized in the 1950s by such popular books as *The Lonely Crowd* (1950), *The Man in the Gray Flannel Suit* (1955), and *The Organization Man* (1956), Goodrich saw that individuals were, in fact, growing more and more reliant upon big government and large corporations for their subsistence.

Furthermore, the world in his later years was driven by technology. It was constantly moving toward standardization and larger operations, as well as consolidation and centralization of power and influence. The individual was no longer front and center, but a cog in the larger machinery driving society. The term *mass* seemed to be used to describe many new phenomena: mass communication, mass transportation, mass marketing, mass destruction. Goodrich also believed (despite his vehement protestations to the contrary) that the average person's behavior was continually being adapted to meet others' expectations, to win approval, to fit in.

Moreover, despite being warned about the dangerous and growing role of influence peddlers—by, for example, Vance Packard's books *The Hidden Persuaders* (1957), *The Status Seekers* (1959), and *The Waste Makers* (1960)—many Americans were content to be told by slick marketers (the press, Madison Avenue, Wall Street, Capitol Hill, Hollywood, and so forth) what to think about politics, business, economics, virtue and morality, the good life, and freedom. This manipulation of thought angered Goodrich, particularly because of the average person's unwillingness to examine critically the bombardment of hype. Pierre did not appreciate that many people are not interested in challenging the status quo or in doing more than scratching the surface of ideas. Moreover, the 1960s were even worse than the 1950s for libertarians such as Goodrich, for during that decade many of their values were held up to ridicule.

Finally, Goodrich was disappointed that he had not found greater truths than he had; through all his reading and scholarship, he had come to realize that there were limits to understanding that he could not overcome. As important as liberty, learning, and other fundamental human values and aspirations were to Goodrich, they were not a substitute for spiritual understanding. Spiritual understanding has to transcend reason, and Pierre had a difficult time letting go of his rational side after having worked so hard to develop it. It is interesting how little Goodrich discusses spiritual matters in his writings. I think that was the case not because he thought that religious faith was not tremendously important, but because the notion that man can know anything absolutely, as God knows, seemed to him highly presumptuous. Perhaps he believed that discussion of such matters should not even be attempted.[9]

Goodrich's discontent is perhaps best summed up by his good friend, Wabash College president Byron Trippet. In June 1959, Trippet wrote the following for the dedication of the Goodrich Seminar Room in the new Lilly Library:

> The Goodrich Seminar Room symbolizes the timeless pilgrimage of man toward truth, goodness, and beauty. It also exemplifies the part of one man in particular in this historic quest. Pierre F. Goodrich, an alumnus and trustee of Wabash College, is a lawyer, industrialist, and a financier. By the standards of the contemporary world, in all of these capacities he is a successful man.
>
> By his own standards of what is important, however, he is a discon-

9. Goodrich does discuss religious beliefs in the *Basic Memorandum,* but he devotes little space to them. One of the passages most relevant to the author's observation is the following: "Religious beliefs and theories must be commented on. Certain rational processes often take place in arriving at the religious beliefs and theologies which each individual holds. However, man's ignorance and imperfection, as herein referred to, are so extensive that in the end the particular belief enters the area of mysticism and pure belief. This is distinguished from anything which is completely arrived at by observation and reason" (pt. 3, p. 60).

> tented man, aware of his own imperfections as well as the imperfections of others, eager through study and reflection to understand the human drama, and to act as wisely as he can in his own interests and in the interests of others. The highest expression of appreciation those who use this room can make is to emulate his intellectual curiosity, his skepticism of expedient answers, and his resolute effort to act on principle supported by sound knowledge.[10]

On his seventy-fifth birthday, in October 1969, Pierre was honored in Indianapolis at a testimonial dinner given by Ben Rogge and several of his other close personal and business associates. Frank Barnett, a long-time friend, former Rhodes scholar, and then president of the National Strategy Information Center in New York, could not attend the dinner, but he sent his birthday greetings. He wrote, in part:

> I am sure you are spending this evening, not wholly in frivolity, but in the company of other Renaissance Men whose discourse on the nature of power, freedom, God, man and government you find provocative. From pleasant experience, I know that, wherever you sit, there also is a Seminar—say, rather, a Colloquium—on the first order of things.
>
> Since Birthdays are a time for reminiscence, I am moved to recall vivid impressions of the past: standing together on the sidewalks of Chicago, during the 1952 Republican Convention, to practice "street agitation" in the cause of civic virtue; nibbling cheese at Wabash College with the man who was shortly to become Chancellor of West Germany; watching the face of the sommelier at the great restaurant Pavilion as he began to realize that a lawyer from Indiana knew more about rare vintages than the masters; explaining to my wife that a midnight telephone call, that lasted an hour, was only from a friend who wanted to know if the English version of Clausewitz had lost something in translation.
>
> Happy Birthday, Pierre! May your integrity, and non-conformity, and probing intelligence, and sheer decency continue to ennoble others as those qualities have animated so many who have known your friendship and kindness in the past.

10. The quotation comes from "Goodrich Seminar Room," the program that was prepared for the dedication, which took place on June 4, 1959.

> Let me raise an imaginary glass to propose an earnest toast: "In America, some men *do* still dare to dream the Impossible Dream; and one of the most engaging . . . complicated . . . impish . . . and innovative Dreamers and Darers lives in Indianapolis!"[11]

Goodrich's health and stamina deteriorated slowly in the early 1970s, but he continued to go to the office daily, conducted business, and read for hours. Ben Rogge was very concerned about Pierre's taking on any more obligations. He intervened, for instance, to see that Goodrich did not accept an offer to serve again on the board of directors of the Institute for Humane Studies (IHS). Goodrich had been a founding trustee of IHS in 1961.

Shortly after Labor Day in 1973, Pierre was admitted to Methodist Hospital in Indianapolis. He had not been particularly ill, but he remained in the hospital with a weakened heart and a blood disorder that had caused clotting. For the first few weeks at Methodist, he continued to conduct business from his private room much as he had done before: He talked incessantly on the telephone and kept several secretaries busy taking dictation.[12] He was very concerned with labor problems that had developed at the Indiana Telephone Corporation. He knew that no one would win if relations between management and employees worsened.[13]

On the evening of October 25, 1973, Pierre Goodrich died in Methodist Hospital. Ben Rogge delivered the eulogy at Pierre's funeral. The music of the great German composer Johann Sebastian Bach, Goodrich's favorite, was played at the service.[14] Pierre was buried near his father and mother at Fountain Park cemetery in his hometown of Winchester. His final resting place was among the gravesites of several fami-

11. Barnett's letter is attached to a memorandum that Ben Rogge sent to Thaddeus Seymour, then president of Wabash College. See memorandum to President Seymour, November 17, 1969, and the attached letter from Frank Barnett, dated September 19, 1969, Ben Rogge Collection, Archives, Wabash College.

12. Ruth Connolly, interview, October 25, 1991, and July 30, 1993.

13. Frank Jessup, telephone interview, February 27, 1993.

14. This information was provided by Roseda Doenges Decker, a board member of Liberty Fund who attended the memorial service (letter to author, September 3, 1996).

lies with whom he was closely associated as a young man—the Edgers, Jaquas, Macys, Moormans, McCamishes, Kitselmans, and Millers—names that were forgotten long ago. Ironically, Pierre was buried in the same cemetery that saw the humble beginning of the Goodrich family's fortune, the cemetery where, some ninety-three years before, eighteen-year-old James Goodrich earned ten cents an hour moving dirt and planting trees.

After Pierre's death, the governor's mansion in Winchester, which Pierre had inherited from his parents, remained unoccupied for three years. The future of the mansion became the source of considerable controversy in Goodrich's hometown. The house fell into disrepair despite attempts by Pierre's widow, Enid, to maintain it. Within a short time, the house was besieged by vandals and thieves. They damaged the walls of the structure and stole valuable copper guttering from the roof and outside walls. A citizen's group called Save the Governor's Mansion was formed in an attempt to keep the majestic house from total destruction.[15]

In the spring of 1976, the architectural school of Ball State University presented a proposal to the Winchester Chamber of Commerce. The plan made the mansion the centerpiece of a community revitalization program. Steps were also taken to place the house on the National Register of Historic Places. The future of the mansion, which had been visited by a former president, Herbert Hoover, a Russian princess, and other American and foreign dignitaries, became such a local contro-

15. The Reverend Richard Merriman, then minister of the Winchester Main Street Christian Church, was the unofficial leader of the citizens' group that sought to keep the governor's mansion from being torn down. What transpired in the fall of 1976 is rather sad. Apparently, Pierre's widow, Enid, could not understand why all of a sudden there was such a great interest in the Goodrich mansion, when the house had remained essentially empty for the previous thirty-five years. Pierre was the only one who ever used it during most of that time, and after his death the mansion remained unoccupied for three years. Moreover, apparently Enid had no love for the house, since she had never been welcomed into it while Pierre's parents were alive. Therefore, although it was apparently structurally sound, the beautiful mansion was torn down in the winter of 1976, and a community landmark was lost (Richard T. Merriman, telephone interview, March 19, 1993).

versy that Indianapolis television station WRTV aired a report on its evening news about the community's efforts to save the local landmark. Despite the citizens' group's intervention, a decision was made to raze the mansion in late 1976. At a three-day auction in October 1976, most of the Goodrich family's home furnishings and personal belongings were sold.[16]

The destruction of the mansion and the sale of the family's possessions left little physical evidence to remind the community of the significant influence the original five Goodrich brothers had in Winchester. There is still the park that Elizabeth Goodrich donated to the town in honor of her husband, John B. Goodrich, and Pierre's cousins Perce Goodrich and Elizabeth Terry had a lovely chapel built in the cemetery where most of the Goodrich family members are buried. Yet within one hundred years, a small town's family dynasty has come and gone.

Pierre's influence, however, is still felt in his home community in nonmaterial ways. The Winchester Foundation remains in operation, supporting local community art, music, and literary projects, as well as national organizations.[17] Also, the Pierre F. Goodrich Scholarship Fund, benefiting graduates of the local high school, was established in 1988 by Enid Goodrich in memory of her husband.[18] Of course, Goodrich's most important legacy, Liberty Fund, continues to have an important influence nationally and abroad.

It is a shame that Pierre Goodrich did not live to see the successes

16. Most of Pierre's possessions were sold at a public auction that took place on October 25, 26, and 27 at the Randolph County 4-H fairgrounds south of Winchester. See "Goodrich Sale Begins," *Winchester (Ind.) News-Gazette,* October 26, 1976, p. 1, col. 3.

17. Moreover, the foundation has helped fund construction of a new addition to the local library, which includes a room named for James P. Goodrich. See Janet Fuller, "Library Is Given Foundation Grant," *Winchester (Ind.) News-Gazette,* April 15, 1993, p. 1, col. 5.

18. The award provides nearly a full college scholarship to at least one graduating senior annually from Winchester Community High School. Winners since the inception of the scholarship are Jeffrey Chalfant (1988); Steve McCord (1989); Charles Stonerock and Karine Oswalt (1990); Catherine J. Hall, Katrina E. Horner, and Brian N. Peters (1991); T. Meeks Cockerill (1992); Molly C. Smith (1993); Melanie L. Martin (1994); Gary Campbell (1995); and Scott K. Stranko, Wendy R. Holder, and Dawn M. Love (1996).

that have been achieved by Liberty Fund. At the time of his death, Liberty Fund was still very much in its infancy, having held only a handful of seminars. But in another way Goodrich is fortunate: How many people have their most important work continue after they have died?

Through his contributions, Pierre Goodrich has helped us realize that we know too little to be dogmatic and too much to remain passive in the protection of our cultural heritage. Pierre Goodrich knew a great many things, and we can benefit from his example if we are prepared to pursue rigorous study and take appropriate action. The essence of the Goodrich family's legacy is an abiding faith in man's ability, through concerted effort and reflection, to bring about and maintain social progress. As for Pierre, he believed deeply that staunch individualism was the necessary foundation for a flourishing Western democratic society. Clearly, the Goodriches were an original American family.

Shortly after Pierre's death, many testimonials were written. The board of trustees of the Foundation for Economic Education, on which he served for more than twenty years, paid a fitting tribute, which read, in part:

> We remember [Mr. Goodrich] as a man of ideas who demanded hard and straight thinking of himself and everyone else. . . . He loved good music, good food, and good books. He was a true individualist, whose occasional irascibility was that of a man who does not suffer fools gladly. He believed in freedom without compromise. His absence will be felt, and we mourn his loss.[19]

In a memorial resolution by the Indiana Telephone Corporation, the board recognized Goodrich's pioneering contributions to the telephone industry, concluding:

> Pierre F. Goodrich saw that the world of his abstract philosophizing and the world of his business decision-making were, in fact, but one

19. "Tribute to Pierre Frist Goodrich," December 3, 1973. Pierre F. Goodrich file, Foundation for Economic Education, Irvington-on-Hudson, N.Y.

world. . . . [He] contributed his time, his energy and his talents to his community, the state of Indiana, his country and mankind.[20]

But perhaps the most fitting remembrance was written by Anna Marie Gibbons, a reporter at the time for the *Winchester News-Gazette.* Ms. Gibbons had known Pierre ever since she was a young girl, asking precocious questions of him when he would visit her father, John Macy, Jr., Pierre's first law partner:

> Pierre Goodrich, who died at Indianapolis Thursday evening at 79, was probably the most remarkable Hoosier of this century in terms of intelligence, range of interests and financial acumen. . . .
>
> Pierre was difficult to talk to or listen to, partly because he spoke in a soft, hesitant voice and partly because his mind darted from thought to thought with such dazzling speed it was too much for the average person to follow. But if you followed, you found the tour both fascinating and rewarding.
>
> If you tried to catalogue all the things he became interested in in his lifetime, you would find the list amazing. And whatever he became interested in he learned about from the inside out, totally and entirely. Just to name a few of Pierre's interests:
>
> . . . He became interested in coffee, and immediately found out all there was to know on the subject. His interest in education resulted in much support and encouragement on his part for Wabash College. It also resulted in the prominent part he played in the Great Books movement. Here again, he not only read the books but became a prime student of the philosophies of all the writers—and from Great Books he wandered into the field of oriental philosophy and became an A student there.
>
> . . . Pierre was so totally engrossed in the world of ideas that he often lost complete track of time when he became involved in a conversation or discussion that interested him—and had to be reminded by a tug at his sleeve or coat-tail that it was time to be going.
>
> The tug that told him Thursday evening that it was time to be going, was one he couldn't disregard. But I'm sure he left as reluctantly as

20. See "Pierre F. Goodrich Memorial Resolution," *ITC Highlights,* November 12, 1973, p. 6.

ever—not because he was so tied to the things of this world, but because he had a few thousand ideas which he still had not had time to explore and think about, and a few thousand questions his amazing brain had still not had time to find answers for.[21]

21. Anna Marie Gibbons, *Winchester (Ind.) News-Gazette,* October 28, 1973, p. 1, col. 1.

Appendixes

APPENDIX A

The Goodrich Family

Edmund B. Goodrich
m.
Amy Watkins

- John Baldwin
  1783?–1828
  m. 1802
  Rebecca Pearse
  1789–1876

  - Thomas Watkins
    1803–1839
  - Edmund Baldwin
    1805–1843
    m.
    Ellen Bell
    m.
    Mary Robinson
  - Celestina St. Pierre
    1808–1875
  - John Fletcher
    1810–?
  - Carey Seldon
    1811–1865
  - Carolina Louise
    1813–1854
  - George Whitfield
    1815–1873
  - Rebecca Pearse
    1816–1853
  - Alfred Keiling
    1818–1912
  - Calvin Gibson
    1820–1880
  - Martin Luther
    1822–?
  - Jane Alexina
    1824–1906
  - Ann Eliza
    1826–1906
  - Charles T.
    1828–1901

John Baldwin
1831–1872
m. 1859
Elizabeth Edger
1840–1917

William Wallace
m.
Kate Bond

- Percy Edgar
  1861–1951
  m.
  Susan Engle
  ?–1934
  m. 1940
  Ethyl Jones Kuhner
  ?–1973

- James Putnam
  1864–1940
  m. 1888
  Cora Frist
  1861–1941
  - Jean
    (stillborn)
  - Pierre Frist
    1894–1973
    m. 1920
    Dorothy Dugan
    1896–1987
    m. 1941
    Enid Smith
    1903–1996
    - Frances "Nancy"
      (Poniatowski)
      1921–

- John "Jay" Baldwin
  1866–1937
  m.
  Charlotte Martin
  ?–1941
  - John
    1894–1971
    m. 1964
    Helen Cummings
  - James P.
    1887–1901

- Edward Shields
  1868–1953
  m.
  Elizabeth Neff
  1866–1958
  - Florence
    1897–1994
    m. 1921
    Francis Dunn
    1896–1976
    - Wesley
      1922–
    - Edward
      1925–

- William Wallace
  1871–1948
  m.
  Charlotte Moore
  ?–1899
  m.
  Louise Gordon
  1879–1964
  - Elizabeth
    1906–
    m. 1939
    Phillip Terry
    1896–1967
  - Perce ("Bud")
    1908–1996
    m. 1932
    Gaynel Graber
    - Elizabeth P. (Orrill)
    m. 1939
    Frances Ann Hawkins
    - Janice G. (Gerson)
    - John B.

APPENDIX B

Liberty Fund Book List

Hesiod	*Works and Days*
Aeschylus	*Prometheus Bound*
Sophocles	*Antigone*
Thucydides	*History of the Peloponnesian Wars*
Plato	*Apology, Crito, Gorgias, Meno*
Aristotle	*Ethics, Poetics, Politics*
Marcus Tullius Cicero	*De Legibus, De Officiis, De Republica*
Bible	Old Testament, New Testament
Tacitus	*History of Germany*
St. Augustine	*Confessions, Concerning the Teacher, On Music*
St. Anselm	*Proslogium*
St. Thomas	*Of the Teacher, Treatise on Laws*
Gerard Zerbolt of Zutphen	*The Imitation of Christ*
Thomas á Kempis	*The Imitation of Christ*
Machiavelli	*The Prince*
Martin Luther	*Ninety-Five Theses, Commentary on Galatians, Of Christian Liberty, Babylonian Captivity of the Church, The Christian Nobility of Germany*
John Calvin	*Institutes of the Christian Religion* (especially "The Letter to the King of the French" and "The Twentieth Institute"), *Commentary on Romans, Commentary on Daniel, Commentary on Galatians*
John Milton	*Areopagitica*
James Harrington	*Oceana*
John Locke	*Second Treatise on Civil Government, Letter on Toleration*
Montesquieu	*The Spirit of the Laws*
David Hume	*Political Essays*

Adam Smith	*The Wealth of Nations*
William Blackstone	*On the Nature of Laws in General*
Immanuel Kant	*Foundations of the Metaphysics of Morals, Perpetual Peace, Critique of Pure Reason*
Johann Wolfgang von Goethe	*Faust, Egmont*
	Declaration of Independence, United States Constitution and Amendments
Max Farrand, ed.	*The Records of the Federal Convention of 1787*
Alexander Hamilton, James Madison, and John Jay	*The Federalist Papers*
Daniel Webster and B. H. Liddell Hart	*Conscription*
John Stuart Mill	*On Liberty*
Jacob Burckhardt	*Force and Freedom*
Lord Acton	*Freedom in Christianity, Freedom in Antiquity, Letters to Bishop Creighton, Massacre of St. Bartholomew, Protestant Theory of Persecution*
Eugen von Bohm-Bawerk	*Capital and Interest*
Hugo Leichtentritt	*Music, History, and Ideas*
Roscoe Pound	*The Development of Constitutional Guarantees of Liberty, Jurisprudence*
Ludwig von Mises	*Human Action, Socialism*
Leonard Read	*Government, an Ideal Concept*
Dean Russell	*The Conscription Idea*
Richard M. Weaver	*Ideas Have Consequences*
F. A. Hayek	*The Constitution of Liberty*
Henry Hazlitt	*The Failure of the "New Economics," The Critics of Keynesian Economics*
Felix Morley	*Freedom and Federalism*
Wilhelm von Röpke	*A Humane Economy*
Pierre F. Goodrich	"Why Liberty?" "Education Memorandum"
Gottfried Dietze	*The Federalist*

APPENDIX C

The Gods of the Copybook Headings

Pierre F. Goodrich often gave a copy of Rudyard Kipling's poem "The Gods of the Copybook Headings" to friends and associates. The pamphlet he gave, which contained the poem, also included the following introduction.

What are the foundations of our beliefs and actions? History has built the civilization we enjoy by accumulating small pebbles of wisdom based upon experience. Every once in a while, some misguided action tears down years or centuries of progress by ignoring or misunderstanding the basic truths that underlie all that has gone before.

Rudyard Kipling, with his gift as a poet and prophet, has put this into focus in his poem, "The Gods of the Copybook Headings." Although written in 1919, it is pertinent to the conditions that exist in the world today. His "Gods of the Copybook Headings" are, in effect, those rules of human conduct that are so well defined by centuries of experience that they have become immutable. To disregard them, says Kipling, will inevitably lead to failure and destruction.

As I pass through my incarnations in every age and race,
I make my proper prostrations to the Gods of the Market-Place.
Peering through reverent fingers I watch them flourish and fall,
And the Gods of the Copybook Headings, I notice, outlast them all.

We were living in trees when they met us. They showed us each in turn
That Water would certainly wet us, as Fire would certainly burn:
But we found them lacking in Uplift, Vision and Breadth of Mind,
So we left them to teach the Gorillas while we followed the March of
Mankind.

We moved as the Spirit listed. *They* never altered their pace,
Being neither cloud nor wind-borne like the Gods of the Market-Place;

But they always caught up with our progress, and presently word would
come
That a tribe had been wiped off its ice-field, or the lights had gone out
in Rome.

With the Hopes that our World is built on they were utterly out of
touch.
They denied that the Moon was Stilton; they denied she was even
Dutch.
They denied that Wishes were Horses; they denied that a Pig had Wings.
So we worshipped the Gods of the Market Who promised these
beautiful things.

When the Cambrian measures were forming, They promised perpetual
peace.
They swore, if we gave them our weapons, that the wars of the tribes
would cease.
But when we disarmed They sold us and delivered us bound to our foe,
And the Gods of the Copybook Headings said: "*Stick to the Devil
you know.*"

On the first Feminian Sandstones we were promised the Fuller Life
(Which started by loving our neighbour and ended by loving his wife)
Till our women had no more children and the men lost reason and
faith,
And the Gods of the Copybook Headings said: "*The Wages of Sin is
Death.*"

In the Carboniferous Epoch we were promised abundance for all,
By robbing selected Peter to pay for collective Paul;
But, though we had plenty of money, there was nothing our money
could buy,
And the Gods of the Copybook Headings said: "*If you don't work you
die.*"

Then the Gods of the Market tumbled, and their smooth-tongued
wizards withdrew,

And the hearts of the meanest were humbled and began to believe it was true
That All is not Gold that Glitters, and Two and Two make Four—
And the Gods of the Copybook Headings limped up to explain it once more.

. . . .

As it will be in the future, it was at the birth of Man—
There are only four things certain since Social Progress began:—
That the Dog returns to his Vomit and the Sow returns to her Mire,
And the burnt Fool's bandaged finger goes wabbling back to the Fire;
And that after this is accomplished, and the brave new world begins
When all men are paid for existing and no man must pay for his sins,
As surely as Water will wet us, as surely as Fire will burn,
The Gods of the Copybook Headings with terror and slaughter return!

Bibliography

Primary Sources

MANUSCRIPTS

AMAX Corporation, Englewood, Colo.
History of the Ayrshire Collieries Corporation
History of Patoka Coal Company

Foundation for Economic Education, Irvington-on-Hudson, N.Y.
Leonard Read Papers
Pierre F. Goodrich Papers

Hanover College, Hanover, Ind.
Percy E. Goodrich Collection

Harvard University Law School Archives, Cambridge, Mass.
Roscoe Pound Collection

Herbert Hoover Presidential Library, West Branch, Iowa
Felix Morley Collected Papers
James P. Goodrich, "Diary of Various Trips to Russia"
James P. Goodrich, "Manuscript on Various Trips to Russia, 1921–1922."
James P. Goodrich Papers

Hoover Institution on War, Revolution and Peace, Stanford University, Stanford, Calif.
American Relief Administration Personnel Records
Frank A. Golder Collection
Friedrich A. Hayek Collection
Mont Pelerin Society Papers
Pierre F. Goodrich Collection

Indiana Commission on Public Records, Indianapolis, Ind.
Dissolved Corporations of Indiana

Indiana Historical Society Library, Indianapolis, Ind.
Down in Indiana (newsletters of Percy E. Goodrich)
Indiana State Library, Indianapolis, Ind.
James E. Watson Collection
James P. Goodrich Collection (Years as Governor, 1917–1921)
William Harrison Hays Collection
Liberty Fund, Indianapolis, Ind.
Minutes of the Board of Directors of Liberty Fund, Inc.
Pierre F. Goodrich, "Education Memorandum," May 12, 1969
Pierre F. Goodrich, *Liberty Fund Basic Memorandum*
Various files of Pierre F. Goodrich
Wabash College, Crawfordsville, Ind.
Benjamin A. Rogge Collection
Frank Sparks Collection
Great Books Foundation Collection
Pierre F. Goodrich Collection
Roscoe Pound Papers
Wesleyan University (Mansfield Free Center for East Asian Studies), Middletown, Conn.
China Institute of America Collection

PUBLIC DOCUMENTS

Presidential Papers of Franklin D. Roosevelt, Franklin D. Roosevelt Presidential Library, Hyde Park, N.Y.

Presidential Papers of Herbert Hoover, Herbert Hoover Library, West Branch, Iowa

Presidential Papers of Warren G. Harding, Ohio Historical Society, Columbus, Ohio

Report of the Committee on the Conservation and Administration of the Public Domain. Washington, D.C., 1931.

U.S. Congress. House. Committee on Foreign Affairs. *Russian Relief Hearings.* 67th Cong., 2d sess., December 13–14, 1921.

U.S. Congress. House. 67th Cong., 2d sess., 1921, H.R. 9458 and 9459.

U.S. Congress. Senate. *Roscoe Pound's Analysis of Chinese-American Affairs—Hits United States Aims for Compromise, Misconception of Red Role.* 81st Cong., 1st sess. *Congressional Record* (April 2, 1949), vol. 95, pt 3:3765–3767.

U.S. Congress. Senate. *St. Lawrence Waterway Project.* 69th Cong., 2d sess., 1927. Rept. 183.

Secondary Sources

"AMAX Today: How It Came to Be." *Engineering and Mining Journal,* September 1972.

Anderson, Martin. *Impostors in the Temple.* New York: Simon and Schuster, 1992.

Andrews, William H. "Ayrshire Collieries Corporation—Profit with Ecology." Research paper, Indiana University, n.d.

The Annals of America. Chicago: Encyclopaedia Britannica, 1987.

Association Book of Indiana. Indianapolis: James O. Jones Company, 1929.

"The Ayrshire Story." *Mechanization,* July 1959.

Bales, Miriam Halbert. *We Pass the Words Along: A 300-Year Chronicle of the Bales Family.* Muncie, Ind.: privately printed, 1984.

Ball, Clayton G. "The Ayrshire Story: A Detailed Analysis of the Management, Engineering, and Operating Technics Involved in the Growth and Progress of a Large Modern Strip-mining Company." *Mechanization,* March 1947: 57–66.

Bellah, Robert N. *Habits of the Heart: Individualism and Commitment in American Life.* Berkeley: University of California Press, 1985.

Bellah, Robert N., et al., eds. *Individualism and Commitment in American Life: Readings on the Themes of Habits of the Heart.* New York: Harper and Row, 1987.

Berlin, Isaiah. *Four Essays on Liberty.* Oxford: Oxford University Press, 1969.

Beroff, Joseph, Elizabeth Douvan, and Richard Kulka. *The Inner American: A Self-Portrait from 1957 to 1976.* New York: Basic Books, 1981.

Biographical Sketches of Adams County, Indiana, Citizens. Indianapolis: Citizens Historical Association, 1977.

Blee, Kathleen M. *Women of the Klan: Racism and Gender in the 1920s.* Berkeley: University of California Press, 1992.

Boettke, Peter J. "Friedrich A. Hayek (1899–1992)." *The Freeman,* August 1992: 300–303.

Bowers, Claude. *The Life of John Worth Kerns.* Indianapolis: Hollenbeck, 1918.

———. *Beveridge and the Progressive Era.* Cambridge, Mass.: Houghton Mifflin Co., 1932.

Brand, H. W. *The Reckless Decade: America in the 1890s.* New York: St. Martin's Press, 1995.

Brislin, Richard W. *The Art of Getting Things Done: A Practical Guide to the Use of Power.* New York: Praeger, 1991.

Brooks, Sidney. "Russia as a Hoosier Banker Sees Her." *The Independent,* November 21, 1925: 583.

Buckley, William. *God and Man at Yale: The Superstitions of Academic Freedom.* Chicago: Regnery, 1951.

Burleigh, Anne Husted, ed. *Education in a Free Society.* Indianapolis: Liberty Fund, 1973.

Carr, Edward Hallett. *The Bolshevik Revolution, 1917–1923.* Vol. 2 in A History of Soviet Russia. New York: Macmillan, 1951.

Clutter, Richard M. "Indiana and the First World War." *Indiana Military History Journal* 1 (July 1976): 20–22.

Coe, John Y. *On These Walls: Inscriptions and Quotations in the Buildings of the Library of Congress.* Washington, D.C.: Library of Congress, 1995.

"College Professor New Board Member." *ITC Highlights,* June–August 1971: 2.

Cornforth, Carol L. "Reclamation Commitment Proves Rewarding." *Coal Mining and Processing,* March 1973.

Cottman, George S. *Centennial History and Handbook of Indiana.* Indianapolis: State of Indiana, 1917.

Crawford, Hazel E. "Indiana's Victory Celebration of World War I." *Indiana Military History Journal* 4 (October 1979): 16–20.

Cummins, Cedric C. *Indiana Public Opinion and the World War (1914–1917).* Indianapolis: Indiana Historical Bureau, 1945.

Dietze, Gottfried. *America's Political Dilemma: From Limited to Unlimited Democracy.* Baltimore: Johns Hopkins University Press, 1968.

Dionne, E. J. *Why Americans Hate Politics.* New York: Simon and Schuster, 1991.

Dunn, Jacob Piatt. *Indiana and Indianans—A History of Aboriginal and Territorial Indiana and the Century of Statehood.* Chicago: American Historical Society, 1919.

Ellis, Frances H. "German Instruction in the Public Schools of Indianapolis, 1869–1919." *Indiana Magazine of History* 50 (1954): 372, 374–78.

Encyclopedia of Indiana. New York: Somerset Publishers, 1993.

"Erhard, Ludwig." *The New Encyclopaedia Britannica* 4 (1992): 540.

Esarey, Logan. *A History of Indiana.* Indianapolis: Hoosier Heritage Press, 1970.

Finer, Herman. In preface to *Essays on Freedom and Power,* by John Emerich Edward Dalberg Acton. Boston: Beacon Press, 1948.

Fisher, Harold H. *The Famine in Soviet Russia, 1919–1923: The Operations of the American Relief Administration.* New York: Macmillan, 1927.

Franklin, Benjamin. *Poor Richard's Almanack.* Mount Vernon, N.Y.: Peter Pauper Press, n.d.

Freeman, Walden S. *Their Infinite Variety: Essays on Indiana Politicians.* Indianapolis: Indiana Historical Society, 1981.

Friedman, Milton, and Rose Friedman. *Free to Choose.* New York: Harcourt Brace Jovanovich, 1979.

Furlong, Patrick J. *Indiana: An Illustrated History.* Northridge, Calif.: Windsor Publications, 1986.

Gallahue, Edward. *Edward's Odyssey: An Autobiography of Edward Gallahue.* New York: Doubleday, 1970.

Gas Boom of Gas City, Indiana. Indianapolis: Department of Geology and Natural Resources, 1892.

Geelhoed, Bruce E. *Indiana's Investment Banker: The Story of City Securities Corporation.* Muncie, Ind.: Ball State University, 1985.

General Grain, Inc. v. Pierre F. Goodrich, 221 N.E.2d 696 (Ind. Ct. App. 1966).

General Grain, Inc. v. Pierre F. Goodrich, 227 N.E.2d 445 (Ind. 1967).

General Grain, Inc. v. Pierre F. Goodrich, 233 N.E.2d 187 (Ind. Ct. App. 1968).

"Going, Going, . . . Gone." *Forbes,* February 15, 1969: 55.

Goldberg v. Kelly, 397 U.S. 254 (1970).

Golder, Frank Alfred, and Lincoln Hutchinson. *On the Trail of the Russian Famine.* Calif.: Stanford University, 1927.

"Goodbye to Old Jim." *Passing Parade,* August 4, 1948: 47–49.

Goodrich, Calvin, and Percy Goodrich. *A Great-Grandmother and Her People.* Winchester, Ind.: privately printed, 1950.

Goodrich, James P. "Can Russia Come Back?" *Outlook* 130 (March 1, 1922): 341–44.

Goodrich, Pierre F. "Why Liberty?" Paper presented at the annual meeting of the Mont Pelerin Society, Princeton, N.J., September 1958; later reprinted as a pamphlet by Central Newspapers, Inc., Indianapolis, Indiana (reprint page numbers cited).

———. "Monetary Inflation, Growth and Accounting." *Public Utilities Fortnightly,* October 28, 1971.

"Goodrich Brothers' Company, The 90th Anniversary of the", County Elevators, Shippers, and Feeddealers' Luncheon (brochure). Columbia Club of Indianapolis, Ind., January 23, 1950.

Hamilton, Alexander, James Madison, and John Jay. *The Federalist Papers.* New York: Signet Classics, 1961.

Hardness, Georgia. *John Calvin: The Man and His Ethic.* New York: Henry Holt, 1931.

Hartwell, R. M. *A History of the Mont Pelerin Society.* Indianapolis: Liberty Fund, 1995.

Harvey, Robert S. *These Fleeting Years: Wabash College, 1832–1982.* Crawfordsville, Ind.: Wabash College, 1982.

Hayek, Friedrich A. *The Collected Works of F. A. Hayek: The Fortunes of Liberalism.* Chicago: University of Chicago Press, 1992.

———. *The Constitution of Liberty.* Chicago: University of Chicago Press, 1960.

———. *The Counterrevolution of Science: Studies on the Abuse of Reason.* Glencoe, Ill.: Free Press, 1952.

———. *The Road to Serfdom.* Chicago: University of Chicago Press, 1944.

Hays, Will H. *The Memoirs of Will H. Hays.* Garden City, N.Y.: Doubleday, 1955.

Heller, Dick D., Jr., ed. *1979 History of Adams County, Indiana.* 2 vols. [Decatur, Ind.]: Adams County Historical Society, 1979–89.

Heyman, David C. *Ezra Pound: The Last Rower.* New York: Viking, 1975.

Hofstadter, Richard. *Anti-intellectualism in American Life.* New York: Alfred A. Knopf, 1963.

Hoover, Dwight W. *Magic Middletown.* Bloomington: Indiana University Press, 1986.

"How Inflation Warps Accounts." *The Economist,* January 16, 1971: 58–59.

Ice, Harry T. *History of a Hoosier Law Firm.* Indianapolis: privately printed, 1980.

Ideas on Liberty: Essays in Honor of Paul L. Poirot. Irvington-on-Hudson, N.Y.: Foundation for Economic Education, 1987.

"Indiana's Masonic Governors." *The Indiana Freemason* 40 (October 1962): 9.

Indiana State News Bulletin. August 1, 1928.

"ITC Memorandum No. 1 Re: Employees; Good Citizens; Good Supervisors; Good Customers." Indiana Telephone Corporation, March 5, 1970; rev. May 30, 1973.

Jacobi, Jolande. *The Psychology of C. G. Jung.* New Haven, Conn.: Yale University Press, 1973.

John Beals et al. v. General Grain, Inc., and Acme Goodrich, Inc. (Boone County, Indiana, Circuit Court, unpublished decision).

Johnson, Paul. *Modern Times: The World from the Twenties to the Nineties.* New York: Harper Collins, 1991.

Jung, Carl. *Psychological Reflections: A Jung Anthology.* Princeton, N.J.: Princeton University Press, 1973.

Keynes, John Maynard. "Soviet Russia—III." *New Republic,* November 11, 1925: 301–2.

Kipnis, David. *The Powerholders.* Chicago: University of Chicago Press, 1976.

Kjetsaa, Geir. *Fyodor Dostoyevsky: A Writer's Life.* New York: Fawcett Columbine, 1987.

Knowland, J. H. B. "Internal Improvements in Indiana." *Indiana Magazine of History* 3 (1907): 20.

La France, Ernest. "Winchester and the Great Books: Indiana Town Reads the Classics for Recreation and Self-improvement." *Parade,* August 1, 1948, 5–7.

Libbey, James K. *Alexander Gumberg and Soviet-American Relations, 1917–1933.* Lexington: University Press of Kentucky, 1977.

"The Liberal Education." *The Wabash* 37 (October 1912): 21–23.

Lieber, Emma. *Richard Lieber.* Indianapolis: privately printed, 1947.

Locke, John. *Treatise of Civil Government and A Letter Concerning Toleration.* New York: Appleton-Century Co., 1937.

Luther, Martin. *Basic Theological Writings.* Minneapolis: Fortress Press, 1989.

Lutholtz, M. William. *Grand Dragon: D. C. Stephenson and the Ku Klux Klan in Indiana.* West Lafayette, Ind.: Purdue University Press, 1993.

Lynd, Robert S., and Helen Merrell Lynd. *Middletown: A Study in Contemporary American Culture.* New York: Harcourt, Brace, 1929.

McLean, Edward B. *Law and Civilization: The Legal Thought of Roscoe Pound.* Lanham, Md.: University Press of America, 1992.

Madison, James H. *The Indiana Way: A State History.* Bloomington: Indiana University Press, 1986.

Meltzer, Allan H. *Keynes's Monetary Theory: A Different Interpretation.* Cambridge: Cambridge University Press, 1988.

Meng, Chih. *Chinese American Understanding: A Sixty-Year Search.* New York: China Institute of America, 1967.

Mises, Ludwig von. *Human Action.* New Haven, Conn.: Yale University Press, 1949.

Mises, Margit von. *My Years with Ludwig von Mises.* New Rochelle, N.Y.: Arlington House, 1976.

Moley, Raymond. *The Hays Office.* Indianapolis: Bobbs-Merrill, 1945.

Monks, Leander J. "James P. Goodrich." In *Courts and Lawyers of Indiana,* vol. 3. Indianapolis: Federal Publishing Company, 1916.

Montgomery, M. W. *History of Jay County, Indiana.* Chicago: Church, Goodman and Cushing, 1864.

Moody's Public Utility Manual. 1979.

The Morality of Capitalism. Irvington-on-Hudson, N.Y.: Foundation for Economic Education / Freeman Classics, 1992.

Morley, Felix. *The Power in the People.* New York: D. Van Nostrand Company, 1949.

———. *For the Record.* South Bend, Ind.: Regnery/Gateway, 1979.

Morozanov, A. "Famine in the Volga Region." *Ekonomicheskaya Zhizn,* June 30, 1921.

Morrow, Barbara Olenyik. *From "Ben-Hur" to "Sister Carrie": Remembering the Lives and Works of Five Indiana Authors.* Indianapolis: Guild Press of Indiana, 1995.

The National Cyclopaedia of American Biography. New York: J. T. White and Company, 1926.

Nelson, Jacqueline S. *Indiana Quakers Confront the Civil War.* Indianapolis: Indiana Historical Society, 1991.

The New Encyclopaedia Britannica. Chicago: Encyclopaedia Britannica, 1992.

Nolan, Jeannette Covert. *Hoosier City: The Story of Indianapolis.* New York: Julian Messner, 1943.

O'Brien, Brice. "Coal Industry: Atomic Power." *Vital Speeches* 35 (April 1, 1969): 379–84.

O'Donnell, John L. "The Financial Operations of a Regional Investment Bank." Ph.D. diss., Indiana University, 1954.

Osborne, James Insley, and Theodore Gregory Gronert. *Wabash College: The First Hundred Years, 1832–1932.* Crawfordsville, Ind.: R. E. Banta, 1932.

Parker, Mrs. Albert G., Jr. "Percy Goodrich Was Our Friend." *Hanover Alumni News* 5 (October 1951): 3.

Parker, Katharine McAfee. "In Gratitude for P. E. and Ethyl L. Goodrich." *The Hanoverian* 2 (August 1970): 3–7.

Parker, Lowell. "Winchester, Indiana: Literary Guinea Pig." *Indianapolis Star Magazine*, September 28, 1947: 16–17.

Peat, Wilber D. *Portraits and Painters of the Governors of Indiana, 1800–1978.* Indianapolis: Indiana Historical Society, 1978.

"P. E. Goodrich—A Good Trustee." *The Bulletin of Hanover College* 43 (September 1951): 6.

Persico, Joseph E. *Casey.* New York: Viking, 1990.

Phillips, Clifton J. *Indiana in Transition: The Emergence of an Industrial Commonwealth, 1880–1920.* Vol. 4 of *The History of Indiana.* Indianapolis: Indiana Historical Bureau and Indiana Historical Society, 1968.

"Pierre F. Goodrich Tours Company." *ITC Highlights*, July 1971: 1–2.

Plato. *Republic.* Middlesex, England: Penguin Classics, 1972.

Post, Margaret Moore. *First Ladies of Indiana and the Governors, 1816–1984.* Indianapolis: Pierson Printing Company, 1984.

Pound, Roscoe. *The Development of Constitutional Guarantees of Liberty.* New Haven, Conn.: Yale University Press for Wabash College, 1957.

———. *Jurisprudence.* St. Paul, Minn.: West Publishing Company, 1959.

Pulliam, Russell. *Publisher Gene Pulliam, Last of the Newspaper Titans.* Ottawa, Ill.: Jameson Books, 1984.

Rafert, Stewart. *The Miami Indians of Indiana: A Persistent People, 1654–1994.* Indianapolis: Indiana Historical Society, 1996.

Randolph County History: 1818–1990. Paducah, Ky.: Turner Publishing, 1991.

Rauch, Georg von. *A History of Soviet Russia.* New York: Praeger, 1967.

Read, Leonard. *Government—An Ideal Concept.* Foundation for Economic Education: Irvington-on-Hudson, 1954.

Regnery, Henry. *Life of a Dissident Publisher.* New York: Harcourt Brace Jovanovich, 1979.

Reiss, Irwin H. "We Are Farmers, Not Miners." *Coal Mining and Processing*, May 1974.

Remy, Charles F. "Governor Goodrich and Indiana Tax Legislation." *Indiana Magazine of History* 43 (March 1947): 43.

Rhodes, Benjamin D. "Governor James P. Goodrich of Indiana and the 'Plain Facts' About Russia, 1921–1933." *Indiana Magazine of History* 85 (March 1989): 1–30.

———. *James P. Goodrich, Indiana's "Governor Strangelove."* Selinsgrove, Pa.: Susquehanna University Press, 1996.

Robertson, James O. "Progressives Elect Will H. Hays Republican National Chairman, 1918." *Indiana Magazine of History* 64 (September 1968): 173–90.

Rogge, Benjamin A., and Pierre F. Goodrich. "Education in a Free Society." *Education in a Free Society.* Indianapolis: Liberty Fund, 1973.

Roll, Charles. *Indiana.* Chicago: Lewis Publishing Co., 1931.

Rothbard, Murray N. *Ludwig von Mises: Scholar, Creator, Hero.* Ludwig von Mises Institute: Auburn, Ala., 1988.

Rudolph, L. C. *Hoosier Zion.* New Haven, Conn.: Yale University Press, 1963.

Sayre, Paul. *The Life of Roscoe Pound.* Iowa City: College of Law Committee, 1948.

Schaller, Lyle E. *Twenty-one Bridges to the Twenty-first Century.* Nashville: Abingdon Press, 1994.

"Senator James E. Watson: The Professional Public Servant." *Atlantic Monthly,* February 1932: 183–90.

Sennholz, Mary. *Leonard Read: Philosopher of Liberty.* Irvington-on-Hudson, N.Y.: Foundation for Economic Education, 1993.

Smith, John L., and Lee L. Driver. *Past and Present of Randolph County, Indiana.* Indianapolis: A. W. Bowen and Co., 1914.

"A Statement of the Gifts of James P. Goodrich to Wabash College." *The Wabash Bulletin* 39 (October 1940).

Stigler, George. "The Intellectual and the Market Place." University of Chicago *Select Papers,* February 1967: 7.

Tocqueville, Alexis de. *Democracy in America.* New York: Doubleday-Anchor Books, 1969.

Trippett, Byron K. *Wabash on My Mind (Wabash College 1932–1982).* Crawfordsville, Ind.: Wabash College, 1982.

Tucker, Ebenezer. *History of Randolph County, Indiana.* Chicago: A. L. Kingman, 1882.

Ulam, Adam B. *A History of Soviet Russia.* New York: Praeger, 1976.

VanderMeer, Philip R. *The Hoosier Politician: Officeholding and Political Culture in Indiana, 1896–1920.* Urbana: University of Illinois Press, 1985.

Wabash—A Record of Honor. Crawfordsville, Ind.: Wabash College, 1924.

Wabash College: Pure American. Crawfordsville, Ind.: Wabash College, 1918.

Walker, Michael. *The Revolution of the Saints: A Study in the Origins of Radical Politics.* Cambridge, Mass.: Harvard University Press, 1965.

Walsh, Warren B. *Russia and the Soviet Union.* Ann Arbor: University of Michigan Press, 1958.

Watson, James E. *As I Knew Them.* Indianapolis: Bobbs-Merrill, 1936.

Weber, Max. *The Protestant Ethic and the Spirit of Capitalism.* New York: Charles Scribner's Sons, 1905.

Wigdor, David. *Roscoe Pound: Philosopher of Law.* Westport, Conn.: Greenwood Press, 1974.

Williams, T. Harry, Richard N. Current, and Frank Freidel. *A History of the United States: Since 1865.* New York: Alfred A. Knopf, 1959.

The World Book Encyclopedia. Chicago: World Book, 1989.

Index

This book is set in Minion, a typeface designed for Adobe in 1989 by Robert Slimbach. Minion is inspired by the highly readable typefaces of the Renaissance.

Printed on paper that is acid-free and meets the requirements of the American National Standard for Permanence of Paper for Printed Library Materials, z39.48-1992. ♾

Text design by Sandra Strother Hudson,
Athens, Georgia
Case design by Erin Kirk New,
Athens, Georgia

Typography by G& S Typesetters,
Austin, Texas
Printed and bound by Edwards Brothers, Inc.,
Ann Arbor, Michigan